# SEGREGATION

# HISTORICAL STUDIES OF URBAN AMERICA

*Edited by Timothy J. Gilfoyle, James R. Grossman, and Becky M. Nicolaides*

*Additional series titles follow index.*

A Global History
of Divided Cities

# SEGREGATION

Carl H.
Nightingale

The University of Chicago Press

Chicago and London

**Carl H. Nightingale** is associate professor of urban and world history in the Department of Transnational Studies at the University at Buffalo, State University of New York. He is the author of *On the Edge: Poor Black Children and Their American Dreams*.

The University of Chicago Press, Chicago 60637
The University of Chicago Press, Ltd., London
© 2012 by Carl H. Nightingale
All rights reserved. Published 2012.
Printed in the United States of America

21 20 19 18 17 16 15 14 13 12     1 2 3 4 5

ISBN-13: 978-0-226-58074-6 (cloth)
ISBN-10: 0-226-58074-1 (cloth)

Library of Congress Cataloging-in-Publication Data

Nightingale, Carl Husemoller.
  Segregation : a global history of divided cities /
Carl H. Nightingale.
      pages ; cm. — (Historical studies of urban
America)
  Includes bibliographical references and index.
    ISBN 978-0-226-58074-6 (cloth : alkaline paper) —
ISBN 0-226-58074-1 (cloth : alkaline paper)
1. Discrimination in housing—History.
2. Segregation—History.  3. Urban policy—
History.  4. Minorities—Housing—History.
5. Discrimination in housing—United States.
6. Segregation—United States.  7. Urban policy—
United States.  8. Minorities—Housing—United
States.  I. Title.  II. Series: Historical studies of
urban America.
  HD7288.75.N54 2012
  305.8009173′2—dc23

                                    2011050362

⊗ This paper meets the requirements of ANSI/
NISO Z39.48-1992 (Permanence of Paper).

to Mbali, Martha, Skhumbuzo,
and our tricontinental extended family of relatives and friends

for your loving reach across long distances
and urban color lines

# Contents

## PART THREE: SURGES OF SEGREGATION IN THE COLONIES

## PART FOUR: THE ARCHSEGREGATIONISTS

# Acknowledgments

This book tells a story about powerful institutions and intellectual networks and how they spread coercive practices of residential segregation to cities around the world. The book came into being, however, because of a very different sort of intellectual network, one that reached across both color lines and long distances and that was powered by the generous support of dozens of institutions, hundreds of suggestions for improvements, and thousands of individual acts of collegiality, kindness, political courage, faith-building, and friendship.

Within that beneficent community, there are a few people who have given this book close scholarly attention from its earliest inception to its finish. Martha T. McCluskey shared seventeen years of conversations with me exploring the relationship of ideas, politics, law, and institutions. These, combined with inspiration from her own wide-ranging work on legal theory and economic justice, infuse all aspects of the book's conceptual architecture. As a graduate student long ago, I was lucky to have Daniel T. Rodgers as an advisor. Since then, he has become a lifelong academic councilor and voracious reader of pages I send him. He scoured the manuscript, both in portions and in its entirety, several times along the way, refreshing it with his own deep experience of writing border-crossing history. On the repeated occasions that I hunted Michael B. Katz and Mike Frisch down in their adjoining cabins in Maine's western woods, they took time from their own academic pursuits to encourage this project and push it toward more productive aims. Since meeting Thomas Bender at his pathbreaking conference on global approaches to American history, he has relentlessly encouraged my travel beyond the geographical boundaries of my professional training. Paul Kramer has been willing on multiple occasions to repeat the founding event of our friendship, a casual encounter in St. Louis that turned into a five-hour conversation on empires and other macrohistorical subjects. I was similarly lucky to encounter Aims McGuinness, this time in Milwaukee, also a granter of enormous amounts of conversation time. Among many other things, I am grateful for his deep understanding that very big historical things are made up of the very smallest things. Thanks too for his thoughts on his students' reactions to various drafts of the work. Throughout the writing of this book, I have also benefitted from a half dozen long conversations with Robert O. Self, this time on entanglements between urban, national, and international politics. My Buffalo colleague Theresa Runstedtler has been another great source of inspiration, especially on questions of race and turn-of-the-twentieth-century global popular culture. The results of her willingness to share ideas and resources, as well as her critical reading of the manuscript, are particularly patent in the chapters on South Africa and the United States. Jeanne Nightingale's encouragement and advice over the years included not only the usual support one hopes for from a parent, but also numerous suggestions on the book's scholarship, many useful references, and several in-depth critical readings of drafts of the book's introduction.

The origins of this book date back to the time when I was a faculty member in the History Department at the University of Massachusetts Amherst. During writing workshops, departmental colloquia, and a five-college seminar that brought together faculty from other nearby institutions, the book benefitted from the thoughts of Kevin Boyle, Kathy Peiss, Max Page, Alice Nash, Brian Ogilvy, Stephen Nissenbaum, Laura Lovett, Gianpaolo Baiocchi, Mary Wilson, David Glassberg, Bruce Laurie, Gerald McFarland, Frank Couvares, Mary Renda, Neil Salisbury, Victoria Gettis, Joye Bowman, Todd Crossett, Paula Chakravartti, Neta Crawford, Dean Robinson, Barbara Cruikshank, John Higginson, and Jack Tager. Thanks to Dick Minear for urging me to teach world history for the first time, a habit that has stuck with me ever since. Thanks also to members and associates of the country's most incisive economics department, especially Gerald Epstein, Nancy Folbre, Carol Heim, Gerald Friedman, Robert Pollin, James Heintz, and Stephanie Luce, for glimpses into the mysteries and politics of their craft.

During the early years of the project, the American Council of Learned Societies granted me a fellowship. In conjunction with generous release time from teaching at UMass, I was able, among other things, to explore the connections between American urban segregation and that practiced in colonial cities.

This book took its current form while I was visiting faculty member at the University of Wisconsin-Milwaukee in 2002-3. That was due in no small part to the extraordinary confluence of interest in urban and global history at UWM, involving not only professors McGuinness and Self, but also Merry Wiesner-Hanks, William Jones, Jasmine Alinder, Bruce Fetter, Amanda Seligman, Anne Hansen, Margo Anderson, Mark Levine, Michael Gordon, Kate Kramer, Patrice Petro, and Jeffrey Merrick. Especial credit goes to Mark Bradley, whose vision and institutional savvy was largely responsible for enticing all of us into the friendly atmosphere of Holton Hall. The fruits of my chance to bask in the cartographic dreamland of UWM's American Geographical Society Library will be evident from the book's illustrations. It was there that I began my study of early modern politics of color lines in Madras.

My current academic home, the University at Buffalo's Department of American Studies—now renamed the Department of Transnational Studies—has provided a unique and generous interdisciplinary environment for the book's growth from proposal to final manuscript. In addition to pervasive inspiration from UB professors McCluskey, Frisch, and Runstedtler, the book received large infusions of critical reading, ideas, expertise, and encouragement from Erik Seeman, Victoria Woolcott, Keith Griffler, David Herzberg, Gail Radford, Ellen Berrey, Camilo Trumper, Dalia Muller, Robert Adelman, Christopher Mele, Jason Young, Sarah Robert, Aaron Bartley, David Fertig, Carole Emberton, Hal Langfur, Donald T. Grinde, Kristin Stapleton, and Robert Silverman. Thanks too to Angela Harris, Susan Cahn, Theresa McCarthy, Teri Miller, Robert Steinberg, Gwynn Thomas, Frank Munger, Bruce Jackson, Athena Mutua, Shaun Irlam, Greg Dimitriadis, Erin Hatton, Y. G.-M. Lulat, Samina Raja, Munroe Eagles, Claire Schen, Douglas Koretz, Stephanie Phillips, Susan Mangold, Patrick McDevitt, Jose Buscaglia, Janina Brutt-Griffler, Henry Taylor, Kari Winter, Ruth Meyerowitz, Cynthia Wu, Piyasuda Pangsapa, Ramon Soto-Crespo, Quan Hoang, and Lillian Williams. I am also grateful to Paul McCutcheon, Adrianna Hernandez-Stuart, Marta Marciniak, Robert Starzinsky, Stephanie Bucalo, Christopher Atkinson, Matt DiCristofaro, and Makeda Greene, all of whom read parts of the final manuscript for my class on the politics of urban space and subjected it to a thorough review, with especially consequential results for the final chapter.

At the vortex of UB's commitment to interdisciplinary conversation is the Christopher Baldy Center for Law and Social Policy. Under the leadership of Lynn Mather and Rebecca French, the Baldy Center supported this book in numerous ways, most importantly by awarding me an annual research grant (twice extended), which funded much of the research in South Africa and the United States. Under the aegis of these grants, the book benefitted enormously from the extensive and very able research assistance of Mark Lempke and Skhumbuzo Mthethwa. A small research grant from the center also covered expenses for the original maps in the book, created by Kailee Neuner. In addition, the center supported numerous meetings of the Buffalo Seminar on Racial Justice, including a pathbreaking transborder conference on race and politics at the University of Toronto that allowed me to share some of the book's ideas. Finally, I am deeply grateful for Professor Mather's invention of an institution unique to UB, the Faculty Manuscript Workshop. In the workshop devoted to the manuscript of this book, I benefitted enormously from comments from Boston University sociology professor Zine Magubane, McMaster University geography professor Richard Harris, and Professor Runstedtler. Three hours worth of subsequent discussion involving colleagues from across the university brilliantly illuminated my path toward final revisions.

Numerous other scholars generously offered guidance as I trespassed onto fields of their expertise. Thanks to Peter Biehl and Gwendolyn Leick for thoughts on ancient cities. On India, I benefitted enormously from telephone, e-mail, and personal exchanges with Peter Marshall, Durba Ghosh, Partho Datta, Stephen Legg, Preeti Chopra, Swati Chattopadhyay, Robert Frykenburg, Prashant Kidambi, Richard Harris, Robert Lewis, Susan Nield-Basu, Veena Oldenburg, Vijay Prashad, Rajani Sudan, Antoinette Burton, Robert Gregg, Madhavi Kale, and the late Pradip Sinha. Profesor Sinha also gave me a splendid tour of Kolkata. Richard Harris and Robert Lewis organized a panel at the conference of the International Planning History Society, which gathered together many of these luminaries. At the same conference I met David Pomfret of the University of Hong Kong and began a very valuable and lengthy e-mail exchange that helped me refashion much of the narrative in chapters 5 and 6. Cecilia Chu provided tips on archival sources that were invaluable as well. Elsewhere in the colonial world, Leonhard Blussé and Remco Rabin helped me fathom early modern Dutch colonial urban policy; Malyn Newitt and the late Glenn J. Ames helped with the Portuguese; Jeremy Mumford, with the Spaniards; Bruce Fetter, with the Belgians; Robert Tignor, Robert

Home, and Rinaldo Walcott, with the British; Zeynep Çeylik and Michael Vann, with the French; Olavi Fält, with the East Asian Concessions; Eric Roorda, with Cuba; and Aims McGuinness, with Panama.

For guidance on matters of South African and Johannesburg history, I am grateful to Susan Parnell, Charles van Onselen, Keith Beavon, the late George Fredrickson, Alan Mabin, Patrick Bond, Lindsay Bremner, Gary Baines, Paul Maylam, Philip Bonner, Christopher Saunders, Howard Philips, Christoph Strobel, Zine Magubane, James Campbell, Johan Bergh, Clive Glaser, and my original teachers of the subject, Robert Shell and Robert Tignor.

On the United States and Chicago, thanks for help and inspiration from Daniel Rodgers, Michael Katz, Michael Frisch, Robert Self, Kevin Boyle, Gary Gerstle, David Freund, Becky Nicolaides, Thomas Sugrue, Eric Schneider, Nayan Shah, Laura Lovett, Max Page, Robert Gregg, Wendy Plotkin, Roberta Moudry, Amanda Seligman, Peter Agree, Guy Stuart, Gregory Squires, Thomas Jackson, Steve Fraser, Michael Kahan, Kenneth Kusmer, Alice O'Connor, John Wertheimer, Roger Levine, Tim Gilfoyle, Arnold Hirsch, Loïc Wacquant, Marc Stern, Julia Foulkes, Pierre Gervais, Michan Connor, Samuel Kelton Roberts Jr., Audrey McFarlane, Robert Devens, Marc Egnal, Marc Stein, Jerry Ginsburg, and Molly Ladd-Taylor. I am also grateful for help from transborder urban historians Robert Fishman, Pierre-Yves Saulnier, Nancy Kwak, and Christopher Klemek, as well as for Patrick Manning's call for a world history of urban segregation.

On contemporary cities outside the United States, I benefitted from conversations with Stefan Kipfer, Eric Fong, Larry Bourne, Robert Murdie, Michèle Dagenais, Simon Gunn, Richard Harris, Hilary Silver, Loïc Wacquant, Ola Uduku, Jay McLeod, Stephen Read, Christine Lelevrier, Brigitte Guigou, Robert Lafont, and Anne-Marie Chavanon. Especial thanks to Hervé Vieillard-Baron for the chance to lecture on these topics as a visiting professor at the University of Paris 8 and for introducing me to much of the literature on segregation in France. Warm thanks to Bruno Voisin and Gilberte Hougouvieux for sending still more materials my way, for our many urban adventures together, and for their splendid guided tours of Lyon.

Among the many archivists I worked with over the years, several gave me especially extensive help. Thanks to Michelle Pickover, Carol Archibald, and Gabriele Mohale of Historical Papers at the University of Witwatersrand; Malini Roy and Jennifer Howes of the British Library; and the late Walter Hill at National Archives II. I am also most appreciative of the labors of Jill Ortner and the staff of the University at Buffalo's Interlibrary Loan Office for the countless titles they ordered for me.

For assistance with expenses involving the illustrations for the book, I am grateful for a grant from the Graham Foundation for Advanced Studies in the Fine Arts.

The project transformed from a manuscript into a book under the encouraging and always incisive guidance of my editor, Robert Devens at the University of Chicago Press. "Onward!" he always signed his emails; it was a call that seemed to make all the usual obstacles of book production disappear into thin air. Thanks too for the very able assistance of Anne Goldberg, Russell Damian, Katherine Frentzel, Levi Stahl, and Yvonne Zipter. As part of the peer review process, James T. Campbell and an anonymous reviewer provided enormously helpful insights. Becky Nicolaides went far beyond the call of duty as editor for the Historical Studies in Urban America series and provided me with dozens of pages of thoughtful commentary on the manuscript. Her comments helped me reshape and clarify large sections of the text. Please note that any remaining errors are entirely my own responsibility.

As the book's dedication page suggests, the scholarly network that sustained this book is nestled in a tricontinental community of urban activists, friends, and family in North America, Europe, and Africa who helped me and this project navigate what was otherwise a pretty depressing period in world history—whether by demonstrating irrepressible political faith, organizing all kinds of wonderful diversions and pleasurable times, providing a place to rest while I was traveling, or remaining willing (often inexplicably) to keep on sending their love.

To sustain my own hope for better futures for our cities, I owe a tremendous amount to the activists who have taken me under their wings over the years: from the youth activists of Kids Against Violence and Drugs in Philadelphia; to Maurice Taylor, Mara Dodge, and Michaelanne Bewsie at ARISE for Social Justice in Springfield, Massachusetts; to Mary Regan and her many friends in Boston and São Paulo; to Kye Leung; to the fabulous community organizers of Boston's Dudley Street Neighborhood Initiative; to Sparrow Village in Johannesburg; to Anina van Zyl and other devoted staff of the Edendale School in Culinan, South Africa; to Rick French of Journeys of Solutions; to Scott Gehl of the Housing Opportunities Made Equal, New York; to Diane Picard, Jesse Meeder, Zoe Hollomon, and Erin Sharkey of Buffalo's Massachusetts Avenue Project;

and most of all to the tireless visionaries associated with PUSH Buffalo: Aaron Bartley, Eric Walker, Whitney Yax, Clarke Gocker, Maxine Murphy, Sara Gordon, Sergio Uzurin, Aminah Johnson, Ishmael Johnson, Anna Falicov, Kevin Connor, and the late Ray Jackson.

For friendship, spiritual regeneration, political discussion, readings of difficult pieces of the book, and invaluable observations on city life from many angles, thanks that transcends words to Jon Liebman, Anne Fine, Alex and Eli Fine-Liebman, Andrea Raphael, John Reilly, Susan Meeker, Todd Crosset, Anne Richmond, Gerry Epstein, Fran Deutsch, Julie Cristol, T. L. Hill, David Dorsey, David Herzberg, Wayne Jortner, Marianne Ringel, Giovanni Banfi, Beth and Vanessa Adel, Don Kreis, Jenny Keller, Julia Foulkes, Brian Kane, Dan Wyman, Jane Eklund, Taylor Flynn, Roxanne Amico, Anne Beckley-Forest, Michael Forest, Sharon Treat, Bob Collins, Tressa White, Paul Zanolli, Val Anderson, Mark McLaughlin, Jody Hansen, Nicolas Penchaszadeh, Sarah Robert, Jo Freudenheim, Peggy and Dennis Bertram, the Georgette Brown family, and all the great kids that live with them.

Thanks for the many warm welcomes in Soweto, Thaba Nchu, and Naturena from my extended South African family: Sifiso Dubazana; Queen and Ntombizodwa Mageseni; Lizzy and Nthabiseng Mohao; Lucia Dubazana; Nozipho and Opa Bhele and their children; Lindiwe, Xoli, and Sphiwe Maduna and their children; Albert Thanduyise Mthethwa and the late Angelina Ntombinhle Mthethwa; their daughters Setukhile, Busisiwe, Similosenkosi, Ntokozo, and Nnana; and their grandchildren.

For keeping hearts and hearths open and for inspiring me by pursuing diverse and challenging life paths, deep thanks to my siblings, Anna Jeretic, Erich Husemoller, Kurt Husemoller, and Greta Lichtenbaum; to my grandparents, Barbara and Philip Nightingale; to my fabulous in-laws, Patricio Jeretic, Alison Sinkler, Peter Lichtenbaum, Chris and Pete Jensen, and Peter McCluskey; to my eleven nieces and nephews; to Nancy Schwab; to Ann and Norm Farr; and to Christiane Geisen. I could not wish for more generous parents-in-law than Donald and Dorothy McCluskey; the warmth of their spirit has touched every aspect of my life. I am blessed to have been brought up by Jeanne Nightingale and Dale Husemoller. Thanks for providing me a home that fostered adventure, travel beyond boundaries, and love of learning—and thanks for your abiding scholarly example, friendship, and love in my adult life.

In dedicating this book to the communities that nurtured it, I have singled out three people whose spirit and specific decisions touched the project most profoundly. At the very kernel of my heart—and of all my communities of the heart—stands my closest intellectual colleague, supporter, friend, and partner-in-life, Martha T. McCluskey. Her acute understanding of the political economy of scholarship begins with the view that families and households play as crucial roles as universities, institutes, and research foundations in the production of knowledge. No evidence for this argument could be more persuasive than Martha's own multifaceted contributions to this book, which range beyond her scholarly inspiration and her companionship amid the emotional ups and downs that attend all academic work. She was also willing to funnel family resources directly into this project by paying for time off from university responsibilities that allowed me to write, travel, research, and present ideas from the book. This project depended on her bread-winning and slow-tracking other priorities, and I am deeply grateful for her generosity.

Our daughter, Mbali, who came into our lives at more or less the same time as the book, provides additional grist for Martha's thesis. Though having a youngster about the house should in theory have slowed her parent's scholarly output, this particular child positively impelled me to invent all sorts of time-management techniques that moved the book forward more efficiently and gave me great times with her. Moreover, any feistiness or ironical energy readers may detect in the text very likely derives from a recent conversation—or a raucous game of backyard basketball—with her.

While working on the book, I also had the great pleasure of building a friendship with Mbali's first father, Skhumbuzo Mthethwa. Skhumbuzo and I collaborated in a series of high-efficiency raids on the National Archives of South Africa, where his skills with digital cameras and old documents proved enormously handy. Soon he was combing other archives in the Johannesburg area on my behalf and shipping big packages of photocopies and CDs back across the ocean, many containing documents that are identified in the footnotes to chapters 8, 9, and 11. Getting to know Skhumbuzo and Mbali's other South African relatives—and exploring the New South Africa through their eyes—was one of the greatest inspirations for writing this book.

# Introduction

"Segregation," the preacher paused to let his congregation absorb the full solemnity of his message, "is apparent everywhere." It was December 4, 1910, in Baltimore, Maryland. Members of the largely African American crowd that had gathered in the sanctuary and overflowed onto the steps of the John Wesley Methodist Episcopal Church were grimly aware of what the Reverend Dr. Ernest Lyon was talking about, at least as far as the United States was concerned. The country's black slaves had been emancipated less than a half century before. But now white people in Baltimore and elsewhere, even in cities outside the formerly slave-owning South, were clamoring for new ways to assert political supremacy. They had devised a new technique of racial control—segregation.[1]

Since about 1900, whites across the United States had been outdoing each other shouting these four dread syllables from the political rooftops. In the name of segregation, they had passed laws that relegated blacks to inferior Jim Crow schools, train cars, railroad station platforms and waiting rooms, restaurants, theaters, public bathrooms, amusement parks, and even public water fountains. Employers and white workers imposed color bars that kept certain higher-prestige jobs off limits to blacks. Laws that prevented blacks from voting helped to reinforce the system.

Earlier that year, on July 5, 1910, a group of angry whites in Baltimore decided it was time to take a step further and extend segregation to the city's residential neighborhoods. As a result, Lyon reminded his congregation, "the city fathers of Baltimore are having under advisement at this time a measure which seeks to deprive free men ... of their right to live and own property anywhere they can." Two weeks after Lyon's sermon, on December 20, 1910, Mayor J. Barry Mahool signed the city's pathbreaking segregation ordinance into law. The ordinance divided every street in Baltimore into "white blocks" and "colored blocks" based on the race of the majority of their inhabitants at the time of the ordinance's passage. It set a penalty of one hundred dollars and up to a year in the Baltimore city jail for anyone who moved to a block set aside for the "opposite race," except black servants who lived in the houses of their white employers.

Members of Reverend Lyon's congregation knew this bad news all too well. But the preacher wanted to stretch the minds of his flock even further. Segregation may have come to Baltimore, and it was definitely spreading across the United States, but it was also crisscrossing big expanses of the world beyond. White people almost everywhere had decided it was worth the effort to put into place the types of color lines that are the central focus of this book—those that involve the difficult and complicated process of rearranging whole cities into separate, unequal, and compulsory residential zones for different races.

As Reverend Lyon pointed out, the surge of enthusiasm for urban residential segregation resonated "not only in the United States, but even in Africa, the natural habitat of the black man." On this matter he could speak from firsthand experience. He had just returned from Africa's west coast, where he had been the US resident minister and consul general to the nation of Liberia. Lyon reported that in the nearby city of Freetown, capital of the British colony of Sierra Leone, "the whites have vacated the valleys, leaving them to the blacks, while they have escaped to the mountains." He was speaking of Hill Station, an all-European residential zone that British authorities developed on a small mountaintop a few miles from Freetown's all-black downtown—a downtown that, ironically, they had built earlier in the nineteenth century as a haven for freed slaves.[2]

"This method" of segregation, Lyon went on, "applied all across that vast continent," wherever in Africa whites "could be found." Here, the preacher was doubtlessly referring to new segregationist measures in the cities of the Union of South Africa, where English- and Afrikaans-speaking settlers had agreed to form a whites-only colonial government earlier that year. But he could just as easily have been alluding to events in colonial cities elsewhere in Africa, whether they were run by the British, the French, the Germans, the Belgians, or the Portuguese.

Moreover, segregation was not by any means limited to America and Africa—nor to the newly dawning twentieth century. Urban segregation designed to enhance elite groups' power and wealth extends back to the most ancient of cities in Mesopotamia, and it was practiced in most other ancient civilizations as well. European colonial segregation dates at least as far back as the Middle Ages, when English colonists in Ireland

and Italian merchants in the eastern Mediterranean reserved separate parts of overseas colonial towns for themselves. Similar practices went into the ghettos that the Christian rulers of Venice and other Europeans cities established for Jews. The idea of separating a "black town" from a "white town" dates back to 1700, when British officials decided that color designations were crucial to governing their southern Indian colonial city of Madras (today's Chennai). Race first entered into the conversations about urban segregation in the late 1700s in Calcutta (Kolkata), the capital of British India. British officials coined the phrase "hill station" in the early 1800s to describe dozens of segregated cities they built in the highlands of India, such as Simla—but the Dutch had built a similar place in Java a hundred years earlier. Baltimore's 1910 segregation ordinance was not the first; experiments with legalized urban color lines arose in the mid-1800s in cities in China and around the Pacific Rim; they were designed to keep Chinese people from living in the white sections of cities like Shanghai, Hong Kong, and San Francisco. The word "segregation" itself was first used for techniques of racial isolation in Hong Kong and Bombay (today's Mumbai) in the 1890s. From there it inspired a nearly worldwide spread of what I call "segregation mania" across Asia, Africa, and the Atlantic world. The mania even resonated in Latin American cities like Rio de Janeiro and Buenos Aires, where distinctions between black and white were typically murkier than elsewhere. Monumental segregated colonial capitals went up in places like Rabat, in French Morocco, and New Delhi, in British India, signaling new arrogant ambitions for urban planning based on separate racial zones. The most radical of all forms of urban segregation arose during these same years in two rapidly industrializing white settler societies. In South African cities like Durban, Cape Town, and Johannesburg, imperial officials and white settlers put in place the precedents for what would be called "apartheid" after 1948. In the United States, Baltimore's segregation ordinance was soon followed by a subtler and ultimately more durable system of segregation, this one designed in Chicago and based above all on racial dynamics in the real estate market.

The tide of urban racial segregationism reached its high-water mark worldwide during the twenty years following Dr. Lyon's warning in Baltimore. However, members of Dr. Lyon's congregation took his warning seriously. They helped lead a massive social movement with the goal of stopping whites' segregationist ambitions. By the 1930s, this African American civil rights movement had created loose alliances with simi-

3

lar movements for national liberation in colonies across Africa and the world. After World War II these movements succeeded in widely discrediting both racism and segregation, and they also forced whites to give up many of the practices they used to draw urban color lines.

Still, the early twentieth-century mania for racial segregation left a terrible legacy for the cities of today's world—and for the larger human communities in which they are located. Some aspects of the system of residential segregation that operates in the United States can be detected in otherwise quite different cities in the world's other wealthiest countries, such as London and Paris, the ancestral hometowns of the world's most influential white segregationists. The cities of Latin America and the colonial cities that Europeans and Americans ruled more recently in Asia and Africa have transformed into massive megacities sharply divided by class. There, new pressures from international financial institutions have enhanced the legacies of colonial-era segregationist urban policy. American Jim Crow fell during the 1960s and South African apartheid finally collapsed in 1994, but settler-led urban segregation continues to play a dispiriting role in some of the world's most excruciating political conflicts, most notably in Belfast, Northern Ireland, and in Jerusalem and other cities of Israel-Palestine. In many places, the explicitly racial component of segregationism has been supplemented—or disguised—with talk of class, culture, ethnicity, and, most dangerously, religion. But much of the underlying logic and many of the techniques bear unmistakable legacies of the forces Reverend Lyon warned his congregation about in 1910.

Today, more than half of all human beings are city dwellers. We need our cities more than ever. Their comparatively rich economic, political, and cultural opportunities and their potential for a relatively small per-capita environmental footprint may well make them crucial to our very survival as a species, as our many billions rapidly multiply and as we just as rapidly diminish our planet's resources. But segregating our cities diminishes their promise—it makes them less equal, less democratic, less livable, less safe, and less able to sustain us all.[3]

* * *

This book offers an update and an elaboration on the themes of Lyon's sermon a hundred years after he delivered it in Baltimore. It asks us to expand our minds even further, to consider not only the idea that residential color lines have proliferated across the world but also the book's main point: that such movements to segregate cities spread because they were interconnected.

Wherever and however they went about their business, urban racial segregationists always worked within three kinds of institutions that were critical to the West's rise to global dominance in the modern era. These were: governments, networks of intellectual exchange, and the institutions associated with the modern capitalist real estate industry. Segregationists everywhere relied on such powerful institutional connections because they alone could import and export the people, ideas, money, and specific practices and policy tools that were essential to the success of their projects to divide cities.

We must be very clear about how these institutions operated, however. No seamless, secretive global conspiracy was at work in spreading segregation, nefarious though segregationists' beliefs and actions often were. Putting a coerced residential color line in place is fundamentally a political act—it involves enormous amounts of power. But wielding that power always involves negotiation and conflict. Urban racial segregation rises and falls amid dramatic contests over power. Historically, the most important of these contests pitted segregationists against opposition movements, usually led by people of color. But conflicts between different factions of white urban residents were also important—and so were conflicts between and within the three most powerful segregationist institutions themselves.

Governments have been the most important of all city-splitting institutions, most often acting as colonial empires. Of these, the empires of Britain, France, and the United States supported and replicated—by far— the largest numbers of local movements for racial segregation across the world, though they have always relied on smaller-scale national, colonial, or municipal governments as well. All styles of government have been involved, from authoritarian regimes to racially exclusive republics to nominally nonracial democracies. The politics of urban segregation has always related to some of the most fundamental questions facing any government: Who gets to be a citizen? Who gets which rights and privileges? Where should territorial boundaries run? Who will be permitted to cross those boundaries? How should different-sized jurisdictions be administered? In too many cases, urban color lines have also been directly related to government-led violence and atrocity: warfare, conquest, racial cleansing, and genocide.

Western intellectuals, racial theorists, scientists, doctors, lawyers, urban planners, and urban reformers of all types have also always played crucial roles in legitimating segregationist ideas and practices. Beginning in the late 1700s they developed ever-denser institutions of intellectual exchange that soon reached across the world. At international conferences, on long-distance lecture circuits, in professional journal articles, newspapers, large-market magazines, and bestselling books they debated the idea of race and racial segregation furiously. Not all white intellectuals and reformers advocated residential segregation, but those who did were often able to gain tremendous influence over government urban policies.

To successfully divide cities by race, whites also needed to control far-flung urban real estate markets and minimize the power of darker-skinned people who could undercut segregation by purchasing property in zones that whites wanted to keep for themselves. That meant expanding the reach of several institutions central to modern capitalism: government agencies such as property courts and title registrar's offices; profit-making businesses such as real estate agencies, surveyors' offices, assessment companies, land development firms, and financial institutions; and, in larger settler societies, grassroots organizations of white property owners.

Other types of multinational capitalist corporations—which otherwise shaped cities in profound ways—only sometimes played important roles in urban racial segregation. Whenever capitalist employers sought to divide multiracial workers' movements by spreading racist propaganda or whenever they drew rigid occupational color lines in workplaces, they may also have inspired residential segregationists to do the same in neighborhoods. Media companies had a driving interest in spreading popular culture that contained racist imagery, and that too played into the hands of segregationists, especially in white settler societies. In industrializing capitalist societies like South Africa and the United States it is possible—but by no means easy to verify—that the general anxieties caused by massive social transformation heightened the racial anxieties that underlay many whites' support for segregation.

Overall, though, the direct role of multinational corporations in drawing urban residential color lines was inconsistent. At different times and places, their owners' various interests in trade, in gaining access to large consumer markets, in recruiting and controlling large labor forces, or in passing the social costs of their operations on to governments could lead them to a range of positions on the issue, from eager support to apparent ambivalence to outright rejection.

By looking at residential segregation from a global perspective, therefore, we confirm neither materialist theories that hold capitalism solely responsible for segregation nor "free-market" theories that hold that capitalism is "colorblind" and will inevitably make segregation obsolete. However, we do learn one thing very clearly: land markets are the one capitalist institution in which race-infused economic interests became consistently and increasingly important to the division of cities, even arguably becoming the single most important segregationist force in cities today. Manufacturing or mining capitalists who had ambivalent corporate interests in residential segregation were usually ardent segregationists when it came to their own land market interests. In urban real estate markets where whites believed that darker-skinned neighbors posed a threat to their property values, racially determined economic interests in segregation (often combined with similar economic interests in class segregation) became devilishly difficult to counteract.

The role that governments, intellectual networks, and land markets played in segregationist dramas varied in importance from city to city, and sometimes governments were forced to retreat from the central role they usually played. It is important to note, however, that this book's approach rejects the oft-drawn distinction between de jure segregation, made compulsory by government legislation, and de facto segregation, which is not institutionalized or based solely on cultural beliefs or customs. First, governments could use many instruments other than legislation to impose segregation. Second, in cities where governments could not take a central role, segregationist efforts always relied on intellectual networks or land market institutions for leadership—precisely because those institutions offered their own forms of coercion. Segregation never comes about because it "just is," as the term "de facto" might also suggest. The bottom line is this: segregation has always involved some form of institutionally organized human intentionality, just as those institutions have always depended on more broadly held beliefs, ideas, and customs to sustain their power.

No matter how they imposed their urban color lines, white segregationists have always had to combat political opposition. Segregation might have weakened the political power of darker-skinned people confined to inferior urban zones, but it never erased all their power, and they rarely accepted their exclusion from important urban advantages. In some cases excluded people have actually needed relatively little institutional coordination to wield their power. They could informally but collectively ignore segregation as they went about their daily lives. Small numbers of wealthier people of color who bought homes in white neighborhoods, usually acting without any coordinated plan of integration, historically presented one of the most important threats to residential color lines. At other times, people of color could launch more formal grassroots protest organizations and movements. If successful, they could seize slices of power within parts of the complex formal institutions that were otherwise committed to segregation—even within governments, the world of ideas, or housing markets. Finally, they could completely disrupt the segregationist order with massive street riots, rebellions, and sometimes urban warfare.

* * *

In addition to exploring the role of institutions, this book also rests on arguments about the role of color and race in urban and global history. Until about 1600, these concepts were relatively obscure, and the words "black," "white," and "race" played little role in either urban or global politics. After 1600, notions of blackness, and later whiteness, grew more important within the politics of the Spanish Empire, the Atlantic slave trade, and the American plantation system, but it was only in 1700 that British colonial officials in Asia first linked such color-based concepts to efforts of urban residential segregation. Neither blacks nor whites were considered "races," however, until the late 1700s, when the concept of race itself was transformed from a vague synonym for "ancestry" to a universal system of categorizing different types of human beings. When that happened, race became one of the most important concepts in global politics, and urban racial segregation was born.

Urban segregation by race was the first type of urban residential segregation created by representatives of a single civilization and then spread across the planet. As Western white segregationists began dividing cities by the new category of race, they both borrowed and reinvented ideas and tools from other genres of city-splitting politics. Especially important for race segregationists in the colonies were tools designed to divide the classes that were first developed in the land markets of seventeenth-century London. By using these techniques to divide cities in the colonies by race, they in turn created favorable contexts for the worldwide spread of class-based residential segregation, especially after colonial cities became part of independent nations. However, Western racial segregationists also found uses for practices that originated in other regions of the world and that sometimes went back to ancient times—the separation of districts for gods and mortals, the spatial division of city dwellers from country dwellers, and the segregation of nations, religions, classes, crafts, clans, castes, and the sexes.

\* \* \*

My hope is that this world history of urban segregation will shed new light on debates about cities that have become increasingly important around the world in recent years. Typically these debates are framed around questions such as: Are cities like London, Paris, Amsterdam, Hamburg, Toronto, Sydney, and Johannesburg developing racial ghettos like those in the United States? What about the slums or shanty towns of Kolkata, Delhi, Mumbai, Djakarta, Algiers, Cairo, Lagos, Mexico City, Rio de Janeiro, or Buenos Aires? Are they "just like the Bronx," as one youngster from a Buenos Aires slum once asked a visiting sociologist? Conversely, have "Third World conditions" come to the United States and other wealthy societies? And what about apartheid—has it "gone global," as some have argued, even after its demise in South Africa in 1994?

For some, answering these questions depends on quantifying *how much* segregation can be found in any given city, and social scientists have invented a variety of segregation indexes that measure just how divided any city really is. For others, the big question is terminology—that is, how to categorize different kinds of segregated urban neighborhoods. Scholars have sought to answer that question, too, by debating what characteristics make up the "ideal-type" of a "ghetto," a "slum," an "enclave," a "township," a "colonial city"—or even "segregation" itself. Still others compare cities across the world by modeling the processes of segregation. The most famous of these models includes the "invasion and succession" process, which describes how whites flee neighborhoods when nonwhites move in; and the "voluntary segregation" model, sometimes dubbed "good" segregation, which accounts for instances when people from the same ethnic group cluster in culturally familiar neighborhoods. Most of these concepts arose in research on cities in the United States, but they are pertinent to the world at large. This book relies heavily on the results of such social scientific research, especially when it is necessary to compare cities at any one given time.[4]

By insisting that segregation is above all a political animal, however, this book focuses most of its attention on aspects of city-splitting that are harder to count, type, or model. Real people, not mechanical processes, make segregation, and the ideas, interests, and practices people mobilize for or against segregation are complex. The political dramas that result never stop to rest in one spot; they are always dynamic, shape-shifting, unpredictable, and internally contradictory. What I hope to show is that if we emphasize these messier aspects of segregation, we actually get a clearer picture of the long-distance connections between different cities' experiences with racial dividing lines, and we can also offer richer contexts for comparisons between cities.

To embrace the complexities of urban residential color lines, this book returns repeatedly to the intrinsically paradoxical nature of segregationist politics. The very concept of urban segregation, after all, is self-contradictory. Cities are places where many different people come together, congregate, and create great agglomerations—where geographical distances between people are diminished, not increased. For whites who dominate multiracial cities, this contradiction often translates into a real political dilemma. Urban growth can help them build political prestige, create great wealth, and inspire cultural and intellectual innovation. But when the advantages of urban growth arise from the gathering of large numbers of people of color in cities, growth can also pose perceived political, economic, and cultural threats to white rule. Some whites, notably those in South Africa, responded to such threats by constraining growth, imposing what they called "influx controls" against potential black migrants to the city. But most, starting with the British founders of Madras and later including many diehard proponents of influx control, saw residential segregation of dark-skinned people as a necessary tool to resolve their political dilemma: to have the fruits of the growing city and tame its threats too. Even then, segregationist politics rested on further paradoxes. For example, growing populations of color could threaten the very color lines designed to contain them. Conversely, movements to impose color lines often relied on strength gained from whites' heightened fears of being "swamped" by dark-skinned migrants. But however the paradox cuts, the basic contradiction remains: despite centuries of segregation, cities have always been the site for the largest-scale interactions between people from different part of the world, and they are responsible for most of the mixing of peoples and cultures in world history. If there was no segregation, cities would be even greater sites of such potentially beneficial interaction.

Another paradox arises from the relationship between segregation and power. Residential segregation by race is a means to expand white racial power. But to put segregation in place, whites also need to expend power. To accomplish the difficult task of splitting a city, leaders need to give up some of their political capital, or pay dearly for the deployment of armed force, or invest the resources necessary to build systems of labor control and exploitation, or to put discriminatory voting systems in place, or to fight for power within the world of ideas, or to arouse white-led grassroots social movements, or to support systems of proprietary access to money, finance capital, and landed property. Residential segregation also often relies on other forms of segregation that require enormous political efforts to put into place, such as segregation in the voting booth, on the job, in schools, in public amenities, in small towns and villages, between different areas in the countryside, or between countries. Faced with these costs, segregationists have to make a strategic calculation that all the trouble of splitting a city is worth it—that expending the power necessary will give them more power than they had before. This calculation essentially involves a test of whites' faith in segregation, and it is a main reason why conflicts can arise within white urban communities and their institutions. In both South Africa and the United States, where segregation took especially radical forms, such internal conflicts may have been—paradoxically—essential to the success of urban color lines.

Movements opposed to segregation face painful paradoxes too. If underprivileged peoples destroy urban color lines and disperse themselves everywhere in the city, they may undercut the urban territorial base that gives strength to their own collective and institutional power in a hostile world. Jews faced this dilemma in their early modern ghettos; so, in a different way, did American blacks during the civil rights movement. In these instances, whites can lay claim to an additional political benefit from segregation, namely that their opponents cannot claim to be strictly antisegregationist and thus seize the higher moral ground that might come from such a principled stand. Dismayingly, many successful antiracist movements, including many anticolonial movements in Latin America, Africa, and Asia, have turned to segregation themselves once they won power. That said, we should always hesitate before we equate the spatial tactics of antiracist movements with "voluntary" segregation—

let alone assert the "goodness" of any form of "self-segregation"—even if it creates successful cultural havens. The word "voluntary" should never substitute for a close analysis of the relative institutional strength, and the changing and often narrow range of political options, available to antisegregationist movements or nondominant groups in different cities at different times in world history.[5]

In the midst of dramatic conflicts over urban space, still another paradox arises within whites' justifications for segregation. Whites often justify segregation in terms of their racial supremacy. But just as important are justifications based on whites' vulnerability—the growth of the city's dark-skinned population can be spun as a story of mortal political, economical, cultural, physical, and even sexual threats to white people. In fact, whites' moral outrage about injustices they claim to face arguably played a larger role than arrogant expressions of white supremacy in justifying the most authoritarian forms of racial city-splitting. Such claims are powerful because they divert attention away from the injustices segregation imposes upon people of color. Some segregationists, notably those in the United States, survived their greatest political opposition—the anticolonial and civil rights movements of the mid-twentieth century—by taking a different but related tactic: they attempted to camouflage their intent to support racial privilege. More recently, they have simply denied the existence of racial inequalities in cities, or even posed as egalitarians and antisegregationists themselves.

The very practices of racial segregation, finally, contain their own paradoxes. On the one hand, segregationists strive to make residential boundaries compulsory and watertight. A quick survey of the wide range of tools (and local natural features) they have used to split cities includes: walls, palisades, battlements, bastions, fences, gates, guard shacks, checkpoints, booms, railroad tracks, highways, tunnels, rivers, canals, inlets, mountainsides and ridges, buffer zones, free-fire zones, demilitarized zones, *cordon sanitaires*, screens of trees, road blocks, violent mobs, terrorism, the police, armies, curfews, quarantines, pass laws, labor compounds, building clearances, forced removals, restrictive covenants, zoning ordinances, racial steering practices, race-infused economic incentives, segregated private and public housing developments, exclusive residential compounds, gated communities, separate municipal governments and fiscal systems, discriminatory access to land ownership and credit, complementary systems of rural reservations, influx control laws, and restrictions against overseas immigration.

On the other hand, segregation-based assertions of white power always, just as fundamentally, rely on keeping color lines semiporous—that is, by authorizing very specific forms of urban boundary-crossing. To meet some whites' economic interests, for example, segregation laws (such as the one passed in Baltimore) nearly always exempt domestic servants; sometimes other workers or commercial partners of color can cross as well. Due to the wide circulation of workers of color, streets in whites-only commercial and residential neighborhoods often give the impression of neighborhood integration. Gendered interests matter too: white people, typically men, always have tacit permission to cross color lines in search of sex. Perhaps most importantly, white-run police forces and armies must have authority to cross color lines just to keep segregation intact.

* * *

To follow the connections between these paradoxical dramas in different places and to compare them, we need to keep a final messy thought in mind: the politics of segregation always plays out on multiple stages at once. Much of the action, of course, occurs in cities themselves and their suburbs, and much smaller spaces within cities—neighborhoods, streets, and inside households. But those smaller metropolitan, local, or intimate dramas are always connected to broader ones that unfold on political stages that are much larger than cities—in provinces or states, nations, regions, continents, oceans, and hemispheres, even sometimes the world as a whole.

It is within these larger contexts that, after 1700, the globe-spanning institutions of Western expansion first made their entrance onto the stages of urban segregationist politics. As part of their bid for global power, imperial governments, cross-oceanic intellectual networks, and the Western land business helped support movements for urban racial segregation across long distances by importing and exporting all of the basic elements of urban political drama: the main characters, the institutional influence, the ideas, the money, and the specific city-splitting policy tools. Everywhere they went, though, these institutions were also forced to play on cities' smaller stages, adapting plotlines of political dramas they developed in one place to the conditions they found in others. In yet another paradoxical twist, the obligation for local flexibility helped make the wide spread of segregation possible.

This book attempts to bring all these political dramas of urban racial segregation—the most enormous, the most minute, and the many sizes in between—into a single, wide-ranging, always changing, and always paradoxical narrative. In a kind of geographical counterpoint, it asks us to watch the theater of segregationist politics on many stages at once, by continually switching from wide-angled lenses, to various kinds of telescopes and binoculars, to highly focused microscopes. Meanwhile the narrative also moves chronologically across time, retelling the sweeping story of human history with the politics of urban segregation at its center.

The book begins by exploring the historical contexts of urban color lines in ancient and medieval practices of city-splitting. From there, the story follows the stainlike spread of color- and race-based residential segregation as it engulfed urban politics, city by city, across the planet from 1700 to the present.

The geographical path that the narrative charts out is striking. Most histories of race begin in the Atlantic world, where the slave trade inspired the first political uses for color and racial distinctions. Instead, this book's central plotline begins in the Indian Ocean, to explore why it was that British colonial officials in Madras and Calcutta adapted concepts of color and race for the specific purpose of dividing cities. There, officials, reformers, and land speculators also invented some of the most enduring justifications for their policy of racial segregation: that it could demonstrate the grandeur of the Western imperial mission; that it allowed officials to administer multiracial colonies efficiently; that it could reduce the dangers of epidemic disease and race mixing; and that it could protect the value of white people's urban property.

From these colonial capitals, race segregation and its guiding doctrines spread to other places. To follow the first large-scale surge of racial city-splitting politics we must visit the so-called stations of the British Raj (rule) in India—segregated military and administrative outposts that multiplied across the vast expanses of the subcontinent during the early nineteenth century, culminating in the glamorous hill stations. Meanwhile, a second surge of expansion began in connection with the so-called opening of China. That process caused race-infused practices of city-splitting to travel still further east, to Southeast Asia, China itself, and—in a huge burst across the Pacific—to white settler colonies in Australasia and western North America.

When the bubonic plague broke out in Hong Kong in 1894 and

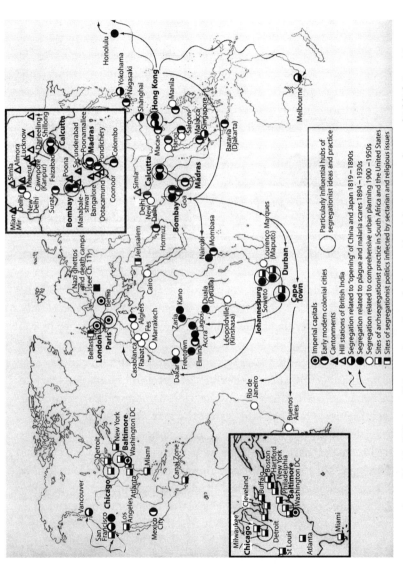

**FIGURE 0.1** The worldwide diffusion of ideas and practices of urban residential segregation by race, highlighting cities discussed in the book. Map by Kailee Neuner.

Bombay in 1896, the two cities became new crucial nodes in the spread of segregationist practice. As the plague spread via shipping routes across the world, the stage was set for the largest, planetwide surge of racist city-splitting practices, largely under the guise of urban public health reform. These reforms, now for the first time explicitly known as "segregation," spread to hundreds of cities across Asia, Africa, and the Americas.

This age of "segregation mania" lasted until the early 1920s. Amid all the excitement, the international city-planning movement also endorsed segregationist practices. Colonial governments sponsored ever more sophisticated, comprehensive, and architecturally elaborate practices, resulting in another surge of city-splitting that radiated from Europe (and most importantly from France) to all the colonies and even to Latin America.

During the mania, the stage was set for the rise of more radical and comprehensive forms of what I call "archsegregationism" in South Africa and the United States. To see how these practices became central to national urban policy in both countries, and to see how they outlasted the era of worldwide triumphs of antiracist civil rights crusades and anticolonial movements, this book makes extensive visits to Johannesburg and Chicago as they became pivot points in city-splitting politics during the 1920s. It also shows how related and loosely connected forms of radical urban segregationism came to the heart of Europe, where they played an important role in hastening the horrors of the Nazi Holocaust.

In our own time, the many legacies of early twentieth-century segregation mania continue to bedevil all the cities of the planet—despite warnings like Reverend Lyon's, despite widespread revulsion against the racial atrocities of our era, and despite the many important victories of antiracist, antisegregationist social movements. Still, the book closes with a bittersweet paradox: even amid new, enormously powerful planet-crossing surges of segregationism, more people than ever before have joined the fight to build cities that provide justice, opportunity, equality, power, sustenance, and a warm welcome to all people who seek a life in them.

# PART ONE | ANCESTRIES

# I     Seventy Centuries
## of City-Splitting

*Before Race Mattered*

When did we first start dividing our cities into separate, unequal, and compulsory residential zones? And when did we start to spread such practices across the world?

The answers to these questions cannot simply be chalked up to a human instinct to distance ourselves from those we find unfamiliar. Throughout our history, we have defined the boundaries between in-groups and out-groups—the "us" and the "them"—in many ways. Our cities' politics have reflected changes and variations in those definitions, each of which gave rise to a different type of segregationist politics. The idea that humanity is divided into separate "races," for example, is relatively young. It was not until the 1700s that Westerners first used race as a universalized category to explain human differences, and it was only then that it became important to the practice of dividing cities.

Sadly, though, people did not need to wait for the invention of race in the West to start dividing cities, nor to replicate urban segregation over large regions of the world. In fact, for about seventy centuries—arguably since the invention of cities themselves—we have repeatedly committed acts of inequitable and forcible city-splitting. Along the way, we have justified our actions in the name of just about every other concept of human difference imaginable, marking off separate residential territories for different classes, clans, castes, crafts, nations, religions, civilizations, and even sexes. The most successful forms of ancient segregationist politics were based on more complex and specific combinations of these ideas: that the gods should live in separate, more splendid places than mere mortals; that city dwellers should live separately from those in the countryside; and that foreigners should live apart from local people.

Unlike the case of racial segregation, no single civilization was responsible for the invention and replication of these ancient forms of city-splitting. Instead, each of humanity's urban civilizations adopted these segregationist practices for the most part on their own. They did this at approximately the same time that they built their first cities and that they invented three institutions crucial to segregationist politics: authoritarian governments, castes of elite religious intellectuals, and institutionalized inequalities of wealth that included efforts to monopolize control over urban land. These were the direct ancestors of the institutions that would spread racial segregation worldwide during the modern era.

## The Long Shadow of the Ziggurat

Sometime around 5000 BCE—seventy centuries ago—the Mesopotamian god Marduk is said to have commanded his priests and worshipers to build a temple at a place called Eridu. Archaeologists uncovered this city, which many consider the oldest of all, under a mound of windblown desert sand in 1854 in today's Iraq. Long before that, though, in 600 BCE, a gaggle of Babylonian poets had already identified Eridu as the birthplace of segregation by claiming that the city came into being when Marduk ordered his followers to surround "his holy house ... of the gods in a holy place" with separate dwellings for ordinary mortals charged with the place's upkeep.[1]

Human settlements contained all sorts of dividing lines long before Marduk's power move into Mesopotamian real estate. On the most elementary level, of course, the walls and roofs of all dwelling places intrinsically "segregate" sheltered spaces from exposed ones. Towns and cities, for their part, have no existence without their honeycomb-like built environment, made up of clusters of such walls and roofs. But it is certainly possible to imagine a settlement without the type of segregation that Marduk proposed. In fact, archaeologists found exactly such a "protocity" during the 1960s at a place in Turkey called Çatalhöyük. The interiors of Çatalhöyük's houses, more than a thousand years older than Eridu's, were themselves subdivided in simple and familiar ways. Cooking space was marked off by hearths; food-storage areas contained dugout grain bins; prayer, sleep, and lovemaking happened elsewhere; and there was also a separate place for the dead—buried under the floor. The status of men and women was apparently much more equal than in later cities, and they seem to have shared the same spaces, though some may have been closely associated with the daily activities of one sex more than the other.

Outside, Çatalhöyük was divided into separate cells by the walls of its houses. But within the honeycomb of the town there was little evidence of the separation of the diverse activities or functions that help distinguish a city from simpler settlements. All of Çatalhöyük's residents did more or less the same thing: they farmed. Some townsfolk moonlighted as artisans, but their workshops seem to have occupied yet another space inside their houses. The only clear large-scale dividing line was that which separated the town itself from the surrounding fields and wild places. Çatalhöyük's builders never even set aside space for streets between the town's buildings, which snuggled right up next to each other and shared each others' walls (to get around, people probably climbed a ladder through a door in their ceilings and walked on the rooftops). All of the houses also looked more or less the same. A few were a little bigger than others, and some had more bodies buried under their floors than others, a hint that some might have been more important ritual spots than others. But all of them had approximately the same sized bins for storing grain, implying rough economic equality. Questions about dividing space may have led to some complex political dramas. Exactly which spaces belonged to different members of the community could have caused quarrels, for example—the kind of conflicts that in some societies could result in boundaries between pieces of private property. Whether or not Çatalhöyük's residents engaged in such conflicts, though, they did little to use the separation of urban space as a means to differentiate between the rich and the poor—or the powerful and the subordinate.[2]

Then, so say the Babylonian poets, Marduk changed world history by demanding a special space for gods to live—a "dwelling of [their] hearts' delight"—as the poets called the temple of Eridu, that would set divine urban zones apart from those for mere mortals.

Needless to say, it actually took more than the snap of godly fingers to bring urban inequality and segregation into being. Despite Eridu's mythic status as the birthplace of Sumerian kingship (other narratives name Enki, Marduk's father and creator of the earth, as the city's

FIGURE 1.1 "Then Eridu was made … in order to settle the gods in the dwelling of [their] hearts' delight." This painting shows the city as it might have appeared in 3000 BCE when it was about two thousand years old. By then, the separate house of the gods, the ziggurat, had grown to monumental proportions. Similar exclusive palace-temple districts arose in most other urban civilizations across the world, whether in imitation of Mesopotamia or independently. Balage Balogh, *Eridu Sunrise*, used with permission from Balage Balogh/ Archaeology Illustrated.

founder), its temple was quite a modest affair for more than a thousand years, and its floor plan suggests it was quite accessible. Nor did ancient forms of urban inequality always depend on segregation, or vice versa. During Eridu's first millennium, people elsewhere in the region built both exalted sacred places without separate towns nearby and towns without sacred districts that appear nonetheless to have been increasingly unequal.[3]

That said, it is clear that, after 4000 BCE, at the dawn of the written historical record, separate temple districts in Sumer modeled on those of Eridu had become the site of crucial political conflicts between cities' elite officials and intellectuals—the local priests—and these conflicts ultimately resulted in the rule of authoritarian factions that, in turn, founded the first lines of divinely ordained urban kings and queens. In these cities, a larger "sacropolitical" district grew around the temple that included the royal palace and, crucially, the city's granaries—indicating the development of centrally controlled food-distribution systems. Fearsome walls also surrounded the god-kings' urban territories for the first time, signaling a deliberate effort to exclude all but the city's elect.

As the authority of governments and court intellectuals intensified, and as they assumed growing power over the allocation of urban land, measures of urban segregation grew severer. Monarchs and priests, eager to meet the gods' apparently increasing needs for residential splendor, repeatedly ordered the palace-temples rebuilt over the centuries, usually enlarging them and making them more grandiose each time. Since the rubble of dismantled older buildings, often carefully stacked in a giant pile, served as the foundation for the new ones, the exclusive homes of the gods also began to grow upward toward the heavens.[4]

In this way, Mesopotamia's famous ziggurats grew, and monumental urban architecture was born, assuming a crucial role in the politics of city-splitting that has lasted well into our own age. By the time of the legendary tyrant Gilgamesh, sometime around 3000 BCE, the city of Uruk's temple district of Eanna, home to the goddess Inanna or Ishtar, was hoisted high on its own human-made hill and surrounded by a massive wall—sublime in its mountainous separation from the rest of the city. The evidence of egalitarianism is long gone:

> He built the walls of ramparted Uruk,
> The lustrous treasury [or storehouse] of Eanna!
> See its upper wall, whose facing gleams like copper,
> Gaze at its lower course, which nothing will equal
> Mount the stone staircase, there from days of old,
> Approach Eanna the dwelling of Ishtar,
> Which no future king, no human, will equal.[5]

From down below, the ziggurat and its surrounding buildings offered a vision of heaven itself, floating in its majesty above the rest of the city. As such, the sacred precinct became a crucial mass medium of the day, beaming down brick-and-mortared propaganda that the gods and their royal servants would assure everyone good harvests, prosperity, health, and peace—or at least victory in war.[6]

With war very much in mind, rulers like Gilgamesh enhanced a second fundamental form of monumental urban separation, that between

the city and the countryside. The walls that surrounded the whole city of
Uruk measured nearly ten kilometers around, and they too proclaimed
the city's link to the divine.

> Go up, pace out the walls of Uruk,
> Study the foundation terrace and examine the brickwork
> Is not its masonry of kiln-fired brick?
> And did not the seven masters lay its foundations?[7]

City walls had been around since before complex cities themselves. A
hundred centuries ago, Jericho, the earliest of all known protocities, was
already surrounded by the ancestor of the famous wall that came tumbling
down to the blare of Joshua's trumpets. By contrast, Uruk was a thousand
years old before it acquired its walls, sometime around 3000 BCE. The
advantages of walls for urban royalty, however, were many. In addition
to providing military defense and reinforcing the propaganda of divine
rule, city gates provided a convenient place to levy tolls on commerce
from outside. Protection could ensure the loyalty of the city's residents;
those deemed disloyal could be banished beyond the walls. Walls could
flaunt the wealth of the city—as Gilgamesh's chronicler noted, those were
*kiln-fired* bricks, not the cheap ones merely left to dry in the sun! More
abstractly, walls also could contrast the superior civilization of the city
with that of the hinterland. Inside, city dwellers could acquire unheard
of wealth and leisure and look down on the farmers in the surrounding
fields. In their epic poems, Mesopotamians contrasted city life—filled
with feasting, conviviality, and cutting-edge sexual experimentation—
with the wild lands beyond, peopled with bumpkins, drudges, barbaric
hordes, wanderers, tent dwellers, half beasts, and bandits.[8]

The two oldest forms of urban segregation also brought into being
the most enduring of its many paradoxes. If monuments and city walls
offered a tremendous boost to divinely ordained royal power, their very
creation required huge expenses of both power and resources. Uruk's
temples contained tens of millions of bricks and its walls maybe even a
hundred million. Firing each of them required vast amounts of scarce
fuel. Tens of thousands of hands were needed to mortar them in place.
Yet such monuments also spoke just as eloquently to the vulnerability
of the god-kings who built them—above all their need to fend off countless powerful enemies, ranging from rival members of the royal family to unhappy taxpayers to the hordes of mounted pastoralists who

sometimes did indeed emerge from the wild lands to storm the walls of cities.

The biggest threat, though, came from other cities. As places like Uruk grew, they reached ever further into the countryside to feed their populations, thus increasing the likelihood that they would impinge upon the territories of other urbanizing settlements. Rival god-monarchs responded to these threats by building their own glorious monuments and fearsome ramparts and by waging their own campaigns of conquest, sometimes unifying large numbers of cities under the control of a single empire.

In this way, governments and their priestly castes did something else completely new in world history: they began to diffuse urban segregation over large distances. First, the ziggurats in the southern Mesopotamian region of Sumer grew more numerous, taller, and more fearsome (the one at Ur was dubbed the "house whose foundation platform is clad in terror"). Then they spread northward and westward into the Fertile Crescent. In Nineveh, for example, the Assyrian emperor Senacherib built a "palace without rival" (700 BCE). A century later the Babylonian emperor Nebuchadrezzar countered with a massive two-tiered ziggurat for Marduk that he called the Foundation of Heaven and Earth and that we call the Tower of Babel. In the meantime, these ancient structures helped inspire other monumental markers of urban division further afield—the Pharaonic sanctuaries of Egyptian cities; the acropolises of Persia, Asia Minor, and Greece; and Rome's Temple of Jupiter on the Capitoline Hill. Of all direct descendants of the ziggurat, the most important for subsequent world history was the one built sometime around 950 BCE on Jerusalem's Mount Zion by King Solomon of the small, unified kingdom of Israel and Judah. It housed a royal palace and a temple to the biblical god Yahweh. Mount Zion was destined to become a monumental urban sanctuary for all three of the world's most powerful monotheistic faiths: Judaism, Christianity, and Islam.[9]

As monumental segregation spread outward from Sumer, similar political dramas began in other less closely connected parts of the world. These new traditions of monumental segregation radiated outward across large regions, in a few cases intersecting with others radiating from somewhere else. The somewhat less fearsomely divided cities in the Indus-Saraswati valleys of today's Pakistan, which date from after 2600 BCE and which include Mohenjo-Daro and Harappa, traded with contemporary Mesopotamian cities and may have imported some aspects of Sumerian urban politics. The cities of sub-Saharan Africa's first urban civilizations, such as Kerma, Meroë, and Napata, which arose in the Middle Nile Valley after 2200 BCE, almost certainly influenced the urban practices of the pharoahs of Egypt.[10]

By contrast, the first sacropolitical districts that developed later in cities elsewhere in Africa—such as Ile-Ife, the "navel of the universe," in West Africa (500 to 800 CE) or the stone palaces at Great Zimbabwe and elsewhere in southern Africa (1000 to 1500 CE)—developed in relative isolation from outside influence. So did the much older cities of the Americas, such as Caral in today's Peru (2600 BCE), from which exclusive districts devoted to the exaltation and propitiation of the gods traveled northward to Mesoamerica, culminating in the great city of Teotihuacán, which later influenced the many monumental cities of the Maya, and the Aztec capital of Tenochtitlan, on the site of today's Mexico City.[11]

Meanwhile, a similarly independent tradition of monumental city-building began in China under the Shang dynasty after 2000 BCE. There, cosmologists wrote the earliest extant tracts of urban planning, the most famous of which is known as the *Chou li*. Its authors insisted that the emperor live in a central, walled "Forbidden" or "Imperial City," and that the rest of the city should be enclosed with a larger, square-shaped, walled perimeter precisely oriented to the points of the compass. This basic form, with some variations, provided the models of dynastic capitals throughout three millennia of Chinese history, culminating in medieval Peking (Beijing) after 1421 CE. Similar patterns of urban division spread to Korea, Japan, and what we now call Vietnam.[12]

In Southeast Asia, Chinese traditions overlapped with the more diverse traditions of monumental architecture that had arisen meanwhile in India. The Hindu epic *Mahabharata* extols ancient Indraprashtra—the city of Indra, the god of war and storms, probably located within the city limits of today's Delhi—for "walls reaching high to the heavens" and "gateways looking like clouds and as high as the Mandara mountain." Delhi's subsequent sovereigns, whether they were Hindu, Buddhist, Persian, Muslim, or Afghan, always seemed bent on building their own monumental Indraprashtra, each in a different section of the same area on the banks of the Yamuna River. The Mughal emperor Shah Jahan outdid all of them in the seventeenth century when he crowned his version of Delhi—which he called Shahjahanabad—with the giant Red Fort. Similar monumentality can be found in cities across India. But the most impressive capital of any line of Hindu and Buddhist emperors was undoubtedly Angkor, in today's Cambodia. The city's soaring lotus towers, festooned with intricate gilded carvings, were meant to evoke the mountains where the Hindu gods were thought to dwell.[13]

Most of the world's largest empires seem to have found urban monumentality and its attendant politics of urban division an irresistible means of expressing their power. But the spread of segregation was not a foregone conclusion. In some places alternative possibilities arose, at least for a time. Within Muslim culture, for example, a strong strain of more modest, open, and egalitarian urban imagination held sway at different periods that oriented cities around the mosque, a place where all could worship and where the ruler was bound to hear the complaints of his subjects. As Islam expanded across three continents, however, the caliphs increasingly resorted to urban expressions of their might, building monumental cities in places like Baghdad, Cairo, Istanbul, Algiers, Fez, Rabat, and Cordoba.[14]

In Europe, Germanic invaders sacked many of the cities of the Roman Empire, and monumental architecture disappeared during the so-called Dark Ages. When it reemerged, authorities built sacred monuments like the cathedral and political monuments like the lord's castle-fort apart, in uneasy rivalry with one another. During the Crusades, this architectural rivalry diminished as Christian warriors built fearsome hilltop fortresses in the areas of the Holy Land they conquered. These *citadella* (little cities) later appeared in greater numbers across war-torn early modern Europe. When Europeans expanded into the Americas and around Africa to Asia, they brought their mania for citadels with them, to places as far afield as El Morro of San Juan, Puerto Rico; the high fort of Quebec City; the gold and slave-trading forts of West Africa; and the walled European districts of the colonial towns of Asia—Spanish Manila, Dutch Batavia (on Java), and British Madras. There, officials unified the political and sacred once again—at least in name—for they often called their severe walled districts the "Christian Town."[15]

## Segregating Strangers

The officials in these European colonial cities were merchants who had traveled far from home. The separate districts they built for themselves in Africa and Asia represented variations on another ancient tradition of urban politics: the practice of segregating strangers. As historian Philip

Curtin explains, separate urban "colonies" of foreign merchants and moneylenders are "one of the most widespread of human institutions," continually created and re-created across "the long period of history that began with the invention of agriculture and ended with the coming of the industrial age."[16]

The wide spread of urban mercantile districts was a product of the uneasy relationship between merchants and monarchs. Merchants' wealth could rival that of monarchs, but monarchs also depended on merchants—as wealthy taxpayers, as sources of loaned money and luxury items from abroad, and as conveyors of tribute from far-off places. For their part, merchants relied on rulers for protection, and were willing to pay to acquire it. Because disputes over protection deals arose constantly, it behooved monarchs to stack their cities' political decks in their royal favor by stoking popular mistrust, if not outright contempt, of merchants. All of the world's cultures contain seams of antimercantile sentiment, most often based on the idea that merchants were unproductive members of society who leeched off others' work. Foreign merchants were even easier targets than local ones, and they made great scapegoats for local problems, allowing rulers to deflect criticism from their own rule and consolidate their power in times of crisis. However, violence against foreign merchants could also arise spontaneously, threatening the monarch's grip on the social order. To give themselves a lever against such passions, monarchs often forced foreigners to live separately from the rest of the city's inhabitants. For their part, merchants themselves often asked rulers for the right to wall off a separate district as part of their protection deals. The political dramas involved thus contained a highly ambiguous mix of coercion and consent. As such, their plotlines varied and changed over time and place.

The origins of foreign merchant districts may date back to residential neighborhoods archaeologists have unearthed near the port areas of Sumer's river cities. Harappa and other ancient cities had spaces outside the walls that might have been caravanserais—resting places for cross-desert traders. Later, after 1850 BCE, we know that a group of Assyrian merchants known as the *kārum*, or "the wharf," lived in their own section of town in the Anatolian city of Kanesh. There, for the first time, sources give us an inkling of the forceful politics involved: authorities at Kanesh obliged all arriving merchants to pass through the palace before heading to the *kārum*, so they could guarantee payment of protection money.[17]

Cities throughout the ancient eastern Mediterranean set aside way stations or inns for merchants, first referred to in the Bible as the *pandocheion*, a Greek word meaning "accepting all comers." Arab rulers translated the word as *funduq* for a similar institution; the Byzantines called it the *foundax*; and after about 1100 CE Italian merchants translated it once again as *fondaco*. In the process, the institution itself spread across the Mediterranean and became gradually more elaborate. In medieval Alexandria, for example, the Venetian and Genoese *fondachi* consisted of entire neighborhoods of warehouses, bathhouses, Christian churches, special ovens that were not subject to Islamic regulations on the preparation of food, and brothels. Local Islamic authorities first acceded to the Venetians' demand to be in charge of the key to the gates of their own *funduq*, but by the late Middle Ages, local officials had retrieved the key and hired a guard to open and close the gate from the outside. A welcoming home away from home thus took on the trappings of a nighttime semiprison. In Constantinople, Byzantine authorities locked Arab, Jewish, Venetian, Genoese, Pisan, and Greek merchants into gated quarters called the *mitaton* in Pera, north of the Golden Horn (as the city's famous harbor is called) and once massacred all of its inhabitants. During the Fourth Crusade (1204) the Italians took revenge, sacking the city and setting fire to the Jewish and Muslim *mitaton*. The Genoese took over Pera (or Galata, as they called it), ruling it themselves as an independent city-state long after the Byzantines returned to power, and the Venetians moved into the walled city proper, assuming an important role in the Byzantine court. After 1453, when the Ottoman Turks took the city, the Italians once again negotiated for advantageous separate residences in Muslim Istanbul.[18]

In Persia, the Savafid Shah Abbas the Great laid waste to Julfa, the capital of Armenia, as part of a campaign against Muslim rivals. But he later allowed homeless Armenian merchants to settle outside the wall of his capital Isfahan, where they founded a Christian city they called New Julfa. Later, European merchants secured separate enclaves in Persian cities, establishing their own sub-enclaves in New Julfa. The Armenians used their position at New Julfa to run a loose mercantile empire that stretched from Europe to China and that later rivaled the Europeans in some parts of India.[19]

In China, Confucian doctrine was especially contemptuous of merchants, and the *Chou li* counseled rulers to place marketplaces in the least favored parts of the city. But overseas merchants poured into China, most notably into the southern port of Canton (Guangzhou), where officials confined Arabs, Armenians, Jews, Persians, and South Asians to a quarters called the *fanfang* between the sounding of the sunset and noon drums. Authorities in the more trade-friendly port cities of Southeast Asia developed a tradition of setting aside separate *kampungs*, or "villages," for dozens of merchant communities from all over Asia. Similar neighborhoods existed all along the coast of India. Sometimes foreign merchants used their separate district as source of considerable influence in local affairs. When, in 758 CE, the Arab merchants of Canton did not get their way in negotiations with local authorities, they burst out of the *fanfang*, sacked the city, and seized its riches. The Muslim traders of Calicut in India dominated the politics of the town.[20]

Meanwhile, West African commercial cities like Kumbi-Saleh, Mali, Djenné, Gao, and Timbuktu were often divided into a royal town and a merchant town. The Hausa of what today is northern Nigeria established separate wards for foreign merchants called the *Sabon Gari* or *zongos*, and they later established *zongos* for themselves in cities across West Africa. There, policies toward foreign-merchant enclaves were embroiled in the complex process by which some rulers adopted parts of Islamic teaching and others rejected it as potentially subversive to their rule. At Kumbi-Saleh, the Ghanaian king ordered Muslim merchants to settle six miles out of town; elsewhere, such as in Timbuktu, Muslims were welcomed with more open arms.[21]

For the subsequent history of racial segregation, perhaps the most important variation on the politics of the foreign-merchant quarters came into being when the foreigners themselves simply seized control of the overseas cities where they did business. The Phoenicians and Greeks had accomplished this feat in ancient times by conquering colonial cities elsewhere in the Mediterranean or by founding new overseas port towns themselves. Later the Venetians and the Genoese established similar colonial cities on Cyprus and in the Black Sea. Constantinople's Galata was only one of many urban enclave colonies of the Genoese empire. But it was the English conquerors and settlers of Ireland who set the most important medieval precedents of this sort. English practices of discrimination against the Irish were more virulent—and more focused on physical and cultural separation—than anywhere within Christian Europe. The infamous Statutes of Kilkenny of 1366 made it illegal for English people to marry, foster, or be godparents to Irish people and prohibited settlers from speaking Irish or adopting distinctive Irish clothing and hairstyles. In the 1400s, the English king ordered farmers to plow some seventy miles of earthworks around the entire English-speaking hinterland of Dublin to keep the "wild Irish" out of what was soon called "the Pale"— from the Latin world *palus*, or stake. English merchants also built some divided port towns. Limerick, for example, had two sections, divided by the Abbey River: the Englishtown and the Irishtown. Later, during the 1500s and 1600s, the Tudor and Stuart monarchs completed the conquest of Ireland, now in the name of spreading Protestant power in a bastion of Catholicism. Embarking on what amounted to an early large-scale project of demographic engineering, English monarchs encouraged Protestant settlers to displace Catholics on the island's most fertile land. They also ordered settlers to wall numerous Irish towns—most notably Derry and Belfast in the heavily Protestant northern province of Ulster—and for a while even forbade Catholics from living in any of the island's cities. The fortified Castle in Dublin, meanwhile, became the monumental political-religious symbol of Britain's harsh grip on Ireland.[22]

In these European overseas colonies, new concepts of difference arose that justified the link between dominance over strangers and their physical separation. Western overseas-merchant communities and their hosts alike had often used the words "nation" and "people" (*gente or jente*) to describe their distinct origins. Both words derived from Latin concepts related to birth (*natus* and *gens*), and they were often linked to biblical ideas about kinship and ancestry such as seed and blood. Those eager to sow contempt for foreign merchants or colonized peoples could thus rely on at least a hazy sense that strange customs or religious practices were grounded in innate and sometimes even subhuman physical differences. English separation decrees in medieval Ireland also took some of their force from a contrasting idea, that settlers' proximity to Irish "barbarians" tempted them to adopt customs that could only result in moral "decay." Variations on both of these strands of thought would later enter into the modern concept of race. Meanwhile, Europeans (most notably the British) took the related practices of migration engineering, native dispossession, and urban division with them when they set their imperial ambitions on the Americas and the trade routes to the East. As such, the separation of "nations" and "peoples" was the most direct conceptual forerunner of urban separation of colors and races.[23]

## Scapegoat Ghettos

Another crucial concept to arise from practices of stranger segregation was the word "ghetto." Though it was not coined until 1516 by the
Venetians to designate a coerced section of town for the city's Jews, the
history of religious-based segregation had much earlier roots that were
tied to conflicts going back to the biblical Holy Land. At stake was the
rise of religious faiths based on worship of a single god. This spiritual
innovation often provoked harsh responses from ancient polytheistic
god-kings. Later on, seismic frictions developed between the three great
monotheistic faiths themselves, the adherents of which often congregated in the same cities. Throughout the ebb and flow of these conflicts,
representatives of rival religious camps never shared the very top position of power in any city. But ruling urban religious communities did
sometimes negotiate a subordinate status for their rivals that allowed
for some autonomy and periods of peaceful coexistence. Residential segregation, involving varying degrees of coercion, could be part of those
deals. When agreements broke down, however, dominant religious communities sometimes subjected their rivals to long periods of forced expulsion, and sometimes to orgies of mass killing.

Jerusalem—the city of Mount Zion, where many believed the god Yahweh subjected Abraham to his famous biblical test of faith—was the most
fraught urban stage for these changing dramas. The epic began in the
early sixth century BCE, when the Babylonian emperor Nebuchadrezzar overran Mount Zion and destroyed Solomon's temple to Yahweh. To
keep a closer eye on the rebellious Judean elites, he moved them (along
with their weapon makers) to Babylon. There, they lived in several parts
of Marduk's city, though many settled permanently in a neighborhood
called Tel Aviv. When King Cyrus of Persia conquered Babylon and
ended the exile, some Jews returned to Jerusalem, soon to rebuild their
temple on Mount Zion. There, the kings Nehemiah and Ezra for a time
transformed the old capital into a more exclusively Jewish enclave. This
contrasted with the more cosmopolitan visions elsewhere in the ancient
world, including that of Cyrus's successors in Babylon and that of the
Greek Ptolemaic pharaohs of Egypt, who allowed a large Jewish community to live throughout the capital city of Alexandria and enjoy considerable privileges.[24]

When Rome conquered the eastern Mediterranean, tolerance eroded and the Jewish kingdoms were crushed. In 39 CE, Alexandria's gentile majority turned against the Jews, fearing that worship of a single God threatened the cult of the Roman emperor Caligula. They stormed the city's Jewish households and synagogues, confiscating the community's wealth and forcing the refugees to live in a crowded and more starkly delineated enclave called Delta—arguably the world's first Jewish ghetto. A few years later, the Romans turned on Jerusalem, subduing two major Jewish revolts there. During the first campaign, in 70 CE, they destroyed King Herod's magnificent Second Temple on Mount Zion. After the second campaign, in 137 CE, they banned Jews from Jerusalem altogether.[25]

When the Roman emperors adopted Christianity in the fourth century CE, they renewed the decree banishing the Jews from Mount Zion. It was only annulled when the Muslim caliph 'Umar captured Jerusalem in 638. The Muslims built the Dome of the Rock and the Al-Aqsa Mosque on Mount Zion and renamed it the Haram-al-Sharif, both in recognition of Islam's reverence for the god of Abraham and to sanctify the destination of the prophet Mohammad's dreamlike voyage to Jerusalem to meet Allah. However, 'Umar allowed both Jews and Christians to live in the city as subordinate but semiautonomous citizens, and a long period of relatively peaceful coexistence ensued. Then, in 1099, Christian crusaders stormed the city, interrupting the Islamic peace. They slaughtered the city's Muslim and Jews and refashioned the Dome of the Rock as a Christian "Temple of the Lord." When Saladin reconquered Jerusalem in 1187, he restored the Haram-al-Sharif as a Muslim shrine. He famously desisted, however, from his original plan to exact murderous revenge upon the city's Christians. For the next eight hundred years, until the dawn of the twentieth century, all three faiths lived together within the city walls under Muslim leadership, each occupying a separate quarter whose boundaries changed and varied in exclusivity over time.[26]

Jerusalem's religious politics mirrored broad patterns that played out in other cities of the Mediterranean and Europe. Muslim rulers tended to be most welcoming of fellow monotheists; Christians grew increasingly intolerant; and the world's many diverse communities of Jews almost always had to negotiate some kind of subordinate status, often in a separate zone of the city. The most important medieval stages for these politics were Spain and Portugal, which were home to Europe's oldest Islamic emirates, Christendom's most fervent crusader kings, and the largest Jewish population in the medieval world.

For many centuries, Christian kings on the Iberian Peninsula followed the example of neighboring Muslim rulers, committing themselves to a policy of *convivencia* or "cohabitation" between the major faiths. Even when the crusaders destroyed Jewish communities elsewhere in Europe on their way to Jerusalem, Spanish Jews were allowed to prosper, often by agreeing to live in secure, separate zones called *aljamas* in Muslim towns and *juderías* in Christian ones. In the countryside, Jews also sometimes lived in separate villages.[27]

*Convivencia* began to unravel in the 1300s, when Spain and Portugal became flashpoints for Catholic extremism. Conspiracy theories spread about the role of Jews in the Black Death, and Iberia's Christian monarchs fanned crusading passions for a *reconquista* of Muslim territories in the south. Firebrand preachers raised latent suspicions about Jews' power and wealth and about their role in the crucifixion of Christ. In 1391, mobs burned down the large, well-fortified *judería* of Seville, unleashing terrible massacres of Jews across Spain. Local authorities throughout the country forced Jews to shave their beards and wear special costumes, and they tightly restricted Jews' use of urban space. They prohibited Jewish ownership of real estate, even in the *juderías*, and Jewish landowners had to sell at ruinous prices.[28]

The idea was to make life so intolerable that Jews would leave Iberia or convert. Some did leave and many others converted in fear for their lives, but as the number of formerly Jewish *conversos* grew, scapegoat politics became even more vicious. Christians doubted the sincerity of the *conversos'* piety, and their status as Christians opened them to persecution by the Spanish Inquisition, which often branded them "Judaizing" heretics. To prove their piety, *conversos* often stepped up as leaders of the persecution of the Jews, sometimes with the help of Christian Spanish grandees of part-Jewish heritage who wished to escape the taint of Jewish "blood." Jews then defended themselves by trumping up charges of heresy against the *conversos* in the Inquisition's courts. Meanwhile, Queen Isabella's war against Muslim Granada drained her treasury and forced her to seek favor with often fiercely anti-Jewish local authorities. Her lingering commitment to *convivencia* collapsed after the Jews of Toledo were accused of ritually murdering a young Christian child, and anti-Jewish violence once again raged across the country. In 1492, as Granada fell, Isabella and Ferdinand of Aragon celebrated the unification of a powerful Catholic Spanish kingdom by permanently expelling the Jews from their realms, claiming that Jews would ever tempt the *conversos* into impiety if they remained. That year, the wharves of Cadiz were so crowded with

Jews boarding ships for safer havens that Christopher Columbus had to delay setting out on his westward voyage to China.[29]

In Spain, and shortly afterward in Portugal, the politics of scapegoating Jews meant the end of urban segregation. By contrast, in Venice, scapegoating and segregation found a much more subtle, if still nefarious, common cause. The Jews of Venice, like those in most of the European cities that allowed Jewish communities to exist, were limited by law to commercial pursuits and moneylending, a pursuit that was technically forbidden to Christians as sinful. Venice depended heavily on money borrowed from Jews to finance its mercantile ventures, and Jews were ordered to operate pawnshops and issue low-interest loans to keep the poorest Venetians afloat financially. "The Jews," one of the city's oligarchs opined (more honestly than most), became "as necessary as bakers in a town."[30]

Under pressure from some of the same anti-Jewish mania that had

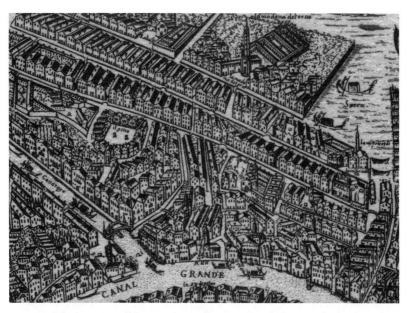

FIGURE I.2 "The Jews must all live together in the Ghetto." With these words, the oligarchs of the Most Serene Republic of Venice decided in 1516 to crowd the city's Jews into a separate quarter surrounded by walls and canals. Segregation gave the oligarchs a convenient scapegoat for the city's problems. As such, the ghetto represented a new twist on ancient traditions of separate districts for cities' foreign residents. Source: Giovanni Merlo, *Pianta prospettiva della città*, from *Piante e Vedute Prospecttiche di Venezia (1479–1855)*, by Giocondo Cassini (Venice: Stamperia di Venezia, 1982), 116–17.

35

spread across Spain, the Venetian Republic twice expelled Jews from the city in the late fifteenth century. However, the city's gentile merchants and the poor suffered from this policy, and in a momentous decree of March 29, 1516, Venice officially forswore expulsion and embraced separation. Jews could live in the city, proclaimed the city council, but they "must all live together in the Ghetto near San Girolamo, and in order to prevent their roaming about at night: Let there be built two gates, on the side of the Old Ghetto where there is a little Bridge, and likewise on the other side of the bridge, . . . which gates shall be opened in the morning at the sound of the Marangona [the bell of Saint Mark's Cathedral] and shall be closed by four Christian guards appointed and paid by the Jews." The ghetto, named after the neighborhood's abandoned cannon foundry or *gietto*, lay on an island surrounded by several of Venice's famous canals. Later, authorities walled off an adjacent neighborhood and added it to the ghetto. To get through its gate, Jews had to pass through a tunnel under one of the buildings that was so low they were forced to bow down to the Christian city as they emerged. Four patrol boats, also paid for by the Jews, were supposed to ply the waters of the surrounding canals at all times. Once in town, all Jews were supposed to wear a yellow badge to distinguish themselves, and later a yellow hat.[31]

To be useful as long-term scapegoats, Jews had to be present, visible, active in society, and in some way appear ridiculous—all of that in addition to being walled up at night. The act of Jew-blaming became nothing less than a central keystone to the Most Serene Republic's social order. Any threat to the ruling oligarchy from below could be redirected against the supposedly bloodsucking, corrupt, anti-Christian, and even hyper-sexed inhabitants of the ghetto, who, on their best days, also doubled as hated creditors to thousands of poor people.

Jewish writers, it is important to note, did often call for self-separation as a way to preserve the purity of the community's religious beliefs. Despite the hostile climate, the Ghetto of Venice prospered and became an enviable center of learning, like some of the more fortunate foreign merchant districts elsewhere in the world. In addition, at about the same time that Venice created its Jewish ghetto, the city's oligarchy also locked the Muslim Turks and other Christian foreigners into separate *fondacchi*, and the city occasionally convulsed in hatred against these groups.[32]

Still, though, in early modern Western Europe, threats of expulsion and even annihilation generally hung more heavily about the necks of Jews than other segregated foreign communities. We need to remember that even when Jews appeared to accept ghettoization, it was only in a universe of alternative "choices" with consequences direr than cultural dilution alone. In 1555, the fiercely anti-Jewish Pope Paul IV decided, after much harrumphing about expulsion, that Rome's Jews could remain in the very capital of Christendom, but his ghetto was much more miserable than the one in Venice. Prague had a walled Jewish section as early as the thirteenth century—the burgomaster possessed a massive gilded chain to close the neighborhood down, if necessary. From the fifteenth century on, Frankfurt consigned its Jews to a tiny *Judengasse* (Jew alley) in the shadows of its outer walls. The neighborhood's three thousand inhabitants made it "surely the most densely populated district in the world." A demeaning set of laws called the Stättigkeit subjected Jews to even more picayune humiliations than those in Venice. In Hamburg and Amsterdam, the Jewish alleys were somewhat more privileged than elsewhere, but in Vienna, a seventeenth-century Austrian emperor decided summarily to expel the population of the city's prosperous Jewish ghetto.[33]

In the years after the Spanish expulsions, the world's largest Jewish communities lived in Eastern Europe. In the Commonwealth of Poland and Lithuania, Jewish communities differed in two major respects from those who lived further west. Most lived in small towns know as *shtetlekh* (the plural form of *shtetl*) spread throughout the countryside, and Jews spoke their own language, Yiddish, rather than adopting the language of local Christians. Nonetheless, Jews lived in relative peace in the *shtetlekh*, which often had majority Jewish populations but were not officially segregated. Some Eastern European Jews lived in larger cities, also with few restrictions.[34]

In the late 1700s, Europe's momentous democratic political revolutions suddenly reversed the geography of Christian Europe's regard for the Jews, at once spawning more tolerance in the West and increasingly violent hatred in the East. In Western Europe, the Enlightenment gave rise to ambiguous calls for religious tolerance and equal rights for Jews. When the French revolutionary armies reached Venice in 1797, flying wild banners of secularism and the universal rights of man, one of their first acts was to declare the Jews emancipated. Soldiers ripped the ghetto's gate from its three-hundred-year-old hinges. A few years later, the revolutionary emperor Napoleon Bonaparte's General Jourdan bombed the wall at one end of Frankfurt's crowded *Judengasse*. Within a few decades, most other ghettos elsewhere ceased to be, and though bursts of hostility continued, officials in countries that had once expelled the Jews now allowed small emancipated communities to grow in their midst.[35]

Clouds of foreboding, however, descended across the *stetlekh* of Eastern Europe at almost exactly the same time. From 1772 to 1795, the fiercely antirevolutionary monarchies of Prussia, Austria, and Russia conspired to rip Poland-Lithuania to pieces. Russia gobbled up the biggest haunch of territory, which also encompassed the largest number of Jewish inhabitants. In 1835, to forestall commercial competition with Russians, Tsar Nicholas I confined Jews to a "Pale of Settlement," a wide corridor of western Russian territory stretching from the Baltic to the Black Sea. In the Pale, Jews continued to live alongside Russians and other Christians, but some cities were also declared off-limits to Jews, and others settled in loosely defined separate zones of cities like Vilnius, Warsaw, and the culturally diverse Black Sea port of Odessa. In Odessa, most Jews lived near an old overseas Greek community. Each year, during Holy Week, when the Greeks and other Christians ritually relived the passion of Christ, resentment against the descendants of his supposed Jewish killers arose, sometimes explosively. The first of the notorious anti-Jewish *pogroms*—a Russian word with the same root as the word for "thunder" and usually translated as "destruction" or "devastation"—raged in Odessa in 1821, followed by even more destructive anti-Jewish riots there in 1849, 1859, and 1871. In 1881, when a small group of revolutionaries assassinated Tsar Alexander II, rumors abounded in Odessa and elsewhere that the new Tsar had given license for violence against Jews, and soon hundreds of pogroms thundered across the southern Pale, usually starting in larger cities and radiating out along new rail lines into the *shtetlekh*.

Another even severer storm of pogroms crested during the years 1903 to 1906. Despite a spirited defense of Jewish communities by the armed worker's party known as the *Bund*, over three thousand Jews were killed, most savagely in the cities of Kishinev, Kiev, and, once again, Odessa. Still thousands more would die in pogroms during the civil war that followed the Russian Revolution of 1917, when the Bolsheviks officially abolished the Pale.[36]

Already in 1905, the politics of the pogroms had taken a new and ominous turn. That year, anti-Jewish activists had published the incendiary *Protocols of the Elders of Zion*, a document that passed itself off as a call for a Jewish conspiracy to dominate the world. The *Protocols* raised scapegoating politics to a new level at a moment when Europeans across the continent were reinventing religious-based anti-Jewish thought in secular form, bringing the racist ideology of anti-Semitism into being. This ideological shift presaged more horrific forms of segregation and expulsion, culminating in Adolf Hitler's plan to exterminate all Europe's Jews. The more general act of combining racial and national ideology with religious and sectarian rivalry continues to cast a pall over urban and world politics today.

## Quarters for Classes, Crafts, Clans, Castes, and the Sexes

Underlying both the ancient politics of monumental city-splitting and the separation of strangers and scapegoats were more elemental forces of social division: those of class, craft, clan, caste, and sex. All of these social cleavages also had wider, if usually ambiguous, effects on the politics of urban segregation by color and race in the modern era.

The story of class segregation—defined broadly as the impulse to separate those with power over a society's economic resources from those with little power over those resources—is the most complex and widespread of these dramas and is connected to all the others. Sacropolitical districts, city walls, merchants' quarters, and scapegoat ghettos all contain elements of class segregation. Inequalities of wealth in early modern cities were, after all, staggering. In many places, laws forbade anyone but aristocrats from owning land, and the wealthy often signaled their status by living in the best-ventilated, poshest parts of town, often nearest the temple or palace, and by erecting ostentatious (if smaller) copies of the palace. The housing for the poor, meanwhile, was often self-built, unsanitary, sometimes piled high in tenements, and a sure enabler of disease and early death. The unluckiest of all lived in shanties beyond the walls, amid the noxious smells of leather tanners, cloth dyers, and the renderers of livestock fat. In a few cities dating as early as ancient Egypt, large-scale employers built separate workers' villages in cities designed to control their workforces. Meanwhile sumptuary laws, which decreed the kinds of clothes and personal adornments deemed appropriate to different ranks of people, could be found in just about all the world's major premodern civilizations; outlandish clothing was not reserved for Jews alone. These laws aimed precisely to highlight class distinctions and make social hierarchies more visible and legible in the anonymous hubbub of urban life.[37]

On the other hand, plenty of evidence also exists that class lines in urban neighborhoods could just as often be poorly marked and quite permeable. In fact, some cities' richest residents often actually tolerated, even preferred, to live alongside the poorest. For example, on the Palatine Hill, Rome's richest neighborhood (it gave us the word "palace," after all), it was commonplace for an opulent Roman *domus* to share a city block with countless tiny one-room flats, bakeries, artisan shops, and even a few of the city's many wine shops and brothels. In a city where most people walked or got around by sedan chair, elite control over the city's resources could mean insisting on having such shops close at hand. In the words of Marcus Tullius Cicero, the most famous observer of Roman streets, "there is no baker or cellar at home; the bread is from the bakery, the wine from a wineshop."[38]

Wealthy people's speculation in land could also just as easily create forms of class "integration" as segregation. This was the case of the most common structure in ancient Rome, the five-story apartment buildings known as *insulae*. To make these buildings pay, owners of *insulae* typically rented the lower floors to wealthier people and the less convenient upper stories to poorer tenants. Trash and human waste from the upper floors would often rain down past the posh lower-story windows on its way to the street; noise and stench abounded, yet this was all part of the urban ambience the rich shared with the poor.

Rich people's pursuit of class prestige could also lead to neighborhood integration. One sign of status was being surrounded by large numbers of lower-status clients, flatterers, and servants. Wealthy patrons often saw to it that such a retinue lived close by. In Rome, they typically allowed their clients to enter the *domus* at will; they even set aside public sections of their homes specifically to cement these cross-class relationships. The most important violation of residential class lines, though, arose because of wealthy people's desire to control another crucial economic resource—the labor of personal servants. The *domus*, like aristocratic households across the world well into our own times, functioned as kind of factory producing leisure and pleasure for the rich. Aristocrats typically lived with dozens of their social inferiors: cooks, gardeners, personal guards, musicians, dancers, and other specialized servants, most of whom were slaves. Though the slave quarters in Roman households were usually shunted to outer corridors, few doors or gates—if any—separated them from the most intimate spaces of the elite family.[39]

Efforts to control economic resources could thus just as easily lead to

residential class integration as segregation. Moreover, other lines of social cleavage could further complicate the picture. One was rich people's
desire for occasional relief from the rough-and-tumble ambience of the
city. The rich have always been able to afford second houses on the urban
fringe, most often at a distance from the smellier industries and shantytowns they also relegated beyond the walls. The anonymous Babylonian
who expressed his love for the suburbs on a clay tablet in 532 BCE sounds
uncannily close to us in time: "our property seems to be the most beautiful in the world. It is so close to Babylon that we enjoy all the advantages
of the city, and yet when we come home we are away from all the noise
and dust." It was Cicero himself who coined the term *suburbium*; his and
other rich people's second villas dotted the countryside around Rome, as
around many other large cities across the world. The processions of clients and slaves that accompanied their Roman patrons on suburban holi-
days admittedly guaranteed only an ambiguous degree of increased class
segregation. However, when the wealthy residents of late seventeenth-
century London organized world history's first concerted movement to
create a legally bounded class-exclusive residential district, they located
it on a swath of land in the suburbs—the West End—not one within their
local version of the monumental, wall-protected downtown.[40]

The politics of craft, clan, caste, and sex, meanwhile, could push and
pull the spatial politics of class in even more contradictory directions.
Most well known is the tendency of people working in different artisanal pursuits to clump together on separate streets, many of which still
have names associated with those crafts today. Historians have expressed
some skepticism about how long any one of these streets ever had majorities of their eponymous craftspeople. However, artisans' attempts to
secure control over their economic pursuits did sometimes mean that
their guildhalls were located on the appropriately named street, and
some guilds regulated the conduct of business on their streets. To this
day there are some types of business that do best when competitors for
the same market concentrate their shops in the same part of town.[41]

In cities where the politics of clan determined residence, class lines
melted further into ambiguity than elsewhere. In West Africa's Yorubaland, for example, the streets that radiated from the central palace of
the *oba* (king) divided cities into wedge-shaped districts occupied by the
sprawling compounds of separate lineage groups. Wealthier members of
the lineage showed their prominence precisely by offering their less for-

tunate kin economic sustenance, which included making space for them in the compound. Certain lineages were more privileged than others, and their quarters may have reflected that difference to some degree. But even the heart of the city, the area around the palace of the *oba*, was kept largely free of concentrations of wealthier people, as the *oba*'s kin group was forbidden to enjoy the riches or status his office gave him.[42]

By contrast, the politics of caste as practiced in parts of India and other Hindu societies may have tightened class boundaries somewhat. Caste politics arose in ancient times, probably when the religious idea of *varna* fused with a clan-based social category, *jati*. *Varna*, sometimes confusingly translated as "color," more accurately denotes people's capacity for ritual purity in relation to the gods. The three upper *varnas*, or "castes," of Indian society were purest in their devotion—the Brahmans (priests) were the purest of all, followed by the *Kshatriyas* (rulers and warriors), and the *Vaishyas* (landholders and merchants). Lower castes, or *Shudras*, were often deemed completely incapable of ritual purity. Outcastes, or untouchables, were deemed an unspeakable source of pollution. The idea of *jati*, or "birth," may have originally referred to the clan ties of early Indian society, but it may also have helped to fix one's level of ritual purity as an inherited trait. *Jati* also doubled as a word for the multitudes of subcastes within each *varna*, usually defined by separate craft and occupational groups, also seen as determined by birth.[43]

Since members of upper castes had to avoid contact with lower castes to avoid pollution, *varna* and *jati* required spatial separateness. Even the shadow of an impure person passing over the path of a Brahmin could touch off elaborate rituals of cleansing; upper castes were often forbidden from breaking bread with people lower in the caste hierarchy, and intermarriage was anathema. One text on caste from 300 BCE offers precise advice to the king on how to separate the city into various caste neighborhoods, and in many places, the caste leaders, or *panchayats*, would negotiate with the ruler for separate neighborhoods, among other privileges.

That said, premodern Indian society never had anything approaching a single caste system. Hundreds of local traditions of *varna* and *jati* existed across the vast subcontinent. Caste could be just as difficult to ascertain in the anonymous space of the city as class. Migrants from other cities could further complicate the picture, as could wartime disruptions. Sex and marriage that transgressed taboos continuously created new caste subgroups. The *panchayats'* best-designed patterns of separation could succumb to the vagaries of housing markets. But to the extent that caste groups had connection to economic status, the dramas of caste politics represented a more thoroughgoing and explicit project of residential segregation by status and class than existed anywhere else in the early modern world.[44]

Residential segregation of the sexes also intersected with the politics of class in cities. The system of *purdah*—or the "curtain," which refers at once to the veiling of women, the provision of separate amenities for the sexes, and the confinement of women to separate zones of households—dates back to ancient Assyria and Babylon. Early and medieval Christian societies, including the Byzantine Empire, also practiced female sequestration and covering, as did the Portuguese in India well into the 1600s. Islamic societies adopted purdah during the Middle Ages, and it was within a long band stretching from North Africa to Southeast Asia that the sharpest forms of gender separation persisted into our own time. Purdah's most important consequence for urban residential separation was within the space of households, where women were often confined to separate apartments, known as the *harim* (harem) in Arabic-speaking areas and the *zenana* in South Asia. There is no record of efforts to create exclusively separate neighborhoods for men and women in cities, though the large *harim* within the Ottomans' Topkapi Palace in Istanbul comes close—it was home to the sultan's many dozens of imperial consorts.

The sultan's *harim* illustrates another point even better—that the domestic seclusion of women could also act as yet another ostentatious architectural mark of the divide between the classes in urban space. In that way, purdah reflects a bigger trend in the history of urban gender and class segregation. In all civilizations, the invention of cities seems to have coincided with a sharp increase in male domination of society, certainly in comparison to less hierarchical proto-urban settlements like Çatalhöyük. But the wealthy were most able to express that dominance spatially, by separating the public male-identified spaces of work and statecraft from private, female spaces centered above all on the home. For most ordinary city dwellers, by contrast, work and home were much less segregated. Men certainly ruled, but spatial boundaries between the sexes in most of the premodern world's urban markets, shops, and streets were less severely drawn.[45]

## Ancient and Medieval Legacies

In the vast, seventy-centuries-long course of urban politics, the three-hundred-year history of modern racial segregation represents but a blip in time. It was only after 1700 that Europeans injected the concepts of color and race into the political dramas of urban space.

When they did that, they began something new and unprecedented. The new politics reflected new sorts of planet-crossing connections, new institutions, new ideas, and even new practices of city-splitting.

No world historical change, however, obliterates all legacies of the past. As new as the concepts of color and race certainly were, they also drew heavily on old notions of birth, lineage, and "blood" that were linked to all the social categories of ancient and medieval societies. Balefully innovative as they were, racial segregationists also drew heavily on the logic of the sacropolitical district, the city wall, the stranger's district, and the ghetto. Like all forms of segregation, color and race segregation are inherently forms of class segregation, designed to supplement privileged groups' control over material resources. Today, national and religious segregation has fused itself with racial segregation in some places, with dismal effects.

Perhaps it was no coincidence, then, that segregation by color and race emerged in two Indian cities where wealthy people from the new suburban class-enclaves of London, accompanied by their less-advantaged but all-male British employees, built monumental walls around restricted foreign merchants' districts—which they first named "Christian Towns" and which they later supplemented with exclusive suburbs—all with the goal of separating themselves from local people who themselves practiced urban segregation based on premodern concepts of class, craft, clan, caste, and sex. It is time to see what happened in Madras and Calcutta, for new institutions, ideas, and city-splitting tools arose there amid political dramas that both hearkened back to earlier centuries and soon transformed urban politics the world over.

# PART TWO | COLOR AND RACE COME TO THE CITY

# 2 ⋮ White Town/Black Town

*Governor Pitt's Madras*

"The White Town." "The Black Town." To discover the first time some-one used these words in an official capacity, you have to hunt among the tiny houses, churches, streets, squares, and city walls that two surveyors painstakingly etched onto a 1711 woodcut map of Madras, today known as Chennai, in South India. The surveyors' orders came from the British governor of Madras himself, Thomas Pitt (the grandfather of the more famous William Pitt, the "Great Commoner"), and from Pitt's bosses, the court of directors of the East India Company in London. Take a glance at the map, and your eye is drawn to a fearsome stone wall at the heart of the city, bristling with miniature bastions, artillery points, and cannons. It surrounds White Town and divides it from Black Town, a less monu-mental but much larger part of the city.[1]

Why did such a city come into being? Some of the most ancient dra-mas of urban segregation are evident on Thomas Pitt's map. The monu-mental central district is there; so is the surrounding city wall; and White Town is a district for foreign merchants. But contemplate Madras a little longer, and revolutions wrought by two and a half centuries of European expansionism come into view. The foreigners run the place, not the lo-cals. Their mercantile enclave *is* the city's ziggurat. The walls look funny too. The strongest ones run around White Town; those that circle the rest of the city look like an afterthought, and indeed a big swath of Black Town is completely unwalled. Then there is the matter of color: Why have terms like "white" and "black"—which seem to have so little relationship to the gods or royal power, let alone the wealth of merchants—become so important?

In fact, the invention of White Town and Black Town required three

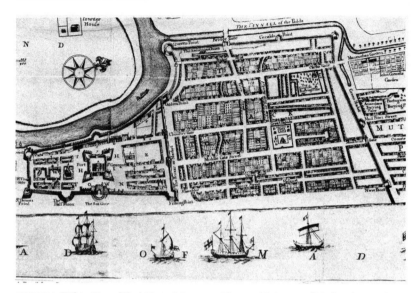

FIGURE 2.1 "White Town/Black Town." Governor Thomas Pitt's map of Madras (ca. 1711) illustrating the first explicit instance of a government-sanctioned urban color line. The older names for the districts, Christian Town and Gentue (Hindu) Town, have been replaced with names that demonstrate the rising importance of color designations to urban politics. From H. Davison Love, *Vestiges of Old Madras* (Government of India, 1913), vol. 1.

new dramas of urban politics, two of which spanned the hemispheres, and one that operated locally, within Madras itself.

The first hemisphere-sized story came from the West. In the Americas (and in a sort of echo at the Cape of Good Hope in South Africa), Europeans initially tried divided cities but abandoned the idea once they decided to import large numbers of African slaves (largely Asian ones at the Cape), who were instead obliged to live in the households of their masters. Over time, though, the rulers of these forcibly "integrated" slave cities found concepts like "black" and, later, "white" increasingly essential to sustaining their authority.

The second hemispheric drama played itself out along the sea routes from Europe to new Western colonial cities in the East. There, beginning in 1482, Europeans developed a lasting tradition of foreign-ruled divided cities—so lasting, in fact, that these cities would provide a model for the hundreds of segregated colonial cities that Western imperialists later built across the world in the 1800s and 1900s.

Then there was the local stage, Madras. There, East India Company officials connected the contrasting genres of urban politics from the two hemispheres. Essentially, they demonstrated for the first time how the politics of color from the Americas could be useful to divide a commercial city in the East. The increasing ties between Company officials in London and colonialists active in the Americas made this blending possible in Madras. But, ironically, it was local political concerns that compelled Madras officials to import color politics there. As we explore that story, we will need to keep our eyes at once on enormous, planet-spanning developments, starting with those in the Americas, and on more parochial changes affecting a single city in Southern India, its walls, neighborhoods—and even inside the little houses those surveyors painstakingly etched on Governor Pitt's map.

## The Rise and Fall of American (and South African) Segregation in Colonial Times

A few basic contexts distinguished the conquest of the Americas from colonialism in the East. First were the political contexts: formidable as Amerindian governments were, none was able to stop European conquest for long. Even the most technologically advanced empires of the Mexica (Aztecs) and Inca did not possess the iron weaponry, the horses, or the combination of sailing ships and printing presses that gave the Spanish conquistadors an unbeatable edge in war. Second were the demographic contexts: world history's worst-ever episodes of mass death followed on the heels of contact, since native peoples were isolated from the environmental factors that would have given them childhood immunity from diseases Europeans brought with them. In the aftermath of the disaster, Europeans settled in the Americas in much larger numbers than they ever would in the East, and they imported captive Africans in larger numbers as a labor force. Finally, there were the economic contexts: plantation slavery became the dominant means of exploiting the lands Europeans appropriated from native peoples in the Americas.

Upon the ruins of Mesoamerican and Andean cities, the Spaniards built brand-new palaces and cathedrals of their own, often using the remains of the magnificent pyramids of the native god-kings. In the port cities of the Caribbean islands and the Spanish Main—San Juan, Santo Domingo, Havana, Cartagena de las Indias—new cities went up that were completely surrounded by massive fortifications. Their walls hardened as soon as rival European nations began sending their own merchants

49

and—more famously—hired pirates into the same waters. Indigenous peoples in those places had no previous urban traditions, and their numbers declined so quickly that little was done in these cities to provide separate quarters for them.[2]

In the interior of New Spain, by contrast—at Mexico City, Oaxaca, Antigua, and many smaller cities—thousands of Mexican and Incan city dwellers survived conquest and disease. There, threats to Spain from other Europeans were less acute, and authorities dispensed with city walls. However, they fortified many of their houses in case of Indian revolt and established a system of urban separation for their conquered subjects. City officials forced local Amerindians into areas known as *reducciones* or *barrios*, far outside of the central gridiron of the *ciudad de españoles*—the Spanish city. In Lima, Peru, the Indian quarter was a fenced neighborhood inside the walled city known as El Cercado. The remaining Indian nobles, whom the Spaniards called *caciques*, were charged to look after the local secular affairs of these districts under a legal code designed exclusively for Indians.[3]

King Philip I of Spain himself took a keen interest in urban affairs in his New World colonies. In a 1573 decree, he made clear that he intended divided cities to act as keystones of his overseas empire: "[Spanish] settlers shall try as much as possible to avoid communication and intercourse with the Indians and shall not go to their towns and shall not amuse themselves nor give themselves up to sensual pleasures in the land. Neither shall the Indians enter the precincts of the [Spanish] town until after it has been built and placed in a condition of defense, and the houses so built that when the Indians see them they shall wonder and understand that the Spaniards settle there for good . . . and so that they may fear them."[4]

Even before Philip's decree, urban segregation had served Spanish religious goals. Shortly after conquest, Catholic priests and Franciscan friars began to convert people they deemed heathens and idolators. In Mexico, as elsewhere, this process was quite a delicate one, as many supposedly Christian Mexican *caciques* tried to keep alive at least some version of the cycle of festivals and rituals upon which the indigenous Mexican empire once stood. Ordinary Spanish settlers, many of them single men, sought business, laborers, entertainment, and sex in the Indian *reducciones*, disrupting efforts to engender Christian piety among the Mexica. Since these Christians' behavior often corresponded poorly to that preached by the Franciscans, the friars pushed for separation laws that ordered all Spaniards, as well as *mestizos* born of Spanish and Indian parents, out of the Indian towns. In this way, they also imported to the New World the preoccupation of Spanish nobles with any unclean Jewish blood in their ancestry. When African slaves arrived in New Spain, the *mulatto* offspring of African-Spanish and African-Indian sexual encounters were added to the shameful catalog of mixed-blood outcastes.[5]

The secular authorities of New Spain did set up largely separate legal systems for the Spanish and Indian *republicas*, but as time went on, they had greater trouble enforcing the decrees to keep the two republics physically separate in the cities. Not only did "blood mixture" make people increasingly difficult to identify as Spanish or Indian, there was also no clear or quick way to distinguish which part-Indians had truly embraced Christianity and Spanish culture. Meanwhile, many Indian *caciques* did become Christians and sought a status similar to Spanish noblemen. Some of them bought African slaves and brought them to live in the *barrios*, thus dubiously accomplishing the aims of Christianization and Hispanization, but clearly violating the separation laws. Even by the mid-sixteenth century, the boundaries between Mexico City's Spanish and Indian quarters began to blur. Elsewhere, Indian barrios gradually disappeared by the seventeenth century or, as in the capital, filled up with mixed-heritage people and thus became indistinguishable from the rest of the city.[6]

As segregation waned, officials instead developed a system of *castas* aimed to register people by the varying amount of Spanish, Indian, and African blood in their heritage. In doing so, they confirmed that the sharp distinctions between Spaniards and Indians had broken down. By the 1600s, cities like Mexico City were marked above all by small-scale class separation within buildings. Poorer, mixed-blood plebeians, most of them of highly ambiguous *casta* status, tended to live in the musty and more dangerous downstairs apartments of the city's buildings. Their higher-bred patrons—many of whom had increasing difficulty proving the "cleanliness" of their own blood—occupied the more commodious, better-protected, and better-ventilated upper floors.[7]

In the French and British colonies, similar but much smaller separate districts for Indians were established, called "praying towns" in New England, or "Indian Town" near Savannah, and *"missions"* in New France. At New Amsterdam (New York) Peter Stuyvesant put up a wall (which later gave its name to Wall Street) along the northern border of town to keep Indians out, and the British later supplemented it with a law that forbade Indians from "tarrying ... during the night" in New York. But most native coastal settlements across the Americas changed seasonally. European settlers forced some of these inland, others declined due to war and disease, and many communities of "praying Indians" assimilated into colonial society. Nowhere in the Atlantic were the city walls that were raised against natives as formidable or long lasting as further east in the divided cities of the Indian Ocean. Although historians have argued that schemes like the New England praying towns prefigured segregated rural Indian reservations, the spatial politics of American coastal cities were decreasingly affected over time by the otherwise complex ongoing diplomacy and warfare between Europeans and native peoples of the interior.[8]

Urban residential segregation waned quickly in the Americas, but it was slavery that killed it outright. As New World cities became increasingly enmeshed in the Atlantic slave trade and the plantation economy, local officials had to institutionalize their suppression of what they saw as slaves' nearly constant insubordination. To those officials, virtually all of whom were slave owners in their own right, it was utterly unthinkable to control slaves by creating separate neighborhoods for them. To sanction any kind of congregation of Africans out of white people's eyeshot was seen as nothing less than an open invitation to slave conspiracy, revolution, and possibly the downfall of the whole Atlantic plantation system. To control a "slave city" internally, authorities preferred a technique that went back to ancient times: they forced slaves to live in the households or on the properties of their masters. In practice this amounted to separation on the level of the household, with slaves living in garrets and closets in the house or in the "black houses" (*cases á nègres*) sited in back courtyards next to the kitchens and stables where slaves worked. To enforce that system, authorities supplemented it with draconian measures to limit slaves' movements and actions and above all to keep any independent social or political life to an absolute minimum, especially between slaves and free blacks. In other words, blacks had to be segregated from one another.

The Spanish were the pioneers in using such policies in the Americas. In Mexico City and in port cities throughout Spanish America, sixteenth-century slave codes forbade the arming of blacks, imposed curfews, banned gatherings of more than a few slaves, forced slaves to live in the houses or on the properties of their masters, and forbade mestizos and mulattos from living outside the Spanish sections of town.

Similar laws regarding the control of slaves' movements and residence were passed in the cities of the French and British Caribbean and at slave cities throughout the Atlantic from Charles Town to Kingston and New York to Rio de Janeiro.[9]

When separation did occur, it was in defiance of slavery, not because of it. The Spanish established the separate free-black city of Mose on the outskirts of Saint Augustine, Florida, explicitly to entice slaves to run away from the British plantations of South Carolina and thus weaken a colonial rival. Black people themselves built separate settlements in places like Charleston's Neck, Savannah's Bluffs, the yards of Kingston, and on Rio's steep hillsides by exploiting weaknesses in the enforcement of slave laws and grasping small whiffs of freedom to associate with each other. In Spanish Town, Jamaica, and Bridgetown, Barbados, the self-built slave yards got out of hand. Authorities mandated that slave houses in these yards have only one door, and they ordered clusters of houses to be surrounded by eight-foot fences, preventing slaves from escaping through the back door and into the next yard whenever the local constabulary made searches. Slaves often broke laws forbidding them to gather, to walk about at night without lanterns, and to organize Sunday revelries and the like, and colonial legislatures responded by enacting still more laws. All across the Americas slaves defied efforts of control by repeatedly organizing insurgencies, often in allegiance with radicalized poorer whites. But the universality of slave holders' desire to keep blacks away from each other is best demonstrated by the only officially sanctioned color-segregated spaces in any slave city—the so-called African cemeteries. Black people only got a legal "neighborhood" of their own when they were dead.[10]

At the Cape of Good Hope, in the far corner of the Atlantic, the city of Cape Town followed many of the dynamics of slave cities in the Americas. The city's history belongs mostly to that of the Eastern trade routes. The Dutchman Jan van Riebeeck founded the place in 1652 as a revitalization station for United East India Company ship crews heading from Amsterdam to the Spice Islands, and it was for that reason that most of the city's slaves came from Asia, not Africa. But, like many American cities, Cape Town occupied a spot where local inhabitants, the pastoralist Khoikhoi people, had no traditions of permanent city building. Also, large numbers of Dutch migrants soon settled the Cape hinterland permanently, in a pattern not dissimilar to the North American settlement at New Amsterdam. Slavery also persisted in the Cape of Good Hope colony, like in New Amsterdam, despite the lack of large slave plantations. At Cape Town, van Riebeeck famously planted an almond hedge at the city limits to keep the Khoikhoi out. For this act, a few scholars anointed him a kind of great-grandfather of apartheid. But like the many slim city walls around American cities (including Peter Stuyvesant's wall around New Amsterdam), van Riebeeck's hedge hardly compares with those that separated urban Europeans from Africans or Asians elsewhere along the trade routes to the East.[11]

The United East India Company, which was an unusual large-scale urban slave owner, did build a segregated slave lodge in Cape Town, and that building could be seen as the precursor to the segregated mining compounds of later South African cities. But laws that applied to slaves not owned by the Company specified that they should be confined to their owners' homes. The population of the slave lodge itself—which was a single building, not a neighborhood, and which could just as easily be interpreted as a large version of the outbuildings that existed on many other slave owner's properties—also decreased in the late eighteenth century, when segregation elsewhere in the colonial world increased. By the time of abolition of slavery at the Cape in 1834, the city—like those in the Americas at the same time—had developed no discernable residential color line. Only in the late nineteenth century would Americans and South Africans develop a new hankering for separating the races in their cities.[12]

## Eastward Connections

Meanwhile, things were going very differently in the Eastern Hemisphere, as attested by a letter from a British merchant in India to the court of directors of the British East India Company in London. "Without . . . defensible places," wrote the merchant, "your goods and Servants among such treacherous people are in Continuall hazard. The just feare whereof hath induced the Portugalls [and] Dutch to frame themselves in more safe habitations." Citing the precedent of their rival imperialists, the directors agreed, and as they built their new fortress—christened Fort St. George—outside the little southern Indian fishing village of Madraspatnam (soon shortened to Madras), a new divided city grew, much like the dozens of European colonial towns that stretched along the coasts from Morocco to East Asia.[13]

In the East, the demographic, political, and economic circumstances of colonialism contrasted sharply with the Americas. Tropical disease and long distances from the metropole generally kept European populations in Africa and Asia small. Surrounding them were vast and increasing indigenous populations with longstanding urban traditions of their own. Some of the world's richest and most powerful governments held sway, in great part because they possessed some of the most advanced weaponry of the day—the Mughals in India, the Savafids in Persia, and the antiforeign Qing in China and Tokugawa in Japan. Powerful foreign merchant communities—the Swahilis, Arabs, Armenians, Jews, Indians, Indonesians, Chinese, and Japanese—dominated many port cities. On top of that, rival European commercial imperialists in Asia were often under royal obligation to export the nearly constant dynastic, national, and religious wars from Europe to the far corners of the earth.

In addition to such external threats, European authorities in Eastern colonial cities had to contend with complex and tense internal conflicts. Though they had to scare away potential attackers, they also had to grow their cities by convincing local merchants, craftspeople, and laborers to settle nearby. Only in this way could aspiring European monopolists get dependable access to the local products that would make them rich. The British East India Company needed to prevent its European employees from siphoning its potential wealth by engaging in personal trade on the side. Natives had to be prevented from spying for the city's enemies. Slavery thrived in the Indian Ocean world, and Europeans used slave labor extensively, sometimes even to build the very walls around their cities. But the hemispheric and urban economies of the East depended less on slave labor than on goods like spices, porcelains, and cloth. Europeans did generally force their non-European slaves and servants to live within their households, as in the West. But the politics of defending and controlling most colonial cities in the Indian Ocean was focused on separating the places where Europeans and local non-enslaved Asians or Africans lived.[14]

As the British merchant suggested in his letter to London, it was the Portuguese who had first shown the way. In 1482, the Portuguese king sent his general Don Diogo de Azambuja with five hundred soldiers, a hundred top stonemasons, four ships full of precut stone blocks from Portuguese quarries, another ship filled with lime cement, and several fearsome bronze cannons (designed to avoid rust in the tropical humidity) to a small village at the mouth of the Benya River in present-day

Ghana. Their mission was to build a "strong house" where a Portuguese "factor" could acquire gold and thus outflank the Muslim merchants who carried it across the Sahara. What they had in mind by a "strong house" was the massive stone fortress of Elmina (named after the gold mines). Its high walls soon loomed on a rocky promontory above the African village. The fortress itself became the world's first *feitoreia*, or "factory," a new kind of overseas merchant *fondacco* so heavily infused with royal and godly power that it could rule an overseas city and its commerce outright.[15]

The more famous Portuguese conquistador Vasco da Gama widened Azambuja's strategy during his two epic voyages around the Cape of Good Hope to the pepper markets of southwest India's Malabar Coast. There, in the city-state of Calicut, he faced strong opposition from the Hindu *Samudri Raja* (the Lord of the Seas, often called the *Zamorin*) and a foreign-merchant community dominated by the city's Arabs and local Muslims, all of whom had every interest in obstructing the trade of "infidel" Christian merchants in the Indian Ocean. After getting an eyeful of this opposition on his first trip (1497-99), da Gama returned (in 1502-3) with a fleet of war ships to bombard Calicut and rout its Muslim fleet. He was followed by a succession of viceroys who established the *cartaz* system, forcing all non-Portuguese ship captains in the Indian Ocean to buy a pass or risk forfeiting their cargoes to the King of Portugal. To enforce that system, the Portuguese took over key cities across the region and built fortified *feitoreias* there. In a flurry of activity between 1510 and 1515, the merciless conquistador Afonso de Albuquerque captured the wealthy city of Goa, north of Calicut, which became the Portuguese capital in the East; the storied entrepôt of Malacca; and Hormuz at the entryway to the Persian Gulf. Over the next fifty years an empire of urban fortifications, known as the *Estado da India*, stretched around the coast of Africa and Asia as far as Japan. One special prize was the only foreign-run port on the Chinese coast, Macao.[16]

Though the Portuguese built dozens of overseas mercantile citadels, they were less systematic overall about turning them into segregated towns. This was not out of any tolerance toward non-Christians, least of all toward Muslims. The ruins of temples, synagogues, and mosques can be found in many places the Portuguese settled. Afonso de Albuquerque committed what he called "a great deed and well carried out" at Goa by slaughtering six thousand of the city's Muslim merchants after they briefly recaptured the city from him in 1510. Not long after the conquest,

Goa became home to a Catholic archbishop, officers of the Inquisition, several powerful religious orders, and even the great proselytizer Saint Francis Xavier. They set up a religious establishment that made Goa a kind of "Rome of the East," and in 1572 church authorities pressured the viceroy to sign decrees that would have effectively forbidden Christians to interact with Muslims or Hindus in the cities of the empire.[17]

In practice, though, urban spatial policy varied from one place to another, suggesting that local political concerns were largely at stake. In places like Elmina, Malacca, Hormuz, and Colombo, fortress walls separated the Portuguese settlement from those for local people. But the capital Goa was among the least clearly divided of all the Portuguese cities. Some streets were set aside for different groups of Hindu and Muslim merchants in a pattern that might have reflected India's traditional geography of caste and religion. In public, the Portuguese also seem to have insisted on an etiquette of superiority and deference. Portuguese noblemen would walk about with exaggerated formality, followed by large retinues of slaves, musicians, and umbrella carriers. Native people, derided as *Canarins*, had to back off the roadway in deference or risk being hit with a hard stick called a *stochado*. The Luso-Goanese also practiced what might be seen as a syncretic version of purdah. Portuguese men were known to sequester their wives back home, but at Goa, where they often married Eurasians familiar with the Indian system, upper-class women universally seem to have been kept out of sight inside the city's mansions and were even transported to church in special covered sedan chairs.[18]

That said, no walls divided Goa into European and native districts. Secular authorities there did not make a priority of enforcing the separation decrees, no doubt mostly because they would have stifled the city's commerce. The great marketplace in the central Rua Diretta was a vast meeting of the continents, lined with European artisan shops and filled with merchants from all over Asia as well as African "caffres," some selling their own artisanal wares and some for sale themselves as slaves. At Goa, one contemporary visitor wrote, the Portuguese "dwell . . . among . . . Indians, Heathens, Moores, Iewes, Armenians, Gusarates, Benianes, Bramenes, and of all Indian nations and peoples."[19]

When the Spanish took Manila in the Philippines in 1570, they divided the city's space by official word and deed much more quickly and thoroughly than anywhere in the Portuguese empire. The conquistador Don Miguel Lopez de Legazpi, who arrived from Mexico across the Pacific, brought Philip I's policies for separate native districts with him. His first act was to burn the trading village of Manila to the ground, along with the small community of Muslim merchants who lived there. Next, he ordered a palisade built around the smoldering remains. In the countryside nearby, Franciscan clerics set up a version of the *reducciones* of New Spain by pushing rural and village Filipinos into scattered fenced locations—here called *cabaceros*—where they could receive the good word. The most pressing question, though, concerned the Chinese and Japanese merchants who flocked to Manila after the conquest. Some were eager to trade silk for the Spaniards' American silver; others set up shop to serve the bustling town. Still others, like the Chinese corsair Limahing and the Japanese *wako* pirates, had less friendly ways of doing business, and they made short work of Don Miguel's wooden stockade.[20]

By the 1590s, Don Miguel's successors had poured large quantities of American silver into building a gigantic fortress around the Spanish part of town, which they now called Intramuros. Already in 1581 the governor forced the "Sangleys," as the Spanish called the Chinese (probably after the city of Xiamen, where many originated), out of Intramuros to a marshy place called the Parian, or silk market. This Chinatown soon held upward of twenty thousand inhabitants and became the economic nerve center of the city, providing Intramuros with provisions and artisanal wares and even attracting Spaniards to its Chinese eating houses. Officials then set aside another quarter called Binondo to protect Chinese Christian converts from their "infidel" countrymen—something in the manner of the Mexican *ciudades de indios*. The Japanese and Filipinos got their own neighborhoods (*arrabales*) as well. Ever more stringent laws were enacted in the 1590s, proscribing the penalty of death to any Chinese, Japanese, or Filipinos (other than household servants) who were found in Intramuros after dark and restricting Filipinos to within two leagues of the city at all times unless they got a special pass.[21]

The main reason for segregation was the fear of a Chinese rebellion. Cannons were continually trained on the Parian and Binondo from the heights of the city walls. Governors flagrantly scapegoated the Chinese for social problems in the Intramuros, and in 1603 and 1639 their rhetoric inspired fierce anti-Chinese riots that destroyed the Chinatowns. Such policy ran directly against the economic interests of all merchants in the town, for it effectively depressed the local economy, as well as the trans-Pacific one, until the Chinese felt safe enough to return and rebuild the Parian. A key aspect of official scapegoating rhetoric, repeated endlessly to heighten the sensation, involved accusations that the Sangleys were consumed by urges to practice sodomy, and that they threatened to contaminate the morals of the Spaniards with such "unspeakable" practices. Manila may have pioneered the forced separation of urban Asians, but it thus also gave birth to a kind of antihomosexual segregation too.[22]

Meanwhile, in the 1590s, the Dutch arrived in the Indian Ocean flying the banners of the world's first private multinational corporation, the United East India Company. The Dutch brought their war of independence against Spain and Portugal overseas with them and wielded the most formidable guns in the Indian Ocean. In 1603 and again in 1643 they blockaded Goa, eventually sending the "Rome of Asia" into an economic tailspin and onto a path of gradual abandonment (sewage seeping into the drinking water helped). The Dutch also picked off some of Portugal's key fortresses, including Elmina in 1637, Malacca in 1641, and Colombo in 1656, in addition to founding their refreshment station at Cape Town. They got their big start, though, as early as 1619 when a Company merchant, Jan Pieterzsoon Coen, turned conquistador and stormed the little Javanese town of Jacatra (the origin of today's Jakarta) to establish a "rendezvous" for the trade in spices and Chinese luxuries to rival Macao and Manila. This town they renamed Batavia, after the Latin word for Holland, and its imposing "Casteel" soon became the new capital of the Eastern trade routes.[23]

As the Dutch built their own empire of seaside fortified merchant citadels, they too instituted a variety of official policies regarding separation, which both reflected the geopolitical situation at each locality and the Company's generally more frugal policy toward wall building. The system they developed at Batavia qualifies them as the most thoroughgoing segregationists of their day, at least in terms of the sheer volume and innovation of residential legislation and in terms of the hefty bureaucratic machine they built to enforce it. Again, local concerns of defense and control were paramount. Batavia quickly became a very powerful and wealthy colonial outpost, but officials there seem to have felt the sheer terror of the city's geopolitical and internal social situation more acutely than perhaps anywhere else. The sultan of Mataram in central Java had repelled previous European attempts to establish a fortress on the island, rightly fearing threats to his sovereignty similar to those the Portuguese had inflicted upon India. He and the sultan of Bantam, Batavia's neighbor on the far western point of Java, repeatedly besieged Batavia throughout the seventeenth century. Merchants from across the Indonesian archipelago came to the city too, many of them from places involved in other wars with the Dutch. Then, servants of the Dutch Company's rival, the British East India Company, got permission from the sultan of Bantam to establish a mercantile enclave in his small city, and they began coveting Batavia. The Dutch Company's most steadfast ally was the city's overseas Chinese mercantile community. As at Manila, the Chinese both ran Batavia's local economy and allowed trade with Chinese ports that were off-limits to the Dutch themselves. Also as at Manila, however, the alliance could sour on very short notice.

The separation system at Batavia closely attended to these security threats and alliances. A town grew up around the castle on the east side of the Cipang River, and it was soon walled too. The Dutch lived there and even built a system of canals to remind them of Amsterdam. Unlike the Spaniards at Manila, authorities at Batavia allowed the Chinese into the privileged precinct, though for some time their street was gated at both ends, perhaps also in imitation of Amsterdam's "Jew-Street"; later there would be Manila-like massacres. Other members of the "Eastern nations" of the archipelago were allocated separate villages known as *kampungs* outside the walls and on the east side of the river. This reflected the age-old tradition of the region, but the Dutch reinforced the system by appointing both an indigenous army captain and a Dutch neighborhood watchman (*wijkmeister*) over each kampung. Then, in periodic censuses administered by the watchmen, all of the city's population was registered according to different national and religious categories.

The Javanese, whom the Dutch repeatedly denounced as a particularly "murderous and faithless people," were given the harshest treatment. As of 1638 they were ordered to carry "a certain mark" while in town to better supervise their movements, and they were expelled from the city for a time in 1656. In 1688, the sultan of Mataram once again threatened the city. As a "powerful means to check in the future the theft, robberies, and murders, as well as other crimes inflicted by the daily encroaching and intrusive Javanese, Malays, Balinese, Makassarese, Bugis, Saeyrese, Butonese, Birmanese and suchlike pernicious peoples," every inhabitant was supposed to pick up a lead chit called a *loodge* from the local watchman with their name and nation written on it. This pass system was also meant to form the basis of separate national companies of soldiers under their own captains to help defend the city.[24]

Meanwhile, in London, officials of the British East India Company observed and debated the merits of these precedents. Many held the idealistic view that the Company should engage in "trade not war" and engage in diplomacy rather than expensive, belligerent fortress building. Others, by contrast, had grown frustrated with the "fenceless factory" the Company maintained in the western Indian port of Surat, where the Mughal emperor and his officials had visited numerous depredations upon British merchants and even once forced them to delay business for a whole season and ferry pilgrims to Mecca on Company ships. It is significant that the merchant who wrote to the Company's court of directors in London advocating Portuguese- and Dutch-style "defensible places" was stationed at Surat. His implication that the Dutch could make enormous and enviable profits despite investments in walls was particularly persuasive to the directors. Knowledge of London merchants' recent project to fortify the towns of Londonderry, Belfast, and other Protestant mercantile outposts in northeast Ireland may also have entered their strategic equation. When a ragtag band of Company agents acquired Madraspatnam in 1639, the Company agreed to spring for the expenses of building Fort St. George.

Madras's precarious local geopolitical situation on southeast India's Coromandel Coast also helped make the case for the advocates of fortification. Far from an all-powerful colonial power, the Company acquired the town under an agreement that made it an only somewhat privileged vassal to a petty local official of the long-crumbling Vijayanagar Empire, the naik Damarla Venkatappa. Local sovereignty over the region shifted continually and unpredictably over the next seventy-five years, and Company officials at Madras had to fend off several besieging armies as well as spies who mingled among the many Indians and other Asians who settled near the new commercial outpost. The Portuguese occasionally harassed Madras from their nearby town of São Thomé; the Dutch had a fort a few miles up the coast; and the French would soon threaten from just to the south, from what would become a resplendent capital at Pondichéry (Puducherry).[25]

As the town grew around Fort St. George, Europeans appear to have built their houses closest to the fortress walls. By the mid-1650s, they built yet another wall, which formed a much larger trapezoidal perimeter around the whole European settlement, enclosing what was then called "Christian Town."[26] Meanwhile, it also became clear that the rapidly growing Indian city beyond those walls posed its own security threat because it provided easy cover for enemy armies. For five decades, authorities at Madras tried to cajole the city's wealthiest Asians to finance a wall around Black Town as well. In 1687 the Company's powerful court director Josiah Child, an anti-Parliamentary royalist at home, even insisted that the Hindu and Muslim merchants of Madras as well as the resident Armenians and Portuguese be encouraged to participate in a unique local "Corporation" (municipal government) as aldermen, and in exchange pay a wall tax. When they saw right through the bargain and refused to join, Madras's most famous governor, Elihu Yale (1687-92), used company money to build a mud wall around Black Town, which mostly washed away in the ensuing monsoons. Furious about that and other things, the court of directors deposed Yale and made him pay for the wall personally. (Yale had meanwhile gotten so rich from speculating in the legendary diamonds of Golconda that, after paying up, he had plenty left over to endow a college in Connecticut so lavishly that it took his name.) Finally, in 1706, after seven years of periodic sieges from a particularly mercurial local sovereign, the Nawab Da'ud Khan of the Carnatic and Gingee, Governor Thomas Pitt, Madras's most ruthless colonial official, used British arms to confine the "heads of the castes" of Black Town in a local pagoda until they came up with the money. A stone wall finally went up around Black Town in the next few years, as can be seen on Pitt's map.[27]

Indians played important roles in the politics of dividing Madras, and not only by threatening the city with armies. In fact, the subcontinent's traditional openness to outsiders, which contrasted so markedly with China, Japan, and Java, made the Company's initial deal with the naik conceivable in the first place. Indian practices of caste segregation may have also made the dividing of Madras easier. Many Hindu residents of Madras no doubt preferred to live far from what were seen as the sacrilegious practices of the British, like eating beef or hiring "untouchable" *Pariars* as household servants—though mercantile interests just as doubtlessly led many to suspend some of these pieties. As in other South Indian cities, Madras's rival "Right-Hand" and "Left-Hand" Hindu caste alliances lived on separate streets in Black Town, as did Muslims and the *Pariars*. This soon made it possible for the British to enhance their conquest by encouraging Asians' differences.[28]

British authorities' relationships with Indian merchants at Madras, like elsewhere in the Indian Ocean, were based on delicate push-me, pull-you power dynamics. As a local government interested in the settlement's security, the Company needed to keep locals at a distance. As a profit-seeking would-be monopoly, though, its interests required exclusive access to middlemen, called *dubashes* at Madras, to make business contacts, help with trade negotiations, and provide financing for purchases. At Madras the Company's dependence on locals was especially acute, as cloth production required an elaborate cottage-industry infrastructure and thousands of artisans to make it work. The city grew dramatically in response to these needs, possibly topping two hundred thousand inhabitants, thus increasing the throb both of its commerce and of its security headaches. Separation grew all the more necessary to resolve the Company's dilemmas.[29]

The walls also allowed Company officials to control white people, an essential task for both profit making and security. The Company forbade its own employees from traveling outside of the small territory around Madras, and early governors even expected all British officials to be present every night at dinner in their own residence. The idea was to minimize private trading on the side—something that, of course, proved impossible. In addition, soldiers were given strict curfews to avoid drunken quarrels with locals in Black Town. As in all premodern walled towns, banishment was an easy punishment for social deviancy.[30]

Still, it would be a mistake to take any of this evidence to mean that the double city of Madras amounted to a case of voluntary, mutual, or de facto separation. The walls themselves were, of course, the work of the East India Company, and they communicated commanding superiority over Indian subjects. As we know from Pitt's map and the accompanying

FIGURE 2.2 "Without … defensible places, your goods and Servants among such treacherous people are in Continuall hazard." This "prospect" of the British East India's Fort St. George illustrates the connection between fortifications and color lines. White Town bristles with armaments trained on potential threats from the sea, from the land, and from Black Town. From H. Davison Love, *Vestiges of Old Madras* (Government of India, 1913), vol. 1.

"prospect," the architecture of the European section radiated might: parapets and cannons festooned the roofs of the walls, gates, and houses. By the eighteenth century, most buildings in White Town were plastered with *chunam*, a substance made from the crushed shells of a local mollusk, which gave a marblelike appearance to exteriors and, from out at sea, made White Town shine *whiter*, literally, than Black Town. Proclamations from the Company's governor were traditionally issued to the sound of cannon shots from White Town and large processions that passed from the fort through the massive Choultry Gate into Black Town. In support of the walled division of residences, governors felt it necessary either to pass or propose laws in 1680, 1688, 1690, 1698, 1706, 1743, 1745, and 1751 that regulated where various groups could live, sometimes ordering English residents to restrict the resale of their houses to other Englishmen. As with slave laws in the Americas, the frequency of these laws suggests even more frequent violations. But they did help ensure that a dual housing market, and what South African historian Paul Maylam calls "fiscal segregation," developed in Madras by the eighteenth century, if not before. Property values were deemed much higher on average in White Town—even taking into account Indian merchants' palatial dwellings and temples in Black Town—and tax rates for European property were set lower than those levied in Black Town to avoid excessive burdens on Englishmen.[31]

To seal its stamp of supremacy, the British East India Company used divisive Indian caste politics for its own ends. For many years governors relied primarily on members of the higher-status Right-Hand caste alliance as its principal middlemen and suppliers. When the British sought better prices by allowing merchants from the Left-Hand alliance to bid on contracts, they provoked an enormous battle that centered on fights over the overlapping neighborhoods that each alliance claimed for itself in Black Town. In this case, segregation and capitalist economic interests went hand in hand. Governor Pitt finally forced caste leaders into seclusion to negotiate a clear division of Black Town, complete with a system of boundary stones, into separate Left- and Right-Hand zones. When the dust settled, the British made off with their cheaper cloth.[32]

As in divided cities throughout history, the color lines at Madras were semipermeable, regularly transgressed by Indian servants, mercantile collaborators, and, as we shall see, many Englishmen in search of sex and marriage partners. Separation proclamations tended to arise in moments of crisis and languish in a less-enforced state during more stable times. But the walls of White Town and the color inequalities they created continuously served as a primary instrument in institutionalizing what became a color hierarchy—as well as a grand stage for the theatrics of an emerging colonial authority. In the 1740s, as Britain's wars with France and Spain took on transhemispheric dimensions, the process of fortified and legalized separation by color intensified dramatically at Madras. In 1746, the French seized the city, leveled the historic Black Town (wall and all), and resettled its inhabitants four hundred yards from the gates of White Town. When the British regained Madras two years later, they forbade any building in the intermediate zone, which became a military cordon sanitaire forcing besieging armies into the open. Officials then filled in the languid Elambore (or Cooum) River to the west of White Town, allowing for a doubling of White Town's area and making room for a bristling, state-of-the-art, Vauban-style fortification system. Later in the eighteenth century, when security threats faded, the Company subsidized the growth of White Town beyond its walls. The Company's methods, which evoke those of twentieth-century South Africa and the United States, included grants of land for suburban "garden estates" and the construction of wider roads to accommodate increased numbers of horse carriages carrying commuters into the city's business center.[33]

## The Cross-Colonial Color Connection

So now we know why Madras was divided in two, but that alone does not clear up another mystery: How did its rulers get the idea to call its separate sections "Black Town" and "White Town"? The answer is not self-evident. As European colonial officials scattered across the hemispheres and as they plotted policies of defense, control, and residence in their new cities, they also spread a variety of European ideas about human difference. Strangely, as time went on, these officials began to grow weary of words that had long served them well—the idea of "nation" (or "people"), which tied them to the kings and homelands they served; and religious categories, like "Christian," which identified their colonial exploits with the will of God. Instead, they began to call non-Europeans "black" and Europeans "white"—words that had at best ambiguous historical connotations. More puzzlingly, this embrace of color categories cannot be explained by the idea that Europeans had deemed white people a superior "race." Colonial officials rarely, if ever, used the word "race"—even though it did exist in all European languages at the time. In fact, race would not become an important concept in political thought until the late 1700s.

To solve our mystery, it behooves us to take each of these terms— "black," "white," and "race"—one at a time. As we do, we need to contemplate how each spread not only *within* hemispheres, but also *between* them. At the same time, we need to think about how they fit into the dramas of urban politics.

Of the three terms, "black" is the oldest. In Europe, it reaches back to classical times. The most complex premodern vocabulary of color, though, developed within the Muslim world. When the Portuguese began slaving on the West Coast of Africa, they adopted Muslims' convention of using "white" for local Arabs and "black" (*negro*) for Africans. The Spaniards also used *negro* for the slaves they imported into New Spain, and that word was absorbed, along with *mulatto* and *mestizo*, in various Iberian-inspired forms into Dutch, French, and English throughout the Atlantic.[34]

European travel writers to the East, meanwhile, used a variety of colors for Asians—white, yellow, brown, and black. The Dutch, English, and French did not, however, transliterate the word "Negro" for Asians; in the Indian Ocean, even Africans were most often called "Caffres" or "Kaffirs" after the Arabic word *qafr* for "unbeliever" (in modern South Africa, "Kaffir" would be used much like the severest American racial insult, "nigger"). When Europeans did use color terms, it was as descriptions for people they met, not as official political categories for their subjects. Moreover, though the segregation of colonial cities in the East had a history going back to the 1480s, authorities never officially designated these sections by color before the East India Company began calling the Asian section of Madras "Black Town" in the 1660s.[35]

Even at Madras, the designation of "Black Town" was not automatic. The inhabitants of the city included many people who were usually described as black by travelers—sometimes even "black as pitch."[36] However, British officials at Madras most often used national or religious designations such as "Malabar Town" (the word for Madras's majority Tamil population) or "Gentue Town" ("Gentue" being a word that either referred to the city's large minority Telugu population or Hindus in general) to designate the Asian section of their outpost. Locals preferred to call the Asian section of Madras Chennaipattnam (the root of today's

Chennai) in honor of Naik Venkatappa's father, and they avoided "Black Town" in their petitions to the British governors.

Only after 1676 did the phrase "Black Town" enter British officials' vocabularies, and it appears to have been a derogatory term. Some of this disdain may have come from the increasing association between blackness and slavery in the Atlantic, but agendas within Madras's local politics of defense and control were clearly more important. From the city's earliest years, the British there saw local inhabitants as "treacherous people," and they most often used the word "black" as a way to express their frustration with Indians' refusal to submit to Company commands. The phrase "Black Town" arose in the context of one of the fruitless efforts to get Indian merchants to pay taxes for the wall around their section of the city. Writing from London, the Company's court of directors' language fluctuated. At one moment it issued thundering directives to tax the "black merchants" by force, and at another it advised "gentleness and perswasion" to entice the "Gentues and Moores" to take seats as aldermen of the Madras Corporation and pay the tax voluntarily. By contrast, the Company's local agents, such as Governor Elihu Yale, had more at stake in being consistently respectful, since they engaged heavily in illegal trade with Asian merchants to supplement their low salaries and were thus dependent on good personal relationships with the *dubashes*. Their tendency was to use "Gentue Town" and "Malabar Town" and even "Chennaipattnam," though "Black Town" grew in frequency. By the first decade of the eighteenth century, "Gentue" and "Malabar" disappeared from local usage after Pitt finally forced the "black merchants" to pay for the Black Town wall.[37]

The history of "white" as a self-designation for Europeans has a completely different chronology and even a different global geography than that of "black." The Spanish and Portuguese occasionally used it for themselves, in obvious contrast to *negro*, but like the Muslims they used it more systematically as a descriptive term for Arabs or other light-skinned Asians. In the realm of official categories, Iberians in Asia much preferred to call themselves "Christians" or by their respective national designations, and other Europeans copied this practice in both the East and the West. In the *sistema de castas* of New Spain, *negro* was the bottom category, but the top category was almost always designated by the term *Español*. In Portuguese India, top place in a similar system was given to the *Reinois*, those born in Portugal, not to "whites." The Dutch appear

to have almost entirely dispensed with "white" in the population registration systems of Java, preferring "European." At Madras, throughout
almost the entire 1600s, the European section of the city was consistently
called the "Christian Town."[38]

It was not until the 1660s that authorities in any European colony began
widely using the term "white" as an official category. The practice probably
began in the sugar colonies of the British West Indies. The first government censuses there, which date from 1661, universally use the dichotomy
of "white" and "black."[39] The earliest sustained use of "white" on the mainland comes from the slave laws of Virginia. In 1691 the legislature updated
an earlier law forbidding sex between what they now called "English or
other white women" and black slaves. After about 1700, and especially after
1710, "white" appears in colonial documents with what, in the slow pace of
cultural historical change, must be called sudden profusion.[40]

In Madras, the increased use of "white" occurred at approximately
the same time as on the North American mainland. "Whyte town" first
occurred in an isolated incident in 1693 and then not again until 1711,
on Pitt's map. Authorities were nevertheless very comfortable contrasting "Black Town" with "Christian Town" from the 1670s until about 1720,
after which "White Town" took over as the most widely used designation.
Again, Madras was the first place in Asia where this was the case.[41]

Why would colonial authorities abandon "Christian," a term that for
centuries had marked them as instruments of God's will, and instead
start calling themselves by the color white? Neither the idea that whiteness generally has positive connotations in Western culture nor the idea
that Western society was becoming more secular explains why "white" so
suddenly became a powerful term of group pride and solidarity, nor why
that happened successively in a series of specific British colonies.[42]

A more likely answer involves political conflicts between Europeans over class, religion, and nation. These grew during the years when
the British formalized slavery in their American colonies. They began
in a series of political dramas that tied Parliament in London with the
West Indies, the first place where "white" displaced "Christian." There,
the sugar revolution transformed islands like Barbados into the wealthiest colonies of the British Empire. That brought into question the status of European indentured servants. Many observers in London and
the islands were worried these servants had been reduced to "Christian
slaves"—a term that was increasingly rendered as "white slaves." That,
one observer warned, threatened to make "our lives ... as cheap as ne-

groes." Meanwhile, various clerics and later the Crown put increasing pressure on slave holders to convert Africans to Christianity. Many slave holders were reluctant to do so, fearing that conversion would entitle Africans to emancipation. Morgan Godwyn, a prominent propagandist for slave conversion, complained about this reluctance, noting that "*Negro* and *Christian, Englishmen* and *Heathen*, are by idle corrupt Custom and Partiality made *Opposites*; thereby as it were implying, that the one could not be *Christians*, nor the other *Infidels*."[43]

While no one ever made it an explicit policy, adopting "white" as the designation for free people instead of "Christian" clarified such matters. It diffused looming conflict between the Crown, the missionaries, and the slave holders. More importantly, it helped to cement political support among European colonists of different classes and persuasions in defense of slavery. This alliance between whites in the British colonies also reflected different demographic conditions and gender politics than existed in New Spain. In Spanish colonies, the larger native and smaller European female populations led to a "plebeian" class of mixed Indian, black, and European heritage. Elite power rested on segmenting plebeians into dozens of *casta* categories. In British colonies, larger white female populations created a larger unmixed population. By resorting to a politics of whiteness, authorities could purchase the allegiance of poorer European colonists by offering the compensatory illusion of sharing elite status with slave holders. Indeed, the term "white" arrived in mainland British North American colonies more or less at the same time that slavery became central to the local economy and legal system.[44]

That still begs our main question: Why would anyone bring this newfangled black-white dichotomy to a city in the Indian Ocean? Though it is hard to pinpoint exactly how this happened, it is likely that whiteness made its way from the Americas through London to the East. Many East India Company directors, Josiah Child included, invested in American ventures, and some served in Parliament, so they would have been familiar with the growing use of "white" and "black" in English discussions of slavery. Some of the governors of Madras, including Elihu Yale, were born in the Americas and had extensive family contacts there. Ship captains and sailors could have also brought the new vocabularies with them. Color politics, like slavery, was of course alive in early modern Britain itself, and the growing persecution of blacks there in the early eighteenth century may have also influenced the mindset of officials who spurred concepts of whiteness in the East.[45]

Whatever the case, though, officials at Madras imported white and black politics for their own specific needs, and these were much different than in the Atlantic. At Madras, the designation "White Town" in particular was not aimed to forge a new political alliance between whites, nor did it have much to do with blacks. Instead, it helped British officials renegotiate an arrangement unique to Madras, an alliance between the Company and the city's important communities of Portuguese and Armenians. Both of these groups had been allowed to live at Madras since the city's origins, the Portuguese to shore up the small British army, and the Armenians because of their connections to Indian courts and long-standing trade contacts with the Middle East. Among other things, the name "Christian Town" helped to welcome these two groups and encourage their loyalty. At one point, in fact, the Company even circulated a plan to double the size of Christian Town to allow more Armenians to settle there.[46]

By the early eighteenth century, the Company had grown impatient with its Christian allies. British officials had long been wary of the Portuguese. Their Inquisition-minded priests lurked in the nearby settlement of São Thomé, and Portuguese soldiers would often desert in moments of danger, or even spy for rivals. The Armenians fell behind on their taxes; traded with the French, Dutch, and Danes; ignored the authority of Madras courts; and were often suspected of treachery during wartime. Though both groups were clearly Christian, the Company seemed unsure about what color they were. Sometimes it pigeonholed them as white, sometimes it called them by the Portuguese *casta* term *musteez* (*mestiço*), and sometimes it put them in a long list of Indian castes. In this context, the name "White Town" seems to have fit a general strategy among British authorities to cool their welcome of the Portuguese and Armenians and keep disloyal members of both communities on notice.[47]

True to that pattern, the British used "White Town" more frequently as more of them called on the Company to kick its Christian allies out of the more privileged section of town. A long period of prosperity and relative political peace began in Madras during the 1720s, attracting more resident British merchants and soldiers. That put pressure on the finite space in White Town. Competition over real estate, especially with Armenians, exacerbated tensions. In 1749, when the East India Company regained Madras after the French occupation, local Company officials fulfilled the veiled threat contained in the words "White Town." Some

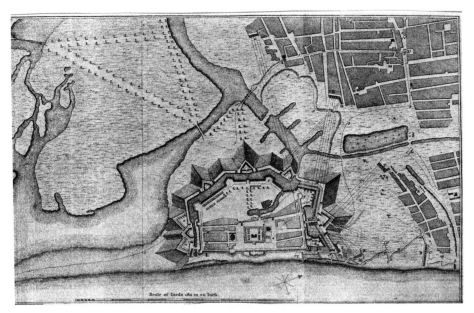

FIGURE 2.3 Were Madras's Armenians and Portuguese white or black? When the British East India Company regained Madras after the French occupation, they resolved this question by forcing both groups of ambiguously colored Christians to live in Black Town. Meanwhile, the French had widened the city's color line by leveling the houses outside the wall, creating a four-hundred-yard free-fire zone. A state-of-the-art fortification system replaced White Town's original walls. From H. Davison Love, *Vestiges of Old Madras* (Government of India, 1913), vol. 3.

Armenians and Portuguese had sided with the French and enriched themselves through the occupation. In response, the British passed new ordinances that for the first time explicitly forbade Armenians and Portuguese from settling in White Town without exception. Houses were confiscated, a pitiful sum was paid in compensation, and both groups were sent to live in the new Black Town four hundred yards distant from the fort. While this latest spasm of separation lasted, it rested upon the most exclusive possible interpretation of local color categories.[48]

## Color before Race

With the help of hindsight, we can see that early European colonial cities in the East at once looked backward for inspiration, possessed unusual new qualities, and sparked innovations that changed urban politics globally. Their monumental architecture and foreign mercantile districts represent their most striking continuities with earlier centuries of urban form. These reflect the overwhelming focus of segregationist politics on military defense and control in the service of colonial expansion. Naturally, quests for profit, commercial monopoly, and control over labor and land also underlay the very foundations of these cities. In fact, the especially strong role armed companies of merchants played in founding and running many of the European colonial cities represents the most unusual characteristic of their politics. However, in residential matters, even economic concerns were sometimes subordinated to military and geopolitical imperatives. This is clear both in slave cities, where the forced residence of Africans on their owners' property conflicted with the hiring-out system—and in Asian and African double cities, where segregation conflicted with merchants' need for contact with native merchants and financiers.

Merchants' waxing power in colonial cities and the strength of their increasingly transhemispheric networks resulted in one of early modern colonial cities' biggest innovations, a secularization of the central political ideas involved in the splitting of cities. Spanish-style segregation, focused on the conversion of non-Christians and the preservation of converts' fragile morality, waned during the seventeenth and eighteenth centuries—even before the segregation of Jews in Western Europe itself. Independent, largely Protestant-run mercantile companies helped this process along, for the dominant view among Dutch and British East India Company officials was that Spanish and Portuguese practices of Catholic intolerance were misguided. Certainly, they obstructed profit-making collaborations with non-Christians.

The color line, of course, was the clearest example of the secularization of urban spatial politics—most graphically attested by the replacement of "Christian Town" with "White Town" at Madras. Color lines were also such cities' biggest legacy to the future, especially when Madras's black-white urban boundaries were adopted by officials in cities like Calcutta and Bombay that achieved greater prominence than Madras during the late eighteenth century.[49]

That said, it is very important to distinguish early modern *color* segregation from *racial* segregation, which only came into being later in the eighteenth century. The word "race" does not appear in any of the official documents pertaining to Madras or other early modern colonial cities before the 1770s. The medieval concepts of "nation" and "people" sufficed for most colonial urban officials when they went about the business of winning support for their residential policies. Later, "color" and "complexion" also surfaced as more general containers for "white" and "black." Most European languages did have some version of the word "race" as early as the sixteenth century, but its commonest contemporary meanings had limited use for colonial urban officials. Mostly it was a word for aristocrats to describe the purity of their families' descent, a synonym for "blood," "seed," "progeny," "posterity," or "lineage."[50]

That would soon change. Already in 1683, François Bernier, a French man of letters who had spent some time at the court of the Mughals, returned to Paris to publish what is often seen as the first effort to transform the word "race" into a conceptual anchor for a system to categorize different strains of humankind based on their skin color. Many years later, in the late eighteenth century, other scientists and philosophers took up Bernier's scheme. A growing number of Enlightenment thinkers argued that Christian theologians were wrong to think that all humans were made equally in God's image. Instead, they concluded, humanity was divided into separate categories, some of which were superior to others. This gave race meanings that were far more elaborate and universalistic than those borne by the color categories of the early 1700s, which functioned to meet a growing number of still quite specific political expediencies. Once scholars began to think in these more elaborate ways, they transformed race, and color along with it, into some of the most important words in global—and urban—politics.

There was also the growing question of cross-color sex, particularly in the British Empire, a question that leads us both to large-scale global movements of people and ideas and to the smallest, most intimate spaces of colonial cities. Ironically, in "segregated" places like Madras, British officials, including court director Josiah Child himself, actually encouraged European men to marry and have children with Asians. Because few European women could be persuaded to migrate halfway around the world to Asia, he argued (once again citing similar practices at Dutch Batavia) that intermarriage with locals would be the only way to guarantee a loyal population in the city. By contrast, in the forcibly "integrated" cities of British America, where white women were much more common, officials increasingly considered all cross-color sex an abomination, declared it illegal in many places, and they consigned all children of black mothers, including "mixed" ones, to slavery. In this way slave cities contributed other key ideas to the intellectual arsenal of later urban segregationists—taboos on cross-color sex, and the black male sexual peril. Those ideas too would soon arrive in Asia and Africa, whether through London, Paris, and Amsterdam, or along the increasingly direct transhemispheric connections between all colonial cities. In that way, divided colonial cities transformed from places where color lines largely arose from needs for defense and control to cities consumed by the grander "natural" obligation to separate the races.[51]

# 3 : Race and the London-Calcutta Connection

## *The Modern Way to Split a City*

The modern politics of urban racial segregation owes its origins—and its capacity to spread almost everywhere—to the relationship between two cities: London and Calcutta. The ever-denser lines of contact between these two places brought into being all three of the institutions that in later years made it possible for segregationists to replicate their ideas and practices worldwide. The London-Calcutta connection allowed Britain to administer the world's first modern colonial empire; it nurtured innovative, ocean-crossing intellectual exchanges among professional scientists and urban reformers; and, as increasing numbers of people shuttled back and forth between the two places, money began to flow in an early version of a multicontinental market in urban real estate. Once the concept of race acquired its universalistic meanings in the late 1700s, it found fertile uses in the epic debates about how to govern London, Calcutta, and the three wide-stretching institutions that the two cities sustained. New race-infused plotlines of urban segregationist politics absorbed Madras-style practices of color-based separation, elaborating their ideological underpinnings. Older genres of city-splitting—associated with god-sponsored monarchy, religious conflict, and overseas commerce—continued to have relevance. But these older themes gradually submerged into new concerns related to race, imperial administration, urban reform, and the global trade in urban land.

The birth of racial segregation occurred within the context of much bigger stories, those of world history's great modern transformations: the slow death of Atlantic slavery; the violent lurches of the great democratic revolutions; the scientific, technological, and industrial revolutions; the "great gap" that the factory system opened up between the wealth and military power of the West and that of Asia, Africa, and Latin America; the Western scrambles for empire in Asia and Africa; the explosion of human migration; the invention of modern concepts of gender and sexuality; and—perhaps above all—the dilemmas caused by the sheer and exponential growth of cities.

Urban birth, rebirth, and explosive, chaotic growth often lay at the heart of the flows of ideas, people, money, and even the disease-bearing bacteria that drove the new, connected institutions and political dramas of London and Calcutta. By 1800 the two cities were the first- and second-largest in the British Empire, and they would remain so until India's independence in 1947. In 1800, London's population of nearly nine hundred thousand was four times larger than it had been in 1600, and it now vied with Peking as the world's largest city. From 1800 to 1850 it more than doubled, and by 1900 it had tripled again, to over six million. By 1950, despite the bombardments of World War II, eight million people clustered near on the banks of the Thames. Calcutta's growth was only somewhat less spectacular: three small Hughli River villages in 1690 became a very large city of two hundred thousand by 1800. The city quintupled in size by 1900 to become the world's fourteenth-largest, and it quadrupled again by independence in 1947, when it was the world's tenth-largest city with over four million inhabitants. In both cities, explosive growth also started earlier than elsewhere. By 1800, only Paris, with a half million people, was as preoccupied with the dilemmas of rapid growth as London and Calcutta; the City of Light contributed its own large part to the new story of segregation, including the dividing of Calcutta.[1]

Historians usually attribute the modern explosion of cities to the Industrial Revolution. In that interpretation, industrial capitalists and the working class were the city's principal characters, and their bitter class struggles were the main drama in town. Certainly that story was important, especially in London but also in Calcutta by the late nineteenth century. From the beginning, though, both London and Calcutta grew for two other reasons. They were imperial capitals that housed large corps of government administrators and military people, topped off by the empire's political elites. And they were two of the world's very largest commercial centers, swarming with wealthy merchants, financiers, middlemen, shipbuilders, marine suppliers, and sailors—and, to meet all their needs, a vast population of craftspeople, petty merchants, laborers, and servants.

An empire, and the trade that helped create that empire, was thus critical to both cities' growth. In turn, the growth of cities redounded to the glory of the empire and its increasing economic dominance over the globe. But cities that grew that fast also gave the empire and its wealthy urban elites enormous political headaches. In part those headaches were about morality and control—how to deal with the anonymity of such complicated spaces and the "vice," crime, and, above all, anti-imperial opposition movements that proliferated in cities. Arguably the biggest immediate problems, though, concerned the basic biological and ecological regime of the city—how to feed and house so many people, move their waste out of town, and, in particular, contend with the causes of disease.

Modern empires became deeply invested in solving these problems, but to do so they had to depend ever more heavily on professionals, especially doctors, medical researchers, and public health experts (later, housing reformers, architects, and town planners would join the effort). These professionals—some of them imperial officials, others reformist gadflies, and most of whom moved back and forth between those two positions—believed that the greatness of the empire and the progress (if not the very survival) of civilization meant that cities had to be remade even as they exploded in size. Because many of their prescriptions—for sewer systems, public water supplies, new streets, and the like—were politically very bitter pills involving substantial taxation and sometimes large-scale land seizure, much of reformers' work involved harping on government, whether municipal or imperial, for more unpopular action. In addition to using their official positions, they built their own power by establishing their own influential and independent transoceanic institutions—professional associations, conferences, lecture circuits, books, scholarly journals, and personal travel. Meanwhile, their use of the new mass market press also grew savvier. From the beginning, one of the most well-worn long-distance routes traveled by these networked urban reformers was between London and Calcutta. Ironically, their ability to command the ear of those in power grew when a microscopic bacteria they knew nothing about—the cholera bacillus—itself traveled from Calcutta and its environs by ship to London and elsewhere in Europe.

The birth of modern segregation was also the work of cities' builders and owners. As empires swallowed up new land, and as democratic institutions came in and out of being in Europe, the right to own, buy, and sell land spread unevenly and haltingly—from an aristocratic privilege to a middle-class prerogative, and from Europe to some of its colonies.

The transnational capitalist urban real estate market was one result. With it came the rising influence of financiers, developers, estate agents, surveyors, property lawyers, law courts, and homeowners, all of whom could form their own organizations. While they shared concerns with imperial officials and reformers, their focus never wavered from a single priority: to protect their investment and make property pay. Because so many people led lives that alternated between residences in London and Calcutta, the institutions and ideas that governed the real estate markets in both cities took much of their shape from each other, and the money and the investment decisions people made in the two cities grew increasingly connected as well.

That said, the innovations that arose within the London-Calcutta connection were due as much to the differences in the two cities' politics as to their connections. Put much too baldly, the politics of urban space in London began with differences between the classes. The city was the site for the world's first use of government-protected legal instruments— restrictive covenants—to divide neighborhoods for the rich and "respectable" (the West End) from the poor, the "paupers," and the "unrespectable" (the East End). In Calcutta, by contrast, color was the driving edge of the political theater, and, after about 1770, race. There, official policing of the color line between White Town and Black Town actually grew less consistent over time, but the imperial and local governments did pioneer crucial tools later used elsewhere for race and class segregation— peacetime, sanitation-driven building clearances and forced removals.

Even so, the dense connections between London and Calcutta ultimately meant that the language and tools of urban space in the two cities melded somewhat over time. London's East End poor, and its Irish poor especially, became racialized as the "darkest England." White Town Calcuttans learned to suffer a handful of "respectable natives" as neighbors, just as London's aristocrats found ways to live alongside merchant commoners. In both places race and class distinctions grew up alongside a more pliable concept, one that soon became a kind of frosty-polite disguise for both: the idea of "civilization." The question of housing for servants and other essential people from across the class or color line rankled separationists in both cities, forcing boundaries between neighborhoods to be porous in order to survive. In both cities, monumental architecture was redesigned for use as a symbol of the new political priorities. And in both cities the urban fringe was where the "civilized" spaces lay. Modern segregation, at least in the orbit of the British Empire, was typified by the vilification of the "slum" and the glorification of the exclusive suburb.[2]

## How London Conquered and Divided Calcutta

The foundation of Calcutta in 1690 by the maverick East India Company employee Job Charnock marked the culmination of three decades of efforts by the court of directors of the British East India Company in London to replicate the commercial success of Madras, this time in the far richer region of Bengal. Some of the same mercantile and geopolitical concerns that created the White Town and Black Town of Madras applied to Calcutta, the big difference being that Bengal was, at time of Calcutta's founding, part of the Muslim Mughal Empire under the rule of the mighty Aurangzeb. His powerful local governor, or nawab, had long forbidden Europeans to fortify their settlements on his territory—and he had the weapons and the armies to back up his command. Only after the Company helped the nawab suppress a Hindu rebel, and then paid a bribe that "made a large hole in our cash" to Aurangzeb's grandson, Prince Azimush-Shah, did London get its wish for a fortified factory. In 1702 the British flag was hoisted over Fort William in Dihi Kalikata, one of three villages (*dihi*) on the eastern shore of the Hughly River granted to them by the prince. The village of Calcutta eventually became known as the White Town. To the north, the cloth-weaving village of Sutanuti became the nucleus of Black Town, and to the south lay Govindapore, home of the Seths and Bysacks, some of Bengal's richest Hindu commercial and money-lending families, who quickly became the Company's main commercial go-betweens, known as *banians* in Bengal.[3]

The power of the nawab of Bengal ultimately made a walled boundary between the Black Town and the White Town, like that at Madras, impossible. During two prolonged periods, the court and the local governor and council actively vacillated over the possibility of such a wall, sometimes fearing that the nawab would take offense if they built it and sometimes worrying that he would attack the town anyway and thus make it essential. In their first bout of indecision, from 1708 to 1714, London pushed an idea of taxing the "blacks" to dig a defensive ditch around the English part of the town and "to color over our reall design of making the place tenable against . . . the Moors [the Mughals] by alledging that the Ditch was to drain the Townes &c." The governor in Calcutta dragged his feet

79

for some years, and the idea went out of circulation, though London was sure that a good military threat would change local minds.[4]

That threat came during the tumultuous 1740s, when raiders of the Maratha Confederacy of Western India, which had been seizing large chunks of territory from the now-tottering Mughals, appeared on the opposite shore of the Hughly. The French took Madras a few years later and threatened Calcutta from their own redoubt at Chandernagore, a few miles up the Hughly. Still, at Calcutta, another long period of vacillation ensued. Fort William, which was never much of a stronghold anyway, was now crowded on all sides by houses of wealthy merchants who did not want them pulled down and a church whose steeple was much higher than the fort's walls. The outer boundaries of White Town itself had become ambiguous. A dozen engineers and surveyors proposed a total of seven different plans of defense over the next sixteen years, including a wooden palisade that zigzagged around the furthest-outlying English houses. The city's wealthy Hindu financiers, seeing that the English were only willing to fortify their own neighborhoods, seized the initiative and began digging a kind of moat, later called the Mahratta Ditch, around the whole city, Black as well as White. The English helped with a loan for the ditch, then added a few dozen gates at the many entry points to the White Town. Finally, in 1756, a fiercely anti-European nawab of Bengal, the famous Siraj-ud Daula, assembled an army of fifty thousand soldiers, swept across the unfinished ditch, past the feeble gatehouses and remaining palisades, into the heart of the city. He commandeered the church steeple that peeked over Fort William, made quick work of the fort's walls, took the place by evening, and imprisoned 120 British defenders in their own dungeon—the storied "black hole" of Calcutta—where most suffocated to death by next morning.[5]

As every British schoolchild knows, everything changed after that. Under Robert Clive, the Company's forces defeated Siraj-ud Daula at the battle of Pallashi (Plassey) a few months later, and they deposed the nawab in favor of a succession of puppets. In 1763 the Company discarded the last of these puppets and received the Mughal emperor's permission to take over the governorship of Bengal outright. In London, Parliament passed the Regulating Act of 1772 and the East India Act of 1784, making Calcutta an imperial subcapital, the seat of a British governor general who oversaw the Company's possessions in the two other "presidencies" at Madras and Bombay. As capital, Calcutta became the nerve center for the ensuing hundred-year British conquest of India, and thus the urban incubator of modern Western imperialism.[6]

In the heat of wartime, authorities at Calcutta acted much more quickly than they could before to rearrange the defense of the city. They tore down many of the merchants' houses that the nawab had left standing south of the old fort and opened up a vast open field known as the Esplanade. To do that, they ordered the leading Hindu families of the southern village of Govindpore to move north into Black Town. On the ruins of their houses, British engineers built an enormous citadel that became the new Fort William. English merchants began plowing the proceeds of their newfound wealth into ever more elaborate, columned mansions along the east side of the Esplanade, clearing the jungles and filling the swamps of the Chauringhi district. In the 1780s, Governor General Warren Hastings convinced the Company to spring for a mansion called Belvedere, intended for his "refreshment," which was located on a slight rise south of Chauringhi, outside the old Maratha Ditch, in a village called Alipur. Others soon followed, and white Calcutta spread to suburbs in several other villages, such as Garden Reach, Kidderpore, and Ballygunj. Then, in 1798, Governor General Wellesley signaled Britain's intention to remain permanently in India by building an imposing government house for himself at the north end of the Esplanade, where it dominated a European administrative and business district.

Calcutta had become the City of Palaces. The view of the city by ship from the south, which was how most Europeans approached it, was a monumental vision—the wide Esplanade surrounded by a halo of blinding white *chunam*. The enormous, multiplying Black Town, with its narrow lanes, shrines, and its large merchant houses surrounded by thousands of thatched huts, lay behind this wall of white, far out of sight.[7]

To police the color line, authorities in Calcutta had issued periodic wartime orders, much like those at Madras, expelling Indians, Portuguese, and Armenians from the White Town. For some time after 1763 the Company sought to avoid problematic entanglements in the hinterland by ordering British citizens to remain *inside* Calcutta city limits. This was ineffectual, given the enormous profits that became available in Bengal's inland trade after the defeat of the nawab. But as imperial officials fastened their rule more deeply upon Calcutta, the diminishing military threat allowed them to pull back from policing the boundaries of White Town and Black Town. The first racialized urban color line was

FIGURE 3.1 The City of Palaces. Looking north from Chowringhee Road across the Esplanade, Government House is visible in the distance. In the foreground, neoclassical villas in European styles are set inside walled compounds. In White Town's streets, Indian servants dominate foot traffic, and English men and women seal themselves in their carriages. Engraving by Robert Havell, from James Baillie Fraser, *Views of Calcutta* (London: Radwell, Martin, and Smith, Elder, 1824–26), plate 3. © The British Library Board.

thus a notoriously fuzzy one. The new White Town and its suburbs to the southeast did become the residence of almost all the city's Europeans of means, and its lower density and imported architectural style contrasted with that of Black Town. But a large mixed district also developed around the ill-famed Burra Bazaar between the white and black towns, filled with castoff white soldiers, sailors, and petty merchants; their Indian colleagues, lovers, and wives; and their mixed-race offspring. A number of wealthy Indians also lived in White Town itself, and so did thousands of servants who staffed the elaborate households of the rich and whose families filled the city's notorious "bustees"—the self-built, thatch-roofed slums of Chauringhi's marshes. In the daily life of White Town's streets, the color line was most clearly demarcated by the doors of white peoples' horse carriages, which sealed them off from the thousands of Indians going about their business on foot.[8]

London's conquest and division of Calcutta thus did not give the world a model for government-coerced racial zoning. What it did was much more important, though: it set into motion the underlying insti-

FIGURE 3.2  Burra Bazaar. Calcutta's Black Town and White Town bumped up against each other in this teeming market district east of Government House. To the right (south) are what might be the offices of a British mercantile firm. To the north are houses of Indians and Eurasians. Because British rule depended on alliances across this color line, no government coercion kept it in place. However, the city is the birthplace for many of the ideological justifications for urban racial segregation that would later radiate across the world. Engraving by Robert Havell, from James Baillie Fraser, *Views of Calcutta* (London: Radwell, Martin, and Smith, Elder, 1824-26), plate 24. © The British Library Board.

tutions and ideologies needed for the replication—and the increasingly coercive politics—of white and black town systems across the world. If modern empire was the first of these institutions, race, which also came to Calcutta via London, was the driving ideology.

## Race and the Imperial City

Race was not the exclusive invention of people working in the London-Calcutta orbit, but the growing numbers of those who lived their lives between the two imperial capitals did introduce this increasingly influential concept into the politics of two modern phenomena: divided colonial cities and the practice of imperial domination more generally.

83

To put this point in context, we need to recall that beginning in the late eighteenth century, race rapidly became one of the most successful concepts in global politics, if not *the* most successful of all. Not just cities and empires, but *all* of the key institutions of the modern era were deeply marked by the political uses they found for race. In the crusade against slavery, race was critical to both abolitionists and slave holders who wanted to justify their "peculiar institution." In the industrial class struggle, capitalists used race to divide and control their restive work-forces, and white workers used it to preserve privileged occupations for themselves. Leaders of nations and nationalist movements used race as a gauge for who belonged in the nation and who did not. In countries that loftily espoused "universal rights," race offered a supposedly scientific benchmark that defined who was, practically speaking, truly "fit" for citizenship. Elite political parties used race to convince newly enfranchised white workers that they faced their biggest threat from powerless black people and that they should support the programs of their social superiors, no matter how oppressive or anti-egalitarian. Race, of course, became essential to the conquest and genocide of the native peoples of the Americas and Australasia, as well as to the control of mass migrations of people. It also more subtly sustained the Victorian middle-class family by making defense against race-mixing and black rape the outer measure of masculine honor and of female respectability—thus also helping to rewrite the rules of patriarchy and to sanctify sex within marriage.

People who built each of these institutions used race for their own reasons. But much of the blame for its grim political success should go to its scholarly reinventors. As we know, the word "race" has existed in most European languages since the sixteenth century, but it had been used relatively rarely and narrowly, mostly by noblemen to describe the purity of their family's lineages or clans and by literary figures in a variety of similar, but more flowery, ways. Then, in the eighteenth century—following earlier suggestions by the Frenchman François Bernier—Enlightenment scholars like the French ethnologist George Louis Buffon, the German anthropologist Johann Friedrich Blumenbach, and more well-known philosophers like David Hume, Voltaire, and Thomas Jefferson gave the word a much more encompassing meaning by turning race into a universal system of categorizing human difference. All humankind could be divided into races, they argued, marked by their contrasting physical characteristics, such as skull shape, facial features, hair texture, size of reproductive anatomy, and, above all, skin color. Such physical charac-

RACE AND THE LONDON-CALCUTTA CONNECTION

teristics explained cultural characteristics, such as each race's level of "civilization"—another Enlightenment invention. From there, scientists proposed a hierarchy of the races, with the white races at the top, the darkest ones at the bottom, and others somewhere in between. Cross-racial reproduction, some thought, could create less viable mixed races and even threaten the superior races with degradation. Finally, race became a theory of human geography. Each race was seen as inhabiting a "natural homeland" whose natural features, climate, soil, and vegetation were uniquely suitable to it. This idea—and its arrogant, all-embracing scope—proved enormously adaptable and debatable, and race propelled itself into politics in great part precisely because it could be remolded to justify virtually any form of social injustice.

Pieces of this potent conversation about race began to appear in the thoughts of people in the London-Calcutta circuit at about the time of the conquest of Bengal. In the 1760s, Robert Orme, who had served the East India Company in Calcutta and Madras for two decades before returning to London, began writing a series of popular volumes on the history of British rule in India. The newly fashionable idea of race crept into his writings by the 1770s—and its main goal was to justify British dominion. "We see throughout India a race of men," he wrote, "whose make, physiognomy, and muscular strength, convey ideas of an effeminacy which surprizes when pursued through such numbers of the species, and when compared to the form of the European who is making the observation." This racial "effeminacy" (another example of the many ways gender and race could be linked) derived from the warm climate and natural plenty of the land, and it left the many millions of Hindus at once a "tricking, deceitful people" and ever-corruptible, willing to live supinely under the rule of a small minority of Muslims. The British could be satisfied, Orme implied, that India's lot was to be subject to outside rule.[9]

Other important officials and scholars in Calcutta took a somewhat more sympathetic view of the Indian races. Governor General Warren Hastings was the most prominent of these; in 1784 he helped found Calcutta's Asiatic Society and tapped the scholar William Jones as its first president. Jones's research on ancient Sanskrit texts had convinced him not only that India possessed a long tradition of law that undercut the theory of Hindus' natural receptivity to "Oriental despotism," but also that the close linguistic connection between Indian and European languages suggested some commonalities of heritage. Today's scholars have rightly criticized such "Orientalist" thinking for imagining India to be unchanging and lost in the mists of time and for imposing En-lightenment-era obsessions with the systematizing of knowledge upon ever-changing and widely debated Asian concepts, such as caste. But race theory in the early years of British India rarely took on the harsh edge it did in the contemporary Atlantic world, where a school of British and American "polygenists" argued that Africans had a completely separate origin and an unchangeably inferior physical and moral makeup from whites. British imperial thought, at least until the Great Uprising of 1857, was virtually unanimous that India was a stalled civilization that was nonetheless changeable and even improvable—though only with a good shot of the energy of the British race.

By holding out the possibility of change, the British Empire could appear benevolent and progressive even as it fastened its racial dictator-ship upon India's hundreds of millions. Even William Jones argued that no matter how much he "wish[ed] for universal liberty," the Hindus "are incapable of [it]; few of them have an idea of it; and those, who have, do not wish it. They must . . . be ruled by an absolute power." Governor General Hastings had envisioned an empire that would include Indians among its higher officials, but this vision was rejected by his successor, Charles Lord Cornwallis, who arrived in Calcutta in 1786 (a few years after he surrendered Britain's thirteen North American colonies by los-ing the battle of Yorktown). Cornwallis's sentiments were closer to those of Robert Orme. "Every native of Hindustan," he once groused, "I verily believe is corrupt." The Indian Civil Service he founded to administer the empire was off-limits to all natives—and also, pointedly, to anyone of mixed race as well.[10]

In point of fact, nothing had so jangled the lines of connection be-tween London and Calcutta in the late eighteenth century as sensational stories of race mixing. The great irony of the White Town–Black Town system, from it origins, was that it was actually based on official encour-agement of marriage between Englishmen and native women—in great contrast to the slave cities of North America, where cross-race sex of any kind was looked upon as an abomination. The difficulties of long sea voyages to the Eastern Hemisphere had proved an obstacle to sending Englishwomen to India in any great numbers, and many prominent British men at Madras, Bombay, and Calcutta had longstanding relation-ships with Indian and Indo-Portuguese women, even if they were some-times prevented from marriage. Elihu Yale of Madras actually sent his English wife back to London in part so he could spend more time with his Portuguese Jewish mistress. The otherwise not very tenderhearted Job Charnock, Calcutta's founder, famously married his Indian wife after rescuing her from a *sati* (widow burning), and then later honored her grave by regular sacrifices of roosters. From the late eighteenth century and well into the nineteenth, officials at Calcutta and elsewhere in India maintained numerous wives and lovers in separate apartments (*zenanas*) of their households, following the custom of upper-caste Indians.[11]

Race theorists in India began warning of the perils of mixing as early as the 1770s, if not before. But such behavior in Calcutta literally went on trial in London in 1786, when Warren Hastings was recalled to face impeachment for corruption. Edmund Burke's famous, fiery, often over-the-top speeches highlighted the proceedings, which Londoners followed eagerly for more than a decade. In part this spectacle expressed the feeling that the "British nabobs" of Calcutta had descended to the level of corrupt "Oriental despots" through their commercial, cultural, and sexual contacts with Indians. (As Burke put it, Hastings's "heart [was] blackened to the very blackest, a heart dyed deep in blackness"). There was much fuel for such sentiments in England at the time. Aristocrats were envious of the conspicuous riches that merchants brought home with them, and in the years after Pallashi those fortunes were enormous. Mrs. Hastings herself, a European, caused a scandal in both India and England when she left her first husband for the governor general on the outbound ship voyage to India. When she returned to gossipy London, her jewelry, studded with enormous Indian diamonds, became a symbol of ill-gotten gain, and her title of "Nabobina" endowed her with a hint of none-too-honorary blackness. All of this racial uproar was enhanced by a rising Evangelical movement focused on moral perfection—which glowed with the early successes of its crusade against slavery in the Americas and was led in Parliament by the formidable William Wilberforce. Evangelical spokespersons spun Calcutta as a kind of Gomorrah of dark-skinned dancing girls, hookah-smoking Englishwomen, polygamy, palm-tree liquor, and peculation.[12]

Though Hastings was eventually acquitted in his trial, the merchants who had invented black town–white town segregation had now been declared guilty of too much race-crossing. Parliament took increasing oversight over the East India Company after 1784. With the appointment of Cornwallis, a tradition began of giving the governor generalship to aristocrats over merchants. Cornwallis's civil service regulations, in turn, were designed to create a corps of professional administrators who were forbidden from commerce with natives and discouraged from any personal contact or experiments with Oriental customs. The aloof rule of the "conquering race," ensconced in its gleaming City of Palaces, had begun.[13]

## The London-Calcutta Sanitation Connection

Once the British East India Company defeated the nawab of Bengal, the new empire could give more attention to another, more mysterious, and much deadlier enemy—what early English Calcuttans knew as their city's propensity for "Agues, ffevers and ffluxes." In the opinion of one early traveler to Calcutta, Job Charnock "could not have chosen a more unhealthful place" for the city. The town clerk's record books, the traveler pointed out, contained records of 460 burials of Englishmen within the first six months of the arrival of 1,500 Company employees. The historian P. J. Marshall has calculated that during the eighteenth century, well over half of all Company servants in Bengal died while in India, cutting short the dream most cherished of returning to England as rich men. The death rates of European soldiers were particularly distressing for an empire based on military force. After going to pains to recruit soldiers and to pay the expense of shipping them halfway around the world, the Company buried a quarter of their total in India *every year*. Only five of the 230 soldiers Robert Clive brought with him to Bengal from Madras, a somewhat healthier spot, were still alive a year after their victory at Pallashi. The new Fort William, its fearsome battlements notwithstanding, became a notorious deathtrap for soldiers who lived within its fetid barracks.[14]

Why was this? European medical researchers, and London doctors in particular, had developed explanations that proved more promising for public health than they might sound. A revival of Hippocrates's classic text *Air, Water, and Places* in the seventeenth century inspired some of these scholars to focus their attentions beyond explanations for disease located within the body, and toward environmental causes. Following the lead of the London doctor Thomas Sydenham, the "miasmatic" theory gained currency; it explained sickness as the result of heat, putrid air, foul water, rotting vegetation, and "emanations" from the soil. Certain places had more of these things—for example, cities like London, swampy areas, and especially the world's steamy "tropical zones." Calcutta contained all of these threats in one urban ecology: it was brutally hot nine months of the year; it was surrounded by a rainforest whose profuse vegetation needed to be constantly hacked back; it was deluged by monsoons that flooded most of the town for five months of the year, leaving behind pools of standing water and swampland during the remaining months; and it was occasionally overwhelmed by the smell of rotting fish on the shore of the Salt Lake to the east of town when its waters receded. To top it off, decomposing human bodies would often float by on the Hughly, mostly those of poor people who could not afford the ritual cremation at special riverside peers (*ghats*) set aide for the purpose.[15]

In the late eighteenth century, European medical researchers who tested miasmatic theories in the West Indies and India helped to develop a crucial aspect of contemporary racial theory, the notion that the different races of humankind had different natural homelands. The native races of the tropics, they noted, were affected by the dangerous disease environments there, but much less so than Europeans. Much of the project of imperialism thus hung on the big question of whether the races could change as they moved from one racial homeland to another. Could Europeans, most importantly, adapt to life in the very places they had colonized? Many of these researchers were optimistic, suggesting that if Europeans were careful over several years, they could achieve a level of immunity to local disease approaching that of natives.[16]

By the early 1800s, though, that optimism was beginning to wear off. The lead pessimist was James Johnson, one of the most influential researchers on tropical medicine. His experiences of life in Calcutta inspired the seminal book *Influence of Tropical Climates on European Constitutions* (1813) in which he argued that the "tender frame of man" was "incapable of sustaining that degree of exposure to the whole range of causes and effects incident to, or arising from the vicissitudes of climate." The best one could do in India was to adopt some of those very customs that imperial officials had been discouraging, even including moderate hookah smoking. "The untraveled cynic may designate these luxuries by the contemptuous epithet of 'Asiatic effeminacy'; but the medical philosopher will be disposed to regard them as rational ... salutary precautions, rendered necessary by the great difference between a temperate and torrid zone." But, Johnson argued, no behavior change whatsoever could stop the tendency of Europeans to "droop" in hot climates, to slowly degenerate both morally and physically, and—thus sickened into a daze—even seek out "vicious and immoral" cross-racial sex.[17]

That said, there was another path. In addition to changing white people's behavior, medical professionals argued, it was also possible to rebuild their environment, at least in a city. London itself, to some degree, showed the way. Like Calcutta, it too, after all, was a "great wen"—nearly a million people in 1800 stacked on top of ground suffused with their own waste and the decomposing bodies of their shallowly buried forebears—and it was watered by the Thames, easily as stinking and pestiferous as the Hughly. Authorities in Britain were by no means in the forefront of European public health practice at the time, and they had not effectively followed up on the opportunity opened up by the Great Fire of 1666 to rebuild the city center much more salubriously than before.

Yet some improvements were in the offing, for miasmatic theory, while wrong in itself, did suggest some useful public health measures. The city built an extensive sewerage and water supply system, for example—even if the reliance on the Thames for both waste removal and drinking water was a major defect! Advanced medical research using statistics had confirmed that people in overcrowded districts succumbed to fevers and other ills more severely. Little had been done about neighborhoods that would later be called "slums," like St. Giles and the Seven Dials, but authorities did widen a few streets for ventilation purposes. Laws designed to clean the smoky air had also had some effect. A system of hospitals and dispensaries acknowledged the public obligation to provide health care to the city's poor and ordinary people.[18]

From early on, the court of directors of the East India Company sought to export some of these public health advances to Bengal. The ditch they ordered the governor to dig around Calcutta's White Town in 1708 was mostly an excuse for defensive outwork, but they had the system under London streets explicitly in mind; the rainwater collected was to be directed into "proper Drains" that "might be made to run under ground Archt and built with brick like our common sewers." Over time, authorities also invested in projects based on Bengali traditions of public engineering, which involved digging large square tanks, or reservoirs, to store storm and ground water and using the excavated dirt to fill stagnant pools and swampy areas.[19]

It was the ruthless Governor General Richard Wellesley who, in 1803, truly set into motion the rebuilding of Calcutta, squarely on the model of British public health practices. Furthermore, by putting the power of his office behind his proposals, he allowed authorities in Calcutta to leapfrog the progress made in London, invent novel financing schemes for their work, and then envision more comprehensive projects of slum clearance and avenue building decades before sanitary reformers could manage them back home in the imperial capital—or, for that matter, anywhere in Europe. The world travels of the cholera bacillus, which lurked in profusion in Calcutta's swamps, ditches, and tanks, would soon help drive this transoceanic commerce in sanitation-based urban spatial politics.

Wellesley's plan for Calcutta envisioned remaking the entire town in the image of the City of Palaces. His intention was to introduce "a greater degree of order, symmetry, and magnificence in the streets, roads, ghauts [piers], and wharfs, public edifices and private inhabitations." Both public health and military goals would drive the plan; it would "meliorate the climate and ... secure ... a just and salutary system of police." His most ambitious goal was to ventilate "those quarters of the town occupied principally by the native inhabitants" where "houses have been built without order or regularity and the streets and lanes have been formed without attention to ... health."[20]

Wellesley appointed a committee to oversee these plans in 1804. It and its successors, the Lottery Committee (organized in 1817 during the city's first deadly cholera epidemic) and the Fever Hospital Committee (first convened in 1837), pioneered aspects of authoritarian urban planning usually credited to much more famous projects in Europe. Though the Lottery Committee got its name from its unique funding source, the town lottery, the amateur planners who populated it hoped to pay for new straight streets in the city by "excess condemnation"—that is, by seizing more land than they needed and financing the work by reselling those larger plots at a price enhanced by their location on the new avenue. This plan predated that of Baron Haussmann in Paris, who made the practice famous, by over thirty years. The committee's work in clearing what its members thought of as degraded housing in Black Town began a quarter century before the razing of London's St. Giles slum for Oxford Street (1847).[21]

Such techniques would later be used repeatedly in the service of more thorough plans of urban segregation of dark-skinned people and the urban poor than those at Calcutta. The most important thing about the schemes in Calcutta was the subtle change in ideas about race and disease that underlay them. On the one hand, the rather unimaginative grid of widened thoroughfares that the Lottery Committee successfully drove through the small lanes of Black Town was meant to facilitate military and commercial traffic through town and also to allow the prevailing winds to clear the city of foul air held responsible for cholera and other diseases like malaria (literally "bad air"). But the new racial thinking operated as well: an overriding goal was to "render the seat of [British India's] government a place where Englishmen, having the usual constitutions of their race, can live in the full possession of their faculties, and their vigor." More importantly, they also increasingly saw natives, their dense neighborhoods, and their cultural practices as a main reason for urban disease—and thus a major racial threat to white people.[22]

The surgeon James Ranald Martin laid out this new line of thought most clearly and influentially. Martin arrived in Calcutta in 1817 in the midst of the chaos brought on by the world's first large-scale epidemic of cholera, which he witnessed while attending to Europeans at the city's segregated Presidency General Hospital. Later, he endured the first Burmese campaign as a military surgeon. There he was at constant odds with his commanders, for his professional duty to protect soldiers from miasmas made it impossible for him to abide officers' repeated decisions to locate camps near swamps. Memories of many deaths of soldiers due to illness—as usual, far exceeding the toll of combat—stayed with him, as did his own recurring bout with malaria. Back in Calcutta, he entered private practice and by the mid-1830s became the white town's most sought-after physician, on close terms with the governors general of India William Bettinck and Lord Auckland.[23]

In addition to his engagement with worldwide debates on tropical disease, Martin was also a utilitarian, a follower of the British philosopher Jeremy Bentham's theory that the laws of a society should promote the maximization of "utility," that is, "the greatest happiness for the greatest number of people." This philosophical school had itself developed along the London-Calcutta axis. James Mill, Bentham's close ally and later an employee of the East India Company, wrote a history of British India (1818) that argued that Hindu civilization offered little if any utility to the mass of its inhabitants and that the British needed to reform it according to Benthamite principles. By the 1830s, in Britain, other close associates of Bentham, like James Philip Kay, Thomas Southwood Smith, and (most famously) Edwin Chadwick, had used utilitarian arguments to bring the Victorian era's infamous workhouses into being. In their enthusiasm, they blurred some of the lines between race politics in the colonies and class politics in Britain. In 1832, Kay, a doctor, wrote an influential pamphlet describing his frenzied work during Manchester's

**FIGURE 3.3** J. A. Schalk's *Plan of the City of Calcutta*, 1823. To the north is Black Town. The Lottery Committee pierced a few straight avenues through its dense maze of streets, inherited from former villages such as Sutanuti. Government House and the European business district lie along the Hughly River on the site of Kalikata village. The Esplanade is dominated by the new Fort William (built on the cleared site of Govindpore). East of the fort are the widely spaced compounds of White Town, carved out of the jungles of Chowringhee. Courtesy of American Geographical Society Library, Milwaukee.

cholera outbreak—widely seen as an unwelcome if mysterious gift from Calcutta's swamps. A "squalid and debilitated race" had grown in England, he argued, further contaminated by "hordes" of "savage" Irish immigrants, whose neighborhoods had become an "excrementitious" source of miasmas that threatened the public health of all. By the late 1830s, poor law administrators like Chadwick, Smith, and Kay launched a sanitarian crusade, lobbying the central government to take a driving role in preventing ill health in cities, in part to relieve the suffering of the poor, but above all to safeguard the lives of respectable classes.[24]

In Calcutta, James Ranald Martin followed and anticipated many of these reformers' moves, though with an even greater attention to racial threats. His *Medical Topography of Calcutta* (1837) added to a growing genre of similar studies of the healthfulness of certain places in India, and it brought into grave doubts the possibility of any long-term health for Englishmen in their capital. In the book, Martin combined Mill's critique of Hindu civilization with Kay's concern about the moral roots of disease and poor people's threat to the wider society. His survey of the mud and thatched huts that surrounded the native mansions of Black Town exasperated him: "when I mention the customs of the Hindus that are injurious to health, I should write a respectably sized book." Caste "superstitions" and Hindu traditions of charity topped the list, followed by the building practices, overcrowding, and the convoluted layout of the native city. All of this, he warned, posed a great threat to Europeans. Natives' "health and character will doubtless be felt in their own persons, but it is undeniable that they must ultimately operate on their visitors."[25]

The only redeeming thing about the site of Calcutta was that Charnock had placed "the black town to windward during the monsoon"— otherwise "must the Europeans have tried their fortunes somewhere else." Still, anticipating Edwin Chadwick's famous mantras, he had faith that prevention of "the most fatal scourges of the human race" could be traced to the "free exposure of the streets of London to the sun and wind, a hard regular pavement preserved clean by proper scavengers; the construction of common sewers and privies, and the advantage of a flowing stream." On the basis of the *Medical Topography*, Martin persuaded Governor General Auckland to establish a Fever Hospital Committee in Calcutta to pick up the work of the Lottery Committee, which London had abolished in 1830 under pressure from Evangelicals who deemed its financing scheme unseemly. Over the next decade the new committee hashed out a new design for the city's sewers (this one recognized Calcutta's tilt toward the Salt Lake, not the pestiferous Hughly, though it focused on draining White Town). It rammed laws through the supreme council forbidding the erection of thatched huts. And, most ambitious of all, it unveiled a revised plan for straighter, parallel, air-clearing boulevards through Black Town.[26]

At the peak of his influence in Calcutta, another bout of malaria forced Martin to recognize his own racial frailty in the tropics and retreat to London. His reputation arrived home before him, though—courtesy of his book and his trans-imperial professional connections—and soon he joined forces with the luminaries of the sanitation-reform movement, eager to accomplish in Britain and ultimately the empire at large some of the things he had helped set in motion from India. As such, he became a transnational force in his own right.[27]

Would the Fever Hospital Committee's wrecking crews actually plow even more new radial avenues through Black Town's alleys? More pertinently, would Martin's racial theory of disease lead where it seemed to be leading, to more intense state-sponsored segregation of black and white? The answers to these questions were bound up in another transnational force, one that Martin had neglected in his *Medical Topography*: the capitalist real estate market.[28]

## The West End–White Town Connection

The modern capitalist urban real estate market, and the industry that profited from it, came into being because of two major developments in the world history of cities. One was the first sustained effort to segregate a city by class: the creation of London's West End. The other was the increased role of overseas merchants in buying and selling urban land for temporary use in Asian colonial cities like Calcutta and Madras, and the reinvestment of some of their trading and real estate profits in more permanent residences in places, such as back home in the West End. As people and money moved between White Town and the West End, so did ideas about exclusive suburban residence and architectural style and so did the institutions that made a capitalist land market possible—more secure property rights, more accurate land surveys, title deeds, official registries, property courts, and profit-hungry corporations devoted to development and finance.

As this market came into being, London land speculators invented the driving intellectual principle of class segregation, the idea that having poor people as close neighbors brought down the property values of the rich. The same speculators also invented a tool to prevent the invasion of wealthy neighborhoods by unrespectable elements, namely the restrictive covenant in title deeds. As Europeans and Americans grabbed increasing swaths of urban land worldwide during the nineteenth century, such segregationist ideas and tools would be imported elsewhere and translated into a language of race. In Calcutta, that was not politically possible. Some of the ideas about class threats to property values entered the real estate market of White Town, but white landowners did not widely adopt a position that Indians posed a racial threat to housing values, and authorities' early efforts to impose racial restrictions on European land-selling were abandoned. Instead, by the nineteenth century the city's housing market actually became a source of political power for Bengali landholders and other wealthy Indians who stood squarely in the way of any formal racial zoning legislation and later used their wealth in land to help launch an anticolonial movement in the heart of the imperial capital.

More broadly, the story of the West End–White Town connection is the story of the bicontinental invention of modern-era exclusive suburbs. While the outskirts of cities had often been seen as disreputable places, elites going back to ancient Babylon and Rome had often lauded the Arcadian pleasures of exclusive semirural retreats. When, in the 1500s, Europeans embarked on a major reappreciation of their classical past, they revived a taste for the villas of Cicero's Roman *suburbium* as places to retire during the summer or once a week or even as one pole of a daily commute.[29]

The Venetian architect Andrea Palladio led the way with his famous Villa Rotondo, the archetype of the classically inspired suburban villa, with its four equally columned sides surmounted with a perfect dome. It was not long before a British aristocrat built his own Villa Rotondo in the London suburb of Chiswick, sparking a mania for a version of "Palladian" architecture along the banks of the Thames to the west of the city. At the start, this was exclusively an aristocratic fad. The king of England himself sold some of his land to noble families who built an enclave around Pall Mall in Westminster, just west of London City, a somewhat more urbanized version of the aristocratic country seat in which several prominent people's villas abutted on the same patch of green. As time went on the first of the West End's famous residential "squares" were developed in imitation.[30]

During the same period, in colonial Asia, European merchants also sensed the newfound prestige that aristocrats were attaching to the suburbs. The earliest evidence of this is from the 1620s, in Manila, where Spanish government officers, generals, and merchants took advantage of improved security to build a widely spaced parade of houses "more sumptuous than those in the city" along the banks of the Pasig River and its tributaries, each of which was surrounded by magnificent gardens, orchards, and "decorative enclosures to keep out the crocodiles." Similar development occurred outside Batavia's Casteel beginning some fifty years later. By the late 1600s, British merchants at Madras were itching to get their hands on open land outside the city walls too.[31]

British merchants' entry into the suburban land market occurred more or less at the same time in London and in Madras, and somewhat later in Bombay and Calcutta. In London, a plague epidemic in 1665 and, more importantly, the Great Fire of 1666 were the major stimulus for the more intense development of the West End. The owners of that land—the Crown and a handful of aristocrats and high ecclesiastical officials—were eager to increase their revenues but reluctant to give up their feudal monopoly on land ownership. They thus offered plots in and around the squares on ninety-nine-year leases, a tenure that merchant-class property buyers felt was secure enough that they could invest in buildings as well. For aristocrats, the risk was that these new profit-hungry leaseholders would build shoddy buildings on the land and allow the West End to be run over by "lackeys and pages" from the city. Soho Square had already become a working-class district in this way, a development that led to the growth of the notorious St. Giles slum in the very heart of the West End.

After some failed attempts to launch legislation in Parliament to zone the West End for the rich, individual developers took matters into their own hands, using a different type of legal power, one built into the very contracts between buyers and sellers of land. Many of London's late seventeenth-century lease titles contain what amount to the world's first class-based restrictive covenants. Those for Leicester Square, for example, obliged leaseholders to "build in such a manner and form and with such proportions ... as those houses in the Pal Mal." Such practices grew more common and more precise over the course of the next century and a half, eventually receiving state sanction in the court case *Tulk v. Moxhay* in 1848. As such, restrictive covenants became a key legal underpinning for suburban exclusivity—and a spur to the worldwide spread of urban residential segregation by class.[32]

Meanwhile at Madras, rich merchants had more difficulties buying suburban land, despite the fact that the place was run by merchants themselves. The East India Company controlled a growing circle of Indian villages around the city, but it stubbornly forbade its employees to live there for fear of independent trade and other entanglements that might jeopardize the city's security. It did, however, wish to ease the Gradgrind existence it forced upon its employees in the confines of White Town and established a company garden outside the walls as a way to promote health and offer amusements. Many Company employees, including Elihu Yale, found ways of getting around company strictures on suburban real estate ownership as early as the 1690s, and by the 1730s private garden houses had proliferated in the farmland between the Indian villages to the west and south of White Town. By the 1760s, the Company had given up on its prohibitions and actually encouraged suburbanization by widening a network of carriage roads that connected the villas with downtown.[33]

As it did so, the Company imported many of the institutions needed to manage an urban land market, adapted them somewhat to fit the political situation in India, and ended up creating a kind of hybrid set of arrangements, Indian in name yet recognizably British in substance. When the Company acquired the three villages of Calcutta, for example, it assumed the Mughal title of *zamindar* (a combination of landholder and tax collector) for the new settlement. The British reinvented the zamindar's office, called the "Cutcherry" or the "Collectorate," so that it issued British-style leases, once again called by their Bengali name, *pattas*, to people who wanted to purchase land. As in London, the Cutcherry collected a small ground rent in exchange. To avoid confusion and corruption, the company hired surveyors, using technologies brought from England (such as Gunther's measuring chain) to accurately fix the metes and bounds of each plot, and pattas were registered at the Cutcherry following British rules, to ensure accurate information on any financial obligations attached to the land. Finally, a court of Cutcherry, and later a supreme court, also both modeled on British institutions, decided disputes. In 1774, the Calcutta Supreme Court decided the Company could not annul such *pattas*, even with compensation. In so doing it signaled that Indians would benefit from a strikingly more liberal land policy than natives in other parts of the empire. The penal laws in contemporary Ireland, for example, had kept many of the harsh seventeenth-century constrictions on Catholic landowning in place. In fact, Indians could arguably claim a more solid title to land in Calcutta than British merchants could in London.[34]

British landholders in Calcutta did not go as far as those in the West End in using their title to property as a means to exclude people from White Town by either class or race. To signal the neighborhood's exclusivity, they did, however, import a few things from London. One was the Palladian villa. Most of the facades of the City of Palaces were based on the same architectural pattern books used in London, and at least one Venetian architect plied his trade in town. In Calcutta, moreover, these villas got an added feature, a surrounding wall enclosing what became known as a "compound"—a word derived from the Malay *kampung*, but now shed of the negative associations the Dutch had given to the term at Batavia and redefined as a space of British privilege.

By building these walls, private landholders took on themselves two tasks that government authorities had neglected. One was a defensive wall around White Town. Even in the climate of improved security after Pallashi, wealthy households were often the targets of bands of thieves known as *dacoits*, and political unrest and even rioting in Black Town continued to be a source of fear. The compounds created what we might call a "privatized" version of the town wall against such threats—even a forerunner of today's gated communities. Another was attention to public health. Long before Wellesley's improvement committees, private landholders used their location apart from Black Town, the slight rise in altitude that could be found in some of the White Town suburbs, and their compound walls to create a more salubrious private environment for themselves. Within the compound, Calcutta's miasmas could be controlled to some degree: the land could be drained effectively, kept free of rotting vegetation, and assured of ventilation and some protection from the heat. As time went on, following some of James Johnson's and James Ranald Martin's prescriptions, some landholders built "bungalows"—that is, houses in the Bengali style—on the same grounds as their Palladian palaces, or sometimes as their main residence. To these they attached broad-roofed *verandahs*, another local term, which allowed both freer circulation of air and protection from the sun's rays. *Punkas*, large pieces of cloth suspended from the ceiling, which a servant, the *punkawalla*, could move back and forth with a rope, also helped air circulate. And *tatties*, grass screens on the windows periodically moistened by a *bheestie*, or "water bearer," acted as a kind of air-conditioning system.[35]

For Calcutta property owners, the advantages of compound living, the prestige it offered, and therefore its market value required these compounds to be located among other similar exclusive developments. Advertisements for White Town real estate often referred to a plot's location in a "highly eligible neighborhood," the size of grounds, walls, and the salubriousness of the site—and for good measure they also mentioned the names of some of the illustrious people who lived nearby. However, there is no evidence that London-style class restrictions were ever added to Calcutta's pattas. Nor were there any racial covenants, which came into being elsewhere and later. In 1748, during the Maratha scare, the court of directors had declared that henceforth "Houses belonging to our Servants or any English must not be sold to Moors or Any Black merchants whatsoever." But this was a military measure designed to protect the city from the Marathas and their spies, not a business proposition designed to protect property values.[36]

The old registries of pattas from this period are in terrible shape—Calcutta's humidity and its paper-eating white ants had left a "hole large enough for a well-fed ferret to run through" by the time the historian Walter Firminger looked at them in 1917. The records he was able to transcribe from 1780 to 1834 show that in the area east of the Esplanade, for the most part Europeans did, in practice, sell most of their property to other Europeans (73 percent of all pattas). However, a full quarter of all transactions occurred between Europeans and others, and about half of those involved an Englishman selling to an Indian, Portuguese, or Armenian. Over half of the title-transfer records describe the property in question as bordering that of an Indian neighbor. What is more, large "bustees," filled with the self-built thatched-roof huts of Calcutta's poor, grew up in several places in Chauringhi on land owned by Indians, much of it swampy.[37]

Why did the boundaries of White Town remain so porous? One reason was that only a minority of the relatively tiny Calcutta British elite invested in real estate at all. Cornwallis's reforms discouraged civil and military officers from trade and investment in India, and thus most of them lived in rented facilities, generally for short periods before they were reassigned elsewhere. A few wealthy "nonofficial" Europeans, many of them not English, became large landholders in the city and came close to what we think of as developers—the Venetian architect was one of them. But none of these people would have had the political influence to mount a campaign for state-coerced segregation even if they wanted to.

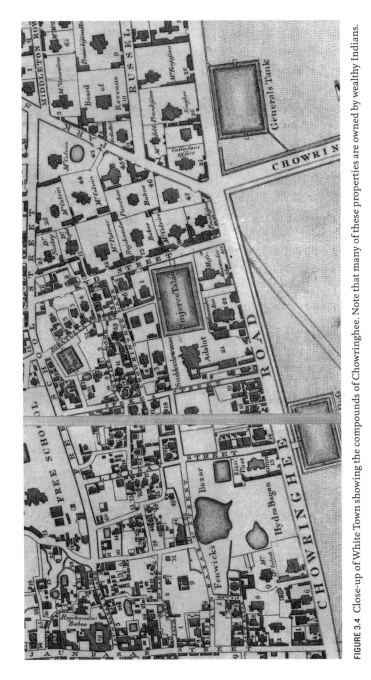

**FIGURE 3.4** Close-up of White Town showing the compounds of Chowringhee. Note that many of these properties are owned by wealthy Indians.

Of the minority of Englishmen who did invest in real estate in British Indian cities, most did so as a means to diversify wealth largely gained in other lines of business.[38]

Most who invested in India at all did so as a temporary measure before reinvesting the profits in real estate back home in England. Some, like the Governor General Warren Hastings, opted for an aristocratic country seat when they came home, but many more preferred the West End and the London suburbs. Elihu Yale of Madras set that pattern early: in addition to endowing his college in Connecticut, he plowed a large chunk of his fortune into a lease and a mansion on London's Queen Square, at that time existing as a small cluster of similar properties surrounded by open fields. There, his neighbors included another former governor of Madras—and the court director Josiah Child himself. Thomas Pitt, a great amateur of the suburban company gardens at Madras while he was governor, acquired a leasehold to a house in Pall Mall when he returned to London, which he used when he was not living in his country seat in Hampshire. Robert Orme, the company servant and historian, reinvested part of his wealth from Bengal and Madras in the new London suburb of Marylebone and later retired further out in a country villa in Ealing. Seventy years later the pattern continued: James Ranald Martin, the Calcutta doctor and "medical topographer" bought a house near Grosvenor Square on his return to London and then retired to the suburb of Cheltenham. In the early years, the transoceanic reach of modern real estate institutions and the money that flowed within them may have helped foster separation within colonial cities, but it also created a transoceanic pathway for whites to flee those cities for more restricted investments in England.[39]

A second reason for the loose color line in Calcutta was the sheer size of the service staff in English households in White Town. Whites in all race-segregated cities throughout history made exceptions for dark-skinned servants—even those imagined as dire threats to white health. But in Calcutta they probably made the biggest exception of all. Even the most modest households could count as many as a hundred people on staff, including specialized retinues in charge of dressing, bathing, and shaving the English "sahib" and "memsahib," as well as cooking, cleaning, laundry, child supervision, stable and horse management, gardening, and palankin (sedan chair) bearing—in addition to the water bearers and *punkawallas* we have already met. The festering bustees of Chauringhi came into being as living quarters for the families of servants and other tradespeople, making it hard, in the days before public transport, for English property owners to agitate for clearance. On top of that, as the historian Swati Chattopadhyay has demonstrated, British homeowners depended on Indian masons to lay out the interiors of the Palladian houses of Chauringhi. Local builders may have followed English pattern books for the facade, but in the interior, they followed local preference for an open plan that maximized ventilation. That allowed for little segregation between masters' quarters and those of servants, who were present everywhere in the house. Such arrangements struck new European arrivals to India as strange, in particular because English suburban houses of the time were increasingly designed to create separate rooms, passageways, and stairwells for servants.[40]

The most important reason for the growing fuzziness of Calcutta's color line, though, was the influence of Indians themselves within the land market. Cornwallis's reforms may have closed off all but the most menial positions of government service to Indians, but his famous "Permanent Settlement" of Bengal's land tenures guaranteed the economic strength of a class of rural Bengali landowners, many of whom had their primary residences in Calcutta. There, these landowners soon eclipsed older mercantile families, such as the Seths and Bysacks. The new Bengali Hindu "famous families," the Debs, the Roys, the Mitras, the Ghoses, the Sens, the Banerjees, and (most famous of all) the Tagores (Thakurs), formed an aristocracy of a much larger group of urban landholders known collectively as the *bhadralok* (well-mannered people).

Even before the rise of the bhadralok, wealthy Indians had used their secure property rights to build a city that reflected their own class status. Calcutta's Black Town came into being as a series of villages that grew up around the core of Sutanuti, the village to the north of the original Dihi Kalikata, and then fused together. In the process it became a dense and complex fabric of larger neighborhoods known as *tolas*, further subdivided into *paras*, many of which were named after the occupational group or caste that predominated there. The city's wealthier families bought large pieces of land in the midst of this complex fabric and built large mansions. Though some of them actually came from lower-caste backgrounds, their wealth allowed them to build alliances of supporters from various castes, inviting many of their members to rent land around the house and enter into the rich family's service. In this way they replicated a pyramidal pattern of residential class and caste "integration" that was similar to that of many other premodern cities. The

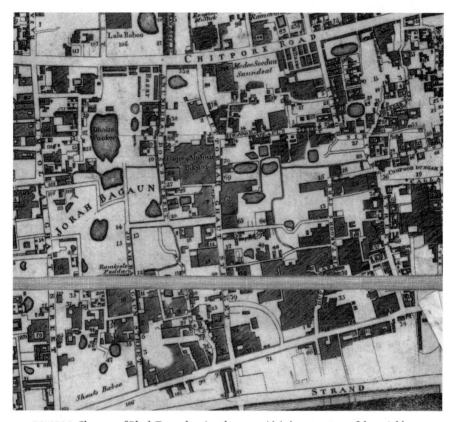

FIGURE 3.5 Close-up of Black Town showing the pyramidal class structure of the neighborhood surrounding the Tagore (Takoor) family mansion. We know from others sources
that, in addition to the many smaller buildings that surround the mansion, dozens of huts
built by the family's servants and clients covered the areas that appear vacant on the map.
Soon, however, many Indian elites—like Calcutta's Europeans—moved to the city's fringes,
thus creating a more class-segregated city.

mazelike alleyways and internal courtyards of the *tolas* were considered
an ideal environment to promote the various communities and families
that made up these alliances, and the open-air shrines allowed for a collective and public spiritual life. Though James Ranald Martin did not
appreciate this fact, Hindu culture was deeply focused on ritual purity
and avoidance of pollution, and many of the larger houses and streets
also contained facilities for daily ablutions considered important for
physical and moral health.[41]

In the early nineteenth century, the "famous families" used their land-based wealth to sustain an independent Bengali press, educational institutions, and political movements—the basis of what we now sometimes call the Bengal Renaissance. Many strands of thought animated this movement, but all of its supporters felt it crucial to marry Indian culture with at least some Western ideals. By the 1830s, they also demanded increasing Indian participation in the administrative and judicial systems of the empire. The hybrid nature of the Bengal Renaissance was reflected in its leaders' land-development strategies. Although most of the bhadralok aristocracy owned mansions in Black Town and thus occupied the pinnacles of its pyramids, some began to imitate the European model of class segregation and built gigantic houses in the suburbs adjacent to Black Town. Some even appropriated the classical facades of White Town palaces, such as Dwarakanath Tagore's Jorasanko mansion (the childhood home of his more famous grandson, the Nobel Prize-winning writer Rabindranath Tagore). Others, of course, simply invested in White Town itself and even moved there, though Bengalis continued to recognize the area's European character by calling it Sahibabagan (sahib's place) or Ingroitollah (*tola* of the English). There, their wealth could hardly excite any white racial worries about declining property values; indeed, many European developers relied on Indian capital, and many even worked with Indian business partners just like other merchants. It is worth noting that despite, and probably even because of, these breaches of the color line, British investors did very well in the Calcutta land market. Lots belonging to Europeans, which made up 12 percent of the total in the city, accounted for over 40 percent of Calcutta's assessed value. In 1806, the average plot owned by a European was assessed at three times that of the highest-status segments of the Indian population. Among whites, housing in White Town was known to be among the most expensive in the world, rivaling that of London's West End.[42]

As Calcutta's various European-run improvement committees began implementing their efforts to drive avenues through Black Town's dense fabric, they encountered a variety of responses from its inhabitants. Some of the bhadralok were persuaded by Martin's sanitary arguments and offered support. Others took a businessman's perspective that the wide avenues could raise their property values, just as similar avenues had in White Town. But others were vociferously opposed. Some may have acted in defense of the prestige they gained from the traditional urban fabric or in defense of what they saw as highly developed Hindu sanitary practices. Many worried that sanitary projects threatened the low tax rates they enjoyed. Others did not want to give up the handsome profits they derived from renting plots of ground in the bustees the British wanted to raze. Still others reacted to the dictates of arrogant British sanitary officers with newly developing nationalist pride. Always, though, the power of the bhadralok rested at heart on their landed wealth and thus on British recognition of their property rights. Later, that led to the vote as well: in 1875, hoping to get the bhadralok to agree to higher taxation for improvements, the Raj extended representative government to Calcutta. Some ten thousand wealthy Indians, a tiny aristocracy, got the vote in municipal elections.[43]

## London's Calcutta Problem

At the midpoint of the nineteenth century, there were some, like the British collector of Calcutta Reginald Sterndale, who could look back at a century and a half of London's rule of Calcutta and wax proudly about the "seat of justice, learning and commerce" the British had created out of a "place of mists, alligators, and wild boars"—even if all the enormous "labor and expenditure incurred" was taken into account.[44] But the vast majority of European imperial administrators, reformers, and real estate investors looked at Calcutta with increasing skepticism—and even racist disgust. The London-Calcutta connection had never been a peaceful affair, of course. As both cities swelled in size to the point where both harbored multiple millions of people, the struggle within their connection grew more agonized.

The empire itself was the first to distance itself from its City of Palaces. As early as the 1830s, Governor General Bentinck proposed to move the imperial capital to some place less hot, less swampy, and less full of clamorous "Bengalee baboos," as Europeans derided the bhadralok. His preferences included places with more ancient and splendid imperial cachet like Agra or Delhi—or possibly Simla, a new British hill station perched high in the Himalayan foothills, where the climate was cool and where the mountaintop views better gratified the empire's sense of aloofness. Soon the Raj would decamp for six or even eight months of the year to Simla to avoid Calcutta's summers. In 1911, fed up with Bengal's increasingly radical, anti-imperial politics, the Raj would finally remove permanently to Delhi, where the British conquerors could bask in the reflected glory of their predecessors, the Mughals.[45]

Sanitary reformers had also grown increasingly dissatisfied with Calcutta. James Ranald Martin was willing to support grand plans for improvement, but he ultimately grew less optimistic about Calcutta's viability as a location for permanent European settlement. He began warning of the dangers of transshipping soldiers through what he saw as the stinking, miasmatic maul of the Hughly, and he led the movement to relocate the infrastructure of British control to higher, cooler elevations. His racial critique of Calcutta was adopted by others, and it took an increasingly nasty tone as the century went on, especially as reformers contrasted Calcutta's belabored sanitary politics with London's supposedly dramatic progress. In London, they claimed, new sewers, experiments in model worker housing, and soon a growing town-planning movement had transformed the world's greatest "wen" into a cleaner and healthier place. Bengali opposition to London-style improvement schemes only exacerbated the negative racial comparison. Rudyard Kipling spoke for many in the 1890s in the increasingly racist "nonofficial" white community of Calcutta when he famously scowled that "all India has heard of the Calcutta Corporation"—meaning the liberals' showcase experiment in Indian democracy—"but who has investigated the Calcutta stink?" In 1899, in the wake of the great plague epidemic, viceroy Lord Curzon had his governors dismantle that corporation, opening the path for the most powerful and authoritarian sanitary town-planning body in the city's history, the Calcutta Improvement Trust (CIT), founded in 1911.[46]

One of the dreams of CIT officials was to promote a "social advance on present Calcutta conditions" by demarcating "separate areas for the various races." But long before 1911, European buyers and sellers of land, like imperial officials and sanitarians, had cast their own negative vote on the city. Calcutta's European population grew somewhat throughout the period, led by the city's relatively settled "nonofficial" business class, but white Calcuttans invested less and less in urban real estate. As early as the 1820s they had begun to pull out of parts of Chauringhi. Almost half of the White Town "palaces" that fronted the Esplanade were owned by Indians as early as 1832. In 1856, the number of European-held pattas in the city proper had dropped to half the level of twenty years before, and the percentage of these that were residential properties declined even faster. The same trend could be seen even in the city's suburbs. One period of white exodus began in the 1840s, when the British forced the fabulously wealthy nawab of Oudh into exile in Garden Reach, along with his enormous retinue. The port of Calcutta expanded across Kidderpore, and the city's cotton and jute mills encroached on places like Alipore.

By the turn of the century, most of the emblematic European-style mansions in the southern reaches had been sold to wealthy Indians. At that same time, the Bengali writer Nirad Chaudhuri reminds us, "there was complete racial segregation" in clubs, railway carriages, public conveniences, churches, beaches, parks, and at public events—sometimes enforced by Jim Crow-like signs and the police. But furiously racist as Calcutta's nonofficial Europeans became, they did not succeed in officially zoning off neighborhoods for whites only. The wealth and power of the bhadralok and the relatively slim clout nonofficial Englishmen possessed within the institutions of the Raj left them without the will or power they would have needed for a city-splitting movement. So they elected instead to rent rooms in segregated clubs rather than buy, putting their money into other lines of investment, or into real estate ventures elsewhere—in the hill stations, other colonies, or, as always, back home in London's West End and other British suburbs. Calcutta's residential color line retreated southward and grew less restrictive. Already by the census of 1901, the entire city and its closest suburbs was 4 percent "Christian," a total that included Indian Christians and Eurasians. The population of the five *tolas* that had composed the historic White Town remained at 12.8 percent Christian, but former white citadels like Alipur and Garden Reach had almost completely emptied of the people who had given White Town its name.[47]

In the years after Indian independence, the "stink" stuck to Calcutta's reputation like a plague flea on a sewer rat. Calcutta became everyone's favorite symbol of "third world" urban dystopia, especially once its population surged past London's, to 16 million, and its bustees swelled exponentially. In the process, the city regained some its influence within global currents of segregationist ideas and practices, this time as a bastion of "megacity"-style class segregation.

Over the course of the 1800s, by contrast, a local contingency—the British-supported power of Bengali landowners—had caused white Calcutta's seminal commitment to racial segregation to dwindle and then virtually disappear. Calcutta, the preeminent—the original—modern colonial city became as much an example of what city-splitters should avoid as a model to imitate.

Paradoxically, that doubled-edged legacy only increased the influence of institutions, ideas, and policy tools that originated along the London-Calcutta axis. But when people working within those institutions began inventing new, more coercive forms of segregation, they did so elsewhere. The avant-garde of the world's modern-era dramas of racial segregation had shifted to other cities in India and to other cities across the world.[48]

# PART THREE

## SURGES OF SEGREGATION IN THE COLONIES

.

# 4 : The Stations Raj

*Paradoxes of Detachment and Dependence*

Not far from Madras, there is a place called Poonamallee. The British built a military station there, one of many that cemented their raj, or rule, of India. In 1836, an Englishwoman named Julia Maitland spent some time there with her husband. One day, she noted in her diary, "I asked [a] lady what she had seen of the country and the natives since she had been in India. 'Oh, nothing!' said she: 'thank goodness, I know nothing about them, nor do I wish to: really I think the less one sees and knows of them the better.'"[1]

What should we make of such supreme, airy detachment? On the one hand it perfectly reflects life in a British station. Colonial authorities in India designed these strange quasi-cities—some one hundred seventy-five of them, from Afghanistan to the Malay Peninsula—with spatial, social, and even mental distance in mind. Part military base, part Victorian suburb, part resort, part provincial capital, part Indian market town, part open sewer—these variations on a white town were built three to six miles from the Indian cities that gave most of them their names. An important subcategory of stations, the hill stations, functioned as the Raj's hot-season resort capitals and were meant to be even further removed from Indian life. Most of these were built in remote places in the mountains, precisely to distance themselves from their cousins in the Indian *mofussil*, as the dusty, hot, flatland districts and their teeming Indian cities were called.

Within the stations, moreover, as one historian put it, "segregation was everything." Much of the space in the mofussil stations was taken up by soldiers' barracks in the army's cantonment (pronounced "cantoonment")—in fact, the words "cantonment" and "station" were often used interchangeably. Special boundary pillars demarcated separate lines for different regiments of the European infantry, artillery, and cavalry. The more extensive "native cantonment" or "native lines" occupied yet another clearly delimited space, filled with huts for the Indian troops (known as *sepoys*) and their families. Bearers of the army's luggage and camp followers of other kinds also had their separate "hutment" areas, as did the different types of beasts of burden employed in military campaigns—elephants, bullocks, camels, and horses.[2]

Even larger than these soldiers' and animals' quarters were the sprawling bungalow and compound districts for European military officers, as well as the similar and usually adjoining "civil lines" for nonmilitary administrators. "Wheresoever in Hindostan Englishman make their homes," wrote one observer of the station at Cawnpore (Kanpur), "no regard is made to economy of space." A wide parade ground typically lay at the center of this privileged part of the station, sometimes next to a horserace track, a polo field, a golf course, racket courts, skittles alleys, a picnic ground, and a space for genteel evening carriage rides. The station's official buildings, the officers' mess, the clubs, a theater, the Anglican church, some racket courts, the post office, a rail station (after 1850 or so), and, in some places, European-style hotels clustered near the bungalows. To keep morale up, the wives of the station officials played a key role—their job was to rival each other in concocting evening "entertainments" packed with as much fashionable London-style sociability as could be mustered in a bungalow in the furthest corners of India.[3]

That said, the English lady of Poonamallee who saw and knew "nothing" of India was also coyly dissembling. The stations of the Raj were also great illustrations of the paradox that the privileges of racial segregation depended as much on institutions and people that crossed color lines as those that drew them. Whites' very real power and their equally real vulnerability went hand in hand.

To grasp why, we must first remember just how small a speck Europeans represented within the vast millions of India. Their total number, a midcentury British royal commission noted, "would be less than the population of the London Parish of Marylebone," a tad above 125,000 people (note that this number did not include an equal or larger number of Eurasians). If the white community of Calcutta represented a highly skewed version of its British counterpart, that which inhabited the stations was even less diverse. Soldiers predominated, representing the closest thing there was to an urban working class. Their commanding officers and a much smaller number of civilian administrators represented the middle and upper classes. If there was anything resembling Calcutta's "nonofficial" population of businessmen and professionals, it was extremely small. The most striking change over the course of the nineteenth century involved gender and age: as long-distance sea travel became easier, more white women and children made their way east. By 1900, they made up about a third of the European community in the Indian stations.[4]

That such tiny British islands could exist at all was due to the much larger Indian population that built the stations, defended them, served them, and ran virtually their entire local economy. Thousands of Indian "coolies" constructed all the stations' barracks, bungalows, and buildings—except the huts in the native lines, which the sepoys had to build for themselves (with a "hutment allowance" provided by their white officers). The overwhelmingly martial flavor of the stations' small white population should not deceive us: the security of British stations rested above all on the loyalty of the Indian troops. During the first half of the nineteenth century, Indian sepoys made up 80 percent of the British army and were indispensable to the success of Britain's conquest of the subcontinent. That they formed the keystone of the empire was amply demonstrated in the so-called Sepoy Mutiny of 1857-58 (often called the Great Uprising or even the First War of Indian Independence) when the Indian regiments of northern India turned their muskets against their British officers, flocked to the heir of the Mughals in Delhi, and from there sparked a general uprising of peasants and landholders throughout large portions of the Gangeatic Plains. Britain regained control, but, once again, they relied heavily on sepoys who remained loyal. Even after the mutiny, when fearful military commanders increased the size of their European regiments, the British army was still two-thirds Indian.

While the coolies and soldiers could be kept at some distance in a station, the hundreds of Indian servants who assured the comfort of their white sahibs and memsahibs could be found everywhere in the European districts, from the very bedrooms of the swankiest bungalows to the lowliest soldier's barracks. One advice manual for "griffin" (rookie) officers suggested a personal-service staff of a dozen or two (even more if an English wife was involved) and counseled them to avoid playing with firearms at night—for fear of killing "boys" who might be sleeping anywhere on the grounds of the compound, even on the verandah.[5]

Whites' nearly thorough dependence on local Indians for their daily needs also further complicated the stations' racial geography. A few white furnishers of "European goods" from Calcutta, Madras, or Bombay set up branch stores in the larger cantonments to purvey such luxuries. But most food, furniture, clothes (even soldiers' uniforms), and other domestic necessities were provided by hundreds of Indian merchants and artisans whose households made up the majority of the stations' inhabitants. Cantonment officials needed to set aside space in the station for native bazaars to accommodate these "nonofficial natives" with shops and places to live. Each of the enlisted soldiers' lines had its own regimental bazaar, which also included the "chaklas" or "lal bazaars" of the Indian prostitutes. These were a key destination in the painfully dull daily lives of the largely unmarried white enlisted soldiers. Their commanders saw the chaklas as an indispensable evil in the maintenance of an army that ruled so far from home. A much larger "sadar bazaar" (central market) was also set aside, which, among other things, supplied the elite bungalows with everything necessary for their more respectable and typically uniracial nightly entertainments. From the small station of Faizabad in North India, the cantonment magistrate H. H. Ozzard reported—without noticing the sheer irony of the thought—that the farther the station was set apart from the historic Indian town it was meant to supervise, the more white residents needed the services of the bazaar. In other words, in the stations, a greater degree of segregation was predicated upon a greater degree of racial boundary crossing and the presence of a larger Indian population in the midst of the European zone.[6]

## Beyond Calcutta

What brought this enormous archipelago of paradoxical white places into being? Modern-era segregationist practice, as first elaborated in Calcutta, had begun its initial great burst of expansion, in this case across an entire subcontinent. All three of the cross-oceanic institutions and many themes from the political dramas that divided London by class and Calcutta by race were just as much in play in the stations. In fact, Fort William and Calcutta's White Town were considered stations in their own right, as were the other two "presidency towns" of Madras and Bombay, whose imperial, reform, and real estate politics followed scripts very similar to those at Calcutta.[7]

As the archipelago of stations expanded, though, it was amply clear to actors in all of these institutions that neither the predominantly military stations of the mofussil nor the hill stations could achieve their reasons for being if they merely replicated the politics of the white towns of Calcutta or the other presidency capitals. By all accounts, most Anglo-Indians' racial attitudes hardened over the course of the nineteenth century, most notably after the Great Mutiny. In part this reflected the worldwide expansion of social Darwinism, the belief that human history could be explained by the inevitable competition of "fit" and "unfit" races for world dominance. More immediately, though, many British Indians saw the mutiny as evidence that the empire would only hold onto its "crown jewel" through irrepressible racial conflict with a treacherous adversary. Memories of mutineers' massacres of British women and children in the stations of Lucknow and Kanpur left behind especially long-lingering senses of racial retribution. The word "nigger" entered British Indian vernacular speech, a gift from the vocabulary of American slavery.[8]

While that hardening trend predominated, there was something of a countercurrent as well. Even as the mutiny inflamed racial hatred, it also put just as much pressure on British officials to demonstrate the grand and benevolent promises the Raj offered to its Indian subjects. At the same time, Indians' calls for a voice in the affairs of the Raj only grew—especially in Bengal and the presidency towns. Thus, harsher lines of thought—that India's backwardness and inability for self-rule was predetermined by nature—coexisted uneasily with older liberal reformers' dreams that Britain could and should reawaken what they saw as India's somnolent "civilization." In official pronouncements, British authorities preferred words like "European" and "native" and avoided even "black" and "white" for fear that such color terms would seem insulting. Madras's Black Town, for example, was renamed Georgetown during this period, both in honor of the current British Crown prince and "in deference to the sentiment of some of the inhabitants." Calcutta's nonofficial European population developed a reputation for being particularly racist, but it was forced to suffer through liberal experiments like nonracial municipal government. Madras, Bombay, Delhi, and other places put in place similar arrangements.[9]

Within these contradictory currents, the politics of the mofussil and hill stations for the most part followed the more conservative trends in racial belief. Their designers even seemed to recoil in horror at instances of liberal experimentation. This racialized rejection of the "baboo"-dominated politics of Calcutta can be seen in all of the main innovations in segregationist practice in the stations: the use of military cantonment law, not civilian municipal corporations, to run cities; the heightened imperial aloofness embodied in the hill stations; the ever-rawer insistence that urban disease among whites was caused by racial proximity to natives; the increasing use of spatial segregation as a public health measure; and a halting state-run effort to restrict Indian real estate investments in the white areas of some stations.

## Stations of the Empire

Provincial, petty, and pompous though British station life could be, the founding purpose of these white towns was ambitious, far-reaching, and deadly serious: to rule ever-bigger chunks of India. As early as the mid-eighteenth century, during the wars with France, British officials and military officers established separate residences in the cities of India's interior. It was then that the East India Company first struck deals with some of the increasingly independent provincial governors of the Mughal empire—such as the nizam of Hyderabad in South India and the nawab of Oudh, Bengal's near neighbor up the Ganges—to train and officer local armies so they could better fight off the French and the Marathas. As the power of the Mughal Empire and the Maratha Confederacy declined, the British used their control of these Indian governors' armed forces to command further power, ultimately reducing the governors to puppets under the control of a British resident minister. At Hyderabad, the British used the word "cantonment" (from the French word *cantonner*—to quarter) to describe the military base they set up twelve miles north of the old walled city for one of these mercenary forces, the core of one of the first sepoy contingents. The British resident minister also lived in a separate residency, closer to the walls but still outside them, with his own military detachment. Then, in 1798, the Nizam Sikander Jah agreed to set aside some lakeside ground to the north of the city at a place the British named after him. Secunderabad would become one of the largest of the British stations, four square miles by the 1860s. In North India, the large cantonment of Cawnpore (Kanpur) was similarly established by treaty with the nawab of Oudh in 1770 as a forward base for the war the nawab and the British waged against the Marathas over the next three decades. After the British defeated the Marathas in 1818, the Maratha capital Poona (Pune) got its own British station, also situated several miles from

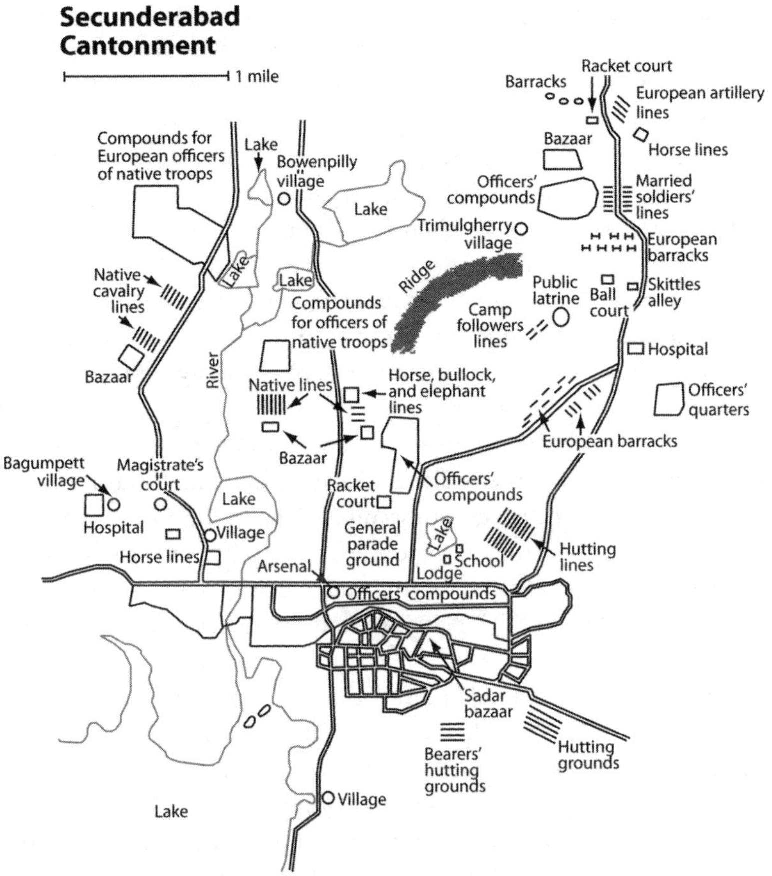

**Secunderabad Cantonment**

|——————————————| 1 mile

Racket court

Barracks

European artillery lines

Compounds for European officers of native troops

Lake

Bowenpilly village

Bazaar

Horse lines

Lake

Officers' compounds

Married soldiers' lines

Trimulgherry village

European barracks

Ridge

Native cavalry lines

Lake

Public latrine

Ball court

Skittles alley

Lake

Compounds for officers of native troops

Camp followers lines

River

Hospital

Bazaar

Native lines

Horse, bullock, and elephant lines

Officers' quarters

Bazaar

European barracks

Bagumpett village

Magistrate's court

Lake

Racket court

Officers' compounds

Hospital

Village

Horse lines

Arsenal

General parade ground

School

Lodge

Hutting lines

Officers' compounds

Sadar bazaar

Bearers' hutting grounds

Hutting grounds

Lake

Village

FIGURE 4.1 This map shows the layout and many of the features of a large British station, or "cantonment," in India. Adapted from *Plan of the Cantonment of Secunderabad* (1884), from the British Library. Map by Kailee Neuner.

the Indian town. So did many other cities previously captured from the Mughals by Maratha armies, including the Mughal capital of Delhi.[10]

In Delhi, the British established a cantonment in the 1820s on the famous Ridge northwest of town. Thomas Metcalfe and David Ochterlony, the British resident ministers in charge of the puppet Mughal court, acquired land from villagers of the Gujar tribe, who inhabited Delhi's northern suburbs, and built mansions there for themselves. Delhi's wealthy residents found it strange that the British preferred such wild lands in the suburbs over what they saw as the achingly gorgeous streets and palaces of Shahjahanabad, Delhi's walled town. However, in

Metcalfe and Ochterlony's case, spatial distance was not meant to seal off a separate space for British sociability, as it was in most other stations. In all other ways, the resident ministers imitated Mughal life and its many splendors. They hosted enormous festivities in honor of local courtiers and the emperor himself; patronized the city's renowned artisans, artists, and Urdu poets; planted Mughal-style gardens; and set aside large wings of their house as zenanas for their many Indian wives and lovers.[11]

Still, British governors general—and, after the mutiny, their successors, the viceroys—struggled to imbue their colonial stations with majesty befitting a conquering race. Various types of separation could play a role in this effort. Governor General Richard Wellesley, who spent enormous sums outfitting Calcutta with its Government House, was never quite satisfied with the results of his labors. In the spirit of European monarchs who maintained palaces like Versailles and Windsor outside their capitals, he hoped to build a second palace for the governor general fifteen miles upriver at Barrackpore—which, as its name suggests, was also the site of one of Britain's early cantonments (established 1772). The Company nixed Wellesley's plans after a quick look at the price tag, and a later governor general settled for a more modest structure.[12]

Indeed, the architecture of most of the provincial stations, which one historian derided as "petrified camps," did little to inspire awe, despite the lavish use of real estate and the wide parade grounds. The palaces and forts of the puppet Indian sovereigns, built in the spirit of the most ancient forms of monumental segregation, were much more effective as symbols of authority. During the nineteenth century, the historian Narayani Gupta writes, British "never ceased to covet" the "stupendous remains of power and wealth" on display at Delhi, especially in the Mughal's Red Fort—which, after all, symbolized the legitimacy of another foreign dynasty that had successfully conquered India. Ochterlony and Metcalfe, happy as they were personally in their suburban mansions, often called upon Calcutta for authority to move the powerless emperor somewhere else so the British Raj could take over his magnificent fort and its many palaces. As a compromise, they stationed many of their subofficials—and even the main body of the army for a while—inside Shahjahanabad itself, in districts directly to the north and south of the fort.[13]

Meanwhile, in 1814, Ochterlony commandeered his hybrid detachment of the British army in conquest of another potential source of imperial majesty—the Himalayas. Already in 1819, word filtered back to

Calcutta of a spectacular ridgeline in the foothills north of Delhi, where the cool, foggy summertime weather reminded its first British real estate prospectors of England, and where the views of snowcapped mountains outshone those of Switzerland. In 1827, Simla was honored by the first of many visits from a governor general of India, Lord Amherst. Officials at Madras, meanwhile, discovered Ootacamund, a beautiful spot eight thousand feet up in the Nilgiri hills of southern India, and those at Bombay scouted out Mahabaleshwar, high in the Western Ghats.[14]

By the 1830s, the British love affair with the hill stations had blossomed, and Governor General Bettinck began to contemplate moving the capital of the Raj away from the "Vast Pestilential Vapor bath" of Calcutta. In the 1860s, one of his successors, viceroy John Lawrence, a notorious hater of Calcutta, only accepted the top job in India on condition that he get to work for eight months out of the year at Simla. There, he insisted, he could get more work done in one day than in five days in Calcutta. By then, Simla's steep slopes sprouted mansions, hill cottages, and Swiss-chalet-style public edifices. Each May, as the southwestern monsoons turned their drenching, then scorching, then moldering attentions on Calcutta, the entire bureaucracy of the British Raj, its enormous army of personal servants, and several detachments of soldiers decamped in an enormous procession of bullock carts and palanquins on the multiple-day journey up to Simla (later they would take the train). High in the hills, an exuberant, showy, gossipy, backstabbing, duel-filled social season began in the unofficial playground-capital's mansions and along its celebrated main street, the Mall. British India's provincial governments and several military commands also treated themselves to similar yearly migrations to their own hill stations—including places like Darjeeling, Shillong, Naini Tal, Almora, Dharamsala, and Coonoor—whose names rang with exotic splendor all the way back in England.[15]

"Government by picnic," the nonofficial business community of Calcutta sneeringly called Simla's season, when the hills sucked their main customers away every year. "Snooty Ooty," their counterparts at Madras called Ootacamund. However, for the Raj, the Elysian hills not only offered a break from the weather—and a chance to play house in a make-believe English country getaway—they also provided the most monumental of segregated perches for a condescending ruling race. At Simla, high above the haze that blanketed the steaming mofussil, that race of conquerors could prove its superiority precisely by transcending its only built-in weakness, an inability to deal with heat and tropical disease. Moreover, in the British imagination, the hill stations offered the safety of the ultimate in impregnable fortresses. These were cities from which the conquerors could imagine ruling without any compromises with quarrelsome Indians.[16]

That was all a fantasy, of course, as the British discovered to their terror and international embarrassment in 1857, when the real keystone of their power in India, the sepoy troops, began burning the white bungalows at Barrackpore, then at Meerut cantonment near Delhi, then at Delhi itself, then at dozens of stations across the northern mofussil, including Cawnpore and Lucknow—the capital of Oudh and the site of another residency and station. Though the British managed to pull together enough soldiers to restore their power over the course of the next fourteen months, the Great Uprising taught them, among other things, that the measures of urban segregation they had taken in earlier years were not enough.[17]

The empire's first impulses were particularly murderous. By the time British soldiers and officers finally retook Delhi, they had built up an enormous sense of vengeance—for the sacking of English mansions, including Metcalfe's, during the early days of the mutiny; for the enormous amount of blood spilt in battles on the Ridge; and for the deaths of comrades during the storming of the old city's Kashmiri Gates. Once inside the walls, commanders and soldiers went on a rampage of looting and pillaging, killing hundreds of Shahjahanabad's inhabitants and forcing many more to flee, some to squalid tents among the city's surrounding ancient ruins. A few officials argued that the entire rebel city ought to be razed for its treachery. British generals contended themselves by flattening many of the Red Fort's pleasure palaces and reducing to ornate rubble a large district surrounding the fort of elegant homes and streets that mostly belonged to the city's wealthy Muslims, many of whom had supported the mutineers. In their place they built a "howling desert of barracks" in the fort, a vast parade-grounds-like esplanade in front of its gates, and an elevated railroad trestle across the neighborhoods to the north, all designed at once to finally seize the city's monumental center and make further mutinies there impossible. "Where is Delhi?" wailed Mirza Ghalib, the city's greatest poet. "By god it is not a city now. It is a camp. It is cantonment."[18]

At Lucknow, meanwhile, the British wrath left behind even less poetic results. There, the army engineer Robert Napier (later commander

FIGURE 4.2 "By god it is not a city now. It is a camp. It is cantonment." When the British recaptured Delhi during the Indian mutiny in 1857, they destroyed many of the city's Mughal palaces, leaving behind a five-hundred-yard security zone around the Red Fort (on the far right). The railroad, visible further to the north, involved further destruction. The tree-filled civil lines lie in the distance beyond the north walls. In the foreground is a buffer zone that separates Old Delhi (Shahjahanabad) from New Delhi, inaugurated just as this photo was taken in the 1930s. Used with permission from Getty Images.

in chief of India) avenged wounds he sustained during the siege of the residency and a brutal campaign of urban warfare in the city's maze of winding streets by destroying about 60 percent of the city and piercing it with a series of soulless, wide, and dead-straight diagonal avenues suited above all to the tromping of troops. At Lucknow—unlike Delhi, but much like other places across the plains—he moved the station and cantonment several miles further out of town to better ensure its defense.[19]

Large-scale urbicide was not the most pervasive way that the heavy hand of the imperial military shaped the stations. More of the work was accomplished by pounding new tensile strength into military law. Cantonments were useless if their design did not continue to facilitate military authority, hierarchy, discipline, and preparedness, and for this reason, civilian institutions were never considered appropriate means to govern them. Only the civilian-dominated hill stations like Simla were granted town corporations like those of Calcutta and other big cities. The original legal system of the cantonments, dating from their origins as army camps in hostile territory, consisted simply of the sum of their commanders' orders. It was these officers who first set up the pillars between each regiment's camps, just as they would have done at the end of any day's march. Their insistence on separate units for British and Indian troops also created the stations' first color lines. In his memoirs, Field Marshall Roberts remembered with a chuckle the old days before the mutiny when native troops at the cantonment of Mian Mir near Lahore were given a spot between two white regiments. Such practices would have been deemed strategically idiotic after 1857; henceforth, wary commanders placed the potentially explosive native lines at a much greater distance.[20]

After the mutiny, officials began to formalize commanders' many rules for behavior at camp in a special body of regulations known as cantonment law. These codes empowered a civilian official (who usually had a military background) known as the cantonment magistrate to arrange and maintain the broader plan of the station, though it left officers in charge of the various regimental lines. Among other things, cantonment law allowed local magistrates more legal power to draw residential color lines than anything available in contemporary Calcutta—or, for that matter, than anything available to any British official since the walls of Madras's White Town. The station magistrate "should rule with a benevolent but absolute despotism," wrote Captain H. H. Ozzard from the small station he commanded at Faizabad. New cantonment codes were passed in 1864, 1880, 1887, 1889, 1912, and 1924, which gave station officers what one commission called "the most comprehensive powers of minute interference" over who could enter the British city and where they could live. Though those powers derived from military needs, the magistrate only used them in his primary civilian roles, which, in any normal city, would be distributed to a range of municipal officials and bureaucracies. The most important of these roles included the magistrate's job as the station's chief sanitary officer and as its chief adjudicator of property disputes and regulator of land sales. In this way, the long reach of urban reform politics and Western real estate markets also deeply shaped the station's role in extending the power of empire and the division of its space.[21]

## "Bring Your Cities and Stations within the Pale of Civilization"

Several strains of Victorian English reform politics made their way through the London-Calcutta connection across the Indian plains and even up into the hill stations. The mutiny intensified this traffic in ideas and offered the reformers a variety of new calls to arms. One strand derived from the evangelical movement led by William Wilberforce and its ideas about the salubriousness and practicality of life on the urban fringe. The massacres of the Indian mutiny had amply demonstrated that the mofussil stations were certainly not the "havens in a heartless world" that evangelicals imagined the London suburbs to be. In India, therefore, concerns about white racial survival and race mixture fused with early Victorian beliefs about gender, age, and class. The Anglo-British elite increasingly imagined the hill stations, in contrast to the mofussil stations, as "cradles of the ruling race," in the words of one historian—places where white women could keep their moral purity and health and British children could grow up without losing any of their ruddy-cheeked Anglo-Saxon racial vigor to the sapping torpor of the lowlands. Accordingly, English boarding schools sprouted up in the hills, as did communities of year-round "grass-widows" (those whose husbands were stationed in the plains).[22]

Related to this gender-inflected racial segregationism was the public-health-based city-splitting of the British sanitarians. By the mid-nineteenth century, sanitarians had found that the scientific knowledge they had assembled in the era's massively growing cities and in the tropical colonies was also useful to army camps. In England during the 1840s and 1850s, London's Edwin Chadwick and Thomas Southwood Smith joined forces with Calcutta's James Ranald Martin and a new international star in sanitary reform circles—Florence Nightingale, fresh from the Crimean War. Her legendary reportage of the siege of Sebastopol from a nurse's perspective vividly reminded everyone that the empire's soldiers died of sickness far more often than from enemy bullets and that the perfectly awful conditions of army camps were at fault. When equally depressing mortality statistics filtered back to London from the Indian mutiny campaigns, Nightingale and Martin successfully lobbied for a royal commission to take a hard look at the stations of the Raj.[23]

The commissioners, led intellectually by Martin, distilled evidence gathered from station commanders from all corners of the subcontinent. They folded in observations from British and colonial practices around the world. They concluded with a bleak "medical topography" of the white archipelago, focusing on the soldiers' barracks. Some of the litany of problems they found could just as easily have come from any city or slum in Europe: nonexistent sewer systems, impure drinking water, inadequate ventilation, overcrowding, and the dissolute behavior of the disrespectable classes—which in India meant enlisted soldiers' drunkenness and visits to diseased native prostitutes. To one sanitarian, the cantonment looked like a scale model of the class geography of London: "the preventative qualities of the well-ventilated, airy, capacious and comparatively cool, bungalow . . . Are contrasted with the too often ill-positioned, imperfectly ventilated, and contaminated barrack rooms . . . of the ranks, as the palatial residences of Belgravia are with the wretched hovels and polluted cells of St. Giles, Whitechapel, or Bermondsey." The commission's recommendations for more sanitary barracks and the moral uplift of soldiers both echoed and presaged discussions about model worker's homes in Europe and North America. The commission's suggestions for an Indian Sanitary Service, staffed by municipal officers of health, derived from the British Public Health Act of 1848, a law that Chadwick, Smith, and Martin had done so much to promote. Edwin Chadwick's mania for state-of-the art sewers (oval pipes and glazed brick), fresh water, and wide streets was also palpable in the commission's report.[24]

But to reform stations in India, the commissioners also had to wrestle with race. In doing so they put forward a slightly more elaborate sanitary argument for urban segregation than Martin had developed earlier in Calcutta. Since they never debated that argument with any precision, though, its racial logic remained somewhat twisted, and its implications ambiguous. Martin, as in his Calcutta report, was most pessimistic about ameliorating British health in India at all. No matter how far the stations were set apart from Indian cities, "the numerous camp followers always connect the cantonment with the city and they exist in a community of suffering." Furthermore, sanitary reform could only at best mitigate "the union of heat and malaria"—this term referred to miasmas—which was "the most powerful" cause of disease among Europeans in the tropics. His one hopeful recommendation amounted to a Raj-spanning, city-based scheme of racial and spatial management: to rotate as many of the British troops as possible through the white hill stations on a regular basis every twelve months or so.[25]

In separate comments on the commission's evidence, Florence Nightingale cast some doubts about her friend Martin's plan, since it was clear from hill station commanders' reports that the mountaintops were no less immune than the plains to cholera and other deadly diseases. Still, Nightingale did worry about the racial boundaries within the stations themselves and the extent to which barracks areas were "mixed up with unhealthy native towns and bazaars abounding with nuisances." Some years later she wrote to viceroy Lord Mayo that "filthy towns and bazaars, or foul native houses and inhabitants *inside cantonment* boundaries, or too close to them, are constant sources of danger. Of course the only real safeguard is to keep such population out of cantonments and at a safe distance to leeward. This, we are told, is not always possible."[26]

Still, over time, Nightingale and other reformers turned away from the commission's exclusive focus on European soldiers, arguing that empires could only be justified if they brought "civilized" standards of public health to all races under their control. "Bring your cities and stations within the pale of civilization," Nightingale argued, pushing Martin and other tropical-sanitation thinkers hard, "they are the life destroyers, not the climate." Most debates about public health in India and Britain focused not on segregation, but whether to invest in other, much more expensive policy tools: sewers, water supplies, vaccination, sanitary education, regulation of prostitution, sanitary policing, and better collection of vital statistics. Like at Calcutta, these debates involved conflicts between imperial officials as well as between officials and prominent Indians. New questions about the origins of disease and concerns about sanitary measures' impact on caste traditions animated these debates, but above it all hovered the question of who would pay.[27]

From the perspective of cantonment magistrates, Martin and Nightingale's crusades seemed to have heightened the importance of much more down-to-earth matters. "If I were asked, 'what is the most important work a C.M. has to do?'" wrote the wry Captain Ozzard from Faizabad, "I should reply without hesitation 'visiting latrines and filth and rubbish trenches.'" Nightingale's essay on Indian camp conditions derived much of its rhetorical pungency from detailed accounts of the vast fields of human waste that seem to have been universal scourges of the stations. Without any facilities, she noted, both native and European soldiers "resorted" to any available open ground they could find convenient to their lines. The standard solution to this problem were latrines, most consisting of a line of movable bamboo cabins built above a set of trenches dug across convenient fields and attended to by a corps of sweepers. As the trenches filled up, the sweepers would slide the cabins onto a new trench, repeating the maneuver until a now fully fertilized field could be given over to cultivation of some kind. Natives were of course most often blamed for the sewage problems of cantonments, but magistrates also had to face the delicate reality that even the European officers' compounds were hardly sanitary. To keep miasmas out of the bungalows, private latrines in the compounds were outlawed, but few resident European or native servants found it convenient to walk all the way to the public trenches. Thus the grounds of many compounds developed their own open cess-ponds.[28]

That said, no sanitary reformer, no matter how egalitarian, explicitly condemned the already existing White Town–Black Town divides, and all assumed they would persist. Few sanitarians objected when the army took up the commission's suggestion to rotate as many as a fourth of the European troops at a time up to the hill stations, even though, as Nightingale had predicted, minimal health benefits came out of such an expensive, militarily incautious practice.[29]

Meanwhile the Government of India came under blistering criticism from the delegates to a series of new international sanitary conferences for doing too little to stop cholera that originated in Calcutta and other Indian cities from reaching Europe. These critics' theories of disease transmission contradicted Martin's squarely. Cholera was a contagious disease, not a "meteorological" one carried by air currents, and it invaded Europe from Asia because people—that is, travelers, but especially Asian religious pilgrims—had become increasingly mobile, and they spread disease from one person to another over large distances. These travelers, contagionists concluded, not spaces, had to be better monitored. Over time international conferees developed regulations aimed at using inspection points on the Suez Canal to seal Europe off from Asian travelers without impeding commerce. Such a system of continental or oceanic segregation had its roots in other practices dating back to medieval times, the quarantine and the sanitary cordon. The Government of India was opposed to such measures because of their negative effects on commerce, but they loomed large in the imagination of increasing numbers of sanitary officials. Yet another theory, the waterborne theory of the spread of cholera, first put forth by John Snow in 1854 during his investigations of an epidemic in London's West End, also slowly made inroads on traditional miasmatic notions—once again, against strong resistance by hidebound public health officials in India. That resistance continued even after the German bacteriologist Robert Koch found the comma-shaped cholera bacillus in a Calcutta tank in 1883. Neither discovery did much to alter the view that natives' behavior threatened disease in whites.[30]

That basic racialized assumption inspired a few miscellaneous efforts to intensify segregation within the Indian stations in the name of public health. The broadest of these efforts concerned the cantonment codes, the earliest versions of which were based in part on Chadwick's Public Health Act of 1848, especially its provisions for professional sanitary officers in towns. In the 1880s, authorities revised the cantonment codes to give increasing power to magistrates to "remove and exclude from Cantonments any person whom they may deem it expedient to so exclude" and to summarily seize natives' property if they failed to keep their property up to sanitary snuff. Following time-honored contagionist practices, local officials sometimes placed temporary cordons sanitaires around whole bazaars and other native villages to quarantine surrounding areas from cholera epidemics. Inspired by Britain's Contagious Diseases Act of 1866, the Government of India also dusted off the early modern institution known as the "lock hospital"—at its worst a kind of jail for sick people—to confine Indian prostitutes who, upon compulsory examinations, were deemed likely to spread venereal disease among European troops. Indians stiffly resisted the cordons sanitaires, as those measures sometimes detained merchants in their bazaars for up to ten days. Quarantines also disrupted Hindu pilgrimages, causing further protest. Vice reformers in England and missionaries in India, meanwhile, denounced lock hospitals both because they officially condoned prostitution and because they subjected women to unjust confinement. Fearing unrest, officials tried to minimize local officials' use of sanitary cordons, and lock hospitals were officially disbanded for some time. But similar controversies would arise again, much more explosively, in the 1890s, when cities across India and throughout the colonial world confronted a global outbreak of the "black" plague.[31]

## Stations for Sale?

Of all the cross-oceanic institutions that produced racial segregation in cities, the international real estate market played the smallest role in the politics of India's stations. European officers and civilian officials who worked at the stations had little incentive to buy property there, especially in the more out-of-the-way places. For them, the stations were just that: waystations in an existence that was fundamentally peripatetic. Most Europeans in the stations were either on the march toward a theater of war or they were following the typical career path in India in which advancement involved transfers from station to station at a moment's notice. Others were headed to the hills as part of the government's seasonal migration, to visit family, or to recover their health. Some desperately counted the days until their promised yearlong furlough back in Britain. Most residents received lodging as part of their pay and were assigned bungalows for the period of their stay by the station authorities, a system that helps account for the fact that the cleanliness of the grounds was not always well attended to.[32]

Any desire by other overseas investors to buy and sell real estate in the stations was certainly not whetted by the Raj's constant worries about a second mutiny, the mofussil's climate, the primitive facilities, or the bad press about life in the midst of carousing, often sick, soldiers and miasmatic native bazaars. Even more importantly, the Government of India owned all of the land in most mofussil stations—that is, British authorities had either appropriated the land from local landlords or "inherited" land that previously belonged to the Mughal emperor or another local ruler. In stations where Europeans were allowed to buy land in the officers' districts or the civil lines, cantonment regulations stipulated that the commanding officer could appropriate any property at a moment's notice, with compensation, but without giving any reason.[33]

Despite these disincentives, a small nonofficial population did grow in some of the more desirable stations, especially in the late nineteenth century. Bangalore (today's Bangaluru)—which, at three thousand feet, has a climate some Englishmen compared favorably to Italy—attracted a community of retired officials once the cantonment officers relaxed land restrictions. Elsewhere, traders in European goods and hotel owners who catered to transient Europeans bought restricted properties. Indians also bought property in the stations from Europeans, thus working their way around laws that confined them to the bazaars. "Native landlords are the curse of a Cantonment," griped Captain Ozzard of Faizabad, who advised the Raj to give magistrates greater powers to "check ... the transfer of immovable property." When it came to this matter, Ozzard contradicted his earlier observations on the parlous state of European bungalows. Europeans, he now claimed, were happy to listen to magistrates' demands for sanitary improvements, because they knew this would raise their property values. The native landholder, on the other hand, "cannot understand anything except getting his monthly rent." Indeed, it appears that transient officers could increasingly acquire housing within a private rental market largely run by Indian landlords. When that happened, it was because of dynamics that resembled those in the white town of Calcutta more than conscientious local officials would have liked.[34]

The press of Indian land acquisition was especially evident in the nominally white sections of Delhi. After recapturing the city, the British felt it necessary to purchase the loyalty of the local elite who had not joined the mutiny. One way they tried to do this was by allowing suitable candidates to buy property in the civil lines that authorities had marked out north of town between the hallowed Kashmiri gate and the Ridge (the area where Ochterlony and Metcalfe lived before the mutiny). Here, British administrators often rented land from Indian landlords, giving rise to many bitter complaints. "The natives have begun to behave as though the Europeans have left the country," one European tenant groused when an Indian landlord demanded that he water the gardens. Some Europeans owned land in the civil lines, but the political situation still hardly fostered any kind of racial zoning or restrictive covenants. Wealthy Indian landlords were not the only rival for control of residential space. Recall that the civil lines lay astride the ancestral lands of the Gujar tribe. Imagine the harrumphing that ensued when officials of the most powerful empire in the world learned the tribesmen had issued a standing threat to burgle the house of any British resident who did not hire Gujars as night watchmen! All of this would change after 1911 when the British moved their capital to New Delhi and imposed a more elaborate variant of cantonment law on a new, much more monumental European district, this time to the south of town.[35]

As might be expected, a much livelier housing market arose in the hill stations. Simla attracted a large segment of Calcutta's nonofficial population—eager to keep connected to its clientele during the hot season—in addition to the seasonal waves of government officials. Some of these businessmen set themselves up as developers who rented space to the government during the social season, often repatriating their money to real estate markets in England. Cantonment law did not apply here, for the hill stations were meant to be "an extension of John Bull's island." Wealthy British residents thus benefitted from representation

FIGURE 4.3 Simla, the most important of the hill stations of the British Raj and the summer-weather capital of India. Race and class segregation followed from the vertical terrain, with highest officials living in large mansions along the ridge, near the Anglican Church, lesser officials on the slopes, and Indians in the Bazaar Ward far below and out of sight. Samuel Bourne, "Simla, 1883–84," photograph in the McNabb Collection. © The British Library Board.

on the town council and also from British-style property law, surveying, titles, and registration systems. Over four hundred homes in the city's "Station Ward" were owned by British officials or were rented by officials from nonofficial British owners. The vertical dimension of the hill stations made segregation somewhat simpler in general, as higher-priced plots tended to concentrate on the ridges, where the best views could be found. It was there that the top officials congregated; middling bureaucrats rented in areas in between; and Indian clerks were consigned to rooms in the valley. Several giant native bazaars grew up to support British Simla's needs for servants and consumer goods, but they could mostly be kept out of sight and mind far below in the "Bazaar Ward." When one bazaar did spread up the hill behind the Ridge and perched "insolently" above the Mall, local officials tore it down. That was in 1875, when a cholera epidemic gave them the political opening to do so. Town authorities even built a tunnel under the Mall to divert Indian foot traffic from the European section, and constables were placed at the end of the Mall district to prevent some classes of Indian laborers to walk there during high promenading times in the evening.[36]

Because the British endowed the hill stations with such prestige, it was not long before wealthy Indians got interested in living there too. By the late nineteenth century, in the areas of India that Britain ruled indirectly, the Raj had offered hundreds of princes nominal independence and a lavish ongoing court life in exchange for subservience to the British queen-empress. Many of them bought summer homes in the most desirable areas of the hill stations. Unlike at Calcutta, British landowners and government officials at Simla actively tried to slow this influx, invoking a number of rationales: the right of conquest, a shortage of government housing, and even health concerns about the large retinues of servants the princes brought with them (given the size of British servants corps, this was hardly credible). Concerns about racial threats to property values were apparently not a big theme in the records from Simla, but it is clear that one of the hill city's attractions for overseas real estate investors was its claim to exclusive Britishness. In 1890, the viceroy Lord Lawrence personally drew the color line when the wealthiest of all the Indian princes, the nizam of Hyderabad, tried to buy Snowdon, one of Simla's most prestigious addresses and a former residence of governors general. Later, the authoritarian viceroy Lord Curzon, a great lover of Simla, considered banning all Indian land purchases in the station, but even he had to admit that such a course would be too risky politically. Later, an attempt to impose cantonment law in Simla to rid it of Indians also failed. By the 1910s and 1920s, faster steamship service to Europe gradually weakened whites' attraction to the hill stations. Simla faded, like so many of the world's other Victorian resorts, but the hill stations remained playgrounds for wealthy Indians.[37]

## Beyond India

In the stations of the Raj, the British were able to push back against the counterforces that limited segregation in Calcutta and the other presidency towns—but only somewhat. The use of cantonment law, the "benevolent but absolute dictatorship" of cantonment magistrates, more elaborate racist sanitary practices, and the geographic isolation of the hill stations represented real innovations in the dour business of splitting cities by race. Such tools were effective in creating urban spaces of relative privilege and comfort for whites, and they helped to sustain the political inequalities that were central to the business of imperial control. However, they neither created the level of exclusivity many Anglo-Indians wanted or that some—like the lady from Poonamallee— off-handedly imagined they actually had. That was because none of these tools yet provided enough of a counterpoint to what emerged as the most important forces in the political dramas of urban space everywhere in India: the sheer numbers, the sheer wealth, and the established legal rights of Indian property buyers. It follows that, though the same British institutions were involved in splitting all the cities of the Raj, the expansion of the urban white archipelago in India was never a clearly linear, inevitable process. In each city and in each station, the Raj, the reformers, and the European real estate investors met slightly different types of measures of political opposition to white residential exclusivity.

As the quest for exclusive white spaces spread eastward from India into Southeast Asia, China, and the Pacific, European (and North American and Australian) city builders found themselves acting on other types of stages. There, the local political calculus was sometimes quite different, and in some places it was possible to imagine even stronger tools of urban segregation.

# 5 : Segregating the Pacific

## Incomings and Outgoings

"We must come in and you *shall* come out." Thus Britain promised China while storming its great port cities in the 1840s. To many Chinese, good things had come out of bad. Westerners had brutally flung open the long-closed trade routes to China, humiliating the emperor, but in the process, they had made it possible for the Chinese to move out into the rest of the world as a free people.

Now it was 1879, and Lowe Kong Meng, of Melbourne, Australia, re-called the British promise with bitter words. Less than thirty years had passed, and already the West had renounced its commitment to Chinese freedom. White access to China was well and good, but the Chinese needed to stay at home. That was because, to white settlers of the Pacific Rim, Chinese migrants had become the "yellow peril."

For Meng and for other Chinese people who had left their homeland for promises elsewhere, the change was chilling. Their small overseas urban communities, the Chinatowns, were under siege, vilified in the press and in the halls of power, and threatened by white mobs. Many feared for their lives. "Where is your justice?" Meng reproached Austra-lian authorities and their superiors in London, "where your morality? ... Where your love of liberty?"

The answer, Meng well knew, lay within two strands of Western impe-rial policy in East Asia and the Pacific. The first, which was mostly the work of British imperial officials and merchants (though the Ameri-cans and the French helped as well), involved the use of state-sponsored opium smuggling, soon followed by warships, to end the Chinese Qing dynasty's Canton (Guangzhou) system, which put limits on Westerners' access to China's riches. As a byproduct of the "opening" of China, larger numbers of Chinese people left their homelands for new opportunities in Southeast Asia and even the far sides of the Pacific Ocean.[1]

The second policy involved British and American support for another tide of migration, that of white settlers flocking to gold fields and other opportunities in remote places all around the rim of the Pacific Ocean, like Australia's Victoria Colony, Canada's British Columbia, and the US state of California. There, as in Ireland and the Atlantic colonies of North America, English-speaking settlers hoped to create permanent large-scale colonies. Only this time, many whites fantasized, no bedeviling racial "questions" would arise: the settlements on the Pacific Rim would be exclusively "white men's countries."

As the tide of white imperial expansion crashed into the tide of Chinese migration in Asia and the Pacific, urban racial segregationist politics expanded to new shores and spawned two new variations. One of these variations played out in new colonial cities like Singapore, Shanghai, and Hong Kong—the crucial gateways for Westerners' penetration of China. There, small, transient European populations moved into white enclaves in cities that were otherwise overwhelmingly populated by Asians. In some ways, segregationist practice in these cities resembled that of Calcutta and the stations of the Raj. But imperial and sanitary justifications for segregation grew more elaborate in East Asia, and they were supplemented by some of the earliest theories linking race and property values. The practice of urban segregation relied on more stringent forms of government coercion than were possible in India—including experiments in segregationist urban planning and even explicit racial segregation laws.

The second new strand of city-splitting politics arose in cities in Australasia and along the west coast of North America. There, urban populations were the reverse of those in Asia: white settlers were in the majority, and their intention was to remain permanently in their new towns, to raise families and future generations. Asians, by contrast, were a small though significant immigrant minority, living far from their homelands, and many were understandably unsure about permanent settlement in cities where their survival depended on living in separate Chinatowns. That is because white settlers in cities like Melbourne, Vancouver, and, above all, San Francisco were prepared to defend the urban color line with violence backed by a new, more racially sensational sanitary rhetoric and by more potent references to the idea that Chinese people brought down the value of white property. More importantly, the settlers' imperial ambitions drove them to supplement urban color lines with a much-larger-scale form of racial segregation, the unequal division of an entire ocean. The goal of the first race-based immigration-restriction laws was to prevent Chinese people from moving across the Pacific to the coasts of North America and Australasia.

The geographical trajectory of nineteenth-century urban racial segregationist politics—from India eastward to China and the Pacific—is striking. Race, after all, is usually deemed a product of the much-denser connections that spanned the Atlantic Ocean. In fact, the all-important invention of social Darwinism in the 1860s and 1870s did at first stem from intellectual conversations that spanned the Atlantic. An important corollary to the belief in the inevitable conflict between "fit" and "unfit" races was Anglo-Saxonism, the idea that the world's English-speaking diaspora belonged to an especially vigorous Anglo-Saxon race destined to dominate the darker races and probably all other white races too. However, it was in the East and in the Pacific that this newly imagined Anglo-Saxon race drew its first urban residential color lines. Ironically, as discussions of urban racial segregation made their way eastward and spawned the idea to divide the Pacific, white segregationists also played a role in intensifying human contact—unequally, to be sure—across the world's largest body of water.

## Segregating China's Gateways

The story of how the Anglo Saxons and other whites forcefully entered China is a famously sordid one. For two centuries, Western merchants and imperialists had been frustrated with what they saw, not incorrectly, as the Qing dynasty's arrogant disregard for foreigners. The Canton system of urban segregation was especially galling. It forced all foreign merchants interested in Chinese goods to conduct their trade in a tightly restricted zone of a single port, Canton, negotiating with a single company of Chinese merchants, and only during certain months of the year. The demand for Chinese tea had rocketed in Britain as hundreds of thousands of mill workers in Manchester and other new industrial towns began drinking it (with Caribbean sugar stirred in) in order to stay alert throughout their grueling workdays. But because the Qing would only accept silver in return for their tea, the tea trade threatened to suck Britain's stocks of precious metals dry.

Undaunted, the British first turned to the mofussil of India, where opium poppies could be grown in abundance, and then to the ports of Calcutta and Bombay, where British and American merchants could be found who would happily smuggle chests of processed opium into southern China in exchange for tea. Meanwhile, in 1819, a young man named Stamford Raffles persuaded Calcutta and London to give him the authority to establish a new port city at Singapore to offset the monopolistic power of the Dutch in Southeast Asia—thus smoothing the way for British commerce through the Straits of Malacca into the China Seas. As Chinese authorities protested in horror at the rising numbers of opium dens and addicts in their cities, warships from the British navy soon sailed up the Pearl River, guns blazing. The one-sided Opium War (1839-42) ended with the forced Treaty of Nanjing, which gave Britain the islands of Hong Kong as well as permanent "concessions"—a new name for foreign-merchant quarters—in five "treaty ports," which included Canton and Shanghai. There they could trade with all interested parties, and they could live in an urban zone that gave them privileges, not a long catalogue of frustrations.

As they engaged in this drug-laced trade imperialism, first Britain and then the United States also urged the Chinese to "come out" into the rest of the world. More treaties, in 1860 and 1868, required Peking to drop centuries-old restrictions on Chinese emigration. Chinese merchants had long defied their emperor's travel bans; as we know, they formed some of the most powerful foreign mercantile communities in the world, at places like Spanish Manila, and Dutch Batavia and Malacca. British Singapore immediately attracted yet another large community of expatriate Chinese, as did Hong Kong. Since contacts with these merchants helped Europeans get wealthy, the imperial powers were interested in expanding the number of contacts. The free-migration treaties also coincided with increased turmoil in China, as the Qing Empire's hapless effort during the Opium War encouraged many Chinese to join movements against its rule, including the massive Taiping Rebellion (1850-71). Upward spikes in the Chinese population had already placed added pressures on the land. From 1800 to 1914, as uncounted millions of Chinese people were dislocated within the Celestial Empire, somewhere between three and seven million left their homeland. Most went to other places in Asia, but when gold was discovered at one Pacific outpost after another, the Chinese diaspora burst its traditional bounds and spread all around the ocean's immense rim.[2]

The founding of Singapore, Britain's first if still remote gateway to China, indirectly made comings and goings in the Pacific possible. The event also stands out in the early history of race segregation for the sheer clarity with which its founder planned a city's color lines from the very beginning. We might even say that Sir Thomas Stamford Raffles made urban segregation into a sort of political philosophy—though he, like others during this period, did not use the word "segregation" itself when he divided up Singapore.

In 1819, to undercut Dutch influence in the Southeast Asian seas and among the expatriate Chinese merchants who traded there, Raffles acquired the seafront of the ruined medieval Hindu town of Singhapura from its ruling Temungong, as the local official of the Malaysian sultanate of Johor was known. There, in exchange for a yearly payment from Government House in Calcutta to the sultan's court, he proposed to create a tariff-free port at the very tip of the Malay Peninsula that would lure Chinese foreign merchants from Batavia and Malacca. This would allow Britain to command the Straits of Malacca, which would in turn give East India Company merchants increased, though still indirect, access to the commerce of China itself and East Asia in general. The Singapore gambit, Raffles knew, required both military protection—from both the Dutch and the "ferocious races" of pirates in the region—and a system of internal social control for a city whose "population ... will necessarily consist of a mixture."[3]

For external defense, Raffles—who was himself an East India Company employee taking orders from Bengal—borrowed features of both Calcutta and the early Indian stations. Singapore thus got its own Government House, in this case on the top of a low hill. The city was also protected by a smaller version of Fort William, and a nearby cantonment housed separate lines for British soldiers and Indian sepoys, surrounded by bungalows for officers.[4]

To make sure, however, that the foreign-merchant communities within the city behaved themselves, Raffles felt he needed something more clearly divided than Calcutta. For that, he turned to the Dutch at Batavia. From 1811 to 1816, India's governor general Lord Minto had entrusted the thirty-something Raffles to administer the British occupation of Java. At that time in Europe, Napoleon had conquered Holland. Fearful of French incursions in Asia, the British had landed several thousand troops at Batavia. In the Dutch colonial capital, Raffles and his charismatic wife, Olivia, used their positions as entertainers-in-chief to signal a Cornwallis-style disdain for Java's hybrid *Indische* culture. Though they frowned on cross-racial marriages, they invited Dutchmen's Eurasian wives out of their segregated women's quarters and exposed them to the civilizing influence of lavish, London-style, mixed-gender parties. Olivia Raffles even personally forbade the women from bringing along the fancy brass cuspidors they used, in local fashion, for spitting out chewed betel-nut leaves. Subsequent Dutch governors followed the Raffles's lead when Batavia was returned to Holland after Napoleon's defeat at Waterloo, and intermarriage at Java waned. While at Batavia, Thomas Raffles studied Javanese cultures and wrote a book about them—a classical Orientalist text that earned him an appointment to London's Royal Society during a subsequent triumphal tour of England. While in Java, Raffles also had plenty of time to observe what was left of the Indo-Dutch kampung system of segregation at Batavia. When he picked up a nasty Javanese bug, he also spent considerable time at Buitenzorg, a hill station on the slopes of a volcano founded by a Dutch governor in 1744, more than eighty years before Simla.[5]

To lay out his new port city at Singhapura, Raffles used the mouth of the Singapore River as a racial boundary. On the northeast side lay prime land for the station and mercantile district, which were "set aside exclusively for accommodation of European . . . settlers." Across the river in a swampier zone he envisioned two Batavia-style "campongs," one for the Chinese majority and a smaller one for the "Chulia" or the "Kling," as South Indian merchants were known on Malay Peninsula. At the other end of the European zone to the northeast he set aside separate campongs for Muslims—the city's Arab and Buginese traders and Malay communities of fisherfolk—near the palaces of the Temungong and the sultan, who moved down from Johor to be nearer the new action of Singapore. Within each of Singapore's campongs, Raffles thought, the "respectable classes" should be given choice land, and the various "tribes" of Chinese people should also be separated as much as possible from each other.[6]

Raffles's philosophy of racial separation aimed to maximize the "comfort and security of the different classes of inhabitants," but what he had in mind mostly concerned matters of imperial administration, not sanitation or the land market. As at Batavia, each campong would appoint its own leaders to regulate behavior according to customary laws. The goal was to avoid confusion in legal disputes that crossed community lines, and for that, "mutual intercourse" of different groups needed

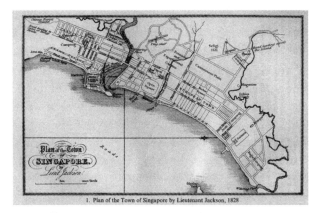

1. Plan of the Town of Singapore by Lieutenant Jackson, 1828

FIGURE 5.1  Raffles's plan for Singapore called for the division of the city into a Chinese campong, a Chuliah campong for South Indian merchants, a government district to the north of the Singapore River, a European town, a racially divided army cantonment, a Malay campong near the palace of the sultan of Johor, and a Bugis campong. From Brenda S. A. Yeoh, *Contesting Space: Power Relations and the Urban Built Environment in Colonial Singapore* (Kuala Lumpur: Oxford University Press, 1996), 42.

to be minimized. More abstractly, separation also enabled Raffles to thread a compromise between those British imperial theorists, such as his friend the evangelical abolitionist William Wilberforce, who wanted to impose what they saw as the universal superiority of British law on natives of the colonies, and those who thought it better to work within native institutions, a system later known as "indirect rule." If any native law was "contrary to reason, justice, or humanity," Raffles argued along universalist lines, British law could be imposed, though with "a patriarchal friendliness." At the same time, the Orientalist in him noted, native laws showed that Asian races were capable of "honorable feelings" and even "reasoning," no matter how "peculiar" it seemed to Europeans. This "germ of civilization . . . should not be checked," and urban segregation could allow the benevolent British Empire to foster it.[7]

Raffles's official capacity soon called him away to a station on Sumatra, several days' sail from Singapore. Still, he left detailed town-planning instructions in the hands of the less competent local officials who succeeded him at Singapore, and he made a point to visit his growing city twice afterward to make sure these officials followed his orders. On these visits, he repeatedly ordered that nonconforming residences be destroyed to maintain his racial boundaries and that their owners be given compensation money to rebuild where they were supposed to. At

141

the same time he recognized that "advantage may arise from deviating from the rule in special cases where the commercial interests of the Settlements are concerned." In one of these cases, Raffles allowed Europeans to take choice land on the Chinese side of the river for warehouses; later wealthy Chinese allies bought houses in European districts. Other than the early clearances and painstaking instructions to his "Allotment Committee," Raffles left no set of laws to keep his color lines intact. In poor health, he left for London in 1823. There, like other returnees from Asia, he settled in a London suburb—in this case Mill Hill, next to his friend Wilberforce, where he died young. Over the course of the century, Singapore's Europeans, like those at Calcutta, fled to their own suburbs, away from the congestion and the growing Chinese community in Raffles's downtown. The cantonment soon followed. By the mid-twentieth century, Singapore's "European" districts were majority Chinese. Still, as the city's campongs radiated inland, the Raffles doctrine still dictated the general direction in which the city's different groups settled.[8]

Meanwhile, on the mainland of China, in the years following the Opium War, the press of Chinese migration into segregated European colonial towns was even stronger. In treaty ports like Shanghai, Qing authorities originally intended to create facsimiles of their traditional foreign-merchant districts in what became known as the British Concession (founded in 1845 and later called the International Concession, when merchants from the United States joined the British there) and the neighboring French Concession (established in 1848). The only difference was that the emperor would waive the restrictions on seagoing trade and daily life. The result was a unique, mutually enforced hybrid arrangement, one part Western racial segregation and the other part based on medieval Chinese traditions forbidding urban interactions between Chinese people and "foreign barbarians." Here, unlike in Singapore, the law did reign. Qing and European authorities agreed to a set of Land Regulations for Shanghai under which foreigners could rent land (in effect in perpetuity) in the Concessions from the emperor, who would remain the nominal sovereign. The regulations also annulled all leases held by Chinese Concession residents. Tangible government coercion was involved. For several years Qing, British, and French officials from the two empires cooperated in evacuating the Chinese residents from the Concessions, and European developers began assembling plots. During this period, Europeans lived an exclusive life in many ways resembling that of Indian stations, complete with clubs, entertainments, carriage promenades, race course, amateur theater companies, and large retinues of Chinese servants. The population was small, and, apart from business headquarters on the Huangpu riverfront, building was sparse; the Concessions' inhabitants even went on hunting expeditions within their small territory. Similar arrangements existed in other Chinese cities and soon at the Japanese port of Yokohama, also forcibly "opened" by Westerners.[9]

Shanghai's mutually enforced system of residential separation may have been thorough, but it was also short-lived. In 1851, as the Taiping Rebellion began to sweep across large parts of interior China, a secret society called the Small Swords took over the old city of Shanghai, which bordered the French Concession to the south, then raised an army and began attacking towns in the vicinity. Chinese refugees streamed into the Concessions by the tens of thousands, and the expulsions ground to an abrupt halt. European leaseholders, who had been disappointed in the sluggish demand for land among white buyers from overseas, suddenly had a bonanza on their hands, and convinced Concessions officials to annul the racist Land Regulations. In the particular political and demographic circumstances of Shanghai, the international land business thus became a powerful force of residential *integration*. Soon, greater numbers of Europeans arrived, many of them eager to make money renting to Chinese refugees. But the Chinese share of the city's population gradually eclipsed all others': by 1930, the Concessions' population was 97 percent Chinese. At that point, though, people of all nationalities could be found strolling the Concessions' bustling "Bund," the wide bend in the Huangpu River where the city's foreign-run banks and merchant houses lined up in monumental fashion. Exclusive Euro-American clubs, parks, and other amenities reflected the ongoing racist side of the city's life. But that occurred in a city where, a bit like Calcutta, color lines between neighborhoods had blurred into virtual nonexistence.[10]

In Hong Kong, the political drama took a sharper racist edge than in any of the Concessions. Unlike the treaty ports, Hong Kong was manifestly British territory, seized in 1841 by the British navy as a base in the Opium War, ceded by the emperor to the Crown under the treaty of Nanjing, and equipped with a permanent garrison of white troops. While hostilities were still underway in the Pearl River, eager British authorities proclaimed the sparsely inhabited main island—with its soaring, treeless mountain range—a free port like Singapore. As elsewhere in Asia, Chinese migrants and refugees quickly outnumbered whites by a large margin. However, at Hong Kong, the paradoxes of white politics embodied a more polarized set of contradictions. Along with a heightened sense of white power and entitlement came an edgier sense of vulnerability, especially because the little British island lay so close to places like Canton, teeming with what many imagined as hordes of antiforeign Chinese people.

This haughty edginess may have helped fuel more insistent demands for more coercive, unilateral enforcement of residential color lines. Amid the wartime chaos, no extensive, Raffles-style urban planning was possible, especially after two typhoons in quick succession leveled most of the new city's buildings. British officials at first encouraged a settlement of Chinese shopkeepers in a spot called the Upper Bazaar. As soon as British land seekers expressed an interest in the area, however, the officials revoked the flimsy titles granted to the Chinese, paid them a pittance in compensation, and destroyed their shops. The Upper Bazaar became a European zone, and the increasingly diverse Chinese community was relegated to an area called Taipingshan, which became a dense slum next to the Lower Bazaar.[11]

Early on, officials deputized a land officer with the unenviable task of sorting out title disputes that arose during the rush to grab stakes in the new city. Wealthier property owners grudgingly accepted seventy-five-year property leases. Like some of their ninety-nine-year cousins in London, these leases contained land-use clauses that specified the minimum amount of money that owners had to spend on buildings over the course of a few years. In the white district, they also stipulated that houses had to be built in "conformity with the character ... of other houses in their neighborhood"—both to discourage traditional Chinese architecture and to keep out Chinese residents without technically violating their property rights.[12]

In 1877, the liberal governor John Pope Hennessey began relaxing these restrictions to attract more wealthy Chinese residents to Hong Kong. An activist surveyor general led the countercharge, supported by a group of angry white property owners. They gave voice to an early and explicit claim about the link between race and property values: "experience teaches us," the surveyor admonished the governor, "that a European house standing next to or between Chinese properties, will not let as profitably as one standing among buildings of its own class."[13]

Sanitary rhetoric was also abundant in the political dramas of Hong Kong. Chinese speculators built hundreds of tenements for the poor in Taipingshan; some of them went up right near the walls of the army barracks. For Hennessey's opponents this proved that "Chinese were not fit to live near Westerners." In the 1880s, Osbert Chadwick, son of the most famous of all sanitarians, Edwin Chadwick, sailed out from London to referee the escalating uproar. His recommendations, much like those of his father in London, focused on improving sanitary infrastructure, building codes, policing, record keeping, and health education—not segregation. He acknowledged that the dwellings of the Chinese working class were unhealthful, but he also rebuked local whites for "condemn[ing] them as a hopelessly filthy race till they have been provided by means for cleanliness."[14]

Unconvinced, Europeans continued to flee their Chinese neighbors up Hong Kong's steep slopes in search of less congested perches. In 1888 they passed a European District Reservation Ordinance aimed to draw a line around one area they favored. The law did not forbid Chinese people from living in the district, though the designation "European Reservation" and the law's vague ban on "Chinese tenements" revealed an intention to lay down more stringent color lines. The ordinance was not strong enough, however, to stop the chase up the hillsides.[15]

In 1904, a new Hill Reservation Ordinance drew a more explicit color line near the summit of the island's Victoria Peak. In tortuous wording, it forbade all owners of property on the peak from letting any "land or building ... for purposes of residence of any but non-Chinese." In London, however, Joseph Chamberlain, the secretary of state for the colonies, added a clause allowing the governor to make exceptions. At the time, the Colonial Office, which actively supported segregation elsewhere, was eager to avoid Chinese dissent at a moment when British liberals were raising a fury over a scheme to import thousands of Chinese mine workers through Hong Kong to South Africa.[16]

After considerable deliberation and with some internal dissent, Chinese notables, led by Ho Kai, a Western-educated doctor, landowner, and member of city council, finally signed off on the official arguments for the ordinance. These included the now-shopworn idea—dating from the work of Calcutta doctor John Ronald Martin—that an open, high-altitude station was necessary for "those who are accustomed to a temperate climate," specifically noting the needs of European women and children.

FIGURE 5.2 The Peak District of Hong Kong. In 1904, after numerous failed attempts, white residents convinced Chinese elites that proper governance of the colony depended on setting aside a reservation at the top of Victoria Peak, where only Europeans and their families could live—far from the congestion of the Chinese city and at an altitude supposedly more appropriate to European constitutions. "Peak District, Hong Kong. Probably taken abt. 1885," photograph in the Crofton Collection: Hongkong and Canton, 1880-90. © The British Library Board, photo 1116/1(8).

A version of the imperial administration argument also came into play, linking the prosperity of the colony as a whole with the contentment of its British administrators.[17]

Though Ho Kai gave lip service to such nostrums, his assent may have actually hinged on an unusual real estate deal. In 1898, Britain added a substantial piece of the Chinese mainland to its Hong Kong colony, including the city of Kowloon. Chinese speculators, whom Ho may have informed in advance about the acquisition, started buying up parcels there. In 1903, alarmed Europeans passed a law aiming to reserve twenty thousand acres of the so-called New Territories for themselves. The colonial office had insisted, however, that the Kowloon law exempted "Chinese of good standing"—a loophole big enough to allow the Chinese real estate juggernaut to continue rolling. The sturdier Hill Reservation Ordinance may thus have represented a mutual understanding that Chinese investors would have relatively free access to the New Territories in exchange for a guarantee that they would stay out of the zone back on the Reservation at Victoria Peak. There, an official noted, the ordinance would "free" the British "from the speculative builder." British authorities also agreed to relax restrictions on Chinese landowners' infamous practice of subdividing buildings into tiny apartments called cubicles. In all these ways, geographical variables—Hong Kong island's verticality and its tight space, combined with the addition of lucrative new territories across a natural barrier—may have combined with intense demographic pressures on the city's land market to give legislated segregation a comparatively smooth political road that outflanked the usual objections of local elite landowners. During the same years in Singapore, where the geography did not offer opportunities for similar compromises with Chinese elites, white agitation for a segregation ordinance went nowhere.[18]

At Victoria Peak, like at Simla, "Britannia" could "[look] down with emotion of pride on the great Babylon which her sons have built." An exclusive, first-class-only, funicular tram allowed its residents to get back and forth to work in the rest of the city. A few wealthy Eurasians who lived at the Peak before the ordinance were allowed to stay, but in 1918 the colony's governor closed that remaining loophole by bombarding the colonial office with the ill-meaning argument that British children were vulnerable to the negative influences of mixed-race peers. Despite growing protests against discrimination in the 1920s, only a very small number of Chinese ever took up residence at the Peak before the ordinance was rescinded in 1946. British locals could boast with plausible accuracy that "no where in the East is the color line so strictly drawn as in Hongkong."[19]

## Two Tides in the Pacific

Meanwhile, in cities on the far shores of the Pacific, self-styled "Anglo-Saxon" settlers gave the world another style of urban segregation. The distinct attribute of this new politics was, in fact, the central role played by communities of white people who planned to live permanently in the colonial cities they founded. While the white settlers of the Pacific Rim were deeply connected to the three big ocean-spanning institutions that drove all modern urban segregation—empires, reform networks, and the land business—they also built institutions of their own that could wield power over large distances. Settlers' local colonial or territorial governments, for example, could both influence and conflict with imperial policy back in the home capitals—London, Washington, Ottawa, and later Canberra—and they held sway in other local colonial governments elsewhere in the Pacific and beyond. Whenever settlers felt blunter instruments of race war were necessary, they could also send shockwaves across the continents by assembling themselves into angry urban mobs. In addition, settlers' newspapers and other popular media could disseminate and reinterpret the ideas of reformist thinkers and academic researchers on race, sometimes giving them new rhetorical force. And Pacific settlers played a much more vital role in the politics of the real estate market than whites in Asia—as the most numerous buyers and sellers of the vast, continent-sized tracts of land seized by Western empires over the course of the nineteenth century. That included land in towns and cities, where both their ownership of real estate and their political power were most concentrated. Finally, in all settler colonies, segregationist politics more deeply reflected intrawhite class conflicts, dramas that mirrored, in a rawer sort of way, similar ones that raged all across the contemporary world's newly industrializing societies.[20]

Like many large-scale historical events, the connected segregation movements in Pacific Rim settler towns owed their origins to a geological accident: easily discoverable and workable surface deposits of gold happened to exist in many dispersed places along the ocean's coasts. Uncannily, much of this gold was discovered in virtually the same historical eye-blink: in 1848 in California, in 1851 in Australia's Victoria and New South Wales colonies, in 1856 on the Fraser River in what later became Canada's British Columbia, and in 1861 in Otago, New Zealand. New gold strikes led to the arrival of new white settlers, and that in turn increased the number of new gold strikes. As prospectors rushed from one Pacific bonanza to another, an ocean that had seen much less seagoing commerce than the Atlantic was suddenly crisscrossed by the activities of a sort of transoceanic community of fortune seekers.[21]

Everywhere white gold-seekers went, communities of similarly peripatetic Chinese prospectors, most of them whom were born in southern China and who shipped out from Hong Kong, followed. Miners from Latin America and free black communities of the US South added to the diversity of the North American mining sites, where small numbers of people could be found from many other regions of the world as well.[22]

The backcountry gold-mining camps established by these handlers of picks and pans became the birthplace of Pacific-settler-style urban segregation. There, in similar incidents repeated over and over again in gold towns otherwise separated by tens of thousands of miles, white mobs wielding firearms, projectiles, and even high-pressure water hoses (normally used to loosen gold from gravel beds) expelled Chinese miners from claims deemed too close to whites or too desirable for "Orientals." Four California towns passed laws excluding Chinese from their gold fields altogether. In other places Chinese prospectors were forced to work in separate areas, a solution that received the endorsement of an Australian royal commission in 1854. A separate "Chinese Protectorate" arose on the fields at Bendigo, Victoria Colony. Often the segregationists were whites who had brought both their weapons and their hatred for Asians from other parts of the Pacific. A group dominated by recent migrants from California, for example, burned down the camp of Chinese miners during a riot in Lytton, British Columbia, in 1883; Californian-led mobs did similar things earlier in Australia.[23]

Once the gold strikes petered out, both white and Chinese prospectors joined larger communities of white settlers in faster-growing coastal towns, bringing some of the same mining-camp rawness to the local politics of places like San Francisco, Melbourne, and Vancouver. The cross-oceanic scope of grassroots settler segregationism persisted when these gold-rush towns became railroad terminuses, burgeoning industrial centers, and commercial nodes for the growing trans-Pacific trade. As larger numbers of Chinese migrants arrived, racial conflict over the goldfields was replaced by competition over jobs and wages in railyards, docklands, canneries, sawmills, and other factories. In cities on both distant shores of the Pacific, small, white, frontier working classes and their political parties developed a habit of blaming periods of high white unemployment on low-wage Chinese competition for jobs. Groups like the Workingmen's Party of California, led by the notorious Chinese-baiter Denis Kearney, blamed their employers and other big businessmen for encouraging this racial threat to their livelihood. Many Pacific-coast capitalists were indeed eager to expand migration from China, India, and other areas of Asia or Oceania to obtain cheap labor for large-scale ventures in railroad building, fruit growing, and the like. But elites in all of these settler cities could also be just as vociferous in their condemnation of Chinese immigration and Chinese neighborhoods.[24]

Local and colonial government officials were foremost among these anti-Chinese elites. So were doctors and sanitary reformers, who brought with them training from Europe, the North American East Coast, and the colonies, thus stretching the orbit of their professional networks to the Pacific. Newspaper editors and journalists represented another institutionalized force of settler-style racial segregation. As telegraph cables began encircling the earth, the power of journalists' long-distance megaphones was enhanced. The local European press had played its part in supporting white supremacy in mainland Asian colonies, but in the Pacific settler colonies, newspapers were an even more strident force. The white press also kept these far-flung communities in touch with each other even after the gold-rush-era migrations waned. In Melbourne and later in Vancouver, pressmen kept an eager eye on events in California, to see how Americans would take care of their "Chinese problem." In California, papers repeatedly carried stories about Australian "solutions" to that same problem; Dennis Kearney got big laughs when he ominously quipped that Californians ought to mimic Australians and resort to the Gatling gun. The California congressman Horace Davis kept press clippings not only on Australia, but also about supposed Chinese threats to whites in Singapore, Batavia, and Manila—all with the idea of persuading his colleagues in Washington DC that white Californians were right: the Chinese had to go.[25]

The segregation of Pacific Rim Chinatowns was largely the work of settler-run institutions: white urban mobs, harassment by public officials, and an unrelentingly hostile local press. Their pressure also affected the pattern of Chinese migration and settlement more generally. Many Chinese migrants in fact decided against permanent settlement in white settler cities. Quite a few returned home, and others made the trip back and forth across the Pacific several times. Those who did remain were overwhelmingly single men or married men living across the ocean from their Chinese families. Though most were manual and industrial laborers, their livelihoods were quite diverse. Many who stayed brought capital from Canton and Hong Kong and founded small businesses or cross-Pacific trade houses. Regardless of class, though, most Chinese migrants felt it prudent to live in houses, shops, flats, and dormitory-style rooms on the same streets as their countrymen, most of the time in areas whites thought undesirable. San Francisco's Chinatown, with a population of twenty-two thousand in 1880, was the largest Chinese city outside Asia; it radiated for fifteen square blocks around its historic core on Sacramento Avenue. In Melbourne a smaller Chinatown developed along Little Bourke Street near a back alley dubbed Celestial Avenue. In Vancouver after 1887, the city's small Chinese population clustered along a swampy creek-bed known as Dupont Street after a mob chased them out of several smaller disconnected neighborhoods.[26]

"The Chinese live in aggregation," wrote one unusually sympathetic white observer of Vancouver's Chinatown, "but this is more a matter of necessity than choice." Won Alexander Cumyow, a Chinese resident of the city's muddy Dupont Street clarified the "necessity" involved: "The Chinese know that the white people have had no friendly feeling towards them for a number of years." "A large proportion" of the Chinese, he thought, "would bring their families with them were it not for the unfriendly reception." A key piece of evidence supporting Cumyow's mutual-protection theory was that Chinese merchants in North America and Australia, unlike those in Singapore or Hong Kong, chose to live in neighborhoods priced far below what they could easily afford.[27]

Chinatowns may have offered some safety to their residents, but whites were quick to seize upon these small communities as symbols of everything that was wrong with the presence of an "alien race" in a white man's country. Far from acknowledging their own responsibility in creating Chinatowns, whites portrayed the isolation of these enclaves, their relative squalor, and their transient all-male populations as evidence of the hateful flaws of the "Mongolian race." A vitriolic scapegoat politics arose from that impulse. It was as harsh in many ways as that employed against the Jews in Europe; it was similar in other ways to the anti-Chinese politics of early modern Spanish Manila and Dutch Batavia; but it was also markedly inflected with a particularly nasty social Darwinist version of nineteenth-century urban-reform rhetoric. In the Pacific settler colonies, unlike in India or even Hong Kong, there was relatively little of the softer (if still archly condescending) Orientalist view that whites could improve Chinese civilization. To blame the Chinese for urban disease in San Francisco was to say that their incapacity for basic morality was an unchangeable attribute of their race, built into their very biological being.

The campaign to vilify San Francisco's Chinatown was probably the most elaborate and was certainly the longest lasting. It began as early as 1854 when the common council and the public health board, responding to angry calls from a prominent doctor, the local newspaper, and its burgeoning post–gold rush white populace, declared all of the area around Sacramento Street an "unmitigated and wholesome nuisance" and called for the "immediate expulsion of the whole Chinese race from the city." The courts stepped in to prevent that from happening, but a many-barreled strategy of rhetorical attack took shape. The biggest guns in the arsenal were loaded with racist public-health rhetoric, and the first shots in the campaign were delivered by the municipal government's sanitarians. As Chinese businessmen and the courts also pointed out, it did not seem to matter to whites that such attacks involved a false accusation against the whole Chinese community for the sins of a few and that whites altogether ignored the role of white land owners in Chinatown who were responsible for maintaining the healthy state of their buildings.[28]

In the hands of San Francisco's particularly acerbic director of public health, Dr. John Meares, who served from 1876 to 1888, a period when

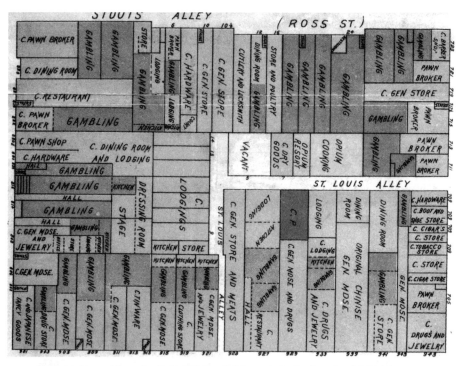

FIGURE 5.3 Excerpt from the "Official Map of Chinatown in San Francisco" (1885), produced by the San Francisco Board of Supervisors. The map helped give an official stamp to a widespread belief that the city's Chinese residents were the source of vice and disease and that their neighborhood posed a threat to the city as a whole. "C" is short for "Chinese"; "C. P." is short for "Chinese prostitution." Courtesy of the Bancroft Library, University of California, Berkeley.

three smallpox epidemics raged through the city, mortality statistics and figures on overcrowded housing became evidence of the "hereditary vices" of the Chinese race. During his tenure, the city's board of supervisors produced an elaborately surveyed "Official Map of Chinatown in San Francisco," which highlighted the district's "opium resorts," whorehouses, and gambling dens. Eyewitness accounts by officials and journalists—one of which was entitled *Horrors of a Mongolian Settlement*— led readers on nighttime tours into subterranean "labyrinths" beneath Chinatown's streets that connected a series of "pens," "dungeons," and "lairs" filled with smallpox, smoke, sex, and the darkest of sins. Meares and others overlooked whites' own responsibility for the predominantly male profile of Chinatown's population and represented Chinese men as sex-starved gatekeepers of a hell that swallowed innocent white women into prostitution. Single Chinese men who crowded into dormitories, they hinted, were also prone to such "beastly corruptions" as sodomy; in the process Meares and others breathed new life into a strand of anti-homosexual, anti-Chinese thought that began in sixteenth-century Spanish Manila. Capping this line of argument, Chinese people's efforts to protect themselves in enclaves was interpreted—in a way very similar to European anti-Jewish thought—to reflect their inherent "clannishness," their conniving secrecy, and their fundamental disinterest or racial inability to assimilate into white society. Sanitary rhetoric also helped raise the specter of racial threats to property values, which could contain their own trans-Pacific imagery. In 1876, for example, a California state senator testified in Washington that landlords in white blocks near Chinatowns often rented "a single house . . . to Chinamen," then watched as "the atmosphere becomes fetid, and a sickly smell pervades the neighborhood. . . . The rents fall, and finally the Chinese get possession. . . . The property has fallen in value, becomes dilapidated and offensive, and the street is as much dedicated to Chinese uses . . . as if it were a street in Hong Kong or Canton."[29]

White San Franciscans' campaign against Chinatown continued off and on for at least a half century. Like anti-Chinese agitation elsewhere in the Pacific, it lost a little steam during the 1860s when the gold rushes ended, but it picked up again in the 1870s and 1880s. A mob of working-men threatened to incinerate the neighborhood in 1877. In the 1880s, the city's common council, egged on by Dr. Meares, several more times sought authority to evacuate the residents of "this great reservoir of moral, social, and physical pollution." In one case a city official who was frustrated by court injunctions halting such summary expropriation explicitly threatened to do the job by once again unleashing "the Workingmen." In 1890 the city council decided that the on-again, off-again segregationist actions of white mobs, the press, and official harassment were not enough to sustain the color line, and it passed a municipal segregation ordinance.[30]

The short-lived law was one of the first to use race explicitly as the basis for government-coerced segregation. It ordered all the inhabitants of Chinatown to move to an area outside the city, alongside other nuisances like "slaughterhouses, tallow factories, [and] hog butcheries." Its sanction of forced removal set it apart from Hong Kong's 1888 and 1904 segregation laws and more closely resembled those establishing "native locations" outside South African cities, which had arisen in rudimentary form some years earlier (see chapter 8).

In the end, though, no Chinese "township" came into being in San Francisco. During earlier decades of experience with white attacks, Chinese activists had learned how to forestall expulsion by appeal to the courts. In 1890, the federal judge Lorenzo Sawyer ruled in favor of Chinese plaintiffs in the case *In Re Lee Sing et al.* In his opinion he invoked the universal civil rights doctrine embodied in the Fourteenth Amendment to the US Constitution, but his main argument was that the city had not shown how a wholesale violation of property rights would solve any specific matter of municipal health or morality. Once again, Asian landholders parried the segregationists—in this case with good lawyers operating in the courtrooms of conservative judges who held private property sacrosanct. In 1901, San Francisco's whites again tried to level Chinatown, but once again Chinese plaintiffs and sympathetic judges foiled the attempt (see chap. 6).[31]

## Segregating All Oceans

The creation of Chinatowns in Pacific-coast cities was intrinsically linked to white settlers' more ambitious innovation in segregationist politics, the effort to keep Chinese migrants from crossing the Pacific in the first place. Whites' interest in drawing an ocean-spanning color line arose from a crucial distinction in social Darwinist racial geography, that between Asia and the rest of the Pacific Rim. In tropical Asia, whites had to justify their presence in a part of the world most thought inhospitable to them. By contrast, in western North America and Australasia, most whites imagined themselves as inhabiting places that were "white man's countries." In the United States, settlers even believed that a "manifest destiny" propelled their claim to the continent's West. The dictates of racial struggle, they imagined, made the mass killing of native peoples, or their forced relocation, inevitable. It followed that further measures would be needed to keep other "darker races" from setting foot on racially exclusive shores. Race theorists from North America to Australia reminded their readers that African slavery had caused no end of racial conflict in the United States east of the Mississippi. Further west, the choice was clear: "Either the Anglo Saxon race will possess the Pacific slope," as the US senator James Blaine warned in 1879, "or the Mongolians will possess it." By then, the restriction of Chinese cross-ocean migration had grown from a crackpot idea of frontier settlers living in distant outposts to a rallying cry heard at once in London, Washington DC, Ottawa, and in colonial capitals across white Australasia.[32]

For white settlers in the Pacific, this was a hard-won achievement, for there were powerful obstacles to the restrictionist cause. Both London and Washington were eager to promote trade with China. The Qing court was hardly pleased by the treatment its subjects were receiving abroad, and it was even less happy about white settlers' calls to renegotiate the free-migration treaties it had signed with the West. Meanwhile, throughout the Pacific and beyond, railroad companies, mining companies, and plantation owners clamored for cheap "coolie" laborers. As a result, the Asian diaspora soon encompassed places across the Pacific world—including Hawaii, the western coast of Latin America, and all the colonies of Australia—and stretched into southern and eastern Africa as well as the Caribbean. For white settlers in many of these places, the lower wages white employers paid to Asians and Pacific Islanders gave inferior races an unnatural advantage in the global war of fit against unfit.[33]

Whites in the Pacific took the lead in tamping down the "rising tide of color" they saw surging forth from Asia. The city of Melbourne began the oceanwide campaign for Chinese immigration restriction in 1855 by charging a stiff landing tax for arriving Chinese passengers and limiting the number of passengers that ships of various sizes could land on the docks. London disallowed the law as a violation of treaties and an obstacle to labor recruitment; Washington did the same to an imitation of Melbourne's statute passed in California. Once again, colonists responded by gathering into mobs, this time to offer their hate-filled greetings to ships that arrived in port with large cargoes of Chinese or Indians on board. Even more electrifying international sensations arose when a single ship received hostile reactions at a succession of ports, linked by telegraphed advanced warnings that were reprinted as screaming headlines in settler newspapers.[34]

By the 1870s, anti-Chinese violence in Pacific cities had ironically resulted in the spread of Chinatowns elsewhere, as Chinese migrants left hotbeds of white hatred for what they hoped were safer places, like Chicago, New York, Philadelphia, Toronto, Perth (Western Australia Colony), and Auckland (New Zealand). As more whites encountered the supposed "Chinese menace" firsthand, the profile of the exclusion movement rose on the national scene on both sides of the Pacific, and also in places like Honolulu, where a sizeable Chinatown came into being when large numbers of Asian plantation workers moved to the islands. Propagandists and race theorists across North America and Australia warned of the perils that befell white societies when they let their racial guard drop, and some pointed to Singapore as an example of a white place overrun by Orientals. As shining counterexamples, exclusionists also lauded Dutch and Spanish authorities' stringent anti-Chinese regulations in the East Indies and the Philippines. Then, during the otherwise dull US presidential election season of 1879, James Blaine made the restrictionist clamor of the California Workingmen's Party his own, in an effort to bait race all the way to the White House. He failed to get there, but the Chinese Restriction Act passed Congress in 1882 and then got sharper teeth in 1888. Similar restriction legislation passed during the next few decades, as movements calling for a White Canada, a White Australia, and even a White New Zealand crested in influence.[35]

Pacific settlers' segregation of the world's largest ocean would soon have wide-ranging implications for urban politics in many other parts of the world. The political success settlers achieved on two continents in stopping Chinese immigration—followed by similar efforts to restrict the movements of Japanese and Filipinos—emboldened anti-Asian restrictionists elsewhere. In Africa, British settlers sought to draw new lines across the Indian Ocean, restricting Indians from entry into the South African colonies of Natal and the Transvaal as well as into Rhodesia, Kenya, and Uganda. In the United States in 1924, the Anglo-Saxonist movement to restrict immigration of the "suspect" white races of southern and eastern Europe effectively segregated the most trafficked of all oceans, the North Atlantic. In the process, race became a *practical* theory of world history and world geography. The American racist theorist Lo-throp Stoddard lauded immigration restriction as "a species of segrega-tion on a large scale." South Africans would refine the concept for inter-nal use as "influx control," the basic principle of its notorious pass laws. For urban segregationists, the engineering of global demographic flows became part of a growing kit of tried and tested tools.[36]

As one tide of segregationism washed from the Pacific outward, two even more pervasive waves of city-splitting politics engulfed East Asia and the Pacific, both from within and without. The first originated in Hong Kong, whose uncontested 1904 Hill Reservation Ordinance now marked it as the most radically segregated city in the East. Even before the law's passage, the city became the epicenter of another aggressive form of sanitary segregationism, this one linked to the spread of bubonic plague. Soon its effects would not only engulf both Pacific coasts but also the rest of Asia, Africa, and even across the Atlantic to the Americas.

The second wave of segregationist politics was driven above all by the politics of land markets. One important eddy in this wave first arose in the Pacific world. In 1858, a registrar of deeds in the colony of South Australia named Robert Torrens developed more secure procedures for property-title registration that soon spread across the Anglo-Saxon world and beyond. As beliefs about racial threats to white property values began to pervade the cities of settler colonies elsewhere, including the United States and South Africa, real estate agents and their lawyers began to fill the new "Torrens titles" with adaptations of London's restrictive land-use covenants that now explicitly forbade people of Asian, African, and Latin descent from buying or occupying white property. In the pro-cess, Pacific white settlers' interest in using legislation to segregate did not completely die. In 1918, Vancouver passed another anti-Asian racial segregation law, soon disallowed, that aimed to give whites "relief from encroachments of Asiatics into business and retail sections." But the overall trend among white Pacific-coast settlers, especially those in the United States, was to put their faith in what proved to be a much hardier and even court-sanctioned system of dividing cities. It would rely less on government statutes and more on race-infused economic incentives.[37]

# 6 : Segregation Mania

## A Call to All Continents

Everything changed for the word "segregation" just before the dawn of the twentieth century. Before then, the word had evolved glacially, from its ancient Latin roots—referring to shepherds' practices of culling livestock from their flocks (*gregis*)—into a staid, nineteenth-century bourgeois professional's synonym for "separation." Scientists, for example, used it to describe the loosening of chemical bonds between one substance and another, and when hospital officials placed contagious patients in a special ward, they too spoke of "segregation." Then, suddenly, in the late 1890s, segregation escaped from the laboratory (as it were) and transformed itself into an electric political rallying cry. You could hear it in cities almost everywhere.[1]

The main reason for this sudden metamorphosis? The bubonic plague—the so-called Black Death. In 1894 it broke out in Hong Kong, where thousands died gruesome deaths. Two years later it appeared in Bombay, only worse. Public health officials, in sheer panic, started yanking people from their homes and forcing them into hospitals, tent cities, or onto ships. This technique they called isolation, or, increasingly, segregation. Race mattered: the main goal was to protect Europeans, and local Asian people got the roughest treatment. Tens of thousands of natives fled town, in part from fear of the plague, but more from fear of segregation itself.

From there, the plague, with segregation as a kind of twin dark shadow, spread across big expanses of the world. Eastward the germ and the urban practice sailed together, across the Pacific as far as San Francisco and westward across the Indian Ocean and Africa as far as Dakar in Senegal, on the continent's westernmost tip, before jumping the Atlantic to southern Europe and the Americas.

In Africa, new fears of disease added fuel to segregation mania. Colonial public health officials—sometimes the very same people who dealt with the plague in Asia—fought with each other about another sensational medical discovery. Billions of the tropical zone's swarming mosquitoes, it turned out, carried the deadly malarial plasmodium in their guts. "The only means of escape," some of these new mosquito-hunting reformers declared, was the "segregation of the Europeans"—at least a quarter mile from "any African hut."[2]

From there—as *ségrégation, segregación, segregação,* or *segregazione*—the word was quickly picked up by the French, Belgian, Dutch, Spanish, Portuguese, and Italian conquerors of Africa and Asia. The instigators of Jim Crow in the US South jumped on the original English usage, as did city dwellers everywhere in North America, including the authors of Baltimore's 1910 segregation ordinance. Even speakers of the newly named Afrikaans language of South Africa quickly embraced *segregasie.* Only the Germans, who acquired their own colonies in Africa, abjured the Latin roots of the word; they translated the concept as *Rassentrennung* or *Absonderung*—literally, city-"sundering."[3]

For some historians, segregation's new, edgy, turn-of-the-century political meanings signify that the practice of dividing races in spaces had reached a new level of political existence—when segregationists first married a "coherent ideology" to a "de jure system." In urban politics, that is simply not true, as we know. From the Black Town–White Town separation policies of Madras and Calcutta, to cantonment law, to the Raffles doctrine, to Hong Kong and San Francisco's racial zoning ordinances, the earlier history of city-splitting had provided plenty of examples of government-sanctioned or legislated practices that reflect ever more clearly worked-out doctrines. It is true, however, that the word "segregation" gave racist city-splitters a clearer slogan than they had before. It is also definitely true that white supremacist rhetoric rose to its shrillest pitch during the years of segregation mania. Western science more fiercely than ever confirmed the idea that humanity was divided into races, and social Darwinism, racial craniology, and the rising science of eugenics enjoyed its greatest-ever respect among scholars and researchers. The African American historian, philosopher, and activist W. E. B. DuBois warned about the rise of a "new religion of whiteness" during these years; Mohandas Gandhi later called it whites' "fetish of . . .

pre-destined superiority." During these same years, an unprecedented wave of new, radical experiments in state-run racialized city-splitting got under way. Perhaps most importantly, it was during the era of segregation mania that practices of racial separation spanned the globe for the first time. Even Latin America and Europe were touched.

But it was not the crystal clarity of the slogan nor the elaboration of segregationist doctrine that guaranteed this malefic achievement so much as the growing strength of Western empires, reform networks, and land markets—the three institutions that have become so familiar as we travel to segregated cities across time and place.[4]

Empires, of course, provided much of the mania's political energy. The years after 1880 witnessed the largest-ever burst of Western imperial expansion—the near-crazed "Scramble for Africa" above all, but also the French, British, and Dutch conquests in Southeast Asia and Oceania, and the Europeans' and Americans' ever-deeper interference in China. The United States, meanwhile, completed its conquests of continental North America and extended its power throughout the Caribbean basin and across the Pacific to Hawaii and the Philippines.

Perhaps even more important to segregation mania was the work of a new generation of public health reformers. While some of them grew ever more insistent that dark-skinned people presented a threat to white health, they had now divided into two camps, some insisting that the threat came from natives' contributions to deadly miasmas in the atmosphere (the "infectionist" camp), others countering that deadly poisons spread directly from black bodies to white ones (the "contagionists"). After about 1870, rival public health experts were forced to square their beliefs in infections or contagions with a third theory of disease. In laboratories of Europe and then across the colonies, the evidence grew unassailable that people got sick because of microscopic organisms, some of them conveyed into human bodies by other small animals. Plague and malaria germs, along with rats, fleas, and mosquitoes, played starring roles in the new, terrifying drama of racial public health segregationism that resulted—though in some cities they shared the stage with yellow fever, smallpox, tuberculosis, and influenza.

As in the years before the new era of segregation, city-splitting also depended on the nature of urban land markets. There was plenty of mania to go around here too. For one thing, the scrambles for colonies represented world history's largest-ever landgrab. On top of that, a new generation of housing reformers arose, most notably in Britain. For them—

like for Florence Nightingale in the Indian stations, Osbert Chadwick in Hong Kong, Lawrence Veiller in New York, and, most famously, Octavia Hill in London—the key to stopping disease was not the avoidance of uncomfortable climates but the transformation of cities' built environment, starting with the slums, or, as some were soon called, the "plague spots." For some housing reformers, this could be accomplished by forcing slumlords to abide by stringent building codes. For many others, though, a different kind of landgrab was necessary: they believed government should use its powers to forcibly purchase the plague spots from the slumlords, raze them, and rehouse their inhabitants either on the same land or in more salubrious low-rent surroundings, perhaps even on the edges of cities, so prized by the middle class. Though officials in Calcutta had experimented with this idea much earlier, the practice had gained increasing legal respectability, especially in the wake of the passage of Britain's pathbreaking Housing of the Working Classes Act in 1890. In the colonies, urban officials picked up the call for slum clearance from the imperial center. Winding it together with racist ideas about public health and the right of conquest, they began dramatic worldwide escalation of one of the most controversial tools of urban segregation: forced removal. In many cases the expensive obligation to rehouse those displaced was honored only in the breach—intensifying the overcrowding of slums adjacent to those recently cleared. In other cases, rehousing itself served to tighten urban color lines, as reformers pushed slum dwellers of color into separate districts far out on the urban periphery.[5]

As in colonial cities from Calcutta onward, though, other Western land market institutions could also slow down segregation mania and even empower outright opposition to it. Wealthy Asian and African landholders proved again and again that it was possible to buy one's way out of racial segregation in colonial cities, thus often rendering residential color lines virtually meaningless. No segregated city came into being without people entering into very messy and enormously varied conflicts and negotiations over land rights. Indeed, segregationist dramas did not even always hang solely on conflicts between whites and blacks—sometimes they arose between multiple groups of people— often of multiple colors—whose shifting alliances, rifts, and claims to land sometimes crossed color lines. As before, some white merchants could oppose segregation. So could colonial governors, if they had the mind and the moral fortitude to do so. No imperial regime ever created fully "dual" cities whose two parts had nothing to do with one another, no matter how starkly divided those cities looked on the map or in the law books. Though efforts to impose and resist imperial control were always present, so were interdependence, compromise, and constant, more or less regulated boundary crossing.

As the call for segregation rose to a manic pitch, the internal contradictions of segregationism ground against one other more shrilly. While the mania most certainly reflected whites' greatest moment of imperial triumph, it also revealed their increasingly jittery sense of racial vulnerability. The broader field of imperial rule meant that the energies of Western empires were spread that much thinner, and it meant that whites faced racial insubordination in a wider array of places. The era's most emblematic paradox was that the "highest stage" of race segregation in the colonies coincided exactly with the entry onto the urban stage of a political counterforce of even greater world historical import. As the rise of a new generation of anticolonial leaders like DuBois and Gandhi suggests, the most fervent age of the "white religion" also spawned the first great calls for colonial self-rule and for racial and economic equality. Because of the forces arrayed against them, most colonial urban segregationists had to camouflage their racial ideologies at least to some extent. In particular, they found themselves administering the bitter medicine of segregation with spoonsfuls of what they hoped were sweeter concepts, like civilization, culture, healthfulness, racial peace, and white men's "burden" to ensure what they called the "uplift" of their so-called inferiors.[6]

## The Germ Theory of Segregation

English-speaking public health reformers invented the idea of sanitary-based housing segregation. They and their Anglo-Saxon successors would continue to be its greatest champions throughout the colonial world. But these English speakers were not the only ones to play their game. Sanitary thinking in Britain and North America—like racial thinking more generally—had always drawn inspiration from continental Europe, especially from Paris but increasingly also from Berlin and other fast-growing cities of the European industrial belt.

In Europe, the cholera epidemics that lasted from the 1830s through the 1860s provided one of those great periodic shocks to Western civilization's faith in the ability of humankind to make progress in its efforts to conquer nature. As such, they ignited a burst of cross-national sanitary debate. Imperial rivalries also began to fester again at about the same time, for France invaded Algeria in 1830 and Indochina in the 1860s, in part as way to make up lost ground against Britain in the business of seizing colonies. Such political enmities added spice to public health discussions, as when the French took the lead at international sanitary conferences in lambasting the British Raj for its poor performance in stopping the worldwide spread of cholera.

But nationalist posturing and cross-national inspiration could coexist. Edwin Chadwick's classic work on sanitation in London, for example, borrowed heavily from the work of Paris's great sewer expert Alexandre Parent-Duchâtelet. In one diatribe, James Ranald Martin, formerly of Calcutta, laughed out loud at the idea that Frenchmen could ever settle permanently in fever-ridden Algeria. Shortly afterward, he set out on the English sanitarian's obligatory pilgrimage to Paris to consult with such luminaries as Dr. Louis-René Villermé, the world's greatest authority on the diseases of working-class districts. Meanwhile, on the other side of the world, in Shanghai, even as French and British colonialists jostled each other in their neighboring Concessions, their public health officials traded ideas and collaborated on sanitary projects. Multiplying specialized public health journals and the international sanitary conference movement meant that Anglo-Saxon public health professionals conversed cordially with their rival colleagues from the Continent on a regular basis.[7]

Competition, cross-fertilization, and the reach of Western sanitary discourse all increased during the 1880s, when the French scientist Louis Pasteur and the German doctor Robert Koch confirmed the theory that microscopic organisms caused disease. Koch found the culprit for the deadliest of them all, tuberculosis, in 1882 in Berlin. A year later Koch was in Alexandria, Egypt (by that point under Franco-British supervision), to search for the "comma" bacillus that causes cholera. Later, to the Government of India's dismay and stubborn denial, he also found it swimming in the tanks of Calcutta. Meanwhile, in 1880, the French doctor Alphonse Laveran discovered the plasmodium that causes malaria in the blood of sick soldiers at an army hospital in the city of Constantine, Algeria. In the Caribbean, the Cuban doctor Carlos Finlay found in 1881 that mosquitoes transmit the germ that causes yellow fever. Later, in experiments conducted in a half dozen stations of the British Raj but that culminated in 1898 in research on birds in Calcutta, Ronald Ross established that mosquitoes were also responsible for a key part of the life cycle of Laveran's malaria-causing plasmodium: the insects ingested immature forms of the germ from one person or animal on a first bite and then, with a second bite, infected other people with the debilitating mature form. Finally, in 1894, in a panicked Hong Kong, the Saigon-based French-Swiss doctor Alexandre Yersin, a student of Pasteur's, isolated and described the microbe that causes bubonic plague. He also theorized that it might be transmitted by rats, and his suggestion inspired further experiments that connected the germ with fleas that live on rodents' blood.[8]

These discoveries had revolutionary, if not immediately obvious, implications for public health. It took several decades for the germ theory to make inroads into the debates between miasma-obsessed infectionists and their contagionist opponents. Members of the infectionist school, like the followers of Chadwick and Martin, continued to press for expensive changes in sanitary infrastructure like sewers and water supplies. If they took any notice at all of Koch's confirmation of John Snow's waterborne theory of cholera, it was to say that it reaffirmed the measures they had always advocated. Those who thought that disease was predominantly caused by person-to-person contagion—and who favored more ad hoc countermeasures like ship quarantines and cordons sanitaires—also took germ theory to confirm their practices. Both schools meanwhile faced continuing opposition from colonial officials and many colonial subjects. The expense of bringing purer water to Calcutta, for example, was more than taxpayers and officials were prepared to pay, and some high British officials simply denied that a microbe (especially one discovered by a German) caused cholera. Quarantines fared no better politically: they went against dominant free-market theories, they interfered with religious pilgrimages, and no one who was engaged in commerce, whether European or native, liked to have their business disrupted.[9]

The arrival of the plague in Hong Kong in 1894 and in Bombay in 1896 stormed these torpid waters of trans-oceanic public health debate. As the plague spread, killing off millions, public health officials summoned new authoritarian energy to force old-fashioned Western remedies down the throats of the inhabitants of their colonial cities. Even as Yersin and others worked largely off stage to discover plague's bacterial causes, these measures set off political explosions that rocked the foundations of the British Empire and continued to ricochet throughout the colonial world for two decades.

## Segregation Sails East with the Plague

The pandemic of bubonic plague that raged from 1894 to 1950 was the third quasi-global visitation of this disease (the first occurred during the sixth century CE, the second was the famed Black Death of the fourteenth century). When plague broke out of western China in the 1890s, the new field of bacteriology had yet to convince many of the world's public health officials of its usefulness. No one knew what caused the plague's ghastly symptoms and the swift death it delivered. Even when Yersin discovered the bacillus shortly after its arrival in Hong Kong, it was a long time before anyone knew for sure how the germ spread. In retrospect, it became clear that the actual deadliness of the disease varied tremendously in each city it visited. We now know that plague death tolls largely depend on whether infected rats and fleas from elsewhere can find a niche in varying local rodent and insect ecologies. Officials also discovered that Asians and Africans died in much larger numbers than Europeans, but they did not know until later that this was because most whites lived and worked in places where they were less likely to encounter those scurrying carriers of plague.[10]

For colonial officials who had to respond to plague, fear understandably filled the space left by this absence of knowledge. But their antiplague measures were even more panicked than those they devised to stop deadlier but equally misunderstood killers like tuberculosis and cholera. The especially terrifying prospect of a recurrence of the medieval Black Death seemed to have seized their imaginations. Whether or not the "blackness" of the death mattered, racial theories of disease clearly had something to do with the panic as well. Universally, Western plague responders reserved their most extreme and invasive measures for colonized natives, especially the poor.[11]

In Hong Kong (1894) and Bombay (1896), those draconian measures were largely the work of the same man, Dr. James A. Lowson—though the officials who hired him in each of the two cities roundly supported him. He opted for classic contagionist remedies, aimed above all at separating sick people from healthy ones. The interpersonal transmission theory appeared to be borne out when a Japanese researcher, Kitasato Shibasaburo, who had studied under Koch in Berlin and who was in close contact with Lowson, claimed to have isolated the plague bacillus in one of Hong Kong's clinics (three days later Yersin made a more accurate description and later received credit for the discovery). Once local officials declared the outbreak of an epidemic, their counterparts elsewhere placed quarantines on all ships arriving from that port. Lowson mobilized his small staff, soldiers, and later even gangs of convicts to remove sick and dead people from their homes, along with potentially infected belongings. They buried the dead unceremoniously in pits and covered them with lime or thick slabs of cement. In Bombay they pumped the city's sewers with three million gallons of seawater mixed with carbolic acid. But, as Bombay's health officer explained, "the greatest attention was paid to . . . the segregation of the poor." Thousands of residents of plague spots, like Hong Kong's working-class Taipingshan and the slums of Bombay's Native Town, were forced into "isolation hospitals" and "segregation camps." In Hong Kong, the main camp was on a converted hospital ship called the *Hygeia* anchored far out in the harbor. Officials then destroyed hundreds of houses in the emptied districts and even considered burning large swaths of Taipingshan to the ground.[12]

In practice, most of these measures were disastrous to the cities' public health, or at least highly ineffective—though of course we can never know precisely whether the plague would have killed more people without the responses. Officials who enforced quarantines of ships from plague ports usually lifted them once they were cleared of human plague cases, but often those ships still had rats on board whose resident fleas brought the disease on shore. Thus the plague quickly transported itself eastward across the Pacific to Sydney, Honolulu, and San Francisco, and westward to points all along the shores of Africa and South America and even to a few cities in southern Europe. Meanwhile, destruction of houses and the cleansing of sewers forced rats out of their nesting places into wider areas of the city, thus exposing greater numbers of humans to deadly flea bites. In Bombay and western India as a whole, where the ecology was especially well suited to the most efficient types of plague-carrying fleas, a staggering twenty million people died over the next two decades, accounting for the large majority of people killed during the pandemic. Death rates at Bombay and Hong Kong were particularly elevated among all stricken cities; only Cape Town's came close a few years later. The only bright light in the story was that Yersin's discoveries led to an antiplague serum, and in Bombay a Ukrainian scientist named Waldemar Haffkine even invented a cumbersome vaccine. To their credit, Lowson and others put these to use as soon as they were available, thus saving some lives.[13]

Meanwhile, the political revolt against antiplague measures led many to fear that Hong Kong Colony would collapse and that a second mutiny was on its way in India. In Hong Kong the local Chinese hated the segregation measures—they violated the sanctity of the household and made it impossible for family members to give respectful attention to sick and dying loved ones. In India some Muslims and Hindus ironically lashed out at race segregation for its violations of purdah and caste segregation: house searches forced sequestered women into public, and the segregation camps brought incompatible castes together. Summary, undignified burials violated Confucian, Hindu, Jain, Jewish, Buddhist, and Muslim norms—not to mention Christian ones. Property confiscation and damage from acid and other disinfectants led to years of angry claims concerning adequate compensation. When public health officials sought to deploy Yersin's serum or Haffkine's vaccine, more storms of protest arose, either in defense of traditional medical techniques or over worries about the often disturbing side effects and the use of prohibited animal products in the injections. Almost a hundred thousand people fled Hong Kong. Nearly two hundred thousand left Bombay, many unwittingly transporting the plague into the countryside.[14]

Amid this chaos, it's worthwhile to make a quick stop in Calcutta, to meet the city's Medical Officer of Health, the abrasive Dr. W. J. Simpson. Soon he would earn his nickname "the stormy petrel of tropical hygiene," for his exceptionally extensive travels around the colonial world and his seemingly uncanny ability to arrive in town when sanitary matters looked direst. He inaugurated his contentious career as a plague responder by singling out Calcutta's mixed-race Burra Bazaar as the city's likeliest plague spot. He left town for England on convalescent leave in 1897, but only after he diagnosed a few local cases and endorsed Lowson's techniques. Amidst fears of Bombay-style segregation camps and defiling vaccination campaigns, 150,000 people fled Calcutta to avoid antiplague measures.[15]

Those who remained behind in Hong Kong, Bombay, and Calcutta staged tumultuous protests, attacked beleaguered sanitary crews, and invaded hospitals in search of loved ones victimized by forced segregation. In Calcutta, crowds of the city's new industrial workers succeeded in forcing the government to disavow any intention to follow in Bombay's footsteps. The plague uprisings inspired the emergence of a more radical wing of the Indian National Congress. In 1897, two radical opponents of the Raj assassinated the health officer of the city of Poona (Pune). The

Congress leader B. G. Tilak was imprisoned in connection with this event. On his release, he raised some of the first calls for "Swaraj," or Indian self-rule. Bombings and other violent acts of resistance began reverberating in the streets of Calcutta and other Indian cities.[16]

Ironically, in Hong Kong and India's biggest cities the explosive use of racial segregation measures to combat the plague had relatively little direct long-term influence on urban residential color lines. Osbert Chadwick returned to Hong Kong in 1900, accompanied by Calcutta's Dr. W. J. Simpson himself, who had by now become the empire's foremost plague expert. Faced with the task of rebuilding most of Taipingshan, Chadwick and Simpson suggested a new housing code but no new segregation measures. By the time whites began to agitate for the Kowloon Ordinance (1903) and the Hill Reservation Ordinance (1904), the plague had receded. To the extent that segregationists relied on public health concerns to make their case, they took their stand based on newly fashionable malaria-based arguments in the first case, and then dusted off old-fashioned hill-station-style climatological arguments to support the reservation at the Peak.[17]

In India, widespread anger at Lowson's property seizures gives us something of a sense of how poorly any kind of race-based residential segregation ordinance would have fared there. Though urban Indian elites did lose significant measures of power in the crackdown that followed the plague revolts, they used the influence that they retained to push for class-based segregation measures aimed at the poor. At Bombay, the British founded the empire's first urban Improvement Trust in 1898, in part to restore the power of what one official called "a large leaven of Englishmen who have no vested interests in property in the city" over the local elite landowners who ran the town corporation. In its schemes, however, the Bombay Improvement Trust (BIT) prioritized Indian elites' desire to raze the slums that lay closest to their own swank districts. When the BIT tried to relocate cleared slum dwellers near a prestigious, largely Indian beachfront neighborhood, its wealthy inhabitants successfully cancelled the idea. In any case, the BIT was lackadaisical at best about providing rehousing for the poor, let alone public transport—in marked contrast to obligations under London's Housing of the Working Classes Act. For poor people ejected from their homes who needed access to work in town, the only option was to crowd into those central-city slums that had yet to be destroyed, worsening conditions there. In Calcutta, the plague rebellion aggravated whites' long-standing complaints against the city's bhadralok-dominated municipal government. In 1899, the governor of Bengal, with Viceroy Curzon's approval, restructured the city's government to restore European control, despite the determined protest of the local Congress leader Surendranath Banerjea and others. Soon Calcutta too had its Improvement Trust, which operated in a similar manner to that at Bombay.[18]

The biggest effects of plague politics on urban residential color lines occurred elsewhere, in the Pacific and especially in Africa. In the Pacific, plague-infected fleas quickly made their way from Hong Kong to, among other places, Honolulu (1899) and San Francisco (1900). In both cities, health officials instinctively identified the plague as "a disease of locality and place"—that place, of course, being Chinatown. In Honolulu, three doctors, led by Clifford Wood, effectively became "dictators of Hawaii" for a period of three months. They investigated the acid-based plague-abatement methods of Bombay, but rejected them for their expense and

FIGURE 6.1 Fighting plague with fire. Residents of Honolulu's Chinatown flee the blaze set by American public health authorities to eradicate the plague. Because plague was deemed a "disease of place"—and of racially determined habits—the global pandemic of 1894-1930 became a major force in the worldwide spread of segregation mania. "The Exodus From Chinatown, January 20, 1900," photograph in the C. B. Wood Collection, Hawaii State Archives, Honolulu.

instead settled on a method first contemplated by British officials at Hong Kong: fire. On January 20, 1900, Wood was busy setting fires in several "contaminated" buildings in Chinatown when sudden winds that are common during that time of the year on Oahu whipped the flames out of control. By the end of the day, all of Chinatown was reduced to cinders. The neighborhood's Chinese, Japanese, and native Hawaiian residents were all forced into plague camps outside the city, where they were placed under guard for three months.[19]

In San Francisco, after a single suspected case of plague surfaced a year later, the board of health roped off Chinatown and placed police officers around it to forbid ingress and egress. While lurid journalistic exposés of the "Horrors of the Plague in India" played in the background, one of Clifford Wood's Honolulu colleagues urged the board to repeat the feat of destroying Chinatown by fire. A fervent supporter of this idea was Dr. James Kinyoun of the San Francisco office of the United States Public Health Service, who trained in Berlin with Koch and in Paris at the Pasteur Institute. Awaiting final orders, he made arrangements for a housing scheme outside town to resettle Chinatown's residents. The town's white press once again renewed its sensational attacks on Chinatown. Land speculators, eager to acquire the prime real estate underneath Chinatown for themselves crossed their fingers that the plague would constitute a sufficient emergency to overcome court objections that had scuttled the 1890 segregation ordinance.[20]

It would not. Once again Chinatown residents of both Honolulu and San Francisco were successful in preventing the permanent relocation of their communities. In Honolulu, where US civil rights laws did not yet apply, Chinese owners of burned shops and houses were rarely able to get adequate compensation for their losses, despite federal funds that flowed into town once the United States annexed Hawaii shortly after the fire. Still, many refused to sell to developers, and a smaller Chinatown grew up in the same spot as the old one and remains there today. In San Francisco, a Chinese grocer and a cook successfully filed motions in federal court for an injunction against Kinyoun's resettlement plan on civil rights grounds, and the board of health had to back off. The plague scare dwindled owing to natural factors in both cases. But for the time being, white settlers had left Chinese residents with yet another bitter memory of the surrounding society's hatefulness, and thus with stronger reasons to continue seeking protection in a separate neighborhood.[21]

## Hunting Rats, Fleas, and Mosquitoes in Africa

Meanwhile, the plague traveled westward from Asia to Africa—arriving as the thirty-year imperial scramble for the continent began to wind down. In Africa's many port cities, the Black Death opened up a much wider range of options for residential segregationists. The most successful, enduring, and complex plague-related city-splitting efforts occurred in South Africa. The plague reached Cape Town, Port Elizabeth, and Durban during the height of the Anglo-Boer War (1899–1903). British troop convoys moved flea-infested rats inland with war supplies, so the disease also broke out in inland cities like Johannesburg. In all of these places, medical officers of health, supported by white town councils and invoking precedents in India, China, and the Pacific, made liberal use of summary expropriation and even fire. All of them forcibly removed blacks, mixed-race "coloreds," and Indians to segregation camps. Those they set aside for blacks quickly became permanent. Most of them formed the nuclei for the infamous segregated townships of the apartheid era, though a much more complicated politics of segregation replaced that focused on plague scares shortly after the epidemic burned itself out (see chapter 8).

In tropical Africa, the plague arrived somewhat later—in Accra, the capital of the Gold Coast Colony (today's Ghana), in 1909; Nairobi in 1911; and Dakar, Senegal, in 1914. Despite growing awareness of the cause of the disease, public health officials prolonged the segregation mania there and ultimately engaged in some of the more radical segregation measures in all of the colonies outside South Africa. In Africa, officials made little distinction between emergency policies to separate the sick from the healthy and permanent policies to divide the city by race. In some places, the South African example helped smooth the tortuous logical reasoning involved—most tangibly in Nairobi. But the bigger factor in the drawn-out mania was a growing international consensus that splitting cities could solve another dread disease as well—malaria.

The malaria argument for segregation, like the plague argument, had its origins in professional networks that linked colonial administrators, public health reformers and officials, and the discoverers of bacteria themselves. In Africa, both discoveries and public health measures took some of their shape from experiences in Asia. In 1898, at Calcutta, Ronald Ross discovered the role of *Anopheles* mosquitoes in transmitting malaria. That discovery quickly gave rise to a sharp debate among two of the biggest names in the germ-hunting business about how to eradicate the disease. Ross himself believed in mosquito eradication—draining the swamps where the insects bred, spreading kerosene and other larvicides on ponds, and filling low-lying ground that could otherwise become mosquito-breeding puddles during rains. Robert Koch, who immersed himself in malaria research soon after Ross's discovery, believed that mass delivery of quinine offered the more practical route. He claimed to verify this theory during trips to German East Africa, the Dutch East Indies, and New Guinea. These titanic debates, along with ongoing issues related to plague, led to the foundation of two research institutes in England. In 1898, merchants who traded along the West African coast founded the Liverpool School of Tropical Medicine, which hired Ronald Ross away from the Indian Medical Service. Then in 1899, Ross's mentor, Dr. Patrick Manson, most recently of Hong Kong, and the "stormy petrel" W. J. Simpson helped found the London School of Tropical Medicine. As one of its first acts, the Liverpool School sent Ross to Freetown, Sierra Leone, to test his eradication theories. A year later, the British Colonial Office arranged to send two other scientists from Liverpool, J. W. W. Stephens and S. R. Christophers, to Freetown, Accra, and Lagos, Nigeria. Simpson himself would follow soon after.[22]

These destinations, like other cities on the western African coast, owed their origins to the slave trade, and most had grown up around fortified European warehouses or factories and their surrounding African villages. After the abolition of the trade in human beings, Europeans had shown less interest in the region. Only a few mercantile houses, such as those from Liverpool, continued doing business there. Africans took over the reins of power in some cities, as at Accra, where the Ga people ran their own city-state, largely ignoring the British outpost in their midst. Sierra Leone, like neighboring Liberia, was founded as a colony for freed or escaped slaves from the Americas and Britain, who later formed the local elite. In Senegal, the French had granted a qualified right to vote to Africans in four towns, including Dakar and St. Louis. St. Louis had a black mayor as early as the eighteenth century. The powerful Duala people of Cameroon dominated the commercial life of their region's main port town, named after them.[23]

During the scramble for Africa, British, French, and German colonists sought to transform these cities into bases for conquest and then capitals of new colonies. Malaria was an enormous problem for these would-be colonists. The type of *Anopheles* that lived in West Africa was a particularly efficient propagator of the disease. Its larva could survive in puddles as small as those left behind by a cow's hoof, and it was exceptionally long-lived, so the malaria plasmodium had plenty of time to mature in its gut. It is no coincidence that Europeans originally coined the phrase "White Man's Grave" on the West African coast. One out of every seven European officials in the Gold Coast colony died in their first year of service, most due to malaria, and the death rate for soldiers was much higher.[24]

When Ronald Ross arrived in Sierra Leone, he immediately set out on his new life mission—the mass killing of mosquito larvae. But he had other antimalaria strategies on his mind as well. Ross had lived nearly all of his life shuttling between dozens of European stations in India, from his birth in the hill station of Almora to his malaria work in Bangalore, Secunderabad, and Ootacamund. In the midst of his climactic discovery during the looming hot season in Calcutta, Ross had instinctively sent his family to the Himalayan station at Darjeeling. When Sierra Leone's governor mentioned to Ross that he too was considering building a hill station a few miles outside of Freetown on a small mountain for European residence, Ross was astounded. "I ... wondered for what conceivable reason this had not been done years ago."

On further inquiry he found that: "opinions were divided on this point. Liverpool merchants generally wished their agents to live near their offices in the town, for business reasons; and others thought it wicked for white men to segregate themselves from their brothers, being quite regardless of the fact that the former died so frequently in consequence of the proximity. I was in favor of the new settlement being higher up the hills; but a railway was required, and [governor of Sierra Leone] Sir King-Harman finally chose the spot referred to—about 500 feet above sea level."[25] Note that Ross's argument for segregation turned on a striking point, coming as it did from the world's greatest mosquito eradicator: in a sense, he was saying, Africans could transmit malaria to white men as effectively as *Anopheles* itself. Even more ironically, it was Ross's rival Robert Koch who had actually "proven" this point. While the blood of African adults, Koch had observed, contained few malaria germs, the blood of native children was filled with them. This was because adults acquire a partial immunity to malaria, but only from repeated infection during their childhood. It followed that Europeans living within the range of mosquitoes who had bitten African children were at highest risk of death by malaria.[26]

In their travels through West Africa and India from 1900 to 1903, Ross's colleagues, the doctors Stephens and Christophers, went one step further: rejecting *both* Ross's mosquito-eradication schemes and Koch's quinine programs, they successfully established the segregation of Europeans as the only official malaria-prevention policy of the British Empire. "To stamp out native malaria is as present chimerical," they wrote to their sponsors at the Colonial Office in London, "and every effort should rather be turned to the protection of Europeans." The segregation they had in mind, furthermore, was of the severest kind: European residences should be placed at least a half mile from any African hut, and (here was the hard part) even "the native quarters for servants should be removed as far as possible." Allowing themselves a moment of supreme racial chauvinism, they predicted that the inconvenience was worth it, because "in Africa, a complete isolation of Europeans would, we believe, render malaria a comparatively rare disease."[27]

In London, the colonial secretary Joseph Chamberlain—nicknamed

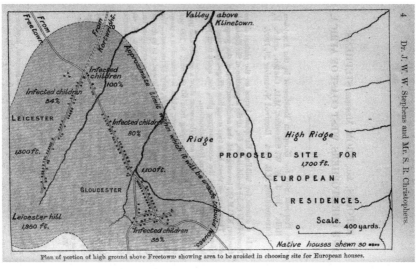

FIGURE 6.2 Freetown, Sierra Leone. Plan for a white-only hill station on a five-hundred-foot rise one mile outside of town. Ronald Ross's discovery that malaria was spread by mosquitoes helped fuel segregation mania, most notably in West Africa. Drs. J. W. W. Stephens and S. R. Christophers, who drafted this plan, were the most effective proselytizers of the idea that malaria prevention among whites depended on residential segregation from Africans, particularly African children. From S. R. Christophers and J. W. W. Stephens, "The Segregation of Europeans," in *Further Reports to the Malaria Committee of the Royal Society* (1900).

"radical Joe" because of his strong support for sanitary reform and slum clearance during his early career as mayor of Birmingham—bought Stephens and Christophers's segregation argument. The two doctors subsequently sailed on to India, where they oversaw an experiment in mosquito eradication at Mian Mir, the cantonment of the comparatively dry city of Lahore. Even with relatively few mosquitoes to kill, the experiment was miserably unsuccessful. Quinine dispensation had also failed—even European soldiers could not be trusted to take the medicine regularly. Segregation, by contrast, had a long track record behind it, Chamberlain reasoned, ignoring the political struggles that had made dividing Indian cities and the stations difficult. He quickly dispatched confidential letters to all the governors of West African colonies, ordering them to scout out areas that could be reserved for European residence.[28]

In Freetown's hill station, prefabricated bungalows arrived from England by ship in 1904, then made their way up the mountainside near town, along with the Portland cement required for the foundations. Crews set them up in a pattern that allowed local winds to bring in fresh air. Officials were more ambivalent about the prohibitions of servants' quarters. Despite Stephens and Christophers's advice, they put a number of these in, but forgot to make room for the latrines that went with them. Later, servants were allowed into the bungalows themselves, though with instructions to make their quarter "mosquito-proof." Thus officials backhandedly admitted that the wisest antimalaria policy involved segregating mosquitoes from people, not blacks from whites. Soon an eight-kilometer Mountain Railroad ferried civil servants up to the hill station after their day's duties, which of course involved frequent trips into the malarial town they were supposed to be avoiding at the risk of death.[29]

Perhaps unsurprisingly, not everyone was pleased with the Colonial Office's malaria theory of segregation. Wealthy African landlords, like their counterparts in India and Hong Kong, were the most vocal opponents. Their arguments against the expropriation of their lands for the health needs of a handful of Europeans—who then proceeded to live with lower-class African servants, mistresses, and even sometimes their mistresses' supposedly deadly children—were even persuasive to colonial governors. A few of these governors refused to follow orders from London and confronted both the Colonial Office and the colonies' increasingly well-organized municipal officers of health.

The most formidable opponents were governors William MacGregor of Lagos (1899-1904) and Hugh Clifford of the Gold Coast (1912-19).

At Lagos, MacGregor wrote to Chamberlain, "segregation from the social point of view would be disastrous. . . . There is . . . no racial question [here]. It would be unwise to start one." Borrowing from Rudyard Kipling, he went on, "I do not see how the 'White-Man' can shirk any part of his 'Burden.'" MacGregor, who was a doctor, had a particularly humanitarian view of that "burden." He rejected the idea that Africans did not suffer from malaria, pointing to high infant-mortality rates and continuing suffering among adults, who were supposedly immune. With meager resources, he instead developed a corps of African medical officers and nurses, engaged them in both mosquito destruction and quinine distribution, and encouraged the use of nets and wire screens to keep mosquitoes out of homes. He also gave more attention to general sanitary procedures in town and developed a public education campaign explaining ways to avoid malaria. In response, the Colonial Office sniffed that MacGregor's efforts betrayed "a curious view of sentimentalism" and transferred him to a post in Newfoundland. His successor was more willing to follow orders from London and expropriated seven acres of property belonging to elite Africans near the Lagos racecourse. He tried to create a European zone there, but many of the previous landholders protested vehemently and were able to remain in their houses.[30]

At Accra, meanwhile, the governor of the Gold Coast passed a Towns Amendment Ordinance (1901) that allowed him to expropriate land, and he began laying out a European reservation at an old Swedish mercantile installation called Victoriaborg on a higher ridge inland from the African town. The racial restrictions earned the usual complaints from African landowners, and subsequent governors dragged their feet for fear of the political consequences. Then, in 1909, plague arrived in the city. So did Dr. W. J. Simpson, this time with the principal medical officers of all the West African colonies, who met in their first-ever joint conference. Their report back to London reinforced the Colonial Office's call for segregation. With the fires thus lit under their feet, authorities began to expropriate more land in Accra and eight other towns in the Gold Coast. As the bungalows went up, another agnostic governor, Hugh Clifford, arrived in Accra and immediately tried to put a stop to the scheme. It was unconscionable, he argued, to use taxes raised from Africans for the sake of a few Europeans' health. The Colonial Office responded this time with a somewhat more tightly argued letter, this one containing elements of one of the arguments that had been deployed in favor of the Peak Ordinance at Hong Kong. The racial friction and the costs were a problem, London admitted, but other things needed to be considered. The motive for segregation was health, not race, and the high political price was outweighed by efficiencies of administration that depended on healthy European bodies positioned in Africa. Such efficiencies were central to the main purpose of empire—to serve Africans. Clifford had to go ahead with the segregation schemes, though he found ways of slowing them down.[31]

## The High Tide of Segregation Mania

In the bigger picture, MacGregor and Clifford represent the exceptions rather than the rule. European officials elsewhere in tropical Africa were much more enthusiastic about translating the fear of mosquitoes, rats, and fleas into large-scale residential segregation schemes. Within the British Empire, governors of the large colonies of Northern Nigeria and the East African Protectorate embraced the Colonial Office's doctrines with greater fervor. The French and Germans were also ardent public health segregationists, as they demonstrated in two key cities of their respective empires, Dakar, in French West Africa, and Duala, German Cameroon. Viewed together, the political fireworks that arose in these four places give a good measure of both the sheer breadth and the outer limits of early twentieth-century segregation mania in colonial cities.

Sir Frederick Lugard, governor of Northern Nigeria, gave segregationists in the Colonial Office much more confidence than MacGregor or Clifford. Lugard was one of the most prominent colonial conquerors and administrators of his day. He led Britain's scramble for East Africa in the 1890s and founded a divided capital for the colony of Uganda at Kampala. That city provided the template for other divided Ugandan towns, with their European central districts surrounded by open spaces that separated them from African zones. From 1896 to 1906 Lugard brought Northern Nigeria under what he famously called "indirect rule," a policy similar to the princely states of India, which kept the traditional leaders of the region's Muslim city-states in their positions on condition that they submitted to the guidance of British resident ministers. After a stint as governor of Hong Kong (1907–12), he returned to Northern Nigeria as governor. His first official act was to pass legislation segregating Nigeria's cities along the strict lines suggested by the Accra conference. In his famous Memorandum 11, he formulated his own, highly elaborate version of Indian cantonment law. At places like Zaria and Kano, he blended the cantonments and civil government stations that dated from his conquest and called them "European Reservations" using the term current in Hong Kong—later he renamed them European Residential Areas, or ERAs. These, he ordered, were to be surrounded by four-hundred-yard "Building-Free Zones," or BFZs, which kept natives and the mosquitoes who fed on them downwind and far away. The native towns

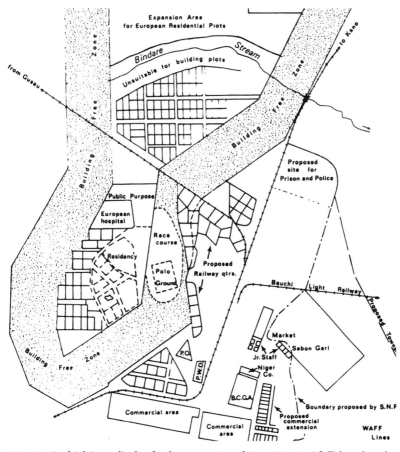

FIGURE 6.3  Fredrick Lugard's plan for the segregation of Zaria, Nigeria. Of all the colonial governors of tropical Africa, Fredrick Lugard of Nigeria was the most thoroughgoing segregationist. His Memorandum 11 outlined a strict town-planning regime that not only called for "Building Free Zones" (BFZs) between European Residential Areas (ERAs) and black neighborhoods, but that also made an unusual attempt to segregate European and African commercial areas. Map from Robert Home, *Of Planning and Planting: The Making of British Colonial Cities* (London: E and FN Spon, 1997), 131.

were themselves divided, comprising an old town (if there was one), a section for African clerks and other artisans, and a traditional separate *Sabon Gari*, or "strangers' district," where poorer laborers also had to live. A further ordinance in 1917—which one breathless supporter dubbed the "Europeans' Sanitary Magna Charta"—actually imposed fines on Europeans, including businessmen, who lived outside their reservations. The thrust of this provision was that European and African commercial activity ought to take place in different parts of town—European in the ERA, and African in the Sabon Gari. This was another idea from the Accra conference. Though the segregation of commerce was also meant to give Europeans an advantage over their savvy West African competitors, it stood in the way of crucial cross-racial business contacts. Two British merchants made it clear they would not move their operations from the old town of Kano unless liberally compensated. Much like Singapore's Stamford Raffles almost a century earlier, Lugard saw urban segregation not only as a sanitary or commercial measure, but as a way of creating separate juridical zones for city residents based on race and culture, a policy that squared well with the broader idea of indirect rule.[32]

In the British East African Protectorate, meanwhile, the governors of what later became known as Kenya elaborated segregation plans for their capital at Nairobi that were at least as ambitious as Lugard's, though they took South Africa rather than India as the primary model. Unlike the rest of equatorial Africa, the cool highlands of Kenya had attracted a sizable community of British settlers, some of whom had previous experience in South Africa and Rhodesia. As in southern Africa, early governors of the protectorate had set aside rural reserves for Africans, similar to Indian reservations in North America, to keep them from competing with settlers for the choicest land.

Nairobi originally came into being as an isolated rail station on the route to Uganda, but it blossomed as the commercial gateway to the white highlands. Immigrant Indian railworkers, who lived near the station in the town's bazaar, made up the majority of its inhabitants until as late as 1920. White settlers built bungalows in the higher wooded areas to the north of the station when the city became the capital. Five African villages also grew on the outskirts. Plague rats and their fleas rode into Nairobi on railroad cars on several occasions in the first decade of the twentieth century, culminating in larger outbreaks from 1911 to 1913. When the plague kept coming, the Colonial Office once again dispatched its doom-speaking stormy petrel, Dr. W. J. Simpson, this time on the last flight of his career, a grand tour of East Africa.

The report Simpson filed on his return contained his most sophisticated defense of residential segregation yet. Reflecting on the growing town-planning movement in Europe and especially the "Garden City" ideals of the visionary Ebenezer Howard, he lauded planners' efforts to separate the city's different functions from each other—keeping work, commerce, and industry away from residential zones. But, he went on, "something more is required where the races are diverse and their habits and customs differ from one another." The diseases "to which these different races are respectively liable are readily transferable to the European," especially "when their dwellings are near each other." "It is absolutely essential that . . . town planning should provide well defined and separate quarters or wards for Europeans, Asiatics and Africans . . . and that there should be a neutral belt of open unoccupied country at least 300 yards in width between the European residences and those of the Asiatic and African."[33]

Simpson wanted to carve up older Swahili-coast cities like Mombasa and Zanzibar into multiple racial zones, a task that proved difficult in places where Europeans were so few and African polities—as in coastal West Africa—too strong. But in recently founded, blank-slate Nairobi, with its teeming white settler population, the municipal government felt more emboldened in 1921 to begin expropriating Nairobi's African villages and removing their inhabitants to Pumwani, a South African–style native township near the railyards and the sewage outlet. The colonial government also began enforcing a pass law system aimed to regulate the numbers of Africans who could leave the rural reserves for the new capital and the protectorate's other growing towns. By the 1930s, the colonial state felt strong enough to simply abrogate Africans' property rights, also much like in South Africa, and even the wealthiest remaining villagers were forced into Pumwani.[34]

The towns' Indian merchants presented a more difficult political issue. Their bazaar—like the Chinatowns of Honolulu and San Francisco—was located on choice real estate near downtown. A town engineer had burned it to the ground once before during a plague outbreak. Simpson now recommended razing the place again and relocating it out of town. Though authorities did level the bazaar once again, Indians were able to leverage growing unease among British officials about the nationalist movement in India itself to rebuild on the same spot. By the 1920s whites began to complain that wealthier Indians were also starting to buy real estate in all-white areas.[35]

British authorities nevertheless made greater progress in dividing cities in Northern Nigeria and Kenya than in West Africa. In Nigeria this was in part, no doubt, because there had been relatively little earlier commercial contact between Africans and whites; in Nairobi the African elite had little foothold in local commerce at all, and even its wealthiest members had little political leverage. Local officials there could also rely on the support of a larger and more powerful white settler community to segregate Africans, even if they could do less to undermine the power of Indians.

By those measures, the French and Germans pushed the political envelope of malaria and plague-based segregation even further than the British, for both Dakar and Duala were cities that more closely resembled Accra, Lagos, or Mombasa, where small groups of mostly transient white officials and more permanently invested business agents lived within African communities run by established, wealthy, and relatively powerful commercial elites.

Dakar, situated on the westernmost point of Africa at Cape Verde, was the capital of the enormous confederation of colonies known as French West Africa. It was also the largest of the "four towns" (*quatre communes*) of Senegal, which are often seen as evidence of France's commitment to the "assimilation" of natives to French norms. Anyone who lived in the four towns for five years could vote. At Dakar, voters included whites; the Catholic *métis* ("mixed race"), who spoke French and whose French citizenship went back to the eighteenth century; French-speaking African clerks known as *évolués* (literally, "evolved ones"); and a handful of the wealthiest of the Lebu, the original inhabitants of Cape Verde, a mostly Muslim people who lived in a crescent of thirteen villages overlapping the edges of the French town. The city's large majority of poorer African Muslims were either ineligible for the vote or opted out of infidel colonial institutions. In May 1914, the *évolués* combined forces with the Lebus and other African voters and shocked the French Empire by electing an African man, Blaise Diagne, to represent them in the Parliament of the Third Republic in Paris.[36]

African Dakarois' celebrations of this unprecedented triumph were barely underway when the bubonic plague came to town, along with its traveling companion, segregation mania. By July, with the death toll climbing rapidly, the city's hygiene committee determined that the only way to stop the epidemic was "the destruction of all shacks and huts not susceptible to disinfection" and a "*camp de ségrégation*" where the "native population" could be resettled at "a point far removed from the European city." The formidable governor general of French West Africa, William Ponty, supported the plan, and within a month a new African section was under construction on a low-lying sandy wasteland to the north of the city. The Lebus referred to the place as Tilène, or the "place of the jackals." The French called it Medina, after the Arab word for the walled towns of North Africa. Whatever its name, by autumn, authorities had moved 2,900 people—about a tenth of the city's total—to what amounted to the closest approximation of a South African native township in West Africa.[37]

French segregationism at Dakar was deeply entwined in the same cross-colonial webs of sanitary thinking that had propelled segregation mania across the British Empire. France had its own traveling public health researchers, people like Gustave Reynaud and Alexandre Kermorgant, who had visited West Africa and who wrote influential hygiene manuals that included references to the debates over malaria eradication between Ross, Koch, Stephens, and Christophers. When yellow fever made appearances in Dakar in 1901 and 1905, first Kermorgant and later a commission from Paris floated the idea of segregating the city. Local sanitary officials seethed when colonial officials instead timidly allowed blacks who built their houses of brick to live in close proximity to whites. In 1913 yellow fever returned, and Governor General Ponty laid out his own homespun version of Koch's "native reservoir" theory of malaria. "The presence of natives," he began, "in close proximity to Europeans exacerbates yellow fever and malaria." A bit of improvisation followed: "Black children ... conserve and sustain the *amaryl* [yellow fever] virus." The rest he pulled from thin air: "It is as if the *anopheles* absorbs from black blood a renewal of its strength, a new vitality."[38]

Other motives for the forced removals to Medina are also evident in records of the time. Many of the Lebu houses lay in a zone near the bay that whites coveted for exclusive development. African customs were also seen as nuisances, as we can tell by the words of one sanitary official who wandered off the strict lines of the official public health script. Relocation to Medina, he wrote, would allow Africans "to play the tom-toms all night, and to pound millet from four in the morning on"—far from where they would bother Europeans.[39]

For Africans, by contrast, the real reason for their forced removal to the jackal-infested wilderness was clear: they were being punished for Diagne's victory. For several years, Ponty had, in fact, begun to whittle away at the citizenship rights of the évolués and the Lebu. His actions were one of the reasons for the strong African turnout for Diagne's election. Rumors circulating in white and métis circles that the plague had come as a punishment to rebellious Muslims (the Lebu were the disease's primary victims) did not quiet these sentiments. The Lebu also worried that authorities were scheming to restrict Africans' right to own land, and the expropriations of 1914 seemed to herald just that.[40]

Resistance to the plague removals in Dakar was as fierce as anywhere outside India. In May, 1,500 Lebu entered city hall with canes and clubs, demanding the halt of expropriations. They won some concessions from Ponty, but in October and November, when the bulk of the remaining Lebu villages were scheduled for removal, another crowd of three thousand to four thousand massed in the streets and put a halt to the destruction of shacks and straw huts. Ponty readied his troops for a siege of the city, then backed down, fearing the consequences of a major disruption in the colonies just as the German army threatened Paris early in World War I. At that moment, the Germans, who were allied with the Ottoman sultan, the caliph of the Islamic world, hardly needed more ammunition against the French in their Muslim colonies. Blaise Diagne himself was in Paris by this point and had grown aware of such sensibilities. He, like many Asian, African, and African American leaders of the time, hoped whites would improve the lot of colonized peoples as a reward for their service as soldiers in Europe. He thus urged the Lebu to act with restraint. Things calmed down, but the expropriations continued, if on a slower schedule.[41]

As in Dakar, the drama of segregation in German-ruled Duala came to a blazing climax in 1914 as the world war began, and it too sent shudders to a distant European capital. In Duala there was no plague emergency, but both the repression and the response were more dramatic than anywhere else in tropical Africa. The story began in 1910 when the Duala district commissioner, Hermann Röhm, declared his intention to move all twenty thousand of the Duala from their homes along the Wari River, where many had pursued a livelihood as regional merchants, to a native town one kilometer from the coast. A mere four hundred European merchants would take title to the shoreline land instead and develop a port that would dominate the business of transporting central Africa's vast riches to Europe. The one-kilometer buffer zone, of course, was meant to keep mosquitoes with African blood in their guts from reaching European houses. An unusual racialized land-value argument also overlay the sanitary one: Röhm argued that the Duala were mere economic parasites who benefitted from Europeans' improvements and that the fruit of these investments ought to be returned to those who deserved them. Finally, there was the matter of race relations more abstractly. Elsewhere in Africa, Röhm declared implausibly, the British had made the mistake of allowing "social and political equality with the natives." The German Reich would instead build cities in ways that furthered "the opposition of the white *race* to the black."[42]

The Duala did not hesitate to oppose the plan. Their leader, Manga Bell, unearthed a treaty signed by a previous German governor that guaranteed them rights to their land. Then he hired a German lawyer, presented a petition signed by most of the Duala elite to the Reichstag in Berlin, and courted support from among the German leftist deputies. Sadly, this was hardly a moment for advances in participatory government in Germany, and the kaiser's officials encouraged outrage in the conservative press that people of an inferior race should presume to exercise citizenship rights. Trumped-up indictments soon followed against Manga Bell and his personal secretary, Ngoso Din, which accused them of conspiring to turn Cameroon over to the British. Their case went to trial during the heated days of July 1914, as war broke out. Bell and Din were quickly convicted and executed.[43]

## The Long End of the Craze

In the years between 1914 and 1923, segregation mania peaked across tropical Africa, signaling a slow end to the strategy of segregation based on plague and malaria worldwide. From the exclamation point of Manga Bell's execution to William Ponty's abandonment of a siege of Dakar later that year, from Lugard's frenetic term as governor of Nigeria to the British Colonial Office's official change of heart in 1923 on Indian segregation in Nairobi, sharp moments of radicalism eased into drawn-out moments of adjustment and compromise. A long, much less eventful denouement began.

Just about everywhere in Africa, as in India, China, and the Pacific before that, the drama of de-escalation contained the same political elements. In the flush of plague crises and the early mosquito scares, blaming the "inferior races" for deadly disease and proposing separation as a solution came relatively easily in most places. The cutting edge of Western science confirmed it, researchers' international networks gave it credibility, and some of the first winners of the Nobel Prize in medicine added authority. But the argument's integrity quickly fell apart in the rough and tumble of politics that ensued. The diminishing threat to health helped this process. Plague never made the inroads in tropical Africa or the Pacific that it did at Bombay or Cape Town, and the high death rates soon became stale news, at least for the purposes of politics. Malaria deaths diminished among whites even in the direst of White Man's Graves as MacGregor-style education campaigns took effect and as mosquito netting, wire screens, and quinine became more widely used (mosquito killing would have minimal effect until the invention of DDT in the 1940s).

Capitalist economic interests also played their usual contradictory roles in the drama of segregation. Imperial officials who segregated colonial cities may have been building sustainable bases for longer-term schemes to exploit their colonies for the benefits of industry back home. But the interests of other capitalists in those cities drove residential policy just as firmly in the opposite direction. Like urban landholders everywhere in the colonial world, African ones had no interest in giving up the source of their wealth and political power for resettlement schemes. But in Africa, white capitalists too could oppose segregation, especially white merchants who thought any sanitary benefits of segregation negligible compared with the advantages of proximity to African business partners. Neither of these interests completely stopped the progress of segregation, but they always slowed it down considerably, forcing segregation's supporters to use other, sometimes less noticeable tools to keep color lines intact.

By 1920 or so, public health officials who supported segregation had to labor on with less and less resounding support from their champions in the world of science or even their patrons in imperial capitals. Public health might still animate the desire to split cities, but whoever tried to push segregation further had to do so in the face of an ever more enormous challenge: anticolonialism.

District Commissioner Röhm's partial retreat from radical segregation in Duala illustrates many of the features of this denouement well. Even as a burst of imperial authoritarianism transformed Manga Bell into one of the antisegregation movement's first martyrs, Röhm and other higher German officials quietly softened their expropriation and resettlement plan. The area they had earmarked for exclusive German use was far bigger than four hundred European merchants could possibly use. Many of those white merchants had already purchased enough land for their purposes, and they were happy to forgo the dubious kilometer-wide barrier against mosquitoes to make deals with the Duala more easily. Though Röhm had much bigger economic plans for the city of Duala in mind—to build a port that would allow Germany to outdo Britain, France, and Belgium in the exploitation of central Africa—he agreed to limit expropriations from Africans to meet immediate European needs, and the Duala people retained their land in one of the more desirable, elevated, and thus healthiest neighborhoods of the city. He also recognized that many of the richest Duala were perfectly able to build in solid materials that met sanitary codes; those who did were allowed to live in the German zone.

As the process of expropriation continued more slowly during the war, imperial rivalry intervened. The French and British milked the execution of Manga Bell for all it was worth: it demonstrated without a doubt, they claimed, that Germany was not morally qualified to run colonies. At the 1918 Versailles conference, German Cameroon was transferred to France. Then, after years of accusing the Germans of using their segregation scheme as part of a nefarious plot to take over all of central Africa, with Duala as its New Hamburg, the French decided they wanted such a megaport themselves. Respelling the name of the city and its inhabitants "Douala," they went ahead with Röhm's plan themselves. The Douala people did not miss a beat. As they reconfigured themselves as a major force in the Cameroonian nationalist movement, they repeatedly accused the French rulers of being more grasping and authoritarian than even the Germans who had killed Manga Bell.[44]

In Dakar, meanwhile, the plague wore itself out by the end of 1914, and forced removals to the Medina proceeded much more slowly. The official connection between race and health grew less stark. Ponty had promised the Lebu early on that they could return to Dakar city and claim their land as long as they rebuilt their houses à l'Européenne. By 1919, a new governor general was taking pains to explain that "the word 'European city' should be understood as meaning 'city for people willing to accept submission to sanitary rules applicable to Europeans.' . . . We shouldn't imagine that this separation of the two cities entails a political effort to oppose the races against one another, and no restrictive tendency against the rights of the native population." Such rhetoric, of course, did nothing to encourage the French to develop any adequate sanitary infrastructure in Medina. Throughout the 1920s Medina became an increasingly over-crowded and poorly equipped place, filled with varied migrants from the countryside. Many Lebu eventually gave up the fight and moved there as well, as large-scale development projects in downtown Dakar slowly nibbled at the remains of their thirteen villages. Downtown continued to have its pockets of African and *métis*-owned houses throughout the remainder of French rule. As Ponty had planned, however, Medina was exclusively black.[45]

Sir Frederick Lugard's radical plans for divided cities in Nigeria, de-tailed and painstaking as they were, also proved politically vulnerable, as well as confusing and impractical. When Lugard retired in 1918, the Colo-nial Office replaced him with none other than Hugh Clifford of the Gold Coast. This appointment reflected a slow change of heart at the Colonial Office: many there, like Ronald Ross himself, had lost faith in the malaria argument for segregation and were beginning to ask whether the politi-cal and even economic costs were worth it. Lugard's European residential areas, filled with widely spread bungalows and compounds, and his wide building-free zones required government to purchase enormous pieces of real estate and to leave much of it unproductive. It grew harder to keep African notables out of the ERAs or to deny either white or black merchants the right to build in BFZs—especially because some of the European commercial concerns created nuisances and sanitary threats to ERA residents. Lugard's byzantine regulations on the rights of differ-ent types of African "strangers" also tied local administrations in knots. Clifford suspended many of the clauses in Lugard's "Magna Charta," re-fusing to move Africans, businessmen, or missionaries who contravened them. The decline was not uniform. Winston Churchill sought fervently to revive racial segregation in West Africa during his brief tenure as co-lonial secretary in 1921–22. At Lagos, despite Governor Clifford's oppo-sition, local officials managed to set up a largely successful segregated European reservation east of town in a previously unsettled marshy spot known as Ikoyi. Still other segregationists made sporadic attempts to re-kindle Lugard's legacy well into the 1930s. However, the Colonial Office gradually abolished the ERAs, finally opening Ikoyi to educated Africans in 1947. To compensate, white ERA residents' committees drafted build-ing leases that specified high housing standards for Africans who lived in European zones. In 1945 the Colonial Office mollified segregationists by recommending cheaper rents for Europeans who were forced to live next to Africans. Still, by that point, Britons living in West Africa had to swallow the fact that the overall drift in colonial residential policy was toward separation based on class not race.[46]

At Nairobi, the segregation of Africans proceeded at a more rapid pace after World War I than before. The razing of African villages around the city accelerated in the 1920s and 1930s, and by the 1940s the municipality had built several large "estates" to house Africans in and around Pumwani Native Township. The pass laws were also extended during this time. In that sense, Nairobi's politics looked much like a simplified version of Johannesburg's or Southern Rhodesia's, where cities like Salisbury and Bulawayo had similar arrangements.[47]

By contrast, efforts to segregate Nairobi's Indians hit numerous political roadblocks. It was they, not Africans, who composed the local merchant class, and, as in Johannesburg, many were wealthy enough to buy in white areas. The independence movement in India, now under the leadership of the Mahatma Gandhi, had made the status of overseas Indians an important concern, and the British Raj put considerable pressure on other colonial administrations not to make trouble that would boomerang back to Delhi. In 1923, the Colonial Office published Command Paper No. 1,922, in which it came down unequivocally against formal segregation of Indians from whites in Kenya, pointing out that "it is now the view of competent medical authorities that as a sanitation measure, segregation of Europeans and Asiatics is not absolutely essential for the preservation of the health of the community.... Enforcement of sanitary, police and building regulations ... will suffice." White settlers seethed at this ruling, but unlike in South Africa, where their counterparts could slowly whittle away at Indian land rights despite pressure from Delhi and London, Kenya was a Crown colony whose whites had a much more limited voice.[48]

In 1948, L. W. Thornton, a South African architect who specialized in the design of suburban estates for Europeans, was charged with compiling a master plan for Nairobi. He and the Europeans he interviewed in Nairobi were still gritting their teeth about Command Paper No. 1,922 a quarter century after it was issued. With some asperity, Thornton noted that "many people have expressed to the Town Planning Team their desire to see segregation a reality" and that "it is not difficult to see why there is a drawing away of the ... Europeans, from other groups." He only gave a subtle hint as to how Europeans achieved this "drawing away." On a map he supplied showing Nairobi's population distribution, most of the enormous stretches of the city's European districts were described as "restricted by private estates"—that is, by racial covenants that developers inserted into property deeds. White South Africans had long complained that such restrictions were too weak to guarantee permanent color lines, and by 1950 they got comprehensive racial zoning courtesy of the apartheid-era Group Areas Act. In Nairobi, by contrast, at least in matters relating to whites and Indians, white settlers had to content themselves with a segregation system more closely resembling the one in the United States.[49]

## Legacies of the Mania

Though the most radical moments of disease-scare segregationism in colonial cities had passed by 1920, the underlying principles by no means died out. Even as the wave slowly receded, other Europeans in Africa built capitals of their own that bore the imprints of rat-, flea-, and mosquito-based color lines. The Portuguese, not usually seen as big segregationists, developed the central business district of Lourenço Marques—after 1907 the capital of Mozambique—as a "European, Continental City in Africa" within a circular drive that was meant to act as a color line (the old slave port of Luanda, Angola, with its large and powerful mixed population, was more difficult to divide by race). In 1930, the Belgian government moved the capital of the Congo from Boma to Léopoldville (today's Kinshasa). They built a golf course, a zoo, and botanical gardens around the European quarter of Kalinga to separate it from the Cité Indigène and prohibited both Africans and Europeans from being in each others' zones after 9 p.m. each night, when mosquitoes were at their most active. When chemical insecticides became available in the 1940s, authorities at Léopoldville promoted life in the city to potential Belgian settlers with photographs of a municipal airplane flying low over the sprawling cité indigène, antimalarial mist billowing in its wake. Finally, the Italians, who, under Mussolini, reentered the scramble for Africa very late in the game, also announced segregation schemes in Tripoli and Addis Ababa during the 1930s; these did not get off the ground before World War II crushed Italian colonialism for good.[50]

Even though the excitement of plague and malaria scares receded, the bigger historic marriage between segregation and sanitation continued to thrive throughout the interwar years and even beyond. At least two other waves of urban reform gave lift to its continued fortunes, sometimes both at the same time. One was the movement against urban slums, which went back to the beginning of the nineteenth century in India and Europe and which had become a multicontinental phenomenon by the turn of the twentieth. Public health campaigners had long known that lurid descriptions of the slums were just as effective as disease panics in raising political sympathy for expensive and unpopular expropriation and forced-removal schemes. Though the Improvement Trust movement in the British Empire spread this practice from Bombay and Calcutta across the widest stretches of the colonial world, the most extensive use of slum clearance for racial segregation would take place in South Africa and the United States during the 1930s (see chapter 11).

The second wave was the town-planning movement, or, as its influential French proponents called it, *urbanisme*. For the new breed of comprehensive city planner who led this movement, the connection between sanitation and segregation was the stuff not of fear or disgust, but of the grandest hopes of Western empire and civilization. From this exalted inspiration arose the colonial era's most extravagant monuments to urban segregationism.

# 7 : The Outer Limits of Colonial Urbanism

## Imperial Monuments, Imperial Tombstones

In 1911 and 1912, high officials of the British and French empires made a pair of decisions that inaugurated both the climactic final act and the swansong of the drama of modern-era colonial urban segregation. In 1911, King George V of England himself arrived in Delhi, as emperor of India, to reenact the Mughal tradition of the *durbar*, an elaborate reception of India's princes. The quasi-medieval pomp and circumstance was meant to celebrate the timelessness of India's ancient civilization and, implicitly, to contrast it to the fast-progressing culture of its Western conqueror. The climactic moment in the king's address to the princes also evoked both tradition and sudden change: India's viceroy Lord Hardinge, the king announced, had decided to move the capital of the British Raj from Calcutta to Delhi.[1]

A year later, on the other extreme of the Islamic world, the resident general of Morocco, Hubert de Lyautey, made a similar surprise decision to move the capital of the new French protectorate from Fez, one of the traditional seats of Moroccan power, to another imperial city, Rabat. There he hoped to tell similar stories about the inequality of the races and the civilizations.

Once the formalities were over, both Hardinge and Lyautey hired two of their respective countries' most innovative architects—Edwin Lutyens from Britain and Henri Prost from France. In their plans for the new capitals, both architects mixed an old concept from the colonial urbanist past, that is, racial segregation, with what they saw as a transformational goal, to build white towns whose monumentality and beauty would express nothing less than the highest aspirations of Western empires.

To do that, both took inspiration from the new urban-planning movement that had swept through Europe and the Americas during the 1890s and the first decade of the twentieth century. City planners, proclaimed Lutyens and Prost—drawing on the visions of Britain's Ebenezer Howard, Raymond Unwin, and Patrick Geddes, Germany's Camillo Sitte, Belgium's Charles Buls, and the American Daniel H. Burnham—must imagine the future of cities *comprehensively*, that is, by treating them as organisms that are at once social, economic, circulatory, military, political, hygienic, and—not least—aesthetic. Such endeavors constituted both a new field of knowledge and a new form of "social art": the French, who were arguably its most ardent supporters, called it *urbanisme*.

At Rabat and New Delhi, the new breed of city planners brought their most advanced thinking to the colonies. There, they adjusted the roles of all three institutions that drove colonial urban politics and segregation. While they relied upon imperial might—and upon enormous flows of cash from the imperial treasury—to get their job done, their city plans celebrated what they saw as the benevolence of Western empires' civilian administration more than the gruff military power that lay behind it. While they shared the ardent goals of sanitary reformers, they sought to achieve those goals not just by sowing fear of disease, tunneling new sewers under the ground, or clearing slums, but by convincing people in power that truly comprehensive planning was needed to guard against the pitfalls of these piecemeal solutions. Finally, in an ambitious bid to increase their own influence within the dramas of city politics, the *urbanistes* honed legal tools that would give them a handle on that least tractable part of the urban organism—the land market.

As they marshaled these political, economic, and ideological resources, they also rethought the mission of segregation itself. In addition to all the old justifications, the distinction between the white town and the black town would now also serve as a kind of parable, one that would set in stone lessons like those of the Delhi *durbar*. The new white town would amaze all as a symbol of the dynamism and progress of the West. The old black town would sometimes actually need to be spared from the slum clearer's wrecking ball. Preserved in its own kind of glory, it could both symbolize Western benevolence and offer a kind of backhanded Orientalist salute to the unchanging ancient civilizations the Occident had permanently conquered.

Such racial fantasies, of course, burst apart as quickly as the urbanistes dreamed them up. Even before they constructed their new capitals, the empires those cities were designed to rule were beginning to collapse under the weight of anticolonial insurgency. At the same time, the monumental capitals themselves grew at a rate that overwhelmed their supposedly comprehensive planners' visions. The first indications of the megaslums to come started to appear on the fringes of the new cities' painstakingly rendered Beaux-Arts landscapes. By the 1930s, places designed as triumphant monuments to the West were on their way to becoming Western empires' grandiose tombstones. When that occurred, two centuries of colonial racial urbanism reached its theoretical, political, geographical—and finally historical—outer limits.

## French Connections

Monumentality had been a feature of Western colonial city-splitting ever since the fifteenth-century Portuguese fortress of Elmina. Calcutta's City of Palaces, which the British planned to abandon in 1911 for a mightier place, was another of its most elaborate expressions. But to fully understand the innovations in urban monumentality that the urbanistes had in mind for places like Rabat and New Delhi, we have to follow a set of cross-oceanic connections that date from the earliest origins of urban color lines, but that, up to now, we have only seen from afar.

These connections involve the global trade in architectural thinking and innovation. That trade was implicated in the final burst of racial segregation in African and Asian colonies, but, along the way, the architectural traditions involved also influenced the politics of city-splitting in Europe, both North and South America, and Australasia. Though these innovations took inspiration from urban politics in many places, France led the way, exporting an evolving tradition of urban architectural practice that linked the eighteenth-century fortifications engineer Vauban with the nineteenth-century urban planner Haussmann with a twentieth-century rebellion within Paris's famous École des Beaux-Arts.

For some, the big role of France might come as a surprise. Though the French have proudly embraced their own reputation for monumentality, some Francophiles have encouraged the idea the separation of the races was more of an Anglo-Saxon conceit than a Gallic one. Paris's reputation as a kind of racial utopia helps make their case. Starting in the 1910s, famous African American sportsmen, musicians, writers, and artists flocked to the City of Light to gulp air many deemed free of Jim Crow's menace. There is also evidence that, unlike white men in the English-speaking world, Frenchmen were less likely to object to cross-racial sex and were less likely to be haunted by fears that black men were out to rape white women. If the French had a fault, it was that they exoticized and romanticized (even sometimes adored) black people for such stereotyped attributes as physicality and hypersexuality; certainly Frenchmen resorted to lynch mobs far less frequently than did Americans. A more dubious line of argument about French racism relies on warmed-over propaganda about the country's "civilizing mission" in the colonies. Since French imperial officials, goes the persistent myth, were more committed to universalistic republican principles, their racism was more pliant than the British sort—more focused on making Asians and Africans into Frenchmen than in assigning a permanent inferior status to the "darker races."[2]

Theories of French exceptionalism only go so far. The history of Paris contains plenty of racial violence—and plenty of urban segregation—and so did that of the French Empire as a whole. French imperial rivalry with the British involved much more mutual imitation than either rival was ready to admit. The modern concept of race itself, after all, owed its oldest origins to Enlightenment-era Frenchmen like Bernier and Buffon. Later French thinkers like Cuvier, the Count de Gobineau, Gustave le Bon, and Paul-Pierre Broca developed many of the arguments central to biologistic Anglo-Saxon visions of racism—as well as those in other European countries and Latin America. France imported influences as well. Racially enlightened French republican and "assimilationist" principles, after all, hardly helped Africans in Dakar and Douala when they faced some of the largest-scale expropriation and removal schemes in the colonial world. Those schemes drew freely on the inspiration of racist British public health researchers.

In the realm of architecture and urban planning, the French influence on British and other colonial cities went back to the earliest, formative connections between London, Madras, and Calcutta. In French history, that was the era of Louis XIV (1643-1715)—the self-anointed "Sun King." Under his aegis, France became a font of architectural style-setting for the rest of the world, most notably exporting innovations in two fields of city building: fortification systems and urban planning devices meant to show off royal magnificence. The name of one of the military defense systems, the *citadelle*, betrays earlier Italian inspiration; the city-glorification devices—which included the esplanade, the glacis, the boulevard, the avenue, and the cordon sanitaire—all took their French names with them into English when the British, among others, started using them to spruce up their colonial cities and enhance their color lines.

Louis XIV's wars of conquest opened a vast field of creative possibility for his indefatigable military engineer, Sebastien Le Prestre de Vauban, whose name became synonymous with a new generation of indomitable citadels. To design one, he found a high place, marked off a perfect pentagon, hexagon, or octagon, then walled each of the sides with overlapping rows of triangular bastions that pointed outward like so many fierce spearheads. All around the walls he arranged for the glacis, a wide unbuilt space that sloped downward from the fortification and forced besieging enemies to approach the walls uphill in the open, under the full force of fire from the city. Vauban built about 150 of these war nests in France; many of them still glower over the towns they were designed to protect. They set off their own arms race in Europe, and soon jagged creations like Vauban's appeared everywhere in Europe and in the colonies as well.[3]

Vauban's insistence on geometry as a guide to the layout of cities fit into a bigger theory of urban planning, one that Enlightenment-era French civil architects also found particularly appealing. It went back to ancient Romans, but the more immediate inspiration came from sixteenth-century Italian and Spanish architects who had resurrected the classical era's fondness for right-angled street plans and large triumphal avenues. For many eighteenth-century French thinkers, what they saw as the "regularity" of classical urban space became an important signal of a society's ability to conform to natural laws of beauty and to embrace the highest possible level of civilization. The existing helter-skelter streetscapes of most French towns, by contrast, represented a deviation from such true principles that dated from the Middle Ages—that is, after Rome fell. Vauban himself had made some attempts to counter the medieval trend, for some of his fortifications involved laying out completely new polygonal towns. These he planned with military precision, with rifle-straight streets that intersected at a *place d'armes*, an ideal arrangement for parading troops and distributing them to their siege stations. In most towns, the old, mazelike urban fabric was simply too entrenched for any such rectilinearity, but in those places Vauban and others built extensions to the medieval town that conformed more closely to what he saw as the classical ideal.[4]

Straight avenues, of course, could serve the needs of the state in other ways too, by provoking a sense of awe at the monumentality of royal power. The best example of this was the new town of Versailles that Louis XIV's architects built around his famous château. Instead of a gridiron, a more stylish, symmetrical fan of straight avenues and reflecting pools placed at exact thirty-, forty-five-, and ninety-degree angles made the royal seat appear to radiate power, just as the house of a Sun King should. To promote the expansion of such classical precepts in building, Louis burnished the international reputation of Paris's Académie des Beaux-Arts by establishing the famous Prix de Rome, an all-expenses-paid five-year stint at a palace in Rome awarded to France's most promising young artists. The architects who won the prize were instructed to closely study human civilization's greatest urban creation so they could recreate classical perfection and "regularity" back in France—and, of course, throughout its empire.[5]

In the French colonies, these architectural forms also helped to separate cities by color. The earliest example of this was Pondichéry, a hundred miles south of Madras, which was founded in 1674 as the capital of the French Compagnie des Indes. During the peak of French influence in South India, Governor Joseph-François Dupleix (1742–54) transformed Pondichéry into a city whose magnificence easily outshone the then dowdier Madras and Calcutta. A pentagonal Vauban-style citadel and a straight canal to its north separated the rectangular street grid of the French town from the less regular native town inland. Like at Madras, separation proclamations supplemented the walls during particularly difficult times.[6]

London and Calcutta quickly brought the glamorous potential of the Paris-Pondichéry connection to an end. In 1761, the British destroyed the capital of French India, indomitable citadel and all. Dupleix's successors rebuilt Pondichéry soon after, but on a much less grandiose scale. More than seventy years passed before the British gave the French enough space anywhere in the world to build another triumphant colonial capital. During that time, as we know, the British did more than the French to employ—or at least to aspire to import—French-inspired architectural techniques overseas: the new Vauban-style Fort St. George at Madras and its fiercer cousin, Fort William at Calcutta; their surrounding glacis-esplanades (the French themselves, remember, laid out Madras's esplanade during their occupation of the city); Wellesley's plans for monumental avenues in Calcutta; and his unfulfilled dream for an Indian quasi-Versailles at Barrackpore.

## A French Calcutta?

From the 1750s until 1830, French expansion overseas repeatedly came to naught. Along with other royalist allies, British forces defeated France's revolutionary armies in Europe and in Egypt and even—after enormous effort—destroyed the great hosts of Napoleon Bonaparte (1814). Only in 1830 did France successfully capture a new colony overseas, when King Charles X, facing the threat of a second French revolution in Paris, sought to distract his restive people by shipping thirty-five thousand troops across the Mediterranean to conquer the city of Algiers.[7]

Algiers was a notorious place in the European imagination. It was one of the capitals of the so-called Barbary Coast, whose ruling *deys*, as the semi-independent Ottoman governors were called, had until recently encouraged pirates to seize European and American sailors and sell them into slavery along with Africans. Walls surrounded the city; they climbed the steep slopes from the sea and culminated in a fortress known locally as the *qasbah*. As in other Islamic cities, the houses were tightly packed together. They had windowless outer walls that concealed private courtyards and kept the women's apartments, or *harim*, out of public view. Between the houses ran a maze of alleyways that occasionally opened into marketplaces known as *suqs*. Palaces, domed mosques, and minarets punctuated the cityscape. The district closest to the harbor contained the palaces of officials, including the Dar-al Sultan, the dey's primary residence, and the *funduqs* (or *fondaccos*) of the city's foreign merchants, who hailed from all around the Mediterranean.[8]

When the French army captured Algiers, soldiers and officers stormed through the city. They raped and killed inhabitants who could not flee, and smashed houses and shops, even toppling one prominent minaret. Commanders ordered mosques and funduqs to be used as barracks, and the army engorged itself on the dey's treasury in the qasbah. The news quickly reached Europe that free wealth was available just a short boat ride away. French, Italian, Spanish, and Maltese immigrants flocked to the French lines. Some of these *colons* claimed urban real estate in Algiers and other cities; others fanned out into agricultural areas occupied by French troops and beyond, seizing farms and estates. Within a short time France possessed a new settler colony, which in 1838 took its name from the city: Algeria. In 1848, after years of bloody war against a pan-Algerian countergovernment led by Abd-el-Kader, Algeria was divided into three French-style *départments*, which the conquerors treated as an integral part of France.

Most commentators on cities, including many subsequent French imperialists, agree that the French army's reconstruction of Algiers during the 1830s and 1840s extended the rapacity of the conquest. "The Christian commercial town," one military engineer sniffed in 1839, "cannot preserve the form of a pirate capital." But what such engineers really offered was a divided town largely designed for the needs of the French military—"a war place," as one put it more candidly. On a map, the transformation of Algiers looks striking similar to that of Delhi a quarter century later, after the suppression of the Indian mutiny. The eastern third of the Muslim city became a European town. Somewhat broadened, largely rectilinear streets replaced narrow, winding ones. The remaining two-thirds of Algiers, severely depopulated during conquest, were left to recover slowly as the native town.

In contrast to English Delhi's bungalows and barracks, Algiers's European zone developed a denser texture, more redolent of a French provincial town than a Victorian suburb or an Anglo-Indian cantonment. The most drastic change was the broad, Vauban-style Place d'Armes, which army engineers hollowed out of the heart of the city in the 1830s as a point to muster the troops (they soon renamed it Place du Gouvernement to take some of the edge off of military rule). As they widened the square into a classical rectangle, one beautiful mosque fell to the wrecking crews and a second one survived miraculously even though its placement forced one side of the Place d'Armes to wobble a bit. From the central square, officials also widened three streets into avenues, running north and south to the city gates and east to the harbor. The fabric of the Islamic city forced these otherwise straight roads to change course at certain points, but architects lined them with uniform arcades, and sympathetic observers noted a close similarity to Paris's Rue de Rivoli. Over time, hundreds more Ottoman-era houses, shops, and even gravestones fell, and something closer to a right-angle grid stretched out from the main three axes, which covered most of the European zone. The Marine Quarter, as it was called, was soon filled with apartment buildings typical of French towns. Students from the École des Beaux-Arts sent along designs for staid, classically proportioned government offices.[9]

A song dating from this period gives a good sense of how many Muslim inhabitants perceived the transformation of their city:

FIGURE 7.1 This satellite photograph shows the impact of French rule on the urban fabric of Algiers. The narrow maze of lanes in the hillside Casbah is visible on the left. On the right, in the city's lower reaches, the French created straight avenues reminiscent of their provincial towns. Vauban's influence is visible in the Place du Gouvernement, center right, whose shape has been nonetheless altered to preserve a mosque, to its right. The monumental Haussmann-style Boulevard de l'Imperatrice is raised on an arched embankment along the bay. Courtesy of e-Map and Digital Globe.

O regrets for Algiers, for its houses
And for its well-kept apartments!
O regrets for the town of cleanliness
Whose marble and porphyry dazzled the eyes!
The Christians inhabit them, their state has changed!
The have degraded everything, spoiled all, the impure ones! . . .

They have taken away the marble, the balustrades and the benches;
And the iron grills which adorned the windows
Have been torn away to add insult to our misfortunes
O regrets for Algiers and for its stores
Their traces no longer exist! ...
They have rummaged through the tombs of our fathers,
And they have scattered their bones
To allow their wagons to go over them
O believers, the world has seen with its own eyes.
Their horses tied in our mosques ...[10]

The French found less use for the two-thirds of the city that climbed the hillside behind the Marine Quarter, and it remained almost exclusively Muslim. Its inhabitants called it *el-Djabel* (the mountain). The French called the whole area the "Casbah," after the hilltop *qasbah*. Over time that place name would evoke a sealed-off world that kindled fantasies of Orientalist sensuality, exoticism, timelessness, mystery, and squalor.

Colonial officials, however, never felt it necessary to pass laws that zoned the city racially. Why was this? After all, French rule of Algeria was rife with discrimination—that despite the fact that officials did technically stick to universalistic principles and never used race as an official classification in the colony's laws. As French generals brutally suppressed waves of dissent throughout the mid-nineteenth century, imperial officials seized ever larger parcels of agricultural land from Muslim clans and gave them over to European *colons* and large French development companies. After 1870, the *colons* themselves took greater authority in the running of Algeria. To shore up their power, their representatives in Paris supported laws that granted French citizenship for Spanish, Italian, Maltese, and even Jewish inhabitants but that imposed nearly impossible conditions on Muslims, including an obligation to publically disavow Islamic religious law. Settlers also helped draft a special code of native laws, the *indigénat*, that was designed to subject Muslims to arbitrary treatment by colonial police forces. As French officials in Morocco would later demonstrate, republican universalism posed no insuperable barrier to legalized segregation. The record of French racism in Algeria, and its far more powerful settler population, suggests that the same should have held there, even in a colony that was supposed to be part of the republican France itself.[11]

Paradoxically, however, French Algeria's harsh anti-Muslim policies may have made urban segregation laws politically unnecessary as a tool of white rule. Repression left Muslims politically embittered, and land dispossessions undercut the main source of wealth holding. The Muslim population of coastal cities only recovered slowly after the conquest, remaining less than half the size of the European population throughout the era of segregation mania. European settlers in Algiers thus faced less rivalry in urban property markets from a wealthy local landed elite than whites in other colonies. The vast majority of Muslim migrants to town were too poor to afford housing in European neighborhoods. For those who could, cultural questions may have come to play: most seem to have preferred to settle in districts adjoining the Casbah, where the remaining Ottoman-era housing was better suited to traditions of domestic privacy and gender segregation. Whatever the main cause, the color line in Algiers remained largely intact without a specific law designed to keep it in place. Even as the Muslim hill districts grew increasingly overcrowded after 1900 and expanded somewhat, the Marine quarter remained overwhelmingly European.[12]

Meanwhile, the amount of destruction involved in the creation of European Algiers bothered many French officials. One government commission in Paris even went so far as to admit that the army of the most civilized nation on earth had "outdone in barbarity the barbarians we have come to civilize." This attitude only increased over the years, especially as the military built enormous installations outside the old walls of the city, with the goal of transforming the city into the "citadel of Algeria" to better fight Abd-el-Kader and his successors in the countryside. Already by the 1860s, under Emperor Napoleon III, Algiers held a place in the French imperial imagination that was similar to Britain's Calcutta— the colonial city that had gone wrong. The drastic rebuilding had deeply embittered France's new colonial subjects. And, for all that, the French got even less from their white town than the British did from Calcutta's. No "city of palaces" rose at Algiers, and the Place du Gouvernement hardly passed as an esplanade. The military's influence had allowed the glowering legacy of Vauban to overshadow the radiant potential of Versailles.[13]


## Planet Haussmann

For the Baron Georges-Eugène Haussmann, appointed by Napoleon III to supervise the rebuilding of Paris in 1852, the triumph of classical "regularity" envisioned by Louis XIV's planners had been delayed too long, not only in peripheral places like Algiers, but in the very capital of France itself. In fact, he thought, nineteenth-century commercial and sanitary concerns only heightened the need for a less congested urban fabric. But visions of imperial grandeur also clearly danced in his dreams—as they certainly did in those of his patron, the emperor. Urban defense was also a priority, though the enemies he worried about most were not Vauban's besieging armies but Paris's own revolutionaries. Twice they had struck since the first Napoleon was consigned to exile. In 1830, they had seen right through Charles X's Algerian sideshow and overthrown him despite his glorious victory. Then, in 1848, as just about all of western Europe smoldered in revolution, restless Parisians once again barricaded the capital's labyrinth of streets, confused the royal army, and inaugurated a Second Republic.

Napoleon III, the grandnephew of the greater Bonaparte, brought France's second republican adventure to a swift end in 1852, and one of his first acts of authoritarian rule was to unleash Haussmann upon Paris. Haussmann's legendary *grands travaux* (great works) focused above all on destroying big chunks of the medieval fabric of the city and driving through its ruins the wide boulevards that still stir the imagination of visitors today. Lined with apartment buildings of equal height and complementary design, Haussmann intended his great thoroughfares not just to be barricade-proof, but also to draw amazed eyes to the city's monuments and symbols of imperial power (his wide sidewalks also left lots of space for the city's famous cafés). Many of Paris's most elegant "green lungs" also came into being under Haussmann's direction: the Bois de Boulogne and Vincennes, the Champs de Mars (later home to Eiffel's tower), and the jewel-like Parc des Buttes Chaumont. To clear the way for these projects, Haussmann—like the Lottery Committee in Calcutta hoped to do before him—condemned more land than he needed with the idea that plots on the boulevards would rise in value enough to pay back his expenses and more. Conditions of resale also guaranteed architectural regularity.[14]

His clearances of working-class and slum neighborhoods, combined with skyrocketing rents along the elegant new avenues, forced the city's poorer residents to gravitate toward the urban fringe—especially to the east. Thus Paris's famous *banlieues rouges*, the "red suburbs," came into being. As in London, supporters of Parisian slum clearance often equated the urban poor with the natives and blacks of the colonies. When, in the twentieth century, Paris began to draw larger numbers of immigrants who actually came from those colonies, the red banlieues became disproportionately brown and black. Haussmann thus set Paris on a course of interlinked class and racial segregation whose roots sometimes get obscured today when Parisians debate whether American-style ghettos have appeared in their midst.[15]

Meanwhile, Haussmann's audacity captured other imaginations, especially those of authoritarian elites, sanitarians, and new generations of urban planners. His signature wide, straight, diagonal boulevards and parklands became standard practice in all turn-of-the-century schools of modern urban redevelopment. Outside of France, Haussmannian regularization brought even swifter combinations of class and racial segregation along with it. Examples can be found all across the continents, but the most important were the largest cities of South America, Buenos Aires and Rio de Janeiro, and Africa's largest city, Cairo. In all three of these places and elsewhere as well, the stage was set for the importation of Haussmannian planning when elites committed to "Europeanizing" their societies came to power during the 1850s and 1860s, rejecting regimes that called for greater isolation from the imperial heartland.

In Buenos Aires and Rio, the embrace of Haussmann went hand in hand with an importation of social Darwinism and eugenics. None of this cross-oceanic influence was straightforward, however. Westernizing elites in Latin America had to contend with the fact that their nations (and in some places the elites themselves) were made up of people of mixed African, European, and Amerindian heritage—and thus, according to the most fashionable racial theories, doomed to a long process of racial degeneration. To Europeanize their countries, the elites made three audacious intellectual and political maneuvers. First, they invented a kind of eugenical countertheory, which posited that race mixing could actually create a stronger race, not a weaker one. If enough whites migrated into South America, black and mixed-race people would slowly meld into the dominant group and "whiten" themselves out of existence. Second, they enacted state policies to encourage large waves of white immigration and they quietly closed the door on black immigration to guarantee that racial whitening, rather than darkening, actually occurred. Third, they poured forth a torrent of propaganda, fashioned in part by local race theorists, that argued that the black population of their countries was in irrevocable decline.

All of these strategies were remarkably successful. Millions of European immigrants poured into both Argentina and Brazil in the late nineteenth century. The population of black and mixed-race people continued to grow as well. But in the midst of the propaganda of "whitening," a variety of socially attractive intermediate color categories became available to darker-skinned people. As a result, census takers across Latin America recorded ever-smaller numbers of self-described "black" people. Argentine intellectuals had mused about the decline of the black population since the 1830s, even though census returns suggested otherwise, but by 1900 they declared it virtually gone. Brazil, with the largest black population of any country outside Africa, now reimagined its dark-skinned people as a benign component of a "racial democracy," still obviously in existence, but inexorably headed toward whiteness.[16]

The cities, however, presented a paradox for the essentially antisegregationist program of whitening. In urban politics, a fourth imported policy tool was needed: a massive Haussmannian makeover of cities that was nothing if not ruthlessly segregationist. As poor European immigrants and people from the South American countryside flooded into Buenos Aires and Rio during the last few decades of the nineteenth century, the cities became two of the world's largest, and among the fastest-growing in world history up to that time. Newcomers from Europe packed themselves into slum housing known as the *conventillos* (little convents) in Buenos Aires and *cortiços* (beehives) in Rio, where they lived with mixed-race and black people; in Rio many of these black neighbors were recently freed slaves. Sanitary officials with credentials from Paris, London, and Berlin labeled Rio's tenement districts as prime sources of the city's notoriously murderous outbreaks of yellow fever, malaria, and other diseases—all of which threatened to sabotage elites' plans to lure more European immigrants. To deal with this problem, immigration advocates gave themselves license to have their racial cake and eat it too. While proclaiming the advantages of race mixing as a path to whiteness, they called for the wholesale destruction of the *conventillos* and *cortiços* as dens of "primitive miscegenation" and white racial degeneration. A "civilized" European city would take their place—and Haussmann would show the way. Plague scares in both cities at the dawn of the twentieth century further encouraged their schemes.[17]

From the 1880s through 1910, massive state-sponsored slum-clearance and construction projects remade the centers of both Buenos Aires and Rio with broad Parisian boulevards and monumental squares (similar, somewhat less spectacular schemes also went forward in Mexico City and other Latin American capitals). Slum dwellers, as in Paris and London, were forced to the urban fringes. But since the displaced poor in Latin America were disproportionately dark-skinned, class segregation and race segregation occurred simultaneously. In Rio, sharp hikes in downtown rents pushed most of the city's poor and darker-skinned people to the northern industrial zones of town or into informal housing in the famous *favelas* that grew on the plunging slopes of its mountainsides. The city's generally lighter-skinned elites had long been used to a kind of self-segregation: during yellow fever season they flocked up the nearby escarpment to Petropolis and other resort towns—Brazil's version of the hill stations. The new city plan gave these elites even more options. While it made little provision for transit systems that would allow working-class people easier commutes from the northern fringes to their jobs downtown, it did lay out a nice network of trolleys for the well-to-do that led southward to the gorgeous, still sparsely inhabited beachfronts of Ipanema and Copacabana.[18]

In Cairo, fewer flights of racial theory and much less destruction and displacement were involved in the Hausmmanization process, but a divided Cairo emerged just as rapidly. The whole process also bankrupted Egypt and left it at the mercies of France and Britain. Here the grands travaux were the work of the Khedive Ismā'īl the Magnificent (1863–79). Ismā'īl had studied in Paris as a young man. He returned there in 1867 as a guest of Napoleon III and Haussmann himself and was awed by the city's transformation over the previous fifteen years. Faced with the humiliating prospect that crumbling, medieval Cairo would soon have to host all of Europe's heads of state at a celebration of the opening of the Suez Canal, Ismā'īl hired the project director of Haussmann's Bois de Boulogne, paired him with a French-educated Egyptian architect named 'Ali Mubarak, and ordered a Haussmann-like remake of the former capital of the caliphs.

Out of respect for the Nile's annual floods, the walled city of Cairo had developed a kilometer and a half to the east of the mighty river. Ismā'īl, however, had begun the process of taming the Nile through diversionary canals and higher embankments, and thus an enormous piece of real estate had became available for his plans. In the former flood plain, Ali Mubarak laid out the avenues of Ismailiya, the nucleus of Cairo's new town, while Haussmann's architect added a facsimile of the Parc des Buttes-Chaumont. From there, Ismā'īl borrowed heavily from European banks to lay out a plan of radiating boulevards, some of which he drove into the old town as well. As the debts mounted out of control, France and England took over the finances of the country, then deposed Ismā'īl, and by 1882 jointly took over the government of Egypt in an "indirect-rule" arrangement with grudging Ottoman assent.[19]

In the meantime, Egypt had become a magnet for European investors—people involved in Suez Canal-related projects or in the Egyptian cotton boom, which dated from the US Civil War years, when British industrialists needed a replacement for the cotton embargoed from American plantations. During the early colonial era of the 1880s and 1890s, Europeans from across the Mediterranean flocked to Cairo much as they had to Algiers. So did enormous numbers of Egyptians from the countryside, pushed off the farms by the consolidation of land into cotton production. The old town filled up, and the European-style section grew dramatically, filling the spaces along Ismā'īl's boulevards, and then bursting across the Nile to the west bank and onto islands in the river. Though the political circumstances allowed no legalized racial zoning, the new town became the exclusive residence of wealthy Egyptians and Europeans. White immigrants made up one-seventh of Cairo's population in 1907. The British built a classic bungalow district on the island of Gezirah, and exclusive clubs sprouted up, just as in Calcutta and Shanghai. Old Cairo, meanwhile, remained exclusively Muslim and disproportionately poor, like the Casbah of Algiers.[20]

Then, in the 1890s, the Baron Édouard Empain, a Belgian who had gained a fortune in Congo's forced-labor rubber plantations, developed a giant Orientalist residential fantasyland called Heliopolis (Sun City) in the middle of the desert northeast of Cairo. Empain borrowed his street plan from the "garden city" ideas of the visionary socialist English planner Ebenezer Howard. But the quasi-suburban, quasi-resort "oasis"—festooned with *Arabian Nights*-style onion domes and even an imitation Hindu temple—was one of the era's most elaborate capitalist boondoggles. Even the American banker J. P. Morgan shook his head in disbelief at its success. Heliopolis attracted wealthy European vacationers and second-home buyers, including a clutch of British Indians who had given up on Simla. Like other developments in Cairo, Heliopolis tied the city's real estate market to the fortunes of European and American banks. During the 1907 panic on Wall Street, Cairo's real estate bubble burst, slowing development until well into the 1920s.[21]

## Splitting Cities, Beaux-Arts Style

While French urban design achieved triumphs abroad, influential commentators in France began to worry that French civilization as a whole had begun to lose its capacity for innovation in the years after Haussmann. In 1870, Napoleon III's Second Empire collapsed after a humiliating military defeat to the Germans. Haussmann's boulevards did nothing to stop Paris's ungovernable crowds from taking the city once again. First they proclaimed a commune, then a Third Republic came into being—this one longer-lived but politically unstable. The population of the City of Light, meanwhile, doubled in size during the second half of the nineteenth century, most of it in its poorly planned, sprawling, working-class banlieues.

Housing reformers like Jules Siegfried and Maurice Halbwachs decried the inequalities leftover from Haussmann's schemes and complained that the new republic lacked the legal machinery necessary to prevent speculators from building ugly, insanitary workers' housing—often placed cheek-by-jowl alongside the suburbs' noxious factories. Fearing the revolutionary discontent that could grow under such conditions in the banlieues rouges, they banded together to form the influential Musée Social (Social Museum), dedicated to lobbying for housing and planning legislation in France that would allow Paris to catch up with other European capitals.[22]

Then, during the years immediately after 1900, a rebellion brewed in the architectural division of Louis XIV's august École des Beaux-Arts. Three Prix de Rome winners in architecture, Tony Garnier, Ernest Hébrard, and Henri Prost, pointedly refused to spend their five-year stints in the Eternal City solely contemplating the universality of classical beauty. In reports they sent to their shocked professors in Paris, each in his own way argued that architecture must develop not according to preordained aesthetic laws but within the complex and unique social contexts of the city of which it was to be a part. Once again, their goal was to bring French architectural practice up to date and embrace advances in urban planning from elsewhere in Europe: Germany's Camilo Sitte, Belgium's Charles Buls, and Britain's Ebenezer Howard. Like Haussmann they rejected the rigid, impersonal, rectangular grid favored by Vauban and embraced diagonal boulevards—as well as the more relaxed British-style curved lanes suitable for parks. To be sure, urban planning needed to concern itself with questions of defense, commerce, sanitation, control, beauty, and even triumphalism, but it was also obligated to serve a broader, more humane ambition as well, to solve the social problems that led to unrest and inspire a new level of urban civilization.[23]

Accomplishing this grand mission, agreed the Musée Social reformers and the Beaux-Arts rebels, would require lots of power—perhaps even more power than Haussmann wielded under the Second Empire. In particular, the fledgling urbanistes began calling for truly comprehensive legislation to give planners wide authority to condemn and seize private property in the name of their larger social goals. In France, such a call ran up against the power of large developers and liberal supporters of property rights. By 1910, with planning legislation repeatedly stalled in the French Assembly, the country appeared to be falling even further behind other European countries in civilizing its cities.[24]

It was then, though, that the urbanistes' fortunes changed. The resident general of the new protectorate of Morocco, Hubert de Lyautey, called Henri Prost to North Africa to design a capital city that would not only demonstrate France's superior capacity to bring civilization to the world, it would also show France itself—and the rest of its empire—how to remove the shackles of its own hidebound ways.

Lyautey (1854–1934) was one of France's most famous imperialists. Conquering general, colonial administrator, man of letters, and one of his era's foremost conservative intellectuals, Lyautey had grown deeply disillusioned with France's turn to republicanism. He had also become a prominent critic of what he saw as the inflexibility and the sheer brutality of the French army, which he thought hindered the empire's ability to convince the colonized natives of the glorious promise of French civilization. To back up his complaints, Lyautey echoed other urban-planning critics by pointing to the sorry state of French colonial cities. In Algeria, and later in Indochina, the rigid influence of Vauban and the military engineers remained intractable. Haussmannian planning was rudimentary at best, but even when improvements came in the 1880s and 1890s, they seemed to Lyautey to emphasize superficial bombast over more elevated planning goals.

Lyautey's critique picked up on the ongoing dissatisfaction with the city of Algiers. The most influential of the city's critics had been Napoleon III himself, who visited the city twice during his reign and appointed a commission aimed to bring some of the virtues of Parisian-style planning to the colonial capital. The commission's report chided earlier planners for their lack of ambition: the new streets in the Marine Quarter were too narrow to be sanitary or grandiose, and the military engineers' Vauban-style wall systems made it impossible for the city to grow southward, where there was more open land and a gorgeous bay setting. Planners had found space within the Marine Quarter for the city's trademark Boulevard de l'Impératrice (named in honor of Napoleon's wife, then renamed for the republic after 1870), raised upon an elaborate arched embankment above the sea. But in 1881, while Lyautey was stationed at Algiers, the military remained opposed to the extension plans. The white town was as cramped and uninspiring as ever, and the Casbah was turning into an overcrowded slum. "It is we," Lyautey wrote, "who have the air of barbarians in the midst of barbarians. . . . How would an Arab not feel exasperated?"[25]

In Indochina, Vauban's legacy went back further than at Algiers. During the eighteenth century, French merchants and adventurers had peddled their protection services to rival Vietnamese rulers, much like Dupleix in India. They designed a Vauban-style citadel for one ruler at Saigon in 1790 and another for the Vietnamese emperor at Hanoi in 1803.[26] When the French took Saigon outright in 1859, they destroyed the old citadel and replaced it with a smaller one. The gridiron of streets within the old fort, though, set the pattern for the European town, which encompassed the relatively high ground known as the Plateau. Over time, some of these streets were widened to form boulevards, and one of these linked the new citadel with a large palace for the governor general, set in a park. Elegant villas rose up along smaller avenues that were flanked by sweet-smelling tamarind, frangipane, and teak trees. The heart of town was the Rue Catinat, which later visitors compared to the Rue de la Paix in Paris. In the north of Vietnam, at Hanoi, the old citadel likewise dictated a rectangular street pattern, though here an old city known as the Thirty-Six Streets remained intact after the final conquest of the city in 1883. Like at Algiers, though probably not in direct imitation, the French planner Paul Bert arranged the white town so that it completely surrounded this small native town—the citadel on one side, the right-angled streets of the administrative and villa districts on the second and third sides, and the Red River on the fourth. At Hanoi, the Rue Paul Bert performed the same function as the Rue Catinat in Saigon. Colonial officials could mark the end of their workdays there by living the *vie large* at languorous cafés where they could sip real pastis and absinthe, shipped directly from France via the Messageries Maritimes. Lavish local opera houses in both cities allowed their ersatz Parisian life to continue into the evening. In Saigon, seekers of more exotic cross-racial adventures could traverse the "bamboo curtain" to the sex houses and gambling dens of the nearby Chinese mercantile city of Cholon.[27]

For Lyautey, who passed through Saigon on his way to his earliest missions as a high-ranking army commander in the Vietnamese countryside, the results, even with the larger measures of Haussmannian flair, were not much better than those at Algiers. "Ah!" he exclaimed sardonically of his visit to what he called the "cream tart" of Franco-Asian cities. "Monumental cafés, would you believe! And hotels, dance halls, and restaurants....All this cardboard decoration in the midst of magnificent vegetation satisfies the eye. One quickly senses that it would be dangerous to scratch the surface, though, for if we removed the bureaucrats, military types, and their enormous privileges, everything would fall apart." By contrast, the British at Singapore, which Lyautey had visited a few days earlier, had brought European culture to Asia more humanely, and it had thus sunk much deeper roots. Even Singapore's cantonment had sent Lyautey into rapture: "My head is swimming at the sight of all my ideas put into practice; these are not just utopias; somewhere there really does exist the cheery, welcoming, open quarter which furnishes a complete life, where things are done with a smile, where men are humans and not ragged convicts stuck endlessly sweeping deadly courtyards under the curses of warrant officers."[28]

Over the next two decades, Lyautey had more opportunities to put his ideas into practice himself. Taking time out from his command of the conquest of Madagascar, he personally plotted out two new colonial towns, one of them the European town of the island's second-largest city, Fianarantsoa. There, he prefigured Beaux-Arts adaptations of Haussmann by lining his avenues with features of the English colonial city, like "cottages and assymetry," aimed to "avoid...uniformity or any sense of the prison or barracks."[29]

Lyautey's chance for truly grands travaux, though, came in 1912. As a reward for instigating the conquest of Morocco, he was named resident general of the new French protectorate there. One of his first acts was to call upon French planners to build *villes nouvelles* for Europeans outside each of the principle Moroccan cities' impressive fortified zones, known there as the *medinas*. An eager Henri Prost raced to Morocco from Paris in response to Lyautey's call. The resident general seemed ready to make himself into the urbanistes' very own Napoleon III, the authoritarian political patron they could only dream of back in republican France.

The plum project in Morocco was to design the controversial new capital at Rabat. Lyautey chose this seaside city in pointed opposition to other possibilities. Though Rabat had a history as an imperial seat, it was distinctly *not* the more lustrous Fez, where Moroccan potentates seethed at the conquest and presented greater dangers to French rule. Rabat was also not Casablanca, a relatively small place under Moroccan rule that since the conquest had become a booming port town. Very much like Cairo twenty years earlier, "Casa" had been overrun by European merchants and land speculators. But most of all, Lyautey dreamed that Rabat would become the very opposite of Algiers, an uninspiring capital built upon the ruins of a Muslim civilization.[30]

To show he was serious about avoiding that fate, Prost pulled out all the planning tricks he and the urbanistes had devised since their rebellion at the École des Beaux-Arts: wide diagonal avenues à la Haussmann, of course; monumental government structures that, unlike Haussmann's, were built in a variety of styles drawing from French, English, and Maghrebian models that took the local climatic and architectural context into account; delightful public spaces and parks; a full infrastructure of sewers; a rationally planned transport system; and separate administrative, residential, industrial, and military zones. To this day architectural critics have universally praised Prost's aesthetic and urbanist conception of the Moroccan villes nouvelles as a work of Beaux-Arts genius. At Rabat, the shadow of Vauban finally lifted.[31]

Underlying the splendor, though, was a tawdrier drama, one that was not quite as far removed from Algiers as Lyautey and Prost claimed. As Lyautey and Prost rebuilt Moroccan cities, they developed one of the most elaborate theories of racial segregation in the history of city-splitting. For Prost, "*complete separation of European and indigenous agglomerations*" was an "essential condition" of planning in colonial cities. Without it, none of the other considerations of a comprehensive plan could be realized, whether they be "political, economic, sanitary, . . . [or] aesthetic."[32]

The political concerns, first of all, reflected Lyautey's own theories of race and empire, which involved what he saw as a deep respect for the unchangeable differences in culture between the races. Rejecting the idea that natives would "assimilate" quickly into French culture, Lyautey

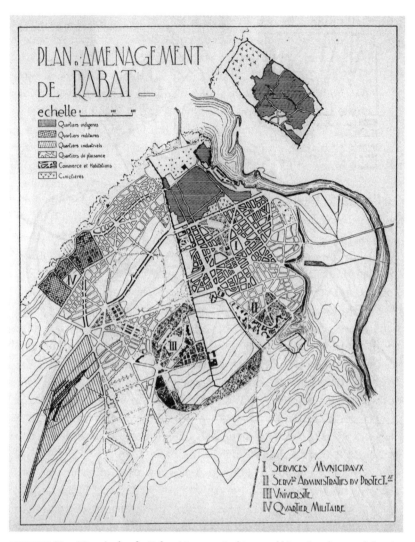

FIGURE 7.2  Henri Prost's plan for Rabat, Morocco. Architectural historians have acclaimed Prost's *ville nouvelle* for its elegant street layout and gracious architectural fusion of French and North African styles. Prost's particularly elaborate and comprehensive segregationist vision grew out of the idea that the city's historic native quarter, the Medina, needed to be preserved as a means to contrast the static civilizational glory of the Arab world with the more progressive West. From Henri Royer, *L'Urbanisme aux Colonies* (1932), 63.

preferred to run his protectorate in "association" with the Moroccan sultan and other native institutions, much more in the manner of Frederick Lugard's "indirect rule" in British Nigeria. Urban segregation—as in Lugard's Kano and Zaria or Raffles's Singapore—allowed parallel forms of local governance to operate simultaneously and without colliding at cross-purposes. Differences in gender politics, Prost also argued, made segregation indispensable. Muslims built their houses without outward-facing windows to keep the porches of the women's quarters out of view. Such restrictions could not apply to Europeans, so a completely different town was needed for them.

The economic and sanitary reasons for segregation were self-evident to Prost: the cramped, winding streets of Morocco's medinas would simply not do for modern commerce or sanitation systems. In all of his plans, Prost called for a building-free cordon sanitaire between the medina and the new city, which could protect Europeans from inevitable contagion and also free up a corridor for commercial traffic.

Finally, Prost and Lyautey's aesthetic reasons for racial separation represented their most striking contribution to the history of city-splitting. The Moroccan medinas, they thought (unlike the military engineers of Algiers) ought to be lovingly conserved—once again, as monuments to a noble, if unchanging culture. Segregation thus got a new mission: historical preservation. For Lyautey this respect for Muslim culture resonated deeply with his conservatism. Islam, he thought, sustained an aristocracy that France had unwisely cast aside. Only by taming and working with the Moroccan elite could France maintain its control over the colony. Preservation of the medina had other political and economic benefits—it avoided the lingering Muslim bitterness that had arisen over the destruction of Algiers's Casbah. What is more, the medina itself could become a tourist destination that would lure Europeans and their money to Morocco, possibly permanently. Though Lyautey despised European *colons* for their racism (which he apparently deemed harsher than his own), the encouragement of European colonization also became an increasingly important justification for expending lavish sums on Morocco's beautiful "new cities." A sustained influx from Europe, some thought, was needed so that the protectorate could build a counterforce to the natives' "nationalist tendencies and Bolshevik propaganda."[33]

If the theoretical justification for segregation was elaborate, so was the authoritarian legal apparatus that put the theory into practice. Unlike the conquest of Algiers, that of Morocco did not involve widespread destruction of cities, and much urban land remained in the hands of the local elite. Legal measures were thus more clearly necessary to bring color lines of this ambitious scope into place, and Lyautey was willing to use his power of decree to make up for his relatively restrained use of military force. Indeed the planning regime he and Proust put together represents one of the most extensive legal efforts to undercut the power of the landed interests that had foiled segregation schemes elsewhere in colonial cities. The villes nouvelles required large amounts of land—at Rabat, Prost's European city was to be ten times the size of the old medina. To assemble it, Lyautey ignored his own principles about working through Moroccan institutions and imported three tools from abroad. One was the Australian Torrens system, which made proof of landownership dependent on the ability to produce a written, state-certified title. Under this system, traditional Muslim titles were often deemed invalid in French courts, which were called upon to settle land disputes. The white judges who presided over these courts tended to rule in favor of European titleholders, no matter how fraudulent their claims. At Saigon, a similar system had been used to clear the Plateau for European ownership in the 1860s—and the process was repeated in Madagascar and Tunisia as well. The second tool was a comprehensive urban-planning law assembled by Musée Social housing reformers from provisions passed in numerous European municipalities. Lyautey proclaimed this law by decree in 1914, long before much less sweeping planning laws came to France. Under the legislation, every city was to produce a comprehensive plan that would be legally binding. Borrowing an expropriation scheme from Maurice Halbwachs of the Musée Social—who in turn borrowed his from a controversial scheme in Frankfurt—Lyautey further decreed that private owners of land that lay in the way of Prosts's grands travaux had to cede the most useful portions of their property to the state, then negotiate with other land holders in the same district to divide up the plots that remained after construction. Only Torrens titleholders could participate in these negotiations or receive compensation. The decree thus effectively allowed the state and other European speculators to rob large tracts of property from their Moroccan owners. Finally, Lyautey also passed separate building codes for the medinas and the villes nouvelles making it illegal to build structures that did not conform to the architectural and sanitary standards in each racial zone. Unless Moroccans were willing and financially able to buy Torrens-title land and build European-style houses, they would not be permitted to live in the ville nouvelle.[34]

How well did this system work? Prost did build his resplendent new capital at Rabat largely according to plan, and Fez, Meknès, and Marrakesh also sprouted less completely rendered villes nouvelles. As Lyautey predicted, speculation-mad Casablanca proved a more difficult nut to crack, and planners were forced to build a "New Medina" there to supplement the much smaller old Muslim town. Still, the city's magnificent boulevards have remained intact, much in the way Prost and his assistants imagined them. Beaux-Arts-style planning also revived the influence of French architecture throughout the empire and beyond, though planners met with varying degrees of success: at Hanoi, Prost's Prix de Rome colleague Ernest Hébrard had less powerful planning tools at his disposal and wrestled less successfully with the city's gridiron (Saigon's remained largely in place). However, he did plan out a resplendent Beaux-Arts *station d'altitude* (hill station) for the government of French Indochina at Dalat. According to French critics, it far surpassed Dutch Buitenzorg and British Simla in glamour. Meanwhile, features of the ville nouvelle could be found in extensions of Cairo's Heliopolis and in plans for European Dakar and Madagascar's capital, Tananarive. They even made their way to Algiers, where the southern zone beyond the old walls of the Casbah became a more elegant center of French life than the Marine Quarter.[35]

How about the segregation of the races? In Morocco, Lyautey's ruthless legal tools were essential to the creation of separate European towns and the cordons sanitaires that divided them from the native towns. Those laws, however, only created separate European and Moroccan "agglomerations": following colorblind scruples much as in Algeria, they did not explicitly forbid Moroccan people from living in the white town. Some European-educated Moroccan Muslims and Jews (who had lived in separate quarters under Moroccan rule) could and did acquire land and proper titles, then built houses for themselves along western lines in the European towns. Lyautey and Prost both also acknowledged that their cities, like all supposedly dual cities in world history, depended on extensive daily traffic across the residential color line: they were, one of their colleagues put it, "Siamese sisters." The parks that made up part of the cordon sanitaire of Rabat became a kind of leisured cross-racial meeting place. Despite the heavy-handed techniques involved, this was not, as one critic called it, a North African version of apartheid.[36]

In 1931, French-speaking colonial urbanists met in the first and only International Congress devoted solely to the planning of colonial cities.

There they fêted their now retired hero Hubert de Lyautey and his amanuensis Henri Prost. Conferees lauded the pair's Moroccan achievements as a "master lesson" for future generations of colonial urbanistes.[37] Prost rose to the podium to deliver his most definitive statement yet on the fundamental link between Beaux-Arts planning and the separation of the races. In the discussion that followed, though, it was clear there was some unease about what he and Lyautey had wrought. A delegate from the Dutch Indies angrily compared French segregation to the old Chinatown system of Batavia and called it "medieval" and even "ancient," with no sanitary justification whatsoever. In response, Ernest Hébrard vehemently (and mendaciously) puffed that it would be "completely erroneous" to call the policy of "rescuing the medinas" of Morocco an instance of "deliberately intended racial segregation." Separate racial districts in the French Empire, he argued furthermore, "correspond, in essence, to the business districts and working-class residential neighborhoods of our own modern cities, ... separated ... without a definite line being drawn on the map." In matters of segregation, another speaker concluded, the French temperament differed fundamentally from the British one: Prost's plan used "separation for sure, but not radical separation," the kind that "involved disdain for the native town ... [like] the English method."[38]

These sweeping defensive remarks not only overstate imperial France's commitment to racial universalism but also ignore both the variety of French practices across the world and their close connections with equally variable British ones. They also reveal a bigger theme in late colonial urban politics that was not limited to its Beaux-Arts practitioners. As nationalist movements called ever more credibly for an end to empires, elaborate segregationist theories became less and less relevant. The actual political survival of the urban color line depended increasingly on colonial authorities' ability to plausibly deny its existence.

## Sunset at New Delhi

Something strange happens as you drive westward along the vast, rifle-straight stretch of New Delhi's Kingsway and approach the monumental "acropolis" of Raisina, surmounted by the inscrutable dome of the Viceroy's Palace, the work of the famous British architect Edwin Lutyens. The great dome commands your eye from almost two miles away, where the

Kingsway—also designed by Lutyens—begins at the All-India Arch. But just as you reach the ramp that leads up to the acropolis, the palace suddenly begins to fall away from sight, obscured by the ramp itself. Then, finally, the dome itself virtually disappears, like a setting sun.

Edwin Lutyens was reportedly apoplectic that nothing could be done to change this outrageous error in planning. The ramp had to have such a steep pitch in order to allow enough frontage along the last stretch of the Kingsway for the equally magnificent twin Secretariat buildings, designed by his colleague Herbert Baker, which flank the palace on the summit of the hill. After expending years of creative energy laying out New Delhi as a supreme urban monument to the majesty of the British Raj, the most important symbol of all—the palace dome itself—seemed to fulfill the mordant prophesy of the French prime minister Georges Clemenceau, who visited the site of the city as construction began in 1920. "This," he said, looking out at the remains of the many imperial cities that had come and gone on the site, "will be the finest ruin of them all."[39]

New Delhi has often been called the ultimate colonial city. Ultimate it was, in both senses of the word—the most ambitious and, in India,

FIGURE 7.3  New Delhi. The two-mile-long Kingsway and other avenues radiating at ninety- and sixty-degree angles draw attention to the magnificence of Edwin Lutyens's Government House and Herbert Bakers's twin Secretariat Buildings on the top of the Raisina "acropolis." A zone for the bungalows of high-level officials begins to far left. Midlevel officials live to the right of the circular Parliament building. Apartments for Indian clerks lie in the far distance, upper right, closer to Old Delhi, which Lutyens's street plan shoulders aside. Courtesy of Getty Images.

the last.[40] On one level it represents a perfect bookend to the drama of modern British colonial urban race segregation, looking backward to eighteenth-century Calcutta, where the plot began. At the same time— Clemenceau's disdainful comments aside—New Delhi, like Calcutta, also represented a culmination of something distinctly French. London, after all, had nothing quite like the Kingsway or the Viceroy's Palace— New Delhi's inspiration came above all from Paris's Champs-Elysées and Louis XIV's Versailles. Like the Beaux-Arts rebels, Lutyens had made his own journey to Rome (he often referred to the Raisina acropolis as a copy of the Capitoline Hill). Like them, he pored over the Franco-American architect Pierre Charles L'Enfant's plans for Washington DC. In homage to L'Enfant and the architects of Versailles, he plotted out the wide radial streets that intersected New Delhi's Kingsway at perfect thirty-, sixty-, and ninety-degree angles. Like them, he kept up with the work of the American city planner Daniel Burnham and his Haussmann- and Beaux-Arts inspired "City Beautiful" movement in the United States and the Philippines. Of course, there was plenty of room for a British touch at New Delhi as well. Prior to his work in India, Lutyens had served as a design consultant for London's famous Garden City suburb at Hampstead, inspired by Ebenezer Howard. As in many Anglo-American suburbs, the bungalows that lined the Kingsway and other grand arteries were set back far from the road, almost invisible behind the greenery that surrounded them—a clear contrast with Haussmann's six-story apartment buildings on the Champs-Elysées or Prost's denser, sidewalk-fronting buildings at Rabat.[41]

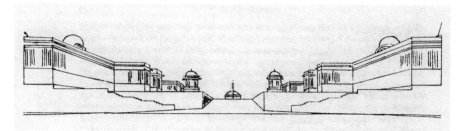

FIGURE 7.4 The New Delhi "sunset." Because of the steep slope of the Raisina hill, the dome of Lutyens's Government House appears to sink below the horizon along the final stretch of the Kingsway. Indeed, the construction of New Delhi was one of the last self-aggrandizing acts of an empire upon which the sun was never supposed to set. Drawing by W. H. Nicholls, "Approach to Government House, New Delhi, as Designed," March 28, 1916, IOR/L/PWD/6/1187. © The British Library Board.

Then there were also the anti-inspirations, the things New Delhi was to avoid. One of these was the cantonment. A top advisor to viceroy Hardinge was clear on this point: now that the British capital had arrived in the old seat of the Mughals, New Delhi would have to become a true imperial city, not a mere army camp. Lutyens's formal planning at New Delhi flew in the face of a hundred years of helter-skelter planning in the empire's stations, whose layout allowed little sense of the triumphant or the monumental.

Another counterinspiration was Old Delhi. While the New Delhi could absorb some of its majesty from the old, it was to be as different as East was from West. Walled, mazelike Shajahanabad should remain intact, like the medina in Lyautey's Rabat, but as a kind of countermonument that contrasted the past glories of Indian grandeur with a new, grandly sprawling, angular expression of the far superior "power of Western science, art, and civilization."[42]

Finally, New Delhi could not, of course, reproduce stinking Calcutta, the quarrelsome city whose streets now echoed with the bomb blasts of Bengali "terrorists" and whose Improvement Trust, for all its slum clearance, could barely keep the rising tide of color from washing over a declining White Town. New Delhi, by contrast, would benefit from the more healthful environs of the North Indian plain, and it would allow the Government of India an easier escape to Simla to boot. Thanks to imperial land expropriations south of Old Delhi, Lutyens would have something of a tabula rasa on which to build. And, as one old India hand assured worried military types, within the political geography of the Raj, New Delhi would be "safer than Clapham Common," London's iconic suburban Evangelical retreat from urban moral pollution.[43]

As at Rabat, racial segregation was the key to making all of this work. Color lines would allow the triumphal planning influences to prevail within New Delhi and keep the undesirable ones out. The very choice of New Delhi's site represented a first act of segregation. Rather than build up the encumbered civil lines to the north of Old Delhi, with its Indian landlords and its blackmailing Gujar tribesmen, the committee settled on the "virgin soil" south of town. Lutyens's plan oriented New Delhi's streets and public squares away from the old city and, like Rabat again, set up a cordon sanitaire between the two towns, reinforced by the south wall of Shahjahanabad. That said, the southern site, which was scattered with the remains of the many other monumental capital cities that had flourished on the spot, allowed Lutyens to elevate "the Delhi of today" by connecting it with these glorious and politically much less trouble-some "Delhis of the past." The Kingsway's grandiosity, for example, was only heightened by the direct connection it drew between the Viceroy's Palace and the site of ancient Indraprashtra. (Several other ruins had to be razed for this to work, but, as Lutyens exclaimed to his wife, "imagine the Place de la Concorde in Paris with tombs anywhere and everywhere about it.")[44]

In 1913, while visiting King George at Balmoral Castle in Scotland, Lutyens went a step further and laid out an intricate plan for dividing New Delhi internally. On a piece of graph paper, he sketched a kind of racial cross-section of his city. In the diagram, the great Jamma Masjid (Friday Mosque) of Old Delhi appeared all the way to the left, down low. To its right appeared a few trees, representing the cordon sanitaire. Then there were two small houses, labeled "thin black" and "thin white." Higher up and further to the right in the diagram was a larger, more ornate house labeled "fat white." Finally, on the far right, at the "line of climax," was the viceregal palace. As the construction of New Delhi slowly proceeded over the next two decades, the Raj and the city's planning committees developed the ideas in this sketch, creating the most complex system of dividing residential space in any colonial city outside of South Africa.[45]

At Rabat, Lyautey had minimized the power of private landholders in the ville nouvelle through registration systems and planning legis-lation. At New Delhi, the Government of India did the same things by simply retaining ownership of more or less all of the land and buildings in the western two-thirds of the thirty-three-square-mile improvement zone as an "official estate." That gave the Raj the power to split the city into no less than five separate residential zones. The least desirable of these, a densely built area in the north, nearest the noisome suburbs of the old town, was reserved for Indian clerks (Lutyens's "thin blacks"). Somewhat to the south of that, and somewhat less densely built up, were the houses of lower-level white government officials ("thin whites"). The "fat whites"—the senior officials—could live in extensive compounds of the third zone, in the triangle just north of the Kingsway, near the acropolis. The elite of the elite got to live south of the Kingsway, where they could get even bigger compounds. A fourth zone, around the eastern stretches of the Kingsway, was designated for the palaces of the Indian princes (Lutyens himself designed the biggest of these for the nizam of Hyderabad). Finally, a fifth zone, for commerce, surrounded Connaught

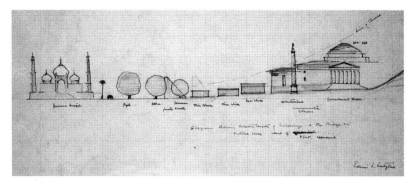

FIGURE 7.5 Lutyens's sketch of a cross-section of New Delhi showing the plan of segregation intrinsic to the new capital city's design. From the far left, the Jamma Masjid of Old
Delhi is kept apart by a tree-filled buffer zone and wall, followed by lodgings for "thin
black" clerks, houses for "thin white" officials, bungalows for "fat white" officials and, at
the "line of climax," the viceroy's Government House. Courtesy of Royal Institute of British Architects (RIBA) Library Drawings Collection.

Circus, another grand meeting point of Lutyens's radial avenues in the
north.[46]

Despite the effort to distance New Delhi from the cantonments, the
system that doled out housing to the city's inhabitants resembled a hyper-
trophied version of the residential provisions of the cantonment code.
Under the "rules governing the allotment of quarters in New Delhi"—
issued in 1927, when the capital was finally ready to receive its first large
wave of government employees—a special estates officer established a
waiting list for the best housing within each broader category of government employee. He was to update this list every fall, when the government returned from the hill stations. Government employees' place on
the list was based upon their salary (emolument), the length of their previous residence in New Delhi, the suitability of their current housing to
their stature, and finally upon their spot within the byzantine "Warrant
of Precedence," a sixty-six-level pecking order that graded all government
posts, from the viceroy at number one to the lowliest clerks at sixty-six (a
similar ranking governed seating at the viceroy's dinner parties).[47]

The rules of allotment created a strong link between the level of racial
residential segregation in New Delhi and the extent of racial discrimination in government hiring. That, in turn, linked residential segregation to the ability of the Indian nationalist movement to convince the
Raj to open the upper levels of the administration to Indians. Under the

movement's increasing pressure, the Government of India Acts of 1919 and 1935 made ever bigger concessions on this point, and by 1940 a few of the most prestigious addresses near the Kingsway were taken over by Indian department secretaries who reported directly to the viceroy. Still, until independence, the ranks of the higher "gazetted officers" remained overwhelmingly white and those of the lower clerks remained overwhelmingly Indian, so the occupational basis of the residential policy only blurred the color line somewhat. But the inequalities were stark nonetheless. As Lutyens and the viceroys were nervously aware, New Delhi involved massive government expense on what was essentially a thirty-three-square-mile public housing project—much of it made up of extremely costly, even palatial, bungalows. When it came to prioritizing outlays for housing construction, the swank bungalow districts always got more than the zones for clerks' apartments. Since the clerks' numbers were the greatest, and since they were most likely to be Indians, they were sharply underserved, and many had to live in Old Delhi. There, job opportunities opened up by the new capital had drawn in tens of thousands of other newcomers to the city. Rents had soared and accommodations were overcrowded to the bursting point. To make matters worse, Lutyens's plan assigned the richest people to residences that were closest to their place of work on the acropolis, and it forced the poorest government employees to pay for the longest and most expensive commutes.[48]

## A Bitter Epitaph

We should return now to 1931 and the international conference on colonial urbanism in Paris, when Ernest Hébrard brazenly denied that he and his colleagues in the urban-planning movement engaged in racial segregation. After all, he asserted, natives could live in the white towns, just as long as they built their houses to code. Thus, the boundary between black and white was just as harmless as the one between the classes in European cities, one that was determined "without a definite line being drawn on the map."

Hébrard's defense of French policy contains a double deception. It is impossible to wish away the power of race in the history of colonial cities, whether it was during moments when planners did draw color lines clearly on their maps or moments when they sought to hide race away. More importantly, though, there is nothing innocent or somehow less insidious about urban class segregation, whose history can never be miraculously excised from that of segregation by race. Remember that the biggest problem with urban racial separation is not that it separates different types of people into different neighborhoods. It is that it does so unequally—creating a maldistribution of resources that disproportionately disfavors those racial groups that the color line also helps to subordinate politically. Racial segregation, therefore, was not only dependent historically on techniques of class segregation. It *is* a kind of class segregation—and its nefariousness arises principally from that fact.

Hébrard's comment is telling in another way, however. By 1940 colonial urbanism had reached its outer limits—in the sheer ambitions of its aesthetic conception, in the reaching conceptual power of race, in the institutional power of empire, in the imagination of colonial reform networks, and in techniques of government control over urban land markets. By then, the practitioners of colonial urbanism had also revealed the outer limits of their self-identification as *comprehensive* planners. In their zeal to build spectacular new cites, they almost completely neglected to plan for one of the main consequences of their actions: the rapidly growing migration of mostly poor people from the countryside into colonial urban centers. In this sense, none of the twentieth century urbanistes learned lessons from either Algiers or Calcutta. At Algiers, the military may have provided room for the European town to spread outward, but the Casbah remained locked behind the citadel walls. When Arabs and other North Africans, thrown off the land in the countryside by a new wave of European settlement in the 1920s and 1930s, began to move to Algiers in enormous numbers, the Casbah quickly filled to capacity and degraded into a slum. With no place to live, poorer newcomers were increasingly forced to build their own shacks and shanties on the surrounding mountainsides, beyond the fringes of the expanding European town. The same happened to Hanoi's Thirty-Six Streets and Rabat's medina, all in the name of "preserving" or "rescuing" monuments of supposedly unchanging Eastern civilizations. Meanwhile, in India, Lutyens's thirty-three square mile zone for New Delhi contained sixty-five thousand people in 1931. In the same year, Old Delhi's seven square miles was home to 350,000. Health and sanitation budgets for the two sections of town were the same despite these enormous differences in population size and density; death rates were three times higher in Old Delhi and than in New Delhi. The sheer size of the Lutyens district combined with the civil lines to the north left only a small corridor to the west of the old city wall for expansion. That area too quickly filled in, and shantytowns soon began to appear on the far outskirts. "New Delhi people have not descended from the heavens," protestors proclaimed at a demonstration at the Old Delhi town hall in 1935, "when the government can spend millions on [New Delhi] why should it treat the Delhi people as untouchables?"[49]

In fact, the class divisions of colonial cities were *not* the same as those of London, Paris, and Berlin. Discussions about governments' obligations to house the poor—problematic as they were in Europe and (even more so) in the United States—did not arrive in colonies until much later, for the most part. But on top of that, class segregation in colonial cities reflected a much bigger, global form of economic segregation. During the course of the nineteenth century, imperial expansion, exploitation, and underdevelopment in the colonies created a widening "great gap" in wealth and economic power between the West and the rest of the world. As colonial cities became the capitals and economic centers of independent "Third World" countries, they were forced to absorb many more people, and much poorer people, than the cities in the imperial home countries. Today's megacities, with their enormous, separate penumbras of self-built housing, are the result—a bitter epitaph written upon the monumental colonial capitals that became the tombstones of Western empires.

# PART FOUR | THE ARCHSEGREGATIONISTS

# 8 ⋮ The Multifarious Segregation of Johannesburg

## Archsegregationism and the Wider World

By the 1960s, officials in Johannesburg, South Africa, had succeeded in putting in place the most ambitious and complex system of urban color lines in world history. Perhaps it was appropriate, then, that those boundaries should come to rest along the crests of not one, but two ranges of mountains.

Parallel to each other and about two miles apart, these two modest but redoubtable ridges, one natural, the other artificial, stretch from east to west along the northern and southern boundaries of the city's downtown and beyond. The northern, natural one is called the Witwatersrand, or the White Watershed. According to legend, South Africa's Afrikaans-speaking Boers (farmers) gave it that name because, from far away, storm water cascading down its slopes seemed to glint white in the sun. But the Rand was white in another way too. Its parallel broken ridges mark the beginning of the city's northern suburbs, a territory for the city's ruling middle- and upper-class elite and a zone exclusively intended for whites. The origins of these suburbs date to the 1890s, when the city's legendary gold barons, the Randlords, discovered that the Rand's rocky summits made excellent perches for their mansions. Looking north from Parktown, as the first of their hilltop neighborhoods was called, they got great views of the rolling waves of South Africa's high veldt. If you strained your eyes a little, the Randlords' wives were reputed to sigh, you could even see all the way "home," that is, to London's Park Row, where many of them owned second palaces. North was the direction of racial privilege in Johannesburg. Like the name of one gold baron's mansion, it was the "Sunnyside."

To the south, things got progressively less glamorous and sometimes even less sunny. The city's busy, workaday downtown, which lies at the foot the Rand's southern slopes, came into being as a dusty mine camp in 1886. That year, gold was discovered in what were then remote stretches of the Boers' independent South African Republic (Zuid-Afrikaansche Republiek, or ZAR). The heart of downtown was the feverish stock exchange on Commissioner Street, where clerks brokered the cross-continental flows of capital needed for the mines. It was not until after 1900, when the British seized the city during the Anglo-Boer War and when imperial officials abolished the ZAR and renamed it the Transvaal Colony, that Johannesburg got a proper town hall, on Market Square. There, the city's all-white elected officials debated the merits of segregationist ideas and tools from across the world and put them into practice locally.

Beyond downtown, things got markedly less pleasant. To the west was a slum that ZAR officials had set aside for the city's poor white Afrikaners, Indians, blacks, and mixed-race people known as coloreds. These "western areas"—along with other slums that ringed the southern underbelly of downtown—would become the city's primary racial battleground throughout the early twentieth century.

To the east of downtown were the city's first white working-class districts, consisting of small houses amid fading neighborhoods like Doornfontein and Jeppestown, which the elite had favored before they left for the ridge.

Along the southern edge of downtown, the city's second mountain range, the artificial one, rose slowly throughout the twentieth century in the form of enormous, bright-yellow piles of waste-earth known as the "mine dumps." For thirty miles in each direction from the city center stretches Johannesburg's reason for being: the outcrop of an enormous dish of gold ore that plunges southward from the surface deep into the earth's crust at a forty-five-degree angle. Amid the mine dumps could be found the pulley towers ("head gear") of the mine elevators, the loudly pounding ore-stamping machines, the busy freight yards, and, as the century drew on, the poisonous tailing ponds known as "slimes dams."

The much less desirable residential real estate on the south side of town made it ideal for dumping things other than mine waste. Amid the mines themselves, for example, the Randlords constructed their "compounds"—severe living places for the tens of thousands of migrant all-male black workers who descended into the mines in shifts every day and night. In 1904, the municipal council also decided to dump all the city's sewage in the southern reaches of town, spreading it across the fields of a "sewage farm" named Klipspruit beyond the mine belt, fifteen kilometers from downtown. Shortly after that decision, council ordered all blacks who did not live in compounds to move out to the farm as well, and the city established a new "native location" smack in the middle of the fields of sewage. This was the first of many black, colored, and Indian locations—later renamed "townships"—in the southwestern outskirts of Johannesburg. In 1962, they became collectively known as Soweto, a compressed version of the phrase "Southwestern Townships."

What created this immovable, mountain-anchored, archsegregationist, north-south divide? The most widely told story is that South Africa's system of segregation, renamed "apartheid" in 1948, was entirely homegrown, unique to an exceptionally racist society and culture. In this version of the story, the Boers, or Afrikaners, are usually cast as the crusty, aberrant villains. By trekking northeast in the 1830s beyond the boundaries of South Africa's original Cape of Good Hope Colony to flee British rule, the Boers isolated themselves from progress, even missing the entire eighteenth century and its age of Enlightenment. A version of Dutch Calvinism compounded their backwardness. Far out on the high veldt, in their two independent republics, the Orange Free State and the ZAR, they began to imagine themselves as a chosen people whose destiny was to rule their part of Africa—and especially the large numbers of Africans who lived there—with the furor of their angry God. When the supposedly more liberal British Empire intervened, the Boers responded only with increasing defiance, backwardness, and, finally, authoritarian ultranationalism. The progeny of this tradition were the grim-faced "architects" of segregation and apartheid: the National Party's J. B. M. Hertzog, the Reverend D. F. Malan, Professor Hendrick Verwoerd, and the "old crocodile" P. W. Botha. They and their ilk, the story goes, bulldozed people into racial pigeonholes, like Johannesburg's white suburbs and black townships, with the ultimate aim to divide the whole country by race, rural as well as urban. The plan was for blacks to disappear from the cities and even from South Africa itself—to their own independent countries in the countryside, carved out of land unwanted by white farmers.[1]

Not so, others argue. The gold-hungry, foreign, mostly English Randlords had laid out the blueprints of South Africa's unique tragedy decades before the Afrikaner nationalists came to power. Because of the steep subterranean incline of the great South African gold seam, the mining capitalists had to pay out ever greater sums for machinery and labor to get their gleaming quarry out of the earth. But the price of gold, unlike any other commodity in the world, remained more or less fixed, since the world's currencies were pegged to its value. Thus, the only way to make a profit was to keep labor costs drastically low by guaranteeing a steady stream of mine workers who would work for ever closer to rock-bottom wages, on ten-month contracts. That meant importing single African men from far away—and, during one bad period from 1904 to 1907, even shipping tens of thousands of Chinese "coolies" to the Rand. To make these migrant workers stay on the job—hammering away at solid rock on all fours, in hot tunnels far underground, amid explosions, collapsing shafts, and lung-wracking dust—the Randlords needed a government willing to enforce merciless labor contracts and pass laws. It also needed to sanction segregated, single-sex, all-black miners' compounds. Apartheid was the eventual result.

Both of these stories contain some truth. Afrikaner nationalists did invent the term "apartheid." And, after 1948—if not during the rule of the first nationalist prime minister, J. B. M. Hertzog from 1924 to 1939—their National Party pushed segregation with greater authoritarian vigor than at least some of their English-speaking (and Afrikaans-speaking) contemporaries found seemly. As for the Randlords, they were indeed unusual among heavy industrial capitalists in that they took a direct role in urban residential segregation, creating some of the most awful features of South Africa's color lines. The anxieties that pervaded a rapidly changing capitalist boomtown may have also created a more general need among whites for a sense of order that they resolved by means of segregation. But neither story comes close to explaining the unusually complex, extensive, and coercive array of government-sponsored measures that distinguished South African urban archsegregationism over the course of its century-long history.

Missing from both stories are the three earth-spanning institutions that split cities by race elsewhere in the colonial world. In the context of South African settlers' racial politics, which were at once especially arrogant and anxiety filled, these three institutions delivered particularly powerful segregationist impulses. The British Empire made the most important early contributions, and its officials are the primary characters in this first act of the drama. From 1900 to 1906, Alfred Milner, the high commissioner for South Africa, ran the Transvaal Colony directly. Milner's handpicked, English-speaking subordinates also directly ruled the city of Johannesburg from 1900 to 1903. Their record on racial segregation is sometimes underestimated, in part because they were not able to come close to fulfilling the expectations they raised. But it is important to remember that it was on Milner's orders that South African whites across all four of the colonies conducted their first in-depth discussions about their governments' obligation to deliver three overweening arch-segregationist goals: the "separate development" of blacks and whites in the countryside, the control of black "influxes" to the city, and the creation of permanently separated racial zones in urban areas.

It was Milner and his acolytes, most notably the energetic Lionel Curtis, who rammed through the first formal legislation to achieve these three goals, and they did so in the face of growing opposition elsewhere in the British Empire. After 1910, when all four of the colonies joined together to form the Union of South Africa, they did so with the expectation that the union's new system of nearly all-white parliamentary governments at the central, provincial, and municipal levels could and should follow up these initial efforts with even more effective legislation in the future.

It is a mistake to say that apartheid was inevitable by 1906, once these early precedents were set. During the ensuing decades, of course, no one knew precisely what that future would bring. A striking consensus did develop among white settlers across the union that segregation was necessary, especially within cities, but whites disagreed sharply about the means to achieve any one of the three abstract goals—and even whether all three were necessary, or even plausible. As a result, many different outcomes were possible along the way, including much less radical ones.

Still, once apartheid's creators began their work after 1948, they relied heavily on highly coercive tools bequeathed to them by earlier generations of government officials. Their toolbox of precedents included the rural native reserve system, the pass laws aimed to control influxes of nonworking black people to the cities, and the native location system in cities. During the Milner years, British officials committed themselves to strengthening all three of these precedents—one result being the fifteen-kilometer buffer, hardened by two mountain ranges, that by the height of apartheid separated the leafy, flower-spangled neighborhoods of white Johannesburg from Soweto and its pall of coal smoke.

The wider world supplied a multifarious array of elements to the segregationist politics of the Milner years. Milner and his subordinates—as well as the race theorists, urban reformers, real estate developers, mining capitalists, merchants, and ordinary Afrikaner and British settlers who helped push his segregationist initiatives along—drew upon ideas and practices from just about all the genres of city-splitting across the colonial world, as well as from the world's other newly aborning archsegregationist society, the United States.

The British Empire's own political objectives in Johannesburg were particularly elaborate themselves. Officials needed to establish basic social control over a place that had turned into a virtual ghost town during the Boer War. They needed to get the newly conquered gold mines back in operation so the local—and the imperial—economy could survive. To do that, they needed to restart the migrant labor system and to control the workers once they got to the Rand. But perhaps most importantly, imperial authorities felt South Africa's future depended on attracting more English-speaking white settlers to the Rand to ensure the Transvaal Colony's loyalty to the empire.

Pressing sanitary issues were also at stake. The plague had arrived in South Africa from Asia during the war, and British public health officials in Johannesburg were quick to import a particularly frenzied version of disease-scare segregation mania from other colonies.

Officials of the Transvaal Colony also self-consciously borrowed Pacific Rim–style legal tools to prevent migrations of Asians across the Indian Ocean to South Africa. That, in turn, enmeshed the colony—and Johannesburg itself—in the political dramas of the British Raj. Local Indians, under the leadership of a young lawyer named Mohandas K. Gandhi, demanded treatment in South Africa that accorded with standards the British granted to Indians living in India, including the right to own land and the right to engage in commerce. In this case, there was an additional twist, for in Johannesburg, European merchants did not collaborate with their local counterparts in overseas ventures as in India or West Africa. In the white settler society of South Africa, as in Kenya and the Rhodesias, Indians and whites competed over the urban white consumer market, and the urban segregation movement in places like Johannesburg took on the additional goal of weakening Indian merchants in favor of white ones.

South Africa's racial politics were also connected, in many contradictory ways, to those of the United States. On the one hand, American racial theorists, like their European counterparts, provided South Africans with much support for segregationist ventures. One of white South Africans' favorite American race thinkers was Booker T. Washington, the enormously successful director of the Tuskegee Institute in Alabama, a black man dedicated to the creed that blacks should "cast down their bucket where [they] are" and avoid the "agitations of questions of so-cial equality" in favor of industrial education aimed to slowly confirm the usefulness of the "Negro race" to society. On the other hand, South African whites deplored the fact that the United States had extended the vote to black people, and they were positively scandalized by other black leaders such as W. E .B. DuBois, who called on his fellow black elites to join with white liberals in a movement for guarantees of equal rights. South African whites even blamed American civil rights activists for racial unrest in South Africa itself. They complained that South Afri-can blacks who went to black universities in the United States brought back unacceptably radical ideas with them. American black mission-aries fomented discontent in South Africa's churches, most notably the forty-thousand-strong Methodist-based independent black church movement that coined the stirring call "Mayibuye iAfrika!" (Let Africa come back!). In the process, secular organizations like the South African Native National Congress (SANNC, later renamed the African National Congress or ANC) also soon came into being at almost exactly the same time as (but independently from) DuBois's National Association for the Advancement of Colored People (NAACP).[2]

South Africans whites, for their part, also shared a crucial legal and economic connection with their counterparts in the United States. Both settler communities played important roles in the British-led globaliza-tion of the world's urban real estate markets, and both drew on their con-nections to British legal institutions, developers, and political traditions to import segregationist tools, money, and even models of grassroots homeowner organizations into their respective societies. Cities like Johannesburg and Chicago became national clearinghouses for tech-niques that reengineered these imported devices in ways that sparked movements for racially exclusive neighborhoods that were unparalleled anywhere else in the colonial world.

In both South Africa and the United States, such movements would prove critical to the defining features of archsegregationist politics: their capability to sustain sharp color lines despite especially acute conflicts between whites; their ability to keep pace with rapid, industry-led urban growth that attracted especially significant migrations of black people toward the city; and their capacity to outlive the dramatic events of the era of decolonization, when racial segregation dwindled elsewhere in the world.

235

## Squaring Race and Civilization

Imperialism was the essential begetter of urban apartheid. It was British imperial officials who first mixed together the multifarious ideological, political, demographic, economic, and institutional ingredients of South African segregationist politics and established crucial, concrete precedents that inspired later, more radical movements.[3] This was most clear in Johannesburg after the British conquest in 1900, when Alfred Milner imported a group of young Englishmen, fresh out of Oxford University, to rebuild the city along British lines. Wags derisively dubbed these young recruits the "Kindergarten," but its members soon embraced the name as a means to promote their brand of imperial renewal. Milner and the Kindergarten were hardly a bunch of time-forgotten Boers lost on the high veldt. What kind of racism, then, went into making what became in its time the most complex and draconian form of urban segregation in the world?

The answer is somewhat surprising. The year 1900, it is safe to say, marked the absolute peak of Western imperial and racial chauvinism, the crest of what DuBois and Gandhi soon dubbed the "religion of whiteness." As the largely English-speaking white refugees from Johannesburg began returning to the newly conquered city during the first months of the Boer War, there was plenty of straight-up social Darwinism, eugenics, biological racism, and John Bull jingoism to go around. However, in the British Empire—as in the French one and even in the American one—the sheer extent of recent Western conquests around the world also provoked fervent crosstalk and even controversy about race and racial theory. Startling doubts began to rise in influential circles worldwide about the ability of the supposedly mighty Anglo-Saxon race to retain its global power and about the central role of race itself in the institutions of empires. For Alfred Milner and the Kindergarten, the local circumstances in South Africa and Johannesburg only reopened and intensified the questions involved.

In North America, the white advance across the continent had at first seemed to confirm social Darwinists' predictions of the survival of the fittest. White settlers had multiplied on the Great Plains, and the numbers of native peoples had drastically diminished, almost to the point, many thought, of extinction. But the same did not seem to be true of American blacks. For a while, the evidence from the United States seemed to show that the black population was actually increasing faster than white. Then, in a spectacular exposé, the New York Life Insurance Company adjuster Frederick Hoffman unveiled new data showing that blacks actually got deadly diseases at higher rates. Those who lived in cities were especially susceptible to the conditions that led to sickness. They were on the fastest road to what would soon be a general disappearance. The "vanishing Negro," though, did not seem to be vanishing all that quickly. For some, what Hoffman really demonstrated was that Africans were naturally a rural race who had no business living in cities, where they had fewer defenses against the urban moral and physical temptations that resulted in disease.

Meanwhile, there was no evidence at all to suggest that Asians were even close to dying out—as Californians, British Columbians, and Australians had long pointed out. From Melbourne, Australia, the bestselling racial theorist Charles Pearson lamented that "we are well aware that China can swamp us with a single year's surplus population." The plague had checked India's population but Indians were moving across the oceans in great numbers, as white plantation owners looked to replace black slaves with indentured coolie laborers, most notably in the Caribbean, in East Africa, and in the sugar cane fields of the South African colony of Natal.[4]

Charles Pearson went on to shock the world with a forthright critique of white racial triumphalism. For white audiences, his was a frightening and globe-spanning prognosis. Few "vacant" places remained in the temperate zones where whites could settle without encountering even larger native or immigrant darker populations. "The day will come, and perhaps is not far distant," he prophesied, with blurry but ultimately accurate foresight, "when the European observer will look round to see the globe girdled with a continuous zone of the black and yellow races, no longer too weak for aggression or under tutelage, but independent."[5]

For Pearson's friend James Bryce, an English politician, traveler, diplomat, and an even more influential racial theorist, Western civilization had brought this "crisis in the history of the world" upon itself. The West's technological advances had brought into being a new "world process—the extreme cheapness of transport due to recent scientific discovery" has made "the world small, and the fortunes of every race and state are now or may at any moment become involved with those of any other." Faced with this crisis of what we now call globalization, Bryce thought, whites in California, Australia, and Natal had shown great forethought in placing restrictions on immigration. But in places where interracial coexistence could not be prevented and where mass deportation was impractical, whites were faced with the alternatives of racial extinction, racial intermixture, absorption, or social separation. Only the last of these choices, segregation, presented any hope for whites' "self-preservation."[6]

For all his talk of segregation, Bryce considered himself a "liberal" in the long tradition that went back to John Stuart Mill. He was deeply concerned with the implications of increased population movement on whites' sacred obligations to develop the "backward" races. In late nineteenth-century London, the Aborigines Protection Society had assumed the mantle of the old abolitionist movement; many dubbed its liberal allies "Exeter Hall," after the venerable meeting place of antislavery activists. The society relentlessly critiqued colonial authorities' failures to make good on the empire's avowed pledge to "uplift" its nonwhite subjects. Imperialists like the colonial secretary Joseph Chamberlain in London and South Africa's Milner both began their careers as fervent liberals, but to them Exeter Hall was a synonym for nettlesome scolds whose critiques of the empire encouraged dangerous causes like the Indian National Congress and the Catholic-led Home Rule movement in Ireland. Such recklessness threatened to further weaken the resolve of what Chamberlain called "the greatest of the governing races."[7]

James Bryce was more sympathetic to Exeter Hall. His liberal credentials rested upon his bestselling book on American democratic institutions, which he hoped Britain would emulate. Three research trips to the United States as well as an earlier visit to India had taught him one hard lesson, however. Advancing the backward races *could* result in greater "friction" between them and their superiors, as darker-skinned peoples gained an awareness of their rights. For Bryce, exhibit A of this friction was the period of Reconstruction in the United States, when liberals, he thought, had mistakenly granted the vote to black men under the Fifteenth Amendment to the Constitution. Echoing contemporary American historians' racist interpretations of those events, Bryce argued that "excellent...intentions" had run into the "teeth of the facts." Most blacks were racially incapable of exercising self-rule. In power they had become corrupt and dictatorial. Then whites' instinct for self-preservation had kicked in, resulting in regrettably but inevitably brutal reprisals and lynchings.

More recently, Bryce was pleased to report, the US state of Mississippi had forged a wiser path by instituting a literacy test for voter registration. Because white registrars administered the test, they could bar blacks from voting, and almost all blacks were struck from the rolls. Most Southern states copied this system during the years that followed, and so did the British Cape Colony of South Africa, centered on Cape Town. There, a so-called Cape Liberal tradition held sway. To qualify for the vote, citizens had to possess property, a restriction that in principle applied to all races. In 1892, the Cape Colony legislature tightened this system by raising the amount of property a person had to own in order to vote, and also made voters demonstrate their intellectual capacity for self-rule by passing a literacy test, the inspiration for which came directly from Mississippi. The other British-run South African colony, Natal, had an even more restrictive "color blind" voting law. In both cases such laws by design disproportionately affected blacks and coloreds; in Natal they essentially disfranchised the colony's large Indian population.

Still, hidden within ideas about property qualifications and literacy tests there was at least a theoretical challenge to the idea of fixed races. The system implicitly denounced the voting laws of the neighboring Boer republics of the Orange Free State and the ZAR, which allowed all whites to vote regardless of property but summarily disfranchised all blacks, coloreds, and Indians. As Bryce put it, "race and blood should not be made the ground of discrimination" in voting. Instead, citizenship in the empire should rest on the degree of civilization. Queen Victoria herself had given official imprimatur to this obligation after the Indian mutiny in 1858, when she proclaimed that all her subjects there should be "freely and impartially admitted to offices in our service, the duties of which they may be qualified, by their education."[8]

That said, the civilization standard did not mean giving up on the concept of race—as Bryce's writings suggested and as the official rhetoric of British India had long maintained. Justifications for empire could be enhanced by juxtaposing talk of races, which did not change—or which changed only over hundreds or thousands of years—and civilization, which, many thought, native peoples could acquire through education. While *race* justified continued white rule, *civilization* gave that rule a sense of grandeur and noblesse oblige. And while "civilization" gave some natives room for personal advancement, "race" could close that advancement down when necessary. Most important, as Bryce calculated, the combination guaranteed racial peace in a world where the racial contact was growing ubiquitous. It cooled whites' racial outrage by denying privileges to most darker-skinned people while at the same time ensuring that the empire did not "wound and alienate the whole of the coloured race by placing them without the pale of civic functions and duties."[9]

In politics, James Bryce had drifted far from Alfred Milner. As a member of Parliament, Bryce, like the Exeter Hall liberals, bitterly opposed the conquest of the Transvaal and the Orange Free State during the Anglo-Boer war. The British Empire, Bryce raged, had once been the greatest force for human good. Now it had embarked on a contrived and greedy grab for some gold fields. Along the way, it crushed two independent white democracies—and only managed that feat by burning thousands of high-veldt farmsteads to the ground and by impounding tens of thousands of Boer women and children in concentration camps. Though Milner, the self-styled "out-and-out imperialist," deeply resented such tongue-lashings from liberal London, he sensed the whiff of practical politics in Bryce's delicate juggling of race and civilization and thought it might be worth trying in the dangerous terrain of postwar South Africa.

## A Keystone of Global Anglo-Saxondom

"A great Johannesburg," Milner proclaimed in 1902 (as Boer farms smoldered nearby), "great in intelligence, in cultivation, and in public spirit—means a British Transvaal." Indeed, the importance of the city went even beyond that, for Milner's mission in South Africa was a global one—restoring the "undivided strength of the British race throughout the world." Echoing Pearson and Bryce, Milner had long worried that the far-flung white colonies of the empire, Canada, Australia, New Zealand, and South Africa, had become "scattered communities." By seeking greater autonomy, they had put a strain on the great mission of British imperialism, that is, "the maintenance of civilised conditions of existence among one fifth of the human race."

Of the British settler colonies, South Africa was the "weakest link in the imperial chain" that Milner hoped to reforge. In the Transvaal, the newest and richest British South African colony, the British "race" itself made up only a minority of the population, outnumbered by a Dutch "race" that was "congenitally" less attached to the purposes of empire. "I attach the greatest importance to the increase of the British population,"

Milner wrote to London in 1900. "If ten years hence there are three men of British race to two of Dutch, the country will be safe and prosperous. If there are three of Dutch and two of British, we shall have perpetual difficulty." Johannesburg, the City of Gold—again, made "great in intelligence, in cultivation, and in public spirit"—would have to shoulder the burden of attracting the British race to the high veldt.[10]

The problem was that in 1902, as one member of the Kindergarten put it, Johannesburg amounted to "simply the veldt with the grass rubbed off by passing vehicles." Strictly speaking, of course, there was much more to it than that: the Randlords' enormous mansions already strutted arrogantly along the Parktown ridge; Milner himself had moved into Sunnyside. The opulent Wanderer's Club had reopened for business and so had the stock exchange and some of the mines. However, before the war, the Boer ZAR, under the redoubtable president Paul Kruger, had tried to keep the largely English-speaking *uitlander* (foreign) population of the city powerless. Until 1898, Johannesburg had no municipal government at all, only a sanitary committee largely staffed by Kruger's cronies. With little taxing power, that mere shred of a political body had done little to keep up a city that still looked, and smelled, a lot like a mining camp.[11]

The worst part of town lay to the west of the central business district, at the foot of the Parktown ridge, barely a mile and a half from Sunnyside itself. This was lower-lying ground, swampy, clayey, and prone to flooding. In 1887, ZAR authorities had selected this unpropitious spot for what they called the "Coolie Location"—named after the country's favorite epithet for Indians—under its Law 3 of 1885, which prohibited "Asiatic" landownership except in "such streets, wards, and locations" as the government chose for "purposes of sanitation." This decision represented the most direct impact of Boer policy on the residential color lines of early Johannesburg. (It should be noted, however, that in enacting Law 3, the republic's Volksrad had borrowed the term "location" from the native settlements established by the British in the Cape Colony. The sanitary justification hardly suggested a people isolated from global currents of urban thought.) In addition to the Coolie Location, the surveyor general also laid out a couple thousand plots in two neighborhoods for destitute "Burghers," the name for Afrikaans-speaking citizens of the ZAR, many of whom made their living by firing bricks from the local clay for use in downtown buildings. Appropriately, these neighborhoods were called Burghersdorp and Brickfields. A little farther out the government also gave land for another Afrikaner neighborhood called Vrededorp (Village

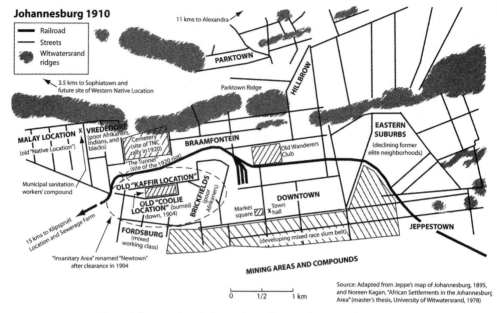

FIGURE 8.1 The racial geography of Johannesburg showing the intensification of efforts to divide the city by race that occurred between the Milner era and the Natives (Urban Areas) Act. Map by Kailee Neuner.

of Peace). Finally, in 1893, the government set aside further blocks of stands for Cape Coloreds and blacks, based upon British precedent—no ZAR law called for them. Consistent with the practice of using racial insults as names for such places, they were called the Malay Location, for coloreds, and the Kaffir Location, for "natives."[12]

On May 8, 1901, Milner issued Proclamation 16 endowing Johannesburg with a British-style municipal government. Over the next two years he appointed twenty-five prominent residents of the city as town councilors, almost all of them men of British descent who lived on the Parktown Ridge. To keep the council on task, he gave the most energetic member of the Kindergarten, Lionel Curtis, the humble title of Acting Town Clerk of Johannesburg.

Curtis's background made him a somewhat unusual candidate to run a town full of right-wingers. As a student he had dressed up in old dirty clothes and for several months wandered amid the country towns of East Anglia in an effort to empathize with the life of England's "tramps." Later, he helped organize a settlement house in London's East End, where he met some of the world's foremost housing reformers, including Octa-

242

via Hill, and thus grew familiar with Exeter Hall society. For a short while he was also personal secretary to a high official at the London County Council, where he deepened his understanding of the worldwide networks of urban reformism at the very source of their greatest legislative innovations.

When the Boer War broke out, however, Curtis followed the path of Chamberlain and Milner and enlisted on the side of the empire just as it embarked on one of its most belligerent crusades. After serving in a bicycle-mounted reconnaissance unit, Curtis approached Milner with his London credentials and quickly received the Johannesburg post. While Curtis's continued liberal scruples and his imperial chauvinism—as well as his energetic use of enormous powers—made him odious to many ordinary white Johannesburgers, he wasted little time in helping them and the handpicked town council organize a white supremacist city unparalleled anywhere else in the world—except arguably in other South African fonts of segregationism like Cape Town and Durban.[13]

Despite the risk of running into stray Boer commandos, Curtis began his new responsibilities by setting out on horseback through the grasslands surrounding the city, plotting out a boundary that would increase the size of the new municipality from five to eighty-two square miles. His main goal derived directly from the housing reforms of Octavia Hill but also fit the racial task at hand: to provide enough space for a "house in its own standing garden" for every British immigrant who came to the city, whether middle class or former London slum dweller.

Meanwhile, the town council declared a big part of the west side of town—including parts of the Afrikaner neighborhoods and the three locations—an "Insanitary Area" and asked for Milner's approval to expropriate the zone in preparation for demolition. At a moment when the plague was killing off thousands in Cape Town, "habitations for Native and oriental races as well as for the poorer classes of Europeans have been allowed to accumulate regardless of . . . health and decency. . . . We have within a short distance of the Market Square a quarter . . . comparable only to eastern cities not subject to European regulation." Finally, as Curtis himself urged in 1901, it was time to overhaul the Boer government's weak commitment to urban segregation: "the Council must set its face against the principle of allowing Natives to remain scattered beyond the limits of the Location." The city should write up clear bylaws for the locations and hire a professional locations manager to enforce them.[14]

The design for the new urban keystone of British South Africa, and the arc of empire, was becoming clear: for Johannesburg to become a global magnet for Britons, the city would have to consist of much more Parktown and much less "Insanitary Area." And a high, bright-shining color line would have to separate one from the other.

## The Birth of "Separate Development"

But what about the empire this keystone was meant to hold aloft? As Curtis and the council got to work, it was the turn of national and global concerns to cast shadows upon the dramas of municipal politics. As the war between the two white races drew to a close, attention shifted to larger-scale solutions to the "native problem" and the "Asiatic problem." Once again people began talking about race, civilization, and the possibility of racial "development."

In Parliament, people like James Bryce, egged on by Exeter Hall, hoped that the blood-soaked victory in the Anglo-Boer War would at least allow the empire to regain a bit of its moral standing through a renewed push for humane treatment of the natives of the Transvaal. On the top of liberals' wish list was the extension of the "nonracial" property- and education-based Cape franchise northward into former Boer territory. At the Vereeniging Peace Conference in 1902, however, the Boer generals Jan Christian Smuts and Louis Botha resisted this demand, and they pushed Milner to postpone the franchise question until after the Transvaal and the Orange River Colony received white home rule. When Milner agreed to this compromise, with Chamberlain's assent, both were fully aware that they had virtually guaranteed a race-based whites-only electorate for the new northern colonies, not just because the Boers would overwhelmingly oppose the Cape system, but because most English-speaking residents of the Transvaal, and probably of South Africa as a whole, were against it too. After all, the first section of the conquered Transvaal to get an elected government was the largely English-speaking city of Johannesburg, in 1903. There, Milner's own appointed council resoundingly opposed admission of black, colored, or Indian voters to the rolls no matter how much "civilization" they could demonstrate. Hoping to resolve this and many other differences on native-affairs policy, Milner appointed Godfrey Lagden head of the South African Native Affairs Commission (SANAC), which toured the four colonies over the next two years, gathering opinions. In so doing he also sparked South Africa's first cross-colonial conversation about rural segregation, "influx control," and urban segregation.[15]

Similar dynamics were at play in Indian affairs. Before the war, the English-speaking residents of the colony of Natal had outmaneuvered a determined protest movement led by Indian merchants and their lawyer, Mohandas Gandhi, and successfully imposed Australian-style immigration restrictions and other discriminatory laws. In defeat, Gandhi had returned to India in hopes of obtaining support from the Indian National Congress, but the organization could do little to help, whipsawed as it was by reprisals after the Bombay and Calcutta plague uprisings. The India Office in London, however, was worried about repercussions of South African Indian politics upon the crown jewel of the empire, and Exeter Hall was taking notice as well. To appease these forces, Milner seems to have hoped at least to soften the provisions of the ZAR's 1885 "coolie locations" Law 3. British merchants on the Rand, however, feared competition from Indians; the Johannesburg Chamber of Commerce pronounced itself dead set against allowing "Asiatic traders" to live and trade anywhere in the city. Milner's subordinates, including Lagden and the Johannesburg Town Council, began discussing a new system of euphemistically named "Asiatic bazaars" for the Transvaal that would be located even further outside the colony's towns and that would put Indian merchants at an even greater disadvantage. Joseph Chamberlain himself came to South Africa in late 1902 to take the pulse of this potentially explosive situation. Gandhi returned from his sojourn in India to South Africa to meet Chamberlain in person. The new opportunities for Indian protest in Johannesburg would keep Gandhi in the city until 1914. Though his main battles would focus on other issues, he repeatedly insisted on Indians' right to freely own land, a right they had enjoyed securely in India under British rule since the 1600s.[16]

On May 18, 1903, seeking to bridge the widening gap between British racial politics in the Transvaal and liberal talk of civilization elsewhere in the empire, Milner delivered his famous Watchtower speech in Johannesburg. After a few laugh lines about the "claptrap of Exeter Hall," the high commissioner went directly to the heart of the matter. There was "an opposite sort of claptrap" coming from Johannesburg, and it began with people basing their politics on "the rotten and indefensible ground of colour." He urged his subjects to raise themselves above this parochial mindset and take up the more elevated, pan-imperial point of view of the "man on the watchtower." From that high perspective, he argued, "there is only one ground on which we can justify" white supremacy,

> and that is the ground of superior civilization. . . . The white man must rule, . . . because that is the only possible means of gradually raising the black man, not to our level of civilization—which it is doubtful whether he would ever attain—but up to a much higher level than that which he at present occupies. . . . if a black man, one in a thousand—perhaps it would be more correct to say one in a hundred thousand—raises himself to the average white level, . . . are you going to put back the whole progress of civilization by banging [him] on the head?[17]

Did Milner himself believe this? Or was he merely burnishing his legacy as a high-minded statesman? It is hard to know, but—its strong theoretical words aside—the Watchtower speech did not proscribe any specific changes in South African municipal policy. Milner quietly accepted the whites-only municipal franchise that his council had just passed, despite his vague request that Transvaal towns accord educated natives, coloreds, and Indians their "municipal rights."[18]

While Lionel Curtis and the council continued to coolly hack away at those very rights, one member of the new ruling group in Johannesburg offered a theoretical basis for what they were doing. Howard Pim had made his living in Johannesburg as a mining company accountant since 1889, and in 1903 Milner appointed him to a seat on the council, apparently hoping to tap his financial expertise. Born in Ireland of Quaker parents, Pim also spent time in Boston, Massachusetts. For all of this, he might have been expected to sympathize more with Exeter Hall than with his white supremacist townsmen. In fact, later in his career, he became known as a major advocate for better treatment of Johannesburg's blacks. But as town councilor, Pim drew on fifteen years of reading on the "native question" to offer a point-by-point refutation of the liberal position on race and civilization. Two months before the Watchtower speech, he rose to the podium of the Transvaal Philosophical Society and began with a veiled warning: "To us in South Africa, the Native question is not an academic one, and to discuss it is not, as the Basutos would say, to go in fabulous pursuit of the birds of the sea. It is a matter for us of very practical politics, . . . of vital importance not only to ourselves but also our children. [Unlike] for the other parts of the Empire, . . . the reponsibility [sic], and the toil, and the danger are ours, and we cannot shirk them if we would."[19] Having stated the case for local knowledge, Pim proceeded to draw freely from the work of racial theorists from Europe, Australia, and above all the United States. Whites' ability to develop the native races was extremely limited, he argued, because the real driving forces involved were physiological. As scientists had proved, "the mental differences between the Native and White man are . . . at least as marked as his physical differences." More important, though, "there is natural aversion far deeper than reason between the Native and the White man," which would limit the contact essential for any long-term development. That aversion would also force whites to compel "the man of colour to his place again" if natives "attain any semblance of equality in capacity or education" or if "his inferiority in any one respect appear[s] open to question." Such white prejudice may not be "admirable," but "no one who has the welfare of this country at heart will attempt to ignore it."[20]

In 1903, Pim was not yet sure whether there really was a "final solution"—as he put it, ominously—to this intractable situation. But a year later, when the South African Native Affairs Commission came to Johannesburg, Pim told Godfrey Lagden that a system of "separate communities" for natives was critical. Impressed, Lagden suggested that Pim give an address to the Johannesburg meeting of the British Association for the Advancement of Science in 1905, the highlight of a prolonged group tour of South Africa by many of Britain's elite academics. There, Pim responded directly to Milner's "rotten ground of color" comment in the Watchtower speech and even upbraided the greatest of all British liberals, John Stuart Mill. "What is meant by civilization?" Pim asked the congregation of luminaries. "Is it what our fathers have worn for us by thousands of years of effort and renunciation, or is it what the individual native acquires who is taken from his kraal and trained for a few years under white teachers?" The escalating race war in the United States was the clearest evidence that South Africa could only ignore fundamental racial inequality and conflict at its peril. To prove this, Pim treated his listeners to a devious collage of quotations from W. E. B. DuBois's just-published book, *The Souls of Black Folk*, which made it seem that even DuBois agreed that blacks naturally sought to develop separately from whites (DuBois explicitly rejected this point elsewhere in the text). Then, quoting another passage in which DuBois calls for a new generation of black leaders, Pim sniffed, "I ask if it can be taken as anything more or less than a cry for the reestablishment of the chieftainship, for a reversion to a modified version of a tribal system." DuBois thus became, for Pim, the embodiment of the false promise of racial development. In another speech he quoted a moving passage from *Souls* about the inner torments of black intellectuals in a racist land. In "such an outburst," Pim retorted, "in spite of its extravagance," DuBois recognized "that in all the essentials of social life the native and white races must remain apart. And he feels it, resents it passionately, and yet knows that the line is laid down by an inexorable fate." Pim's favorite authority by far on race relations was DuBois's rival, Booker T. Washington. Faced with a country inhabited not by one but by many different native races, Pim averred, Washington's "wise and clumsy words come home to us" in South Africa: "'we can begin in no wiser way to develop any race than by beginning just where the race finds itself in the moment of beginning.'"[21]

For Pim, the precedents for a "uniform native policy" in all four colonies of South Africa, based on Washingtonian principles, were already in place. Officials had long set aside rural land for blacks as "native reserves"—a policy that resembled the Indian reservations of North America. Only by extending this system and segregating the entire South African countryside, where most blacks lived, could whites and blacks benefit from a policy of separate racial development. Lagden agreed with Pim, as did the rest of the Native Affairs Commission. Lagden's previous post had been resident commissioner of Basutoland (today's Lesotho), the small mountainous protectorate the British had established in 1884 to prevent the Boers and other African peoples from seizing the land of the southern Sotho (or Basotho, as they were known at the time). Though completely surrounded by the four white colonies and republics of South Africa, the Sotho had retained many of their institutions in an indirect-rule arrangement with the British. Unlike the Zulu, whose territory had been incorporated into Natal and who launched a major rebellion in 1906 that some deemed the work of American-style radical black churches, the Basutos lived in racial peace.[22]

Basutoland, the peaceful and semi-independent racial homeland, helped Pim and Lagden give a patina of humanitarianism to their rejection of racial liberalism. Other members of the Kindergarten jumped on board, as did the rapidly emerging Afrikaner parties. Rural segregation rose to the top of the national agenda shortly after the foundation of the Union of South Africa in 1910. In 1913, the Native Affairs Commission's recommendations for a Union-wide system of separate rural native locations became law under the infamous Native Lands Act, which reserved an overwhelming percentage of the country's best land for whites while confining blacks to the ancestors of apartheid's so-called independent homelands and Bantustans.

In 1906, Pim summed up the drift of his thinking in a paper he delivered to the Fortnightly Club, a gathering of the veterans of Milner's appointed council, the Kindergarten, and their friends, which met every other week in a succession of the members' Parktown homes. In closing, Pim rejected James Bryce and Charles Pearson's worries that disappearance of "physical barriers between nations" meant that "differences of race disappeared with them.... Though the great cauldron of the American Union may seem to be an exception, I am convinced they will reassert themselves, and that the future will lie with those nations that keep themselves clean, independent, self-sufficing, and self-contained."[23]


## From Labor Control to "Influx Control"

Pim's separate development theory left out the matter of cities. In fact, his idea rested heavily on the old Evangelical antiurban cliché that true wholesomeness could only be found in the countryside. White South Africans widely believed that natives were a "rural race" and that they were particularly vulnerable to the temptations and "stimulations" of urban life. To support this point they often alluded to the research of the American insurance adjuster Frederick Hoffman, as Pim did in his 1905 address. For Pim, though, the key was that life on the farm best accorded with natives' particular path of development. "In a [rural] reserve ... the native lives under natural conditions which he understands and has created himself.... Can it be supposed that the [urban] Location is as healthy a dwelling place as the natives' own surroundings? Certainly any interference with his custom is not likely to improve the generations that are to come."[24]

Such ideas did not sit well with urban whites who hired native labor—least of all the Randlords of Johannesburg. As the gold mines geared up for production in the years after the war, their "native problem" was the reverse of Pim's—how to keep natives *in* the city or, more accurately, down in the mine shafts during the day and in the compounds at night. Solving that problem was even more fundamentally important to Milner's grand imperial plans than gussying up Johannesburg. If the mines made no profit, after all, the city would simply sink back into the veldt. In

1902, when one of Lionel Curtis's fellow Kindergarten members was able to acquire a "Memorandum of Understanding" with the Portuguese authorities in Mozambique for a supply of native laborers, Curtis reported in his diary that "the mines are in transports of delight." A year later, though, as black wages declined, thousands of migrant workers voted with their feet, returning to the reserves or their homes elsewhere in Southern Africa. In 1904, Milner and the Randlords engineered a hubristic plan to import several tens of thousands of Chinese coolies through Hong Kong on long-term ultralow-wage contracts to get the mines going full steam again.[25]

These plans naturally made Exeter Hall furious. The Chinese labor scheme smelled much too much like slavery, and the outcry it created in London helped topple the conservative government that had sent Milner to South Africa (Howard Pim opposed importing the Chinese because it created yet another insoluble axis of racial contact). For liberals, though, coolie importation was only slightly worse than the system of passes that the Randlords used—courtesy of ZAR law—to keep track of their African laborers. These laws, whose origins did in fact go back to South Africa's slavery era, forced migrant black laborers to carry a sometimes bewildering array of identifying documents whenever they traveled, or moved between different parts of the city, or went out at night. The passes, which natives had to be able to produce on demand, contained information about their employment status, and they helped police identify and apprehend anyone who "deserted" from their long-term contracts.[26]

In 1901, the Aborigines Protection Society in London sent the colonial office a vehement denunciation of the ZAR pass laws, characterizing them as instruments of forced labor. From South Africa, Milner replied with some exasperation that he had already assigned Godfrey Lagden the task of ridding the system of abuses—which included pass officers who forced applicants into a period of personal service in exchange for their documents, as well as floggings for people who left work before their contracts were up. Still, Milner made it clear that these passes were an essential mechanism of social control, one that went beyond enforcement of labor contracts. "The root idea of the old Pass Law was not a wrong one. If aboriginal natives are to come and go in large numbers in search of labour, and to reside for considerable periods in the midst of a white community, there must be some passport system, else the place will be a pandemonium."[27]

In this way, the pass laws were also meant to complement a practice of urban race segregation that was explicitly designed for the control of migrant laborers: the compounds. These too had roots in slavery-era laws that forced slave owners to provide shelter in their own households for their human property. During the 1870s, municipal laws in the diamond mining town of Kimberley required similar accommodations for black diggers. When large corporations took over Kimberley's mines in the 1880s, they followed these laws by building what they called "closed compounds," large walled facilities containing numerous bunkhouses that were reminiscent, in scale at least, of the Dutch United East India Company's eighteenth-century slave lodge in Cape Town. Employers claimed that these facilities, which may have been also inspired by similar diamond mining compounds in Brazil, allowed them numerous advantages: to keep migrant black workers from fleeing before their contracts were up, to use convict labor, to regulate alcohol consumption, and to strip-search all their workers after each shift to recover stolen diamonds. The compounds also helped the companies' efforts to divide white and black miners, who had joined together in a major strike at the diamond fields in 1884. In subsequent years, mine owners, who had initially hoped to compound white workers as well as blacks, instead helped provide better housing facilities for whites to promote the idea that white workers' interests were different than those of blacks.[28]

In Johannesburg, the Randlords erected similar, if generally more open, compounds all along the gold reef, above all to enforce the seasonal contracts of their low-wage African migrant mine workers. These represent the Randlords' signal contribution, in their capacity as lords of labor, to the residential segregation of the city (they would make other contributions in their lesser-known role as lords of real estate). What was, for the mine owners, an essential cost of doing business became a kind of "best practice" among public officials eager to prevent "pandemonium" in a city dependent upon the labor of "aboriginal natives." The Johannesburg municipality, a large-scale employer of black migrant labor in its own right, erected compounds throughout town for its sanitation workers, construction gangs, gardeners, and maintenance crews, as well as for the "wash-boys" who worked at municipal laundry-washing facilities. The council also required other private employers, from smaller non-mining companies to employers of domestic servants, to provide worker housing on site.[29]

Clearly, though, compounds and other onsite workers' lodging could not be counted upon either to house or to control all of the city's Africans, let alone its Indians and coloreds. Most of the city's smaller-scale employers did not share the Randlords' economic incentive to establish compounds, and few could afford them. They sought and received exemptions from the on-site requirement, and their employees took lodgings in the city's western locations or in the more convenient slum belt that grew just south of downtown. In those places, they were joined by a small number of black, Indian, and colored professionals, a larger number of Indian merchants, other self-employed tradespeople of all colors, cab drivers and other service workers, day laborers, illegal-liquor traders, prostitutes, criminals, and large numbers of unemployed people. All of these categories of people could include recent migrants, and many were in violation of the pass laws.

In 1903, when Lionel Curtis returned to Johannesburg after a trip to attend to his health and relatives in England, he set to work on regulations for precisely this population. He had left the position of town clerk to fellow kindergartner Richard Feetham, and he now worked for the Transvaal colony as assistant colonial secretary for urban affairs. His job was to draft model legislation for municipal governments across the colony, and it was for this purpose that he helped organize the Municipal Conference in May 1903—the one at which Milner delivered his Watchtower speech. Officials at the conference wanted to ensconce into law some of the basic principles of the mining companies' migrant-labor and compound system and to generalize them to all Africans, if not to Asians and coloreds as well. Curtis's first task was to legislate the principle of "influx control," that is, to extend the mission of the pass laws to limit the number of nonwhites who resided in the city to the number needed by white employers. The second task was to write up municipal bylaws for native locations—in effect municipally run, larger-scale, and more distantly segregated labor compounds for "natives not living on the premises of their employer."[30]

The use of pass laws for influx control embodied a kind of compromise between Pim's idea that Africans were essentially a rural race and employers' desire to attract large numbers of native laborers to the city. Section 2 of Curtis's Native Pass Laws for municipalities stated the principle boldly: "No native shall be allowed to reside or remain within the limits of the Municipality ... unless he is in bona fide employment." New arrivals had six days to find work or move on. Later on, this principle would be refined as the so-called Stallard Doctrine, named for Colonel C. F. Stallard, an associate of Curtis and a regular at the Fortnightly Club.

Stallard's 1921 commission report on town government was a kind of magna carta of influx control well into the apartheid years.[31]

Curtis did not invent the Stallard Doctrine in 1902 by himself. In the Cape Colony, urban legislation had long treated natives as "strangers" and as "temporary" residents of towns. Pass laws there had been married to vicious vagrancy laws since at least the 1880s, and municipalities in other colonies had similar provisions. However, Curtis's clause 2 does signal the arrival of an important set of characters on the stage of South African urban segregationism: activist municipal governments answerable to often vigilant ratepayers who regarded excess natives in town as an undue financial burden.[32]

Curtis's 1903 Watchtower conference inspired the foundation of the Transvaal Municipal Association (TMA), which, under the presidency of Johannesburg town clerk Richard Feetham, lobbied Curtis and his colleagues in provincial offices for reforms designed either to reduce local governments' expenses from black influx or increase their revenues from passes. The TMA was unable to get some of its highest-priority wishes. For example, the Transvaal Colonial Office nixed the TMA's call for passes for black women and fourteen-year-olds as a means to discourage families from leaving the reserves. Such a policy, provincial officials thought, was too likely to provoke the wrath of black men and London liberals. Conversely, when the TMA sought to raise more revenue by offering extensions to the six-day work-search limit at a shilling a day, the province rebuked municipalities for even contemplating "loafing certificates" that would encourage more migration. The actual enforcement of influx control was well beyond the capacity of both the fledgling municipalities and the province, and of all the big segregationist principles first formalized during the Milner years, its implementation was the scantiest. However, the TMA and its allied British-style, grassroots ratepayer organizations were only beginning to flex their muscles. In time, Johannesburg would get its more restrictive passes, and much more influx control machinery as well.[33]

Influx control, we must remember, was not solely a South African invention. British, French, and Belgian colonial officials in other parts of Africa also used migrant-labor systems tied to seasonal contracts, identification documents, labor camps, compounds, and *villes indigènes*. South Africa's recruitment networks soon even overlapped with those in the mining districts of Northern Rhodesia and the Belgian Congo.

In addition, influx control was seen as a regional version of much wider efforts to engineer and restrict cross-oceanic and cross-border migration. Lionel Curtis himself embodied the connection between influx control and Pacific-style oceanic segregation. Less than two years after his work on the pass laws, he helped draft the notorious Asiatic Registration Act, known as the "Black Act," which forced all Indians to register with local authorities and submit a full set of fingerprints—a clear effort to supplement the Transvaal's ever stricter restrictions on Indian immigration. Though Curtis complained to his superiors that the law discriminated against people who were British subjects, the demographic engineer in him was won over by arguments that the white Transvaal was in danger of being "swamped." As Mohandas Gandhi began a new passive resistance campaign against the Black Act, he too perceived the connections between the multiplying manias to master regional and global migration. The law, he said uncharitably, "reduced Indians to a level lower than the Kaffirs."[34]

## Grandparents of the Group Areas

If the pass laws were destined to be the most hated aspect of South African segregation, the apartheid-era Group Areas Act of 1950 would become the central symbol of South Africa's uniquely ruthless urban-planning politics. Lionel Curtis's native locations bylaws for the Transvaal, which he hoped to extend to Indians and coloreds, represented an early effort to solidify some of the legal principles that later made their way into the Group Areas Act. In Johannesburg, these precedents were also tied to early experiments in two hallmark practices: forced removals and permanent, government-guaranteed white racial zones.

Thanks in part to Curtis's efforts, the South African concept of the urban native location became ever more intertwined with the systems of compounds and passes. However, the locations had separate and more recent historical roots. If compounds and passes owed their origins to slavery, native locations were instead intimately connected to the British Empire's prolonged and bloody wars of conquest waged against the Xhosa people on behalf of white settlers on the Cape colony's eastern frontiers. The first locations came into being in the two cities closest to the battle lines of these wars and thus suggest some direct influence of South Africa's frontier upon at least one aspect of urban segregation. As early as 1834 in the rapidly growing town of Port Elizabeth, Lutheran missionaries established a location to house and convert black people fleeing from frontier conflicts. In 1847 the town formalized a "Native Stranger's Location," though it took some years before the Cape parliament allowed the municipality to actually move people there. In East London—which lay a hundred and fifty miles further east and much closer to the frontier hostilities—military considerations dictated an effort in 1849 to confine natives to locations. The remotest ancestors of Group Areas thus contain elements both of the praying towns or missions for Indians in New England or French Canada and of divided colonial towns like Madras. Sanitary concerns and the desire to claim choice urban land for whites gave rise to forced relocations in the ensuing decades in both Port Elizabeth and East London. Farther to the east, the town council of Durban, the capital of Natal, also used a sanitary rationale to confine the city's growing Indian population—which consisted of formerly indentured coolie laborers from the sugarcane fields and a growing merchant community—to a location in 1871. These examples probably helped inspire the ZAR's Law 3 confining all Indian landownership in the Transvaal to what the Boers called *locatie*, in imitation of the British.[35]

As elsewhere in the colonial world, it was the arrival of bubonic plague in 1901 that set off the first nationwide bout of urban segregation mania in South Africa. Next to Bombay and Hong Kong, Cape Town was affected by the plague more than any other city in the world. Its segregationist response was also among the most vigorous. There had been relatively little interest in racial zoning in the city up to that point, and the town's mixed residential patterns resembled many other former slave cities in the Atlantic world. Once the first of thousands of plague cases were discovered, authorities rounded up most members of the city's small African community and moved them to a hastily built camp at Uitvlugt (Outflow), a desolate spot nine kilometers from town next to the end of the city's sewage pipe. When the city sought to charge rent there, Alfred Mangena, a local activist and future founder of the SANNC, helped organize demonstrations that at one point involved four hundred stick-wielding residents, demanding better conditions and improved transport to work in town. By 1902, Uitvlugt got a more euphonious name, Ndabeni. Only somewhat better housing was built over the next few years, but native affairs commissioner Godfrey Lagden considered it a "model" permanent native location.[36]

In Johannesburg, members of the appointed town council closely followed these events in Cape Town and similar dramas over the next two years in Port Elizabeth and Durban. As early as 1898 under the ZAR, the city's English-speaking health committee chair reported that "for some years past attempts have been made to rid the Town of the number of Arabs, Coolies, and other colored races which now unfortunately infest it, but without any good results." Shortly after the conquest of the city, British authorities identified the multiracial slum to the west of the city as a plague spot. To prevent the arrival of the disease into the city, the council's health committee, with Lionel Curtis working behind the scenes, invoked Britain's Housing of the Working Classes Act of 1890 as justification for a proposal to expropriate a big part of the dilapidated areas that lay nearest downtown, including the entire Coolie Location and mixed-race Brickfields. This was a bold and expensive act for such a fledgling municipality. For Indians, it would mean the surrender of the only neighborhood where they could legally own land. Milner, not an advocate of government land seizure on most days, sent the proposal to a commission, which delayed the project another year before giving its blessing. In 1903, the council's finance committee, which included mining accountant Howard Pim, signed off on the scheme based on the unlimited future value of the area, and the city became the owner of a festering slum for a staggering 1.2 million pounds.[37]

The use of one of British liberal reformers' favorite pieces of legislation to expropriate a multiracial neighborhood was a bit of a coup for Johannesburg's right-wingers at a time when even London's slum-clearance programs were barely underway. However, they immediately faced a problem that would bedevil later South African segregationists. The Housing of the Working Classes Act forbade municipalities from clearing slums until they provided for adequate replacement housing. A sound reason underlay this provision: without new housing, slum dwellers simply relocated to other neighborhoods, expanding the problems the clearances were meant to solve. For this same reason, Curtis and town clerk Richard Feetham dug into the task of drafting native locations bylaws for the Transvaal, a process that, at Lagden's urging, took them on a visit to Cape Town's Ndabeni in early 1904. Milner and Lagden, meanwhile, had bullied their way past Joseph Chamberlain's nervousness about the ZAR's Law 3—as well as Gandhi's protests—and compiled a list of sites across the Transvaal for something they now called "Asiatic Bazaars" (Lagden came up with the idea of using the word "bazaar," since "Asiatic location" was "supposed to be an offensive term" to Indians). To Gandhi's dismay, most of the sites on the list lay far out of town, just like

Ndabeni. Thus, he complained, they were likely to result in the financial ruin of his mercantile clients.[38]

Where in Johannesburg would the new location and bazaar go? At first the council explored the idea of a new Coolie Location out beyond the current Native Location, which had not yet been slated for demolition. There they ran into another problem that would bedevil South African archsegregationists well into the future: whites living near the site objected to the location, fearing its effects on their property values.[39]

Meanwhile, another solution percolated in the backs of at least some people's minds. Johannesburg, like many cities in the world, including many in Europe and North America, still relied overwhelmingly upon a slop-bucket system of human waste removal. This system involved a large army of two thousand native bucket-emptiers, with their own compound adjacent to Vrededorp and even a migrant-labor system—complete with recruiting agents who combed the rural reserves for men in search of urban jobs. The council was eager to build a first-rate piped sewage system as an additional lure for British immigrants. By 1903, based on the Transvaal engineer's research into sewage systems in India, Australia, Europe, and Los Angeles, California (whose dry climate was deemed similar to Johannesburg's), they decided on a "sewage farm" system in which a pipe would carry the city's waste to a large expanse of farmland, where it would fertilize crops that the municipality could then sell at a profit. The ideal place for such a facility was a 2,640-acre property named Klipspruit Farm No. 58, fifteen kilometers southwest of the city, beyond a line of mine dumps, and outside Curtis's municipal boundary, in one of the lowest-lying and least inhabited areas in the region. There were many geological and "agrostological" concerns involved. At least one mining company executive objected to the plan because he claimed he wanted to make adjoining land into a white suburb (since this constituency was still small, the council ignored the request on this occasion). A small, largely black, settlement called Kliptown had also existed at Klipspruit since the 1890s that may have also encouraged council's continued attention on the farm. Indeed, another question kept arising as well: would it be safe for large numbers of people to live near such a facility?[40]

On that question, a new leading character in the drama entered onto the stage: Dr. Charles Porter, Johannesburg's first municipal officer of health, recently arrived from England, appointed by Joseph Chamberlain himself. Porter was an enthusiastic proponent of the sewage farm. He was "well acquainted with the sewage works of Manchester ... [where]

there are many acres of open septic tanks and there is no perceptible smell, & people live within ½ mile of the place. And there are not the advantages of wide open spaces that you enjoy at Klipspruit."[41]

Upon assuming his duties in 1901, Porter had kept an eagle eye out for cases of plague. At the request of the Insanitary Area Commission, he had visited the Coolie Location with Gandhi and later made a trip up to the Kaffir Location. The sensational language of Porter's report of the visit startled Gandhi, who had thought Porter would solve the problems of the Coolie Location by issuing a few housing-code violations. As Porter put it, conditions were "the worse he'd ever seen" in his career. "Improvement would be quite inadequate," for the Coolie Location was "a great and constant menace to the rest of the town." Because of plague concerns, "it would no doubt be preferable to have the location some miles away in the country, where it would not be in close contiguity to a white population." He even envisioned a "cheap and very frequent rail service."[42]

Lionel Curtis liked Porter's kernel of a plan. To make it possible, he inserted two telling words in the locations bylaws he was drafting, allowing municipalities to establish such facilities "within *or beyond* the jurisdiction of the Local Authority." By the time of his visit to Ndabeni in early 1904, he, like Porter, must have made the connections between the proposed sewer farm and a dumping ground for the town's natives and Indians.[43]

In future years, Porter's cry of "slum!" alone would be enough to set the gears of South African forced removal into action. In 1904, though, it still took a greater emergency. As fate had it, that emergency came quickly, in March of that year, when the plague struck the Insanitary Area. Porter himself was too ill (with typhoid) to work, but his subordinate Walter Pakes had been well coached. Now with Gandhi's assent, Pakes cordoned off the Coolie Location, ignoring plague cases that came from other nearby neighborhoods. Then he issued orders to embark all the inhabitants—a mixture of blacks, coloreds, and Indians—onto a train that took them out to a collection of tents on Klipspruit Farm No. 58. Finally, he ordered the Coolie Location burned to the ground.[44]

As the plague crested and receded over the ensuing months, most of the Klipspruit deportees returned to town to resettle in the still standing Malay and Kaffir locations. But Porter and Curtis's fifteen-kilometer racial buffer had taken hold of the council's imagination. Howard Pim's finance committee reached a final deal on the purchase of Klipspruit farm in October, noting that the profits from resale of the Insanitary Areas would help defray the costs of a new Native Location and Asiatic Bazaar. The public health committee waxed enthusiastic:

> The advantages of keeping the native quarters completely away from the white population, will be obvious to everyone, whether one considers the interests of the native or those of the poorer class of European. Many facilities for keeping order and for efficient sanitary control will be afforded, which the present position of the Location renders far from easy. At Klipspruit, moreover, it would be possible for the sewage from the Location to be utilized by being put on the land, and the greater amount of space available for the Location itself cannot fail to have a beneficial effect upon the health and cleanliness of the natives.

The same fate, the council continued, would be best for Indians. Their removal to the planned Klipspruit Bazaar would have the additional benefit of promoting the livelihood of Johannesburg's white merchants. Once enabling legislation could be passed at the provincial level, the council would also seek to move the colored inhabitants of the equally dangerous Malay Location as well as the city's small Syrian and Chinese populations. As the council's new sewage pipes slowly snaked their way across the veldt toward the new farm, the municipality negotiated a cheap train service to convey the city's human refuse as well—in their case, back and forth between work in town and the new proposed racial segregation zones.[45]

In April 1906, the council finished the business of forcibly removing the black inhabitants of the old Kaffir Location to the Klipspruit Native Location. The first of the city's Southwestern Townships came into being, surrounded by fields that would soon receive a billion gallons of fresh sewage each year. The racial buffer zone they brought into being yawned wider than any during the age of segregation mania—Klipspruit Location lay almost twice as far from downtown as Ndabeni was from Cape Town, and fifteen times farther than later removal schemes in Dakar, Duala, Northern Nigeria, and Nairobi.

The council did not get everything it wanted. In court, Indian merchants successfully defeated the council's efforts to remove them to Klipspruit. Legislation effectively allowing the municipality to forcibly remove the colored and Indian people did not pass until 1934. Even then, Johannesburg did not get the authority to raze the Malay Location, where most of downtown's Indians and coloreds lived, until 1978, when it began to move them too to townships beyond Soweto. In a bow to Exeter Hall, meanwhile, Lionel Curtis had to include a clause in his locations bylaws allowing prominent black people to petition the lieutenant governor of the Transvaal for exemption to allow them to live in town. Some 997 "educated natives" were able to get such an exemption by the 1920s.[46]

In 1898, in the run-up to the Boer War, Milner scathingly called the Boers' ZAR a "medieval race oligarchy" that could not coexist with an industrial society and "had to be removed." By 1906, though, when he headed home to England, he, Curtis, and the other English-speaking officials had in fact transformed a much looser system of race segregation into a more refined system of legal precedents bristling with many elements from across British colonial practice and from the world beyond. Lionel Curtis, who would later achieve fame for his advocacy of the British Commonwealth—a much more liberal descendent of Milner's vision for a unified British Empire—had engineered much of this accomplishment. In the process, at least for the time being, he had transformed from a lukewarm skeptic into an avowed race segregationist, a fact he proudly proclaimed in 1907 in a speech at a Parktown meeting of the Fortnightly Club. For all his efforts, the segregationists on the council could wax optimistic about the future of racial oligarchy: Klipspruit Location, they trumpeted, would bring closer the day when "we are assured the existence and future of Johannesburg as a white man's town in a white man's country."[47]

# 9 ⋮ The Furies Fly in the Settlers' City

## Arrogance and Its Agonies

In the decades that followed the first forced removals to Klipspruit, Johannesburg's multifariously inspired politics of archsegregation only grew more complex—even exponentially so. The main reason was that ordinary white settlers took center stage in the drama. In 1905, amid intensifying pressures for settler rule across South Africa and a resounding liberal victory in London, Britain called Sir Alfred Milner back home, and the influence of the Kindergarten waned. Ordinary white male settlers took over the reigns of government as voters—first, in 1903, in the Johannesburg municipality; then, in 1906, in the colonial government of the Transvaal; and then, in 1910, in the newly minted Union of South Africa (white women did not get the vote in any of these jurisdictions until 1930). The new voters opened a boxful of furious internal conflicts in urban politics. Paradoxically, they also brought fiercer forces of propulsion to the country's segregationist visions.

For the grassroots of the white archsegregationist movement, institutions like the British Empire, international reform and academic networks, and the real estate business were copious sources of imported ideas, people, money, policy tools, legal instruments, and even forms of popular political organization. But they were also bones of fierce political contention. To the more intransigent among the country's defeated Afrikaner Nationalists, who gathered under the leadership of J. B. M. Hertzog, the empire was enemy number one. Even English speakers and the more reconciliation-minded Afrikaners, led by former Boer War generals Louis Botha and Jan Smuts of the South African Party, were tempted to see the empire as the mushy-minded hand-servant of London liberals, Irish Home-Rulers, and the Indian National Congress. As we know, support for segregation among imperial officials in London and Delhi did in fact become less consistent over time. In South Africa, that meant that more of the burden of city-splitting fell onto the shoulders of settlers and their often fractious local, provincial, and national governments.

The politics of urban social reform in a developing industrial society like South Africa were also probably more conflicted than in most other colonies. Sanitarians were of course very active in promoting segregation, but they shared the stage with legions of other social reformers: anticrime crusaders, prohibitionists, vice reformers, anti-immigration leaguers, domestic-service reformists, and liberal housing advocates. Labor conflict also rattled white society to its roots, most notably in the massive miners' strikes of 1914 and the great Rand Revolt of 1922. Though reformers and leaders of organized labor all found something useful in segregation, their differing agendas led to disputes about the details. They also sometimes allied themselves with and sometimes fought with organized white ratepayers (as South African taxpayers called themselves), eager to keep the costs of government policies—including reform initiatives—low. Johannesburg's periodic "Black Peril" scares—fears about black crime, most sensationally assaults on white women—only added fuel to these fires.

Finally, the large size and permanency of South Africa's urban white settler communities gave them an especially high stake in the politics of real estate—much higher than in the more itinerant white colonial communities elsewhere in Africa and Asia. Settlers widely agreed that the value of their investment in land depended upon the need to keep white neighborhoods white. But the enforcement of racial zoning could just as easily pit different sectors of the business community against each other, and neighborhood ratepayers' associations, one of the movement's crucial imports from Britain, disagreed with each other over central issues.

If these internal conflicts complicated the politics of splitting Johannesburg, so did the bald fact that the Milner-era urban segregation measures made no sense at all to South Africa's blacks, Indians, and coloreds. As they collectively sought a livelihood, shelter, and basic dignity, they continually thwarted official efforts to confine them to exclusive racial zones of cities, or even to follow white-imposed racial decorum in the semipermeable spaces necessary for the effectiveness of color lines as a tool of white power. They also became increasingly able to organize large numbers of people to fight against segregationist legislation, often taking to the streets in mass protest.

On the one hand, the furious dramas that arose created real uncertainties and political difficulties for whites. Paradoxically, however, these years of conflict also give us important insights into why such radical forms of archsegregation eventually did come to South Africa. In 1923, after all, settlers and their new national government succeeded in passing the infamous Natives (Urban Areas) Act. No other society on earth had ever produced such a complex government-legislated system of race-based residential zoning. This one, furthermore, aimed to guarantee color lines that were more or less permanently fixed in the urban landscape. It also gave a big boost to the two other archsegregationist ideals from the Milner era, separate development and influx control. And its passage occurred at a time when segregation mania was waning almost everywhere else in the world.

Three features of South Africa's white settler politics explain why its furies ultimately escalated toward archsegregation. One was the emotional intensity of daily encounters between whites and people of color in smaller urban spaces: homes, streets, sidewalks, tearooms, stores, tram cars, parks, and even in the spaces surrounding advertising billboards. Here, whites experienced abstract theories—such as the inevitability of racial conflict and the dangers of race mixing—as personal matters. Their intimate race war also involved gender conflict between white men and black men over sexual and urban territory—and between white men and white women over women's widely worshiped (but just as widely mistrusted) control over their own sexual feelings. Such conflicts infused segregationist politics with a paradoxical mixture of emotions, including arrogance, wounded honor, desire, danger, and an overwhelming sense that it was whites who were the primary victims of racial injustice. Belittling, sarcastic, and vilifying imagery of blacks, as well as expressions of high white moral outrage, could be found anywhere in contemporary Western popular culture. However, in places like Johannesburg (and, as we shall see, Chicago) the social anxieties of a rapidly industrializing society added to the large size and voting power of the settler community to allow whites' daily agonies and arrogances to accumulate into a much more potent political force than in other colonial cities.

The second driving force behind the radicalization of segregationism was the consensus among Johannesburg's white homeowners that their property values were vulnerable to racial threats—another belief they shared with their counterparts in the United States. As larger numbers of working-class whites bought homes, racialized economic incentives for segregation became more pervasive, eventually outweighing conflicting economic interests in the market for urban land. A groundswell of opinion held that blacks and other people of color should have no right to own urban property at all.

Finally, the precedents from the Milner era mattered. Because of public discussions and legal precedents inherited from direct imperial rule, white South African settlers—this time markedly unlike those in the United States—developed an especially strong expectation that their fledgling racially exclusive governments, despite big defects, could and should build the legal, administrative, and financial capacity necessary to implement ever more audacious plans of segregation, and should do so without unduly taxing the white community itself.

This faith was sorely tested during the period from about 1907 to 1920. Because of the vicissitudes of national and imperial politics, the South African Union delegated most of the responsibility for urban affairs to heavily strapped and not always effective municipal governments like Johannesburg's. At many points Johannesburg's segregation movement seemed to languish in stalemate or even to retreat from Milnerian precedents. But the fierceness of settlers' racial arrogance, whether fired by moral outrage, economic interest, or expectation for government action, finally outweighed the fury of their internal agonies. Intrasettler conflict, in fact, may have been an essential ingredient of the escalation toward apartheid.

## The Intimacies of Race War

To explore the connections between the potency of white Johannesburgers' demands for segregation and the sensations they felt in their routine travels through urban space, we should start where most of those daily experiences began—in their suburban homes. An opportune time to begin our exploration is the year 1912, during one of the city's fiercest episodes of "Black Peril." Over the previous two years, the city had been shocked by sensational reports of black men entering white homes and raping white women. The Union of South Africa empanelled a Commission on Assaults on Women to get to the bottom of the matter, and to do this it quizzed white people in Johannesburg about their private lives.

The whole problem was quite plain to one very irritated white man named Mr. Black. "It was altogether a mistake," he raged to the commissioners, "to allow a full-grown Kaffir to work in the homes of white people, and . . . it was unquestionably a great source of the Black Peril." Amid an otherwise blustery speech, however, a more complicated and sheepish thought slipped out. He had "gotten into hot water," he had to admit "with his own wife on this question." Then, struggling to regain his tone of outrage, he capped his testimony with a solemn vow: Mr. and Mrs. Black "would have these arguments" as long as they "had houseboys employed in their kitchens and their bedrooms."[1]

There was a lot going on in this fleeting instant. For one, there was the long reach of race biologists, who imagined black people to possess attributes of animals ("full-grown" Kaffir). There was also the supposition that one of those animalistic tendencies was an uncontrolled sexual appetite—and that white women, as members of the prized race, would be systematic targets of black male lust and violence. There was also a question of economic class—the drama of an employer seeking greater control over a domestic laborer, in this case in a none-too-advantageous context in which the employer could not do without that laborer's services. There was, on top of that, a gender conflict, pitting a man against a woman over final say in the home, traditionally the woman's domain. And then there was the punch line, which is the reason Mr. Black probably regretted the whole "hot water" business when it came out in the newspapers. For all his supreme racial righteousness, Black could barely control his own wife and servant. Worse, he apparently even feared becoming the cuckold of a cross-race, cross-class sexual conspiracy in his own bedroom.

Of course, in Mr. Black's time, these clichés of race, sex, and violence—and the sensations that drove them—had a much more pervasive life. Such stock figments of whites' racial imagination had long traveled the world through popular media that, by the turn of the twentieth century, connected far-flung white settler societies ever more efficiently. Together, these media might be said to constitute a fourth institutional vehicle for the long-distance transmission of segregationist ideas. They included the parade of blockbuster treatises on racial theory that we have already explored; profuse numbers of articles on race and empire in magazines like the *Atlantic*, *Scribner's*, and *Punch*, whose subscribers could be found across the English-speaking world; articles and editorials in local newspapers tied to new cross-oceanic wire services; bestselling novels; Kipling's poetry; advertisements; ethnological displays at international fairs; and even such light amusements as traveling minstrel shows, gospel troupes, early silent films, and international sports events. As the historian Theresa Runstedtler has shown, cross-racial championship boxing matches became some of the first worldwide multimedia spectacles during this period. Promoters relied on print media to build up the sensation surrounding the fights before they occurred, then they broadcast blow-by-blow accounts over telegraph wires, and later they shipped silent films of the fights to theaters worldwide. For many, the meeting of white and black boxers represented a key gauge of the fortitude of white imperial rule. In fact, one of the hallmarks of turn-of-the-century popular racism in all media was the sense that the struggle of the races was a personal matter, one that required individuals, most notably white men, to prepare themselves mentally and physically for day-to-day racial combat that would at once hone and test their true capacity to rule the world.[2]

South African settlers' own perception of their local demographic predicament added further heat to such fantasies of personal race war. As local whites repeatedly reminded liberal "meddlers" from outside, no other place in the world was like South Africa. A large, permanent white settler community had come into being, but amid a much larger, and thus much more threatening, black population than existed anywhere else. "It would be a blessed thing for us," Lionel Curtis had once wistfully told his diary, "if the negro like the Red Indian tended to die out before us." Such genocidal musings aside, Alfred Milner's alternative demographical engineering plan, aimed to stimulate the immigration of English-speaking whites, had relieved the pressure of the black majority to some extent, if only in the cities. Though postwar migrants from Britain never swamped the Boers as Milner hoped, their arrival in modest numbers had ensured that the white population of Johannesburg remained mostly English speaking and that the whole population of the city remained over half white. As anticipated, white Englishwomen had also arrived in much greater numbers than in the early mining-camp days. Married English couples with children fueled a substantial boom in suburban real estate, just as Curtis and the development companies had hoped.

Nevertheless, in 1912, the city's black population, while only 43 percent of the total, remained over 95 percent male, despite a gradually growing number of black women migrants. These black men fell into three groups, each making up about a third of the whole. One group worked in the Randlords' gold mines and lived in the adjoining labor compounds. A second group worked in town and lived in five possible places: at Klipspruit Location; in the municipal compounds; in smaller "private locations" on the premises of their employers; in private downtown dwellings arranged by their employers under a special license from the municipality; or, as was the case for most, illegally in the spreading slumyards south of downtown. The remaining third of the black workforce of Johannesburg, including upwards of thirty thousand young men in 1912, worked in white homes throughout the northern and eastern suburbs, spending the night either in backyard servant shacks, in small rooms within the house, or simply sprawled upon the kitchen floor. As a result, Parktown, the city's quintessential white suburb, actually had as many black residents as white.[3]

As terrifying as those large numbers were to whites, a tiny minority of black men dominated the way whites saw the whole race. This tiny group was made up of the *amaleita*, gangs of black criminals whose ranks had been augmented to some extent by houseboys dissatisfied with the declining wages for domestic service during the recession that began in 1907. Named after their signature hold-up line—they would demand that their victims show a "light" from the insides of their wallets—some also used their knowledge of white homes to run burglary rings. In 1912, members of one gang entered the home of a white woman named Mrs. Harrison in the southern working-class neighborhood of Turffontein and raped her while her husband was working the night shift in the mines. This "Kaffir outrage," which came on the heels of several other similar incidents over the previous five years, sparked the appointment of the commission to which Mr. Black gave his testimony.[4]

For white householders who hired male domestic servants, racial threats always lurked in the corners of the home, but deeper mutual acquaintance between whites and their black servants could also cut through the clichés. This "familiarity" between white and black itself became sensational news during Black Peril scares. The idea, for example, that black house boys could be put in charge of nursing white babies or young children, especially daughters, raised howls of indignation. Speaking to a packed house at the Grand Theater in June 1912, a domestic-service reformer named Mr. Mulligan brought up the instance of a "lady in considerable position in society in this town" who admitted that "when her maid was absent she got the Kaffir boy to button up the back of her dress." Asked how she could have done this, she replied that "I have good boys and this one has two wives at home."[5]

To Mulligan, such naive notions flew in the face of everything that experts taught about separate races and civilizations. Houseboys who migrated to the Rand were "divorced from the ordinary surroundings" and "free from tribal restraint." In "close contact with white women," such black men were in danger of becoming "sexual maniacs." Other irresponsible behavior on the part of white mistresses reported widely in the papers included their use of the same bathroom facilities as their servants, "rubbing shoulders" with houseboys while riding in horse-traps, and their requests that boys hand them golf clubs while out on the course. Stories about women who allowed houseboys to serve them coffee in their bedrooms, to help them dress or even to bathe them drew the biggest gasps, and there were plenty of hushed rumors about full-blown love affairs. "Many white women," Mulligan concluded to "loud applause," "are extremely careless in their conduct with regard to natives."[6]

In addition to raising the consciences of white women, Mulligan and other spokespeople for domestic-service reform sought help from the state. In 1903, in another uncanny anticipation of apartheid-era legislation, the Milner-era Transvaal Colony passed Ordinance 46, an early "immorality act" outlawing sex between white women and black men. In 1912, the Johannesburg Town Council, in a joint resolution with the city's ratepayers' associations and other civic groups, proposed amending the law to forbid white men having sex with black women as well. The joint committee based their recommendation on the strange social Darwinist corollary that black men would stay away from white men's sexual territory if white men were forbidden from encroaching on that of black men. In addition to this suggestion, there were calls to assign police officers to white homes to lecture mistresses on proper comportment toward their houseboys; demands that pass officers affix a complex system of character traits to houseboys' documents ("Is he civil? Is he quick? Is he clean? Is he sober?"); and laws to segregate homes by race and gender—either by banishing houseboys from kitchens, dining rooms, and bedrooms or by forcing householders to build separate latrines for servants. But the main focus of Black Peril-era domestic reformers like Mulligan was to remove black men from white households altogether—to Klipspruit or the reserves. To replace the houseboys, the government could restart immigration schemes for white domestics or it could put pressure on householders to buy American-style stoves and washing machines. If all else failed, mistresses would have to hire black women. It was that last idea that eventually won out, as black women's migration to towns grew during the late 1910s and 1920s. The result was the different but equally complex psychodynamics of apartheid-era "maids and madams."[7]

Beyond the home, in the streets and public places of the city, the personal race war was fought largely between strangers and was governed by a somewhat ambiguous web of sporadically enforced laws. By a law dating to the Boer South African Republic (ZAR), only whites were allowed on the city's "footpaths," as sidewalks were called; everyone else had to share the street with vehicle traffic, unless they had an exemption or unless they were crossing from the street into a building. White tearooms or restaurants were supposed to be off-limits to blacks. For them, the municipality went to great lengths to license a whole subset of businesses, officially called "Kaffir eating houses." The city was also empowered to keep the interiors of tram cars exclusively white and to run separate trams for nonwhites only when enough cars were available. Regulations permitted house servants to ride on the running boards of white cars, or, at mortal danger, up on the roofs. Some tram lines provided a cart of some sort in the rear for nonwhite passengers. Klipspruit residents, of course, rode the train the council had arranged for their trips into town—it was made of converted cattle cars and it frequently derailed. Though some tram lines did less to enforce racially exclusive provisions, most people of color who lived in the city were forced to walk to work in the middle of the street.[8]

The subtext of these laws, of course, was that white people owned urban public space and that people of color could only use that space in a humiliated or endangered state. At any time, plenty of white people were prepared to deputize themselves to enforce their supremacy in the streets, and plenty of blacks, coloreds, and Indians were eager to reject their degradation. Masculine posturing was, not surprisingly, plentiful on all sides. One memoirist remembered a time when he saw "four Kaffir boys" walking ahead of him. Suddenly, three white men "set their dog after them [which] immediately started for the Kaffir boys' heels.... One big boy in the center was really smart.... He gave a back kick so fast,...the dog went up in the air and turned a complete backward summersault and went yelping back to the men. They set him after the boys again, but he would not budge an inch, and the boys went on up the street laughing." The black men in this story were actually following the law and walking in the street, but the newspapers were filled with indignant letters calling for greater enforcement of the footpath laws against "insolent Kaffirs," some of whom cursed whites who tried to move them aside. For a white man named G. E. Wood, the "swinging self-appreciation" of natives in the street and their willingness to "[square] up to the European, using vile language" betrayed nothing less than a "readiness, even eagerness to destroy the character of the European." Blacks' clothing was also sometimes interpreted as a marker of unseemly racial pride. Like the amaleita, many young Westernized black men wore self-tailored bellbottom pants with a flash of brightly colored fabric sewn into the flare. More traditional costumes, which often included sticks or knobkerries, were no less a threat, and some called for regulations to prohibit natives from carrying these potential weapons.[9]

White women too sometimes engaged in such personal street-corner racial warfare. One Englishwoman wrote to the editor complaining that natives "often walk two and three abreast on the paths, and will never move aside." She thought she ought to "be quite justified . . . in hitting the offender across the face with her umbrella." For most men, though, white female sexuality was a weak link in the white male defense of the streets, as in the home. Billboards (known as hoardings) were a common subject of letters to Johannesburg's newspaper editors. "Is it fitting," one man wrote, "that hoardings should display . . . pictures of white women smoking, drinking, or offering intoxicating liquor? What can be the effect on the mind of a savage" when white women appear "so debauched and debauching?"[10]

The suspicion that some white women themselves could be open to cross-racial sex was part of a longer tradition of scandalized talk about prostitution that went back to Johannesburg's early days, when criminal cartels brought thousands of "white slaves" from all over Europe and even the United States into the nearly all-male mining town. Milner's "Immorality Ordinance" of 1903 was, among other things, an early attempt to stop the cross-color sex trade at the more wayward of the city's brothels. The increasing marriage rate of white male Johannesburgers along with a major police crackdown in 1907 severely weakened the international vice cartels, but substantial numbers of poor Afrikaner and black women prostitutes continued to sell sex both ways across the color line in the city's slums. They got their share of the blame for the Black Peril, but so did a segment of the city's tearooms, which did not always enforce the color line at their door. One "government official" walking with his wife reported that he "happened to glance down into a basement" to see a "tea-room waitress lolling about on a table with a cigarette between her lips while three natives stood before her in various attitudes of mirth." This was "an incident in the public interest," he claimed, for "if this sort of free and easy style of talking to Kaffirs were avoided there would be at least less black peril." Another letter writer called for an "all white tea-room society" that would boycott restaurants that skirted regulations and catered to blacks.[11]

Similarly telling attempts to control the racial imagery in Johannesburg's public spaces arose in the aftermath of two notorious prizefights, both of which occurred in Pacific-coast settler communities half a world away. In December 1908 the African American heavyweight boxer Jack Johnson—a man known for flaunting his rejection of white racial etiquette, for his lavish lifestyle, and for his public affairs with white women—defeated the white Canadian champion Tommy Burns in Sydney, Australia. Then, in an even more sensationally marketed match on July 4, 1910, in Reno, Nevada, Johnson annihilated the previously undefeated "white hope," Jim Jeffries. Promoters and the news media, including the Johannesburg papers, had framed both matches as one-on-one versions of the conflict of the races. After Johnson's victory, spontaneous celebrations broke out in black and Asian communities across the United States, the Philippines, and the British colonies, and whites armed themselves for violent reprisals in dozens of American cities. When advertisements for the film of the Johnson-Burns fight appeared all over Johannesburg, whites grumbled about "the revolting spectacle of gangs of natives gazing with admiration on the posters depicting the downfall of the white man." Calls to remove the posters were delayed so long, one commentator thought, that "tremendous amount of harm had been done to the native mind." When Johnson won again in 1910, local blacks reportedly sent telegrams of congratulations to the winner. The *Rand Daily Mail* called on the council to prohibit theaters from showing the fight films—as had governments in many US and British cities—warning that "for the safety of our wives and children ... we should do our best to prevent the natives from getting swelled head and attempting to imitate their champion." In the end, no less a figure than J. B. M. Hertzog, the South African Union's first minister of justice, declared that the films were "against the public interest" and ordered local police forces to enforce a ban on all showings. To compensate, Johannesburg's Automatic Vaudeville Theater offered "miniature bioscopes" showing a few pictures of the defeated Jim Jeffries in some of his "fine attitudes." One disgruntled white sports fan wrote in to "advocate that every white boy ... be taught how to use his fists as part of his education."[12]

"Give them a street," warned the white footpath warrior G. E. Wood of Black Peril–era Johannesburg, "and they will take a city." The best evidence for this theory was Johannesburg's ever-growing slum belt. There, a substantial, mixed-race, African-majority subcity had grown, where people spoke Zulu, Sotho, Xhosa, Tswana, Shangaan, Gujarati, Hindustani, Afrikaans, English, and a variety of mutually understandable mixtures of all of the above. The growth of the slums reflected a number of factors: the council's accommodating attitude toward employers who wanted their black employees to live near work, the difficulties blacks faced getting to and from Klipspruit, the willingness of white and Indian slumlords to ignore the color line in favor of profit, and spurts of black migration that by the 1920s included almost as many women newcomers as men. From the Malay Location, Vrededorp, and Fordsburg in the west, the slum belt

FIGURE 9.1 The slums of Johannesburg. Nothing symbolized South African whites' fear of being "swamped" by the majority-black population better than the mixed-race slum belt that surrounded downtown Johannesburg to the south. These slums were the primary targets of segregationists in the city, but they continued to grow until the 1930s. Ellen Hellmann, "Alleyway with 'Lapa' on the Left," photograph of the Rooiyard slumyard from Historical Papers, University of the Witwatersrand Library, Johannesburg, South Africa, A1419, no. 11.

stretched through Fereirrastown, Marshallstown, and Spes Bona to the south of downtown and crept into Doornfontein, Jeppestown, and Bertrams to the east, threatening the slopes of the northern suburbs as well. If the streets of the white city seemed overwhelmed by groups of three and four black men, the names of these slum neighborhoods brought up images of large black crowds that gathered on weekends for loud mass revels, complete with drums, stick fights, and traditional dances. The amaleita themselves, of course, hid by day in the slums (that is, when they did not repair to abandoned mine shafts in the southern hills), as did the prostitutes, gamblers, unemployed pass forgers, and vagrants. What made the slums especially noxious to whites, though, was the vast village-style beer-brewing industry that had grown up there.[13]

Johannesburg's slumyards consisted of plots of unused land that landlords outfitted with rows of ten-by-ten-foot shacks, then rented out to large groups of single men or whole extended families. Into these fetid urban villages, women had imported the traditional beer-making processes of the African countryside, which involved fermenting various sorts of grain in any container that was available. The Transvaal had forbidden Africans from possessing alcohol ever since the days when the Randlords switched to deep-level mining. Work thousands of feet below ground required a much soberer workforce than in the earlier outcrop-mining days, when employers widely sold liquor to their workers—to keep them penniless and to guarantee they would stay on their job. With the change in policy, almost all black women in the slums had become criminals—"illicit liquor sellers," the drug dealers of their day. Slumlords aided and abetted the business, for their rental income depended on beer sales. To avoid the police, women buried their fermenting vats underneath the dirt courtyards between their shacks. Out the beer would come, though, whenever the mine boys or the municipal slop-bucket crews or the suburban houseboys would knock off work, and on weekends it would flow freely, dispensed from squalid shacks turned into barrooms known as shebeens. If a neighbor had managed to score a castoff piano, a trumpet, an accordion, or a guitar, then the stage was set for the metamorphosis of African traditional cultures into Johannesburg's famous marabi style, the first of South Africa's several waves of response to American blues and jazz.[14]

White temperance reformers saw this cultural phenomenon as an abomination and once again poured copious doses of moral outrage and race-and-civilization theory onto the city's streets. The liquor industry, they argued, was proof that blacks' presence in the city had been too fast and sudden an introduction to civilization for such "native races" to bear. "Was it reasonable," asked Reverend Collyer, "to suppose that a native just emerging from barbarism, who was placed in a city where excitement always ran high, should preserve a placid sobriety? Was it likely that he would in a moment be equal to all the fine adjustments of civilisation which it has taken us 2,000 years to reach?" Yet, as Collyer and many others also noted, traditional African beer, with its relatively low alcohol content, was only part of the story of black intemperance. Whites too profited from selling much harder forms of liquor in the slums and compounds, a fact that helped prove the theory that contact between the races was detrimental to both.[15]

For whites, another swift and frightening development tied to the slums was black people's political metamorphosis. In the streets of Johannesburg's mixed-race Babylon, street-corner-style defiance encountered the organized, more genteel, but increasingly innovative politics of R. V. Selope Thema's Transvaal African Congress (TAC, the local wing of the SANNC), Charlotte Maxexe's Bantu Women's Association, Mohandas Gandhi's British Indian Association, and the colored leader Dr. A. Abdurahman's African People's Organization. Gandhi's first mass meetings occurred in downtown ballrooms, but he soon moved them to the streets of the western slums, drawing the large numbers of Indians who lived in the Malay Location and Vrededorp.[16]

The March 1920 Vrededorp riot illustrates vividly how explosive the mixture of personal, street-level racial conflict and organizational politics could be. That month, inspired by Gandhi's passive-resistance techniques, Selope Thema and Charlotte Maxexe held a rally in the name of the TAC at the municipal cemetery at Vrededorp. Four hundred black residents of the surrounding west-side slums participated in the largest-yet protest against the pass laws. They also demanded higher wages for houseboys, municipal workers, and striking mineworkers. It is important to remember that the ZAR government had intended Vrededorp as an exclusively white neighborhood for poor Afrikaners. Under Milner and then General Botha, the British Transvaal Colony had honored the pledge, and in 1907 it passed the Vrededorp Stands Act, the goal of which was to expel all nonwhites from the neighborhood's small houses and narrow streets. But Vrededorp was also surrounded by the mixed-race Malay Location on one side, the Municipal Scavenging Department's large native compound on another, and a municipal cemetery on yet another (see fig. 8.1). Whites from Vrededorp and blacks from the compound had engaged in sporadic episodes of stone throwing across the street that separated them for some time. Furthermore, the racial-cleansing efforts within the neighborhood had largely failed. Vrededorp was even home to one of Johannesburg's three American-influenced radical black churches.[17]

The only way for whites to get from Vrededorp into town was by passing under a dark railroad trestle called the "tunnel," which was a favorite spot for Indian and African hawkers as well as scavenging boys on break. On March 1, 1920, as the TAC rally dispersed on the cemetery side, a black man tried to hop a tram packed with whites near the tunnel on its way from downtown to the suburbs further west. When he was pushed off, black protestors began throwing stones at the next trams that came through. The mounted police quickly arrived, followed by gun-wielding white Vrededorpers, who collectively stormed the surrounding streets—killing four black people and injuring seventy over the course of the next two hours. Panicked, many blacks ran into the Malay Location and melted into its narrow streets and shacks. The streets of Johannesburg had gotten their first big taste of a type of conflict—stocked with both organized and informal power on both sides—that would, in the very long run, bring the white regime to the ground.[18]

## They Will Buy Us Out of the Country

In the shorter run, blacks got the worst end of the violence in the riot of 1920. But, in the context of the fears that dominated ordinary white people's sense of the city, it did not take much creative imagination on whites' part to think of besieged and infiltrated Vrededorp as a micro-cosm of Johannesburg as a whole. Ever since the council had proclaimed the city "A White Man's Town in a White Man's Country," the teeming, mixed-race, African slum city in Johannesburg's underbelly had grown steadily. Vrededorp was a poor neighborhood, so its racial defenses were weaker, but, on the other side of town, the now slum-infested Doornfontein and Jeppestown had once been the city's swankiest suburbs, filled with Randlords. There was no reason to think the lordly color line along the top of the Rand would hold out forever.

White Johannesburgers' impulse to defend whole neighborhoods was intrinsically linked to their defense of the smaller spaces of the city. But settlers' determination to protect their real estate also contained other ingredients: high-stakes economic interests, questions of property rights, and the nature of title to land. These elements of conflict also came to Johannesburg both through international exchanges and through local adaptations.

For some historians, eager to find a final resolution to the question of whether class-related (or "material") factors were more important than racial (or "ideological") factors in South African history, whites' drive to preserve real estate values in Johannesburg has provided evidence that, underneath it all, segregation was an economic matter. That is far too simplistic an interpretation. The fact that whites deemed black, colored, or Indian neighbors a mortal threat to their property values drew heavily upon the same widely circulating stories of race, gender, and civilization that also drove settlers' defense of the city's more intimate urban spaces. The "racist theory of value" thus represents evidence of the inextricable intertwining of racial belief and the very price of a material thing, not the higher historical importance of one over the other.[19]

As an engine of political mobilization, moreover, the racist theory of property values rested upon other noneconomic contingencies as well. In South Africa, whites may have been outnumbered, but unlike whites in India and most other colonies, they had invested enough in long-term settlement, felt empowered enough within the public sphere, and could make claims based on enough real legislative precedent to use their racial ideas about property values to demand state protection of their neighborhoods. When white homeowners did make property-values claims for racial segregation, however, they sometimes ran up against other powerful whites, namely developers and slumlords, whose economic interests in real estate did not always point toward segregation. Sometimes white homeowners even betrayed the segregationist cause by selling property in white neighborhoods to nonwhites. When they did so, they were following their economic interest just as much as anyone else. Finally, since homeowners were also ratepayers, their own individual economic interests were split: the interest in avoiding the high taxes necessary for building segregated black housing could conflict with their interest in sustaining their property values.[20]

These cross-cutting economic interests were also suspended within questions of legal rights, themselves inextricably bound up with race. The biggest of these questions was whether blacks, coloreds, and Indians should be allowed to own private property at all. One of the ways South

African racial politics contrasted with that of the United States, India, and most other Asian and African colonies was in South African white settlers' ambition to prevent or at least severely restrict the rise of a non-white property-owning class. In fact, many in South Africa supported segregation precisely because it presented an obstacle to landownership for blacks and other people of color, especially Indians. Conversely, actual restriction of nonwhite property rights also helped immensely to make government-supported segregation legally possible and practicable.

Support for a racially restricted system of property rights was not com-pletely universal in white South Africa. Some liberals supported limited property rights for nonwhites on similar grounds to the ones they used to justify limited voting rights: individual ownership of property was ei-ther a beneficial route to civilization or should be accorded to those who had shown a capacity for civilization. As Howard Pim had demonstrated, however, paying lip service to the "civilization" standard could give extra force to claims made purely in white racial interest—precisely by endow-ing those claims with the semblance of a higher moral purpose.

A good example of this ideological feat was the testimony of the land surveyor and Johannesburg city councilman W. K. Tucker to the South African Native Affairs Commission in 1905. Tucker's career also dem-onstrates how people working within the belly of the international real estate business could connect themselves to other segregationist insti-tutional arenas, including government and urban reform movements. Born into a family of British settlers amid the race wars of the Eastern Cape Province, Tucker had sought diamonds in Kimberley and gold in Johannesburg. Along the way he worked for mining and land companies, making inventories of their property holdings and surveying plots for sale. During the Boer War he helped administer one of the concentration camps for British women and children, and he later helped found the Rand Pioneers, a group of prominent Johannesburg settlers dedicated to protection of whites from the Black Peril. Among other things, the Pioneers agitated for enforcement of the footpath ordinances. His perch with the Pioneers gave him the prominence he needed for election to the Johannesburg Municipal Council. While on the council, he served on the Rand Plague Committee, helping to identify Klipspruit as the site for the city's segregation camp. In 1907 his colleagues elected him mayor of Johannesburg, and in 1908 he won office in the new Transvaal Legislative Assembly. Between political campaigns, he founded and became the first president of the Institute of Land Surveyors of the Transvaal and directed a formal survey of the city for the municipality. He was also a member of Howard Pim's Fortnightly Club.[21]

"No individual native," Tucker told Godfrey Lagden's commission, "should own land." In natives' current stage of civilizational development, only traditional forms of communal tenure in native reserves were appropriate. "I do not think the time has come for individualising" natives by giving them "either leasehold or freehold.... We cannot hope to solve things by what I may call a hot-house process of forcing the Native along a line of unnatural development." But woven into those same exact words was a different line of argument—concern that natives would actually benefit from property ownership. When Lagden asked what Tucker "feared" would happen if natives could own land, Tucker responded "that they will become influential, that they will become wealthy, and that they should develop themselves faster than it suits our purposes." What was at stake, then, were the privileges of whites and their very existence in South Africa, not adherence to any fundamental laws of racial development. "The white man came and took the country from the native." If blacks could own land, whites would be "bought out of the country." Such two-pronged theorizing had many uses: whites could at once reassert their supremacy and their outrage at being unfairly victimized, and they could have their law of conquest and feel good about it too.[22]

Actually putting together a racially truncated system of property ownership, though, required dealing with less lofty matters: land titles. As a matter of fact, in Johannesburg, most ordinary white settlers actually had a very weak title to land. In the years after the gold strike, large development companies called township companies, most of which were subsidiaries of the mining companies, bought up virtually all the land along the Witwatersrand, including almost all of the eighty-seven square miles within the Johannesburg municipal limits. These developers had taken advantage of their near-monopoly, as well as land buyers' uncertainty about the mining town's sustainability, by offering residential plots on ninety-nine-year leasehold, the direct ancestor of the miserly titles aristocrats offered merchants in the West End of London during the seventeenth century. This bad deal forced homeowners to pay monthly "ground rent" and recognize that at lease's end, their heirs could face forfeiture of any "improvements" to the land, such as the family house. Once the success of deep-level mining assured Johannesburg's economic future, residents clamored for the outright or "freehold" title to the land, like most people in contemporary Britain, and Milner and Curtis pressured the township companies to convert the leases as another lure to British settlers. Their pressure resulted in the Transvaal Republic's three Townships Acts (1907, 1908, and 1909).[23]

Before that happened, a few township companies had sweetened their leaseholds by slipping restrictive covenants into the deeds. Some of these were very similar to those in use in British suburbs—they aimed to keep a development exclusive by prescribing expensive architectural amenities, by forbidding subdivision of the lot to avoid tenements and slums, and by prohibiting the erection of "any canteen, restaurant, . . . or place for the sale of . . . liquors." The Jeppe brothers, developers of the eastern suburb of Jeppestown, also inserted racial occupancy clauses in their deeds as early as 1895, mandating that "the lessee shall not allow coloured persons other than domestic servants to dwell on the stand."[24]

The companies that wrote these early race restrictions were up to mischief: they usually had no intention of enforcing them. Leaseholders who acquired stands with the impression that their neighborhood would remain all residential and all white often discovered that some of their white neighbors had less interest in protecting other whites' property values than in opening a bar or renting out backyard shacks to blacks. Aggrieved leaseholders who lived next door to such covenant breakers often sued the land companies to enforce the restrictions. As Julius Jeppe himself admitted, the costs companies incurred in taking any one of these breaches to court (£880 in one case) was hardly worth the covenants' marketing value—especially after Jeppestown started to sprout its first slumyards and became a less desirable place to live anyway. The South African courts, for their part, imported British legal precedent to settle the matter. The key case pertaining to such matters involved an architectural covenant in London's Leicester Square. In *Tulk v. Moxhay* (1848), the lord chancellor had ruled that all deed restrictions "followed the land"—that is, that all subsequent buyers of the plot of land had to abide by those conditions whether they originated them or not. A bank of subsequent cases, including *Renals v. Cowlishaw* (1878), had made it clear, however, that previous owners, including developers who owned many other stands under the same conditions in the neighborhood, were not responsible for stopping later violators. On the basis of these English cases, the supreme court of the Transvaal ruled for the land companies, and the burden of enforcing the restrictions fell squarely on the title holder's shoulders.[25]

Under Milner and Curtis, the Transvaal government itself began to take a direct stand on this matter. The ZAR had passed two laws restricting land ownership and occupancy by specific groups of people—Law 3 of 1885, which prohibited "Asiatic" ownership outside locations, and a Gold Law that disallowed all blacks, Asians, and coloreds from living on land that might be valuable for mining purposes. Curtis's locations by-laws forced natives who did not live with their employers to move to the locations, such as Johannesburg's Klipspruit. In addition, Milner's Proclamation of Townships Ordinance (1905) established a townships board whose job was to approve developers' plans for new townships, as Johannesburg's multiplying, square-mile-sized suburban subdivisions were then called. For approval, the board required that deeds to all properties in the township contain clauses against subdivision and nonresidential use as well as a beefed-up racial restriction that would forbid not only occupancy, but also future purchase or lease by any "Asiatic, aboriginal native, or other colored person." By 1912, sixty-five of the city's eighty-eight suburban townships contained these clauses in their deeds; by 1947, on the eve of apartheid, race restrictions covered 345 of the 387 townships in the larger Johannesburg Mining District.[26]

As the municipal council's vision of Johannesburg as a "White Man's Town in a White Man's Country" became more widely shared, ordinary white residents of Johannesburg pressed the government to move toward a comprehensive and enforceable system of racial zoning. In the meantime, they took matters into their own hands by importing another crucial feature of British suburban politics, the ratepayers' association. Most of Johannesburg's many white suburbs had one of these associations at some point. Some came into being for the same reason as their British counterparts—to keep an eagle eye on the ways council spent their members' tax money. Others, such as the one in Turffontein, exploded into being as "vigilant associations" to patrol the nighttime streets against "Kaffir outrages." Almost all of the ratepayers' associations at one time or another led the outcry against the "invasion" of neighborhood land by black, colored, or Indian buyers of property. While a few of them, like the one in Turffontein, engaged in extralegal vigilante activity, their members refused to "take the drastic step taken in the States of America" and resort to "Judge Lynch" or other forms of violence. Most instead focused heavily on expanding their influence within the formal structures of the municipality, once again demonstrating the trust whites held in the segregationist potential of government. In 1916, several of the strongest associations formed the Johannesburg Federation of Ratepayers Associations (JFRA), which took a strong role in formulation of all types of policy, including racial zoning. Later it ran its own slate of candidates, and finally, in 1923, it became a formal party that took a large majority of seats in the municipal council.[27]

If white homeowners' property interests provided segregationism with a strong favorable undercurrent, the economic interests of blacks, coloreds, and Indians led them to find a place to live wherever they could, to take whatever title they could, and to ignore color lines whenever they could or needed to. One of the most basic—informal, yet collective— ways in which ordinary people of color gummed up whites' hopes for an exclusive system of land occupation was simply by moving to the cities in great numbers, above all in search of work. Despite immigration restriction acts, the numbers of Indians rose from around 5,000 in 1911 to 10,000 in 1935. During the same years, the number of colored migrants, largely from the Cape Province, grew from under 8,000 to over 22,500, and the number of blacks increased, despite the pass laws, from 95,000 to 219,000. Of these, about 100,000 were men who needed lodging in the city because they worked outside the mines, 28,000 were women (seven times more than in 1911), and 51,000 were children. Once they were in the city, the driving economic interest for all these new inhabitants, as for working-class people everywhere during this period, was to live close to their jobs—both to get to work on time and to avoid high transport costs. That meant, as we know, that domestic workers needed to live in the suburbs. Other nonmining workers and self-employed hawkers, liquor brewers, and merchants also needed to live downtown, near to most businesses, municipal offices, and customers. It was above all for this reason that the city's slum belt grew inexorably.[28]

The idea of living in a native location or an Asiatic bazaar fifteen kilometers out in the country struck most Johannesburgers of color as absurd, if not downright ruinous. The council had struck a deal with a railway company to provide cut-rate transport between Klipspruit and downtown in exchange for a guaranteed ridership, but the location was so unpopular that the trains were never full. The company then ran fewer and fewer trains, eventually resorting to two per day each way, the last one of which left town at 5:30 in the afternoon, making it impossible for many location residents to get home after work. When Klipspruit was first laid out in 1906, the council variously envisioned a population of somewhere between four and ten thousand people. In 1907, only 1,800 people lived at the location; at most, three thousand lived there during any one year during the 1910s. Most who remained did so because they could supplement their wages with agricultural pursuits, farming small plots and grazing a few head of cattle.[29]

Most blacks, coloreds, and Indians who did not live on their employers' premises simply rented rooms downtown, putting themselves completely at the mercy of slumlords. However, small numbers of blacks and larger numbers of coloreds and Indians held hope that the British would widen opportunities for landownership on the Rand. Instead, Milner bowed to white pressure and placed all black land titles into the name of a government trustee. Five African Methodist Episcopal ministers led by the Reverend Edward Tsewu challenged this system in court and won. Milner responded with a more court-proof version of the trusteeship system, but the same ministers petitioned Parliament and had the system disallowed. In this context, Curtis considered offering thirty-three-year leaseholds in Klipspruit to increase the location's attractiveness, but the council dug in its heels even on that meager concession. The location's inhabitants instead occupied plots on one-year, renewable "stand licenses" that required an annual rent payment.[30]

The ministers' court victory, however, opened a small window for black property seekers to get much better real estate deals elsewhere in Johannesburg. One of these deals was available in a small township laid out by the independent developer Herman Tobiansky, four miles west of town. Sophiatown, lovingly named after Tobiansky's wife, was at first meant for whites of limited means, and its original deeds contained racial restrictions against black purchase. A few whites, though, were willing to buy some of the cheap plots as proxies for black friends. Their white neighbors, finding their "property greatly depreciated in value," formed a "Vigilance Association" that sent out nighttime patrols to catch blacks at home and arrange for their arrest. Some "Vigilants" even pooled funds to buy up lots adjoining those purchased by blacks to set up a buffer zone within the neighborhood. The matter made its way into the courts as well as to the council (which issued a toothless injunction against black occupancy) and even to the minister of native affairs himself, Godfrey Lagden, whose hands were tied by Parliament. Eventually, the courts got overburdened by Sophiatown cases and refused to hear more. The city decided to open a trash-depositing site near Sophiatown, causing property values to plummet further, and whites began to leave. A few remaining Vigilants continued to protest, arguing that Sophiatown had become a major breeding ground of the Black Peril. From black neighbors, one homeowner wrote, white children acquire "a knowledge, the grossness of which will in no way befit them to follow the paths of virtue." The Native Lands Act of 1913 formally prohibited new black purchases of land outside the reserves, but by that point the Union Supreme Court had ruled that all owners of property, even blacks, had a fundamental right to live on the land they already owned. As a result, nothing stood in the way of the growth of "South Africa's Harlem" on Johannesburg's far west side. Soon, blacks also found ways to acquire land in neighboring Martindale and Newclare, further expanding an all-black zone that whites soon called the "Western Areas."[31]

Meanwhile, just to the north of Lionel Curtis's city line, a white farmer turned developer named H. B. Papenfus began renting plots to black relatives of his cook. In 1912, one year before the Native Lands Act made it illegal for blacks to buy land outside of the reserves, Papenfus subdivided his farm, now renamed Alexandra (likewise after his own wife), and advertised it as a township open to all black people interested in owning land free from stand licenses and the threat of displacement. By 1922, blacks and coloreds owned freehold title to 1,300 lots eight miles north of downtown in an increasingly subdivided and overcrowded rectangle. Later efforts of the most determined apartheid engineers to get rid of Alexandra failed, and it remains in place to this day, even as Johannesburg's northernmost and most exclusive white suburbs grew around it.[32]

For Indian land buyers, most of whom were merchants, the need to live close to downtown was paramount. The destruction of the Coolie Location had robbed them of the only place, under Law 3, where they could legally acquire ninety-nine-year leaseholds. As early as the 1880s, Asians had partnered with sympathetic whites to charter limited liability corporations that bought land for the Asians' use under freehold title. This now became an increasingly common practice, to the frustration of white merchants and ratepayers' associations. Jan Smuts, as colonial secretary of the Transvaal Republic, led the way in further restricting Indian landownership. The Vrededorp Stands Act (1907) prohibited Indians and blacks from living in Vrededorp, the neighborhood envisioned by the ZAR as an exclusively Afrikaner working-class zone. A revised Gold Law of 1908 made it a criminal offense for all nonwhites to own or occupy land in officially designated gold-mining areas. Smuts also snuck in a provision within the Townships Act of 1908 to give the government power to confiscate certain types of freehold property if held in violation of restrictive covenants. Since Indians owned land in all of the areas restricted by these laws, Mohandas Gandhi and the Transvaal British Indian Association (BIA) fought back.

Though Gandhi's most well-known campaigns during this time were directed against the Black Act, which forced Indians to carry registration documents similar to native passes, he kept up a steady drumbeat of protest against restrictions on property rights. While it is true that he very ungenerously joined in the call to remove "Kaffirs" from Indian neighborhoods to Klipspruit, he likened the Transvaal's planned Indian bazaars to Jewish "Ghettos," claiming that the logic of segregation "can only result in ruination to hundreds of law-abiding and respectable Indians." The Johannesburg town council abandoned its crusade for an Asiatic bazaar when lawyers hired by an Indian merchant successfully argued in the Transvaal Supreme Court that Law 3 gave the government no powers to actually compel Indians to move. Later, Gandhi brought up the Vrededrop law in his own meetings in London with high-ranking British officials, including then assistant colonial secretary Winston Churchill. In 1914, in the wake of the most successful of his half dozen passive resistance campaigns in South Africa, Gandhi was able to get Smuts to guarantee that the Union government would not appropriate any previously vested Indian-owned property. When Gandhi left for India later that year, he left the window wide open for more purchases by multiracial front companies, some of them owned by the BIA's white lobbyists in London.[33]

## Pandora's Segregationism

White people's race wars in Johannesburg's streets and in the real estate market created tremendous pressures for segregationist action in governments. But the pressures alone did not dictate exactly what kind of action those governments should take. As furious disagreements broke out among white voters, policymaking lost the focus it had under direct imperial rule. The country's new governments, for their part, only inconsistently developed the bureaucratic machinery they needed to follow up upon Milner-era precedents during the 1910s. The result was a decade and a half of shifting experiments with urban racial zoning. The ongoing hubris of white racism was not matched by bold action until 1923.

At the provincial and national levels, the politics of urban segregation embroiled itself in conflicts over South Africa's relationship to the British Empire and also pitted the cities, largely English speaking, against the countryside, where most of the larger Afrikaans-speaking population lived. These conflicts took surprising turns. When the Afrikaner majority took power, first in the Legislative Assembly of the Transvaal Republic, then in Parliament of the Union of South Africa, it actually slowed progress toward comprehensive racial zoning of cities on the national level for over fifteen years. In 1908, the British settler, surveyor, and homespun racial theorist William Kidger Tucker, now a member of the Rand delegation in the Transvaal Assembly, urged colonel secretary Jan Smuts, the former Boer War general, to include a clause in a freehold transfer bill allowing cities "to lay out lots or stands for exclusive occupation of natives, colored persons or Asiatics." This represented another early stab at formalizing a principle later enshrined in the Group Areas Act, but under the Transvaal Constitution, inclusion of racial "disabilities" in legislation meant that the House of Commons in London, now dominated by liberals, would have to review the bill. Smuts, prime minister Louis Botha, and a united Afrikaner majority voted Tucker down to assure passage of the bill's freehold provisions.[34]

After 1910, the constitution of the South African Union no longer required that racist laws receive Parliamentary assent in London. But the Afrikaners' first priority was to resolve their own internal debates about how to keep black laborers on white farms while segregating the countryside by race. They saw the Native Lands Act, which established a nationwide system of rural reserves in 1913, as more pressing than urban segregation, and Louis Botha, now Union prime minister, shelved a draft of an urban bill during those debates. In 1918, Parliament postponed yet another urban racial zoning bill, once again to make way for revisions to the rural reserve system. Soon after, three separate commissions and one select committee of the Union Parliament got to work drafting urban legislation, but their conclusions opposed each other, guaranteeing further delay.[35]

Without grants of power or resources from above, municipalities like Johannesburg had limited options. And it was the city councils that bore the brunt of the escalating local conflicts. One of the most contentious issues in Johannesburg was where to locate municipally owned residential facilities for black people. Most employers agreed with their black workers that Klipspruit was located too far away to serve as an effective dormitory for people who needed to be at work on time. They could point out that most of the council's own black employees lived in compounds downtown or nearby, precisely to keep them near their work. During the Black Peril scare of 1912, domestic-service reformers likewise called on the council to build new locations closer to town, in this case so that houseboys could find convenient housing that did not require them to sleep in the same homes as their employers' wives. At the same time, the growing numbers of black families in town created added pressure for housing outside the municipal compounds, which were reserved for single men. From about 1910 to 1922, there was growing pressure to abandon the fifteen-kilometer racial buffer and replace Klipspruit. Some wanted the city to build four new locations, one at each point of the compass and closer to town. In 1917 W. K. Tucker, now a Union senator, even distanced himself from his own role in the establishment of Klipspruit by spreading the false story that the location had been meant as a temporary measure when it was founded.[36]

Ratepayers and developers may well have shared employers' disappointment with Klipspruit. But the very same ratepayers' associations that called repeatedly on the municipality to protect their housing values by removing black people from white neighborhoods also opposed all plans to build any compound or location anywhere near their own neighborhoods. In this matter, developers agreed with homeowners. The Braamfontein Estate Company, for example, was a subsidiary of the gold mining company Herman Eckstein and Co. and was thus connected to one the biggest compounders of black labor on the Rand. But it fought an effort to build a municipally owned compound in its beloved Parktown development. In exasperation, the council threatened in 1917 to build up native locations in all parts of town "so that any section of the community cannot complain they are being saddled with natives belonging to other portions of the Municipality." By then, though, the city had shrewdly targeted the one part of town whose property values they could sacrifice with the least political impact: Sophiatown and the other Western Areas. Once the council announced a plan for a native location there, the ratepayers of the nearest white suburb, Newlands, put up yet another big fuss. This time, though, the city was ready. In exchange for accepting natives as neighbors, Newlands would get an extension of an all-white tram line into downtown, a guarantee that the native location would be entirely fenced in, and an agreement that the location would not share the name "Newlands." Work on the Western Native Township (WNT) began in 1918.[37]

If the crisscross of employers' and homeowners' internally conflicting interests roiled the drama of settler segregation, so did the politics of
urban reform movements. The biggest issue was the condition of housing in native locations. From even before the founding of Klipspruit,
Milner's commissioner of native affairs, Godfrey Lagden, had urged
Lionel Curtis to avoid "biscuit-tin locations" whose inhabitants built
their own houses out of whatever materials they could find. By building a handful of small houses at Klipspruit, the municipality had—in its
eagerness to rid the town of blacks—jumped ahead of its time in providing public housing. That said, the quality of this housing was abysmal. A
Union commission found that the high rental fees at the native locations
actually made money for the municipalities since local authorities like
Johannesburg's put so little into materials or maintenance. At Klipspruit,
many of the houses amounted to nothing but "v-shaped huts" that looked
like wood or metal tents, just without floors. A resident named Thomas
Mkosinkulu later testified that "in summer the houses were so hot . . . a
bucket of water would boil if placed inside them and in rain the floor
oozed moisture and the roof leaked. In winter the houses were so cold
that one needed 10 blankets to make one warm." Infrastructure was also
minimal: "The water pipes . . . became stuffed with dead frogs and ran
dangerously near foul waters." As for the nearby sewage farm, "it was
no wonder that so many mad people were in the location; because the
brain was suffocated by the smell. [A campaign was needed] against the
fly and the mosquito during the summer months when they infested
the place."[38]

During the 1910s, South African sanitarians and housing reformers,
led by Johannesburg municipal officer of health Charles Porter, waged an
ongoing campaign to acquire more municipal powers over housing and
urban planning—citing new European housing codes, Britain's Housing
of Working Classes Act of 1890, and its successor, the Housing and Town
Planning Act of 1909. For Porter, who defended Klipspruit's healthfulness
repeatedly, the main goal was to be able to remove the white poor from
the slums and place them in English-style garden suburbs. The Union
Parliament helped realize that goal in 1920 with the National Housing
Act. The attention reformers gave to the housing issue, however, also
reverberated within the Union's Native Affairs Department, which was
otherwise generally preoccupied with rural affairs. Liberal officials there
saw improved housing conditions as a means to lure reluctant natives
from the slums into the locations. When Johannesburg began building

the Western Native Township, the housing it offered was hardly palatial. But the budget for the WNT quickly went into arrears, in part because the price of construction materials skyrocketed after the war. For a time, the council reverted to building World War I-style Nissen huts, which it could assemble in a single day for £55 a piece. Even then, white ratepayers' associations, which were otherwise so bent on segregation, howled in protest at the cost. Then, in 1919, the Labor Party won a majority of city council seats on a program of sending blacks back to the reserves and replacing them with white workers. Under their aegis, the city slowed construction on the WNT to a halt and even eventually reneged on the expensive business of providing a separate tram line for location residents. Once again, white ratepayers went up in arms, this time all along the western line to Newlands, complaining that they had to ride "cheek by jowl" with blacks on tramcars.[39]

A nasty argument between different camps of social reformers, meanwhile, cut off another unusual but, to many, promising source of funds for black housing. Since 1908, the municipal council of the city of Durban had built widely admired native locations by using profits it earned from its very own African beer brewery. In 1916, a delegation of councilors from Johannesburg visited Durban to see the system at work, toured the town brewery and the municipal beer canteens, and came home eager to spread the good news. Not only was the beer business making a handsome profit for the city—even after costs for its relatively expensive native housing were factored in—it also allowed the city to regulate the amount of alcohol in the beer. This, officials claimed, lowered the city's crime rate to boot. Back in Johannesburg, however, the delegation was met with vehement outrage that lasted for years. Temperance advocates and outright prohibitionists were much better organized on the Rand than in Durban, thanks in part to the support of the deep-mining companies and in part to popular rage at the imagined role of shebeens in the Black Peril. They also closely followed the success of American prohibitionists, tallying up each new "dry" US state in speeches that blasted the municipality and housing reformers for even considering official support for native drunkenness. The antiliquor leagues that sprouted up along the Rand effectively doused the beer monopoly idea in Johannesburg until 1938, when prohibitionism waned both in the city and worldwide.[40]

In the years after World War I, the internal agonies wrought by archsegregationism rose to a climax in Johannesburg. The numbers of black migrants to town rose sharply during the war, and with postwar inflation, everyone was having trouble making ends meet, not just the municipality. In 1918, the deadly worldwide influenza epidemic swept through South Africa's native locations and Johannesburg's slums, killing thousands. Fears of a Rand-wide mining strike grew, and the "bucket boys" of the Vrededorp compound partially stopped their collections of municipal waste for a few smelly days in a protest over wages. At Klipspruit, Charles James, the council's martinet of a locations manager, had long antagonized residents by seizing houses for unpaid stand rents and by impounding cattle that broke through the location's fence to graze on the greener grass of the municipal sewage farm. On March 23, 1919, after one such cattle raid, a "band" of residents set upon James and his constables with "choppers, picks, sticks, and missiles," injuring several white men and knocking James on the head. James put the location on lockdown, and the next morning the 5:30 a.m. train into town ran empty.

Meanwhile, the Transvaal Native Congress had been escalating its campaigns against the pass laws with mass meetings in Sophiatown and Vrededorp. When the Klipspruit rebels were hauled to trial, TAC protestors began assembling outside the courthouse downtown. A melee broke out there in April, and later a white gunman killed a black man in a scuffle at the Vrededorp underpass that foreshadowed the full-scale riot of the following year. The council appointed a commission to look into the problems at Klipspruit; that spring its report delivered a deeply critical blow to the municipality's management of the facility and recommended firing James. Suspicions grew, however, that local unrest had taken inspiration from any number of sources outside South Africa: anticolonial agitation in Egypt, Gandhi's mass protests in India, radical black church leaders from the United States, roving agitators from the International Workers of the World, and—in a presentiment of an apartheid-era obsession—the Bolsheviks. Meanwhile, the JFRA and the council were scandalized to hear that the Union government was considering a bill to legitimize all the land sales to white-fronted Indian limited liability companies that had taken place since the Gandhi-Smuts agreement in 1914. An enormous anti-Asiatic congress assembled in nearby Pretoria at which radicals gave fiery speeches advocating deportation. Pressure from the Government of India, London, and Cape liberals resulted in more compromises and more resentments.

Back in Johannesburg the Klipspruit rebels got clemency, and white anger in the western slums grew. In early 1920, as we know, Vrededorp

erupted in a four-hour orgy of tramcar stoning, gun shots, and street battles. The fact that blacks had found refuge in the Malay Location enraged
white ratepayers from several nearby neighborhoods, whose tram line
had made such a perfect symbol of protest during the riots. Urged on by
the JFRA, they sent town hall a petition with three thousand signatures
demanding that the Malay Location be razed. Jan Smuts, who had just
become prime minister of the Union upon Louis Botha's death, came
in person to inspect the area. There, city councilmen ruefully informed
the prime minister and angry ratepayers that if the council destroyed
the Malay Location, it could do nothing to stop its residents from taking
over adjoining neighborhoods, possibly including those of the petition-
ers. The archsegregationist movement was choking on its own furies and
needed rescue.[41]

## The Birth Pangs of Nation-State Segregation

In 1920, Jan Smuts's Union government gingerly took on the issue of
comprehensive urban racial zoning at the national level. The "future difficulties," Smuts had once said, "would not be with the raw native in his
village, but in the great centres where there were congregating hundreds
of thousands of these people. There the great trouble is going to arise."
So great were these complexities in Smuts's mind that he allowed discussions of his Native Urban Areas Bill to undergo five years of public scrutiny (from 1918 to 1923), including a nationwide tour that Smuts himself
organized as chair of a new Native Affairs Commission.[42]

Not surprisingly, sharp fault lines from the grassroots quickly ripped
through the national debate. Black opposition to segregation was sharpest of all. As Selope Thema of the TAC explained, "The segregation they
want is one that will make South Africa 'a white man's land.' ... Between
this policy and that of repression there is no difference." Natives must
have "a place in the sun, [and] freedom of thought and action." Smuts's
commission translated its proposed urban areas bill into African languages, disseminated it widely, and heard testimony from large numbers
of black leaders. Clearly, though, Smuts had no interest in pursuing the
obvious trajectory of Thema's line of thought. The very fact that the bill
applied to natives only, and not to coloreds and Indians, unambiguously
communicated whites' assumption that blacks and their leaders were
politically the weakest group in the country.[43]

The commission did, however, include liberal reformers of some stature, such as Charles T. Loram of Durban, who was eager to see the bill address the quality of housing. Liberals like Colonel G. A. Godley also formed the majority on a second commission, this one focused on the pass laws. Johannesburg's slums and Klipspruit came up repeatedly as an example of how bad things could be. In addition, liberals also floated the idea of giving blacks more secure land tenure in locations as an inducement to get wealthier blacks to move out of places like Sophiatown. Smuts himself flirted with the idea of establishing "native villages" next to locations where blacks "who raised themselves up in the scale of civilisation" could get freehold tenure and live apart from those "in a semi barbarous state." Since this would mean that the some 997 black Johannesburgers exempted from the Transvaal's location laws would be forced out to areas near Klipspruit, his idea would have represented yet another instance of the use of civilization rhetoric for racial repression—the carrot of freehold notwithstanding.[44]

For many of Johannesburg's whites, however, all the talk of housing reform and freehold meant only one thing: Smuts was preparing to concede that large numbers of black people could live permanently in the cities. As urban ratepayers and municipal officials contemplated the possibility of more black "penetration" of white neighborhoods and counted up the expense involved in ever more segregated public housing for blacks, a growing number had embraced the idea that urban racial zoning needed to be accompanied by stronger powers of influx control. This idea was implicit in Curtis's municipal pass code and in Pim's widely shared theory about the inherently rural nature of black people. South Africa's all-white Labor Party argued forcefully along these lines as well, maintaining that the Randlords and other employers had created the racial problems of the cities in the first place by refusing to give up their dependence on cheap black laborers.

In 1922, labor unrest suddenly crested, threatening the white Union itself. That year, a group of Randlords tried to replace semiskilled white laborers with blacks willing to work for lower wages. White workers took up arms, formed Boer-War-style guerilla "commandos," shut down the mines, took over several town halls along the Rand, and wrested the streets of two Johannesburg suburbs from the police. Smuts struck back at the workers, sending in troops. Soon, airplanes strafed the rebels and dropped bombs near downtown Johannesburg, killing hundreds. Meanwhile, the strikers went on their own rampages, killing some forty defenseless black miners in their compounds and in the streets. As a corollary to their infamous slogan "Workers of the World Fight and Unite for a White South Africa," the rebels also called for separate neighborhoods and stronger influx controls. Afrikaner Nationalists, meanwhile, watched the great Rand Revolt with great interest. They too wanted to reduce the black population in the cities so that Afrikaner farmers could count on a steady supply of African farm laborers.[45]

"The native should only be allowed to enter urban areas, which are essentially the White man's creation, when he is willing to enter and minister to the needs of the White man, and should depart therefrom when he ceases to so minister." With these words, the dour Colonel F. C. Stallard, chair of the Transvaal Local Government Commission—the third of the commissions Smuts called on to work on the Urban Areas Bill—pointedly rebuked liberals who wanted to relax the pass laws, improve location housing, and grant blacks property rights. Stallard was an Oxford graduate, a veteran of the Boer War and World War I, a constitutional lawyer, a gentleman farmer, and a fierce imperial loyalist. His archsegregationist creed was born in both the loftiest and the most intimate places in Johannesburg society. A Fortnightly Club member with strong ties to Curtis and the Kindergarten, he became a died-in-the-wool Black Peril fighter, once arguing in court for the closing of a white neighborhood's trash destructor because the black men who worked there did not wear shirts. ("A thing that prejudices the honour of women is more important than the establishment of sanitary arrangements.") For Stallard, the civilization standard had no place in public policy, even as a rhetorical sugarcoating. Any exemptions made for "the ... educated native," he complained, let alone granting the right to freehold, would "ensure the ultimate subordination of the most hopeless portion of the white race to the most competent portion of the black race." Uncannily, his farm, Hope Woolith, lay on the boundary of the Klipspruit sewage farm. The municipal council regularly supplied him with manure from his farms for his fields. It also paid for a fence around his property to prevent unwanted visits from the location residents' errant cows.[46]

The Natives (Urban Areas) Act finally became law in 1923. It replaced all existing local and provincial locations bylaws with a nationwide system of voluntary comprehensive urban racial zoning. Municipalities now had the power to "proclaim" sections of the city as white areas and to move all black people who lived there to native locations—as long as authorities could provide those displaced with adequate housing. Liberals were able to keep that last provision in the law, a racialized version of the key provision in the Housing of the Working Classes Act. To pay for the housing, cities could keep a separate "native revenue account" consisting of the money raised by pass offices from employers register-ing native work contracts, or from a beer-hall system like Durban's—if they could get such a system past local opposition. This system of "fiscal segregation" meant that ordinary white ratepayers would not have to pay the tab to keep blacks in the city.[47]

But the act also embodied the influence of C. F. Stallard, the JFRA, the white Laborites, and nationalists like J. B. M. Hertzog. It allowed mu-nicipalities to impose much stricter pass laws to control the influx of "masterless natives" to the city. Moreover, with the approval of Smuts, Hertzog, and Richard Feetham, Curtis's fellow Kindergartner and suc-cessor as town clerk—and to the deep dismay of black leaders like Selope Thema—the act contained no option for freehold title in the locations. Cities could, furthermore, abrogate black freehold in places that they wanted to proclaim as white, such as Sophiatown. The only place for blacks to get a secure title was in the rural reserves. W. K. Tucker's racial theory of property rights was vindicated.[48]

The Natives (Urban Areas) Act certainly represented in its time world history's most extensive, explicit, and complex legal plan for seg-regating the cities of an entire country, far more elaborate than such colony-encompassing schemes as the Raj's cantonment codes, the Colo-nial Office's recommendations for segregation in West Africa, or Lyau-tey's Moroccan urban-planning laws. The political battle to bring the law to passage was also the biggest such epic ever waged in the name of racial city-splitting. And, thanks to the especially fervid forces that drove South African settlers' racism forward despite their many quarrels, victory had come at a moment when white segregation mania was waning virtually everywhere else in the world.

Even so, the 1923 act did not end all of the furies of the settlers' city. Though national in scope, actual segregationist action, such as clearing downtown Johannesburg of its black people, would depend on local gov-ernments' ability to pay for native locations by extracting revenue from employers, from small Union grants, or, if they could, from black beer drinkers. Already in 1924, the Ratepayer Party of Johannesburg, now fully in command of the council and raging with Stallardist arrogance, tried to call the liberal portion of the act on its bluff by proclaiming the entire city white in one fell swoop. The courts just as quickly annulled the proclamation on the grounds that Johannesburg had not provided alternative housing as the act required. Many of the dramas of the 1910s—over the color line's location, African beer, housing finance, and, above all, whether Africans should be permanent townspeople—continued to fester into the 1930s and beyond. Klipspruit survived—though just barely. In a move that would have represented a big retreat from Milner-era precedents, the council almost closed the place down in 1920 after the negative report on conditions there. However, no less an authority than the great American yellow fever eradicator Colonel William C. Gorgas passed through town just in time, and he agreed with Porter that, while smelly and swarming with insects, the place was not unhealthy. Still, blacks kept streaming into Johannesburg, overwhelming the city's ability to build new Nissen huts in the Western Native Township. The city's slum belt continued to grow.[49]

The next steps would be up to J. B. M. Hertzog, whose National Party parlayed its alliance with the Labor Party to victory against the Randlord- and Empire-loving Jan Smuts in the 1924 election. Back in 1911, Hertzog had felt "a feeling akin to horror" about the native question. "Ever since 1903 I have advocated segregation as the only permanent solution of the question and it is, to me, very clear that unless such a policy is undertaken soon, the conditions necessary for its realisation will, as happened in America, vanish."[50]

Hertzog could not have known this, but in 1923, the same year that South African settlers began to clarify the role of their central government in dividing the country's cities, a small group of American reformers and "real estate men" were doing the same, in a very different, much quieter way. Soon both Hertzog and the Americans would develop techniques—some different and some connected to the same currents of cross-oceanic trends in city planning—to further radicalize settler segregationism, even as it waned elsewhere.

# 10 ⦙ Camouflaging the Color Line in Chicago

## A Subtler Sort of Segregation?

To Americans of native, Asian, Mexican, and African descent (and to some eastern and southern European immigrants as well), the South African politician J. B. M. Hertzog's 1911 lament that the "conditions for segregation" had vanished from the United States would have seemed preposterous. Large-scale separation of the races had long been a central objective of white supremacists in the largest, most populous, richest, and most powerful of all Western settler colonies—especially as the United States of America became a transcontinental, then an ocean-spanning empire in its own right, rivaling Britain and France in sheer territorial aggrandizement. Whites in the United States did not look to South Africa for inspiration as often as white South Africans alternatively admired and clucked in dismay over the "great cauldron of the American union." But at different times and places, US settlers and their governments enacted racial segregation policies that were more radical and thoroughgoing than South Africa's. Some of these took forms remarkably like separate development, influx control, and urban racial zoning. At other times, the actions of US segregationists devolved even further, into mass deportation and racial extermination.[1]

Despite this history, the US federal government could not wholeheartedly support urban segregationists in the great cities of its mainland North American empire in the early decades of the twentieth century. In this way, radical though it was, segregation mania in the United States contrasted sharply with Milner-era South Africa and other colonial cities, even including some in the American overseas empire.

Because of the imperial vacuum, segregationist whites in North American US cities were forced to turn to other sources of power to enforce residential color lines. Their quest at first took them downward in the political scale, first to state and local governments, then to neighborhood "protection" organizations, and then to mob violence in city streets. All of these alternatives backfired during the period 1917 to 1920—the same tumultuous years when segregation mania crested across the colonial world and when Johannesburg's racial furies spun out of control. In a stunning defeat for white supremacists, black activists and their allies were able to convince the US Supreme Court to invalidate residential race segregation by government legislation.

In response to this new setback at the federal level and to the spiraling urban violence that followed, a small group of elite segregationists, largely based in Chicago, reformulated the crusade for urban color lines in the United States. They culled a set of ideologies and city-splitting tools from the two other global-scale sources of institutional power used by urban segregation movements elsewhere—urban reform politics and the real estate industry. Unlike segregationists in Johannesburg, who openly drew upon inspiration from other colonial cities, those in Chicago and other US cities had to reinvent the urban color line by cloaking it within multiple levels of institutional and ideological camouflage. Such disguises aimed to keep public racial discourse about city-splitting at a minimum while ensuring a maximum amount of actual racial segregation. As in South Africa, the first successes of this movement on a national scale occurred in the early 1920s, setting the stage for a more thoroughgoing, federally supported—but far stealthier—archsegregationist system for all US cities.

## Segregating the United States

Throughout most of the history of the United States, racism has not been a subtle business at all. In the nineteenth century, large numbers of the country's most influential white people imagined Americans as a particularly energetic offshoot of the Anglo-Saxon race that possessed a "manifest destiny" to conquer and supplant the continent's inferior races and then move beyond. Some hearkened back to the work of the Calcutta Orientalist William Jones, declaring that whites' destiny in the Americas made up a key segment in a providential plan of worldwide racial segregation. The plan began millennia ago, in the supposed central Asian birthplace of the superior Indo-European, or "Aryan," races, and proceeded westward—like the daily path of the sun—along the world's most temperate and fertile latitudes, through Europe, across the Atlantic, and then across North America. Soon the conquest of this globe-girdling racial homeland would return full circle back to Asia. For many American imperialists, that last leg ran through Hawaii and the Philippines.[2]

Such beliefs, along with settlers' voracious appetite for land, led to repeated calls to purge North America of all "inferior races," beginning with Native Americans. If anything, the transcontinental march of conquest resulted in a more brutal series of forced removals and a more extensive system of rural "native reserves" than the Boer and British conquests of southern Africa. In the United States, like in South Africa, there was much ambiguous talk, going back to Thomas Jefferson, that Indian reservations would give their inhabitants a separate, protected space to attain civilization on their own racial schedule. But for many US conquerors, such calls for separate development just bought time for the total dispossession of Native Americans, either by guileful acts of trickery or brutal acts of extermination. Natives' susceptibility to Old World diseases and their vulnerability to the decimation of resources like the Great Plains bison herds eventually allowed the United States Army and groups of armed settlers to defeat their often spirited resistance— sometimes by massacring large numbers of people. Native populations plummeted in the process.[3]

Because of the genocide, the United States' dynamic industrial economy turned much more decisively than South Africa's to extracontinental labor sources—Asia, Latin America, and, above all, Europe. In response, descendants of "older stock" white American settlers—cynically calling themselves "nativists"—joined passionate anti-immigrant movements that called on the federal government to control the influxes of peoples they considered members of "alien" races. Waves of immigration restriction resulted, first against the Chinese (1882), then other Asians (1907 and 1917), then against Italians, Slavs, eastern European Jews beleaguered by the pogroms, and other non-Europeans (1924). These measures effectively diminished large streams of migration across both the Pacific and the Atlantic Oceans—much like South Africa's restrictions on Indian immigration, and certainly more successfully than its internal pass laws against blacks. From the 1920s on, white nativists turned their energies toward deporting Mexicans from the southwestern regions of the country. That movement culminated in "Operation Wetback" of the 1950s, involving millions of people. Meanwhile, during World War II, the federal government confined more than 110,000 Japanese Americans in internment camps, most located in desolate regions of the US West.[4]

To US whites, however, no problem of racial coexistence was more intractable than the "Negro Problem." Though South Africans often compared their own racial questions with those in the United States, the two societies contrasted in some fundamental ways. Slavery and emancipation made up the central matrices of black-white politics in the United States—not, as in South Africa, armed conquest and land dispossession. During the American Civil War (1861-65), large numbers of black slaves left their plantations for the security of Union army lines, helping to push a reluctant federal government, under President Abraham Lincoln, to accept a central role in the emancipation and protection of freed slaves. After Lincoln's assassination in 1865, his Republican Party—acting upon a measure of liberal sentiment derived from the abolitionist movement and a much larger dose of partisan hunger for black votes in the defeated Southern states—pushed through the Fourteenth and Fifteen Amendments to the Constitution, forbidding all governments from abridging civil rights and voting rights on the basis of "race, color, or previous condition of servitude."[5]

Before the war, proslavery activists had often celebrated the continental commingling of black and white, using the paternalist argument that, as slaves to a superior race, blacks had developed much faster than they would if they remained free in Africa. By contrast, antislavery activists often found themselves on the defensive when called upon to explain what they would do with black people once freed. Many, including Abraham Lincoln, the "Great Emancipator" himself, actively supported so-called colonization policies aimed to resettle blacks in Africa or elsewhere in the tropics. Colonization advocates, who included some black leaders, argued that Africans would do better in climates more suited to their racial constitutions and that continental segregation would spare black people from inevitable conflicts with racist whites that could also undermine American society as a whole. The colonization movement's most ambitious venture was the independent country of Liberia in West Africa, the American counterpart to the neighboring British free-black colony of Sierra Leone. In the Northern states, meanwhile, a policy of gradual emancipation began much earlier, but white mob violence against free blacks was endemic in Northern cities, and some of it verged on exterminationism. By the 1830s, most Northern states disfranchised their black populations and segregated a large range of public amenities. The phrase "Jim Crow" was coined in the North during this period. Many western states, including Lincoln's Illinois, also passed laws forbidding black people from entering their territory.[6]

After emancipation, Southern whites too adopted the idea that continental coexistence with blacks was a bane upon the superior race. As black men gained the right to vote, dozens began winning elections in the South, where they were often in the majority in local districts. Many whites retaliated bitterly, launching violent mob attacks and forming organizations such as the Ku Klux Klan, which openly called for extermination. Others appropriated abolitionist talk of colonization, hoping to force blacks to leave North America. Countless thousands of black people died in the mob attacks, and others fled, noticeably diminishing the black population of some towns and cities. However, African Americans ultimately avoided the kind of brutal racial cleansing that devastated Native Americans. Blacks in the United States were not as susceptible to Old World diseases, and though their new economic situation was precarious, it was less vulnerable than the hunting and gathering culture of the plains. In fact, most Southern blacks' new role as sharecroppers, lowly as it was, gave them an essential function in the plantation economy that rendered both genocide and deportation politically impractical.[7]

Still, to leaders like Henry Grady, the apostle of the so-called New South, the Reconstruction-era violence confirmed the social Darwinistic view that different races in the same places inevitably fell into mortal combat. Instead of removing blacks from the continent, he focused on getting rid of the black vote, which he—like James Bryce and many white South Africans—thought exacerbated these "instinctual" racial conflicts. Though some South Africans, like Hertzog and Howard Pim, became convinced that Reconstruction had deeply wounded white Americans' experiments with segregation, Grady and the legislatures of Southern states were undaunted. From 1890 on, these legislatures defied the nonracial principles of the Fifteenth Amendment on voting rights, using a variety of subterfuges, including the state of Mississippi's pioneering literacy tests. By 1901, most Southern states had virtually eliminated the black vote. The US Supreme Court, stacked with racial conservatives, went along with these ploys and weakened the Fourteenth Amendment's civil rights provisions as they went. In *Plessy vs. Ferguson* (1896), the court also declared that governments could provide separate facilities for blacks as long as they were "equal."[8]

Disfranchisement and *Plessy* cleared the path for Southern Jim Crow—ultimately, Southern whites' most politically feasible solution to the racial coexistence problem. Southern state and municipal governments passed a veritable blizzard of ordinances after 1900 to divide the smaller spaces of cities and towns: rail and trolley cars, train station ticket booths, platforms, waiting rooms, public restrooms, water coolers, courtrooms, schools, and city parks (on city sidewalks, a complex racial etiquette governed blacks' behavior, not ordinances as in Johannesburg). Private businesses were either ordered or given license to segregate places like restaurants, theaters, and amusement parks. The triumph of Southern Jim Crow signaled a dismaying reversal of the promises of the Reconstruction and its landmark constitutional amendments: by 1900, thirty years after the revolution against slavery, Southern black people had arrived at a new nadir in their history, besieged by an intertwined conspiracy of hostile statehouses, brutal local authorities, and threatening lynch mobs that would remain in place until the civil rights movement of the 1950s and 1960s.

## Jim-Crowing the Neighborhoods

Even at the nadir, however, and even amid the early years of segregation mania elsewhere in the world, the US federal government was unable to give sustained support to local projects of racial city-splitting in its vast mainland North American territory.

How could this be? Certainly the United States was not lacking in imperial willpower. In fact at this same time the American empire was in the midst of a full-throated expansion, cheered on by such towering tribunes of social Darwinism and eugenics as President Theodore Roosevelt. In addition to seizing Hawaii, the US Army—including Roosevelt's own "Rough Rider" regiment—extended the country's "manifest" racial destiny by occupying former Spanish possessions like Cuba, Puerto Rico, and the Philippines in 1898. In 1903, Roosevelt strong-armed the new nation of Panama to grant the United States control over a ten-mile-wide Canal Zone, soon to be home to the Panama Canal.[9]

In these new overseas colonies, urban segregationist politics was just as varied and eclectic as within the French and British empires. In Havana, Cuba, formal American political control was weakest. There, US developers laid out an expansive "Country Club District" in the exclusive western suburbs of the city for rich members of the local "American colony," but they shared it with wealthy Cubans and diplomats from across Latin America. In the Philippines, where American control also depended heavily on alliances with sympathetic local elites, legalized residential segregation was impossible as well. The Escolta district in downtown Manila did become a kind of American zone, complete with Shanghai-style segregated clubs, bars, and theaters. Many officials also set themselves up in palatial suburban residences in upper-crust Spanish neighborhoods or in the area near the exclusive Polo Club. In 1904, the celebrated urban planner Daniel T. Burnham came to Manila with a lavish Haussmann-inspired plan to adapt "the city . . . to the better conditions of living" expected by Americans, but he did little to further entrench local color lines. By contrast, his design for a hill station five thousand feet up in Luzon's Cordillera Central at Baguio—meant to "be to the Philippines much what Simla is to India"—represented a much more deliberately segregationist urban plan.[10]

The harshest of the federal government's overseas urban color lines came into being in the Panama Canal Zone, where US imperial control was least contested and where a white settler community was more permanently ensconced. There, the infamous gold-and-silver occupational system held sway. It entitled the largely white engineers, contractors, and workers involved in constructing the canal to a far higher pay scale, in gold US dollars, while consigning the largely West Indian, Panamanian, and African American diggers to far lower wages paid in Panamanian silver. The line between gold and silver quickly mutated into a barely disguised statutory system of racial Jim Crow built around an early version of a racialized welfare state. Under its logic, white Zonians were not only entitled to government-provided vacations in the United States, but their own segregated schools, racially exclusive amenities of all kinds, and superior rental housing in separate areas of local cities. Sanitary justifications that took root during Colonel Gorgas's widely celebrated efforts to eradicate yellow-fever mosquitoes in the Zone helped bring this system into being. Soon after the conquest, American planners laid out state-of-the-art developments for whites in small cities like Cristóbal, outside Colon, which one admiring visitor compared to the suburbs of Chicago. Black and mestizo canal workers and their descendants remained in barely modified work camps, one of which was known as Silver City, after the Zone's payment system. Though some government investment trickled into these excluded developments, many were located at the same distance from the white sections of town as some of South Africa's black townships.[11]

In the United States' North American mainland empire, meanwhile, the options for federal experiments in archsegregation diminished over time. The conquest of the continent had allowed white settlers to seize some of the world's richest and most extensive agricultural and mining lands. Dozens of boomtowns and new cities came into being, dedicated to processing and transshipping the new empire's natural wealth—not much different in that respect from Johannesburg. None boomed more explosively than Chicago, Illinois—easily one of world history's most successful colonial cities.

However, because of the genocidal levels of mass death associated with the western conquest, American industrialists were never interested in establishing a South African–style migrant labor system involving native peoples, nor did they think to impose pass laws or to reintroduce colonial-era praying towns as urban native locations. The primary labor force in most US cities, in sharp contrast to South Africa, consisted of the country's millions of European immigrants. Some employers, most notably Chicago's George Pullman, built all-white "company towns" for their workers that, like the Witwatersrand's native labor compounds, aimed to prevent turnover and strikes. In the long term, however, company towns played only a passing role in the spatial or racial politics of Chicago and other major US cities. In 1894, when the "workingman's paradise" erupted in a bitter strike, Pullman dismantled the place. Most new planned workers' quarters in the United States were built in smaller towns.[12]

In 1900, American blacks were, in any case, almost entirely excluded from work in big-city factories and municipal jobs—again, in striking contrast to their counterparts in South Africa. Labor compounds for blacks thus made as little sense as those for Native Americans. Only in the Southern states did any large-scale employers, the region's plantation owners, seek to control black people's movements across space as a way of keeping them at work. The techniques they used—long-term sharecropping contracts, debt peonage, vagrancy laws, and prohibitions on outside recruiters—overlapped with those in rural South Africa. However, planters in parts of the US South with relatively small pools of black labor differed with their colleagues in labor-rich areas about the wisdom of controlling labor mobility more extensively, and no pass system came into being for black people. Later, the influx controls that American nativists passed in 1924 on "racially suspect" overseas immigrants actually opened up opportunities for Southern blacks to move to Northern cities.[13]

The only other precedent for government-coerced urban racial zones within the continental US empire was San Francisco's anti-Chinese segregation ordinances. Here, another institution of American racial imperialism, the *Plessy*-era US Supreme Court, provided the drama with suspense. While clearly a bastion of white supremacy, the court had yet to rule on the matter of the segregation of neighborhoods. The ambiguity was heightened by the fact that property-rights-minded state judges in feverishly racist California had twice disallowed San Francisco's ordinances in court cases brought by ordinary Chinese grocers and laundrymen. Such ambiguities were heightened further within the racial politics of the rest of the country. Even as the court allowed disfranchisement and Jim Crow laws to spread across the South, black men retained the vote in the North. There, in cities like Chicago, black voting power had contributed to the repeal of pre–Civil War Jim Crow laws, though segregation of public amenities persisted well into the twentieth century. Black voters also gave the federal government less room to pursue residential segregation in mainland cities than it possessed in the Canal Zone and much less than Alfred Milner had in Johannesburg. Finally, since the Civil War, urban segregationists could no longer bypass these forces of opposition by simply seceding from the post-Reconstruction-era federal government, as white South Africans did in 1910, when their new Union constitution limited the influence of London liberals in their affairs. In the United States, the only segregationist strategy left was for state and local officials, and ordinary white citizens themselves, to take the lead in goading the Supreme Court to act.[14]

In 1910, in the city of Baltimore, Maryland, a small group of Jim Crow segregationists tried exactly that by successfully agitating for a municipal ordinance to divide the city into black and white blocks. In so doing, they ignited a regional movement across the former Confederacy and beyond that aimed to convince state and federal authorities, including the judiciary, to extend Jim Crow to residential neighborhoods in cities across the country and perhaps even to American colonies overseas that had yet to fully take that step.

Jim Crow had always been first and foremost an urban phenomenon, and in the South it reflected the post–Civil War growth of the region's cities. Like contemporary Johannesburg's early "petty apartheid" ordinances, Jim Crow laws helped whites sustain a sense of black deference in cities, where the white paternalism of the plantation, built upon re-lationships between people who knew each other, worked less well. The ambiguous sexual intentions of anonymous urban strangers suffused the "culture of segregation" in Southern cities, and "antimiscegenation" laws also proliferated during this time, as in the Transvaal. The Witwa-tersrand "houseboy problem" was not as much of a concern since most in-house servants in the urban US South were black women. But the pres-ence of small numbers of black men and women in cities who could sig-nal their economic independence from whites by dressing better (and, later, by driving nicer cars) than many poor whites added to the sense of white victimization and moral outrage that drove Jim Crow and helped spark the region's massive wave of lynchings.[15]

It was the specter of this small but growing class of Southern black professionals, businessmen, better-paid service workers, and their fami-lies that startled whites into extending Jim Crow to the neighborhoods in 1910. A black Baltimorean named Ashbie Hawkins, the star lawyer of a newly founded local chapter of the NAACP, bought a house on the city's northwest side, an exclusive quasi-suburban development dating from the 1830s that had long been all-white. Some of his dismayed neighbors included a group of white lawyers and city officials who were connected to Maryland senator William Cabell Bruce and the mayor of Baltimore, J. Barry Mahool. Though these people hardly qualified as high-flying imperial officials like Lionel Curtis, they were amateur race theorists in their own right who held public forums in their parlors and published manifestoes in the local papers and national news magazines. Ameri-can imperialism inspired them, but their writings took from multiple sources of white supremacist fervor—including segregation in British India; the work of the French racist theorist the Count de Gobineau; the anti-Chinese movement on the West Coast; personal nostalgia for the plantation order; and bitter disappointment at the failure of their own efforts to disfranchise blacks in the state of Maryland. (For a Southern city, Baltimore had unusually large numbers of European immigrants, and like their compatriots further north, they successfully blocked lit-eracy tests and other mechanisms of disfranchisement.) Also important to the local segregationist movement was the black boxer Jack Johnson's shattering victory over Jim Jeffries in the world heavyweight match in Reno, Nevada, on July 4, 1910. The first meeting of Baltimore's ordinance supporters occurred the very day after the world's most visible embodiment of the high-dressing, fancy-car-driving, "uppity Negro" won new bragging rights on his global, mass-mediated stage.

In the fall of 1910, Mahool's cadre of segregationists drafted an ordinance that divided every street in Baltimore into white blocks and colored blocks and made it an offense punishable by a hundred-dollar fine or up to a year in the city jail for anyone who moved on to a block set aside for the "opposite race," except for black servants who lived in the houses of their white employees. Their principal legal argument derived directly from a central social Darwinist contention: mitigating the inherent conflict of the races was an appropriate use of the city's "police power."[16]

Mayor Mahool also saw himself as an urban reformer in the larger global liberal tradition. Like other segregationists he positioned the ordinance as a moderate measure, guarding a rational middle ground threatened by the lynch mobs on one side and the "negro agitators," such as Ashbie Hawkins, on the other. Sanitary arguments also came into play. Baltimore's Johns Hopkins Medical School was an internationally renowned center on tuberculosis research, led by world-famous doctors such as William Osler and William Welch—men who regularly hobnobbed with overseas giants like the malaria expert Sir Ronald Ross and who wrote positively of his segregationist theories of malaria prevention. They helped mount a traveling exposition on tuberculosis whose centerpiece was a map of Baltimore pricked with pins wherever someone had died from the disease. A dense forest of these pins covered the growing black neighborhood on the boundary of the northwest side, amply demonstrating to contemporary viewers that "the prevalence of the disease amongst the colored people is a great menace to our white population." Such scares helped to galvanize a grassroots movement in white neighborhoods for the ordinance.[17]

The most electrifying call to arms, though, was the racial theory of property values. "But, wail the idiots," wrote the NAACP's great tribune W. E. B. DuBois from New York, "Negroes depress real estate values! This is a lie—an ancient and bearded lie. Race prejudice decreases value both real estate and human." Bearded though it might have been, the lie had only recently become significant to the world history of urban segregation, making sporadic and contradictory appearances in colonial cities before whites in South Africa and the United States elevated it to a driving, desperate truth around the turn of the twentieth century. By that time, Baltimore, like other US cities, had spawned "neighborhood protection" associations that shared roots in the Anglo-American political tradition with the ratepayers' associations of Johannesburg. Like their South African cousins, most of these groups came into being for diverse local reasons—as government watchdogs or enforcers of "dry" antisaloon ordinances, for example. However, many took up guardianship of local residents' property values against the "Negro invasion" as their central mission. In Baltimore, several dozen of these associations pressed their support for the segregation ordinance, which Mahool signed in December 1910.[18]

Mahool's office was quickly besieged by letters from across the country, and even as far away as the Philippines, demanding copies of the ordinance. Authorities in dozens of cities, from Richmond to Atlanta to New Orleans to St. Louis, passed copycat legislation. The state of Virginia passed a law allowing its cities and towns to divide their territories into "segregation districts," thus prefiguring key provisions in South Africa's Natives (Urban Areas) Act by eleven years. In one of the few instances in which a South African race theorist directly inspired an American segregationist, the white tenant farmer advocate Clarence Poe—who had conferred with the peripatetic native affairs commissioner of Natal, Maurice Evans—used the Baltimore segregation ordinance to inspire a campaign for rural segregation aimed to consign black sharecroppers to reserves (large planters saw no benefit in this scheme, and it fizzled).[19]

As Jim Crow flexed its new talons, black leaders used the remaining segments of the political space they had won during Reconstruction to stifle the assault. Even Booker T. Washington objected vehemently to the Baltimore-style ordinances, in his case because he deemed them an obstacle to black economic development. In 1917, NAACP lawyers led by Moorfield Storey brought an ingeniously crafted test case against a segregation ordinance in Louisville, Kentucky, before the Supreme Court of the United States. On November 5 of that year, the court ruled in favor of the NAACP in *Buchanan v. Warley*: "The difficult problem arising from a feeling of race hostility," argued the justices, was not enough of a justification to enact ordinances that "directly violat[ed] . . . the Fourteenth Amendment of the Constitution preventing state interference with property rights by due process of law."[20]

A multiracial team of attorneys led by a black professional had forced a white supremacist judiciary to choose between racism and a basic premise of laissez-faire capitalism—and property rights won out, at least in the case of neighborhood segregation. "The city," moaned a despondent white ordinance supporter in Baltimore, "will soon be a second darkest Africa." Mayor Mahool's successor, James H. Preston, could only offer a slim ray of hope. "I have a friend in Chicago," he wrote to some of them, who "told me of a plan they have of keeping negroes out of white blocks. ... Some such plan may be effective here."[21]

## Segregation by Profiteer, Protective Association, and Pogrom

Segregationists in Northern US cities liked to contrast their supposedly moderate racial policies with Southerners' rabidly racist ones. In fact, such comparisons acted as a primary form of camouflage for Northern archsegregationist activism throughout the twentieth century, resembling British imperial officials' efforts in South Africa to claim racial enlightenment in contrast to the benighted Boers. The truth in the US North was likewise more complex and much less flattering, as the increasingly scam-ridden, highly organized, and often ferociously violent grassroots segregation movement of early twentieth-century Chicago suggests.[22]

As the largest cities in the United States burst into industrial powerhouses during the nineteenth century, their wealthy and middle classes gradually forsook the crowded class-diverse urban cores for the suburbs—just as in London and in Asian colonial cities a century earlier. Like the London elite, American suburbanites also spouted the ideology that distance from social inferiors (and factory smoke) gave people moral upstandingness and health—as well as more lucrative investments in real estate. Factory workers meanwhile piled themselves into tenements and slum dwellings closer to downtown and the grimy commercial or manufacturing districts, trading high rents and poor conditions for low transport costs and proximity to the hiring halls. One Chicago housing reformer calculated that the density of the city's slums was "three times that of the most crowded portions of Tokyo, Calcutta, and many other Asiatic cities." But Chicagoans also distinguished their city's various "foreign colonies" by the origins of immigrants they imagined to predominate there: Polonia, Little Italy, Little Sicily, Greektown, Pilsen for the Bohemians, and the Old Ghetto for Jews. These neighborhoods' names may well have reflected the groups whose religious institutions and businesses predominated there, but a street-by-street analysis of census records shows that all of these "ethnic neighborhoods" were in fact vastly intricate patchworks of peoples speaking dozens of languages.[23]

For much of the nineteenth century, Northern US cities' small but growing populations of African Americans sewed themselves uneasily into these urban patchworks. In former East Coast slave cities, many blacks had remained as servants in the houses of former masters; others sought independence, like their enslaved forbears, by gathering in small, loosely bounded neighborhoods farther from downtown, which whites referred to by such names as "Nigger Hill," "New Guinea," or "Little Africa." We know of scattered occasions from the earliest postslavery years when whites complained about blacks' threats to their property values, so the location of such black communities may reflect whites' preferences to some degree. However, black communities remained small, urban color lines remained vague and transitory, and whites made no effort to extend Northern Jim Crow to residential neighborhoods before the Civil War. As the cities split ever more cleanly along class lines, a few blacks with higher professional standing found ways to buy houses in somewhat more respectable, all-white neighborhoods, and of course black live-in servants could also be found there as well. But most blacks lived deep in the slums, where their small numbers excited varying levels of hostility from immigrant whites, many of whose first lesson in becoming American was how to call blacks "niggers." It was in these slums that some of the forces of a fiercer sort of Northern residential segregation began to germinate, beginning on the South Side of Chicago in the 1890s.[24]

Chicago had risen from a marshy colonial trading post in 1830 to a city of a half million in 1880—despite the Great Fire of 1871 that leveled much of the city's historic core. By 1900, as the premier entrepôt and transport center for the fruits of western conquests—lumber, iron, coal, grain, pork, and beef—the city's population had tripled again, to a million and a half. Much of the increase was due to immigration from southern and eastern Europe, but the city's small black population also quintupled during the same years, from about six thousand to thirty thousand. The relative size of these growing numbers meant that the racial dynamics of real estate in Chicago's slum belt differed from those in a city like Johannesburg. Unlike the Witwatersrand's slumlords, whose primary pool of tenants was the city's large black, colored, and Indian population, Chicago's slumlords could see an advantage in excluding blacks from their properties if the much larger and expanding white population objected to them as neighbors. As housing options grew tighter for African Americans, they were forced to take lower quality lodgings at higher prices, often in the districts where black businesses and churches had begun to cluster. In Chicago, there were several of these areas, but the largest soon got the name "Black Belt." This neighborhood lay not far south of the city's downtown, squeezed within a quarter-mile-wide slot between the noisome Rock Island Railroad on the west—beyond which lay the multiethnic white working-class meatpacking district—and the clattering South Side elevated commuter railroad (the "L") on the east, which separated the Black Belt from the 1850s-era, middle-class, quasi-suburban developments of Kenwood, Hyde Park, and Woodlawn. Within the Black Belt itself, immigrant racism handed the area's largely white landlords a winning proposition. Since these slumlords' black clientele was largely captive, they could get away with raising rents while completely dispensing with expensive maintenance crews. Soon the Black Belt became a kind of anomaly: a slumyard of all slumyards that also imprisoned a striving and increasingly unhappy black middle class. As a result, Chicago's slum belt became much more segregated by race than contemporary Johannesburg's.[25]

Into this situation entered another type of real estate profiteer: the "blockbuster." This character's bread and butter depended on two facts about poor Chicagoans, one about whites and one about blacks. The fact about poor white people in Chicago was that while their wages and job opportunities were certainly exploitative, the diversified industrial economy of the city did allow a surprising number of them to build somewhat nicer homes amid Chicago's tenements. To do this they scraped together financing from friends, ethnic associations, and a new breed of banks called building and loan societies. Then, they raised repayment money by renting spare rooms to boarders and by planting gardens to save on food costs. Since their investments were very shaky, they were prepared to be spooked by any potential threat. One of those threats, they became increasingly convinced, was the growing number of Chicago's blacks—the second basic fact that brought blockbusters into being. From 1900 to 1910, the city's black population increased by a half to forty-four thousand; it would almost triple again, to 110,000, during the Great Migration of the 1910s, more or less equaling the black population of Johannesburg—only in Chicago's case within a much larger industrial city.[26]

These circumstances provided an ideal context for Chicago's block-busters to spread the "bearded lie" about property values, then cash in on

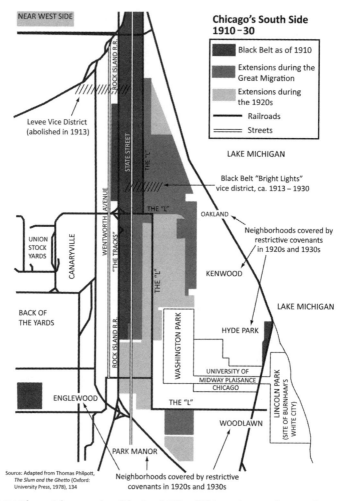

NEAR WEST SIDE

**Chicago's South Side 1910–30**

- ■ Black Belt as of 1910
- ■ Extensions during the Great Migration
- ■ Extensions during the 1920s
- ── Railroads
- ═══ Streets

ROCK ISLAND R.R.

Levee Vice District (abolished in 1913)

STATE STREET

THE "L"

LAKE MICHIGAN

Black Belt "Bright Lights" vice district, ca. 1913–1930

WENTWORTH AVENUE

THE "L"

OAKLAND

Neighborhoods covered by restrictive covenants in 1920s and 1930s

UNION STOCK YARDS

CANARYVILLE

"THE TRACKS"

THE "L"

KENWOOD

LAKE MICHIGAN

BACK OF THE YARDS

ROCK ISLAND R.R.

WASHINGTON PARK

HYDE PARK

ENGLEWOOD

THE "L"

UNIVERSITY OF CHICAGO

MIDWAY PLAISANCE

LINCOLN PARK (SITE OF BURNHAM'S WHITE CITY)

WOODLAWN

PARK MANOR

Source: Adapted from Thomas Philpott, *The Slum and the Ghetto* (Oxford: University Press, 1978), 134

Neighborhoods covered by restrictive covenants in 1920s and 1930s

FIGURE 10.1 The racial geography of the South Side of Chicago in 1930 showing the expansion of the Black Belt during the Great Migration and after, as well as the reaction of neighboring whites. Map by Kailee Neuner.

the fright that resulted. Their scheme often began with a kind of street-corner minstrel show that does not seem to have a precise equivalent in Johannesburg. They hired black men to stage a fight on an all-white corner or black women to push a stroller amid white children playing on the street. Once the theater was over, they followed up with a blizzard of handbills warning whites to leave the neighborhood before the coming onslaught. If the ploy succeeded in sowing enough panic, whites would sell out to the blockbuster for cheaper than they would have otherwise, allowing the blockbuster to rent or sell the same properties at much higher prices to the growing numbers of desperate black lodging-seekers. Some black real estate agents also engaged in blockbusting, though apparently less out of choice than out of necessity, and with less minstrelsy and profiteering.[27]

Whites did not appreciate being caught in blockbusters' stings, but they readily spread the racist firestorm about property values. The two seemingly contradictory forces worked hand in hand. Blacks managed to rent or, in some cases, buy houses from blockbusters west of the Rock Island Railroad tracks, along working-class Wentworth Avenue. Blacks who were more well-to-do liberated themselves from the slums by moving east of the "L," again relying on blockbusters to move into the fringes of the middle-class South Side, first in Kenwood to the north but increasingly into the especially fashionable Hyde Park. There, small shops selling cheap alcohol had already sprung up to cater to black house servants, troubling local temperance activists and property-conscious homeowners. In 1909, the venerable Hyde Park Protective Association, originally founded to clear the neighborhood of saloons, committed itself to fighting the "negro invasion" and the blockbusters who had brought it on.[28]

The ensuing white expressions of victimization and moral outrage contained many of the themes of segregationist movements in urban South Africa and other colonial cities, though there were the usual telling local twists. Social Darwinist clichés abounded in the circulars, newspapers, and public meetings of the Hyde Park Protective Association and its successors. "In every land and clime," intoned one speaker at a meeting of what was then called the Hyde Park and Kenwood Association (KHPA), "man obeys the second law of his nature and seeks his own kind avoiding every other." To prove the point he invoked the words of "that wonderful godlike man" Abraham Lincoln, who once proclaimed, "there is a physical difference between the white and black races [which I believe will forever forbid their] living together on terms of social and political equality." Among neighborhood activists, such hard racist rhetoric was rarely softened by any obligation to take up the "white man's burden" or any need to recognize that blacks' negative racial attributes could be changed for the better if they acquired "civilization." Still, Frederick Hoffman's idea that cities were the worst possible environment for black advancement, a thought that originated in the United States and made its way to South Africa, also inspired South Side segregationists. Like white Johannesburgers, Chicagoans often invoked the name of

Booker T. Washington to justify their cause, while sparing no occasion to discredit the more radical W. E. B. DuBois and other civil rights leaders. One homeowner association newspaper, for example, published a picture of DuBois with the caption "Karl Marx of Negroes. Noted Colored Philosopher Whose Works Are Used by Agitators to Stir Race Hatred." When the Black Belt city alderman Oscar De Priest called a public meeting to respond to the KHPA's segregation campaign, a writer for Hyde Park *Property Owner's Journal* once again dug into the racial sarcasm of the American minstrel show. The typical "negro leader," he wrote, "develops into an overbearing, inflated, irascible individual, overburdening his brain to such an extent about social equality that he becomes dangerous to all with whom he comes into contact.... Their inordinate vanity, their desire to shine as social lights caused them to stray out of their paths and lose themselves.... With much comical oratory, they dangled our association before the spellbound eyes of their sable dupes and after extreme fuming and sweating appointed about fifteen committees to annihilate all Hyde Parkers." The *Journal*'s parting words went straighter to the KHPA's main point: "The place for a Negro aristocrat is in a Negro neighborhood."[29]

White South Siders also poured their agony-laced arrogance upon Chicago's teeming masses of poor black migrants. Here the transoceanic reservoir of sanitary, housing, and vice reform rhetoric got mixed up with whites' personal interpretations of their everyday encounters with blacks in the city. As in South Africa, Black Peril hysteria often added spice to the ideological brew. The boxer Jack Johnson, for example, figured strongly in white Chicagoans' imaginations, all the more so because Johnson actually lived in Chicago for a number of years, and the stories of his various affairs with white women were local news. So was the sophisticated cross-racial camaraderie and sex trade available at the bar Johnson owned in the Black Belt, the Café de Champion. In 1910, an Illinois congressman named James Robert Mann sponsored a White Slave Traffic Act (best known as the Mann Act) in the U.S. Congress that made it illegal to transport women across state boundaries for prostitution and other unspecified "immoral purposes." In 1913, federal prosecutors used the act to trump up a case against Johnson based on a trip he took with a white female companion to a neighboring state. When Johnson was convicted, he fled Chicago into successive exiles in London, Paris, Mexico City, and Havana—ruffling the delicacy of the global color line wherever he went.[30]

In Chicago, meanwhile, vice reformers escalated raids on the city's red-light districts in a campaign to rid the city of its brothels and gambling dens. One police official even publically admitted that the principal goal of the campaign was to chase prostitutes from a largely white area know as the Levee into the Black Belt, and it was there that the new, officially tolerated "Bright Lights" district grew, much to the boiling consternation of the black elite. Whites lost no time in making vice a problem of racial inferiority and race mixing, whipping up fears of "colored" male entertainers and brothel employees "who live with, and in part upon, the proceeds of white women." Throughout the 1920s, as Chicago became a national center for inventive techniques of residential segregation, the "black and tan" clubs of the Bright Lights zone gave the city a national reputation for cross-racial sex. One visiting reporter even wrote a story proclaiming that, in that respect, "Chicago is [a] Worse City than Paris."[31]

As in Johannesburg, black men's supposedly insatiable sexual interest in white women was a primary lens through which whites apprised the intentions of anonymous black people they encountered in public spaces. Such fears were amplified within the racially disordered microgeography of Chicago's streets, schools, parks, and streetcars, including those on one line nicknamed the "African Central." "Sex immorality," one typical informant declared to a commission, "is being contributed to by mixing Negroes and whites in public schools and parks." "Negroes in street cars," we learn from another, "refuse to double up with each other of their race, but seem to delight in sitting beside some dainty white girl ... Often he falls asleep and leans on his white seatmate's shoulder." A third summarized it all with a cliché that lay at the core of popular racial sentiment in most of the world's settler cities: "as you know, a white woman has to fear a colored man."[32]

Reformers of Chicago's slums, meanwhile, had long mixed their denunciations of slumlords with the implication that the racial proclivities of Italian, Polish, or Jewish slum dwellers posed their own threat to the health of the city's more upright, Anglo-Saxon citizens. To many whites, the Black Belt's even worse conditions presaged what would happen to white neighborhoods once the color line was breached. As black migration heightened worries about diseases from the south invading the north, segregationists resorted to truly ancient and bearded metaphors like "miasmatic poison" to describe blacks' "invasion" of white neighborhoods.[33]

In so-called invaded neighborhoods, however, all racial theory—whether social Darwinist, eugenic, sanitary, moralistic, quotidian, or downright idiosyncratic—led directly to one subject: property values. "Every colored man who moves into Hyde Park," spat the *Property Owner's Journal* in 1920, "knows that he is damaging his white neighbor's property. Therefore he is making war on the white man." In Chicago, segregationists expressed their sense of racial vulnerability in the real estate market probably more vehemently than in South Africa, and with more of a sense of race war. The racist theory of property values also more completely dominated discourse about city-splitting, and South Siders elaborated the argument more fully than elsewhere. They trotted out made-up statistics, for example, about exactly how much the black invasion cost the neighborhood as a whole. "Shall we sacrifice our property for a third of its value," the KHPA wanted to know, "and run like rats from a burning ship, or shall we put up a united front and keep Hyde Park desirable for ourselves?" Our job, the association averred, is "to guard that $1,000,000,000 [their calculation of the value of all Hyde Park real estate] against depreciation from anything." No dizzying feats of sensationalism were out of bounds. The "negro invasion" was "the worst calamity that had struck the city since the Great Fire." Or it was theft, pure and simple: "To damage a man's property and destroy its value is to rob him. The person who commits that act is a robber." Finally, blacks not only damaged property, but the image of the city as a whole: "What a reputation for beauty Chicago would secure if visitors touring the city would see crowds of idle, insolent Negroes lounging on the South Side Boulevards and adding beauty to the floricultural display in the parks, filling the streets with old newspapers and tomato containers and advertising for the Poro-system for removing marcelled kinks from Negro hair in the windows of derelict remains of what once had been a clean, respectable residence."[34]

Whites' lack of clear options for a governmental response probably accounts for this especially elaborate, extremist, property-values propaganda. In April 1917, the Chicago Real Estate Board (CREB) tried to step into the breach and remedy this exact problem. The CREB, which described itself, with plausible accuracy, as "the oldest, largest, and most influential Real Estate Board in the world," had grown increasingly worried about the South Side. Blockbusters were threatening to ruin its campaign to improve real estate agents' long-tarnished reputation. Worse, the "promiscuous sale" of property to blacks was threatening to "ruin" property that the board, for its part, first estimated at $100,000,000, then raised to more than $250,000,000. "From thirty percent to sixty percent of that stupendous amount is irretrievable loss ... the moment the first colored family moves into a block." On October 3, 1917, the CREB's "seg-regation committee" demanded that city council "immediately pass an ordinance" that would not only zone the city by race, but use its police power to halt all black immigration into the city until "suitable provi-sions are made and such reasonable restriction of leasing or selling be enforced as to prevent lawlessness, destruction of values and property and loss of life." But city council had no time to act. A month after the CREB's summons, the Supreme Court issued its decision in *Buchanan*. The movement to segregate US cities by government ordinance abruptly lost momentum—right on the verge of what might have been its biggest victory yet.[35]

While the legal contexts for segregation worsened, so did demographic and economic conditions. During World War I, thousands of white male factory workers left their jobs to fight in Europe. White immigration from across the Atlantic slowed to a trickle, just as employers' need for la-borers grew to meet insatiable demands for war materiel. Industrialists, in an unlikely alliance with the Chicago *Defender*, the city's redoubtable black-run newspaper, made an impassioned plea to Southern blacks to come North, and they responded with the Great Migration. Fifty thou-sand newcomers poured into Chicago's Black Belt and then burst over the railroad tracks in all directions, into the packing districts to the west and Hyde Park to the southeast. A smaller black enclave on the city's West Side also grew dramatically; so did a smaller enclave south and west of the Black Belt in Englewood. Since construction of new homes had vir-tually halted during the war, whites had nowhere to flee. When calls for government help fizzled, the war of words that neighborhood protection associations had been fighting for a decade sparked a growing war of ac-tions in the streets of the city.[36]

By World War I, violence and intimidation had played a part in Chi-cago's dramas of residential segregation for some time. Working-class gangs from west of the Black Belt had long made life difficult for blacks who hunted for affordable homes beyond the color line along the Rock Island Railroad tracks. By the 1910s these gangs' ability to scare black tenants from buildings west of Wentworth Avenue, the next logical di-viding line, had become one sign of their members' masculine prow-ess. On the eastern front, the various Hyde Park and Kenwood protective associations had at first used somewhat more peaceful methods, appealing to the CREB to clamp down on blockbusters, calling boycotts of real estate agents who sold to blacks, and pooling association members' money to buy houses owned by blacks with the idea of reselling them to whites. These "offers" were often accompanied by threats of direr consequences.

By 1917, when the Great Migration was in full swing, whatever peace had existed began to crumble. Large crowds of whites assembled outside of houses recently bought by black people, shouting racist slogans and throwing bricks and stones through windows. At night, smaller detachments from the mobs broke in, destroying the furniture that the new owners were just moving in. Soon, someone started exploding homemade bombs. Twenty-four of them went off between 1917 and 1919, including three in the house of one man, Charles H. Davis, who died soon after the third explosion, possibly from a condition aggravated by the stress. Soldiers began returning from Europe after the armistice in 1918, further cramping the housing market. Mob attacks on blacks escalated in other cities in the United States, including nearby East St. Louis, Illinois. Chicago homeowner associations took up the slogan "They Shall Not Pass," General Pershing's famous warning to the Germans on the western front, in this case to halt black people's advance across the eastern front of the growing race war in Chicago. In the summer of 1919, two more black men died in gang killings to the west of the Black Belt, along Wentworth Avenue. Then whites rioted on the city's West Side, killing another black man. A particularly intense rash of house bombings followed. And finally, on a blazing day in late July, a white man threw a stone at a black man who swam across an invisible color line at a Lake Michigan beach, drowning him. Sheer mayhem engulfed the South Side and other parts of the city for a full week.[37]

During the great Chicago race riot of 1919, white mobs made repeated attacks into the Black Belt and other smaller enclaves, sometimes firing guns randomly from cars driving at high speed. Blacks shot back at the intruders. Homegrown systems of neighborhood defense kept most inhabitants of the Black Belt safe. But black residents of largely white neighborhoods like Hyde Park and Englewood were much more vulnerable. Mobs burned many of their houses to the ground, and some were chased and stoned to death. All told, at least thirty-eight people and possibly as many as fifty died, the majority of them black, 537 were injured, and about a thousand people became homeless. Though the Illinois National Guard was able to quell the worst of the disturbances by mid-August, house bombings continued at the rate of one every twenty days into 1921, when black migration temporarily receded, and housing construction picked up, giving whites more options outside the South Side. Well after the riot, though, the KHPA ominously reminded white South Siders that "every owner has the right to defend his property to the utmost ability with every means at his disposal."[38]

## A Time for Camouflage

The Chicago riot was the culminating event of what NAACP executive secretary James Weldon Johnson called the "Red Summer" of 1919. White mob violence broke out in twenty-six other American cities that year, including Philadelphia and Washington DC. Housing pogroms and house bombings too many to count brought angry din, clamor, and sporadic murder to "invaded" white neighborhoods across the United States. Then, in 1921, mob violence erupted with even more fury in Tulsa, Oklahoma, when whites stormed the black business district of the city, burned to the ground thirty-six city blocks containing over a thousand houses, and killed at least thirty-nine people, possibly many more.[39]

Though riotous white street violence also spiked in South Africa during this tense post–World War One period—culminating in forty black deaths on the Witwatersrand during the chaotic 1922 Rand Revolt—it had less connection to the housing market or to residential segregation than in the US South. The half-day mob and police attack on blacks in Johannesburg's Vrededorp (1920) came closest to resembling the violence along Chicago's Wentworth Avenue. It is worth noting that the most important site of segregationist urban street violence during this time was neither in the United States nor in South Africa but in Ireland, a country whose politics many members of the white mobs in Chicago and Johannesburg would have followed carefully. There, in 1920 a largely Catholic Home Rule movement succeeded in winning autonomy for the southern part of the island, leaving six northern counties under control of Protestant settlers loyal to Britain. To tamp down Catholic agitation in Northern Ireland against the partition, Protestant Unionist mobs had repeatedly invaded Catholic neighborhoods in cities like Belfast and Derry during the late nineteenth century, often facing Catholic reprisals. Between 1920 and 1922 the conflict between what some participants called the two "creeds or races" escalated, and isolated minorities in both Protestant and Catholic neighborhoods faced armed eviction squads, house bombings, and even roving assassins. In Belfast alone, 453 people died during those two years, of which two-thirds were Catholics; Unionist mobs forced twenty-three thousand Catholics from their homes. The boundaries between the city's neighborhoods grew ever stricter in the ensuing years, prefiguring the "Troubles" of the late twentieth century.[40]

In Chicago, violence or the threat of violence would continue to undergird the color line in the decades to come. However, it had become clear to the city's nervous elites that mayhem alone could not draw an effective color line. The 1919 riot had certainly done nothing to help sustain property values, and Chicago had sullied itself in the eyes of the world. Like South Africans in the same years, American segregationists had come to a crossroads. Where could a city turn to get legitimate powers to stop the black "invasion"? For South Africans, the choice of path was complex enough, but the precedents of the Milner years, the Natives Land Act, and earlier urban locations bills left little doubt that it ultimately led to some kind of racial legislation sponsored by the Union government. In the United States, things were different: NAACP lawyers had shown that they could mobilize the US Constitution against urban segregation by legislation. As in the case of Southern disfranchisement, the urban color line would have to come into being through subterfuge.

In fact, three camouflaged avenues of power were still open to Chicago's segregationists. One was to pass legislation on behalf of segregation that was, formally at least, nonracial. The federal government helped here by promoting land-use zoning, thus allowing cities and adjoining municipalities to use class restrictions against large-scale "invasions" of unwanted working-class residents, effectively excluding most black people. The second of the two paths involved openly racist but nonviolent action accomplished within government but outside formal legislation, namely, by placing racial restrictions in title deeds, which were guaranteed by the courts, not by explicit ordinances. The third involved action outside government altogether and rested on private sources of power, namely, the real estate boards' own campaigns to enforce racial steering by their members.

By 1920, one breed of suburban real estate developer had already spent considerable effort exploring many of these heavily camouflaged but no less coercive routes toward urban race segregation. These developers were businessmen above all, to be sure, but they also saw their craft as part of a solution to urban problems. Not only did they deal in international capital markets to finance their projects, they also looked to transoceanic reform ideas, especially to trends in real estate law and the urban planning movement. The relative absence of any imperial or government mandate for segregation in US urban politics also gave them a much more prominent role in places like Chicago than their counterparts in South Africa or other colonial cities.[41]

The reformist inspiration that drove these self-styled "community builders" went back a century or more to London's suburban Evangelicals. To preserve the moral and economic integrity of their communities, the Evangelicals used title deeds with land-use restrictions that aristocratic landlords had developed in late seventeenth-century London's West End to keep the city's lower classes at a distance. By the late nineteenth century, after the Lord Chancellor's *Tulk v. Moxhay* decision, such covenants were well established in British law, and developers imported them—and the legal precedents that supported them—not only to South Africa but to the United States as well.[42]

One of the most important importers of land-use restrictions to the United States was Frederick Law Olmsted Sr. As the designer of New York's Central Park and dozens of other similar urban "green lungs" across the country, Olmsted believed that using potentially valuable urban land for parks was critical to improving the morality of the poor and ensuring social peace. The less-well-known corollary to this theory was that middle-class people ought to be able to actually *live* in parks— that is, in their own suburban neighborhoods with meandering lanes, lots of trees, and big yards. In the 1850s, Olmsted visited the exclusive suburban subdivision of Birkenhead Park near Liverpool, England. On his return to the United States, he waxed eloquent about the promise of such suburbs, mixing language from the flighty vocabulary of urban reform with the legal boilerplate of British-style deed restrictions: "Probably the advantages of civilization can be found ... under no other circumstances so completely as in some suburban neighborhoods where each family abode stands fifty or a hundred feet or more apart from all others, and at some distance from the public road." On the basis of these ideas, he developed the first parklike suburb in America—at Riverside, Illinois, just west of Chicago, whose title deeds bristled with restrictive covenants straight out of the London developer's legal handbook. These kept anyone but the very rich out of the development by regulating the minimum lot size, the minimum amount a house could cost, minimum distance from the road, as well as requiring expensive architectural flourishes. Later, Edward Bouton, another developer with a social reformer's bent, took this kind of privatized, contract-based urban planning a step further, working with Olmsted's son Frederick Law Olmsted Jr. on the subdivision of Roland Park near Baltimore. In partnership with a British land company whose business was overseen by a Kansas City–based outfit, Bouton not only built land-use restrictions into his business plan, he also was the first to advertise developments solely on the basis of their restricted nature.[43]

Restrictive covenants had a number of limitations. One of these was that they did nothing to prevent nuisances from springing up just outside the boundaries of the development, potentially ruining its ambience and the value of its property. For this reason, developers like the Olmsteds, Bouton, and his Kansas City partner J. C. Nichols watched the urban-planning movement with great interest as it spread from Haussmann's Paris to Germany, Britain, and the colonies—but especially as it made a big splash in Chicago.

In Chicago, the main mover and shaker in urban planning was Daniel T. Burnham, the personification of the "City Beautiful" movement, whose goals were to import French monumental planning—complete with diagonal Haussmanian boulevards and classical edifices dedicated to high civic ideals—to America's railroad-scarred, grid-ironed, skyscraping, money-obsessed, industrial cities. Burnham's rising star was intimately tied to Chicago's South Side. There, in 1893, for the World's Columbian Exposition in Olmsted's lagoon-filled Jackson Park, he had built the closest thing to a monumental, segregated colonial city in the United States. Within the park itself was the White City, a kind of New Delhi *avant la lettre* rendered in reinforced plaster, complete with columned palaces, obelisks, fountains, and other sensational neoclassical confections, all aimed to showcase the highest attainments of civilization. Off to the west of the park—set apart by the tracks of the Illinois Central Railroad—were the more racy entertainments of the mile-long Midway Plaisance, including such black-town knockoffs as the Moorish palace, the Javanese village, and the street of Cairo.[44]

But, unlike in India or Morocco, the international planning movement never created a permanent White City in the continental United States. Burnham did draw up ambitious plans for Washington DC, Cleveland, and San Francisco, and then, after his trip to Manila, he returned to Chicago to work on what would be his masterpiece. However, most of his focus was on downtowns. Since few of his suggested boulevards were actually drilled into surrounding slums such as those where the Black Belt was located, he displaced fewer poor people or black people than in places like Paris, Buenos Aires, or Rio de Janeiro—let alone Rabat or New Delhi.[45]

That said, Burnham did offer something crucial to American segregationists. The grandeur of his vision galvanized political support among large segments of the landowning urban elite for the idea of planning itself—that is, for collective solutions to urban problems that might depend upon government-enforced limitations on that elite's jealously guarded property rights. In 1909, Frederick Law Olmsted Jr. returned from a trip to Europe to push the case that planning should adopt a more "comprehensive" approach to the city that would take "large question questions of economics and social development" into account, not just urban beauty and civic virtues. In this way he echoed the French Beaux-Arts urbanistes' critiques of Haussmann. But the most inspirational stop on his trip was in Germany, where he witnessed municipal land-use zoning laws in action. Properly adapted to the US context, Olmsted thought, they would give cities the power to separate zones for residential use from industrial and commercial areas—and also to distinguish upper-class residential areas from those for the middling sort and the poor. Unlike restrictive covenants, zoning laws could also give developers a guarantee that their subdivisions would not lose value because of incompatible uses in immediately neighboring areas.[46]

During the 1910s, the movement for comprehensive planning based on zoning gained strength in the United States, as cities like Los Angeles, St. Louis, Atlanta, New York, and Chicago—egged on by their chambers of commerce—held hearings to draw up zoning schemes. Planners and developers meanwhile sharpened the legal argument that zoning's overwhelming civic benefits needed to take precedence over individual landowners' rights. In 1909, Olmsted took control of the newly founded National Conference on City Planning (NCCP), and later his colleagues Edward Bouton and J. C. Nichols forged an alliance between the NCCP and the Chicago Real Estate Board's even more powerful offspring, the National Association of Real Estate Boards (NAREB), whose headquarters were also in Chicago. There, a growing contingent of developers of exclusive suburban subdivisions became especially eager proponents of zoning, and they worked hard to allay concerns about property rights within the organization. Large-scale zoning laws appeared in Los Angeles in 1909 and New York City in 1916, and the CREB put its organizational strength behind a similar ordinance in Chicago, which passed in 1923.[47]

Planners and real estate moguls meanwhile reached out to the broader community of urban reformers. During the early 1920s, the NAREB forged an all-important alliance with America's most famous economist, Richard T. Ely, director of the Institute for Research on Land Economics and Public Utilities at the University of Wisconsin. In 1925, Ely and the NAREB's chief counsel, the Chicago blueblood (and large-scale South Side landowner) General Nathan William MacChesney, engineered the transfer of the Institute from Madison to Northwestern University and eventually to an office on NWU's satellite campus in the Chicago Loop.[48]

A towering figure among Progressive Era reformers, Ely had studied in Germany with some of the first economists to challenge the classical free-market economic theories of Adam Smith and David Ricardo. His training taught him that the value of things depended not solely on supply and demand, but also upon the social factors that determined the shape of the market in which those things were sold. Thus, there was a role for social legislation in regulating capitalist economies. The problem of incompatible land uses was a classic example of the influence of social factors upon the value of a commodity—and zoning was, for Ely, a critical legislative remedy. Capricious swings in the value of land represented a particularly troubling problem for Ely, since they were one of many impediments capitalist society placed in the way of wider access to landownership.[49]

"Under All," preached Ely, "is the Land." For him, the institute had a transcendent mission. "When we establish right economic relations between man and the earth upon which we live, we will have gone far in solving many of the most pressing domestic economic problems, as well as the problem of international peace." His alliance with the NAREB presented a stunning opportunity, since it gave him access to people who had the financial incentive to put the ideal of widespread landownership into action. As for the NAREB, it could point to Ely's work to prove that the business of the real estate agent, and residential zoning, were based upon the most progressive theories of economic science.[50]

Meanwhile, in Washington, the US secretary of commerce Herbert Hoover put the power of the federal government behind urban land-use regulation. Hoover was a hero to Ely and other progressive reformers who admired his technocratic brand of social activism. Business leaders, like the members of the NAREB, also admired Hoover's calls for solutions to social problems driven by an "association" between government and businesses. The NAREB's chief counsel MacChesney later served as the Midwestern spearhead for Hoover's successful run for the presidency, and Ely even switched parties to support the effort. Well before that, in 1921, Hoover created an Advisory Committee on Zoning, which included Fredrick Olmsted Jr., the New York housing reformer Lawrence Veiller, and several luminaries from the NAREB and the US Chamber of Commerce. By the following year, the committee had produced both a *Zoning Primer* outlining strategies to promote zoning ordinances to the public as high exercises in civic cooperation and a Standard State Zoning Enabling Act, which allowed proponents to square their efforts with the latest court decisions. Finally, in 1926, in *Euclid v. Ambler*, the US Supreme Court itself ruled that land-use restriction in an Ohio zoning law represented a constitutionally acceptable use of municipal police power. By 1930, some eight hundred cities across the United States had adopted zoning ordinances; the number would climb into the thousands over the next few decades.[51]

Hoover's Standard State Zoning Enabling Act was the closest the federal government of the United States ever came to South Africa's Natives (Urban Areas) Act. Both were meant as legislation to enable local authorities across the country to zone their cities, and both provided a kind of skeleton for further-reaching policies of national government-directed urban segregation. The big difference was, of course, the place of race in the law. Jan Smuts's Natives (Urban Areas) Act virtually celebrated racial discrimination by explicitly authorizing separate racial zones, degrading black people's title to land, and discouraging black migration to cities. In the United States, decisions like *Buchanan v. Warley* made it impossible for Hoover's committee to include any such explicit racial provisions and even less possible to attack black people's property rights or their freedom of movement. Instead, *Euclid v. Ambler* gave cities the power to divide their territory by land use and, more importantly, by class. The ruling explicitly authorized the shakiest of all legal concepts in the land-use zoning arsenal, the power to create separate areas for single-family homes and apartment buildings. In 1918, Olmsted had noted that creating such separate zones for different grades of residence was "more or less coincident with racial divisions." Class segregation, he was saying, could bolster racial segregation since many black people who crossed the color line into white districts did so by renting apartments. In some places, like Atlanta and New Orleans, blue-ribbon commissions flaunted the implicit racial underpinnings of land-use zoning schemes by explicitly laying out separate areas for blacks and whites, each with their own subdistricts for single family homes and apartments. Such plans failed in the courts, on the basis of *Buchanan*, though their subsequent implementation as "color-neutral" plans often put the desired color lines into place anyway.[52]

For land-use zoning to work more precisely in the service of racial segregation, zoning advocates also turned to extra-statutory legal practices—tools that South Africans saw as inadequate and that Americans saw as legally somewhat more risky than zoning: namely, racial steering by real estate agents and racial restrictions in title deeds. The same people who worked so passionately in public to push a federal mandate for land-use zoning also spread these more explicitly racial practices nationwide during the 1920s—though much more quietly. Racial restrictions existed in US title deeds as early as they did in South Africa, from at least the 1890s. The "community builder" Edward Bouton considered incorporating them into the deeds of Baltimore's Roland Park in 1893 but backed off when his lawyers warned him that they might violate the Fourteenth Amendment. In 1910, though, perhaps emboldened by Baltimore's racial zoning ordinance, he added racial restrictions to deeds for properties in Roland Park's extension, Guilford. Meanwhile, J. C. Nichols and Frederick Law Olmsted Jr. used them to sell plots in other developments, including in Palos Verde, Los Angeles, where the language also forbade resale to Mexicans. In Chicago, the developer Frederick Bartlett inserted language forbidding resale to people with "African blood" in his deeds for the far South Side subdivision of Roseland as early as 1914.[53]

Race restrictions spread much more widely in the wake of *Buchanan* and the Chicago riot. Disappointed in the Supreme Court's verdict, the CREB asked its members to mobilize "owners' societies in every white block for the purpose of mutual defense" to insert the only remaining means of "protecting society and property values" into their deeds. It was probably this "plan" that Baltimore mayor James Preston heard about through his Chicago contact in 1918 and recommended to his own real estate board.[54]

For real estate agents to take leadership in such matters, though, the NAREB had to overcome a strong sense among homeowners that it was the agents themselves who caused black invasion, by engaging in blockbusting. In fact, blockbusters made up only one regiment in the host of unscrupulous "curbstone" brokers and speculators, some of whom occasionally whipped up moments of frenzied land-buying that ended in economic ruin for thousands. In one of his first acts as NAREB chief counsel, Nathan William MacChesney filed for a trademark for the term "realtor" as a designation for more upright members of real estate boards. His purpose was to distinguish the true professionals from the dodgy chaff on the curbstones. The alliance with Ely's Land Economics Institute also aimed to burnish the profession's reputation. Ely, who saw malpractice in the real estate industry as an obstacle to wider investment in land, agreed to edit a series of textbooks, written by his staff economists and NAREB members, that were supposed to train agents on a "simple but suitably scientific" basis, thus giving the realtor some of the professional patina of doctors and lawyers.[55]

Ely, the economics professor and social reform advocate, and MacChesney, the self-designated "conservative progressive" real estate lawyer and military man, forged a close relationship during Ely's Chicago years. Though neither elaborated a full-fledged theory of race in print, both had swum in a similar soup of racialized and imperialist reform politics for most of their careers. Both men knew Theodore Roosevelt personally, and both idolized him; MacChesney even spent some time in the Rough Rider regiment. Like Roosevelt, both men flirted openly with social Darwinism and eugenics. Ely was a close friend of the Christian social Darwinist Josiah Strong; he wrote approvingly of the work of American eugenicists like Karl Pearson, Paul Popenoe, and Roswell Johnson; and several times he advocated measures to slow down the reproduction of people he deemed part of the "sad human rubbish-heap"—the "feeble-minded," welfare recipients, and criminals. In 1922, he congratulated the eugenicist Lothrop Stoddard on the dazzling success of *The Revolt against Civilization* (1922), a book that called for a "neoaristocracy" of the well bred. MacChesney, whose list of board memberships in reform organizations was legendary, likewise wrote a eugenical tract advocating sterilization programs for the mentally ill and for prisoners. He even ominously hinted that similar programs might one day be appropriate for blacks. Meanwhile both Ely and MacChesney endorsed immigration restriction and, like most American eugenicists, also supported "positive" racial breeding policies for whites. Widespread property ownership in single detached homes, they believed—much like their other shared hero, Herbert Hoover—would improve the race by providing the wealth and the nurturing environment whites needed to breed as many sturdily raised offspring as possible.

In the 1910s, Ely did hint at other potential directions in his racial thinking. White prejudice, he wrote in his bestselling textbook on economics, accounted for some of the social problems in black communities that most of his contemporaries simply assumed were part of the physical nature of the "inferior races." He praised black people for improving their racial prospects by moving to Northern cities to take better jobs, and he worried that both white hostility and black people's own "economic inertia and shiftlessness" could slow this progress. In the midst of all his racism, there was room for the idea that property values in changing neighborhoods declined not so much because of any inherent problem with black people, but because of white racism itself—just as W. E. B. DuBois was arguing at the same time in the pages of the NAACP's journal *The Crisis*. But in Chicago, Ely either hardened his position or caved in to his benefactors in the real estate industry. As editor of the series of textbooks the institute proposed for the education of American realtors, Ely never once lifted a finger in protest as his authors repeatedly backed policies that disadvantaged blacks in the real estate market.[56]

With Ely providing a halo of scientific endorsement, MacChesney produced three influential documents that transformed racial steering and restrictive covenants into professional obligations for all upstanding realtors and developers. The first document was the NAREB's professional code of ethics, which MacChesney played a lead role in revising in 1924. The preamble of the new code began by quoting Ely's motto, "Under All is the Land." It went on to list as one of many examples of the realtor's "grave social responsibility and . . . patriotic duty" a strict prohibition against "introducing into a neighborhood . . . members of any race or nationality . . . whose presence will be clearly detrimental to property values in that neighborhood."[57]

The second document was MacChesney's "Standard Form, Restrictive Covenant." His goal in drafting it was to stabilize the legal basis of such clauses. US courts had consistently treated race-based restrictive covenants as matters of civil rights law: the big question was whether they violated the Fourteenth Amendment. As such, they had become a different legal animal than land-use covenants, whose legal standing was solely measured by British precedents in property law. Such legal treatment contrasted with South Africa, where courts used property law alone to adjudicate both class-based and race-based deed restrictions. The key

to MacChesney's legal strategy, like that of other defenders of racial covenants in the courts, was to maintain a stark distinction between racial discrimination by government statute, such as that disallowed in *Buchanan*,
and discrimination by "private contract," as in title deeds. In 1926, the
Supreme Court somewhat ambiguously accepted this line of argument
in *Corrigan v. Buckley*. Sheltered by the legal protection the court gave
to white supremacy in private contracts, MacChesney's "Constitution-
proof" covenant drew upon legal precedents steeped in old-fashioned
racial science, notably Virginia's "one-drop" definition of blackness. To
avoid embarrassing situations in which a covenant breaker's attorneys
forced plaintiffs to prove he or she was black, MacChesney made sure
title deeds specified that a "negro" was a "person having one-eighth part
negro blood" (later covenants would be stricter, raising the bar to 1/32
negro blood). During the late 1920s, the CREB used MacChesney's document in its organizing campaigns among neighborhood associations
throughout Chicago, most notably in South Side neighborhoods like
Hyde Park, Kenwood, and Woodlawn. The NAREB circulated the same
document for use in similar campaigns elsewhere in the country.[58]

Finally, MacChesney wrote a textbook on real estate law, which Ely edited for his series. There, with his academic patron's endorsement, Mac-
Chesney took the final crucial step of wrapping his standard covenant
in a layer of ideological camouflage. Because blacks have "the same prerogative" to exclude whites from their own neighborhoods by restrictive
covenant, MacChesney argued, these covenants involved "no discrimination within the civil rights clauses of the Constitution." Such airy
denials of the existence of institutionalized inequality had their roots
in the "separate but equal" doctrine of *Plessy v. Ferguson*. In the postwar
years, they would become increasingly important in the politics of the
American New Right.[59]

## *The "Iron Ring"?*

So, could this camouflaged compromise of a segregation system actually split cities by race? By 1930, there were 234,000 black people in Chicago, more than double the number in 1920. A mere 10 percent of them,
most of them probably live-in domestic servants, resided in wards whose
populations were less than 50 percent black. More than half of the city's
black people lived in wards that were over 90 percent black, most on the

FIGURE 10.2 The Chicago "L," which for a time served as a boundary to black settlement on the South Side (1940). Middle-class whites in the United States often refer to black ghettos and lower-class white neighborhoods as "the other side of the tracks."

South Side but many in the growing West Side enclaves as well. By any measure, segregation had increased substantially since 1920, when no ward in the city had yet reached the 90 percent threshold.[60]

Elsewhere in the United States, very similar things were happening. In New York City, the segregated "Capital of Black America" had arisen in the northern reaches of Manhattan. In the first decade of the 1900s, when the Lexington Avenue subway made its way toward the three-hundred-year-old former Dutch farming village of Harlem, developers had whipped up a frenzy of speculative building along the line. When the bubble burst in 1905, black people who had lived in slums further south moved in great numbers into the stately, and now very affordable, brownstones and apartment buildings that were left behind. White protective associations could do little to stop the influx, and by 1930, 328,000 black people lived in New York, including fifty-five thousand immigrants from the Caribbean, most of them in central Harlem wards that were over 90 percent black (the growth of Brooklyn's Bedford Stuyvesant dates from this time as well). Similar black urban islands, many of them close to downtown business districts, made up a nationwide archipelago that included Philadelphia's north, west, and south sides; Boston's Roxbury; the west side of Baltimore; Washington's U Street, Cleveland's Hough Avenue district; Detroit's Paradise Valley; North St. Louis; Miami's Overtown; Atlanta's west side; and Los Angeles's Central Avenue.[61]

Clearly, black neighborhoods were not following the pattern of those of other groups of people who had moved to US cities. If Chicago's Little Italy, Polonia, and Pilsen had ever been inhabited by a majority of one immigrant group, their inhabitants had since been able to disperse throughout the city. Some groups of European immigrants had occasionally appeared as undesirable neighbors in the manifestos of neighborhood organizations and in racially restrictive covenants. But the restrictive Immigration Act of 1924 had softened white nativist hatred, and by 1930 covenants targeting foreign whites disappeared. The Jews were one exception—exclusive real estate developers tried to keep them out of their subdivisions well into the 1960s by means of both steering and restrictive covenants. Asians and Mexicans also got second-class treatment in some regions of the country, most notably in Los Angeles, as did Puerto Ricans in New York. But no group ever experienced decades of increasing exclusion nationwide in the way that African Americans did.[62]

For many black people in Chicago, there was only one description for where they lived: the ghetto. As the African American sociologists and activists Horace Cayton and St. Clair Drake noted, this was a term of reproach, meant to promote activism against restrictive covenants and "the iron ring which now restricts most Negro families to intolerable, unsanitary conditions."[63]

Though black lawyers and activists had forced white segregationists to make compromises after their victory in *Buchanan*, those activists now faced a much more difficult system with multiple parts, each with its own camouflage. Restrictive covenants were only the easiest of these working parts to target. In fact, historians have tended to discount their centrality as a city-splitting device—it turned out to be hard for protective organizations to get universal compliance from neighbors, many of whom did not want their options limited if their uncovenanted neighbors sold to blacks or blockbusters, precipitating a general flight of whites from the area. Covenants may have worked somewhat better in new developments, since subdividers could insert them into all deeds before their properties went on the market. Still, the most important role for racial deed restrictions may well have been as a political decoy that allowed the rest of the system to escape the opposition of civil rights activists relatively unscathed. As Fredrick Law Olmsted Jr. once hoped, land-use zoning, which flew lower on the activists' radars, may have been an even more effective force of racial segregation. Most of the jurisdictions that adopted versions of Hoover's standard zoning law came into being in suburban subdivisions that set themselves up as independent municipalities, thus giving themselves the political room they needed to adopt particularly exclusive restrictions. The practice of racial steering, which the real estate boards adopted as a professional badge of honor nationwide, has also been a particularly effective engine of segregation and virtually impossible to eradicate. As for the threat of white housing pogroms and house bombings, they quieted down during the late 1920s and 1930s, but they would soon reappear with great fierceness when the next wartime urban housing crisis struck. Finally, the racial theory of property values that underlay all of these institutions only gained strength and pervasiveness in the white collective imagination.[64]

By 1930, the reinvented conditions of segregation in the urban United States proved arguably more successful than those in the contemporary South Africa of prime minister J. B. M. Hertzog—where, at least for the moment, the Natives (Urban Areas) Act had done little to rid Johannesburg of its multiracial slums. Still, that success came at the cost of still another big compromise for US whites. Unlike their South African counterparts, who still expected government to deliver *permanently* demarcated racial zones to their cities, the US system could offer no such assurances. That was largely because the camouflaged color line of the United States offered no restrictions on black migration to the city and because its creators were not willing or legally able to devote large areas of the city's fringes to South African–style townships. The American color line might be made of iron, but little stopped it from moving across urban space. As long as the black population continued to grow—and it would, well into the 1960s—so would the inner-city ghetto. Within the logic of racial theories of property values, whites who lived in the ghetto's path had to make one of two sacrifices: either they could fight (a physically dangerous business that was rarely successful in the long run) or take flight.

For developers and their reformist allies in the United States, enabling white flight was the next frontier in segregationist policy making.

It turned out that the Great Depression offered American city-splitters an even grander opportunity to put ideas into action on the federal level than the crisis of 1917-19. Not only would they divide American cities even more effectively as a result, but they would help kill many of those cities in the attempt.

# II : Segregation at the Extremes

## Split Cities and the Global Cataclysm

No city in the world and no movement for urban segregation escaped the economic and political cataclysms of the 1930s and 1940s. These were the climactic years of what historian Eric Hobsbawm has called the "Age of Extremes," when the Great Depression devastated the lives of millions worldwide and when Western imperialism's most horrific incarnation, the Third Reich of Adolf Hitler, drew the rest of the world's largest empires into the maelstrom of World War II. Hitler's murder of some six million Jews—and untold millions of disabled people, psychiatric patients, radicals, Roma, and prisoners of war—capped humankind's most horrific period of self-inflicted bloodletting. Then, a year after learning of the atrocities of Auschwitz, the United States demonstrated through bomb blasts at Hiroshima and Nagasaki that humanity possessed an even more precipitous means of self-destruction—atomic and nuclear holocaust. During the ensuing Cold War, the world's new foremost imperial powers, the United States and the Soviet Union, recalibrated the global political order precisely upon the threat of such an unthinkable catastrophe.[1]

Overwhelming as these events were, their impact on the world's urban color lines was as contradictory as it was dramatic. In the overseas colonies of the Western empires, movements for national self-determination and independence grew more potent during the age of extremes. Over the next two decades, they forced the whites of the world's white towns to pack their bags and leave their privileged urban enclaves to the governing elites of newly independent countries.

By contrast, the catastrophes of the mid-twentieth century actually catalyzed the energies of the world's most radical white movements for racial city-splitting—not only among the archsegregationists of the United States and South Africa but also, for a short but merciless period, at the heart of the era of global terror itself, Nazi Germany.

Each of these movements reached toward distinct extremes. In the cities that Hitler's Germany conquered in Eastern Europe, the Nazis devised world history's most atrocious system of urban segregation, marked by the sheer application of deadly state force, the relatively paltry concern for the economic consequences of city-splitting, and, most chilling of all, the final decision to use segregated Jewish ghettos as staging grounds for racial extermination. In the United States, by contrast, the federal government first built urban color lines into the generous-seeming bureaucracies of the country's growing welfare state. Then it camouflaged their driving dynamics within state-sponsored dual and unequal urban housing markets. In South Africa, a contorted synthesis of the two other extremes emerged. Urban apartheid, like the US system, depended heavily on government welfare and housing-market policies. But apartheid's enforcement mechanisms derived much of their character from the South African Far Right's flirtation with fascism. Under Hendrick Verwoerd, minister of native affairs and later prime minister, the Union government morphed into a police state that declared open war on the growing opposition movements that amassed in the black townships.

Despite the differences, important ocean-spanning connections existed between these extreme points in the history of racial city-splitting. In the 1930s, the United States and South Africa continued to rely on mutual inspiration from Britain, France, Germany, and their colonial connections to build the government welfare and development policies that became central driving forces for residential segregation. The transoceanic trade in social Darwinist and eugenical ideas—most notably American eugenicists' strong support for research on "racial hygiene" in early Nazi Germany—was an important source of inspiration to all three systems. The Nazis relied upon American legal precedents—such as disfranchisement, Jim Crow, immigration restriction, and sterilization laws—to bolster their claims to international legitimacy; South Africa's racial laws and British and French colonial policies served similar purposes. In turn, the Nazis and other European ultranationalists inspired the authoritarianism of South Africa's Afrikaner nationalist movements. The United States continued to be both the great foil and the inspiration for the hardening of racial politics in South Africa after 1948. And during the Cold War, when Britain and South Africa at last went separate ways, the United States would become the apartheid regime's most indulgent, if often somewhat troubled, imperial "uncle."[2]

## Hitler's "Death Boxes"

On some level it is correct to see Hitler's mass murder of Europe's Jews as untouched by anything resembling "humanity" or human history—let alone "civilization." Yet historians have made clear that even such an extreme moment of horror could not have happened without all the advanced accouterments of Western civilization: a centralized national state, a rampant European empire, the factory system, the ideas of some of the world's most widely respected academics, and the rhetoric of social reform and public health. The Enlightenment notion of race was also absolutely critical to the Holocaust. By the late nineteenth century, racial thinkers in Europe and the Americas had transformed medieval anti-Jewish thought based on Christian precepts into anti-Semitism, the idea that Jews represented a separate race whose very presence in Europe posed a "Jewish Question" just as suffused in threats of inevitable racial conflict and perilous race-mixing as other racial "questions" elsewhere. If anything, twentieth-century anti-Semites argued, Jews presented a greater threat than blacks, for they were capable of hatching conspiracies to control the highest affairs of capital and the state. Soon, people like Adolf Hitler added a contradictory corollary to this theory, arguing that Jews were also at the heart of the Bolsheviks' takeover of Russia and their Communist designs for the rest of the world. Such threats, Hitler claimed, were built into the very biology of Jews themselves, and one of the führer's most important early acts was to pass the so-called Nuremberg Laws. Like similar laws for blacks in the United States and South Africa, these defined Jews by quantities of racially distinct blood and relegated them to a second-class status designed to engender more widespread anti-Semitic hatred.[3]

Cities, and along with them measures of urban planning and racial segregation, were also part of "civilized" implements that made the Holocaust possible. In fact, in the mad world of the Nazi conquests, the messiness of urban politics even helped make extermination more probable. Most of the mass killing of the Jews, it is true, went on in places outside cities: on battlefronts, in villages, in isolated forests or swamps, and in gas chambers deliberately hidden by trees near small Polish rail-sidings like Chełmno, Bełżec, Sobibór, and Treblinka. Of the death camps, only Auschwitz—forty square kilometers of barracks, slave-labor factories, laboratories, railyards, and top-secret assembly lines for gassing people and cremating their bodies—came close to resembling a city, if a hellish one. Before the mass killing truly got underway, though—when the Nazis first conquered Poland and began to put some of their earliest racial engineering schemes into practice—Nazi Germany reluctantly embraced the old idea of segregating Jews in urban ghettos. Once again, for a few short years, from 1940 to 1942, a conquering European empire—inspired by its own geopolitical appetites and administrative conundrums, by racialized ideas of urban sanitation, and by the desire to inscribe a new racial order in urban landholding—divided cities as a means to consolidate its political and economic gains over subject peoples.[4]

As early as 1935, Adolf Hitler himself had mused that Jews should be "enclosed in a ghetto, in an area ... where the German people may observe them as one observes wild animals." In 1939, during the Nazis' lightning strike into Poland, the führer's security chiefs Heinrich Himmler and Reinhard Heydrich instead came up with an even larger-scale plan of demographic engineering inspired by immigration restriction movements and racial reservation systems elsewhere in the world. It would transform Poland into three strips of racial territory. The Reich would swallow the westernmost and largest of these strips as a new "*Lebensraum*" for Eastern Europe's dispersed ethnic Germans. Poles would live in a smaller strip farther east, in a colony known as the General Government. The third and smallest, easternmost zone, in the swampy region around the city of Lublin, would become a Jewish "super-ghetto." As Heydrich's brutal *Einsatzgruppen* got to work rounding up Jews by the tens of thousands (and killing many thousands, at the very least, in the process), the inadequacy of the Lublin reservation for Poland's Jews became obvious, as did the complications of moving several million people around simultaneously. Later, when France fell to the Nazis, Hitler floated a still more ambitious plan to ship all the Jews to the French colony of Madagascar. British naval power, however, made this scheme logistically impossible.[5]

In the midst of these swings in policy, Heydrich fell back on what he thought to be a more practical short-term plan, a "Jewish deportation from the countryside to the cities." Urban ghettos would allow for "a better possibility of control and later of deportation" elsewhere. In addition to the obvious medieval precedents, Heydrich also undoubtedly had in mind the dozens of concentration camps he and Himmler had built during the 1930s throughout Germany to imprison the multiple enemies of the Reich.[6]

The Nazis fenced off the first of their Jewish ghettos in May 1940 at Łódź, in the slice of conquered Poland envisioned for Germans. The largest ghetto went up shortly thereafter in Warsaw, the capital of the new Polish colony, the General Government. Approximately four hundred other ghettos and camps came into being over the next two years across Poland, most importantly in Kraków, Lublin, and Białystok. When the Germans took over the Baltic republics, Belorussia, and the Ukraine, they also built large fenced-in Jewish ghettos in Vilnius, Kaunas, Riga, Minsk, and Lvov, among other cities. The effort and the destructive force involved were enormous. Most of the larger ghettos contained a third or more of their city's population. To bring the Warsaw ghetto into being, Nazi soldiers removed 113,000 Poles from the zone designated for Jews and forced 136,000 Jews from other neighborhoods into the ghetto at gunpoint, shedding much blood in the process. Over time, the population of the Warsaw ghetto swelled to 450,000—a larger number than all the Jews of France—piled into a fenced quarter that covered only 2.4 percent of the city's built-up area.[7]

To the local officials who were charged with building the ghettos, the physical safety, the economic subsistence, and the health of ghetto residents was often barely a matter of concern. The initial economic presumption of ghettoization was about as rudimentary and barbaric as could be imagined—the Jews would hand over virtually all their wealth in exchange for whatever food the conquerors had left in their storehouses after the Germans and Poles had received what they needed. The conquerors simply erased all Jewish property rights, appropriating for themselves the nicest houses left behind by Jews who had lived outside the ghetto. Nazi officials also regularly justified their actions by claiming Jews posed a threat to the health of the superior races. In Warsaw, local Nazis even tried to trick Jews into believing they were moving to a *Seuchengebeit*, or quarantine zone, to avoid an epidemic. In all cases, though, the ghettos quickly became zones of intense overcrowding, illness, poverty, starvation, and death. To many, including the head Nazi propagandist, Josef Goebbels, this was the simply the point: the ghettos were "death boxes" that would solve the Jewish Question through attrition and save the Nazis the bother of mass deportation.[8]

Not everyone in the multiheaded Nazi regime in Eastern Europe had the same perception, however, and the path from ghettos to genocide was somewhat more complex than Goebbels may have wished. For a brief period from late 1940 through most of 1941, a handful of local Nazi officials successfully pushed the idea that the Jews in ghettos should be kept alive to work. In this way the ghettos could produce goods that would be helpful to the Nazi war effort. By renting the ghetto's inhabitants out as slave-labor forces to German manufacturing companies, the Reich could also fatten its treasury. In both Łódź and Warsaw, officials quickly assembled the machinery needed for rudimentary textile factories and other artisanal workshops. Nazi-appointed Jewish leaders of the ghettos' Councils of Elders sought to leverage the products of their now-industrialized subcities for better rations and to forestall the growing call for deportations.[9]

The hope that ghetto life could be even slightly normalized quickly came to an end in 1942, even as industrial production grew. The previous summer, Hitler had launched his "war of destruction" against what he called the "Jewish-Bolshevik" Soviet Union. As the Germans quickly advanced toward Moscow, Hitler and his security chiefs gave the *Einsatzgruppen* license to slaughter Soviet and Jewish officials, an order that resulted in the killing of a million or more inhabitants of the *shtetls* and cities of the former Russian Pale. Hitler now giddily imagined an immense garden of Eden for Germans in the territories that fell into his hands. The current inhabitants, the führer boasted, would be treated "like the Indians" of the US West. Strangely channeling some of the spirit of turn-of-the-century segregation mania, he proclaimed himself the "Robert Koch in politics" for his discovery of the Jewish "bacillus ... of social decomposition." In July 1941, secret plans got underway to answer the Jewish Question of Europe through extermination. Meanwhile, colonial officials in Poland were growing ever more frustrated with supplying the demands of ghetto residents in wartime. Vigorous smuggling networks grew up on both sides of the fences that were difficult to control, and the threat of disease spreading from the ghetto to surrounding districts grew. Then resistance movements, armed with smuggled weapons, emerged within some of the ghetto factories, most notably in Warsaw. These "untenable circumstances" in the cities, argues the historian Christopher R. Browning, made it easier to find sympathy among local Nazi officials for Berlin's turn toward an even more radical "Final Solution."[10]

In 1941, concentration camp officials at Auschwitz and Majdanek conducted the first experiments in large-scale gassing of inmates. Heinrich

Himmler ordered the construction of the first camps solely dedicated to killing Jews at Chełmno, meant for the inhabitants of the Łódź ghetto, and at Bełżec, for those of Lublin. Later, Sobibór and Treblinka went into operation, designed for the mass murder of the Jews of the Kraków and Warsaw regions, respectively. In January 1943, the Warsaw ghetto's spirited armed-resistance movement managed to stop the deportations for a time, but Nazi forces invaded the ghetto in April and set it on fire, killing most of its leaders. The Germans captured the remaining 56,000 inhabitants and shipped them to Treblinka, where the Nazis murdered more than 750,000 people, all told. By then, even larger shipments of victims began arriving in Auschwitz by rail from all over Europe.[11]

Even at this, the outermost extreme of racist imagination and racial politics, the legacies of cross-oceanic intellectual inspiration were tangible enough. In the 1920s and 1930s American eugenicists like Harry Laughin, Madison Grant, Lothrop Stoddard, and Robert Foster Kennedy had been at the forefront of the movement to encourage German sci-

FIGURE II.I  Evacuating the Warsaw ghetto. In April and May of 1943, Jewish residents of the Warsaw ghetto organized a courageous last-ditch revolt against Nazi authority. In response, the Nazis burned the ghetto to the ground and forced the survivors to the transit square (Umschlagplatz), where they were forced onto trains that carried them to the death camp at Treblinka. Courtesy of the United States Holocaust Memorial Museum and the National Archives and Records Administration.

entists to take up the cause of the Reich's racial betterment; Hitler met Stoddard personally in Berlin and considered Grant's *Conquest of a Continent* his bible. The Americans could proudly point to laws in many US states allowing for sterilization of people deemed racially unfit, including people with birth defects, physical disabilities, and mental "retardation." The American Rockefeller Foundation had helped found and sustain Germany's main institute for eugenical research, the Kaiser Wilhelm Institute. Though support for killing the unfit was more limited among American eugenicists, groups like Kennedy's Euthanasia Society of the United States hardly escaped notice abroad. In the 1930s, German scientists at the institute developed systems to gas people to death whom they deemed threats to Aryan racial health.[12]

In 1939, as Hitler went to war in Poland, he ordered the gassing of thousands of inmates of psychiatric hospitals in Germany. In the fall of 1941, Himmler settled upon this technological precedent for the mass murder of millions of Jews across Europe. In the earliest death camps, the methods were relatively crude, involving the redirection of a delivery truck's exhaust pipe into its victim-filled cargo bay or a diesel engine attached to a sealed farmhouse. Auschwitz's Camp II (next to Birkenau, a neighboring village expropriated for the purpose) offered a more technologically "refined" system involving make-believe bathhouses whose showerheads asphyxiated their naked inmates with hydrogen cyanide. Next on its gruesome factory line were high-powered ovens designed to burn twelve thousand corpses a day.[13]

In a political drama built on the multiplication of horrific superlatives, Camp II also represented world history's grisliest form of spatial segregation, urban or otherwise. Upon arrival at Hitler's quasi-urban killing center, the trainloads of migrants went through a selection process often supervised by "Dr. Death" himself, Josef Mengele. It was his underworldly pleasure to decide everyone's destination within the camp's many sections, each of which was distinguished only by the speed of death on offer. Some headed to eugenical research labs to become live human subjects for Nazi doctors' experiments with often deadly sterilization techniques. Others were selected for the slave-labor factories run by German corporations, where life would end more slowly. For most, though, Dr. Mengele prescribed a much quicker end, in the bathhouses and ovens of Camp II. Over a million people perished there alone before the Soviet Red Army captured Auschwitz in early 1945, a few months before the final Allied victory.[14]

## A New Deal for America's Color Lines

It is often best to turn to W. E. B. DuBois for perspective on matters of race, and this terrible moment is no exception. His assessment, however, was not aimed to comfort. "We have conquered Germany," he noted with asperity after Victory in Europe Day, "but not their ideas." Soon DuBois was at the inauguration of the United Nations in San Francisco, where he confronted General Jan Smuts, of all people—now in his late seventies and once again prime minister of the South African Union—there to unveil the charter he had written for the new organization, aimed to end all wars. But an end to all imperialism, as DuBois eloquently demanded, was still off the table, and racial hatred was on the rise, both in Smuts's own country and in the United States. "We still believe in white supremacy," DuBois pressed on, "keeping Negroes in their place and lying about democracy when we mean imperial control of 750 millions of human beings in colonies."[15]

His criticism could also readily extend to American urban policy. During the years of Hitler's rise and fall, the US federal government took on a new more decisive role in dividing American cities by race. Not only did federal agencies help whites to build bigger black ghettos, they helped city governments and business elites to destroy some ghettos that they deemed too close to downtown and rebuild them in more convenient places with even stronger boundaries. More importantly, those agencies also rebuilt the still comparatively restrictive white section of the dual urban housing market with the goal of opening up huge areas of suburban development for ordinary white homebuyers eager to flee the racial threats they perceived in the cities.

Though eugenics and social Darwinism lingered over the whole business, no dictatorial proclamations, no *Einsatzgruppen*, no deliberate starvation measures, and no gas chambers were involved. Instead, during the age of extremes, the drama of American segregationism took on its new momentum under the much cheerier leadership of Franklin D. Roosevelt, from technically race-neutral legistlation fully debated by representative institutions and from his otherwise benign-seeming New Deal programs designed to expand access to decent housing. Within these programs, segregationists found new ways to whitewash explicitly racist city-splitting practices, this time within the nonlegislated and technical practices of government bureaucracies.[16]

Like other important innovations in the history of US segregationism, the New Deal for American urban color lines was first envisioned during the 1920s in Chicago. It was the work of the same high-powered alliance of reformers and real estate agents that had promoted the nationwide use of zoning and racially restrictive covenants. Everything got started when Professor Richard T. Ely's Institute for Research in Land Economics and Public Utilities (hereafter simply "the institute") and his patrons at the National Association of Real Estate Boards (NAREB) took up a topic that, on its face, seems as far removed from the extremes of racial politics as possible: home mortgages.

For realtors and reformers who wanted to increase the number of people buying and selling real estate, home loans were a crucial subject. That was because, for most Americans in the 1920s, mortgages actually made it almost impossible to buy a house. To get a mortgage from a typical bank, you had to come up with about half of the value of the property as a down payment. Then the bank would give you two, three, or, at most, five years to pay the mortgage off, meaning that you would usually have to take out a second and even a third mortgage to pay off the first one. Interest rates were also very high. It was no wonder that homeownership rates were so low in the United States. In a study conducted with the support of Herbert Hoover's Commerce Department, Ely found, to his alarm, that homeownership rates in some cities actually declined during the early 1920s.[17]

There was some good news, though. Smaller-scale "building and loan societies," which lent most of their assets as mortgages, had begun experimenting in the 1920s with home loans that required smaller down payments and offered longer repayment schedules. These lending societies had historical roots in late eighteenth-century British working-class savings pools, which English immigrants brought to the United States in the 1830s. In the mid-1920s, as housing construction grew dramatically after the postwar slump, the numbers of building societies increased, and they further liberalized the terms of their loans. To promote these trends, as the British government did in the 1920s, Ely lured an expert on home finance named H. Morton Bodfish to the institute. Bodfish published articles and an enthusiastic book on building societies and their international movement to liberalize mortgages. Bodfish and Ely also took leadership roles in the United States Building, Savings and Loan League (USBSLL), which was also headquartered in Chicago. The NAREB, naturally, encouraged the whole business.[18]

In 1929, as Ely's institute trumpeted the good news about building and loans, disaster struck. The New York stock market collapsed, sending the whole country and much of the world into the Great Depression. Incomes and house values plummeted, and hundreds of thousands of homeowners fell behind on their mortgage payments. In 1929, five hundred homes in the United States went into foreclosure every day; by 1933 the number rose to over a thousand. In 1934, more than half of all urban homes were either in foreclosure or in danger of imminent default.[19]

Ironically, the collapse of the housing market actually lifted the political fortunes of the Chicago-based alliance of reformers and realtors. This was because in 1928 Herbert Hoover had been elected president of the United States. Hoover, who believed that social problems must be solved by associations of government and private economic interests, called upon Ely, the NAREB, and the USBSLL, among others, to help him find a way out of the foreclosure mess—despite the big role played by speculative developers, banks, and real estate agents in creating the crisis. In 1931, the president welcomed three thousand participants to his conference on home building and homeownership, reminding them that songs like "Home Sweet Home" were "not written about tenements. ... They are expressions of racial longing.... That our people should live in their own homes is a sentiment deep in the hearts of our race and of American life."

Ely dominated the conference, along with other institute economists and high-ranking NAREB officers. Among its many recommendations, one stood out: the federal government ought to find a way to promote building-society-style mortgages. Hoover tapped the institute's Morton Bodfish to write legislation establishing the Federal Home Loan Bank Board (FHLBB) to protect the assets of mortgage providers. The president did little, however, to shield ordinary homeowners from default, and for this and other similar moves, a tidal wave of voters rejected what they saw as his out-of-touch approach to the Depression. The reformer-real estate alliance, however, extended its hold on federal housing policy. In 1933, the new president, Franklin Roosevelt, ordered Bodfish and the FHLBB to create a new agency, the Home Owner's Loan Corporation (HOLC). One of the pioneer agencies of Roosevelt's New Deal, the HOLC bought up over three billion dollars worth of delinquent mortgages over the next four years and refinanced them on even more liberal terms than the building and loans, allowing over eight hundred thousand people to keep their homes.[20]

In 1934, Bodfish was again at work, this time with the help of the NAREB's former president Herbert U. Nelson, drafting the landmark 1934 National Housing Act, which created yet another New Deal agency, the Federal Housing Administration (FHA). The FHA, whose ranks were also filled with former associates of Ely's institute, insured new mortgages from default with the full weight of the United States Treasury. Its guidelines specified that it would only cover low-interest, low-down payment, long-term loans. Over time, it further liberalized those requirements, decreasing down payments to 10 percent and extending repayment times to thirty-five years. Still other New Deal federal agencies bought up FHA mortgages from banks, pumping capital into the home-finance system, thus encouraging all types of lenders to offer similar loans and allowing ever more homebuyers access to mortgages for the first time. Supporters of the new agencies repeatedly argued that they intervened only minimally in the economy. In fact, though, the New Deal–era federal government completely transformed the real estate market, supporting the emergence of a new financial instrument that allowed for a tremendous expansion of home buying in the United States. The expansion was particularly striking after World War II, when the Veterans' Administration (VA) was also empowered to make FHA-type loan guarantees for returning US soldiers. Between 1944 and 1959, mortgage lending skyrocketed from 4.5 billion to over 32 billion dollars a year, nearly half of that total provided by building and loan societies, now called savings and loan banks. The FHA and the VA insured a quarter of that total. Ely's and the NAREB's dreams of a homeowner society was at hand.[21]

But that dream did not include African Americans. That was because the new federal agencies embraced racial theories of real estate values in their practices, despite the fact that none of the New Deal legislation explicitly endorsed racial discrimination.

The institute-NAREB alliance played just as important a role in putting this racist side of New Deal home-finance policy into place as it did in promoting new kinds of mortgages. Both Richard Ely and NAREB chief counsel Nathan William MacChesney (as well as their hero Herbert Hoover) had long applauded many of the same British and American eugenicist theorists that inspired Hitler and Verwoerd. But black civil rights activists and the courts had rendered Ely and MacChesney's various flirtations with statutory residential apartheid and mass sterilization politically impossible. In the end, Chicago's most tangible gift to

Washington was the alliance's scientific and professional endorsement of antiblack racial steering and restrictive covenants (see chap. 10).

The man who delivered these goods was the Chicago appraiser and amateur economist Frederick Babcock. Even more than MacChesney, Babcock had come of age within the very belly of Chicago's real estate industry. His father, William Babcock, ran a highly respected property appraising firm in the Loop, which he renamed Babcock and Son when Frederick joined the business. The elder Babcock prided himself on the firm's stellar record in the courts, which repeatedly affirmed the logic behind his appraisals. A true assessment of the value of land, he argued in a lecture he gave to the Chicago Real Estate Board as part of Ely's realtor education series, must take into consideration not just what people were willing to pay for it. Speculative fevers, after all, could induce people to pay all sorts of money for worthless land. Instead, a whole variety of contextual factors should be considered, including surrounding land uses, accessibility of transport, planned public improvements, zoning, and so on. The value of residential property, in particular, also depended on the "class" of local residents, and "a tremendous effect on residential values is observable in the racial migrations that take place in cities."[22]

Ely asked William's son Frederick to write up such sentiments in a textbook for the institute's series. Frederick Babcock's book, *The Appraisal of Real Estate* (1924), mixed homespun observations about the racial dynamics of neighborhoods into a thick batter of theoretical language and mathematical formulas. The book marked a major departure in the "science" of appraising, which had previously been based on market models that took no account of social influences. Ely sought to raise money for a permanent post at the institute for Babcock, who was eager to move into an academic career. As it turned out, much higher things were in store for the star appraisal economist. In 1934, Ernest Fisher, a long-term associate of Ely's at the institute and now an economic consultant at the newly minted FHA, called Babcock to Washington to serve as the agency's chief appraiser. His job was to determine what sorts of mortgages the federal government ought to insure.[23]

Babcock's choice was to enshrine racial segregationism within FHA policy. He did so by importing racial theories of property values from the streets of Chicago into the relatively obscure and unscrutinized bureaucratic reaches of the federal executive branch. Again, his instrument was no dictatorial proclamation, as in Nazi Germany, nor a frankly racist act of Parliament like South Africa's Group Areas Act: it was the FHA's rather plodding, technical, and deliberately obscure *Underwriting Manual*, which Babcock revised throughout the 1930s. As in his textbook, the *Manual* treats questions of racial influences on property values more or less the same way as the presence of nearby factories, rail lines, noisy apartment buildings, or other nuisances. But the message to valuators of potential federally backed loans is clear: "The Valuator should investigate areas surrounding the location to determine whether or not incompatible racial and social groups are present, to the end that an intelligent prediction may be made regarding the possibility or probability of the location being invaded by such groups. If a neighborhood is to retain stability it is necessary that properties shall continue to be occupied by the same social and racial classes. A change in social or racial occupation generally leads to instability and reductions in values." Restrictive covenants were among the protections Babcock deemed promising, though he warned valuators to make sure all property deeds from surrounding districts included such clauses, that their terms were uniform, especially regarding race, and that they were adequately enforced. The "FHA Bible," as the *Underwriting Manual* was later called, quickly became the basis of a crucial training program for the agency's valuators across the country. The stated goal was to ensure that all FHA loan guarantees were economically sound, as the National Housing Act stipulated. FHA officials maintained that unprofessional assessments of property had contributed to the mortgage meltdown of the Depression. Henceforth, the standards of a "conservative business operation" would be required.[24]

The FHA's *Underwriting Manual* was not the only source of federally sanctioned segregationism to come out of New Deal agencies. Even as Babcock finished writing his bible, both the HOLC and the FHA engaged in enormous projects to map all the urban neighborhoods of the United States with the goal of identifying the most promising areas for future residential investment. The HOLC's research bureau deemed its reports controversial enough that it stamped their covers "CONFIDENTIAL NOT FOR PUBLICATION." However, to prepare the maps and studies, HOLC field officers and FHA valuators relied heavily upon information they collected from legions of local NAREB-affiliated realtors across the country—as well as officers of savings and loan banks and other mortgage-issuing companies, directors of the many professional organizations that served the real estate industry, and the board members of municipal agencies and commissions. The HOLC also exclusively distributed its reports back to these same sources once it finished the studies. In the process, the federal government set up a nationwide network of exchange that strengthened and vastly expanded the Chicago-based alliance of realtors and economists. Yet, even as these networks grew, the HOLC and the FHA insulated them from any larger public scrutiny by limiting access to their reports. Thus the mapping studies became a kind of proprietary forum for the national dissemination of local information about property values. This forum became the largest of all the United States' many camouflaged institutions for discussions of race and segregationist practices. The hidden interchange that took place there gave those practices yet another quiet but decisive and official federal stamp of approval.[25]

The idea of in-depth community studies of property values may, in part, represent yet another direct legacy of Ely's institute on New Deal housing policy. During the late 1920s Ely had repeatedly called upon the NAREB and the institute's other corporate funders to support such studies. "Color" and "movement in and out of the area" were key questions in the research design he proposed, as were other variables later incorporated into the HOLC's "Area Description" questionnaires and similar FHA materials.[26] The HOLC's "Residential Security Map" for Chicago took five years to complete and involved at least forty-four of the city's most prominent realtors, many local bankers, as well as the Chicago Real Estate Board, the NAREB, Morton Bodfish's USSBLL, and more than a dozen other central pillars of the country's land business. The final map, like those the HOLC and FHA produced for over a hundred other cities across the country, rated all the city's neighborhoods on a now-famous four-step scale, with the "First Grade," or "A," areas marked in blue on the map; "B" areas, in green; "C" areas, in yellow; and the least desirable "D," or "Fourth Grade," areas marked in red. On the final map, a huge, several-miles-wide band of red surrounded downtown Chicago, expanding to cover the entire Black Belt on the South Side and the black West Side, as well as the white slums in between. Only a few areas within the city rated a "green" (Second Grade) designation. One was a small area in Hyde Park around the University of Chicago where evaluators happily reported the existence of a solid phalanx of restrictive covenants—well-known to blacks as "the University of Chicago Agreement to Get Rid of Negroes." The rest of the city was a large sea of yellow (Third Grade), which only gave way to green and blue fringes beyond the city limits.[27]

The "Area Description" forms that the HOLC and FHA used to compile information on each neighborhood began with section on "Population," which asked valuators to fill in lines with information on the predominating "Class and Occupation" of inhabitants, followed by the percentage of "Foreign Families," their "Nationalities," the percentage of "Negro," and evidence of "Shifting and Infiltration." Thus the forms prioritized supposed racial effects on land values even more than the *Underwriting Manual.* At the bottom of the form there was also a section for more open-ended comments. In this last section, valuators offered a complex and contradictory range of sentiments on the topic of race and property values. In more extensive interviews, the study's local collaborators elaborated such ideas even further. Among other things, these documents suggest that, even at this late date, not all European immigrant groups had achieved the same level of "white" status, at least in the minds of largely "old-stock" real estate practitioners. Jews, Greeks, Italians, Poles, and Mexicans evoked the strongest negative sentiments in terms of reliability as renters or mortgage holders, though respondents disagreed over who was the worst. Blacks too fell into this undesirable category, though some respondents also actually had charitable things to say, especially about the "better class" of black people. One even noted that values were actually higher in black districts than for similar properties in white neighborhoods (after all, increasing numbers of migrant blacks were forced into those areas, creating enormous demand for housing and increasing its price).[28]

The HOLC's final report on the study acknowledged the complexity of data about foreigners, but completely brushed aside any nuances about blacks: "Of course not all persons of foreign stock constitute a detrimental influence upon the community. But there are unquestionably large concentrations in Chicago of races which must be so classified. Moreover, there were in 1930 about 234,000 Negroes in the city of Chicago.... A heavy influx of this race continues contrary to the general trend of decreasing immigration into Chicago.... A blight of residential neighborhoods is engendered by the shift and infiltration." Indeed, the agency did not blame blacks and foreigners for property depreciation alone: "The unfavorable concentrations of certain foreign racial groups and Negroes—particularly the latter—are definitely detrimental to the economic future of the community."[29]

The upshot of all of this bad news? "Mortgage lending institutions will continue to withhold mortgage funds at reasonable terms from deteriorating areas thus hastening the expansion of the blighted area." To be clear: neither the HOLC nor the FHA invented "redlining," though their maps certainly inspired this term for the practice. Bankers and savings and loan managers were little troubled by their own longstanding discrimination against blacks, and they felt little compunction in informing federal agencies of their practices. But given the report's contention that redlining made perfect economic sense, and given the fact that the very mortgage-lending institutions responsible for the practice made up the report's main intended readership, it is difficult to see this report—or the many others like it generated by both the HOLC and FHA—as anything but an acknowledgment that the agency was prepared, with perhaps a few guilty tears, to allow its direst prophesies to simply fulfill themselves: "The whole political economic situation involving these races is so complicated that no solution is possible."[30] The city's inner residential zones would die—and the black ghettos in their midst would die quickest of all. America's great rivers of capital and wealth would be redirected toward the overwhelmingly white suburbs.[31]

Not all New Deal-era policy subscribed to such starkly segregated visions. In 1937, at Roosevelt's behest, the US Congress passed a very different sort of Housing Act whose main goal was to funnel federal resources directly toward the urban poor, including black people. Its champions, people like the veteran Chicago housing reformer Edith Elmer Wood and the young cosmopolitan urbanist Catherine Bauer, had indirect connections with Ely and the institute. But their vision of urban development contrasted dramatically with that of Bodfish, Babcock, the FHA, the NAREB, the home-loan bankers, and the HOLC report on Chicago. Instead of looking to the transatlantic building society movement, Wood and Bauer took inspiration from their own tours of Europe's spanking-new public housing projects. Instead of promoting housing within the private market, they began with the assumption that private providers of slum housing had fundamentally failed the poor and ought to be put out of business. Only governments, Wood believed, could level the slums and build decent housing in their place. Bauer went a step further: the federal government ought to build massive new public housing projects for the poor on vacant land—possibly in the suburbs, as in many parts of Europe. Federal competition would force inner-city slumlords to find other uses for their land, allowing government to forgo the expense of clearance. The 1937 Housing Act that Bauer coauthored and shepherded through Congress gave the federal government power to issue highly subsidized loans to local housing authorities. These authorities would then decide where to build the new projects. One of the big questions that hung over such decisions, of course, was race. Would local housing authorities use federal public housing money to promote or to break up the color line that long divided America's slums?[32]

That question—and the bigger question of whether the FHA's or the public housing reformers' vision of urban development would prevail— hung in the balance as Adolf Hitler attacked Poland and as Japan's military regime rained bombs upon Pearl Harbor. In wartime, US industrialists frantically retooled their factories for war production, decisively ending the long-lingering Great Depression. To staff the war plants, they once again heavily recruited African Americans for jobs that would have been off-limits in peace time. Black migrants arrived in Northern cities in numbers that dwarfed the Great Migration of World War I. With both private and public housing construction at a standstill, the ghettos filled far beyond capacity, and the color line began to expand rapidly across nearby white neighborhoods.

As race war raged in Europe and the Pacific, its specter once again haunted the streets of American cities. In 1942 and 1943, two separate race riots ignited in Detroit, the second involving three days of white attacks on black people's homes, gunfights, and arson. Thirty-four people died, the majority of them black, before federal troops restored order. In 1943, Harlem erupted as well, in urban African America's first major rebellion against what ghetto residents saw as the country's largely hostile and nearly all-white police forces. In Chicago, tensions crackled, and Mayor Edward Kelly appointed a Mayor's Commission on Race Relations in hopes of preventing another 1919.[33]

By the beginning of World War II, Chicago's African American population already topped a quarter million. The South Side Black Belt became a "black metropolis" that vied with New York's Harlem as the country's largest, and the West Side ghetto also expanded rapidly. There had been little construction of new housing in Chicago during the Depression, least of all in the older sections where most blacks lived. During the war a renewed flood of people flowed into the Black Belt's groaning tenements. Slumlords celebrated the new profit-making opportunity by chopping their cramped apartments into still tinier units, even throwing up thin walls in mildewed basements to pack more tenants into their properties. By 1950, the black population of Chicago doubled to just under the half-million mark, many crammed in tiny windowless

FIGURE II.2 House in Chicago's Black Belt, 1941. As hundreds of thousands of African American moved north during World War II and the subsequent thirty years, ghettos like the South Side became overcrowded and expanded. Conditions also deteriorated in the face of federally sanctioned redlining practices of banks and other financial institutions. Photograph by Russell Lee for the Federal Writers Project.

and bathroomless "kitchenette" apartments. Housing reformers once again decried the festering "Calcutta" that had sprung up in the American heartland. Blacks who were bold enough began looking for shelter in surrounding white districts. Meanwhile, local civil rights leaders and the redoubtable black newspaper the *Chicago Defender* had embraced the nationwide "Double-V" campaign to gain a "Victory at home against racism as well as Victory abroad" against the Nazis and Japan. One of the victories they hoped to win at home was "open occupancy" in Chicago's housing market.[34]

As Mayor Kelly's commission noted, however, white hostility burned "at the seams of the ghetto in all directions." In 1944, attacks on black households increased, especially on the edges of the South Side Black Belt. As white and black soldiers filtered back from the battlefields of the world war, they found themselves embroiled in a growing urban war against each other over housing in Chicago. Between 1945 and 1950, the commission counted 357 white attacks on black peoples' homes, including a new wave of house bombings and mob riots. When a single black family moved into an apartment building in the city of Cicero, which adjoins Chicago's southwest side, crowds numbering in the thousands attacked the building. The mere rumor that a black family was moving into a house in Englewood, a neighborhood to the southwest of the Black Belt, brought out five thousand angry whites for several straight evenings.[35]

New Deal-era federal housing policies were quickly swept up in this escalating crisis, none so dramatically and visibly as public housing. In most places, local housing authorities had followed the "prevailing composition" rule, explicitly designating new federally funded projects as "Negro housing" or "white housing." In Chicago, a few such segregated projects existed, but in 1937, Mayor Kelly placed the Chicago Housing Authority (CHA) under the charge of two liberal housing activists—Robert Taylor, a black man, and Elizabeth Wood—both of whom supported civil rights activists' nondiscriminatory policy for public housing tenants. Before the war, they were able to house small numbers of black people in two otherwise all-white projects—though only by segregating them in all-black buildings. In 1946, however, they tried to move a black war veteran and his family into the Airport Homes project on the all-white Southwest Side. A rock-throwing mob chased the family away. A month later, when a few more black soldiers tried to move in, hundreds of neighbors threw rocks at the moving vans and the police who escorted them, then fired shots into the families' homes at night, once again foiling the CHA. Even larger hostile crowds greeted the arrival of black soldiers in a temporary CHA project in Fernwood. There the mobs spawned roaming gangs who assaulted blacks in cars and on trolleys, much as in the 1919 riots.[36]

Black soldiers may have helped the United States win victories abroad, but the second victory at home proved much more elusive. In fact, as if raging street mobs were not enough, black home-seekers and the CHA also acquired two new even more powerful enemies: Chicago City Council and downtown's richest business owners. In the council, aldermen responded to the white mobs' demands by securing state legislation that required the CHA to get the council's approval for new sites. In 1947, Taylor and Wood proposed a bold plan to build large housing projects throughout the city, including some on vacant land on the Southwest Side. These projects would have substantially relieved the housing crunch and allowed slum dwellers to escape the crowded conditions near downtown. They also would have given Chicago some of the geography of a European city, with some poorer districts located on the urban fringe.[37]

The council, fearing that incoming black migrants would quickly fill the projects planned for white areas, drastically cut the CHA's list of sites. What remained was a long stretch of land within the Black Belt that required extensive clearances and only offered Chicago's housing reformers enough space to replace the number of cleared units, not add to the city's net housing stock. It was there that the CHA, stripped of influence and facing ever-tighter budget constraints, settled for the least expensive method to house thousands of people on the slim slice of land left over. Over the course of the 1950s, a four-mile parade of brick high-rise housing projects rose up in a straight line along State Street at the center of the Black Belt: the "Chicago Wall."[38]

Meanwhile, back in the Loop, a group of businessmen led by the owners of Chicago's famous Marshall Fields department store, smelled an opportunity to clarify the color line around downtown. For years, they had complained that black slums located nearby had deterred middle-class customers from patronizing Loop-based businesses. In the late 1940s and early 1950s they successfully lobbied for their own state laws that gave them a stronger say in slum-clearance operations. They used this power to funnel new state and federal slum-clearance money toward their own priorities. Soon their bulldozers got to work, leveling additional sections of the historic ghetto that lay nearest downtown. The Loop's pioneering "urban renewal" plan also resettled displaced people further into the heart of the ghetto, in tower developments similar to the CHA's.[39]

Once the mobs, the aldermen, and the businessmen got hold of public housing policy in Chicago and in similar fashion in cities across the country, they transformed it from a tool to solve the housing crisis into a tool that tore down big parts of the historic ghettos and rebuilt them at a slightly further distance from downtown. A big contradiction lay at the heart of this policy: though it was born of white people's desire to remain separate from blacks, it only intensified black people's search for housing in white neighborhoods. For civil rights activists, the "urban renewal" schemes that multiplied across the country amounted to nothing less than forced "negro removal."[40]

As black migrants continued to pour into cities in all regions of the country—a movement that was amplified by the new migration of Puerto Ricans to some East Coast cities—the country's black metropolises continued to swell, even as their historic cores were being shifted away from downtown or destroyed. Some of the country's iconic ghettos first came into being during World War II and the years immediately after: New York's South Bronx; North Philadelphia; Detroit's East and West Sides; Miami's Liberty City; New Orleans's Ninth Ward; and Watts, the core of South Central Los Angeles. Black Chicago, spread across most of the South and West Sides, had over eight hundred thousand people by 1960 and over a million by 1970. During the same years, sociologists invented a way to measure the extent of urban racial segregation. They calculated the percentage of people in a city who would have to move in order for every neighborhood in the city to have the same racial composition as the city as a whole. By 1960, in most American cities this percentage, called a segregation index, approached one hundred. In Chicago the figure was 92.9 percent; in Detroit it was 84.5; in Philadelphia, 87.1; and in Los Angeles, 81.8. Big cities were no longer the only places with rigid color lines: segregation indexes in most smaller Southern cities were in excess of 90 percent, and places like Buffalo, New York; Gary, Indiana; Flint, Michigan; Chester, Pennsylvania; and Omaha, Nebraska were among the most segregated cities in the country. Percentages such as these equaled or surpassed those of South African cities, where Hendrick Verwoerd was busy putting the Group Areas Act in place.[41]

As World War II ended, fifteen years of constraints on new housing construction finally lifted. The NAREB's large, eager armies of suburban developers got to work platting, subdividing, restricting, and throwing up all manner of new residential development, most of it beyond historic city limits. These subdivisions incorporated themselves as independent towns, and the number of new suburban municipalities multiplied exponentially. For most of these new local governments, the first order of business was to pass highly restrictive zoning laws that severely limited apartment buildings and favored low-density developments of single-family homes. For middle-class and many working-class whites in places like Chicago who faced the likelihood of years of race war along the ever-moving color line, mortgage financing was the only obstacle to acquiring a home in these new towns on the outskirts, far from all threats to property values. In the postwar era, the FHA and the look-alike office within the Veteran's Administration worked tirelessly to provide precisely that kind of financing to white people eager to flee the city.[42]

Governments in the United States could never give urban whites

South African-style influx controls to prevent black migration and "invasion" of urban neighborhoods. But the FHA and VA did give whites the world's most efficient system of what we might call "efflux enablement." By handing millions of whites the keys to homes in the suburbs, the FHA and VA gave the country's racial majority the gift of access to relatively affordable shelter that was nonetheless likely to appreciate in value and become a source of personal and family wealth. To this, the federal government added further amenities. The engineers who designed the urban segments of the giant postwar interstate expressway system drove eight-, ten-, and twelve-lane expressway spurs right through the heart of black neighborhoods, often wiping out their struggling business districts, so that suburbanites could have more direct routes to their jobs downtown. The federal government also multiplied the racially skewed advantages of federal mortgage guarantees by giving homeowners a tax deduction on the interest they paid on their mortgages—yet another idea that originated with the NAREB and the institute. Property taxes also tended to be lower in suburban municipalities because they did not have the social welfare and policing obligations of cities. At the same time more revenue was left over for schools and for a wide array of incentives to attract employers to relocate from downtown.[43]

By contrast, federal agencies did little in the postwar period to widen housing options for blacks, including black soldiers and black people who could easily afford suburban homes. Instead, those agencies helped ensure that the ongoing migration from the South would continue to feed an inner-city black housing shortage. Black people had to make do with a ghetto-based market where housing options were limited to older buildings, where bright red lines separated them from mortgages and from especially needed rehabilitation and maintenance loans, and where interest rates on the loans that were available were much higher. When economists actually studied housing values in neighborhoods, they found, as DuBois had long argued, that it was the severity of white reactions to the arrival of black neighbors that determined whether property values declined in the area—not the actual arrival of blacks. In fact, because of shortages, home prices were often initially higher for blacks than comparable properties purchased by whites. However, because credit for maintenance was both scarcer and more expensive, blacks' properties were doomed to lower rates of appreciation. Thus investments in ghetto-based real estate did little to build lasting family wealth. Instead, as the Chicago HOLC report prophesied, federal agencies helped guarantee the gradual deterioration of housing in the inner city.[44]

The dual housing market meanwhile helped undercut American public housing as well. The NAREB and the USBLL continually lobbied against federal appropriations for public housing, since the program took real estate out of the private market, and the program's funding diminished rapidly during the postwar period anyway. In addition, because even the poorest whites had more options for housing than poor black people, and because they fled projects with even a small number of black neighbors, public housing quickly became known as a "black" program. As such, over time it lost other sources of political support, eventually impoverishing authorities like the CHA and transforming them into the very evil they were meant to combat. By the 1970s, the CHA itself had become Chicago's largest slumlord—and a segregationist one at that.[45]

Such an enormous redistribution of wealth to ordinary white people did not go unnoticed by the African American civil rights movement. But discriminatory federal mortgage guarantee policy proved to be a slippery target, even in retreat. In 1948, in the case *Shelley v. Kramer* the NAACP achieved one of its greatest victories when the Supreme Court declared racial restrictive covenants unenforceable under the Fourteenth Amendment to the US Constitution. The FHA reluctantly bowed to this decision—though it only did so two years later—by waiving its requirement that such covenants be attached to title deeds in large-scale suburban projects it helped finance. Soon the *Underwriting Manual* also lost its explicitly racial language. During the 1960s, as the civil rights movement moved from victory to victory, the FHA was forced to give up discriminatory lending and even to refocus its guarantee policies on the poor. But by then it had done its work for the American color line. Not only had it allowed American segregationism to endure its greatest crisis, but it gave enormous numbers of white people the real estate–based wealth they needed to pick up and move to whiter pastures on their own—even after 1970, when larger numbers of black people were able to overcome ongoing racial steering and redlining in the private market and move to the suburbs themselves.[46]

The FHA's most enduring legacy, then, was this: it allowed the US urban color line to persist into a new millennium with decreasing amounts of discriminatory government coercion. The whitewash of the color line

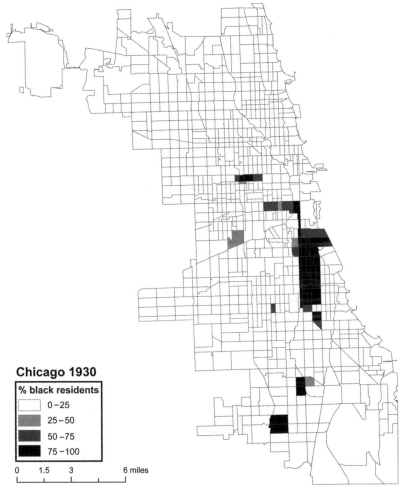

Chicago 1930

% black residents

0–25
25–50
50–75
75–100

0    1.5    3              6 miles

Data sources: Burgess and Newcomb (1933). Census data of the City of Chicago, 1930. The University of Chicago Press. City of Chicago GIS data, retrieved January 28, 2011 from http://www.cityofchicago.org.

FIGURE II.3  A comparison of the progress of archsegregation in Chicago and Johannesburg from the 1930s to the 1970s. Slum-clearance efforts in Chicago removed most blacks living near downtown, but the black ghetto remained in the inner city. Race-infused dynamics in the real estate market, encouraged by the federal government, guaranteed a sharp color line but did not fix it in place. Ghetto boundaries expanded in response to black in-migration and white flight, even reaching some of the least favored suburbs to the southwest by 1970. In Johannesburg, by contrast, government-directed forced removals relocated most blacks, Indians, and coloreds from the central city to disfavored townships on the urban fringe. The Group Areas Act (1950) aimed to fix the color line permanently. Maps by Kailee Neuner.

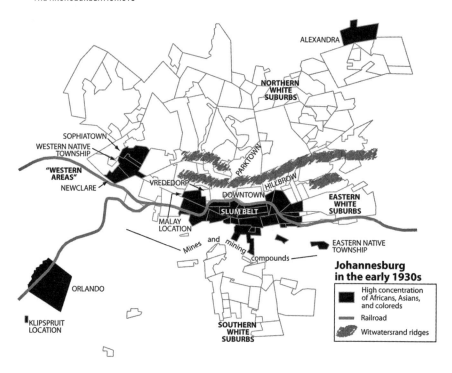

was almost complete. For many Americans, residential segregation had become a de facto part of urban life. It was never made—it just *was*.

## The Sinister Synthesis of Apartheid

In South Africa during the age of extremes, the dramas of city segregation followed a remarkably similar historical pace to those in the United States. Ideas and legislation first proposed in the 1920s inspired a burst of new energy on both the national and local scenes in the 1930s—when prime minister J. B. M. Hertzog pushed hard-line "Stallardist" policies, and when Johannesburg's settlers managed to stuff most of their internal conflicts back into Pandora's box. Then, during World War II, when Jan Smuts returned to power, black migration to the cities increased, painful shortages of urban housing resulted, and black militancy crested. Some argue that for a few fleeting and ambiguous moments, these contexts allowed South Africa's white liberals, like their contemporaries in Chicago, to open the door to less authoritarian racial policies. If that was true,

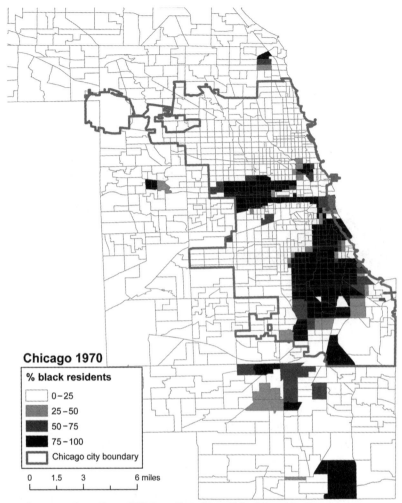

**Chicago 1970**

**% black residents**

☐ 0–25
▨ 25–50
▦ 50–75
■ 75–100
☐ Chicago city boundary

0   1.5   3        6 miles

Data sources: Census Bureau (1970). Census Tracts Chicago, Ill. Population and Housing.
City of Chicago GIS data, retrieved January 28, 2011 from http://www.cityofchicago.org.
Census Bureau TIGER/Line shapefiles, retrieved March 25, 2011 from http:?//www2.census.gov.

the door slammed shut quickly afterward, for the postwar victory of the radical archsegregationists was much more decisive than in the United States. With the election of D. F. Malan's radicalized National Party in 1948, South Africa's apartheid era began.[47]

The global impact of extreme events—the Depression, World War II, the Cold War, and the economic booms of the 1950s and 1960s—was most responsible for the similar timing of the beginnings, middles, and climaxes of these two dramas on opposite ends of the Atlantic Ocean.

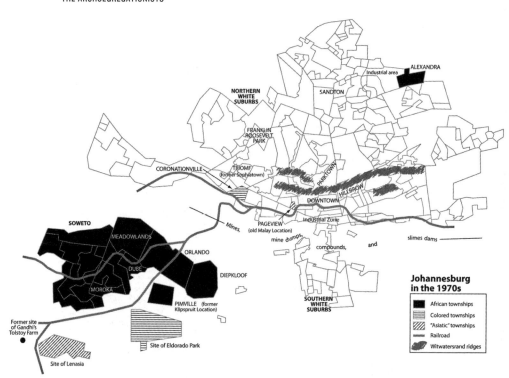

Their many similarities also reflected the fact that both countries' segregationists imported some of the same sorts of reform and real estate institutions from Europe—most notably restrictive covenants, public supports for liberal home mortgages, large investments in public housing, and energetic slum clearances.

But there were big differences as well. While South African segregationists were notorious for their especially Orwellian use of racial whitewash, they also had constitutional permission to shout their cause loudly from the official political rooftops and to explicitly use public institutions toward their ends. They did both of these things continually and ubiquitously: in the legislative debates of the all-white Westminster-style Union Parliament; in city councils; in dozens of segregationist bills, acts, and ordinances; in official government gazettes; in one commission report after another; and from the soapboxes of often electrifying electoral contests between their constantly shifting political parties.

In the process, they created enormous and powerful national bureaucracies whose specific task was to carry out segregationist legislation.

Thus there was no power vacuum such as that in post-*Buchanan* America, where public authorities had to defer to real estate agents and land economists to develop a more camouflaged route for racial segregationism. It is true that South Africa's real estate agents did organize a NAREB-inspired Institute of Estate Agents of South Africa in 1937, and Ely and Babcock's land economics did inspire the work of some South African scholars. Neither played much of a role in segregationist politics, however. South Africa's segregationist Central Housing Board (CHB), for example, the closest South African equivalent to the FHA, was the project of sanitarians and public housing reformers, not real estate agents or their economists. But nothing in the United States even closely resembled Hendrick Verwoerd's tentacular Department of Native Affairs—not to mention the interior ministry's Group Areas Board, the authoritarian Native Resettlement Board, or even the various municipal departments of non-European affairs. It bears repeating as well that some of these agencies were also dedicated to segregationist missions that ranged well beyond the racial zoning of cities—including influx control and "Grand Apartheid," the racial division of the countryside.[48]

The most sinister distinguishing feature of apartheid, however, owes a much larger debt to the other extreme edge of the world's racial politics, Germany's National Socialism. As we have seen, radical segregationists in South Africa did have prior sources of inspiration. British imperial officials like Lionel Curtis and diehard South African imperial loyalists such as C. F. Stallard himself drew from precedents across the world to articulate the general goals and design many of the institutional prototypes that apartheid's engineers later selected and refabricated as national institutions. The postwar radicalization of the segregation movement also drew strength from an otherwise opposing force, South Africa's anti-imperial movement for whites. During the 1930s, Afrikaner Nationalist academics from groups like the Afrikaner Broederbond (the Afrikaner Brotherhood, founded in Johannesburg in 1918) drew upon local Calvinist theology and the world's multiplying national independence movements to imagine the Afrikaners as a divinely chosen Volk, whose century and a half of blood-soaked victimization at the hands of the British could only be redeemed by the creation of an independent white republic with Afrikaans as a principle language. The republic they imagined would, among other things, unequivocally reject outsiders' meddling in South African racial affairs. Yet the racial theories that Nationalists espoused owed much to those that circulated so profusely throughout the rest of the world, especially Britain's contradictory but politically useful juxtapositions of social Darwinism, eugenics, and the separate development of civilizations.

As they declared their separate destiny, the Nationalists also drew increasingly close to Europe's ultra-Right. The Broederbond and important factions of the National Party (NP), including Hertzog himself in his later years, openly identified with the anti-Parliamentary and anti-Semitic shirt movements of Franco's Spain, Salazar's Portugal, Mussolini's Italy, and, most radically, the SS of Hitler's Germany. At the grassroots level, quasi-fascist organizations like the Ossewabrandwag (Ox-Wagon Guard) grew up in the late 1930s by staging lurid commemorations of the hundredth anniversary of the Afrikaners' nineteenth-century Great Trek— complete with torchlight rallies and parades of ox wagons like those that conveyed the *voortrekkers* away from the orbit of British control. In the end, parliamentarians like the NP's no less racially radical D. F. Malan won out. However, when the South African government called upon the "scientific" expertise of an activist professor with substantial training in German universities to design a national bureaucracy that would reshape the country's cities, it did not get the idealistic if eugenicist professor Richard Ely—it got the cynical and authoritarian Broederbonder Dr. Hendrick Verwoerd. As former shock troops from the Ossewabrandwag and the shirt movements filtered into the lower levels of his and other segregationist agencies—most infamously into the security forces—they brought their predilection for *baaskap* (literally, bosshood) along with them. In this way, Malan and Verwoerd synthesized a segregationist welfare state with a fiercely Nationalist police-state. Unlike Nazi Germany, South Africa held on to its Westminster system—racially truncated as it was—and gave lip service to a kind of urban reformism. But that left plenty of space for the country's right wing to swing an iron fist.[49]

To fully understand this story, however, we need to start with one racially circumscribed policy arena in which even South Africa's crustiest segregationists consistently practiced their otherwise duplicitous egalitarian talk. In the 1920s and 1930s, J. B. M. Hertzog gave South Africa's white people of all classes one of the most wide-ranging and generous welfare states in the world. Such racially exclusive but class-egalitarian government activism dated back to before the Anglo-Boer War, when Paul Kruger's South African Republic provided Afrikaner brickmakers in Johannesburg with cut-rate plots of land in Vrededorp. Lionel Curtis, Johannesburg's early twentieth-century British municipal housecleaner hoped—much like his one-time mentor Octavia Hill—that the enormous municipal territory he designed for Johannesburg would enable whites of all classes to find decent housing in uncongested neighborhoods. In 1914, Charles Porter, Johannesburg's plague-fighting municipal officer of health, attended a seminar in London with the great urban planner Raymond Unwin, and he returned to lobby hard for a national public housing program—intended, among other things, to remove poor whites from the "undesirable" influence of their black, colored, and Indian neighbors in the slums.[50]

In 1920, the Union Parliament created a British-influenced Central Housing Board empowered to make cut-rate loans to municipalities for public housing schemes. Local governments could also offer building-society-style loans to first-time homebuyers with 10 percent down payments and twenty-year repayment periods. In contrast to its cousins in Britain, the CHB was poorly funded throughout the 1920s and into the Depression. But it represented one of the first pieces of the country's racially segregated national welfare state. During its first fifteen years it lent more than three times as much for "European housing schemes" as it did for "non-European" ones—amounting to more than seven times the expenditure per individual unit—despite the much stiffer housing crisis for nonwhites. Virtually all of the agency's direct loans went to Europeans. Siting policies were strictly segregationist.[51]

In 1922, Jan Smuts crushed white mineworkers' great Rand Revolt, thus putting his South African Party squarely behind Johannesburg's gold-lords. In response, Hertzog's Nationalists vigorously trolled for working-class votes, and two years later their alliance with the largely English-speaking Labor Party propelled Hertzog into the prime ministership. His "civilized-labor" policy restricted skilled jobs in the private sector and all posts in Union government, including the most menial, to whites only. Still, the increasing commercialization of agriculture, several years of severe drought, and then the Great Depression continued to throw many Afrikaners into the ranks of the poor whites. In the early 1930s, as a study commissioned by the American Carnegie Foundation revealed, tens of thousands of them made their way into the multiracial slums of Johannesburg and elsewhere along the Rand.[52]

By the Depression years, national and imperial politics had changed. Hertzog won cherished victories for the Nationalist cause, including South Africa's constitutional right to secede from the empire. In part to show national unity during the Depression and in part to gain an unassailable majority for his harsh native policy, he negotiated an alliance with Jan Smuts that resulted in the fusion of the two rival major parties into a new United Party. This move angered the died-in-the-wool faction of Nationalists, including the Broederbonders, who broke off to form a "Purified" National Party under D. F. Malan. The Purifieds quickly exploited working-class hatred for Smuts to take the lead on the poor-white issue. Hertzog helped their cause by refusing to follow Britain's example and leave the gold standard, a stubborn move that further aggravated the economic crisis. In 1931, the young professor of applied psychology Hendrick Verwoerd gave the keynote address to the Carnegie Foundation's convention on the poor-white question, in which he lionized the "scientific" practices of New Deal relief programs and urged South Africa to import them as a way to de-pauperize the Afrikaner Volk.[53]

Suddenly, however, in 1933, the Great Depression evaporated in South Africa. International financiers forced Hertzog off the gold standard and a flood of investment capital roared into the country. Johannesburg's small factory belt, located near the mines, grew at a rate that left the city's boosters astonished. Real estate in the suburbs boomed. The Central Housing Board suddenly had much more cash on hand than it had lent out in all its previous years combined. Johannesburg City Council began work on several new CHB-funded housing projects aimed to remove poor whites from the slums and put them in homes explicitly designed to American and British standards. In 1937, the CHB also created an FHA-like partnership with the country's building societies to expand the availability of finance capital for somewhat more affluent first-time homebuyers. Meanwhile, the Purified Nationalists, working with other Afrikaner Nationalist organizations, founded their own bank, the Volkskas, aimed to stimulate a more general economic renaissance among Afrikaans speakers. The National Railroads—now almost exclusively staffed by Afrikaners, thanks to Hertzog's civilized-labor measures—sponsored a cut-rate home-loan program for its employees. After the war, the state-run steel and armaments companies as well as the white labor unions, all dominated by Afrikaners, followed suit. The CHB was reconfigured as the National Housing and Planning Commission (NHPC), and it inaugurated a program of cheap direct loans to ex-servicemen, much like that offered by the US Veteran's Administration. Then, in 1956, under Prime Minister Verwoerd, the NHPC offered a zero-down-payment loan program for all state employees purchasing a home for the first time.[54]

By that time, the Johannesburg City Council owned and managed some 10 percent of the city's white housing, offering a step up into the private market for new migrants from the impoverished high veldt. The municipality also went into the suburban development business, offering affordable plots to returning World War II soldiers and others in leafy subdivisions, one of which bore the name Franklin Roosevelt Park. Superhighways linked the far northern suburbs with downtown, and residential subdivisions sprawled across the veldt, just as they did across Chicago's surrounding prairies. Such strokes of *volkskapitalisme* and racial welfare-statism more than amply solved the poor-white problem. By the time Verwoerd became prime minister in 1958, Afrikaners' standard of living had reached a level equivalent to that of English speakers for the first time. As in the United States, South Africa's public authorities had greatly enlarged the country's middle class by doling out racial privileges to people who had lived in desperation a few years earlier.[55]

Black South Africans got a welfare state of sorts too, and so did coloreds and Indians. But theirs delivered much more brutal repression than wealth, property, or privilege of any sort. The roots of this synthesis went back to the nationwide debates between whites over the Natives (Urban Areas) Act of 1923, when the settler community's many furious quarrels dissolved into a debate between liberals and hard-line Stallardists over the question of whether blacks should be allowed to live in cities at all. When the dust settled, the Stallardists had largely won. Their bottom-line principle, that blacks should only enter cities when they were needed by whites, was reflected in the act's strengthened influx controls, its weakening of black property rights, and new powers it gave to municipalities to proclaim any area of the city for whites only. The law, however, also paid lip service to liberals' demands to give blacks representation in native advisory boards, to create separate revenue streams for the locations, and to ensure that local governments provide housing for all blacks they removed from white areas. The Johannesburg City Council immediately attempted to flout these liberal provisions by proclaiming the entire city white and providing no housing. When the Supreme Court rejected the ploy, frustrated council members from the majority Ratepayer Party, who largely voted for Smuts's SAP on imperial matters, found a receptive ear when they visited Smuts's bitter rival, the new Nationalist Prime Minister Hertzog, in Cape Town.[56]

In 1930, Hertzog pounded an amended version of the Natives (Urban

Areas) Act through Parliament that weakened its liberal housing obligations. Johannesburg now pushed forward more deliberately, proclaiming the city white township by township, starting with the northern suburbs and then targeting the mixed-race slums to the east of downtown that seemed most likely to spread up the slopes into the white zones. In 1934, Hertzog made that project even easier by snatching a particularly vicious slum-clearance law from the Cape Province Parliament and ramming it through the Union Parliament instead. This Slums Act allowed municipalities to expropriate slum land and clear buildings without providing replacement housing. The wording of the act was technically nonracial, but that gave it even more racist force, for it gave council the power to forcibly remove Indians and coloreds as well—a power white ratepayers had been especially eager to acquire.[57]

The Slums Act also coincided with the dramatic swing in the country's economic fortunes. The economy's liberation from the gold standard, like a deus ex machina, suddenly cleared the last of the old obstacles to a unified segregationist movement from the stages of South African urban politics. Most important, cities could now afford to flatten slums and build segregated housing for unwanted groups too. In Johannesburg, the Non-European Affairs Department (NEAD), under the liberal-leaning Graham Ballenden, became a profuse fountain of eviction notices, and by the end of the 1930s, the agency was able to clear almost all black people from the downtown slums. Many of them moved west into Sophiatown and nearby Martindale and Newclare, where blacks actually did own land and where many of those landowners were happy to earn more money renting out crowded backyard rooms. Others found space to live in Alexandra, the other highly congested black freehold township just beyond the city limits to the north.

In the meantime, Ballenden revived the council's long-standing interest in sending blacks, coloreds, and Indians fifteen kilometers to the southwest near the Klipspruit Native Location. With help from none other than separate-development theorist Howard Pim—now a self-proclaimed "liberal" convert—Ballenden gave the old, fly-ridden location a makeover and even renamed it Pimville. Soon the population of Pimville exceeded ten thousand. Then Ballenden received a big CHB loan to build a new, much larger township nearby, named Orlando, after another liberal former councilman. Indians and coloreds also lost homes to downtown slum clearance, though they managed to save the traditional center of their communities, the Malay Location. Still, city council got another CHB loan for a large colored housing scheme at Cor-onationville, eight kilometers out of town along the line to Orlando, and plans got underway for a similar scheme for Indians in the same area.[58]

The long list of once-warring white political interests that now united behind Ballenden can be perceived in the ways council redistributed the cleared land downtown. Northern ratepayers' worries about property values were assuaged. Developers celebrated by erecting a cock's crest of Copacabana-style luxury high-rises for whites along the slopes of the Rand, climaxing in fashionable Hillbrow. Council used more modest open sites for its state-of-the-art white public housing, delighting orga-nized labor and the Nationalists. Manufacturers, including the city's first Afrikaner businessmen, snapped up other cleared plots near the mines for the factories and railyards of the city's new manufacturing economy. Only the city's prohibitionist movement went down in defeat (at the same time as its American role model) when Ballenden persuaded coun-cil to establish a municipal African beer-brewing monopoly to help fund extensions to Orlando.[59]

Meanwhile, Hertzog also rode a tide of white unity in national politics. In 1936, the entire spectrum of the United Party in the House of Assembly broke with tradition and burst into applause for the prime minister after voting overwhelmingly to end the Cape Province's hundred-year policy of limited voting rights for blacks. In churlish compensation, Hertzog offered blacks three white delegates in Parliament and added small bits of land to the reserves to better allow "the native . . . to develop accord-ing to his natural talent and aptitude" far out in the countryside. Then he underlined the fact that he meant no favor at all by tightening influx controls once again. He also diluted the Cape colored vote by enfranchis-ing white women only, and he came down harder on Indian landholding in the Transvaal despite renewed protests from London and New Delhi. Finally, a wave of Jewish immigrants fleeing Nazi Germany sparked anti-Semitic rants by Hertzog, Malan, and Verwoerd. These speeches helped propel the 1939 Aliens Act through Parliament. While it did not restrict Jews explicitly (as Malan wanted), it effectively imposed influx controls upon many who would soon face the death camps.[60]

That same year Britain declared war against Nazi Germany. South Af-rican politics swung wildly in yet another direction, again following con-tingencies of a global scope. The United Party voted to join the Allies, and Hertzog resigned in honor of his Volk's hatred of Britain, of Afrikaners' ancestral affinity for Germany, and of his own growing sympathy for Eu-

rope's authoritarian regimes. The far-right wing of the Nationalist movement was forced into the political wilderness, where its profascist and
paramilitary elements armed themselves for a Nazi victory in Europe
and a coup at home. Smuts returned as prime minister and, in sharp contrast, reoriented national policy single-mindedly upon Hitler's defeat.
Such luxuries as the Central Housing Board closed shop, the pass laws
went into abeyance, and the war industries of Johannesburg welcomed
tens of thousands of new black migrants into town.[61]

From 1936 to 1948, the city's black population grew from 250,000 to
almost 400,000, and the number of blacks surpassed that of whites for
the first time. While some of the newcomers made their way to the freshly
cleared zones of downtown or into bursting Sophiatown and Alexandra, tens of thousands gravitated toward Pimville and Orlando in the
far southwest, where many lived as illegal tenants in backyard shacks. In
1944, an Orlando Native Advisory Board member named James Mpanza

FIGURE II.4 James Mpanza's Shanty-Town, near Orlando Township, Johannesburg. As
thousands of black migrants moved to South African cities during World War II, they
overwhelmed the city's native townships, the only areas most could legally live. Mpanza
urged homeless migrants to join him in tent cities like this one, and he defied the white
municipality by running the government of Shanty-Town on his own. Courtesy of the
Museum Africa, Johannesburg

organized a group of these tenants into the Sofazonke Party (Zulu for "We Shall Die Together"). The party founded a settlement of its own called Shanty-Town, made up of flimsy wood and burlap structures on municipal land to the west of Orlando. There, Mpanza levied taxes, hired police, sold trading and brewing licenses, and went after Johannesburg City Council's goat by claiming to run South Africa's first urban "black self-government." Council responded by evicting the squatters several times, only succeeding in increasing their numbers. The city also attempted to deport Mpanza back to Zululand in 1946, but he beat council's case in court, and his stature rose to messianic proportions. Meanwhile, riots broke out, resulting in several deaths, and similar squatter movements, now involving as many as ninety thousand people, finally forced council to legalize their shantytowns as Moroka Camp, yet another extension of what it now called the Southwestern Bantu Townships.[62]

Mpanza's successes came amid increasing grassroots protest across the Rand. Alexandra's residents boycotted city buses rather than pay increased fares, others protested a resumption of the pass laws, and black mine workers staged a massive strike in 1946 under the auspices of a new union led in part by Communist organizers. Young members of the African National Congress founded the ANC Youth League (ANCYL), which pressured the organization's elders to abandon their polite and long-ineffective strategy of parliamentary petitioning and urged them to embrace the new spirit of protest. Mpanza was particularly inspirational to one twenty-six-year-old member of this group, Nelson Mandela, who at the time lived in Orlando with fellow ANCYL firebrand Walter Sisulu.[63]

For white liberals, events like these confirmed that the days of nationwide segregation through influx control were truly numbered. They pressed this argument within Smuts's United Party, within the newly founded South African Institute for Racial Relations (SAIRR), and in a commission Smuts appointed under a judge named Henry Fagan to study a new course for the country's color lines. In 1948, during the waning days of Smuts's term, the Fagan Commission belatedly emerged from its deliberations to proclaim that the idea of "total segregation is utterly impracticable." It recommended acceptance of a "settled, permanent Native population" in the cities and a gradual phasing out of the pass laws.[64]

It is of course impossible to know whether Jan Smuts, who had been so deeply implicated in South Africa's history of segregation, could have, with a little more time, once again swung the country in such a different direction. By 1948, however, the strongest political winds in South Africa clearly blew from the far right. Ironically, it was Hitler's collapse on the battlefields of Europe that steered the many feuding factions of the Afrikaner Nationalist movement away from various increasingly futile schemes to subvert Smuts's war effort. Instead, they hitched their political ox-wagons to domestic racial politics. One of the impulses came from Geoff Cronjé, a German-trained eugenicist professor of sociology at the University of Pretoria and member of the fascist Ossewabrandwag. In a lecture to a crucial Volkskongress in 1944, Cronjé argued that the fate of the Afrikaner nation to the absolute avoidance of racial mixing and to constant vigilance in racial conflict. Broedbonders like Verwoerd echoed similar sentiments, though, like J. B. M. Hertzog, they also picked up some of the civilization-based discourse of separate development from English authors going back to Howard Pim. Indeed, the Volkskongress's final platform foreshadowed Verwoerd's "Bantustan" policy by declaring that "in order to give the natives sufficient opportunities freely to realize their national aspirations, they must be provided with separate areas which will be administered and developed initially for them and eventually by them as self-ruling native areas in which the whites may have no rights of citizenship." Malan's National Party, meanwhile, appointed its own countercommission under the direction of Broederbonder Paul O. Sauer that scooped the official Fagan Commission in 1947 by announcing the party's commitment to the "eventual ideal and goal" of "total apartheid between whites and natives." The Sauer Report also promised to push influx control hard enough to begin a "gradual extraction of Natives from industries in white areas," though it cautioned "that this can only be achieved in the course of many years."[65]

In 1948, D. F. Malan and the National Party raised the flag of "apartheid"—a word that first arose in discussions among Broederbonders as far back as the mid-1930s—to the top of their campaign standard. In their stump speeches, Nationalists once again revived the *swart gevaar* (Black Peril) and now mixed it with warnings of a native *oorstroming* (swamping) of cities, black takeovers of good white jobs, and the Communist menace on the Rand. Verwoerd lampooned the Fagan Report as the supine "Political Bible of the United Party," and other candidates portrayed Jan Smuts as more interested in doddering schemes like the United Nations than in arresting the country's racial "drift." Though the NP's margin of victory was slim, the apartheid platform convinced just enough English-speaking workers to vote for Nationalists to put Malan over the top. Later, many more whites from all walks of life would join the juggernaut. The Nationalists' majorities steadily increased in every election until 1970.[66]

Though the Sauer Report provided little in the way of a specific legislative blueprint for apartheid, Malan and South Africa's first all-Afrikaner cabinet lost little time in passing radical racial legislation. The Prohibition of Mixed Marriages Act (known as the Immorality Act) of 1949 reflected the influence of Cronjé's eugenics on the NP's racial beliefs. It extended previous bans on white-black marriages to cross-racial unions involving coloreds and Indians as well. The Population Registration Act (1950) created a system of racial identification cards whose primary intent was to clarify the blurry line between the white and colored population, and it toughened penalties on interracial sex outside marriage. The Bantu Education Act (1953) closed mission schools that Verwoerd deemed inciters of black revolt and substituted them with overcrowded township schools guaranteed to foster mass illiteracy.[67]

Amid this growing blizzard of white supremacist ill will, the Nationalists passed world history's most sweeping and complex urban racial zoning measure—the Group Areas Act of 1950. Its goal was more ambitious than anything possible in the United States: nothing less than to provide a "guarantee of future certainty" to urban color lines across the country. The law put the power of declaring urban "group areas" squarely in the hands of the minister of the interior, advised by a Land Tenure Advisory Board (LTAB, or *Grondbesitberaad* in Afrikaans) that had limited obligation to consult with the local authorities who had previously taken the lead in segregation. The law also added Indians and coloreds to the list of groups that could be allotted racial zones. Indeed, the act's complexity reflected the long and tortuous history of South African whites' battle to limit Indian land purchases to specific areas of the city, a battle that went back to the South African Republic's Law 3 of 1885. The LTAB first came into operation under the most recent Asiatic Land Act, Smuts's so-called Ghetto Act of 1946, aimed to assuage white property owners in Durban who were alarmed by the "Asiatic penetration" of their neighborhoods. The chairman of the LTAB, an obscure figure named D. S. van der Merwe, was also a member of such Milner-era real estate institutions as the Rand Registrar's Office and the Transvaal Townships Board. He was thus intimately familiar with all the complications involved in racial restrictions law, including the fine distinctions used in the case of mining and other specially proclaimed lands, the differences between restrictions

on ownership and occupancy, and the complications involved in prohibiting white front companies that bought houses for disallowed groups
in white areas. When Van der Merwe drafted the Group Areas Bill, he
sought to cover all such bases, but Parliament still felt the need to amend
the act a dozen times over the next twenty years, in part to close further
loopholes.[68]

In the debates over the bill, MPs entirely ignored Van de Merwe's legal
hairsplitting in favor of racial grandstanding and political infighting.
Since Malan had not empanelled a customary commission to study the
need for the act, the interior minister T. F. Dönges made a big show of
claiming that large delegations of property owners in the Cape Town area
had demanded "protection against the depreciation of property by . . .
indiscriminate penetration by members of the non-white group." These
"penetrators," he claimed, included Cape coloreds and Indians who had
left Natal and the Transvaal in search of less-restricted land. Since Dönges
did not provide evidence of these demands, we do not know just how
widespread such grassroots white sentiments were at a time when it had
grown extremely difficult for nonwhites to buy in white areas. That did
not stop Nationalist MPs from warning opposition members that they
would face reprisals from English-speaking ratepayers' associations if
they voted against the bill. United Party leaders, for their part, compared
Dönges and Malan to the Nazis for subverting the traditional power of
local governments, and they equated their apartheid slogan to Hitler's
call for *Lebensraum*. In exchange, Nationalists hinted that the UP's liberal
wing was suffused with Communist influence, and they treated the public to a long parade of old shibboleths about miscegenation in the slums,
the natural desire of all groups to live apart, the benefits of segregation
for all races, and the supposed horrors of integration in Brazil and the
United States. Not only did this rhetorical barrage ensure the bill's passage, but Nationalist predictions about the dire electoral consequences
of opposing apartheid seemed to contain some truth. The UP continually
tacked to the right over the next two decades in a vain effort to stanch a
steady leak of support toward the NP. In the process, liberal whites also
left the UP to found their own much smaller Progressive Party.[69]

As apartheid's political road widened, the Group Areas Act began to
infect all elements of South Africa's ever more sinister and ever more
effective segregationist synthesis. The man who made this happen was
Malan's minister of native affairs, Hendrick Verwoerd. Over the course
of the 1950s he expanded the tentacles of what had once been a largely

rural-focused department into a "government within a government" with control over all matters of apartheid policy, including urban racial zoning.[70]

Van der Merwe's LTAB (soon renamed the Group Areas Board) was one of the first offices in other government departments to fall under Verwoerd's sway, and with this shift came control over much of urban planning. Since before the Group Areas Act, the LTAB had attracted the attention of the country's largely European-trained professional planners, many of whom otherwise objected to the Nationalists' authoritarian policies. Once the act became law, lucrative opportunities to engage in what Van der Merwe called *Rassenstreekbeplanning* (racial zone planning) increased. Van de Merwe issued a booklet asking local governments to provide him with maps of group areas in their cities. These maps looked a bit like the redlining maps of the American HOLC and FHA, except that they were completely shorn of camouflage. White areas were to be marked in blue; colored areas, in brown; Indian areas, in red; African areas, in black; and government zones, in orange. Verwoerd was incensed that "liberal" local governments like the Johannesburg City Council and the planners it hired would get even this much control over matters, and he browbeat Van der Merwe into giving Verwoerd's Department of Native Affairs (DNA) the final say over the black zones. Soon the DNA began producing master plans for all the country's black townships that for the first time took future radial expansion into account. The DNA's plans also provided for such security features as wide buffer strips between racial zones (marked in green on zoning maps and later dubbed "machine-gun belts"); screens of trees; single access roads into townships, allowing for regulation of comings and goings; and internal street plans, such as Orlando's, that recalled Jeremy Bentham's utilitarian "panopticon," with administration buildings located at the center of spider webs of straight radial streets that afforded security forces a full view of all activity in their restive realm. Though he gave florid lip-service to the idealistic visions of modern urban planning, Verwoerd's action's resurrected much of the frowning spirit of Vauban.[71]

As part of this power move, Verwoerd also seized control of Union housing policy from the Department of Health. In 1948, Malan appointed a slate of Broederbonders to the National Housing and Planning Commission, and Verwoerd persuaded these old cronies to create a joint commission with the Department of Native Affairs to review all requests for loans from municipalities. At first, this Directorate of Bantu

Housing denied all requests that did not come with DNA-approved Rassenstreekbeplanning maps. Then Verwoerd brought together architects and experts from the building industry to design "scientific" plans for "native houses" and to develop detailed mass-production standards for black townships that were meant to sheer off even the slightest extra cost or inefficiency. The result was the classic township "matchbox house," known in DNA parlance as the "NE 51/6," which stands for non-European model number 6 of 1951. Verwoerd meanwhile raised revenue to build ever more of these matchboxes by getting Parliament to levy a small tax on urban employers, by raising rents on the minority of black people who could pay, and by widening the scope of expenses that municipal beer monopolies could cover to include roads, water, sewers, and streetlights. At the same time, he reduced costs further by persuading Parliament to relax Hertzog's civilized-labor policy, allowing lower-paid black workers to construct township houses. When all of these measures still did not create enough places for blacks to live, he finally resorted to barebones "site and service" schemes, providing concrete platforms for self-built shanties that were equipped with bucket latrines on every plot and water standpipes on every third plot.

Finally, Verwoerd also grudgingly accepted a large loan for native housing from the owners of Johannesburg's gold mines. One morning in 1956, no less a magnate than Sir Ernest Oppenheimer, the chairman of the Anglo-American Gold Mining Company, hopped into his Rolls Royce with a few local officials for a drive out to Moroka Camp. "Aghast" at what he saw there, he returned to the Chamber of Mines, passed the hat, and came up with a cool 6 million Rand at low interest for the municipality. To Verwoerd's chagrin, the city's high capitalists thus made another direct contribution to urban apartheid while smelling like both critics of the regime and black people's greatest benefactors. Such rivalries aside, it took both forces—the penny-pinching Verwoerdian native welfare state and the largesse-spreading Randlords—to finally break through Johannesburg's township housing logjams. Long rows of site-and-service shanties and NE 51/6s matchboxes soon replaced Moroka's squalor. By 1960 a dozen new sprawling black townships had sprouted amid the grasslands beyond Orlando.[72]

To bring a truly segregated native group area into being in Johannesburg, there remained the nagging question of what Verwoerd called the "black spots." Some of these had come into being recently. Servants who worked for whites living in the high-rises of Hillbrow slept at night in small quarters on the tops of the buildings. With little supervision up there, they often brought families and friends to stay with them, creating miniature squatter camps dubbed "locations in the sky." Other black spots had been around for a half century or more, most importantly in Sophiatown and its surrounding western areas. By the 1940s, this "South African Harlem" had become a cosmopolitan center of black urban culture. Its residents included everyone from the King of Swaziland (who owned a few houses there, perhaps for pleasure trips into town); to jazz greats like Dorothy Matsuka, Hugh Masekela, and Miriam Makeba; to the infamous local *tsotsis* and their "Chicago-style" gangs; to a mass of desperate tenants living in backyard shacks. As early as 1937, council announced its intention to evict these tenants, and in 1939 a local MP floated a plan to send Sophiatown's freeholders to new plots near Orlando, as a prelude to redeveloping the area for whites and transforming the neighboring Western Native Township into a new colored district. Nothing came of this plan until 1953, when Verwoerd stepped in. Invoking Le Corbusier's principles of regional planning, he declared a new Western Areas Removal Scheme (WARS), which was also aimed at the "locations in the sky" and other illegally overstuffed servants' quarters in the northern suburbs. In response, the municipality, still majority UP, dragged its feet, making the novel and improbable claim that only local government could truly attend to natives' needs.[73]

When Wilhelm J. P. Carr, Johannesburg's new non-European affairs director, proposed a more liberal voluntary removal scheme that would give Sophiatown's freeholders similar titles in the new southwestern township of Meadowlands, Verwoerd decided he'd had enough. Once again he raged in the Union Parliament for greater powers. In 1954, his Nationalist brethren handed him a new agency called the Native Resettlement Board—nothing less than a fully chartered rival municipal authority for the city of Johannesburg, with power to abrogate freehold and endowed with complete immunity from the court system. The ANC and other organizations began a "We Shall Not Move" campaign to stop Verwoerd's WARS, but they had little chance. The Native Resettlement Board showed up at the crack of dawn on February 9, 1955, two days before the clearance was officially scheduled to begin, along with eighty-six armed vehicles and 1,500 soldiers with rifles. By 1959, the NRB had dispossessed all but eighty-two of Sophiatown's residents, from the shack dwellers to the King of Swaziland himself. To ANC activists' dismay, many of the poorest residents were happy to claim their new 51/6s in Meadowlands,

FIGURE II.5 Forced Removal from Sophiatown, Johannesburg. On February 9, 1955, Hendrick Verwoerd's Native Resettlement Board began forcing all black residents of South Africa's "Harlem" to relocate to new native townships in what would later be called Soweto. Courtesy of Museum Africa, Johannesburg.

which were at least nicer than the backyard hovels many left behind. Meanwhile, UP stalwarts like Carr and the city council shook their heads in amazement and not without a touch of envy. Coolly, the Native Resettlement Board passed Sophiatown's property titles on to Afrikaners. Then, heaping insult upon its rapacity, it renamed the new white township Triomf.[74]

Verwoerd's triumphs did not end there. In point of fact, for an apartheid purist, all of this energy spent on group areas *within* cities represented a kind of compromise. The true goal, after all, was to make cities all-white, not to segregate their neighborhoods. All along, Verwoerd's DNA had made clear that, for the time being, any new native housing in cities was solely meant for black people who could make a very strong case that they belonged there. In 1952, the Native Laws Amendment Act sharply constricted that category to three types of people: those who had been born in the city, those who had lived there for fifteen consecutive years, or those who had worked in the city for ten years. In the same year, the Orwellian Natives (Abolition of Passes and Coordination of Documents) Act actually created an even more severe system of passes called "reference books." Women had to carry them for the first time as well as men, and they contained records of their holder's previous movements, employment, and legal history. The goal of this most dictatorial of all influx-control laws was to finally freeze migration from the countryside to the cities. Its main effect, however, was to transform the Department of Native Affairs into a corrupt and brutal police state. Former fascist paramilitaries pervaded the local labor bureaus, the Bantu Commission courts, and the police and security forces that Verwoerd called on to make the pass system work. The DNA may have slowed urban migration somewhat, but it much more effectively subjected black people to constant and summary pass inspections, hundreds of thousands of arrests, increasingly brutal treatment at the hands of police and prison guards, and summary deportations to the countryside—sometimes for forced labor on white farms.[75]

Verwoerd's grandest dream was to create what amounted to a South Africa without Africans. To get there, he launched his era's most perverse political synthesis—a fusion of apartheid with black liberationism. Turn-of-the-century British officials' concept of separate development provided the rhetorical glue. In 1958, when Verwoerd accepted the office of prime minister, he delivered an unctuous warning to whites that "we cannot govern without taking into account the tendencies in the world and in Africa. We must ... adopt a policy by which we are giving the Bantu as our wards every opportunity in their areas to move along a road of development by which they can progress in accordance with their ability." In 1959, the Bantu Self-Government Act subdivided the black population into eight units and announced that each would be placed on the road to independence within the disconnected checkerboard of national territories defined by their rural reserves. Verwoerd's insistence on the term "Bantu" and his solicitude for black South Africa's ethnic divisions reflected his desire to appear sincerely scientific in his abandonment of race as the basis of apartheid policy and his embrace of more fashionable notions such as culture and nation. Within Verwoerd's fantasies, the Bantustan policy also transformed outsiders' view of South Africa from a country mired in benighted quasi-fascist and white supremacist thought to a modern place on the political cutting edge, akin to Britain and France, both of which were, after all, gingerly parting with their own African colonies at the same time.[76]

Back in the burgeoning black townships southwest of Johannesburg,

FIGURE II.6 Soweto from the air (ca. 1960). A view of the sprawling "matchbox city" of Meadowlands, the destination for most former residents of Sophiatown. Note the radiating street layout designed to allow authorities a "panoptic" view of behavior within the township. Courtesy of Museum Africa, Johannesburg.

few people were remotely fooled by this sinister move. But neither could they deny the extent of Dr. Verwoerd's very real accomplishments. He had come closer than any human being ever had to erecting a seamlessly coercive system of permanent urban racial segregation. Between white Johannesburg and its new native Group Area stretched the vast buffer zone that the creators of Klipspruit Location had imagined back in 1906—now fortified with a "machine-gun belt" of grassland, trees, and intervening colored townships. The bitter recognition of Verwoerd's victories can be sensed in the names black people suggested for their new native city: "Coon's Kraal," "Darkiesuburban," "Thinavuyho" (we have nowhere to go), and, perhaps most appropriate of all, "Khettollo" (segregation). Not surprisingly, city council rejected all of these, and after four years of discussions, Wilhelm J. P. Carr announced the official choice, Soweto, a telescoped version of "Southwestern Townships."

In time, Soweto's residents would transform that bureaucratic abbreviation into a symbol of exuberant resistance—the homeland of the Davids that slayed the Goliath of apartheid. But in 1960, Sowetans, like all South African blacks, Indians, and coloreds—and like African Americans a half world away—faced a troubling predicament. Archsegregationists had put into place the world's two most elaborate systems of racist city-splitting. These systems had survived internal conflicts between whites in two complex industrial societies, in cities that experienced unprecedented in-migrations of people of color. Most stunningly of all, they achieved their greatest victories during the very climax of the era of decolonization, world history's most widespread and pervasive revolution against white supremacy. That was no mean achievement, for it meant defying powerful grassroots urban protest movements led in the United States by Martin Luther King Jr. and in South Africa by Nelson Mandela, both supported by thousands of other brilliant organizers and activists. It also meant promoting racial segregation in the face of the widespread sense of horror that, at Auschwitz, racism had confirmed its potential to turn Western Civilization into a force of mass murder.

Certainly, racial revolutionaries in both countries did not miss the opportunity to equate archsegregationism with Nazi exterminationism. It is no accident that the word "ghetto" entered the vocabulary of protest in both the United States and South Africa during the 1940s. Some antisegregationists went further, dramatizing their causes by comparing racial zoning with Hitler's quest for *Lebensraum*, the FHA's *Underwriting Manual* with the Nuremberg Laws, and apartheid with totalitarianism.

Though very real cross-oceanic connections did exist between all three of these extremes of segregationist politics, their subsequent histories also reveal the importance of the distinct ways they gave practical shape to the continuing thrust of white supremacy. Genocidal racism, we know all too well, did not die with Hitler's demise, and both state and mob violence remained an important part of the segregationist arsenal in South Africa and the United States during the postwar decades and beyond. However, of the two remaining archsegregationist systems, apartheid depended most, by far, on a continual hardening of its Verwoerdian fist. In the United States, racial pogroms, discriminatory behavior by the police, and, after the 1970s, increasingly draconian criminal justice and immigration interdiction systems all helped give shape to persistent urban color lines. But segregationists survived, above all, by developing ever-more ingenious layers of racial camouflage, then using

379

it to call on the white suburbs for the votes necessary to outflank the racial revolution. In the still-murky hindsight of our own day, it appears that it was the subtler of the two approaches that allowed the politics of urban color lines to continue playing on the global stage into the new millennium.

# PART FIVE

# FRAGMENTED LEGACIES

# 12 : Outflanking a Global Revolution

## Age of Liberation, Age of Apocalypse

"It may seem odd," wrote the great African American sociologist Horace Cayton in 1942, "to hear India discussed in poolrooms on South State Street in Chicago, but India and the possibility of the Indians obtaining their freedom from England by any means have captured the imagination of the American Negro."

To Cayton, the buzz in the South Side's poolrooms spoke of historical transformations that arced across the globe. A revolutionary spirit was growing in the world's black towns, medinas, casbahs, townships, and ghettos—from the oldest ones in Madras and Calcutta, to their many variations across the colonial world, to the newest and most intractably delimited ones in Chicago and Johannesburg. "The feeling throughout the colored world," Cayton concluded, "is that there is going to be a change in the status of non-white people, and there is little fear that the change could be for the worse."[1]

It was not long before that political forecast came true—though the changes that came, as Cayton also seemed to expect, were enormously complicated. From 1945 to 1975, the "rising tide of color" of white supremacists' oldest nightmares did, in fact, finally crest upward, riding the force of decades of deferred dreams. For the first time, the world's proliferating antiracist movements became a force to reckon with in global politics. Leaders like Mahatma Gandhi, Jawaharlal Nehru, W. E. B. DuBois, Martin Luther King Jr., Kwame Nkrumah, and Nelson Mandela became planetary icons. Thousands of lesser-known but equally courageous and visionary activists built ties across large regions and between the continents. Transoceanic solidarity funds flowed, at least intermittently. And everywhere, grassroots murmurings like those Cay-

383

ton overheard in Chicago nourished formal movement organizations. With tactics ranging from genteel negotiations to peaceful mass protest to riotous urban upheavals to guerrilla warfare, midcentury antiracist movements launched nothing less than a planetwide revolution against the world of white power and privilege.

The times were ripe for this revolution. The West's extreme orgy of slaughter had left the imperial powers of Europe hobbled, their capitals in rubble. Hitler's Holocaust let loose a rebounding storm of repugnance for racism and anti-Semitism. The ensuing Cold War gave at least some leverage to nationalist and civil rights movements, as the two global superpowers tried to outdo each other in a race to gain the favor of the oppressed peoples of the colonized world.

The victories of the worldwide racial revolution are legendary. India's independence in 1947 signaled the beginning of the era of decolonization, when five hundred years of Western colonial expansion suddenly lurched into reverse in most of Asia and Africa, culminating in 1960, when seventeen new African countries came into being. The legal underpinnings of Jim Crow came undone shortly afterward in the US South, and the American federal government officially gave up its support for residential segregation and racist immigration restriction. Similar advances in civil and migrants' rights came to Europe, Canada, and Australasia, where small urban populations of color grew dramatically. The once-fervid "religion of whiteness" coiled back onto the defensive, in many places hissing and spitting violently, everywhere forced to hunt for new disguises.

Meanwhile, the Great Depression and World War II dramatically shifted the landscape of global capitalism. New possibilities opened up for the fight against urban segregation's boon companion, economic inequality. In 1944, the progressive economist John Maynard Keynes masterminded the Bretton Woods agreements, aimed to keep international financial speculators from disrupting governments' efforts to expand welfare states. Experiments in social democracy flourished in Europe and elsewhere; in most rich countries these far surpassed the scope of the American New Deal. Amid unprecedented economic prosperity and growth, poverty declined in many parts of the world, and for the first time in the industrial age, inequalities between the wealthy and the poor diminished in many countries. So did the yawning disparity in wealth between what postwar analysts dubbed the "First World" and the "Third World."[2]

All of this was good news, and most of it was utterly unimaginable when Horace Cayton first heard murmurings of the "colored world's" revolution in 1942.

So why then do today's urban theorists, faced with the task of describing the cities of the new millennium, cast so breathlessly about for the most apocalyptic superlatives of the word "segregated"? Their conclusions, backed by reams of statistical, cartographic, and architectural documentation, are deeply dispiriting. In an age when cities have become home to a majority of humanity, our urban habitats have become hopelessly "fragmented," "partitioned," "multipolar," "decentered," "segmented," "fractured," even "decomposed." Color lines are deeply tangled, and often deliberately camouflaged, within the political language of class, culture, ethnicity, nation, and—most toxically—religion. Color continues to be the great determinant of residence in the United States, though some American sociologists speak of "hyperghettos" that are both black and poor. Similar ghettos, others worry, have appeared in the more equitable cities of Europe, Canada, and Australia. Meanwhile, the world's suburbs have sprawled "endlessly"—sometimes taking the form of wide, exclusive preserves of the privileged, sometimes of teeming "megaslums" of the very poor, sometimes sharply divided between the two. A "regime" of especially polarized "global cities" has emerged, because the most important capitals of the global economy attract high concentrations of both the wealthiest, whitest, jet-setting elites and the poorest immigrant laborers of color. In many especially polarized places, privileged city dwellers close themselves into gated communities and private compounds, guarded by all manner of high-tech security equipment. Forced removals of vulnerable people, often from "gentrifying" city centers to outlying districts, have become routine; in China they involve millions. Jails and prisons have multiplied, most notably in the United States, where they house a vastly disproportionate population of urban people of color. Walls, barbed-wire fences, and no-go zones divide particularly strife-torn cities like Nicosia and Belfast. Checkpoints and roadblocks riddle the suburbs of Jerusalem and cities in the Occupied Palestinian Territories, and walls and fences spread outward from urban neighborhoods across the surrounding countryside. In much the same way, urban segregation today mirrors a color line that encircles the globe. The world's wealthiest countries have erected new legal and physical obstacles to long-distance migration, targeting people from the poorest and darkest-skinned countries of the global south eager to reach new opportunities in the Global North.[3]

How could this be? How could such an apparent apocalypse of segregation follow so closely on the heels of such promising advances in racial liberation?

In a final sweeping glance across recent world history, we can map out three routes by which urban segregationists outflanked the global racial revolution. First, though opponents of urban segregation achieved their greatest successes by attacking government-imposed residential color lines, they were unable to stop the worldwide diffusion of economic incentives for race and class segregation that were first built into capitalist land markets in the seventeenth century.

Second, though the Cold War provided political room for the world's racial liberation movements to fight against racial segregation in cities, it also severely limited the scope of the egalitarian revolution. Using anticommunism as a justification, Western imperial powers, led by the United States, intervened heavily in the affairs of newly independent nations, among other things encouraging their new leaders to escalate colonial-style, government-driven measures of class segregation against their cities' exploding populations of poor people. Similar global geopolitical conditions helped a handful of settler regimes to sustain elaborate systems of government-sponsored urban segregation, most notably in places where rival nationalist movements used religious sectarian language to make opposing and exclusive claims to the same territory.

Third, and most important, beginning in the late 1960s and culminating in the years after 1980, a nearly all-white "New Right" counterrevolution swept into power, most notably in the United States and Britain. It offered new ways for whites to defend their institutionalized privileges without appearing to embrace white supremacy. On its watch, segregationists operating within governments, global intellectual networks, and land markets gained new political cover for their city-splitting efforts.

Each of these flanking maneuvers led to new bad news for people of color in cities. If these were the only political routes open to us as a majority urban species, we would in fact be well on our way toward a grim future. Fortunately, they are not the only paths we have to follow. But to clearly imagine more hopeful alternatives, we need to first absorb the full range of the fragmented—and too often tragic—legacies of the worldwide spread of racial segregation.

## Have Ghettos Gone Global?

By most measures, the civil rights movement in the United States launched the most elaborate of all the world's assaults on urban color lines. At its broadest base, the revolution against urban segregation in the United States was a movement of ordinary, courageous people seeking housing in neighborhoods where they were not welcomed. Tens of thousands of largely anonymous pioneering black home-seekers willingly walked into the teeth of white violence because housing available in black neighborhoods was hard to find, overcrowded, unhealthful, dangerous, and outrageously expensive. Beyond the ever-moving American color line lay often elusive spaces of urban opportunity, where better deals on housing also came with better amenities for the whole family: schools, parks, public health infrastructure, a less polluted environment, transport, and easier access to jobs.[4]

To help these ordinary African Americans, the NAACP opened up a second front of activism within the law. Its victories in the U.S. Supreme Court are legendary: Moorfield Storey's brilliant maneuvers in *Buchanan v. Worley* in 1917 against racial zoning ordinances and Thurgood Marshall's 1948 defeat of racial covenants in *Shelley v. Kramer*. Marshall also exposed the FHA's proprietary *Underwriting Manual* in 1938, though he had to repeatedly badger a local FHA official from the Long Island suburbs to give him a copy. Thus at least partly decamouflaged, the federal government's complicity in segregation, along with that of municipal public housing authorities, became the target of yet another tactic: persistent petitions and protests in the name of open housing.[5]

From the 1940s through the 1960s, open-housing activists put sufficient pressure on state legislatures to pass a raft of fair housing laws that prohibited practices like racial steering and redlining. Large numbers of liberal white suburban homeowners also entered the fray, some by signing so-called covenants of open occupancy, typically declaring they would "welcome into their neighborhood any residents of good character, regardless of race, color, religion, or national origin." Others went door to door in efforts to persuade their white neighbors to ignore blockbusting real estate swindlers. Still others joined with blacks to persuade real estate agents and bankers to help keep racially changing liberal neighborhoods—like Chicago's Oak Park, Cleveland's Shaker

Heights, and Philadelphia's West Mount Airy—permanently integrated. In 1960, open housing activists pressured the Democratic presidential candidate John F. Kennedy to promise he would end federal housing discrimination "with the stroke of the pen"—a pledge he belatedly fulfilled two years later.[6]

The next step belonged to Martin Luther King Jr. In 1966, fresh from his historic victories in the South, he plunged straight into the maul of American urban archsegregationism by turning his favorite weapon, Gandhian nonviolent resistance, against the color line in Chicago. From his headquarters in a Black Belt housing project he alternately sent black and white testers to white real estate offices to expose the wide spread of racial steering. Then he deployed pickets outside offending real estate agents' offices and personally led a wave of mass marches into the surrounding neighborhoods. There, he ran headlong into the white violence that had long sustained American urban color lines. Enormous crowds of white counterdemonstrators shouted racist epithets, brandished swastika flags, and launched volleys of bricks. After a face-saving truce with Chicago's mayor Richard J. Daley, King left town to nurse his realization that peaceful protest had done little to dislodge divisions deeply rooted in racialized economic interest. Many black home-seekers had similarly disillusioning experiences fighting for housing integration: it was possible, sometimes at great danger, to cross American residential color lines, but no law could forbid white homeowners from making racist calculations about the effects of new black neighbors on their housing values. Once those whites sold out and left, the color line would simply reestablish itself farther off, thus adding a new neighborhood to the city's ghetto and subjecting its inhabitants to the same risks of disinvestment they faced in the all-black zones they had hoped to leave behind.[7]

Two years after his defeat in Chicago, King fell to an assassin's bullet in Memphis. In response, the poorest African American residents of US cities added their own version of mass action to the movement. For five previous "long hot summers," anger and violence had engulfed places like Harlem, North Philadelphia, Watts, Newark, Detroit, and Chicago's South Side. This time, in 1968, the fire once again raged in over one hundred black ghettos, including Chicago's. As before, the most immediate results were scores of people killed and injured and new swaths of burned-out ghetto buildings and businesses. But the din of a hundred riots at once also gave President Lyndon Johnson enough political leverage to persuade the Republican Senate minority leader, Everett Dirksen of Illinois, whose base of support centered on Chicago's white suburbs, to release the votes necessary for the open housing movement's long-delayed federal Fair Housing Act. Discrimination of all kinds in the housing market was now against the law.[8]

In the years following this bitterly won victory, the civil rights movement has continued to champion creative solutions to the problems of the residential color line—despite the limitations of fair-housing legislation and despite growing conservative opposition to civil rights law. In Chicago, activists filed a lawsuit against segregationist practices in public housing. In *Hills v. Gautreaux* (1976), they won another important victory: the US Supreme Court ordered the Chicago Housing Authority to offer thousands of housing vouchers to allow poor African American families to relocate to the suburbs. Though their numbers were comparatively small, the families who were selected for the program did demonstrably better than their counterparts in the ghetto. Meanwhile, a movement also gained steam in a handful of cities for inclusionary zoning laws, which typically require new developments to include substantial shares of affordable housing. Even more promising perhaps, were the Home Mortgage Disclosure Act (1976) and the Community Reinvestment Act (1977), federal laws that required private redliners to reveal information about the location of their mortgage lending and to assume an "affirmative obligation" to lend money in all neighborhoods where they took deposits. Other civil rights–era legislation, the Community Development Block Grants and the Enterprise Zones, unleashed federal funds and tax breaks for the development of neglected areas. Grassroots efforts to channel federal, corporate, and private foundation money into community development corporations (CDCs) or neighborhood-based direct-action organizations have had notable successes across the country.[9]

Elsewhere in the world's wealthiest reaches, gains for the civil rights of people of color have been coupled with more extensive social democratic policies than in the United States. In some cases, these efforts have been explicitly devoted to comprehensive goals of "social mixing." London and Paris are good places to see some of these results. Both cities have long histories of segregation: the historic class boundaries that divide the privileged western side of both cities from the working-class zones to the east remain are still discernible on city maps today. London and Paris also long harbored small polyglot populations of color, either from the slave trade or the colonies. However, the two capitals' histories differed from those of places like Chicago and Johannesburg in that no permanent "Great Migration" of people of color made its way to European cities during World War I. It was not until the Second World War that the racial diversification of places like London and Paris began in earnest. In 1940, the good ship *Empire Windrush* famously disgorged its cargo of West Indian immigrants onto the docks of London. France had meanwhile reasserted Algeria's status as an intrinsic extension of the republic. Two thousand refugees from the impoverished Algerian countryside arrived each month in Paris and began fringing the city with self-built *bidonvilles*, much like those outside Algiers.[10]

By the postwar years, both cities' eastside working-class districts had grown dramatically, spreading around downtown in wide arcs that flanked the smaller bourgeois western suburbs to the north and south (in London, a largely middle-class suburban belt called Outer London surrounded the whole city even further out). Amid postwar housing crises exacerbated by Nazi bombs, London built hundreds of generally small public housing estates (and a few bigger ones) throughout much of the city, including a few in privileged Outer London. By contrast, Paris replaced its bidonvilles and slums with the infamous modernist Habitations à Loyer Modéré (HLMs)—universally monumental and concentrated above all in the poorer "Red Belt" suburbs, now most often known by the medieval term *banlieues*. London's "black" people (a category that soon included large numbers of Indians, Pakistanis, Bangladeshis, and Chinese as well as West Indians and Africans) and Paris's "*immigrés*" (who actually included large numbers of French-born Antilleans and North and West Africans as well as Southeast Asians and Chinese) did what American blacks had done in nineteenth-century Chicago: they wove themselves into the increasingly diverse ethnic patchworks of the city's working-class districts, in their case largely in social housing estates. Soon observers began to trot out a new, incendiary name for these multicolored working-class zones: the ghetto.[11]

Most urban sociologists in Europe, Canada, and Australasia are skeptical of the claim that American-style segregation has arrived in their cities. All-encompassing social democratic safety nets guarantee that income inequality, intergenerational poverty, hunger, and health insecurity are much less acute than in the United States, even if unemployment (especially among youth) in some places approaches that of Chicago's South Side. In all countries of the wealthy world it is possible to find public housing estates that are depressing places to live. But most outside the United States are far more integrated by color and class, sharply contrasting with the desperate towers of Chicago's "Wall," which largely became dead-end social warehouses for the poorest of the black poor, and which the city recently tore down. Such integrated social housing enjoys greater national political support, and the estates are usually better maintained and better provided with amenities. Outside of France's HLMs and a few other gigantic projects in the Netherlands and Britain, most European social housing estates are small in scale and relatively scattered across the urban fabric. The percentage of the housing stock owned by governments in most of the Global North is far higher than in the United States—even after Britain's New Right prime minister Margaret Thatcher sold off a million and a half council houses during the 1980s. Poor people face far fewer difficulties getting safe shelter than the residents of America's rotting ghettos. Stronger gun restrictions keep violent crime and murder rates far lower than in US ghettos.[12]

There are important exceptions to this general rule. The French government, for example, designed a particularly brutal form of state-sanctioned segregation for the Harkis, Algerians who had supported France during the Algerian wars of independence. When the Harkis fled to France to avoid reprisals after Algeria won its independence in 1962, French authorities honored their service by relegating them to squalid internment camps surrounded by barbed wire and guard towers. Some fourteen thousand remained there as late as 1974 when they launched a movement to end the camp system. Though France has since officially apologized to the Harkis, French and other European politicians regularly troll for votes by vilifying the Roma and other traveling people, sometimes ordering the police to destroy their camps and deport them to other countries.[13]

Unlike the United States, however, most other governments in the Global North at least claim to make the fight against urban segregation a high priority. In 1991 and 2000, the French Socialist Party bucked the growing influence of the New Right by passing what were soon dubbed the "antighetto" laws. Their goal was nothing less than a nationwide inclusionary zoning system requiring all municipalities, even the richest ones, upon penalty of steep fines, to ensure that their housing markets contained 20 percent affordable government-owned units. This push for "social mixing" (*mixité sociale*) fit within a larger social democratic urban policy. The state promised to replace the grim postwar HLMs with graceful low-rise developments to make a huge investment in public transport to minimize the disadvantages of Paris's east-west divide and to use

FIGURE 12.1 Have America's ghettos come to Paris? In the "4000" housing project at La Courneuve, one of France's most notorious suburbs, a monumental public housing block serves as the backdrop for a burned-out shell of a car, symbolic of the many riots that have engulfed immigrant neighborhoods since the 1970s. Since this photo was taken in 1999, the French government leveled the 4000 complex and replaced it with more dispersed low-rise public housing as part of a nationwide "antighetto" campaign. Author's photo, 1999.

centralized planning laws to manage sprawl. Similar comprehensive urban policies exist elsewhere in Europe, and some are further subsidized by the European Union. Such policies have helped to guarantee that no vast uniracial inner-city zones like Chicago's South Side have appeared anywhere in the Global North outside of the United States. As in London and Paris, most European, Canadian, and Australian urbanites of color live outside historic city limits in class-segregated neighborhoods that are checkerboarded with people of many different backgrounds, including large numbers of lower-income whites. Many immigrant groups, even those of color, appear to have been able to disperse outward from areas of first settlement into much wider areas of the city, and there are few instances where most people from any one group live in a single area.[14]

In the debate over the spread of ghettos outside the United States, however, two questions remain less fully explored: Have white homeowners and real estate agents made active efforts to defend the residential color and class lines that do exist? And to what extent have racial theories of property values ingrained themselves into white beliefs, bringing dual housing markets into being? Here, the danger signs are more worrisome, but to say that Europe, Canada, and Australia have imported an American style of segregation is only partly correct. The doctrine that high property values depended on neighborhood exclusivity, after all, was born in London. British legal precedents helped developers and homeowners in Canada to argue for the legality of racial covenants, just as in South Africa and the United States. In Europe itself, racial covenants have not played as important a role in real estate politics as land-use covenants, but there is plenty of evidence of white "fight or flight" behavior both along historic class divides and within the working-class racial checkerboards. In Britain, white harassment and mob violence directed at neighbors of color peaked on a number of occasions since World War II, including as late as the 1990s. In France during the 1950s and 1960s, local white mobs were fortified by the so-called *pieds noirs* (black feet), French settlers forced out of Algeria during the war for independence. The *pied noirs* brought their pitched battles with victorious Algerian freedom fighters to the banlieues of Paris and other cities. As in Chicago, European administrators of public housing estates often found themselves forced to bend to segregationist pressures to maintain social peace. Some designated separate towers or stairwells for different groups, following what French officials called whites' "tolerance thresholds" (*seuils de tolérance*). Several majority–North African housing estates in France still have a single building reserved for *pieds noirs* and their descendants off to one side. In France, wealthy suburban *communes* do not have the power to set tax rates and zoning provisions like white-flight suburban municipalities in the United States, but their inhabitants have often pressured local mayors to pay the steep fines proscribed by the antighetto laws rather than accept quotas to build social housing that they think will threaten local prestige, schools, and property values.[15]

These currents of segregationist thought and action were part of a bigger cross-oceanic counterrevolution of white racial privilege that swept across the Global North from the 1940s on. It had many roots across the Global North, but much of what was "new" in the New Right did first arise in the white-flight suburbs of the United States, and to that extent European segregation does take after American-style ghettoization. By 1970, American cities' sprawling outskirts had outgrown the cities they surrounded, in the process becoming home to the country's (and perhaps the world's) single largest and most influential uniracial voting block. Forsaking the balder white supremacist rhetoric of Jim Crow, suburban whites voiced their support for privileges rooted in residential segregation by tapping into traditions of camouflaged racial demands that went back to the work of the National Association of Real Estate Boards and Chicago's Institute for Research in Land Economics and Public Utilities. Already in the late 1940s, for example, suburbanites outside Atlanta, Los Angeles, Detroit, and Chicago articulated their defense of homogeneous neighborhoods in terms of a defense of property rights and the "civil right" to chose one's neighbors. Others fought fair housing laws by appealing to the right of free association or the freedom from unwarranted government interference.[16]

The idea of refashioning white privilege as a defense of rights and liberty was appealing to conservative politicians like George Wallace, Richard Nixon, and Ronald Reagan. Soon, British and French conservatives like Margaret Thatcher and Jacques Chirac laid similar ground. In Europe, American influences mixed with long-standing traditions of imperialist and anti-immigrant racism, such as that of the Tory firebrand Enoch Powell and Jean Marie le Pen, the founder of France's National Front. Wherever it was launched, the New Right electoral strategy had two parts. Veiled promises of support for middle-class white privileges were combined with revived "free-market" attacks on welfare states, labor unions, government regulations, and progressive taxation systems.

394

Meanwhile, a language of racial resentment lured white working-class swing voters away from traditional left-leaning parties and toward those favored by their employers.

Several ill-meaning feats of theoretical conjury were involved. One was the New Right's insistence upon an upside-down narrative of social history in which the black and brown racial revolution and its liberal white allies had succeeded in seizing enormous power—thus transforming white people into the true victims of racial inequality. Accusing civil rights activists of demanding "special rights" for black and brown people, the New Right instead proposed an attractive-sounding "color blind" and ostensibly meritocratic society—concealing the fact that such a society would effectively perpetuate racial subordination by denying its existence. The theme of white vulnerability also allowed New Right leaders to assume the role of the great safeguards of "the nation" or "Western civilization" at a moment when both were supposedly in danger of being swamped by incompatible foreigners. While repeatedly denying any racist intent, New Right leaders could simultaneously channel racial hatred through codewords like "welfare," "taxes," "quotas," "immigrants," "values," "social pathology," and, most of all, "crime."

The word "ghetto" combined all of these coded racial aspersions. The European anti-immigrant Right, in fact, invented the fearsome idea that United States-style ghettos had arrived in places like London and Paris. The times seemed to call for this comparison, for riots resembling American long hot summers became increasingly frequent in Western European cities from the 1970s on. Fears of urban violence and crime have clung to whites' definitions of the word "ghetto" most fiercely of all, replacing segregation mania–era racial panics focused on disease. In recent years, Western Islamophobia has also vehemently entered the fray. Questions of Muslims' supposed cultural incompatibility, symbolized by women's headscarves and urban minarets, have enriched New Right code phrases (and sowed hatred on the left as well), as has the equation of Islam with terrorism. In the years since the September 11, 2001, attacks, the fear of terrorism may very well have become even more important than the fear of black crime to the deep structure of New Right political appeals.[17]

The New Right's "color blind" revival of the once-faltering "religion of whiteness" is one of the most important events in the world history of racial theory. It also represents another example of the impact of crossoceanic intellectual exchange upon the politics of urban space. Once in power, New Right movement leaders (helped by center-left parties that have adopted New Right techniques) combined racial fear-mongering, denials of racial inequality, and free-market rhetoric to blast open a wide political roadway around the flanks of the midcentury antiracist revolution. Three kinds of policy tools helped to drive urban segregation forward and even to give it new forms: authoritarian anticrime and anti-immigration policies disproportionately directed at urban people of color; a willful neglect of fair housing laws that encouraged a variety of segregationist dynamics to persist in land markets; and a campaign to deregulate the financial industry that gave lenders and speculators enormous renewed sway over both global and urban politics.

The New Right's mania for "tough" criminal justice and immigration-control policies created new possibilities for government coercion in the drawing of color lines. In the field of crime, the United States most definitely led the way. Since the Nixon years, successive "wars" on crime and drugs, waged against largely urban, black, low-level drug dealers, has transformed a medium-sized (if already racially unequal) prison system into a massive archipelago of what some sociologists call "carceral ghettos." Now holding over 2.3 million people, the majority of them black and brown city dwellers, these prison ghettos have multiplied across the American countryside, festooning the outskirts of hundreds of nearly all-white small towns with watch towers and barbed-wire enclosures. With the exception of Russia, no other advanced industrialized society has anything of the same size, and no other country has anything so racially skewed (the per-capita incarceration rate in the United States has outpaced that of today's China and of apartheid-era South Africa). Still, other wealthy countries have avidly imported American experiments in private prisons, drug wars, and "zero-tolerance" sentencing. Problems with police misconduct in neighborhoods of color have spread across the Global North. Instances of police abuse repeatedly provide the trigger for urban rioting.[18]

Race-tinged authoritarianism has also crept into New Right–era immigration policy. A reversal has occurred in the general pattern of border opening that occurred in the 1960s, when the United States and Europe repealed racist immigration restrictions, and when White Canada and White Australia policies came to an end. Taken together, the more recent, increasingly militarized influx-control efforts across the Global North have put in place a globe-girdling color line stretching from the two-thousand-mile fence along the US-Mexico border to the patrol boats of the straights of Florida, the Mediterranean Sea, and the Timor Sea north of Australia. In the context of widening desperation in many parts of the global South and increased demand for migrant labor in the global North, such border-interdiction measures do much more than control influxes. They intensify the bureaucratic nightmares involved in acquiring passes and other documentation, encourage racial profiling of both legal and illegal migrants, make it more difficult for migrant workers to protest low pay and bad working conditions, increase the extent of criminal enterprises that exploit migrants, increase the numbers of potentially productive people behind bars, and put migrants at greater risk of death crossing oceans and deserts. All of these discriminatory side effects of the global color line have deep effects on the daily life of black and brown urban communities of the global North.[19]

In the New Right era, increased government coercion of people of color is mirrored by a willful retreat from governments' legal obligations to control segregationist actions by real estate agents, developers, bankers, and privileged white homeowners in the housing market. The racial theory of real estate values is thus left free to continue driving practices of racial steering, redlining, and white flight. Meanwhile, these same real estate market dynamics, helped by big developers and sometimes by governments, have created new forces of coercive segregation, such as gated communities and gentrification.

This trend is also most notable in the United States. In 2008, a bipartisan national commission on fair housing estimated that, in any given year, only about twenty thousand out of four million acts of racial discrimination in the country ever receive official attention. Those that do receive attention receive it largely through a severely underfunded group of independent watchdog agencies that are unable to take more than a handful of cases to court. Surveys of white attitudes in the United States do repeatedly show that whites are more willing than before to consider black neighbors—as long as they are not too numerous and as along as they meet certain class thresholds. White mob violence against black home-seekers decreased once the postwar black migration from the South ended around 1970. Indexes of segregation in US cities have declined somewhat since. Immigrants continue to arrive in large numbers despite restrictions, and many settle in and around the moving color line, often creating much more complex borders and even some integrated checkerboard neighborhoods. In some cities, most notably Chicago and Detroit, the number of people impacted by extreme segregation may be diminishing simply because thousands of ghetto resi-

FIGURE 12.2 Vacant lots on the South Side of Chicago, 2011. Chicago's black ghettos are less affected by property abandonment than the East Sides of Detroit or Cleveland. Many denser neighborhoods remain, and courageous revitalization efforts continue their work. However, Chicago proper lost almost a quarter million black residents between 2000 and 2010. Some have left for the city's largely segregated inner suburbs; others have migrated to cities in the South, reversing the Great Migrations of 1915–70. Author's photo, 2011.

dents have begun to set the Great Migration in reverse, by moving to the somewhat less segregated cities of the US South and Southwest.

Despite all of these changes, though, segregation measures remain extremely high, especially in the largest cities. In Chicago almost 80 percent of the population would still have to move for all of the city's neighborhoods to have the same racial composition (down from about 90 percent in 1960). Ghetto neighborhoods have always been segregated by class, but rates of spatial concentration of poor black people has risen in many cities, including Chicago. Blacks who are able to move to the suburbs are still largely steered to older, inner-ring, "hand-me-down" municipalities with declining values. White flight from those areas continues, if now financed by whites' generally higher personal wealth and by federal income tax deductions more than by direct FHA subsidies. In many suburban rings, racial segregation indexes are higher than in the cities they surround.[20]

Meanwhile, some of whites' outright aggression toward unwanted outsiders and their fear of crime have been rechanneled into the fortified gated communities that private developers began scattering across the suburbs of Los Angeles, Miami, Chicago, and New York during the 1970s.

In a sense, the long history of urban segregation has come full circle in the gated community: though the technology of key-punch entry systems and surveillance equipment is of the late twentieth century, these newer walled residential developments also revive elements of Calcutta's compound districts, Madras's militarized White Town, and the British cantonments. Gated developments are some of the easiest forms of urban segregation to export abroad. Despite considerable debate about the implications for the privatization of public space, they have sprouted up in the western suburbs of many of the worlds' wealthiest cities, including London and Paris, and they have become even more plentiful in post-apartheid South Africa and across the Global South. [21]

Gentrification is another potentially coercive form of market-based segregation that has increased since the 1970s. In the Global North it usually involves well-to-do and often younger people buying up promising old real estate in poorer neighborhoods near downtown that seem more sophisticated, edgier, or simply more convenient to work and play. In the United States it involves a notable, though considerably smaller, reverse-circling eddy in the broader currents of white flight. If gentrification gains momentum, it can work like a market-driven form of forced removal. As renovations push up property values and taxes, poorer residents nearby, often people of color, frequently have no choice but to relocate elsewhere. Gentrifiers, like the worst of government slum-clearance programs, are under no obligation to provide affordable rehousing. Since at least as far back as Haussmann's day, after all, government-directed slum clearances have helped to encourage both downtown gentrification and segregation. In the United States, and especially in Chicago, local housing authorities' ever more zealous efforts to raze the city's rotting public housing towers have in some cases had the effect of opening new areas for gentrification; in any case, the decline of American public housing in general gives poor people fewer anchors of affordable housing that would otherwise allow them to remain in gentrifying districts. Other urban authorities across the Global North organize "business improvement districts" that offer special services to residents of gentrified areas. District officials sometimes replicate some of the fortified feel of suburban gated communities by hiring private security patrols, authorizing periodic roundups of homeless people, and installing bristling networks of surveillance cameras.[22]

As urban segregation persists, it at once reflects and encourages the sharply increasing economic inequalities that have been a hallmark of the New Right era. The most important cause of this increasing inequality was the free-market-driven deregulation of finance. On the global level, US president Richard Nixon's abrogation of key provisions of Keynes's Bretton Woods agreements in 1973 once again gave international financial speculators the power to disrupt government policies they deem inflationary and thus threatening to profits from moneylending. Their capacity to suddenly withdraw short-term investment capital from national economies has cast a pall over efforts to expand welfare states ever since. Combined with attacks on labor unions and free-trade policies that encourage industrial firms to relocate in areas with low labor costs, the machinery that pumped wealth downward in society during the postwar decades has coughed and sputtered. Economic booms no longer decrease poverty rates like they did in the 1950s and 1960s, and even middle-class people have seen their incomes stagnate or decline. By contrast, the increasing returns on speculative activity have propelled the financial sector itself into a commanding position within the global economy. The salaries available to top-flight global financiers have skyrocketed, helping to expand their share of income and wealth, including in urban real estate. Such inequalities are mirrored in cities as well—particularly in those "global cities" where financial firms are concentrated and where high-paid employees of financial firms often play prominent roles in gentrification.[23]

For people of color in the cities of the United States, the deregulation of the global economy has gone hand in hand with the New Right's neglect of fair-housing enforcement to create new disadvantages in segregated land markets and thus new obstacles to accruing wealth. Surveys of mortgage lending repeatedly show tremendous disparities in banks' willingness to lend to whites and blacks all along the spectra of income and education—even as New Right politicians and Wall Street lobby strongly to weaken the anti-redlining Community Reinvestment Act.[24]

Paradoxically, though, big finance's practice of "reverse redlining"—selective targeting of poor people and ghetto residents with predatory loans—may have sown almost as much destruction as redlining itself. This practice, just as paradoxically, first grew widespread in the United States precisely because of legislation accompanying the 1968 Fair Housing Act. That legislation directed the FHA to guarantee mortgages in areas it had previously redlined. Unscrupulous realtors, appraisers, and mortgage lenders took advantage of the new mandate by colluding in schemes to overassess the value of structurally unsound houses, then sell them to often financially insecure ghetto residents with mortgages that were fully insured by the US Treasury. Once the new homeowners ran into insurmountable repair and repayment problems, the predatory sting drew quickly to a close: the banks recouped the mortgage insurance from the FHA and walked away, leaving it up to the federal government to bulldoze the house. It was in great part for this reason that big tracts of the South Side of Chicago and other "rust belt" ghettos first acquired their contemporary bombed-out look, with scores of spectral, abandoned houses dotting large tracts of vacant land that is now returning to its former state of open prairie.[25]

The most devastating of all of the regulatory concessions to big finance occurred in 1998 when President Bill Clinton joined New Right congressmen in support of legislation allowing high-risk investment banks to get into the housing finance business. Wall Street money artists quickly devised or expanded three types of speculative financial instruments: predatory "subprime" loans to poor people; mortgage-backed securities consisting of predatory loans bundled with other loans and resliced into highly lucrative "tranches"; and so-called credit default swaps meant to insure the mortgage-backed securities. The market success of these designer assets pushed piratical mortgage companies, some of them subsidiaries of big banks, to lure ever-larger numbers of poor people into mortgages. The loans they peddled, often using grossly fraudulent practices, virtually guaranteed default. Most contained "adjustable" interest rates that soon increased the size of monthly payments beyond most borrowers' means.[26]

Across the United States, black people were more than twice as likely as white people of the same income—and over three times as likely in Chicago—to be steered into subprime loans, even though two-thirds were eligible for standard mortgages that on average cost $100,000 less over the life of the loan. Racial segregation, noted two eminent sociologists, "created a unique niche of minority clients who were differentially marketed risky subprime loans." The resulting racial disparities in housing foreclosures will clearly do little to improve the large inequalities in wealth on either side of the American color line. In 2008, Barack Obama parlayed his career as a community organizer on Chicago's South Side to become an Illinois senator, then the country's first black president, inaugurating new widespread talk of a "postracial age." That year, as the American mortgage bubble burst, bringing on a global recession, US whites possessed a staggering ten times more wealth on average than blacks of equal income, largely because of the dual housing market's on-going structural depredations.[27]

Elsewhere in the Global North, the deregulation of housing finance never went as far as it did in the United States. Still, the depressing effects of the 2008 financial crisis on the world economy have had severe reper-cussions, particularly in Europe. Once again, speculators have threatened to pull the economic rug out from under countries that do not diminish social spending, including funding for such potentially antisegregation-ist projects as public housing and public transport. Even the world's most egalitarian urban policies have become vulnerable.[28]

## Postcolonial and Neocolonial City-Splitting

If the word "ghetto" dominates the urban politics of the wealthy nations of the Global North, the most important keywords in the exploding cit-ies of the Global South are "slum" and "shantytown." As the language suggests, the main drama in the spatial politics of most former colonial cities is about class—and specifically about the nearly one billion poor people who have made those cities home since 1960. That said, many aspects of colonial White Town/Black Town systems of race segregation continue to help carve the deep social canyons that scar the vast expanses of the megacities. So does the more recent New Right effort to deregulate global finance, which allows banks and wealthy governments to extend practices of predatory lending across the hemispheres. In combination, these forces have brought a new version of colonial segregationism into being.

The great achievement of the mid-twentieth-century racial revolu-tions in urban politics was simple: it forced most white residents of the world's white towns to pack their bags and leave. This historic milestone did not mean an end to urban segregation more generally, however. For one thing, many newly independent countries were enormously diverse in terms of culture, caste, clan, religion, and national origin, and colo-nial powers had often encouraged hierarchical relationships between different groups, sometimes interpreting their differences as racial ones. Longstanding economically privileged Chinese neighborhoods in places like Manila and Jakarta did not disappear with decolonization, for example. In some colonies, independence brought on an intensifica-tion of conflict. The war between Greeks and Turks in formerly British

Cyprus, for example, resulted in a heavily fortified dividing line that still runs directly down the middle of the capital city of Nicosia. The civil war in the former French colony of Lebanon, which pitted numerous sectarian and political factions against each other, resulted in Beirut's Green Line, which for decades divided the city's Christian east from the Muslim west. Similar sectarian hostility, also rooted in colonial times, erupted in Iraq after the American invasion, creating deep geographical fissures in Baghdad and cities across the country.[29]

The most pervasive legacy of racial segregation in the Global South, however, is segregation by class. A taste for London-style class-exclusive neighborhoods made inroads among local elites in British colonial cities as early as the eighteenth century, when the wealthy bhadralok of Calcutta abandoned early modern practices of class integration and built segregated zones for themselves. Since then, Asian elites in Singapore, Hong Kong, and Bombay, as well as African merchants in all of the continent's commercial cities, built similar exclusive districts or else found ways to slip past color lines into White Town itself. In Latin America, nineteenth-century Haussmannian planners cleared central city slums, opening up gigantic class-exclusive zones for generally lighter-skinned elites downtown that remain largely intact today.

During the era of decolonization, the slow conquest of white town accelerated, as all remaining government-enforced racial segregation laws fell into disuse or were repealed: Lugard's Memorandum 11 and the Ikoyi Reservation ordinance, New Delhi's "allotment of quarters" rules, and Lyautey and Prost's system of restrictions in Morocco. Even in Hong Kong, which did not throw off British rule until 1997, the racial revolution rendered the Hill Reservation Ordinance obsolete; it was repealed in 1946 amid British negotiations to regain the colony from the Japanese.[30]

In the process, many of the former white towns became elite districts, just like the cleared downtowns of Latin American cities. In some cases, the new elites put in place equally regressive policies to guard the gates of their new districts. The most extreme case was that of the president of the southern African nation of Malawi, Dr. Hastings Kamuzu Banda, who went so far as to import a clutch of white South African *Rassenstreek* planners to build a new capital at Lilongwe. They designed posh neighborhoods with wide buffers for the president, his cronies, and a relatively large remaining postcolonial white population—while the slums piled up, out of sight, in distant townships. Others were more ambivalent about the legacies of white towns. To Jawaharlal Nehru, independent India's first prime minister, New Delhi was execrable—"a visible symbol of British power, with all its ostentation and wasteful extravagance." To many, the wide lots and sheer extravagance of the Lutyens bungalows seemed obscene in a country with so many poor people living on such tiny pieces of land. The government has since bulldozed many of those bungalows. Lutyens's fans have reacted in horror at the drab modernist government buildings and apartment houses that replaced many of them. At the same time, though, India is by no means above Lutyens's flair for urban ostentation. The president of India still lives in the high and mighty Viceroy's Palace (now renamed the President's Palace or Rashtapati Bhavan), and the Indian military rattles its sabers once a year in giant parades along the Rajpath, the new name for the Kingsway.[31]

In the meantime, exclusive suburban developments and edge cities have also sprung up that more closely mimic British garden cities or American suburbs and even gated communities. Calcutta's planned, rectilinear Salt Lake City (Bidhannagar) is one iconic example of a post-independence garden-city suburb; the glamorous gated, developments in Kolkata West, Gurgaon, near Delhi, and New Mumbai (Navi Mumbai) are more recent. The deserts surrounding Cairo and Giza have also sprouted exclusive suburbs, including one called Dreamland, that eclipse the bombastic luxury of turn-of-the-century Heliopolis. In Brazil, the wealthiest residents of Rio have left Copacabana and Ipanema for the even greater luxury, security, and exclusive beaches available down the shore in Barra de Tijuca and beyond. In São Paulo, developers woo residents out of the busy elite neighborhoods of downtown by promising them gilded condominium complexes "enclosed by walls and iron fences, guardhouses with guards on duty 24 hours a day, intercom, garage. Permanent tranquility."

In many places in the global South, gated zones reflect the ongoing press of Western imperial power more directly. Western corporations build gated compounds for the employees they send abroad to give them a sense of security and a bubble of familiar cultural surroundings. Even more elaborately planned high-security zones surround some of the most recent crop of American embassies and consulates, particularly in the Middle East. The high-tech, walled, 104-acre US embassy compound in Baghdad is the most lavish example: its office buildings, diplomatic quarters, and military installations approximate a twenty-first century version of Madras's White Town. A wider circle of walls that surround both the embassy and the city's central Green Zone (also known as the International Zone) recall those of the foreign concessions of colonial-era East Asia.[32]

The most important legacy of empire in former colonies, however, involves policies toward the poor. Under Western rule, planners like Prost and Lutyens nearly completely ignored the possibility that the native towns of cities like Rabat and Delhi would change and grow through migration from the countryside. Alternatively, the powerful Improvement Trusts, such as those at Calcutta, Bombay, and elsewhere in Asia, repeatedly assaulted inner-city slums without providing sufficient replacement housing thus guaranteeing the persistence of ever denser and more sharply delineated inner-city slums. In the postwar years, as independence movements gained steam, Europe's vast new investments in class-integrated public housing only rarely made their way to the colonies. When they did, they played a role in particularly ruthless forced removal and segregation schemes. In the postwar Belgian Congo, for example, where political and economic conditions in some ways resembled South Africa, officials built large, prefabricated *zones indigènes* around many of their Congolese cities, in part to maintain a large ultra-low-wage migrant workforce in the mines or in household service. The French built some of the first of their HLMs in and around Algiers, explicitly as a measure to supplement their military crackdown on the revolutionary violence that swallowed the Casbah in the 1950s.[33]

Since independence, a billion poor migrants have arrived in former colonial cities. Once in town, they react to the absence of housing by squatting on vacant land, building shacks out of found materials, and scouting out whatever the city can offer in the way of basic necessities. For those who "parachute" into neighborhoods close to wealthy districts, low-paid work is sometimes available nearby in household service, landscaping, and hawking. Further out, people depend more heavily on informal enterprises, whether in small-scale industry or in urban services that help other shantytown residents, like food distribution, construction, transport, and trash recycling. For water and electricity, residents informally tap nearby mains and circuit boxes.

Commentators on the left have idealized the very real and admirable collective action involved in the building and even the planning of informal settlements. Those on the right praise shanty builders' initiative as "bootstrap" individualism—and point to it as conclusive evidence that governments have no need to build public housing. The reality, though,

FIGURE 12.3 Survival in the slums. In the sprawling eastern periphery of São Paulo, migrants from the rural provinces have laid claim to vacant land, founded a Pentecostal church, built brick houses on the site of former shacks, stretched hoses from the water main, and run electric wires from nearby street lights. In this way, they have brought into being yet another new, informal section of one of the world's largest and most sharply divided megacities. Author's photo, 1998.

is that shanty dwellers have always been deeply and multiply vulnerable. Housing conditions in self-built slums are often lethal, especially when settlements are built on unstable ground, flood plains, or steep mountainsides. Sewage removal is typically beyond the ken of informal enterprise, so human waste, as it has throughout most of human history, often ends up in streets or in waterways that double as default drinking sources. Shack dwellers have no legal title to the land, and they are thus vulnerable to expropriation or rack-renting by absentee slumlords and forced removals by the government. For those who live closest to the elite districts, removals can be compounded by loss of employment or drastic increases in commuting costs. Informal employment is just that—completely unregulated, usually involving work in horrific conditions at wages far below the poverty level and with no protections against child labor or various forms of enslavement, sometimes to employers who barely make a living themselves. The dangers of work in criminal enterprises can engulf families and whole communities in violence. With little say in government, shanty dwellers are at the mercy of draconian urban policies of all sorts, including reprisals for any oppositional political activity.[34]

In recent years, the United Nations assembled a remarkable gathering of urban planners, scholars, and shantytown activists from across the Global South in an ongoing global conversation about slums. In *The Challenge of Slums*, a report issued in 2003, they argue forcefully that no slum policy will work if it does not comprehensively address all slum dwellers' multiple vulnerabilities—shelter, infrastructure, land ownership, employment, transport, and political participation. The U.N.'s Millennium Goals for the Human Habitat also recommend on-site solutions that avoid disruptive measures of class- or race-based forced removal.[35]

In the postcolonial era, there has been dismayingly little room for the kind of egalitarian politics that could put such principles into action. The Cold War bears much of the responsibility for this impoverishment of political imagination among most of the Global South's newly independent governments. During the struggle for independence, many nationalist movements depended heavily on the disruptive power of the urban poor. Labor unions and other organized city dwellers staged colonywide strikes; others rioted in the streets against the imperial yoke. As new countries won their independence, however, the same Cold War rivalries that had placed enormous pressure on Western imperialists to free their colonies also intensified the West's fight against potential or imagined Communist sympathizers in the "Third World." Retreating colonial empires supported the most avid anti-Communist elite nationalists with grants and military equipment and encouraged new rulers to use their power to demobilize the most egalitarian forces within the racial revolution.[36]

Far from romanticizing the poor, many new regimes vilified the inhabitants of slums and shantytowns, sometimes using outdated nineteenth-century sanitary rhetoric, but more often by stoking elites' fear of crime. At best, these regimes bought time with showy but piecemeal improvements; at worse, they spent huge sums of money (often borrowed from abroad) on summary clearances, removals, and distant sequestration of the poor. Such urban segregationism could be found across the postcolonial political spectrum. Calcutta's self-styled Marxists continued the colonial-era Improvement Trust's repeated efforts to expel the city's legions of sidewalk and shack dwellers to the periphery, all in the name of what one commentator calls the "gentleman's city." On the right, Brazil's populist military regimes of the 1960s and 1970s waged repeated bulldozer assaults on Rio's hillside *favelas*, especially those on the hills behind the elite southern zones (they burned one behind Ipanema to the ground). Former *favelados* were forced into grim public housing developments like the Cidade de Deus (City of God), two hours away by rudimentary public transport from downtown employment. Even in Senegal, the poet-president Leopold Sédar Senghor, a socialist, stooped to ill-meaning phrases like "human encumbrances" to describe the ninety thousand shanty dwellers he ordered expelled from the areas around downtown Dakar to townships far beyond the Medina and other French colonial segregation zones. During the Cold War, the world's wealthiest countries supported elites in their segregationist urban policies. Money from the US Assistance for International Development (USAID) program, for example, supported Brazil's slum-clearance efforts. Officials in Rio even named a section of the City of God "Vila Kennedy" to acknowledge that fact. France and the World Bank similarly helped finance the creation of distant public housing for cleared residents of Dakar.[37]

Follow-up studies of clearances like these confirm that, for the world's poorest people, the bottom line is clear: urban opportunity depends on class integration. Though Rio's evicted squatters benefited from marginally better housing conditions in the drab City of God, higher rent and transport costs swallowed up their diminished wages. The meager incomes of the residents of Delhi's downtown Yamuna Pushta shantytown fell by a half when their settlement was removed to a spot twenty kilometers outside of the city.[38]

Such ineffective piecemeal or authoritarian "solutions" to the "squatter problem" became even more common across the Global South as the New Right took increasing power in the Global North. During the 1970s and 1980s the influence of Northern governments on urban policy in their former colonies grew even stronger, to the point that an age of re-colonization began.

The deregulation of global finance was the main reason, and—as in the ghettos of the United States later on—predatory loans were the main vehicle. The "Third World debt crisis" came into being after rising oil prices in the 1970s bloated Middle Eastern countries' accounts in European and American banks. Needing to lend this money out again, banks mounted high-pressure, often fraudulent marketing campaigns to sell adjustable-rate loans to generally autocratic regimes in developing countries. When the US Federal Reserve bank sharply hiked interest rates in 1979 to control inflation, debtor countries' payments escalated out of control—and many went into default. To recover the billions of outstanding loans, the banks turned to the International Monetary Fund (IMF), an organization whose founding mission was to help countries extend welfare policies. Instead, the IMF now became the bankers' policeman and a messenger for free markets and government austerity. Among other things, its Structural Adjustment Programs (SAPs) forced governments to divert their revenue from social spending to loan repayment.[39]

Some of the first items to face drastic cuts were subsidies for local farmers, who were forced to compete on the world market with heavily subsidized corporate farms from the wealthiest countries. Accordingly, migration to the cities of the South redoubled, and shantytowns exploded in size. Structural adjustment continues to play an important role in the exploding growth of today's megacities; many of them now count between ten and twenty-five million people. Urbanization in the Global South has dwarfed that of the nineteenth-century Industrial Revolution, this time not so much because of expanding urban industry but because low-paying largely informal jobs in the cities and shantytowns have become more attractive than utter destitution in the countryside.[40]

The megacities have placed escalating pressures on indebted governments for social services. Unable to meet the demand, many governments have turned to the World Bank for new loans, or they have simply off-loaded their obligations to proliferating nongovernmental organizations (NGOs). Neither route promises anything approaching the U.N.'s comprehensive visions for the slums. The World Bank, reflecting its free-market bent and its commitment to structural adjustment, typically aims to achieve change on the cheap. Either its programs focus solely on upgrading infrastructure—as in its site and service programs—or on titling programs based on the idea that once enterprising shanty dwellers become homeowners, they can take care of the rest of their problems on their own initiative. NGOs, meanwhile, typically lack the funds necessary for comprehensive improvements. The pressures for gentrification of slum areas near exclusive former white towns and downtowns are sometimes enormous. Governments have turned increasingly often to mass-scale slum clearances, sometimes by request of elite landholders, sometimes in reprisal against the state's own political opponents. Local authorities removed 70,000 slum dwellers from Bombay in 1976; 180,000 from Santo Domingo in 1986-92; 300,000 from Lagos in 1990; 40,000 from Nairobi in the same year; 500,000 from Jakarta in 2001-3; and no less than three-quarters of a million from the slums of Harare, Zimbabwe, in 2005 during Robert Mugabe's Operation Murambatsvina ("Drive out the Rubbish"). For most, the only place to go was further out from the center of town. Since the 1980s, world history's most extensive slum clearances have been underway in China. These clearances accelerated once the Communist Party reestablished a capitalist real estate market and promoted segregationist incentives in real estate markets. In Shanghai and Beijing alone, over two and a half million people were evicted from downtown areas from 1985 to 2000. Further clearances, coupled with enormous government housing development on the urban periphery, later paved the way for the Beijing Olympics. The vast ranks of residential towers that China has built to house forcibly displaced people on its urban peripheries make such megaschemes as Chicago's Wall or Paris's HLMs seem nearly insignificant in comparison.[41]

Cold War–era, elite-led decolonization and New Right–era financial recolonization both depended heavily on suppressing the voices and institutions of the urban poor. Despite often desperate, violence-ridden circumstances, however, those voices have not disappeared. Sometimes the poor of the megacities articulate their opposition in much the same way as the inhabitants of ghettos in the Global North—by rendering urban streets ungovernable. Two waves of so-called anti-IMF bread riots swept through dozens of cities in the Global South to protest the SAPs—the first in the early 1980s and the second a decade later. Courageous protests against government land seizures in China are ongoing. More hopefully, the United Nations calculates that over two hundred thousand nonprofit grassroots groups operate across the Global South, many of which are explicitly geared to mobilize the poor for greater housing security. To make any headway, though, comprehensive solutions to urban segregation and inequality in the Global South will rely on a new wave of truly democratic independence movements that can remove both the tyrants that continue to run too many developing countries and their crippling yokes of debt peonage.[42]

## A New Century of Settler Segregation?

The midcentury racial revolution had a much more uneven impact upon settler-sponsored segregation. In all cases the racial revolutions and counterrevolutions in settler colonies took bloodier forms than elsewhere, usually involving urban warfare. In some places, racial segregation disappeared at independence. In Algeria, most of the *pieds noirs* were forced to return home after France failed to suppress a decade-long armed revolution. In Kenya, the Mau Mau uprising led to a successful bid for independence, and whites either left or grudgingly accepted African rule. In both Algiers and Nairobi, the legacies of colonial racial segregation were similar to other cities in the Global South. In Rhodesia, whites delayed matters by launching their own anticolonial movement and unilaterally declared their independence from Britain in 1965. In 1979 Robert Mugabe's armed insurgency finally brought the country's milder form of apartheid to an end, but since then he has betrayed any hope that his victory would result in either racial peace, let alone any political voice for the poor African majorities of Zimbabwe's cities.[43]

In two other settler societies, one a very old one—Northern Ireland—and the other much newer—Israel-Palestine—especially tragic conflicts have arisen that have resulted in entrenched government-sponsored segregationist politics. The explosive ingredient in the political dramas in both places consists of rival religious or sectarian groups that have redefined themselves in quasi-secular nationalist or racial terms and have stated their political goals in terms of exclusive occupation of colonized territories. In both places violence has at once responded to and deepened profound spiritual crises for people of faith on all sides of the conflict.

In Northern Ireland, the last remnant of Britain's oldest settler colony, renewed conflict between the Protestant Unionist majority and a growing minority of Catholic Republicans led to intensified segregation of the country's already deeply divided cities. The story began in the late 1960s when Catholic activists, inspired by the American civil rights movement, began a series of protest marches that, among other things, targeted the country's discriminatory public housing system. The resistance they met was unlike that which greeted any civil rights movement elsewhere in Europe, including those led by immigrants of color. In 1969, Protestant mobs—with back-up from the Royal Ulster Constabulary and cheered on by right-wing British politicians—overran Catholic neighborhoods like Derry's Bogside and Belfast's Bombay Street. These attacks gave rise to armed retaliation from Catholic militias and eventually the Irish Republican Army's roving bomb squads. During the "Troubles," the twenty-five years of attacks and reprisals that followed, Catholics and Protestants clustered into ever-more homogenous and separate neighborhoods. The so-called interface areas between sectarian territories became war zones. To stop rock throwing, sniper fire, and murderous cross-boundary raids, beleaguered authorities in Belfast, Derry, and several smaller cities built increasingly elaborate systems of walls through the interface areas. Even after power-sharing agreements in 1998 and 2006 brought the Troubles to a grinding end, these so-called Peace Walls, some of them thirty feet high, still snake through miles of West Belfast and from there into the surrounding countryside—providing at best an ambiguous deterrent to ongoing low-level hostilities.[44]

At the heart of the Israeli-Palestinian conflict lies the Zionist movement's dream to establish a national state for Jews in a land inhabited by a Muslim Arab majority. The ensuing conflicts took strength from epic spiritual crises among both Jews and Muslims. Among Jews, these crises were tied to the experience of the pogroms, growing anti-Semitic persecution across Europe, and above all the Holocaust; among Palestinian Muslims they arose amid British colonialism and escalated after the violent founding of the State of Israel in 1948.

Since the Zionist movement's earliest origins amid the pogroms of the 1880s, the protection of Jews from racist atrocity has been its most resonant mission. However, by linking protection with an imperative for colonial settlement, Zionists also—often quite self-consciously—became a force of conquest and segregation. In fact, the movement's rise to power was connected to many of the same currents of thought and institutional forces involved in urban segregation elsewhere in the world. Early Zionists freely mixed secular ideas about racial hierarchy, the dangers of assimilation and crossbreeding, and providential claims to "natural" homelands with such biblical ideas as the chosen people, the long exile, and the Promised Land. On the one hand, these arguments were meant to spread the Zionist message among the world's diverse Jewish communities. Many Jews, after all, have not experienced their deeply rooted lives outside the Holy Land as "exile." Many others have felt ambivalent about the religious priority of reclaiming what Zionists called the Land of Israel and about linking Judaism with a secular state. Even in the Zionist strongholds of Eastern Europe, most pogrom refugees preferred migration to Britain and the Americas. As time went on, though, Zionists' arguments also served other purposes: to question the validity of Arab Palestinians' claim to their homeland, and sometimes even to deny their existence as a valid people.[45]

To advance their mission, Zionist leaders built influence within the three now-familiar institutions that spread segregationist politics worldwide. The movement's earliest successes stemmed from its leaders' meetings with one of foremost figures of segregation mania, British colonial secretary Joseph Chamberlain, and his senior colleague, the prime minister of the United Kingdom, Arthur James Balfour. Both had experience with large-scale demographic engineering schemes elsewhere in the British Empire. Both were eager to stop the migration of Eastern European Jewish refugees to Britain itself and, as the Zionist founding father Theodor Herzl put it ruefully, to "drain" those flows elsewhere. This explains how Balfour could champion the anti-Jewish Aliens Act in Parliament in 1905 and then, in 1917, issue his famous declaration promising British support for a Jewish "national home" in Palestine. When Palestine became a British Mandate after World War I, Balfour's project got officially underway.[46]

Zionist settlement in Palestine depended heavily on familiar techniques of urban segregation. In 1909, at the height of segregation mania, Jewish settlers in the city of Jaffa founded a British-style building society to finance construction of a "Hebrew urban center in a healthy environment" on the outskirts of the Arab city, which they named Tel Aviv. In 1923, Arab attacks in Jaffa claimed the lives of a dozen Jews, and British officials gave their blessing to the dividing line. In doing so they drew on their own imperial segregationist rationales, claiming the boundary would foster both racial harmony and the settlers' modern urban sanitary experiments. Local officials in Tel Aviv fulfilled this last goal by leveraging their connections with European reform networks and hiring the celebrated British planner Patrick Geddes, who laid out the town as an extensive "garden city." Similar all-Jewish suburbs soon sprouted in the western outskirts of Jerusalem, attracting new waves of Jewish settlers from abroad. In 1929, European Zionists also founded the Jewish Agency for Palestine, which pooled capital to buy large tracts of land for lease to settlers in the Palestinian countryside. Apparently in direct violation of the British Mandate, the agency's leases prohibited later purchase or inheritance by non-Jews and even forbade Jewish leaseholders from hiring non-Jews to work on agency land.[47]

If segregation was supposed to guarantee racial peace, it failed. Palestinian discontent rose, most obviously in the rebellion of 1936–39. In response, different groups of Zionists formed armed brigades. British officials unveiled a series of larger-scale segregation schemes that partitioned the entire Mandate into Jewish and Arab zones. These plans at once forced Jewish and Arab supporters of peaceful coexistence onto the defensive, spurred Palestinians' own exclusivist and violent campaigns to stop Jewish migration, and gave wider resonance to Zionists' claims that only a separate and ethnically exclusive state could offer Jews adequate protection from further persecution.[48]

Then, amid World War II, Adolf Hitler began his appalling effort to destroy Europe's Jews. With refugee escape routes to Britain and the United States largely closed down, the Zionists claimed vindication for their Palestinian solution to the "Jewish problem." Jewish refugees filled Tel Aviv, the western suburbs of Jerusalem, and other settlements. The British were once again unable to stem the ensuing violence committed by exclusivists on both sides. They passed their mandate on to the fledgling United Nations, which tried yet another partition plan. By then it was clear, however, that only military force would determine the final dividing line.[49]

What ensued was what Palestinians call the Nakba—the "great catastrophe." For a long time the official Israeli narrative of these events held that Palestinians voluntarily retreated eastward from their ancestral villages to allow allied Arab armies from newly independent neighboring countries to mount a joint attack on Jews, threatening a "second Holocaust." More recently, revisionist historians have painted a decisively different picture, documenting centrally planned attacks by increasingly well-armed Zionist militias on fully inhabited Palestinian villages and urban neighborhoods across the country. The militias leveled buildings and whole towns, killing thousands, and they expelled over seven hundred thousand people to refugee camps in neighboring Arab countries, the Gaza Strip, and the West Bank. In cities like Haifa, Jaffa, and Acre settlers and soldiers also forced most Arab inhabitants to flee. Later, Israeli authorities allowed only small numbers of urban Palestinians to return, often relegating them to small rundown neighborhoods. In Jerusalem, Zionist forces encountered stiffer resistance, for by the time they reached the city, an armed alliance of neighboring Arab nations had indeed entered the war. Still, thirty thousand Arab residents of Jerusalem's western suburbs were likewise expelled and their property seized. For the next nineteen years, a demilitarized zone—fortified by concrete blocks and barbed wire, and strafed by snipers—divided western Jewish suburbs from the Old City and the majority-Arab eastern suburbs, along the lines where Israeli and Arab armed forces met.[50]

Meanwhile, arms and aid from Britain, France, and soon the United States fortified the new State of Israel's defense forces. Contributions from abroad flooded into the coffers of the Jewish Agency for Palestine—now renamed the Jewish National Fund—which bought up ever-greater swaths of land (including the sites of ruined Palestinian villages) as a permanent and exclusive trust for the Jewish people. Then, during the Six-Day War of 1967, Israel's state-of-the-art army and air force occupied the West Bank, including the Old City and the sacred acropolis of Mount Zion itself, long known by Muslims as the Haram-al-Sharif. Israel abolished the demilitarized zone and vowed that Jerusalem would never be divided again.[51]

As many moderate Israelis feared at the time, cycles of retribution have since entrenched themselves in the politics of the region, reflecting and intensifying sectarian tensions worldwide and becoming more deeply laced with calls for territorial exclusionism. Right-wing Zionist settlers have built fortified hilltop developments in the midst of majority-Arab zones that they claim to be theirs by biblical decree and ancient bloodlines. As Jerusalem becomes an overwhelmingly Jewish city and its Arab population falls deeper into poverty, some radical Zionists call for a new Jewish temple on Mount Zion—thus threatening to end the medieval Muslim leader Saladin's fragile, eight-hundred-year-old vision of a Holy City shared by all three monotheistic faiths.[52]

The Palestinians' two grassroots intifadas, meanwhile, have made little progress in reversing their leaders' inability to rally sympathy among the world's most powerful constituencies. To be sure, the intifadas also face high geopolitical hurdles. Rising Western Islamophobia, the United States' desire for stable regimes in the oil-rich Middle East, and powerful lobbies dominated by hard-line Zionists and fundamentalist Christians in Washington all help keep the doors to peace shut. As a result, the end of Cold War created few pressures to halt Israel's absorption of new Palestinian territory. But the tactics and exclusivist rhetoric of Palestinian radicals also help undermine their cause. Their waves of suicide bombings and their calls for an end to Israel may well express the anger and desperation many Palestinians feel, but they have also enabled new generations of Zionist leaders to keep Israel's vulnerability at the center of debate, especially in the United States, and to cast the Palestinian liberation movement as a central enemy in the American-led "War on Terror." Since the terror attacks on New York and Washington DC in 2001 US weapons shipments to Israel have only increased. The Israeli army continues to periodically pummel Palestinian cities and refugee camps—most notably those of the Gaza Strip in 2008—even when condemned in the ensuing days by its staunchest ally.[53]

The imagination-dulling cycles of violence and retribution have created a perfect environment for the contemporary world's most elaborate remaining government-sponsored system of urban and rural segregation. Contrary to its policy of an undivided Jerusalem, Israel has once again effectively partitioned its capital city's metropolitan area, making it clear that it will never share the city of Zion with a Palestinian state. This time, a wide band of Jewish settlements and a thirty-foot-high concrete barrier separates the remaining majority-Arab neighborhoods of East Jerusalem from Palestinian towns and cities further east, thus effectively choking off the massive amount of daily movement that once passed in and out of the city from that direction. The concrete wall is part of a barrier that twists across hundreds of miles of the West Bank countryside, disrupting access to work and land for thousands more Palestinians. In even more beleaguered Hebron, the once thriving downtown has become a no-man's-land that separates Palestinian residential districts below from a Jewish settlement that looms above. For long periods, Is-

FIGURE I2.4  The Dome of the Rock and early Jewish settlements in East Jerusalem. In 1967, Israel conquered Mount Zion (the Temple Mount to Jews, the Haram al-Sharif to Muslims) and abolished the demilitarized zone that had divided Jerusalem. With government support, Jewish settlers poured into East Jerusalem, building settlements on appropriated Palestinian land. In 2003, Israel began construction of a "security barrier" between these settlements and surrounding Arab towns that also stretched around the entire West Bank. Jerusalem was once again divided. Photograph by Raymond Depardon (1974), used by permission from Magnum Photos.

raeli officials have nearly completely sealed off the bombed-out cities of the Gaza Strip from the outside world. At best, non-Jews who need to cross such boundaries for their livelihood face Kafkaesque ordeals obtaining permits and long waits in lines at military checkpoints. Meanwhile, a network of proprietary highways eases Israeli settlers' access between their jobs in Jerusalem or Tel Aviv and their homes in West Bank settlements. These roads also divide Palestinian territory into some two hundred separate zones, interspersed with Israeli military installations. Roads for Palestinians, by contrast, are forced either into tunnels under Israeli roads or onto flyovers above them, ensuring that the two systems never connect even when they cross. As the Israeli architect Eyal Weizmann has observed, segregation has thus taken on vertical as well as horizontal dimensions as the drive to partition Israeli hilltops and Arab valleys takes ever more elaborate forms.[54]

Today, there are other more caustic regimes in the world, amply willing to undertake much larger-scale authoritarian destruction of outcast neighborhoods, often with naked political reprisal in mind. But nowhere have the legacies of modern-era urban racial segregationism so deeply fused themselves with new versions of the most ancient rationales for splitting cities. Much may ride on the shoulders of people such as the courageous Palestinians and Israelis who, since 2003, have assembled in joint nonviolent protests against land seizures associated with the separation barrier. If they can defy arrest, tear gas, and very real bullets to reimagine the Holy Land and Jerusalem as sanctuaries of faith and social justice, victories may just be possible along dividing lines anywhere upon our deeply scarred planet.[55]

If they succeed, it may well be due to what is by far the most inspiring victory for racial inclusiveness in any postwar settler society—that of South Africa's anti-apartheid movement. For most of the late twentieth century, that movement's dreams looked just as improbable as the one now growing haltingly in the shadows of Israel's security barrier. Those holy-land activists can take hope from the fact that much of the South African movement's success ultimately derived from its largely shared rejection of exclusivist territorial ideas and its embrace of a vision of a single nonracial "rainbow nation"

In 1961, South African prime minister Hendrick Verwoerd returned from London with his biggest triumph yet—independence for a white-ruled republic. A year before, his soldiers had fired on peaceful black pass-law demonstrators at Sharpeville, south of Johannesburg, massacring sixty-nine people. Soon, Verwoerd banned the ANC and other anti-apartheid organizations and drove most of their leadership into exile or, like the ANC's Nelson Mandela, into prison on the infamous Robben Island. Black South Africa thus spent the otherwise vibrant 1960s in a deep authoritarian freeze, warmed only slightly by the low-level guerrilla war of the ANC's military wing, the Umkhonto we Sizwe, or MK, and by Steve Biko's Black Consciousness Movement. As a reward for its stalwart anti-Communism, the white Nationalist regime gained the diplomatic support of the United States, revealing another perverse twist of Cold War-era racial politics. Periodic denunciations of apartheid from Washington did little to stop the system from moving into its most virulent phase.

Following National Party doctrine, Verwoerd declared the country's rural native reserves independent African republics, with the idea of using black nationalist rhetoric to further divide and smother the black movement. Ever more viciously enforced pass laws slowed black influxes to the cities somewhat, all the while filling the jails with hundreds of thousands of violators. Forced removals under the Group Areas Act claimed many of the still-lingering urban "black spots"—Cape Town's vibrant multiracial District Six in 1968 and Johannesburg's Indian Pageview (the smaller successor to the old Malay Location) in 1978. In Johannesburg, white authorities resettled most coloreds in Eldorado Park, adjacent to the old Klipspruit Native Location. The city's "Asiatics" were shipped even farther out, to Lenasia, ironically on land that lay within a stone's throw of the site of Mohandas Gandhi's Tolstoy Farm, an experimental settlement he hoped would "bring East and West nearer in real friendship." After Verwoerd's assassination in 1966, his successors clamped down on new building in the black townships and deferred maintenance as a further deterrent against cityward migration. Despite and because of their efforts, shack cities once again spread amid the townships' endless rows of matchboxes.[56]

The anti-apartheid movement finally ended the political chill in 1976, when hundreds of Soweto's children boycotted their pathetic Bantu schools in protest of a decree forcing them to learn Afrikaans, which they saw as the language of apartheid. In reaction, white South Africa's war against the country's black population began in earnest. Soldiers, guided by helicopters, invaded Soweto and shot at the backs of fleeing children, killing over five hundred protestors and bystanders in the ensuing days. In the aftermath of the slaughter, mass protests of township residents across the country led to the creation of parallel governments called civic associations, or "civics" for short. The Soweto Civic Association (SCA) committed itself to organizing "at the grassroots for the removal of all disabilities that impoverish and dehumanise the residents of this ghetto." Its strategy was to make apartheid finally pay for concentrating so much of its segregationist force in government. Its main target was the official township council, first set up under the 1923 Natives (Urban Areas) Act and now known as the Black Local Authority (BLA).[57]

What followed was world history's most democratic mass movement specifically targeted against urban residential segregation. Under apartheid's segregated urban fiscal system, township residents were supposed to pay house rents and utility fees to the BLA, not to the Johannesburg municipality, which was reserved for whites. The civics played on the vulnerabilities of this system by convincing township residents to withhold payments to the BLAs. By 1986, participation in the boycott reached 90 percent, and the iron fist of the state was forced wide into the open.

President P. W. Botha sent his ungainly Casspir troop carriers (the "hip-pos") into the townships with armed eviction squads. This policy merely solidified the unity of the anti-apartheid movement as well as its ties to antiracist organizations worldwide.[58]

Many more would die at the hand of apartheid during its last days. The battle in the streets against Botha's spies and collaborators was marred by brutal summary executions and later by infighting between the ANC and its government-armed black opponents that lasted well into the 1990s. But the call to free Mandela, lift the ban on the ANC, and turn the country over to nonracial elections galvanized world opinion. Unlike in Israel-Palestine, the end of the Cold War meant that the rationale for US support of apartheid vanished. The Nationalists were thus forced to repeal both the pass laws and the Group Areas Act and to enter into ne-gotiations for a transition to nonracial government.

In Soweto itself, the SCA and other organizations kept up the pressure with rolling mass-action protests and the bread-and-butter slogan "One city, one tax base!" In 1990, after Mandela's release, the SCA successfully negotiated the Soweto Accord with the white municipality of Johannes-burg, forcing it to forgive all outstanding rent and utility payments and to abolish the BLA. Momentously, the negotiators declared that "Johan-nesburg and Soweto must become one non-racial city." A century of seg-regationist precedents vanished from the law books, and a new ANC-run municipality delved into the task of stanching the bleeding racial divide that for so long gashed it in two.[59]

# Epilogue  ⋮  People, the Planet, and Segregated Cities

In 1961, writing amid the waning but still uncertain days of the liberation of Algeria, Frantz Fanon, the Martinique-born revolutionary philosopher, began his famous book *The Wretched of the Earth* with a meditation on divided cities. "The colonial world," he wrote, "is a world divided into compartments." Nowhere was the division more obvious than in the stark contrast between "the settlers' town, . . . a well-fed town, and easygoing town; its belly . . . always full of good things," and "the native town, . . . a hungry town, starved of bread, of meat, of shoes, of coal, of light . . . a crouching village, a town on its knees, a town wallowing in the mire."

Fanon believed that "if we examine closely this system of compartments, we will . . . be able to reveal the lines of force it implies. This approach to the colonial world, its ordering and its geographical layout will allow us to mark out the lines on which a decolonized society will be reorganized." Alas, upon examining that system, Fanon came to a bleak conclusion: Whites—and the elites of "native town"—had so wedded themselves to segregation that only a mind-cleansing, world-spanning bloodbath of urban violence could end it.[1]

Today, we are too many more mind-numbing, city-engulfing bloodbaths the wiser. The long-term benefits of violence to the "wretched of the earth"—whether in Algiers or Chicago, Soweto, London, Paris, Palestine, or in cities across the Global South—seem far from clean or clear. Though violence sometimes seems like the only surefire way for residents of vulnerable urban communities to get national or global attention, and though riots have sometimes been followed by significant policy gains, the price in terms of further community destruction is often staggeringly high, and violence itself builds no promising new futures. If anything it also tends to increase the resonance of segregationists' political ace in the hole: their claim to racial vulnerability. But

Fanon was certainly correct in predicting that imperialists and their elite allies would repeatedly stand in the way of his vision of an egalitarian, anticolonial revolution. As segregation persists in the world's wealthiest societies and marginalized megaslums explode across the poorest ones, humanity looks a lot like a species hopelessly addicted to its seventy-century habit of dividing cities.

Yet it would be a mistake to end the world history of urban segregation upon such a dispiriting note. To do so would be to miss the complex, unpredictable, and—as always—paradoxical reality of urban politics in our own time. While it is amply true that supporters of white and elite privilege remain in charge of the commanding heights of the world's urban politics, it is just as fully true that more people than ever before have come together to imagine and begin to create explicitly antisegregationist urban futures.

Many of these new visions would have been inconceivable even during the headiest days of the postwar black and brown racial revolution. To thrive in the otherwise hostile era since, today's antisegregationist visionaries—who include grassroots activists, academics, public officials, reformers, and planners—have developed cross-oceanic intellectual networks of their own, building upon and refining those left behind by postwar revolutionaries, a process dramatically expanded in the age of the Internet. Though their hemisphere-crossing exchanges have not yet been able to slow the renewed march of segregation, people active within them have been able to acquire real slices of power within governments, the broader universe of intellectual interchange, and even in urban land markets.

The intellectual scope of their endeavor is unprecedented. Elaborating on the thought of such pioneers as W. E. B. DuBois, racial theorists have turned the concept of race on its head, arguing that racial divisions are not a natural phenomenon but a political one, subject both to mystifying rhetorical camouflage and hardened institutional inequalities that must be continually exposed and critiqued. Urban historians have dissected the dynamics of segregation, more fully uncovering some of the most highly camouflaged practices involved. At their best, social scientists who debate the spread of ghettos and slums on all continents have identified and dissected the complex and multidimensional political dramas that underlie color and class lines in cities. Planners and environmental justice activists have soundly rejected old theories that segregation wards off natural threats like disease. Instead, their work shows conclusively that urban division only increases the exposure of cities' most vulnerable residents to environmental perils. More importantly, they point out that the kinds of segregation that depend on sprawl— and thus also upon enormous amounts of habitat destruction and automobile usage—dangerously increase cities' environmental footprints, threatening our survival as a species. Urban activists and theorists, most notably those organized under the United Nations' World Urban Forum, have called upon governments to recognize that all people have a fundamental "right to the city"—that is, freedom from all obstacles to urban opportunities, including freedom from residential segregation.

For these activists and thinkers, there are many ways to fight against urban divides in the interest of all people's rights to the city. In some places, residents persuade real estate agents and local banks that integration and local public housing creates a more stable community than segregation, raising property values. Even where the actual creation of integrated communities is a long-term prospect, residents can revive their own slums and ghettos, attracting job opportunities to locate in closer proximity so that spatial disadvantages are minimized. Transport systems can make color and class lines more porous, thus giving excluded urban residents easier access to opportunities that remain distant while lowering the environmental footprint of the city. Growth boundaries around cities can slow sprawl, thus making white or elite flight more difficult and creating denser cities that also offer environmental benefits while again bringing urban opportunities closer to all. And, even in the absence of major spatial changes, the fight for more just workplaces and for government policies that redistribute wealth more fairly across racial and class lines can create more equality between all urban neighborhoods.[2]

It is in Europe, perhaps not surprisingly, that such antisegregationist political forces have the most sway within governments. There, the strong base of support for social democracy and for centralized and relatively egalitarian urban planning has most successfully weathered attacks from New Right politicians, anti-immigrant racists, and international financial speculators. France is probably the best example, since its cities are arguably the most segregated of any wealthy society outside the United States. There, conservative leaders like Jacques Chirac and Nicholas Sarkozy, both of them well known for their hostility to immigrants, have nevertheless felt compelled to join the call for *mixité sociale* first enunciated by the Socialists in the 1990s. Since 2003, their center-right administrations have pushed a massive, forty-billion Euro urban revitalization campaign to replace French cities' ghastly postwar public housing towers with new estates and to expand the stock of public housing so that even wealthy municipalities reach the 20 percent quota envisioned by the Socialists' anti-ghetto laws. Skeptics have rightly noted that these pharaonic new grands travaux have not yet had much effect on youth unemployment rates, which hover around 40 percent in the most "sensitive" *banlieues*, nor have they had much effect on Paris's larger east-west pattern of segregation. Some suspect the housing program to be a flashy stalking horse for reductions in other social expenditures. But under questioning, Sarkozy's housing minister piously declared that Paris's "ghettos of the rich," as its most conservative Western arrondissements are called, will not be exempt from their public housing quotas. He even endorsed Paris's Socialist mayor's recent moves to buy some of Baron Haussmann's bourgeois apartment buildings in the swank districts near the Eiffel Tower and convert them to public housing. So far, white flight and resistance from wealthy residents and conservative mayors—including in the richest suburban municipality in the country, Sarkozy's own Neuilly-sur Seine—has slowed progress toward increased *mixité*. Still, in the dog days of late 2010, as financiers' speculative attacks on the Euro resounded across the continent and as Islamophobic appeals redoubled, Sarkozy's party voted robustly to refund a program of urban "territorial solidarity" that would be unimaginable, even under a "liberal" administration, in the United States.[3]

Elsewhere in Europe, Canada, and Australasia anti-immigrant forces are just as strong as they are in France, and evidence of creeping race and class segregation can be found in many places. That said, earlier policies of building extensive but generally small-scale and dispersed public housing estates have ensured that color lines are generally less stark. It is true that public housing is an imperfect tool of urban integration: white tenants of public estates do not necessarily want to have neighbors of color any more than middle-class white homeowners, and worries about property values in the private market diminish government's ability to build public estates where they might break up color lines. Still, even in places like post-Thatcher Britain, where governments have sold off many council estates—and even in such a historical heartland of segregation as London's West End—it is still possible to find pockets of municipally owned affordable housing, often filled with immigrants of color, across the street from newly gentrified luxury apartments. Such patterns, which one observer labeled "microsegregation," might actually be among the most successful attempts by any government in modern world history to use residential integration as a tool to at least begin reducing spatial disadvantages. In London and elsewhere on the continent, relatively extensive, cheap, and efficient public transport systems also help diminish some of the harms of segregation. So does London's Greenbelt plan and other efforts to constrain sprawl, most notably in Sweden, the Netherlands, Canada, and New Zealand.[4]

For these reasons, some European, Canadian, and Australasian cities have justly earned their reputation as the most egalitarian, integrated, and environmentally sustainable on earth. But heavy reliance on top-down government policies—no matter how successful—has some critics justifiably concerned. For all the public support that welfare states and egalitarian urban-planning policies enjoy in Europe, many governments' actual implementation of programs too often occurs without much input from racially marginalized and low-income people themselves. The alienation many people feel from mainstream institutions—especially young people—diminishes the work of egalitarian policies. Worse, an important source of creativity and political influence lays relatively untapped.[5]

The potential of excluded peoples' creativity and power, paradoxically, may be easiest to see in places where governments have either given up on the fight for urban inclusiveness or where segregationist forces have most mercilessly outflanked egalitarian public agencies and policies. Such is the case in the United States, where decades of white retrenchment and free-market policies have helped to sustain many of the archsegregationist patterns set in place in the early twentieth century. These have left the country with the least egalitarian, most devastated, and most environmentally damaged excluded urban zones in the wealthy world.

Despite that history, some European antisegregationists have waxed enthusiastically about evidence of "community empowerment" they perceive in some of the least favored zones of American cities. This enthusiasm needs to be tempered, to be sure: in the United States, "empowerment" has just as often served as a cynical rhetorical cover for the weakening of even the most meager of countersegregationist public policies. Conversely, while many of the most creative initiatives in US urban politics have arisen from grassroots organizations that keep the spirit of the civil rights movement alive by mobilizing the residents of segregated ghettos, most have repeatedly demanded that American governments funnel more money into neglected urban areas.[6]

Whatever their methods, it is undeniably true that these scrappy and courageous community-based organizations have done much of the work of desegregation that has occurred in the United States during the New Right era: they shoulder the greatest burden of enforcing fair housing laws, cajoling real estate agents and banks to help preserve the country's few integrated neighborhoods, building affordable housing, passing inclusionary zoning ordinances, pushing for government action under the Community Reinvestment Act, advocating for expanded government support of underfunded schools, combating police brutality and the expansion of carceral ghettos, and drawing attention to urban environmental injustices linked to segregation. Some have been able to make significant inroads into inner-city land markets and finance as well, either by founding community development corporations, or by "banking" vacant urban land for socially responsible reuse, or, as in the case of Boston's Dudley Street Initiative, by acquiring the power of eminent domain from the city government and going into business as nonprofit developers beholden to the community's residents. Though the scale of their operations is often limited, they have not been afraid to take comprehensive approaches to neighborhood revitalization. In Buffalo, New York, for example, People United for Sustainable Housing (PUSH Buffalo) and other allied organizations have linked affordable housing development with green rehabilitation techniques that lower residents' heating and other costs. They strategically acquire some of the city's multiplying vacant lots, resulting in an expansion of urban parkland, an urban farm, small-scale renewable-energy projects, and rainwater-management infrastructure. Indirect action campaigns, the community's residents have leveraged the victories of the global environmental movement and forced open the taps of "green" government and corporate funds. Using those funds, they hope to transform the business of neighborhood revival into a community-managed industry that creates local jobs and small businesses.[7]

As this example suggests, the United States—despite its status as the historic cradle of suburban white-flight and automobile-enabled sprawl—has also recently become home to some of the most extensive discussions of the connections between desegregation, city planning, and the fight against global warming. Inner-city-based movement for environmental and transportation justice helped propel these debates, which have also involved growing numbers of antisprawl activists in the suburbs as well as professional planners attracted to the international New Urbanist and Eco Cities movements. Urban planning built around public transport and walkable spaces has enormous potential to make urban color and class lines more porous and thus create cities that are at once more just and sustainable. It is true that in housing markets where race and class exclusivity determines property values, privileged residents often strongly resist boundary-crossing mass-transit lines. Conversely, successful transit schemes can accelerate gentrification by forcing those who rely the most on the system to live furthest away from stations. In an unusually promising development, the Obama administration opened an exploratory Office of Sustainable Housing and Communities whose mission is to encourage urban transport that is connected to the development of nearby affordable housing.[8]

The movement that perhaps has the greatest chance of erasing color lines in the United States, though, is the movement of millions of people from the Global South to American cities. Recent studies have confirmed that Latino Americans, whose numbers now far outpace those of blacks, are almost as likely to live in segregated neighborhoods and that darker-skinned Latinos are more segregated than their lighter-skinned counterparts. But many new multiracial neighborhoods have also come into being as a result of immigration, not only from Latin America, but from Asia and Africa as well. Immigrants have been an important source of reinvestment capital for many cities and inner suburbs. Their numbers have also transformed many cities—and even entire states—into majority brown and black societies, anticipating a demographic change that will encompass the entire United States later in the twenty-first century. Some bring community-organizing skills honed in opposition to repression in their countries of origin. Already these experienced organizers have helped build the most extensive grassroots protest organizations since the black civil rights movement; these have focused on reversing the militarization of the color line along the United States' southern border. As immigrants' numbers and their disproportionate support for egalitarian, government-led urban policies increase, they may provide the biggest political challenge to suburban strongholds of the New Right and its segregationist legacies.[9]

For the great majority of the world's city dwellers, and especially for the billion people who live in the megaslums of the Global South—now amounting to a third of the world's urban population—hopes for the political future may be dimmest of all. And yet, there, the hemisphere-spanning networks of exchange among antisegregationist visionaries are more firmly ensconced than those in the wealthy world. These networks also benefit from prominent institutional sponsors. Under the leadership of the Tanzanian diplomat Anna Kajumulo Tibaijuka, the United Nation's Human Settlements Program (UN-HABITAT) forged an unprecedented alliance of researchers, leaders of nongovernmental organizations, officials, and grassroots leaders. It was this alliance that, in 2003, produced the the magisterial *Challenge of Slums*. On the basis of research gathered from across the former colonial world, the UN called on governments and international organizations like the World Bank to back comprehensive urban policies that simultaneously address the multiple vulnerabilities of slum and shack dwellers. It also set ambitious "Millennium Goals" to improve the lives of at least a hundred million slum dwellers by the year 2020. That project has spawned policy discussions, including vibrant ongoing Internet exchanges. Out of these discussions arose the UN's World Urban Forum, which brings thousands of people together each year to repeat the call for action on the direst of all forms of urban inequality and segregation. The forum has embraced the concept of the "right to the city," and its participants have fearlessly discussed some of the least tractable issues in the politics of segregation. Some muse, for example, about the effects of the Arab Spring on efforts to bring urban justice to Jerusalem. Others debate how to press for relief from debt and structural adjustment and international financiers' push for government austerity. Still others consider the wisdom of a radical challenge to "the current treatment of land as a private rather than a public good." After all, as one commentator put it ruefully (and in perfect tune with much evidence from this book), the "private market . . . [has] not delivered more inclusive cities."[10]

A very encouraging feature of these discussions is the prominent part played by activists from slums and shantytowns themselves. Some of the two hundred thousand urban grassroots organizations that the UN counts across the Global South have led efforts to develop alliances that span entire countries and, most recently, the Southern Hemisphere as a whole. The most important of these, Shack/Slum Dwellers International (SDI), which came into being in the 1990s, grew out of an effort to re-create the ties between India and South Africa forged by Mohandas Gandhi nearly a century before. The founder of SDI, Jockin Arputham, migrated from the countryside to the Bombay slum of Janata Colony as a child and then cut his teeth as a housing activist in early 1970s Calcutta, helping to settle the million refugees that streamed into the city's bustees during Bangladesh's war of independence. Back in Bombay later in the same decade, he rose to national prominence when he conducted a successful Mahatma Gandhi–style nonviolent noncooperation campaign against Prime Minister Indira Gandhi's plan to raze Janata Colony. Noting that thirty years of nationalist rule had not brought any "milk and honey in the streets," he built an alliance of slum-based organizations across India called the National Slum Dwellers Alliance, renamed the Slum Dwellers International in 1996.[11]

Meanwhile in South Africa, the now-governing African National Congress came under pressure from international investors to begin demobilizing the civics organizations that had brought it to power—much like other nationalist parties during the era of decolonization. Though counterpressures from below have remained strong enough to force the ANC to invest heavily in new housing for the millions of migrants who have poured into South African cities, those who dreamed of a nonracial Johannesburg have made little progress since their revolutionary victory against the Group Areas Act. Whites and the new elites of color have ensconced themselves in sprawling new developments in the northern Johannesburg suburbs whose vast honeycomb of security walls, barbed wire, electric fencing, and gated communities collectively amount to the largest urban fortification system ever built. As for the ANC's social housing for the urban poor, far too much of it is of lower quality than that built by Hendrick Verwoerd and his successors, and almost all of it is located in old townships or on cheap land far from jobs. "When we build low-cost homes," one ANC official droned, "they should be built away from existing areas because it impacts on the price of property." For township dwellers now living in new developments that sprawl even farther beyond Soweto to the southwest, the commutes across Johannesburg's two mountain ranges have become even longer than they were when the fifteen-kilometer racial barrier divided the city by law. While a high-speed train now eases travel within the northern suburbs, southwestern township dwellers still rely on long, often perilous rides in overcrowded Toyota minibus taxis to get to work. Nor is the new housing adequate to meet the demand. Hundreds of thousands of black South Africans live in shacks.[12]

Rose Molokoane grew up in one of the high veldt's shantytowns and got her schooling in the fight against apartheid. In the New South Africa, she has not rested on her laurels. Instead she helped organize the Federation of the Urban Poor (FED-UP), which has repeatedly reminded the ANC of its new constitutional obligation to provide housing for all. In the early 1990s, she took the first plane flight of her life, across the Indian Ocean to Bombay (now Mumbai). There she met Jockin Arputham and toured Dharavi, the world's largest megaslum. Slum/Shack Dwellers International (SDI) arose from this trip and from countless others that its leaders have made since, building the alliance in numerous other countries in Africa and Asia and reaching out to similar Latin American groups as well. The organization builds investment funds out of small contributions from slum dwellers and dispatches local volunteers to collect key information in the streets of their communities. With these assets—money, local knowledge, and organized numbers—the organization leverages influence in government agencies and in organizations like the World Bank for larger-scale improvements and protections.[13]

From her perch in SDI, Rose Molokoane has also become one of the most important spokespeople at the UN's World Urban Forum. There she implores her more technocratically minded counterparts from the World Bank, universities, and NGOs to remember that not all informal settlements are the same—and that listening to poor women should be their first priority. Then she rises to her culminating point: "Please open your doors. Don't call us 'beneficiaries.' Don't call us 'end-users.' Call us 'partners.'"[14]

This straightforward, resonant call is the best way for us to end our trip through humanity's seventy centuries of urban segregation. Today, words like Molokoane's are mostly accorded lip service or honored in the breach. Still, appeals like hers reverberate with greater regularity, clarity, and insistence than ever before. They evoke a simple truth, a basic call to urban justice and democracy—and they get to the very nub of any genuine program of "integration." There is little meaning to reaching across the lines of race, class, gender, culture, and faith that divide our cities, our countries, and our hemispheres if we do so without sharing power. The ability to do just that—and thus completely reorient the dramas of urban politics—provides the only true measure of a world ready to forswear the splitting of its cities.

# Notes

## Introduction

1   "Colored Methodists Should Get Out, Says Dr. Lyon in Forceful Sermon," *Baltimore Afro American Ledger*, December 10, 1910.

2   Ibid.

3   On the consequences of segregation, see, for example, Melvin L. Oliver and Thomas M. Shapiro, *Black Wealth/White Wealth: A New Perspective on Racial Inequality* (New York: Routledge, 1995); Harriet B. Newburger, Eugenie L. Birch, and Susan M. Wachter, eds., *Neighborhood and Life Chances: How Place Matters in Modern America* (Philadelphia: University of Pennsylvania Press, 2011).

4   Quotation from Javier Auyero, "'This Is a Lot Like the Bronx, Isn't It?': Lived Experiences of Marginality in an Argentine Slum," *International Journal of Urban and Regional Research* 23 (1999): 45–69; Peter Marcuse, "The Enclave, the Citadel, and the Ghetto: What Has Changed in the Post-Fordist U.S. City," *Urban Affairs Review* 33 (1997): 228–69; Loïc J. D. Wacquant, "Three Pernicious Premises in the Study of American Ghettos," *International Journal of Urban and Regional Research* 21 (1997): 341–54; Eric Fong and Milena Gulia, "Neighborhood Change within the Canadian Mosaic, 1986–1991," *Population Research and Policy Review* 19 (2000): 155–77; Ceri Peach, "Good Segregation, Bad Segregation," *Planning Perspectives* 11(1996): 379–98. Colonial cities have also been studied in terms of typologies and processes. See Anthony D. King, "Colonial Cities: Global Pivots of Change," in *Colonial Cities*, ed. Robert Ross and Gerard J. Telkamp (Dordrecht: Martinus Nijhoff, 1985), 9–12. The most prominent effort to restrict the definition of segregation itself is by John Cell, *The Highest Stage of White Supremacy: The Origins of Segregation in South Africa and the American South* (Cambridge: Cambridge University Press, 1982), 1–20.

5   In "Good Segregation, Bad Segregation," an essay otherwise dedicated to placing these two types of segregation on the far ends of a spectrum, Ceri Peach is careful to note the possibility of an "an opaque interaction between the two" (391). I believe that all research on segregation should begin by shedding light on the "opacities" of the politics involved, even in situations in which newly arrived ethnic immigrant groups seek out urban zones of their own with little or no immediately detectable compulsion from outside, and even when these groups subsequently disperse.

## Chapter One

1    Gwendolyn Leick, *Mesopotamia: The Invention of the City* (London: Penguin, 2002), 1–29.

2    J. Melaart, *Çatal Hüyük: A Neolithic Town in Anatolia* (London: Thames and Hudson, 1967); I. Todd, *Çatal Hüyük in Perspective* (Menlo Park, CA: Cummings, 1976); Ian Hodder, "Çatalhöyük in the Context of the Middle Eastern Neolithic," *Annual Review of Anthropology* 36 (2008): 109; Leila Ahmed, *Women and Gender in Islam: Historical Roots of a Modern Debate* (New Haven: Yale University Press, 1992), 11.

3    Quote from Leick, *Mesopotamia*, 1; also see 46–55, 126–28, 261–68.

4    Leick, *Mesopotamia*, 54–55, 125–28.

5    Benjamin R. Foster, ed. and trans., *The Epic of Gilgamesh* (New York: Norton, 2001), 3.

6    Leick, *Mesopotamia*, 57–60, 107, 261–70. The image of heaven floating above the city is from 264–65.

7    Foster, *The Epic of Gilgamesh*, 3.

8    K. Kenyon, *Digging Up Jericho* (London: E. Benn, 1957); O. Bar-Josef, "The Walls of Jericho: An Alternative Interpretation," *Current Anthropology* 27 (1986): 157–62; Leick, *Mesopotamia*, 264; Karen Rhea Nemet-Nejat, *Daily Life in Ancient Mesopotamia* (Westport, CT: Greenwood Press, 1998), 113–14.

9    Leick, *Mesopotamia*, 126–28, 224–32, 261–68, quotations on 126, 226; Derek Kane, "Cities and Empires," *Journal of Urban History* 32 (2005): 8–21; Charles Gates, *Ancient Cities: The Archaeology of Urban Life in the Ancient Near East and Egypt, Greece, and Rome* (London: Routledge, 2003), 57, 71, 132, 142, 182–83, 243–46, 331; Karen Armstrong, *Jerusalem: One City, Three Faiths* (New York: Ballantine Books, 2005), 37–78.

10    Jonathan Mark Kenoyer, *Ancient Cities of the Indus Valley Civilization* (Karachi: Oxford University Press, 1998), 55–56, 62–65, 81, 99–100; Timothy Kendall, *Kerma and the Kingdom of Kush, 2500–1500 BC: The Archaeological Discovery of an Ancient Nubian Empire* (Washington DC: National Museum of African Art, Smithsonian Institution, 1997), 46–49.

11    Eva Krapf-Askari, *Yoruba Towns and Cities: An Enquiry into the Nature of Urban Social Phenomena* (Oxford: Clarendon Press, 1969), 39–62, quotation on 40; Jacques Soustelle, *Daily Life of the Aztecs* (1955; repr., London: Phoenix Press, 2002), 2–4, 9–11.

12    Arthur Wright, "The Cosmology of the Chinese City," in *The City in Late Imperial China*, ed. William Skinner (Stanford: Stanford University Press, 1977), 33–74; Paul Wheatley, *The Pivot of the Four Corners: A Preliminary Inquiry into the Origins and Character of the Ancient Chinese City* (Edinburgh: Edinburgh University Press, 1971), 30–36; Paul Wheatley and Thomas See, *From Court to Capital: A Tentative Interpretation of the Origins of Japanese Urbanism* (Chicago: University of Chicago Press, 1978), 109–58; T. G. McGee, *The Southeast Asian City: A Social Geography of the Primate Cities of Southeast Asia* (New York: Praeger, 1968), 1.

13    Catherine B. Asher, "Delhi Walled: Changing Boundaries," in *City Walls: The Urban Enceinte in Global Perspective* (Cambridge: Cambridge University Press, 2000); James D. Tracy ed., *City Walls: The Urban Enceinte in Global Perspective* (Cambridge: Cambridge University Press, 2000), 247–81, quotation on Indraprastha on 250; Dilip K. Chakrabarty, *The Archaeology of Ancient Indian Cities* (Delhi: Oxford University Press, 1995), 194–98, 206–15; Charles Higham, *The Civilization of Angkor* (Berkeley: University of California Press, 2001), 3, 9–11.

14    Nezar al Sayyad, *Cities and Caliphs: On the Genesis of Arab Muslim Urbanism* (New York: Greenwood, 1991), 72, 103, 107–51.

15 Geoffrey Parker, "The Artillery Fortress as an Engine of European Expansion, 1480-1750," in Tracy, *City Walls*, 386-418.

16 Quote from Philip D. Curtin, *Cross-Cultural Trade in World History* (Cambridge: Cambridge University Press, 1984), 3.

17 Nemet-Nejat, *Daily Life in Mesopotamia*, 280-81; Kenoyer, *Cities of the Indus Valley*, 55; Curtin, *Cross-Cultural Trade*, 69-70.

18 Olivia Remie Constable, *Housing the Stranger in the Mediterranean World: Lodging, Trade, and Travel in Late Antiquity and the Middle Ages* (Cambridge: Cambridge University Press, 2003), 1-13, 64-66, 107-57; Curtin, *Cross-Cultural Trade*, 78-80, 111-19.

19 Curtin, *Cross-Cultural Trade*, 182-206.

20 Curtin, *Cross-Cultural Trade*, 109-35, 158-78; Valery M. Garrett, *Heaven Is High, the Emperor Far Away: Merchants and Mandarins in Old Canton* (Oxford: Oxford University Press, 2002), 7-9; Peter J. M. Nas, "The Early Indonesian Town: The Rise and Decline of the City State and Its Capital," in *The Indonesian City* (Dordrecht, Netherlands: Foris, 1986), 18-36.

21 Curtin, *Cross-Cultural Trade*, 39-40, 49-50.

22 Robert Bartlett, *The Making of Europe: Conquest, Colonization, and Cultural Change* (Princeton: Princeton University Press, 1993), 167-96; Roger Crowley, *Constantinople: The Last Great Siege, 1453* (London: Faber and Faber, 2005), 2, 27-28, 48, 53, 62-64, 146, 157; Michel Balard, "Habitat, Ethnies et Métiers dans les Comptoirs Génois d'Orient (XIIe-XVe Siècle)," in *D'une ville à l'autre: Structures matérielles et organisation de l'espace dans les villes européennes (XIIIe-XVIe Siècle)*, ed. Jean-Claude Maire Vigueur (Rome: École française de Rome, 1989), 111-13; Maria Georgopoulou, *Venice's Mediterranean Colonies: Architecture and Urbanism* (Cambridge: Cambridge University Press, 2001), 192-210; Séan Spellissy, *The History of Limerick City* (Limerick: Celtic Bookshop, 1998), 97, 167-68; Steven G. Ellis, "Racial Discrimination in Late Medieval Ireland," in *Racial Discrimination and Ethnicity in European History*, ed. Guðmundur Háfdanarson (Pisa: Edizioni Plus, 2003), 21-32. The text of the Pale decree can be found in Agnes Conway, *Henry VII's Relations with Scotland and Ireland, 1485-1498* (New York: Octagon Books, 1972), 215-16. Thomas Bartlett, *Ireland: a History* (Cambridge: Cambridge University Press, 2010), 58-62, 79-142; James Stevens Curl, *The Honourable The Irish Society and the Plantation of Ulster, 1608-2000: The City of London and the Colonisation of County Londonderry in the Province of Ulster in Ireland, a History and a Critique* (Shopwycke Manor Barn, U.K.: Phillimore, 2000).

23 Constable, *Housing the Stranger*, 116-17; Bartlett, *Ireland*, 58-62; Leonard P. Liggio, "English Origins of Early American Racism," *Radical History Review* 3 (1976): 1-36; Ivan Hannaford, *Race: The History of an Idea in the West* (Washington, DC: Woodrow Wilson Center Press and Baltimore: Johns Hopkins University Press, 1996), 87-126; Nicholas Hudson, "From 'Nation' to 'Race': The Origin of Racial Classification in Eighteenth-Century Thought," *Eighteenth-Century Studies*, 29 (1996): 247-64.

24 Armstrong, *Jerusalem*, 28-31, 39-41, 48-65, 79-103.

25 Armstrong, *Jerusalem*, 125-53; Aryeh Kasher, *The Jews in Hellenistic and Roman Egypt: The Struggle for Equal Rights* (Tübingen: J. C. B. Mohr, 1985), 20 25.

26 Armstrong, *Jerusalem*, 153-370, quotation on 277.

27 The one exception to Jews' subordinate status was in the little-known kingdom of Khazaria. See Shlomo Sand, *The Invention of the Jewish People*, trans. Yael Lotan (2008; repr., London: Verso, 2009), 210-49.

28 Norman Roth, "Coexistence and Confrontation: Jews and Christians in Medieval Spain," in Moshe Lazar and Stephen Haliczer, eds., *The Jews of Spain and the Expul-*

433

*sion of 1492* (Lancaster, CA: Labyrinthos, 1997), 1-24; Heinrich Graetz, *History of the Jews* (1891-98; repr., Philadelphia: Jewish Publication Society of America, 1967), 4:114-22, 166-73, 200-207, 276-78.

29  Marvin Lunefeldt, "Facing Crisis: The Catholic Sovereigns, the Expulsion, and the Columbian Expedition," in Lazar and Haliczer, *The Jews of Spain*, 254-59; Stephen Haliczer, "The Expulsion of the Jews as a Social Process," in Lazar and Haliczer, *The Jews of Spain*, 237-52; Graetz, *History of the Jews*, 4:334-81.

30  Riccardo Calimani, *The Ghetto of Venice*, trans. Katherine Silberblatt Wolfthal (New York: M. Evans, 1987), 8-13, 28, 31-32, quotation on 35.

31  Quote from Calimani, *The Ghetto of Venice*, 1; also see 9-13, 32-33, 39.

32  Calimani, *The Ghetto of Venice*, 31-32, 36.

33  Kenneth Stow, *Theater of Acculturation: The Roman Ghetto in the Sixteenth Century* (Seattle: University of Washington Press; Northampton MA: Smith College Press, 2001), 22-38, 62-66; Otto Muneles, ed., *Prague Ghetto in the Renaissance Period* (Prague: State Jewish Museum, 1965), 17-62; Rachel Heuberger and Helga Krohn, *Hinaus aus dem Ghetto . . . Juden in Frankfurt am Main 1800-1950* (Frankfurt am Main: S. Fischer Verlag, 1988); Marion Kaplan, ed., *Jewish Daily Life in Germany, 1618-1945* (Oxford: Oxford University Press, 2005); R. Po-Chia Hsia and Hartmut Lehman, *In and Out of the Ghetto: Jewish-Gentile Relations in Late Medieval and Early Modern Germany* (Washington DC: German Historical Institute; Cambridge: Cambridge University Press, 1995); Prinz, *Das Leben im Ghetto*, 111-29, 153-276, quotation on 179; Jacob Katz, *Out of the Ghetto: The Social Background of Jewish Emancipation, 1770-1870* (Cambridge, MA: Harvard University Press, 1973), 1-42.

34  Samuel Kassow, "Introduction," in *The Shtetl: New Evaluations*, ed. Steven Katz (New York: New York University Press, 2007), 1-28; Gershon David Hundert, "The Importance of Demography and Patterns of Settlement for an Understanding of the Jewish Experience in East-Central Europe," in Katz, *The Shtetl*, 29-38. On the debate about the origins of Eastern European Jewish communities, see Sand, *The Invention of the Jewish People*, 210-49.

35  Calimani, *The Ghetto of Venice*, 238-47; Cathleen M. Giustino, *Tearing Down Prague's Jewish Town: Ghetto Clearance and the Legacy of Middle-Class Ethnic Politics around 1900* (Boulder: East European Monographs, 2003); Katz, *Out of the Ghetto*, 191-222.

36  John D. Klier, "Russian Jewry on the Eve of the Pogroms," in *Pogroms: Anti-Jewish Violence in Modern Russian History*, ed. Klier and Shlomo Lambroza (Cambridge: Cambridge University Press, 1992), 3-11; Michael Aronson, *Troubled Waters: The Origins of the 1881 Anti-Jewish Pogroms in Russia* (Pittsburgh: University of Pittsburgh Press, 1990), 21-144; Shlomo Lambroza, "The Pogroms of 1903-1906," in Klier and Lambroza, *Pogroms*, 195-247; Peter Kenez, "Pogroms and White Ideology in the Russian Civil War," in Klier and Lambroza, *Pogroms*, 293-313.

37  Gideon Sjoberg, *The Pre-Industrial City: Past and Present* (New York: Free Press, 1960), 91-103; Kathryn Bard, "Royal Cities and Cult Centers, Administrative Towns, and Workmen's Settlements in Ancient Egypt," in *The Ancient City: New Perspectives on Urbanism in the Old and New World*, ed. Joyce Marcus and Jeremy A. Sabloff (Santa Fe: School for Advanced Research Press, 2008), 165-82; Alan Hunt, *Governance of the Consuming Passions: A History of Sumptuary Law* (New York: St. Martin's Press, 1996).

38  Anderson, *Roman Architecture and Society*, 293-336, quotation from Cicero on 335.

39  David Nicholas, *The Later Medieval City, 1300-1500* (London: Longman, 1997), 76-79.

40  Babylonian quotation from Kenneth Jackson, *Crabgrass Frontier: The Suburbanization of the United States* (New York: Oxford University Press, 1985), 12.

41  Nicholas, *Later Medieval City*, 47, 80-83, 274-77; Ira M. Lapidus, *Muslim Cities in the Later Middle Ages* (Cambridge: Cambridge University Press, 1984), 86-87.

42  Krapf-Askari, *Yoruba Cities*, 25-26, 44, 65-75, 141-44; Lapidus, *Muslim Cities*, 88-92.

43  Romila Thapar, *Early India: From the Origins to AD 1300* (Berkeley: University of California Press, 2002), 62-68, 122-36.

44  William L. Rowe, "Caste, Kinship, and Association in Urban India," in *Urban Anthropology: Cross-Cultural Studies of Urbanization*, ed. Aidan Southall (New York: Oxford University Press, 1973), 211-14.

45  Ahmed, *Women in Islam*, 9-124; İlhan Akşit, *The Mysteries of the Ottoman Harem* (Istanbul: Akşit, 2010).

## Chapter Two

1  Henry Davison Love, *Vestiges of Old Madras, 1640-1800: Traced from the East India Company's Records Preserved at Fort St. George and the India Office and from Other Sources* (1913; repr., New York: AMS Press, 1968), 1:593. This chapter is an adaptation of Carl H. Nightingale, "Before Race Mattered: Geographies of the Color Line in Early Colonial Madras and New York," *American Historical Review* 113 (2008): 48-71.

2  See maps in Aníbal Sepúlveda Rivera, *San Juan: Historia illustrada de su desarollo urbana, 1509-1898* (San Juan: Carimar, 1989), 59, 60-63, 84, 152, 192, 226; Adelaida Sourdis de De la Vega, *Cartagena de Indias durante la primera república 1810-1815* (Bogotá: Banco de la Republica, 1988), 16.

3  Charles Gibson, *The Aztecs under Spanish Rule: A History of the Indians of the Valley of Mexico, 1519-1810* (Stanford: Stanford University Press, 1964), 28-37, 99-133; Alexandre Coello de la Rosa, "Resistencia e integración en la Lima colonial: El caso la reducción de indios de El Cercado de Lima (1564-1567)," *Revista Andina* 35 (2002): 111-28. I am indebted to Professor Jeremy Mumford for information on El Cercado.

4  Zelia Nutall, "Royal Ordinances Concerning the Laying Out of New Towns," *Hispanic American Historical Review* 4 (1921): 753. I made a few grammatical corrections to her translation of the document, which she also provides in the original Spanish.

5  Gibson, *Aztecs under Spanish Rule*, 99-133, 147, 502nn41-44; R. Douglas Cope, *The Limits of Racial Domination: Plebeian Society in Mexico City, 1660-1720* (Madison: University of Wisconsin Press, 1994), 13-15.

6  Gibson, *Aztecs under Spanish Rule*, 149-50, 177, 192; Cope, *Limits of Domination*, 22-25.

7  Cope, *Limits of Domination*, 31-32; Gibson, *Aztecs under Spanish Rule*, 376-78, 395-402.

8  Gibson, *Aztecs under Spanish Rule*, 147, 370-81; Cope, *Limits of Racial Domination*, 16-21; Yasu Kawashima, "Legal Origins of the Indian Reservation in Colonial Massachusetts," *American Journal of Legal History* 13 (1969): 42-56; Berthold Fernow, ed., *Records of New Amsterdam from 1653 to 1674 Anno Domini* (Baltimore: Genealogical Publishing Co., 1976), 1:22, 2:51-52, 6:32.

9  For a few examples among many on the residence of slaves in cities, see James C. Anderson, *Roman Architecture and Society* (Baltimore: John Hopkins University Press, 1997), 293-336; A. C. De C. M. Saunders, *A Social History of Black Slaves and Freedmen in Portugal, 1441-1555* (Cambridge: Cambridge University Press, 1982), 96-99, 120-25; Cope, *Limits of Racial Domination*, 15-21; Mary C. Karasch, *Slave Life in Rio de Janeiro, 1808-1850* (Princeton: Princeton University Press, 1987), 59-66; Anne Pérotin-Dumond, *La ville aux iles, la ville dans l'ile: Basse terre et Pointe-à-Pitre, Guadeloupe, 1650-1820* (Paris: Éditions Karthala, 2000), 462-70, 641-718; Pedro Welch, *Slave Society in the City: Bridgetown, Barbados 1680-1834* (Kingston, Jamaica:

Ian Randle, 2003), 39-40, 158-63; Richard C. Wade, *Slavery in the Cities: The South, 1820-1860* (New York: Oxford University Press, 1964), 55-79; Berlin, *Many Thousands Gone*, 58-59, 61-63, 162, 204, 249-50, 287, 318-21, 339. For the exception of Panama City, see Nightingale, "Before Race Mattered," 58n21.

10    Berlin, *Many Thousands Gone*, 156-57, 318; Robertson, *Gone Is the Ancient Glory: Spanish Town, Jamaica, 1534-2000* (Kingston, Jamaica: Ian Randle, 2005), 86-87; Welch, *Slave Society in the City*, 158-59. Leslie Harris, *In the Shadow of Slavery: African American in New York City, 1626-1863* (Chicago: University of Chicago Press, 2003), 1-2, 33, 39-45, 78, 84, 291; Berlin, *Many Thousands Gone*, 156-57; Graham Russell Hodges, *Root and Branch: African Americans in New York and East Jersey* (Chapel Hill: University of North Carolina Press, 1997), 48-50, 59-69.

11    Paul Maylam, *South Africa's Racial Past: The History and Historiography of Racism, Segregation, and Apartheid* (Aldershot, UK: Ashgate, 2001), 32.

12    Robert Shell, *Children of Bondage: A Social History of the Slave Society at the Cape of Good Hope, 1652-1838* (Hanover, NH: University Press of New England, 1994), 143, 172-205; Russell-Hodges, *Root and Branch*, 12.

13    Love, *Vestiges of Old Madras*, 1:39-40, 217.

14    De Souza, *Medieval Goa*, 115-16; Taylor, *Social World of Batavia*, 17, 56, 70-71; Love, *Vestiges of Old Madras*, 1:127-36, 147-49, 545-46, 2:81, 135, 45, 3:382.

15    John Vogt, *Portuguese Rule on the Gold Coast, 1469-1682* (Athens: University of Georgia Press, 1979), 20-29, 205; Christopher R. DeCorse, *An Archaeology of Elmina: Africans and Europeans on the Gold Coast, 1400-1900* (Washington DC: Smithsonian Institution Press, 2001), 1-70; Kwame Yeboa Daaku, *Trade and Politics on the Gold Coast, 1600-1720: A Study of the African Reaction to European Trade* (Oxford: Clarendon Press, 1970), 52-53.

16    Glenn J. Ames, *Vasco da Gama: Renaissance Crusader* (New York: Pearson Longman, 2005), 45-71, 85-102, 108-16; Charles R. Boxer, *The Portuguese Seaborne Empire, 1415-1825* (New York: A. A. Knopf, 1969).

17    The texts of the separation decrees can be found in J. H. Cunha da Rivera, ed., *Archivo portuguez oriental* (Nova Goa: Imprensa National, 1862), 4:14-15, 22-23, 31, 52, 72, 130-31, 187, 191, 214; C. R. Boxer, *Race Relations in the Portuguese Colonial Empire, 1415-1825* (Oxford: Clarendon, 1963), 5, 64; Jose Nicolau da Fonseca, *An Historical and Archaeological Sketch of the City of Goa: Preceded by a Short Statistical Account of the Territory of Goa* (1878; repr., New Delhi: Asian Educational Services, 1986), 136-42; Ames, *Vasco da Gama*, 115-16; Teotonio R. De Souza, *Medieval Goa: A Socio-Economic History* (New Delhi: Concept Publishing Co., 1979), 58, 90; Jan Huygen van Linschoten, *The Voyage of John Huygen van Linschoten to the East Indies*, ed. Arthur Cooke Burnell and P. A. Tiele (1596; repr., New York: Burt Franklin, n.d.), 181-82.

18    No synthetic treatment exists of residential segregation in Portuguese cities, but clues can be found in the essays in Liam Brockey, ed., *Portuguese Colonial Cities in the Early Modern World* (Farnham, UK: Ashgate, 2008); and in contemporary sources like Linschoten, *Voyage*, 45-47, 57-58, 63, 67, 70, 104, 125, 181-84, 222, 228, 230, 285; François Pyrard in *Voyage of François Pyrard of Laval to the East Indies, the Maldives, the Moluccas and Brazil*, trans. Albert Gray (New York: Burt Franklin, n.d.), 2:758; *Voyage de Pyrard de Laval aux Indes Orientales (1601-1611)* (Paris: Editions Chandeigne, 1998), 2:400-402; and in the maps contained in João Teixeira Albernaz, *Plantas das cidades, portos, e fortalezas da conquista da India oriental*, repr. in *Voyage de Pyrard de Laval*, 1:417-41. For a more detailed discussion, see Carl H. Nightingale, "Were Portuguese Colonial Cities Segregated?" (unpublished manuscript, 2006).

19    Linschoten, *Voyage*, 181-84, 193, 205, 222, 228-30, 285, 297; Pyrard, *Travels*, 34, 51, 57, 64-66.

20  Robert R. Reed, *Colonial Manila: The Context of Hispanic Urbanism and Process of Morphogenesis* (Berkeley: University of California Press, 1978), 1-37, 53; Milagros Guerrero, "The Chinese in the Philippines, 1570-1770," in Alfonso Felix Jr., ed., *The Chinese in the Philippines* (Manila: Solidaridad, 1966), 15-39.

21  Reed, *Colonial Manila*, 33-70; Felix, *Chinese in the Philippines*, 40-66, 67-118, 175-210; Edgar Wickberg, *The Chinese in Philippine Life, 1850-1898* (New Haven: Yale University Press, 1965), 3-44; quotations from Domingo de Salazar, "The Chinese and the Parian" (1590), and Franscisco Tello, "Ordinances Enacted by the Audiencia of Manila (1598-99)," both in *The Philippine Islands, 1493-1803*, ed. Emma Helen Blair and James Alexander Robertson (Cleveland: A. H. Clark, 1903), 7:220, 224; 11:56-58, 62-63.

22  See, for example, Tello, "Ordinances Enacted by the Audiencia of Manila," 56-58.

23  C. R. Boxer, *The Dutch Seaborne Empire, 1600-1800* (1965; repr., London: Hutchinson, 1977); Jean Gelman Taylor, *Social World of Batavia: European and Eurasian in Dutch Asia* (Madison: University of Wisconsin Press, 1983); Leonard Blussé, *Strange Company: Chinese Settlers, Mestizo Women, and the Dutch in VOC Batavia* (Dordrecht: Foris, 1986); Leonard Blussé, "An Insane Administration and Insanitary Town: The Dutch East India Company and Batavia (1619-1799)," in *Colonial Cities: Essays on Urbanism in a Colonial Context*, ed. Robert J. Ross and Gerard J. Telkamp (Dordrecht: M. Nijhoff, 1985), 65-85; Raben, "Batavia and Colombo: The Ethnic and Spatial Order of Two Colonial Cities, 1600-1800," (PhD diss., University of Leiden, 1996).

24  Raben, "Batavia and Colombo," 162-69. Blussé, *Strange Company*, 73-96.

25  Love, *Vestiges*, 1:9-24, 34-38, 43, 63-65, 2:149; James Stevens Curl, *The Londonderry Plantation, 1609-1914: The History, Architecture, and Planning of the Estates of the City of London and Its Livery Companies in Ulster* (Chichester, Sussex : Phillimore, 1986).

26  Love, *Vestiges*, 1:204-7.

27  Love, *Vestiges*, 1:204-207, 441-43, 473, 497-98. On Yale's part in the financing debacle, see Hiram Bingham, *Elihu Yale: The American Nabob of Queen Square* (1939; Archon, 1968), 98, 116-17, 137, 174, 215, 238, 275. On Child, see Government of Madras, *Records of Fort St. George. Diary and Consultation Books*, 82 vols. (Madras, 1910-53), "Public Consultations" (hereafter PC), January 4, 1686; Government of Madras, *Despatches from England*, 61 vols. (Madras, 1911-71), PC 8, June 9, 1686, #16, #27, #29. For the wall tax debate, PC 19, January 14, 1692; PC 28, May 10, 1699; PC 29, December 4, 1700; PC 31, August 3, 1702; PC 36, July 6, 1706. Love, *Vestiges of Old Madras*, 1:497-98. On Pitt's resolution, PC 34, October 25, 1705; PC 35, July 6, July 25, and September 12, 1706; Cornelius Neale Dalton, *The Life of Thomas Pitt* (Cambridge: Cambridge University Press, 1915), 214-30.

28  Patrick Roche, "Caste and the Merchant Government in Madras, 1639-1749," in *Indian Economic and Social History Review* 12 (1975): 392-93; Arjun Appadurai, "Right and Left Hand Castes in South India," *Indian Economic and Social History Review* 11 (1974): 245-57; Joseph J. Brenning, "Chief Merchants and the European Enclaves of Seventeenth-Century Coromandel," *Modern Asian Studies* 11 (1977): 398-404; Love, *Vestiges of Old Madras*, 2:617.

29  Susan Nield, "The Dubashes of Madras," *Modern Asian Studies* 18 (1984): 1-31; C. A. Bayly, *Indian Society and the Making of the British Empire*, vol. 2 of *The New Cambridge History of India* (Cambridge: Cambridge University Press, 1988), 45-78; K. N. Chaudhuri, *Trade and Civilisation in the Indian Ocean: An Economic History from the Rise of Islam to 1750* (Cambridge: Cambridge University Press, 1985), 80-118, 203-20.

30  Bingham, *Yale*, 20.

31  PC 2, September 1680, 115-16; PC 14 February 27, 1688; PC 16, July 21, 1690; PC 26,

February 25, 1698; Love, *Vestiges*, 2:25, 308, 395–96, 425–26, 573; J. Talboys Wheeler, *Annals of the Madras Presidency* (1861–62; repr., Delhi, 1990), 3:1–10, 21.

32  PC 38, 1707, 36, 40–41, 52–63, 65–66, 68–80, 84–87, and PC 39, 1708, 3, 5–7, 32, 35–37; Dalton, *Thomas Pitt*, 319–34; Appadurai, "Right and Left Hand Castes," 245–57; Brenning, "Merchants and Enclaves," 398–404; Love, *Vestiges of Old Madras*, 2:25–30; Maylam, *South Africa's Racial Past*, 149.

33  Love, *Vestiges of Old Madras*, 2:347–48, 448–52, 520–38, and map facing 554; Nield, "Madras: The Growth of a Colonial City on India, 1780–1840" (PhD diss., University of Chicago, 1977), 309–36; John Archer, "Colonial Suburbs in South Asia, 1700–1850, and the Spaces of Modernity," in *Visions of Suburbia*, ed. Roger Silverstone (London: Routledge, 1997), 26–54; Kenneth T. Jackson, *Crabgrass Frontier: The Suburbanization of the United States* (New York: Oxford University Press, 1985), 190–218; Susan Parnell, "Slums, Segregation, and Poor Whites in Johannesburg, 1920–1934," in *White But Poor: Essays on the History of Poor Whites in Southern Africa, 1880–1940*, ed. Robert Morrell (Pretoria: University of South Africa, 1992), 115–29.

34  Bernard Lewis, *Race and Color in Islam* (New York: Harper and Row, 1971); Valentim Fernandes, *Description de la Côte d'Afrique de Ceuta au Sénégal*, trans. P. De Cenival et Th. Monod (1506–7; repr., Paris, 1938), 58, 69; Winthrop Jordan, *White Over Black: American Attitudes toward the Negro, 1550–1812* (Chapel Hill: University of North Carolina Press, 1968), 3–43.

35  Linschoten, *Voyage*, 28, 46, 64, 77, 94, 101, 126, 135, 183–84, 255, 261, 269; Peter Mundy, *The Travels of Peter Mundy*, vol. 3, *Travels in England, India, China, Etc., 1634–1638* (London, 1919), 233, 252, 260–66, 312; Laval, *Voyage*, 1:65–66. At Elmina, the African section was sometimes called the "village of the blacks," but not officially. Most other names for sections of cities reflected architectural styles, not color: "Intramuros" at Manila; "Casteel" at Batavia; "Zona da Cimiento" and "Zona da Macuti" ("Cement " and "Mangrove" zones) at Moçambique; Malyn Newitt, "Mozambique Island: The Rise and Decline of an East African Coastal City," *Portuguese Studies* 20 (2004): 31.

36  Linschoten, *Voyage*, 269.

37  Love, *Vestiges*, 1:37, 39, 45, 84–85, 95, 118–19, 198, 206–7, 37, 39, 45, 246, 280, 310, 368, 370–71, 421–22, 432–33, 443, 454, 497–98, 2:52; PC 35, July 25, 1706; quotation from DfE, January 22, 1692.

38  Ilona Katzew, *Casta Painting: Images of Race in Eighteenth-Century Mexico* (New Haven: Yale University Press, 2004), 5–38, 42–53; she documents uses of the word *blanco* (211n32, 231n91), but these are from the late eighteenth century; the word *albino* occurs in a painting on 54–55. Also, Magali Carrera, *Imagining Identity in New Spain: Race, Lineage, and the Colonial Body in Portraiture and Casta Paintings* (Austin: University of Texas Press, 2003), 44–105. Also see references to categories of the color white in Maximilianus Transylvanus, *De Moluccis Insulis*, in Blair and Robertson, *Philippine Islands*, 1:309; Boxer, *Race Relations*, 64–65; Linschoten, *Voyage*, 46, 64, 67, 77, 94, 114, 126, 135, 183–84, 255, 261, 269 (Linschoten uses "white man" [*wit man*] only once, on 216); Mundy, *Travels*, 233, 261; Laval, *Voyage*, 1:12, 17, 65–66; Raben, "Batavia and Colombo," 77–116. The index to Love, *Vestiges of Old Madras* (vol. 4) contains an entry under "Christian Town" on 32–33 that gives numerous references to that naming convention.

39  Nancy Shoemaker, *A Strange Likeness: Becoming White and Red in Eighteenth-Century North America* (Oxford: Oxford University Press, 2004), 129–30; W. N. Sainsbury et al., eds., *Calendar of State Papers, Colonial Series, America and the West Indies*, volume for 1669–74 (Vaduz, Liechtenstein, 1964), 495. Censuses for North American colonies in the Colonial Office Record Group at the Public Record Office, London, include, for Barbados, 29/2/4–5 (1676); for Jamaica, 1/15/192 (1661); 1/45/96–

109 (1680); for the Leeward Islands, 1/42/195-240 (1678); and for Bermuda, 37/2/197-98 (1698). Richard Dunn, *Sugar and Slaves: The Rise of the Planter Class in the English West Indies, 1624-1713* (Williamsburg: Institute of Early American History and Culture, 1972), 155.

40 Nightingale, "Before Race Mattered," 62-63nn31-32.

41 Nightingale, "Before Race Mattered," 63n32.

42 Jordan, *White Over Black*, 7-8; George M. Fredrickson, *Racism: A Short History* (Princeton: Princeton University Press, 2002), 52-54.

43 First quotation from Hillary McD. Beckles, "The 'Hub of Empire': The Caribbean and Britain in the Seventeenth Century," in *The Oxford History of the British Empire*, ed. Nicholas Canny, vol. 1, *The Origins of Empire: British Overseas Enterprise to the Close of the Seventeenth Century* (Oxford: Oxford University Press, 1998), 228-32; second quotation from Morgan Godwyn, *The Negro's and Indians Advocate* (London, 1680), 36. Godwyn uses "white" frequently; see, for examples, 4, 24, 39, 84.

44 Dunn, *Sugar and Slaves*, 238-46; Edmund S. Morgan, *American Slavery, American Freedom: The Ordeal of Colonial Virginia* (New York: Norton, 1975), 327-29; Theodore Allen, *Invention of the White Race: The Origin of Racial Oppression in Anglo-America* (London: Verso, 1997), 2:203-38.

45 Theodore K. Rabb, *Enterprise and Empire: Merchant and Gentry Investment in the Expansion of England, 1575-1630* (Cambridge, MA: Harvard University Press, 1967); Philip J. Stern, "British Asia and British Atlantic: Comparisons and Connections," *William and Mary Quarterly* 63 (2006): 693-712; Bernard Steiner, "Two New England Rulers of Madras," *South Atlantic Quarterly* 1 (1902): 209-23; Roxann Wheeler, *The Complexion of Race: Categories of Difference in Eighteenth-Century British Culture* (Philadelphia: University of Pennsylvania Press, 2000); Kathleen Wilson, *The Island Race: Englishness, Empire, and Gender in the Eighteenth Century* (London: Routledge, 2003); Dror Wahrmann, *The Making of the Modern Self: Identity and Culture in Eighteenth Century Britain* (New Haven: Yale University Press, 2004), 83-156; Folarin Shyllon, *Black People in Britain, 1555-1833* (London: Oxford University Press 1977), 84-114.

46 Nightingale, "Before Race Mattered," 66n39.

47 On the Armenians, see PC 22, November 28, 1695 (taxes); PC 25, May 31, 1697 (interlopers); PC 32, May 7, 1703; DfE April 16, 1697, #5 and #8; DfE February 12, 1713, 94; Love, *Vestiges of Old Madras*, 1:231-32, 308, 425, 573; Wheeler, *Annals of the Madras Presidency*, 1:240, 2:247-48. On Portuguese, see Love, *Vestiges of Old Madras*, 1:183, 376, 387-88, 441, 481, 529, 2:128; PC 17, February 7, 1690, and July 21, 1690; PC 20, October 23, 1693; PC 21, April 19, 1694. On the Armenians, see DfE, April 11, 1688; PC 17, March 6, 1690, and April 26 1690; Wheeler, *Annals* 1:184-85, 204; Wheeler, *Annals* 2:273-76, 247-48; PC 22, November 28, 1695; DfE, April 16, 1697, no. 5, no. 8; PC 35 July 6, 1706; DfE, January 16, 1706; PC 41, June 15, 1710; PC 45, July 29, 1714; Love, *Vestiges of Old Madras*, 2:231-32, 308, 395-96, 425-26, 573.

48 DfE, February 12, 1713, 94; Love, *Vestiges of Old Madras*, 2:308; Wheeler, *Annals of the Madras Presidency*, 1:240, 2:247-48. Love, *Vestiges of Old Madras*, 2:231-32, 308, 395-96, 425-26, 573.

49 C. R. Wilson, ed., *Old Fort William in Bengal: A Selection of Official Documents Dealing with Its History* (London, 1906), 1:28-38, 74-78, 90-93, 158-67, 173-78, 214-22, 2:4-20, 112-18, 129-32; Dulcinea Correa Rodrigues, *Bombay Fort in the Eighteenth Century* (Bombay: Himalaya Publishing House, 1994), 58-59, 72-115; S. M. Edwardes, *The Rise of Bombay: A Retrospect* (Bombay: "Times of India" Press, 1902), 104-9, 138, 146, 152-53, 170-78, 206, 229-38.

50 Nightingale, "Before Race Mattered," 67n44.

51 Child's efforts can be found in DfE 8, April 8, 1687, and 9, January 28, 1688;

quotation from Love, *Vestiges of Old Madras*, 1:247. On Batavia, see Boxer, *The Dutch Seaborne Empire*, 219-30. On later prohibitions of cross-color sex, see Durban Ghosh, "Colonial Companions: *Bibis, Begums,* and Concubines of the British in North India, 1760-1830" (PhD diss., University of California, Berkeley, 2000), 34-80. For North America, see Hodges, *Root and Branch,* 12, 48, 93-94; Edwin Vernon Morgan, "Slavery in New York: The Status of the Slave under the English Colonial Government," in *Papers of the American Historical Association* 5 (1891): 3-16; "An Act to Incourage the Baptizing of Negro, Indian, and Mulatto Slaves," passed October 21, 1706, in *Colonial Laws of New York,* 1:597-98; Thelma Wills Foote, *Black and White Manhattan: The History of Racial Formation in Colonial New York City* (Oxford: Oxford University Press, 2004), 27-28, 152-56.

## *Chapter Three*

1   Tertius Chandler and Gerald Fox, *3,000 Years of Urban Growth* (New York: Academic Press, 1974), 319-37.

2   Zine Magubane, *Bringing the Empire Home: Race, Class, and Gender in Britain and Colonial South Africa* (Chicago: University of Chicago Press, 2004), 40-68.

3   C. R. Wilson, ed., *Old Fort William in Bengal: A Selection of Official Documents Dealing with Its History* (London: John Murray, 1906), 1:13, 23, 28-29, 53, 63-64; Wilson, *The Early Annals of the English in Bengal* (1895; repr., New Delhi: Bimla, 1983), 1: chap. 4. Farhat Hasan, "Indigenous Cooperation and the Birth of a Colonial City: Calcutta, c. 1698-1750," *Modern Asian Studies* 26 (1992): 65-82.

4   Wilson, *Old Fort William,* 1:69-71, 74-75, 76, 78-79, 83, 87, 90-91, 92-93, 95, quotation on 78.

5   Ibid., 1:156, 158-59, 163-64, 166-68, 173-80, 183-200, 224-40; 2:4-22, 27-32, 39-50, 51-52. English eyewitness accounts of the fall of Calcutta are assembled in 2:50-99.

6   Sir Penderel Moon, *The British Conquest and Dominion of India* (London: Duckworth, 1989), 39-133.

7   H. E. A. Cotton, *Calcutta, Old and New: A Historical and Descriptive Handbook to the City* (1909; rev. ed., ed. N. R. Ray, Calcutta: General Printers and Publishers, 1980), 703-12. John Archer, "*Paras,* Palaces, and Pathogens: Frameworks for the Growth of Calcutta, 1800-1850," *City and Society* 12 (2000): 30-34.

8   Peter Marshall, "The White Town of Calcutta under the Rule of the East India Company," *Modern Asian Studies* 34 (2000): 307-31.

9   Robert Orme, *Historical Fragment of the Mogul Empire, of the Morattoes, and of the English Concerns in Indostan* (1782; rev. ed., ed. J. P. Gupta, New Delhi: Associated Publishing, 1974), 270-79, 295-306, quotations on 299, 278.

10  Franklin and Mary Wickwire, *Cornwallis: The Imperial Years* (Chapel Hill: University of North Carolina Press, 1980), 88-92, quotation on 92; Cornwallis quotation from Thomas R. Metcalf, *Ideologies of the Raj: The New Cambridge History of India* (Cambridge: Cambridge University Press, 1995), 3.4:24.

11  Carl H. Nightingale, "Before Race Mattered: Geographies of the Color Line in Early Colonial Madras and New York," *American Historical Review* 113 (2008): 68; Prabodh Biswas, "Job Charnock," in *Calcutta: The Living City,* vol. 1, *The Past,* ed. Sukanta Chauduri (Calcutta: Oxford University Press, 1990), 6-7; Durba Ghosh, *Sex and the Family in Colonial India: The Making of Empire* (Cambridge: Cambridge University Press, 2006), 1-106, 246-56.

12  Burke quotation from Anna Clark, *Scandal: The Sexual Politics of the British Constitution* (Princeton, NJ: Princeton University Press, 2004), 102; Peter Marshall, *The Impeachment of Warren Hastings* (Oxford: Clarendon Press, 1965); Kate Teltscher,

*India Inscribed: European and British Writing on India, 1600–1800* (Delhi: Oxford University Press, 1995); Sara Suleri, *The Rhetoric of English India* (Chicago: University of Chicago Press, 1992), chap. 3; Tillman W. Nechtman, "Nabobinas: Luxury, Gender, and the Sexual Politics of British Imperialism in the Late Eighteenth Century," *Journal of Women's History* 18 (2006): 8–30.

13 Pradip Sinha, *Calcutta in Urban History* (Calcutta: Firma KLM, 1978), 44–47. On Hastings's own mixed-race children, see Cotton, *Calcutta, Old and New*, 725. C. A. Bayly, *Indian Society and the Making of the British Empire: The New Cambridge History of India* (Cambridge: Cambridge University Press, 1988), 2:76–87.

14 Wilson, *Old Fort William*, 75; quotation from Rabindra Kumar DasGupta, "Old Calcutta as Presented in Literature," in Chauduri, *Calcutta*, 122; Robert Travers, "Death and the Nabob: Imperialism and Commemoration in Eighteenth-Century India," *Past and Present* 196 (2007): 84; P. J. Marshall, *East Indian Fortunes: The British in Bengal in the Eighteenth Century* (Oxford: Clarendon, 1976), 217–19; Moon, *Conquest and Dominion*, 58; Royal Commission on the Sanitary State of the Army in India, *Report* (London, 1864), 56–57, 161, 525.

15 David Arnold, *Colonizing the Body: State Medicine and Epidemic Disease in Nineteenth-Century India* (Berkeley: University of California Press, 1993), 28–36.

16 Mark Harrison, "'The Tender Frame of Man': Disease, Climate, and Racial Differences in India and the West Indies," *Bulletin of the History of Medicine* 70 (1996): 68–93. Arnold, *Colonizing the Body*, 36–43.

17 James Johnson, *The Influence of Tropical Climates, More Especially the Climate of India on European Constitutions* (London, 1813), 2–5, 104–5, 462, 465, 479; Mark Harrison, "'The Tender Frame of Man,'" 78–80.

18 Roy Porter, "Cleaning Up the Great Wen: Public Health in Eighteenth-Century London," *Medical History* S11 (1991): 61–75.

19 Wilson, *Old Fort William*, 70; Wilson, *Early Annals*, 1:252.

20 Quoted in J. N. Das Gupta, "Wellesley's Scheme for the Improvement of Calcutta," *Bengal Past and Present* 70 (1951): 82–85.

21 Nandal Chatterji, "Lord Wellesley and the Problem of Town Improvement of Calcutta," *Bengal Past and Present* 70 (1951): 13–17; Archer, "*Paras*, Palaces, and Pathogens," 33–42. I am indebted to personal communications from Professor Partho Datta for clarification of the practices of the Lottery Committee.

22 Archer, "*Paras*, Palaces, and Pathogens," 36–42, quotation on 42. Partho Datta, "Public Health in Calcutta," *Wellcome History* 22 (2003): 2–4.

23 Joseph Fayrer, *Inspector-General Sir James Ranald Martin* (London: Innes, 1897).

24 Metcalf, *Ideologies of the Raj*, 30–31; James Kay-Shuttleworth, *The Moral and Physical Condition of the Working Classes of Manchester in 1832* (1832; repr., New York: A. M. Kelly, 1970), quotations on 21, 37, 47.

25 James Ranald Martin, *Notes on the Medical Topography of Calcutta* (Calcutta: G. H. Huttman, Bengal Military Orphan Press, 1837), 49, 45.

26 Martin, *Medical Topography*, 18–19; Archer, "*Paras*, Palaces, and Pathogens," 39–42; Sumanta Banerjee, "The World of Ramjan Ostagar, The Common Man of Old Calcutta," in Chauduri, *Calcutta*, 1:77–78.

27 Fayrer, *James Ranald Martin*, 99–150.

28 Martin, *Medical Topography*, 63.

29 Kenneth Jackson, *Crabgrass Frontier: The Suburbanization of the United States* (New York: Oxford University Press, 1985), 12; Robert Fishman, *Bourgeois Utopias: The Rise and Fall of Suburbia* (New York: Basic Books, 1987), 44–50.

30 Fishman, *Bourgeois Utopias*, 46–47.

31 Robert R. Reid, *Colonial Manila: The Context of Hispanic Urbanism and the Process of Morphogenesis* (Berkeley: University of California Press, 1978), 49. John Archer,

NOTES TO PAGES 98–106

"Colonial Suburbs in South Asia, 1700–1850, and the Spaces of Modernity," in *Visions of Suburbia*, ed. Roger Silverstone (London: Routledge, 1997), 26–54.

32 Peter Thorold, *The London Rich: The Creation of a Great City, from 1666 to the Present* (London: Viking, 1999), 43, 52–53; Tulk v. Moxhay, Lord Chancellor's Court All ER Rep 9, December 22, 1848. Also see Duke of Bedford v. British Museum Trustees, Lord Chancellor's Court All ER Rep 669, July 6, 1822.

33 Love, *Vestiges of Old Madras*, 2:347–48, 448–52, 520–38, and map facing 554; Susan Margaret Nield, "Madras: The Growth of a Colonial City on India, 1780–1840" (PhD diss., University of Chicago, 1977), 309–36.

34 Wilson, *Old Fort William*, 55–56, 65–66; Reginald Craufuird Sterndale, *The Calcutta Collectorate, Collector's Cutcherry, or Calcutta Pottah Office, from the Days of the Zemindars to the Present Time* (1885; repr., Alipore: West Bengal Government Press, 1958), 11–12, 38–39; Peter Marshall, "Private British Investment in Eighteenth-Century Bengal," *Bengal Past and Present* 86 (1967): 56–57; Thomas Bartlett, *Ireland: A History* (Cambridge: Cambridge University Press, 2010), 163–65.

35 The Venetian architect and developer was Edward Tiretta. Marshall, "White Town," 316; Johnson, *Influence of Tropical Climates*, 458–62. Also see Preeti Chopra, "The City and Its Fragments: Colonial Bombay, 1854–1918" (Ph.D. diss., University of California, Berkeley, 2003), 178–230.

36 The diarist Eliza Fay, for example, wrote that "our house is only 200 rupees per month because it is not part of the town much esteemed; otherwise we must pay 3 or 400 rupees." Quoted in Rudrangshu Mukherjee, "'Forever England': British Life in Old Calcutta," in Chauduri, *Calcutta*, 46. See also real estate advertisements in W. S Seton-Carr, *Selections from Calcutta Gazettes* (1864; repr., Calcutta: Bibhash Gupta, 1987), e.g., 1:34, 41, 44, 49, 109, 113, 117, 118, 166, 183. Also see Swati Chattopadhyay, "Blurring the Boundaries: The Limits of 'White Town' in Colonial Calcutta," *Journal of the Society of Architectural History* 59 (2000): 158–60, 178–79nn26, 27, 30; Sinha, *Calcutta in Urban History*, 8–9n19, 28–29nn49–50; Cotton, *Calcutta, Old and New*, 219–22; 1748 quotation from Wilson, *Old Fort William*, 205.

37 Author's calculations from *patta* registrations reproduced in Walter K. Firminger, "Materials for the History of Calcutta Streets and Houses, 1786–1834," *Bengal Past and Present* 14 (1917): 1–74, 159–222.

38 P. J. Marshall, "British Investment in Bengal," 52–67; Marshall, "White Town," 318.

39 Cornelius Neale Dalton, *The Life of Thomas Pitt* (Cambridge: Cambridge University Press, 1915), 67, 120–21, 131, 461–62; Paul F. Norton, "Daylesford: S. P. Cockerell's Residence for Warren Hastings," *Journal of the Society of Architectural Historians* 22 (1963): 127–133; Hiram Bingham, *Elihu Yale: The American Nabob of Queen Square* (n.p.: Archon, 1968), 310–12, 318–20; Thorold, *London Rich*, 59–60, 128–33; J. P. Guha, "Introduction," in Orme, *Historical Fragments*, xii, xv; Fayrer, *James Ranald Martin*, 99, 180. Also see Marshall, "White Town," 315–16.

40 Swati Chattopadhyay, *Representing Calcutta: Modernity, Nationalism, and the Colonial Uncanny* (London: Routledge, 2005), 109–18.

41 Archer, "*Paras*, Palaces, and Pathogens," 23–25; Mukherjee, *Calcutta*, chap. 6.

42 For "Sahibabag," see Cotton, *Calcutta, Old and New*, 703. For "Ingroitollah," see letter from a correspondent to *Asiatic Intelligence* (1822): 393. Marshall, "White Town," 315–16, 329–30; Chitra Deb, "The 'Great Houses' of Old Calcutta," in Chauduri, *Calcutta*, 56–63. For cross-color business partnerships, Firminger, "Calcutta Houses and Streets," *potta* numbers 742, 764, 765, 1497, 2262, 2631–32, 2637, 2648. On assessments, S. N. Mukherjee, *Calcutta: Essays in Urban History* (Calcutta: Subarnarekha, 1993), 24–26; Marshall, "White Town," 313.

43 Archer, "*Paras*, Places, and Pathogens," 42–49; Christine Furedy, "Whose Responsi-

bility? Dilemmas of Calcutta's Bustee Policy in the Nineteenth Century," *South Asia*
5 (1982): 24-46; Mark Harrison, *Public Health in British India: Anglo-Indian Preventive Medicine, 1859-1914* (Cambridge: Cambridge University Press, 1994), 202-26;
Hugh Tinker, *The Foundations of Local Self-Government in India, Pakistan, and Burma*
(New York: Praeger, 1954), 41-42.

44 Sterndale, *Calcutta Collectorate*, 3-4.

45 Moon, *Conquest and Dominion*, 446, 462.

46 Sanitary Commission, *Report*, 56-57, 525; Kipling quotation from Rabindra Kumar
Das Gupta, "Old Calcutta as Presented in Literature," in Chaudhuri, *Calcutta*, 126;
H. V. Lanchester, "Calcutta Improvement Trust: Précis of Mr. E. P. Richard's Report
on the City of Calcutta, Part I," *Town Planning Review* 5 (July 1914): 115-30, and
"Part II" (Oct. 1914): 214-24; Harrison, *Public Health*, 202-26; Furedy, "Whose
Responsibility?"

47 Quotation from Lanchester, "Calcutta Improvement Trust," part 2, 222. Figures on
declining property investment from Mukherjee, *Calcutta*, 33. Also see Sinha, *Calcutta in Urban History*, 140-59; Marshall, "White Town," 316. On Garden Reach and
Alipur, see Cotton, *Calcutta, Old and New*, 220-22, 703-10. On Indian purchases of
white mansions, Dhrubajyoti Banerjea, *European Calcutta: Images and Recollections
of a Bygone Era* (Delhi: UBS, 2005), 160-263; Nirad C. Chaudhuri, *Thy Hand, Great
Anarch!: India 1921-1952* (Reading, MA: Addison-Wesley, 1987), 62-63. On the size
of the European population, see Marshall, "White Town," 309; Mukherjee, *Calcutta*,
119-21. In 1901, census takers counted 38,515 Christians in the city. J. R. Blackwood,
*Census of India, 1901*, vol. 7, *Calcutta, Town and Suburbs*, part 3, *Tabular Statistics*
(Calcutta: Bengal Secretariat Press, 1903), 11. Author's calculations of Christian
populations for the nine *tollahs* of the historic White Town come from the census
numbers for Bow Bazaar, Puddopooker, Waterloo Street, Fenwick's Bazaar, Taltollah, Colinga, Park Street, Bamun Bastee, and Hastings. Christians made up a mere
1.8 percent of the population of Alipore and 0.8 percent of that of Garden Reach.
Blackwood, *Census of India, 1901*, 2-3, 10-11.

48 United Nations, *State of the World's Cities, 2008/2009* (London: Earthscan, 2008), 6.

## Chapter Four

1 Mrs. Julia Charlotte Maitland, *Letters from Madras during the Years 1836-40, by a Lady*
(London: John Murray, 1846), 26.

2 First quotation from Jan Morris, *Stones of Empire: The Buildings of the Raj* (Oxford:
Oxford University Press, 1983), 90; second quotation from Committee on Prostitution in India, "Report of the Special Commission Appointed to Inquire into the
Working of the Cantonment Regulations regarding Infectious and Contagious
Disorders," in *Report* (London, 1893), 228; third quote and information on pillars
from Captain H. H. Ozzard, *The Cantonment Magistrate's Manual* (Calcutta: Calcutta
Central Press, 1890), 11-12. See also Government of India, *The Cantonment Code of
1899* (Lahore: C&M Gazette Press, 1899); H. W. C. Carnduff, *Military and Cantonment
Law* (Calcutta: S. K. Lahiri, 1904).

3 George Trevelyan, *Cawnpore* (London: MacMillan, 1894), 3. See also the "Plan of the
Cantonment of Secunderabad," map of "Delhi Cantonment, Civil Station, City and
Environs," and other similar maps in the Asian and African Studies Collection,
British Library.

4 Royal Commission on the Sanitary State of the Army in India (hereafter Indian
Army Commission), "Report of Special Commission," in *Report* (London, 1864),

32; P. J. Marshall, "British Society in India Under the East India Company," *Modern Asian Studies* 31 (1997): 89–90; Elizabeth Buettner, *Empire Families: Britons and Late Imperial India* (Oxford: Oxford University Press, 2005).

5   Mrs. Major Clemons, *The Manners and Customs of Society in India, Including Scenes in the Mofussil Stations . . . to which are Added Instructions for the Guidance of Cadets* (London: Smith Elder, 1841), 264–65.

6   Ozzard, *Manual*, 12.

7   Amar Farooqui, *Opium City: The Making of Early Victorian Bombay* (Gurgaon, India: Three Essays Collective, 2006), 51–89; Preeti Chopra, "The City and Its Fragments: Colonial Bombay, 1854–1918" (Ph.D. diss., University of California, Berkeley, 2003), 178–230; Susan Lewandowski, "Urban Growth and Municipal Development in the Colonial City of Madras," *Journal of Asian Studies* 34 (1975): 341–60.

8   Nirad C. Chaudhuri, *Thy Hand, Great Anarch! India: 1921–1952* (Reading, MA: Addison Wesley, 1987), 60–64; Arthur Herman, *Gandhi and Churchill: The Epic Rivalry That Destroyed an Empire and Forged Our Age* (New York: Bantam, 2008), 31.

9   Henry Davidson Love, *Vestiges of Old Madras* (1913; repr., New Delhi: Asian Educational Services, 1996), 3:533n1.

10  There is no comprehensive history of the origins of the British stations and cantonments. I have relied on a variety of miscellaneous sources to assemble this short summary. Shah Manzoor Alam, *Hyderabad Secunderabad (Twin Cities): A Study in Urban Geography* (Bombay: Allied Publishers, 1965), 7–10; Reginald George Burton, *A History of the Hyderabad Contingent* (Calcutta: Office of the Superintendent of Government Printing, 1905), 6; Zoë Yalland, *Traders and Nabobs: The British in Cawnpore, 1765–1857* (Salisbury, UK: Michael Russel, 1987), 30–33; Robert Home, *Of Planting and Planning: The Making of British Colonial Cities* (London: E. & F. N. Spon, 1997), 122–24 (Home mistakenly identifies Poona as the first of the British cantonments).

11  Narayani Gupta, *Delhi between Two Empires, 1803–1931: Society, Government, and Urban Growth* (Delhi: Oxford University Press, 1981), 12–13; Mildred Archer, "Artists and Patrons in 'Residency' Delhi, 1803–1858," in *Delhi through the Ages: Essays in Urban History, Culture and Society*, ed. Robert Frykenberg (Delhi: Oxford University Press, 1986), 270–77.

12  Kathleen Blechynden, *Calcutta: Past and Present* (London: Thacker, 1905), 233–34; Gary D. Sampson, "Unmasking the Colonial Picturesque: Samuel Bourne's Photographs of Barrackpore Park," in *Colonialist Photography: Imag(in)ing Race and Place*, ed. Eleanor M. Height and Sampson (London: Routledge, 2002), 93–94.

13  Morris, *Stones of Empire*, 89; Gupta, *Delhi between Two Empires*, 14–18, quotations on 14, 15.

14  Dane Kennedy, *The Magic Mountains: Hill Stations and the British Raj* (Berkeley: University of California Press, 1996), 20–23.

15  Pamela Kanwar, *Imperial Simla: The Political Culture of the Raj* (Delhi: Oxford University Press, 1990), 13–27; Kennedy, *Magic Mountains*, 1–38, 147–75, 223–30; Sir Penderel Moon, *The British Conquest and Dominion of India* (London: Duckworth, 1989), 446, 462, 799–800.

16  Kennedy, *Magic Mountains*, 150, 170; Kanwar, *Imperial Simla*, 37.

17  Moon, *Conquest and Dominion*, 676–781.

18  Gupta, *Delhi between Two Empires*, 20–45, quotation from Ghalib on 29.

19  Veena Talwar Oldenburg, *The Making of Colonial Lucknow, 1856–1877* (Princeton: Princeton University Press, 1984), 3–61.

20  Field marshall Lord Roberts of Kandahar, *Forty-One Years in India: From Subaltern to Commander-in-Chief* (1897; repr., New Delhi: Asian Education Services, 2005), 65.

21  Ozzard, *Manual*, 11; Indian Army Commission, *Report*, 228.

22  Robert Fishman, *Bourgeois Utopias: The Rise and Fall of Suburbia* (New York: Basic Books, 1987), 18-38; Kennedy, *Magic Mountains*, 117-46; Buettner, *Empire Families*, 1-109; David Pomfret, "Raising Eurasia: Race, Class, and Age in French and British Colonies," *Comparative Studies in Society and History* 51 (2009): 316-25.

23  Jharna Gourlay, *Florence Nightingale and the Health of the Raj* (Aldershot: Ashgate, 2003), 24-50.

24  Indian Army Commission, *Report*, 126-29; quotation from David Arnold, *Colonizing the Body: State Medicine and Epidemic Disease in Nineteenth-Century India* (Berkeley: University of California Press, 1993), 72-73.

25  Indian Army Commission, *Report*, 51.

26  Quotations from Indian Army Commission, *Report*, 160, 161, 333, 297. Nightingale to Lord Mayo, March 24, 1870, in Gérard Vallée, ed., *The Collected Works of Florence Nightingale*, vol. 9, *Florence Nightingale on Health in India* (Waterloo, Ontario: Wilfrid Laurier University Press, 2006), 907 (emphasis in the original). Also see Gourlay, *Florence Nightingale*, 80.

27  Florence Nightingale, "How People May Live and Die in India," in Vallée, *Nightingale on Health*, 192-93; Gourlay, *Florence Nightingale*, 51-106; Arnold, *Colonizing the Body*, 61-199; Mark Harrison, *Public Health in British India: Anglo-Indian Preventative Medicine 1859-1914* (Cambridge: Cambridge University Press, 1994), 60-116.

28  Ozzard, *Manual*, 7-11.

29  Gourlay, *Florence Nightingale*, 51-106; Indian Army Commission, *Report*, 228; Arnold, *Colonizing the Body*, 79.

30  Mark Harrison, "A Question of Locality: The Identity of Cholera in British India," in *Warm Climates and Western Medicine: The Emergence of Tropical Medicine, 1500-1900*, ed. David Arnold (Amsterdam: Rodopi, 1996), 133-59; Arnold, *Colonizing the Body*, 191-99.

31  King, *Colonial Urban Development*, 119; Indian Army Commission, *Report*, 228; Arnold, *Colonizing the Body*, 79, 186-89; Harrison, *Public Health*, 45-47, 72-76, 107-8; Philippa Levine, *Prostitution, Race, and Politics: Policing Venereal Disease in the British Empire* (New York: Routledge, 2003); Kenneth Ballhatchet, *Race, Sex, and Class under the British Raj: Imperial Attitudes and Policies and Their Critics, 1793-1905* (London: Weidenfield and Nicholson, 1980), 10-39, 56-67.

32  Buettner, *Empire Families*, 110-45. For the life of a typical Government of India employee, see Ronald Ross, *Memoirs, with a Full Account of the Great Malaria Problem and Its Solution* (London: J. Murray, 1923). Ross writes about his experiences of several dozen moves during his career, which took him all over India and back to England twice: 10, 14, 18, 40, 42, 44, 47, 53, 57, 64-65, 71, 73, 75, 99, 95, 100, 101, 134, 179, 191, 199, 261, 278. Oldenburg, *Making of Colonial Lucknow*, 176.

33  Indian Army Commission, *Report*, 227.

34  Ross, *Memoirs*, 44; Ozzard, *Manual*, 13-14.

35  Gupta, *Delhi between Two Empires*, 58-60, 93-94, quotation on 93.

36  Kanwar, *Imperial Simla*, 46-71, 90-103, quotations on 104, 58.

37  Kennedy, *Magic Mountains*, 96-98, 196-201; Kanwar, *Imperial Simla*, 90-105, 141-45.

## Chapter Five

1  Meng Lowe Kong, Cheok Hong Cheong, and Louis Ah Mouy, *The Chinese Question in Australia, 1878-79* (Melbourne: F. F. Bailliere, 1879), 4, 29.

2  Dirk Hoerder, *Cultures in Contact: World Migrations in the Second Millennium* (Durham: Duke University Press, 2002), 366-67.

3  Thomas Stamford Raffles, "Proclamation" (1823), reprinted in Charles Burton

Buckley, *An Anecdotal History of Old Times in Singapore* (Kuala Lumpur: University of Malaya Press, 1965), 111–21, quotations on 119, 111.

4  Instructions to the "Land Allotment Committee" (1823), reprinted in Buckley, *Old Times*, 82–83.

5  Maurice Collis, *Raffles* (London: Faber and Faber, 1966), 44–97.

6  Raffles, "Arrangements Made for the Government of Singapore" (1819) and "Land Allotment Committee" in Buckley, *Old Times*, 56–59, 79–87, quotation on 83.

7  Raffles, "Proclamation," in Buckley, *Old Times*, 111, 115.

8  Raffles, "Land Allotment Committee," in Buckley, *Old Times*, 80–81, 85. Brenda S. A. Yeoh, *Contesting Space: Power Relations in the Urban Built Environment in Colonial Singapore* (Kuala Lumpur: National University of Singapore Press, 1996), 40–42; B. W. Hodder, "Racial Groupings in Singapore," *Malayan Journal of Tropical Geography* 1 (1953): 25–36.

9  Hanchao Lu, *Beyond the Neon Lights: Everyday Shanghai in the Early Twentieth Century* (Berkeley: University of California Press, 1999), 25–42; Olavi K. Fält, "European City in Japan: Leisure-Time Activities among Western Inhabitants of Yokohama in 1874 and the Impact of Climate Conditions on Them" (unpublished manuscript).

10  Lu, *Beyond the Neon Lights*, 25–42.

11  Christopher Munn, *Anglo-China: Chinese People and British Rule in Hong Kong, 1841–1880* (Richmond, UK: Curzon Press, 2001), 89–98; Nigel Cameron, *An Illustrated History of Hong Kong* (Hong Kong: Oxford University Press, 1991), 32–39.

12  Cameron, *Illustrated History*, 35, 39.

13  David Faure, "The Common People of Hong Kong, Their Livelihood and Aspirations until the 1930s," in *Colonial Hong Kong and Modern China*, ed. Lee Pui-Tak (Hong Kong: Hong Kong University Press, 2006), 9–38, quotation on 13–14; Osbert Chadwick, *Mr. Chadwick's Reports on the Sanitary Condition of Hong Kong* (London: Colonial Office, 1882), map facing A4 and A8; Cameron, *Illustrated History*, 152–57.

14  Chadwick, *Reports*, 41.

15  *Hong Kong Government Gazette*, 1888, 376–77.

16  *Hong Kong Hansard*, April 19, 1904, 17–20, quotation on 20.

17  Ibid., quotation on 17.

18  Ibid., quotation on 18. During the second reading of the Hill Reservation Bill, the attorney general spoke favorably of Chinese speculators' activities "to Kowloon side." The hypothesis in this paragraph owes much to conversations about this source with Professor David Pomfret of Hong Kong University; any errors of interpretation are my own. See also David Pomfret, "Raising Eurasia: Race, Class, and Age in French and British Colonies," *Comparative Studies in Society and History* 51 (2009): 316–25; David Pomfret, "'Beyond Risk of Contagion': Childhood, Hill Stations and the Planning of British and French Colonial Cities" (unpublished manuscript); John M. Carroll, *Edge of Empires: Chinese Elites and British Colonials in Hong Kong* (Cambridge, MA: Harvard University Press, 2005), 84–107; G. B. Endacott, *A History of Hong Kong* (London: Oxford University Press, 1958), 265; Cameron, *Illustrated History*, 214–15.

19  First quotation from Cameron, *Illustrated History*, 156; Cameron, *Hong Kong: The Cultured Pearl* (Hong Kong: Oxford University Press, 1978), 127–30, 146, second quotation on 127; Pomfret, "Raising Eurasia," 316–25, 328–33, third quotation on 318.

20  John C. Weaver, *The Great Land Rush and the Making of the Modern World* (Montreal: McGill-Queen's University Press, 2003).

21  Marilyn Lake and Henry Reynolds, *Drawing the Global Colour Line: White Men's Countries and the International Challenge of Racial Equality* (Cambridge: Cambridge University Press, 2008), 17–45.

22　Charles Price, *The Great White Walls Are Built: Restrictive Immigration to North America and Australasia* (Canberra: Australian Institute of International Affairs, Australian National University Press, 1974), 53-124.

23　Andrew Markus, *Fear and Hatred: Purifying Australia and California, 1850-1901* (Sydney: Hale & Iremonger, 1979), 1-8, 15-31; W. Peter Ward, *White Canada Forever: Popular Attitudes and Public Policy toward Orientals in British Columbia* (Montreal: McGill-Queen's University Press, 1978), 37-42.

24　Price, *Great White Walls*, 125-277; Markus, *Fear and Hatred*, 45-107, 121-234; Ward, *White Canada*, 3-78; Andrew Gyory, *Closing the Gate: Race, Politics, and the Chinese Exclusion Act* (Chapel Hill: University of North Carolina Press, 1998), 92-169.

25　Lake and Reynolds, *Global Colour Line*, 17-45; Markus, *Fear and Hatred*, 65-66.

26　Nayan Shah, *Contagious Divides: Epidemics and Race in San Francisco's Chinatown* (Berkeley: University of California Press, 2001), 25; Kay J. Anderson, *Vancouver's Chinatown: Racial Discourse in Canada, 1875-1980* (Montreal: McGill-Queen's University Press, 1991), 67-68; Chris McConville, "Chinatown," in *The Outcastes of Melbourne: Essays in Social History*, ed. Graeme Davison, David Dunston, and Chris McConville (Sydney: Allen and Unwin, 1985), 58-68.

27　Kay J. Anderson, *Vancouver's Chinatown: Racial Discourse in Canada, 1875-1980* (Montreal: McGill-Queen's University Press, 1991), 69, 70, 79.

28　Shah, *Contagious Divides*, 17-76.

29　See chapter 2; also Shah, *Contagious Divides*, 26-74, quotation on 74.

30　Shah, *Contagious Divides*, 51, 71-72.

31　Shah, *Contagious Divides*, 72; Charles J. McClain, "*In Re Lee Sing*: The First Residential-Segregation Case," *Western Legal History* 3:179-96.

32　On US "manifest destiny," see chapter 10. Lake and Reynolds, *The Global Colour Line*, 49-113, 137-209; Price, *Great White Walls*, 40.

33　Gyory, *Closing the Gate*, 3.

34　Price, *Great White Walls*, 68, 72, 194-95, 210, 268, 272; Anderson, *Vancouver's Chinatown*, 69; Markus, *Fear and Hatred*, 14-34.

35　Gyory, *Closing the Gate*, 177-84; Price, *Great White Walls*, 127-38, 145-214.

36　Lake and Reynolds, *Global Colour Line*, 137-89, 310-34, quotation from Stoddard on 315.

37　See chapter 10; Anderson, *Vancouver's Chinatown*, 26-27; Shah, *Contagious Divides*, 71-75.

## Chapter Six

1　I borrowed the phrase "segregation mania" from Daniel R. Headrick, *The Tentacles of Progress: Technology Transfer in the Age of Imperialism, 1850-1940* (New York: Oxford University Press, 1988), 164; *The Oxford English Dictionary*, 2nd ed. (Oxford: Clarendon Press, 1989), 14:889-90; Paul Robert, *Dictionnaire alphabétique et analogique de la langue française* (Paris: Société du Nouveau Littré, 1972), 6:192; *Grand larousse de la langue française* (Paris: Librairie Larousse, 1977), 6:5434; Salvatore Battaglia, *Grande dizionario della lingua italiana* (Torino: Unone Tipografico, Editrice Torinese, 1998), 491-94.

2　S. R. Christophers and J. W. W. Stephens, "The Segregation of Europeans," in *Further Reports to the Malaria Committee of the Royal Society* (London: Harrison and Sons, 1900), 23.

3　Heinrich Krieger, *Das Rassenrecht in Südafrika: Ein Rechtspolitischer Überblick auf Rechts-Geschichtlicher Grundlage, Zugleich Andwendung einer Neuen Systematik des Kolonialrechtes* (Berlin: Junker Dünnhaupt, 1945), 347-49, 357-64, 282.

4   Quotations from John Cell, *The Highest Stage of White Supremacy: The Origins of Segregation in South Africa and the United States* (Cambridge: Cambridge University Press, 1982), 1–20, quotation on 20 (emphasis in the original). Cell's analysis arises from his focus on South Africa and the US South. He does little to examine the dynamics of urban segregation in either country.

5   See chapters 4 and 5. J. A. Yelling, *Slums and Slum Clearance in Victorian London* (London: Allen and Unwin, 1986); Daniel T. Rodgers, *Atlantic Crossings: Social Politics in a Progressive Age* (Cambridge, MA: Belknap, Harvard University Press, 1998), 130–59.

6   W. E. B. DuBois, "The Souls of White Folk" (1910), in *W. E. B. DuBois: A Reader*, ed. David Levering Lewis (New York: Henry Holt, 1995), 453–65, quotation on 454; Mohandas Gandhi, "Our Shortcomings" (1921), *The Collected Works of Mahatma Gandhi* (Delhi: Government of India, Publications Division, 1966), 20:257–61, quotation on 260. I am indebted to conversations with Professor Theresa Runstedtler for ideas in this paragraph.

7   Mark Harrison, "A Question of Locality: The Identity of Cholera in British India," in *Warm Climates and Western Medicine: The Emergence of Tropical Medicine, 1500-1900*, ed. David Arnold (Amsterdam: Rodopi, 1996), 133–59; Valeska Huber, "The Unification of the Globe by Disease? The International Sanitary Conferences on Cholera, 1851–1894," *History Journal* 49 (2006): 453–76; James Ranald Martin, *The Influence of Tropical Climates on European Constitutions* (London, 1856), 81, 117; Sir Joseph Fayrer, *Inspector-General Sir James Ranald Martin* (London: Innes, 1897), 118–20; Kerrie L. MacPherson, *A Wilderness of Marshes: The Origins of Public Health in Shanghai* (Hong Kong: Oxford University Press, 1987), 9–10, 27–48.

8   Michael Worboys, "Was There a Bacteriological Revolution in Late Nineteenth-Century Medicine?," *Studies in the History and Philosophy of Biology and Biomedical Science* 38 (2007): 20–42; Mary P. Sutphen, "Not What, but Where: Bubonic Plague and the Reception of Germ Theories in Hong Kong and Calcutta, 1894-1897," *Journal of the History of Medicine* 52 (1997): 81–113.

9   David Arnold, *Colonizing the Body: State Medicine and Epidemic Disease in Nineteenth-Century India* (Berkeley: University of California Press, 1993), 189–99; Mark Harrison, *Public Health in British India: Anglo-Indian Preventative Medicine, 1859-1914* (Cambridge: Cambridge University Press, 1994), 117–38; Philip D. Curtin, "Medical Knowledge and Urban Planning in Tropical Africa," *American Historical Review* 90 (1985): 596–97.

10  Echenberg, *Plague Ports*, 6–9.

11  Echenberg, *Plague Ports*, 1–14, 70–71, 313–14.

12  Echenburg, *Plague Ports*, 28–32, 38–46; Prasant Kidambi, *The Making of an Indian Metropolis: Colonial Governance and Public Culture in Bombay, 1890-1920* (Aldershot: Ashgate, 2007), 49–70, quotation on 65; Arnold, *Colonizing the Body*, 200–218; Harrison, *Public Health in India*, 133–50, 217–26; Sutphen, "Not What, but Where," 101–3. Personal correspondence with Professor Mary P. Sutphen helped me clarify the contemporary usage of words like "isolation" and "segregation."

13  Echenburg, *Plague Ports*, 15.

14  Echenburg, *Plague Ports*, 38–43, 64.

15  Harrison, *Public Health in India*, 213–20.

16  Echenburg, *Plague Ports*, 38–43, 62–68; Arnold, *Colonizing the Body*, 218–39; Harrison, *Public Health in India*, 222–24; Subho Basu, "Strikes and 'Communal' Riots in Calcutta in the 1890s: Industrial Workers, Bhadralok Nationalist Leadership and the Colonial State," *Modern Asian Studies* 32 (1998): 972–83.

17  Osbert Chadwick and W. F. Simpson, *Report on the Question of Housing of the Popula-*

*tion of Hong Kong* (Hong Kong: Noronha, 1902), 20, 36; David M. Pomfret, "'Beyond Risk of Contagion': Childhood, Hill Stations and the Planning of British and French Colonial Cities" (unpublished manuscript).

18 Kidambi, *Making an Indian Metropolis*, 71–113, quotation on 84. Harrison, *Public Health in India*, 184–85, 220–26.

19 James Mohr, *Plague and Fire: Battling Black Death and the 1900 Burning of Honolulu's Chinatown* (Oxford: Oxford University Press, 2005), 83–156, quotation on 197. Echenburg, *Plague Ports*, 200–204.

20 Nayan Shah, *Contagious Divides: Epidemics and Race in San Francisco's Chinatown* (Berkeley: University of California Press, 2001), 121–57; Echenburg, *Plague Ports*, 200–204, 216–17, 225–26. On San Francisco's 1890 ordinance, see chapter 5.

21 Mohr, *Plague and Fire*, 189–94; Echenburg, *Plague Ports*, 209–12, 226–35.

22 Philip D. Curtin, "Medical Knowledge and Urban Planning in Tropical Africa," *American Historical Review* 90 (1985): 597–99.

23 John Parker, *Making the Town: Ga State and Society in Early Colonial Accra* (Portsmouth, NH: Heinnemann, 2000); Curtin, "Medical Knowledge," 608.

24 Stephen Frenkel and John Western, "Pretext or Prophylaxis? Racial Segregation and Malarial Mosquitos in a British Tropical Colony: Sierra Leone," *Annals of the Association of American Geographers* 78 (1988): 211–14; Curtin, "Medical Knowledge," 594–97; Raymond E. Dumett, "The Campaign against Malaria and the Expansion of Scientific Medical and Sanitary Services in British West Africa, 1898–1910," *African Historical Studies* 1 (1968): 155–57.

25 Ronald Ross, *Memoirs, with a Full Account of the Great Malaria Problem and Its Solution* (London: J. Murray, 1923), 449.

26 Dumett, "The Campaign against Malaria," 172; Curtin, "Medical Knowledge," 598–99.

27 S. R. Christophers and J. W. W. Stephens, "On the Destruction of Anopheles in Lagos," *Reports to the Malaria Committee of the Royal Society*, 3rd ser. (London: Harrison and Sons, 1900), 20; S. R. Christophers and J. W. W. Stephens, "The Native as the Prime Agent in the Malarial Infection of Europeans," in *Further Reports to the Malaria Committee of the Royal Society*, 3rd ser. (London: Harrison and Sons, 1900), 19; and Christophers and Stephens, "The Segregation of Europeans," 24.

28 Denis Judd, *Radical Joe: A Life of Joseph Chamberlin* (London: Hamish Hamilton, 1977), 35–76; S. R. Christophers and J. W. W. Stephens, "Malaria in an Indian Cantonment (Mian Mir): An Experimental Application of Anti-Malarial Measures-Preliminary Report," in *Further Reports to the Malaria Committee of the Royal Society*, 8th ser. (London: Harrison and Sons, 1902), 13–22; Frenkel and Western, "Pretext or Prophylaxis?," 216.

29 Frenkel and Western, "Pretext or Prophylaxis?," 217–19.

30 Dummett, "The Campaign against Malaria," 180–85; Curtin, "Medical Knowledge," 602–3; Liora Bigon, *A History of Urban Planning in Two West African Colonial Capitals: Residential Segregation in British Lagos and French Dakar (1850–1930)* (Lewiston, NY: Edwin Mellen, 2009), 125–87; Percival Serle, "MacGregor, William," in *Dictionary of Australian Biography* (Sydney: Angus and Robertson, 1949).

31 Thomas S. Gale, "Segregation in British West Africa," *Cahiers d'études africaines* 20 (1951): 498–501; Curtin, "Medical Knowledge," 601–2; Parker, *Making the Town*, 199–200.

32 Walter Elkan and Roger van Zwanenberg, "How People Came to Live in Towns," in *Colonialism in Africa, 1870–1960*, ed. Peter Duigan and L. H. Gann (Cambridge: Cambridge University Press, 1975), 659–61; Home, *Planning and Planting*, 127–33; Curtin, "Medical Knowledge," 605–6; and Gale, "Segregation," 501–3, quotation on 503.

The text of Memorandum 11 can be found in Frederick Lord Lugard, *Instructions to Political Officers on Subjects Chiefly Political and Administrative, 1913-1918*, 3rd ed. (1918; repr., London: Cass, 1970), 404-22.

33 Elkan and van Zwanenberg, "How People Came to Live in Towns," 661-64; Simpson quotation in Curtin, "Medical Knowledge," 610-11.

34 Luise White, "A Colonial State and an African Petty Bourgeoisie: Prostitution, Property, and Class Struggle in Nairobi, 1936-1940," in *Struggle for the City: Migrant Labor, Capital, and the State in Urban Africa*, ed. Frederick Cooper (Beverly Hills: Sage, 1983), 171-72, 180-81.

35 Dane Kennedy, *Islands of White: Settler Society and Culture in Kenya and Southern Rhodesia, 1890-1939* (Durham: Duke University Press, 1987), 150-52; L. W. Thornton White, L. Silberman, and P. R. Anderson, *Nairobi: Master Plan for a Colonial Capital: A Report Prepared for the Municipal Council of Nairobi* (London: H. M. Stationery Office, 1948), 15-16, 18, 49.

36 Alice L. Conklin, *A Mission to Civilize: The Republican Idea of Empire in France and West Africa, 1895-1930* (Stanford: Stanford University Press, 1997), 151-59.

37 Assane Seck, *Dakar Métropole ouest-africaine* (thesis, Faculté des Lettres, Paris, 1968), 122-39; Raymond F. Betts, "The Establishment of the Medina in Dakar, Senegal," *Africa* 41 (1971): 143-52, quotation on 144; Headrick, *Tentacles of Progress*, 159-67; Elikia M'Bokolo, "Peste et société urbaine à Dakar: L'Épidémie de 1914," *Cahiers d'études africaines* 22 (1985-86): 41; Bigon, *Two West African Colonial Capitals*, 187-216.

38 Betts, "Establishment of the Medina," 143; Gustave Reynaud, *Hygiène des établissements coloniaux* (Paris: Ballière, 1903), 165-71, 207; Alexandre Marie Kermorgant, *Hygiène coloniale* (Paris: Masson, 1911), 30, 154-56; Kermorgant, *Épidémie de fièvre jaune du Sénégal: du 16 avril 1900 au 28 février 1901* (Paris: Imprimerie Nationale, 1901), 94, 110; Alexandre Marie Kermorgant, *L'Hygiène et l'acclimatement à Madagascar* (Paris: Imprimerie Nationale, 1906), 32-33; Georges Ribot and Robert Lafon, *Dakar, ses origines, son avenir* (Bordeaux: G. Delmas, 1908), 160; Ponty quoted in Conklin, *Mission to Civilize*, 141.

39 Quotation from Headrick, *Tentacles of Progress*, 166.

40 Betts, "Establishment of the Medina," 149-50; Conklin, *Mission to Civilize*, 151-54; Seck, *Dakar*, 122-29, 135.

41 Betts, "Establishment of the Medina," 151.

42 Ralph A. Austen, "Duala versus Germans in Cameroon: Economic Dimensions of a Political Conflict," *Revue Française d'Outre Mer* 44 (1977): 477-83, quotation on 483 (emphasis in the original).

43 Richard A. Joseph, "The German Question in French Cameroon, 1919-1939," *Comparative Studies in Society and History* 17 (1975): 72; Austen, "Duala versus Germans," 483.

44 Austen, "Duala versus Germans," 483-84; Joseph, "German Question," 70-73.

45 Betts, "Establishment of Medina," 147; quotation from Seck, *Dakar*, 138 (author's translation).

46 Home, *Planning and Planting*, 129-35; Gale, "Segregation," 503-4; Curtin, "Medical Knowledge," 612; Bigon, *Two West African Colonial Capitals*, 151-53.

47 White, "Colonial State and African Bourgeoisie," 181-85; Carol Summers, *From Civilization to Segregation: Social Ideals and Social Control in Southern Rhodesia, 1890-1934* (Athens: Ohio University Press, 1994), 236-43.

48 Quoted in White, Silberman, and Anderson, *Nairobi Master Plan*, 15.

49 On Indians and whites in Johannesburg, see chapters 8, 9, and 11. Thornton White, Silberman, and Anderson, *Nairobi Master Plan*, 49 (the map is located between 56 and 57); Charton, "Urban Planning and Town Identity," sect. 1.1.

50 Harm J. de Blij, "The Functional Structure and Central Business District of Lou-renço Marques, Moçambique," *Economic Geography* 38 (1962): 58–59; Jeanne Marie Penvenne, *African Workers and Colonial Racism: Mozambican Strategies and Struggles in Lourenço Marques, 1877–1962* (Portsmouth, NH: Heinemann, 1995), 28–43; Whyms, *Léopoldville: Son Histoire, 1881–1956* (Brussels: Office de Publicité, 1956), 21–38; Bernard Toulier, Johan Lagae, and Marc Gamoets, *Kinshasa: Architecture et paysage urbains* (Paris: Somogy, 2010), 51–107; Mia Fuller, *Moderns Abroad: Architecture, Cities, and Italian Imperialism* (London: Routledge, 2007), 151–53.

# Chapter Seven

1 Thomas R. Metcalf, *Ideologies of the Raj* (Cambridge: Cambridge University Press, 1995), 195–99.
2 Tyler Stovall, *Paris Noir: African Americans in the City of Light* (Boston: Houghton Mifflin, 1996), and "Love, Labor, and Race: Colonial Men and White Women in France during the Great War," in *French Civilization and Its Discontents: Nationalism, Colonialism, Race*, ed. Tyler Stovall and Georges van den Abbeele (Lanham, MD: Lexington Books, 2003), 297–322; Petrine Archer-Straw, *Negrophilia: Avant-Garde Paris and Black Culture in the 1920s* (New York: Thames & Hudson, 2000); Elisa Camiscioli, *Reproducing the French Race: Immigration, Intimacy, and Embodiment* (Durham, NC: Duke University Press, 2009), 75–154; Tyler Stovall, "The Color Line behind the Lines: Racial Violence in France during the Great War," *American Historical Review* 103 (1998): 737–69; Todd Shepard, *The Invention of Decolonization: The Algerian War and the Remaking of France* (Ithaca, NY: Cornell University Press, 2006), 19–54.
3 F. J. Hebbert and G. A. Rothrock, *Soldier of France: Sebastien Le Prestre de Vauban, 1633–1707* (New York: Peter Lang, 1989), xi.
4 Roger Chartier, Hughes Neveux, and Emmanuel Le Roy Ladurie, *Histoire de la France urbaine* vol. 3, *La ville classique: De la renaissance aux révolutions* (Paris: Seuil, 1981), 109–16.
5 Chartier, Neveux, and Le Roy Ladurie, *La ville classique*, 116–33.
6 Preeti Chopra, "Pondicherry: A French Enclave in India," in *Forms of Dominance: On the Architecture and Urbanism of the Colonial Enterprise*, ed. Nezar AlSayyad (Aldershot, UK: Avebury, 1992), 107–38.
7 John Ruedy, *Modern Algeria: The Origins and Development of a Nation* (Bloomington: Indiana University Press, 1992), 45–48.
8 Ruedy, *Modern Algeria*, 21–23; J. L. Miège, "Algiers: Colonial Metropolis (1830–1961)," in *Colonial Cities*, ed. Robert J. Ross and Gerard J. Telkamp (Dordrecht, Netherlands: M. Nijhoff, 1985), 171–72; Zeynep Çeylik, *Urban Forms and Colonial Confrontations: Algiers under French Rule* (Berkeley: University of California Press, 1997), 12–21.
9 René Lespès, *Alger: Étude de géographie et d'histoire urbaines* (Paris: Félix Alcan, 1930), 200–246; Karim Hadjri and Mohamed Osmani, "The Spatial Development and Urban Transformation of Colonial and Postcolonial Algiers," in *Planning Middle Eastern Cities: An Urban Kaleidoscope in a Globalizing World*, ed. Yasser Elsheshtawi (London, 2004), 29–58; Miège, "Algiers," 173–74; Çeylik, *Urban Forms*, 26–38.
10 Quotation from Çelik, *Urban Forms*, 27.
11 Ruedy, *Modern Algeria*, 45–113; Charles-Robert Ageron, *Les Algériens Musulmans et la France (1871–1919)* (Paris: Presses Universitaires de France, 1968); Shepard, *Invention of Decolonization*, 19–54; Jonathan K. Gosnell, *The Politics of Frenchness in*

*Colonial Algeria, 1930–1954* (Rochester, NY: University of Rochester Press, 2002), 1–40.

12  Urban historians of Algeria have not explained why a deeply racist settler colony with considerable sway over imperial policy did not pass segregation laws of any sort during the era of segregation mania. The arguments in this paragraph must therefore be seen as hypotheses. Deeper comparative research will be necessary to confirm them. A few other possible factors could include the following. In Algiers, French settlers may also have felt reassured by the loosely defined Spanish, Italian, and Jewish working class and commercial neighborhoods that provided buffer zones along the border between the Marine Quarter and the Casbah as its Muslim population grew and began to put pressure on the color line. New zones opened up for European settlement to the south of the walled town as early as the 1890s, thus opening a safety valve in the housing market for whites that may have lessened the need for segregation laws. The *colons'* comparatively muted anxieties about sexual threats posed by Muslim men may have come into play. So did imperialists' usual concerns to sustain fragile alliances with Algeria's small loyal Muslim elite. Lespès, *Alger*, 493–620; David Prochaska, *Making Algeria French: Colonialism in Bône, 1870–1920* (Cambridge: Cambridge University Press, 1990), 23–24, 156–65; Çelik, *Urban Forms*, 21–26.

13  Quotation from Ruedy, *Modern Algeria*, 50–51.

14  Françoise Choay, *The Modern City: Planning in the Nineteenth Century* (New York: George Braziller, 1969), 15–22; Michel Carmona, *Haussmann: His Life and Times, and the Making of Modern Paris* (Chicago: Ivan R. Dee, 2002), 140–66; Paul Rabinow, *French Modern: Norms and Forms of the Social Environment* (Cambridge, MA: MIT Press, 1989), 73–81.

15  Tyler Stovall, *The Rise of the Paris Red Belt* (Berkeley: University of California Press, 1990), 9–40.

16  George Reid Andrews, *The Afro-Argentines of Buenos Aires* (Madison: University of Wisconsin Press, 1980), 102–6; Theresa Meade, *"Civilizing" Rio: Reform and Resistance in a Brazilian City, 1889–1930* (University Park: Pennsylvania State University Press, 1997), 27–32.

17  Andrews, *Afro-Argentines*, 80; Meade, *"Civilizing" Rio*, 66–74, 116–17; Sidney Chaloub, "The Politics of Disease Control: Yellow Fever and Race in Nineteenth Century Rio de Janeiro," *Journal of Latin American Studies* 25 (1993): 441–63; Ramón Gutiérrez, "Buenos Aires: A Great European City," in *Planning Latin America's Capital Cities*, ed. Arturo Almandoz Marte (London: Routledge, 2002), 45–74.

18  Meade, *"Civilizing" Rio*, 75–101; essays in Arturo Almandoz Marte, *Planning Latin America's Capital Cities* (London: Routledge, 2002); John Lear, *Workers, Neighbors, and Citizens: The Revolution in Mexico City* (Lincoln: University of Nebraska Press, 1996), 23–48.

19  Janet Abu-Lughod, *Cairo: 1,001 Years of the City Victorious* (Princeton: Princeton University Press, 1971), 99–117; Heba Farouk Ahmed, "Pre-Colonial Modernity: The State and the Making of Nineteenth-Century Cairo's Urban Form" (PhD diss., University of California, Berkeley, 2001), 99–145.

20  Abu-Lughod, *Cairo*, 118–31, 144–66; Andrew Beattie, *Cairo: A Cultural History* (Oxford: Oxford University Press, 2005), 170–77.

21  Khaled Adham, "Cairo's Urban *Déjà Vu*: Globalization and Urban Fantasies," in Yasser Elsheshtawy, *Planning Middle Eastern Cities: An Urban Kaleidoscope in a Globalizing World* (London: Routledge, 2004), 134–68. Abu-Lughod, *Cairo*, 132–66.

22  Rabinow, *French Modern*, 168–210, 253–54.

23  Rabinow, *French Modern*, 211–67.

24  Rabinow, *French Modern*, 267–76.

25 Çelik, *Urban Forms*, 31–38; M. Pasquier-Bronde, "Alger: Son développement depuis l'occupation Française," in Jean Royer, *L'Urbanisme aux colonies et dans les pays tropicaux* (La Charité-sur-Loire: Delayance, 1932), 33–40; Rabinow, *French Modern*, 104–25, quotation on 113.

26 X. Guillaume, "Saigon; or, The Failure of an Ambition (1858–1945)," in *Colonial Cities*, ed. Robert J. Ross and Gerard J. Telkamp (Dordrecht, Netherlands: Martinus Nijhoff, 1985), 182; Michael G. Vann, "White City on the Red River: Race, Power, and Culture in French Colonial Hanoi, 1872–1954" (PhD diss., University of California, Santa Cruz, 1999), 24.

27 Nguyen Dinh Dau, *From Saigon to Ho Chi Minh City: 300 Year History* (Ho Chi Minh City: Land Service Science and Technics Publishing House, 1998), 97–105; Guillaume, "Saigon," 188–89; Philippe Franchini, "La Cité Blanche," in *Saigon, 1925–1945: De la "Belle Colonie" à l' éclosion révolutionnaire ou la fin des dieux blancs*, ed. Philippe Franchini (Paris: Éditions Autrement, 1992), 31–35; Vann, "White City on the Red River," 41, 69–83.

28 Hubert de Lyautey, *Lettres du Tonkin et de Madagascar (1894–1899)* (Paris: Armand Colin, 1946), 55, 59 (translation by author).

29 Gwendolyn Wright, *The Politics of Design in French Colonial Urbanism* (Chicago: University of Chicago Press, 1991), 258–61.

30 Janet Abu-Lughod, *Rabat: Urban Apartheid in Morocco* (Princeton: Princeton University Press, 1980), 138–42: Rabonow, *French Modern*, 289.

31 Wright, *Politics of Design*, 85–140.

32 Henri Prost, "Le développement de l'urbanisme dans le protectorat du Maroc, de 1914 à 1923," in Royer, *Urbanisme aux colonies*, 60 (emphasis in original).

33 Prost, "Développement de l'urbanisme," 59–60; final quotation from Vivier du Steel, "Introduction," in Royer, *Urbanisme aux colonies*, 12.

34 Abu-Lughod, *Rabat*, 146–90; Wright, *Politics of Design*, 141–44; Rabinow, *French Modern*, 291–93. The inspiration from Frankfurt was the Adickes law.

35 Hébrard, "Urbanisme en Indochine," in Royer, *Urbanisme aux colonies*, 278–89; Wright, *Politics of Design*, 161–301; Lespès, *Alger*, 528–43, 564–66, 588–620.

36 Abu-Lughod, *Rabat*, footnote on xvii; Wright, *Politics of Design*, 147, 221; Rabinow, *French Modern*, 297–301.

37 Jean Royer, "Compte Rendu Général," in Royer, *Urbanisme aux colonies*, 15.

38 Articles by Prost and others in Royer, *Urbanisme aux colonies*, 22, 29, 30, 276–77, 285.

39 Robert Grant Irving, *Indian Summer: Lutyens, Baker, and Imperial Delhi* (New Haven: Yale University Press, 1981), 142–65, 355.

40 Anthony D. King, *Colonial Urban Development: Culture, Social Power, and Environment* (London: Routledge & Kegan Paul, 1976), 182, 228.

41 Irving, *Indian Summer*, 53–90.

42 Quotation from ibid., 73.

43 Quotation from ibid., 35; Stephen Legg, *Spaces of Colonialism: Delhi's Urban Governmentalities* (Malden, MA: Blackwell, 2007), 31–32, 57.

44 Irving, *Indian Summer*, 39–52, quotations on 46, 80, and from Delhi Town Planning Committee, *Final Report Regarding the Selected Site* (London: H. M. Stationery Office, 1913), 5.

45 Irving, *Indian Summer*, 76–78.

46 Legg, *Spaces of Colonialism*, 27–58 (see maps on 44 and 79 for changing extent of government and private holdings in New Delhi); King, *Colonial Urban Development*, 241–58.

47 Legg, *Spaces of Colonialism*, 45–46; King, *Colonial Urban Development*, 241–43.

48 Legg, *Spaces of Colonialism*, 58–81.

49 Hadjri and Osmani, "Spatial Development of Algiers," 40–43; Çelik, *Urban Forms*,

113–79; Vann, "White City on the Red River," 69–83; Abu Lughod, *Rabat*, 157–61; King, *Colonial Urban Development*, 267–68; Legg, *Spaces of Colonialism*, 162.

## Chapter Eight

1   C. W. de Kiewiet, *A History of South Africa, Social and Economic* (Oxford: Oxford University Press, 1941); Paul Maylam, *South Africa's Racial Past: The History and Historiography of Racism* (Aldershot: Ashgate, 2001).

2   Booker T. Washington, *Up from Slavery: An Autobiography* (Garden City, NY: Double-day, 1922), 218–25; James T. Campbell, *Songs of Zion: The African Methodist Episcopal Church in the United States and South Africa* (Chapel Hill: University of North Carolina Press, 1998), 103–327; Thomas J. Noer, *Briton, Boer, and Yankee: The United States and South Africa, 1870-1914* (Kent: Kent State University Press, 1978), 111–34.

3   Bernard M. Magubane, *The Making of a Racist State: British Imperialism and the Union of South Africa, 1875-1910* (Trenton, NJ: Africa World Press, 1996); Martin Legassick, "British Hegemony and the Origins of Segregation in South Africa, 1901-14," in *Segregation and Apartheid in Twentieth-Century South Africa*, ed. William Beinart and Saul Dubow (London: Routledge, 1995), 43–59.

4   George M. Fredrickson, *The Black Image in the White Mind: The Debate on Afro-American Character and Destiny* (Hanover, NH: Wesleyan University Press, 1987), 228–55; quotations from Marilyn Lake and Henry Reynolds, *Drawing the Global Color Line: White Men's Countries and the International Challenge of Racial Equality* (Cambridge: Cambridge University Press, 2008), 77, 79.

5   Lake and Reynolds, *Drawing the Global Color Line*, 75.

6   James Bryce, *The Relations of the Advanced and Backward Races* (Oxford: Oxford University Press, 1902), 7–8, 33–34; Lake and Reynolds, *Drawing the Global Color Line*, 72–74.

7   Quotation from Alfred Jeyes, *Mr. Chamberlain: His Life and Career* (London: Sands, 1903), 391; Denis Judd, *Radical Joe: A Life of Joseph Chamberlain* (London: Hamish Hamilton, 1977), 35–76; John Marlowe, *Milner: Apostle of Empire* (London: Hamish Hamilton, 1976), 6–25.

8   Lake and Reynolds, *Drawing the Global Color Line*, 62–63; Leonard Thompson, *The Unification of South Africa, 1902-1910* (Oxford: Clarendon Press, 1960), 109–25. Uday Singh Mehta, *Liberalism and Empire: A Study in Nineteenth-Century British Liberal Thought* (Chicago: University of Chicago Press), 77–114, quotation on 196.

9   Bryce, *Relations of the Races*, 42.

10  Walter Nimocks, *Milner's Young Men: The "Kindergarten" in Edwardian Imperial Affairs* (London: Hodder and Stoughton, 1968), 30; Alfred Milner, *The Nation and Empire: Being a Collection of Speeches and Addresses* (London: Constable, 1913), xxxiii–xli; Cecil Headlam, ed., *The Milner Papers: South Africa 1899-1905* (London: Cassell, 1933), 2:242–44.

11  Johannesburg Municipality, *Mayor's Minute*, 1901-3, 3–6; John P. R. Maud, *City Government: The Johannesburg Experiment* (Oxford: Clarendon, 1938), 10–68.

12  D. F. Malan, *Report of the Transvaal Asiatic Land Tenure Act Commission* (Pretoria: Government Printer, 1934), 87–93.

13  Deborah Lavin, *From Empire to International Commonwealth: A Biography of Lionel Curtis* (Oxford: Clarendon, 1995), 11–36.

14  First quotation from Charles van Onselen, *Studies in the Social and Economic History of the Witwatersrand, 1886-1914*, vol. 1, *New Babylon* (Harlow, UK: Longman, 1982), 29–30; see also Lionel Curtis, *With Milner in South Africa* (Oxford: Basil Blackwell, 1951), 342. Second quotation from Johannesburg Town Council Minutes (hereafter CM), March 19, 1902.

15  Thompson, *Unification of South Africa*, 10–12; "Johannesburg Municipal Elections Ordinance," National Archives of South Africa (NASA), Transvaal Archives (TAB), Papers of the Secretary of Native Affairs (SNA), 113 538 02-115.

16  Maureen Swan, *Gandhi: The South African Experience* (Johannesburg: Ravan Press, 1985), 92–98; Mahatma Gandhi, *Collected Works* (Ahmedabad: Government of India, 1960), 3:86–90, 280, 301, 325–29.

17  Cecil Headlam, ed., *The Milner Papers: South Africa, 1899–1905* (London: Cassell, 1933), 2:465–70.

18  Headlam, ed., *The Milner Papers*, 2:468.

19  Howard Pim, "The Native Question in South Africa" (1903), in Howard Pim Papers, Historical Papers, University of the Witwatersrand, Johannesburg (hereafter HPP).

20  Pim, "Native Question," 6, 28–29.

21  Howard Pim, "Some Aspects of the Native Question" (1905), 6, 41–56, 67–68, in HPP; Howard Pim, "The Question of Race" (1906), 5, in HPP; Edna Bradlow, "The British Association's South African Meeting, 1905: 'The Flight to the Colonies' and Some Post Anglo-Boer War Problems," *South African Historical Journal* 46 (2002): 42–62.

22  Legassick, "British Hegemony and Segregation," 43–59; Patrick Duncan, "Suggestions for a Native Policy" (Johannesburg: Central New Agency, 1912), 5–6; SANAC, *Report* 1, 39, 94; Godfrey Y. Lagden, "The Native Question in South Africa," in *The Empire and the Century: A Series of Essays on Imperial Problems by Various Writers*, ed. Charles Sydney Goldman (New York: Dutton, 1905), 539–56; Legassick, "British Hegemony and Segregation," 43–59.

23  Pim, "Question of Race," 3, 5, 7.

24  Pim, "Some Aspects," 37–58, quotation on 39; SANAC, *Report* 1, 935; Sue M. Parnell, "Johannesburg Slums and Racial Segregation in South African Cities, 1910–1937" (PhD diss., University of Witwatersrand, 1993), 25.

25  Curtis, *With Milner in South Africa*, 342.

26  Ellison Kahn, "The Pass Laws," in *Handbook on Race Relations in South Africa*, ed. Ellen Hellman (Cape Town: Oxford University Press, 1949), 276–80.

27  Letters from Milner to Chamberlain, November 29 and December 6, 1901; memo from Lagden on pass Llaws, TAB SNA 13 NA 24/02.

28  Alan Mabin, "Labour, Capital, Class Struggle and the Origins of Residential Segregation in Kimberley, 1880–1920" *Journal of Historical Geography* 12 (1986): 4–26.

29  Parnell, "Johannesburg Slums," 126–32.

30  Correspondence between Lionel Curtis and Richard Feetham from 1903 in TAB TPB TALG 518; [Lionel Curtis], *Native Locations* (Pretoria: Government Printing Office, 1904), TAB LD 269 AG846/04, 1.

31  Lionel Curtis, "Native Pass Regulations," TAB LD 463 AG2801/03, 1; SANAC *Report* 1, 48.

32  Gary Baines, "The Origins of Urban Segregation: Local Government and the Residence of Africans in Port Elizabeth, c. 1835–1865," *South African Historical Journal* 22 (1990): 61–81; Joyce F Kirk, "Race, Class, Liberalism, and Segregation: The 1883 Native Strangers' Location Bill in Port Elizabeth, South Africa," *International Journal of African Historical Studies* 24 (1991): 293–321; Kahn, "The Pass Laws," 276–77.

33  Hugh Windham to Lionel Curtis, November 6 and December 12, 1903; Richard Feetham to Curtis, November 3, 1904; John Dove to H. R. M. Bourne December 10, 1906; and Bourne to Curtis, January 2, 1907; all in TAB TALG 518.

34  Bruce Fetter, *The Creation of Elisabethville: 1910–1940* (Stanford: Hoover Institution Press, 1976); Jeanne Marie Penvenne, *African Workers and Colonial Racism: Mozambican Strategies and Struggles in Lourenço Marques 1877–1962* (Portsmouth, NH: Heinneman, 1995); Garth A Meyers, "Colonial and Postcolonial Modernities in

Two African Cities," *Canadian Journal of African Studies/Revue Canadienne des Études Africaines* 37 (2003): 334–38; Swan, *Gandhi in South Africa*, 101, 118; Lavin, *Curtis*, 59–60.

35  Baines, "Origins of Urban Segregation," 67–81; Kirk, "Race, Class, Liberalism, and Segregation," 293–321; Maynard W. Swanson, "'The Asiatic Menace': Creating Segregation in Durban, 1870–1900," *International Journal of African Historical Studies* 16 (1983): 401–21.

36  Christopher Saunders, "The Creation of Ndabeni: Urban Segregation, Social Control and African Resistance" (typescript of paper in author's possession); Maynard Swanson, "The Sanitation Syndrome: Bubonic Plague and the Urban Native Policy in the Cape Colony," *Journal of African History* 18 (1977): 387–410.

37  CM, March 19, 1902, April 15, 1903; C. A. Wentzel, *Report of the Commission on the Johannesburg Insanitary Area Improvement Scheme* (Johannesburg: Transvaal Leader, 1903); Johannesburg Municipality, *Report on the Work of the Town Council*, 1901–3, 7.

38  Letters from Feetham to Curtis March 26, 1903; Pretoria town clerk to Curtis, April 21, 1903; Windham to Curtis, May 4, 1903; Curtis to Feetham, June 26, 1903; Curtis to Windham, November 25, 1903; all in TAB TALG 518; letters and telegrams from Feetham to Windham, August 24, 1903; Lagden to Windham, October 13 and 17, 1903; Windham to Lagden, January 12, 1904; Curtis to Lagden, January 12, 1904; all in TAB SNA 143 NA 1486/03; Swan, *Gandhi in South Africa*, 94; *Report of the Medical Officer of Health*, 1921–22, 22.

39  Rand Plague Committee, *Report on the Outbreak of Plague on the Witwatersrand*, TAB AMPT PUBS 210, v; *Asiatic Land Tenure Act Commission Report*, 88 para. 27.

40  *Report of the Scavenging Department*, appended to *Report of the Medical Officer of Health*, 1904, 27; CM, July 6, 1904, 540; Johannesburg Municipality, *Mayor's Minute*, 1904, 7–8; engineer's and agrostologist's reports, and letter from Edmund T. Somerset, acting chairman of the Anglian Mining and Finance Company, August 8, 1904, all in TAB MJB 4/2/43 A 307; CM, November 25, 1903. Information on the early history of Klipstown was supplied in personal conversations with Professor Philip Bonner.

41  "Examination of Mr. Charles Porter, MOH," TAB MJB 4/2/43.

42  Wentzel, *Report*, viii–ix; Charles Porter, *Report of the Medical Officer of Health*, 1903, 13–14, and 1904, 16–17; Gandhi, *Collected Works*, 403–5.

43  Curtis, *Native Locations*, 1 (my emphasis).

44  Rand Plague Committee, *Report*; Porter, *Report of the Medical Officer of Health*, 1904, 15–17, 36; Howard Phillips, "Locating the Location of a South African Location: The Paradoxical Pre-History of Soweto," unpublished paper delivered at the biennial Conference of the Southern African Historical Society, Durban, June 28, 2011.

45  CM, February 10 and July 20, 57, 584, respectively, and CM, October 12, 1904, 866–83; quotation on 869 (also in TAB SNA 237 NA 2408/02).

46  Nazir Carrim, *Fietas: A Social History of Pageview, 1948–1988* (Johannesburg: Save Pageview Association, 2000), 126–63.

47  Nimocks, *Milner's Young Men*, 18; CM, October 12, 1904.

## Chapter Nine

1  "Black Peril," *Rand Daily Mail*, August 21, 1912; "Social Problem," *Star*, August 21, 1912; both in University of the Witwatersrand, Historical Papers Clippings Files (HPCF) folders on Native Affairs (NA).

2  Theresa Runstedtler, *Jack Johnson, Rebel Sojourner: Boxing in the Shadow of the Global Color Line* (Berkeley: University of California Press, 2012), chaps. 1–2; Zine

Magubane, *Bringing the Empire Home: Race, Class, and Gender in Britain and Colonial South Africa* (Chicago: University of Chicago Press, 2004), 153-84; Gail Bederman, *Manliness and Civilization: A Cultural History of Gender and Race in the United States, 1880-1917* (Chicago: University of Chicago Press, 1995), 1-44, 170-216; Paul Kramer, "Empires, Exceptions, and Anglo-Saxons: Race and Rule between the British and United States Empires, 1880-1910," *Journal of American History* 88 (2002): 1315-53.

3  Johannesburg Municipal Census (1912), National Archives of South Africa (NASA) National Government Repository (SAB) GG 1349 38/11; NASA Transvaal Archives (TAB) SGJ 17 386; Johannesburg Municipality, *Mayor's Minute*, 1913, xiii; Charles Porter, "Report of the Municipal Officer of Health," July 1, 1903, 30, and June 1904, 42; Charles van Onselen, *Studies in the Social and Economic History of the Witwatersrand, 1886-1914*, vol. 2, *New Nineveh* (Harlow, UK: Longman, 1982), 1-60.

4  Van Onselen, *New Nineveh*, 54-60, 171-201.

5  "The Black Peril and 'Jim,'" *Daily Mail*, June 10, 1912; "Black Peril Commission," *Transvaal Leader*, June 26, 1912; both in HPCF NA.

6  "The Black Peril and 'Jim,'" *Daily Mail*, June 10, 1912; "Black Peril Commission," *Transvaal Leader*, June 26, 1912; both in HPCF NA; "Whites and Natives," *Leader*, June 12, 1912; Van Onselen, *New Nineveh*, 48.

7  "Not Nice, but Necessary," *Transvaal Leader*, September 12, 1908; "Commission on Black Peril," *Leader*, June 26, 1912; "Round Table Conference," *Daily Mail*, June 26, 1912; "Black Peril: Joint Committee Meeting," *Leader*, August 10, 1912; "A Township for Natives?" *Daily Mail*, May 28, 1912; all in HPCF NA; Doornfontein Ratepayers Association, "Recommendations on the Pass Law" (1906), TAB SNA 348 N3919/06; "Ratepayer's Meeting," *Leader*, May 27, 1911, HPCF Ratepayers files (RP); "Black Peril," *Daily Mail*, May 2, 1912; "The 'Black Peril,'" *Leader*, June 16, 1912; "The Black Peril and 'Jim,'" *Daily Mail*, June 10, 1912; all in HPCF NA; *Municipal Magazine*, February 1, 1932. Rebecca Ginsburg, *At Home with Apartheid: The Hidden Landscapes of Domestic Service in Johannesburg* (Charlottesville: University of Virginia Press, 2011).

8  Mahatma Gandhi, *Collected Works*, 4:105-6, 147-48, 220-21, 239, 5:186, 206-7; Johannesburg Municipality, *Council Minutes* (CM), 1923, 578, 628-29. On the train to Klipspruit, see Charles James, "Report to Parks and Estates Committee re: Committee of Inquiry, Klipspruit," 8, in TAB SGJ 78 1557; "Jim's Express," *Star*, June 5, 1920, HPCF NA.

9  Maryna Fraser, ed. *Johannesburg Pioneer Journals* (Cape Town: Van Riebeeck Society, 1986), 225, 228-29; "Natives on Footpaths," *Transvaal Journal*, March 7, 1912; "Johannesburg Kaffirs," *Star*, December 2, 1912; "Natives and Sticks," *Star*, December 31, 1919; all in HPCF NA.

10  "Natives on Footpaths," *Leader*, April 4, 1912; "Tirade against Posters," *Star*, April 4, 1912; untitled letter, *Star*, May 6, 1912; all in HPCF NA.

11  Van Onselen, *Studies in the Social and Economic History of the Witwatersrand, 1886-1914*, vol. 1, *New Babylon* (Harlow, UK: Longman, 1982), 103-62; quotation from "Reasons for Black Peril," *Daily Mail*, July 11, 1912, in HPCF NA.

12  "To-day's Fight" and "The Big Fight," *Star* July 4, 1910; "The Great Fight," *Star*, July 5, 1910; "The Great Fight," "All for the Bioscope," and "Pictures of the Fight," *Star*, July 9, 1910; "The Big Fight," *Star*, July 11, 1910; Hertzog quotation in "Reno Pictures," *Star*, July 14, 1910; "To-day's Great Fight," *Daily Mail*, July 4, 1910; "The Great Fight," *Daily Mail*, July 5, 1910; "Bioscope Pictures of the Fight," *Daily Mail*, July 6, 1910; "United South African Action Called For," *Daily Mail*, July 7, 1910; "The Prize Fight" *Daily Mail*, July 7, 1910; "Jeffries Display," *Daily Mail*, July 12, 1910; first quotation from "The Prize Fight," *Daily Mail*, July 14, 1910; second quotation from "White v. Black," *Daily Mail*, July 15, 1910; Runstedtler, *Jack Johnson*, chaps. 1 and 2.

13  "Native Gamblers," *Leader*, March 25, 1909; "Light on Slums," *Star*, January 7, 1918;

"Lord Buxton Visits the Slums," *Daily Mail*, January 8, 1918; "Native Disturbances," *Star*, March 20, 1919; all in HPCF NA.

14   Susan Parnell, "Johannesburg Slums and Racial Segregation in South African Cities, 1910-1937" (PhD diss., University of the Witwatersrand, 1993), 122-77; Ellen Hellmann, *Rooiyard: A Sociological Survey of an Urban Slum Yard* (Cape Town: Oxford University Press, 1948); Van Onselen, *New Babylon*, 44-102.

15   "The Problem of the Native: Liquor & Gambling," *Leader*, May 20, 1912; "Illicit Liquor Evil," *Daily Mail*, March 8, 1918; both in HPCF NA.

16   Thomas Karis and Gwendolen Carter, eds., *From Protest to Challenge: A Documentary History of African Politics in South Africa, 1882-1964*, vol. 1, *Protest and Hope, 1882-1934* (Stanford: Hoover Institution Press, 1972), 18-29, 39-42, 61-68, 76-82; James T. Campbell, *Songs of Zion: The African Methodist Episcopal Church in the United States and South Africa* (Chapel Hill: University of North Carolina Press, 1998), 249-95; Maureen Swan, *Gandhi: The South African Experience* (Johannesburg: Ravan Press, 1985), 114-22.

17   Karis and Wright, *Protest to Challenge*, 106-7, 118-25; George Frederickson, *Black Liberation: A Comparative History of Black Ideologies in the United States and South Africa* (New York: Oxford University Press, 1995), 140-41; Campbell, *Songs of Zion*, 145.

18   "Natives Want a Board," *Daily Mail*, February 25, 1920; "Municipal Compound Incident," *Daily Mail*, February 26, 1920; "Attack upon Tram Cars," *Daily Mail*, March 1, 1920; "Serious Rioting by Natives," *Daily Mail*, March 1, 1920; all in HPCF NA.

19   The phrase "the racist theory of value" is from Charles Abrams, *Forbidden Neighbors: A Study of Prejudice in Housing* (Port Washington, NY: Kennikat Press, 1971), 158.

20   Paul Maylam, "Explaining the Apartheid City: 20 Years of South African Urban Historiography," *Journal of Southern African Studies* 21 (1995): 25-26.

21   *South African Who's Who* (Derby, UK: Bemrose, 1911); South African Native Affairs Commission (SANAC), *Report*, vol. 4, *Minutes of Evidence* (Cape Town: Cape Times and Government Printers, 1904), 805; Rand Pioneers, *First Annual Report* (Johannesburg: Rand Pioneers, 1904), 2; Johannesburg Municipality, *Mayor's Minute*, 1905, 1; 1907, 1; 1910, 3; Rand Plague Commission, *Report* (Johannesburg: Argus, 1905), 1; *Journal of the Institute of Land Surveyors of the Transvaal* 1 (1905): 1; diary, Fortnightly Club Papers, Historical Papers, University of Witwatersrand.

22   SANAC, *Report* 4:806, 808-9, 812-13.

23   Transvaal Leasehold Townships Commission, *Report* (Cape Town: Cape Times and Government Printers, 1912), 2-8. Sixty percent of land tenures in Britain by 1914 were in freehold. Richard Rodger, *Housing in Urban Britain, 1780-1914: Class, Capitalism, and Construction* (Cambridge: Cambridge University Press, 1995), 13-15.

24   The Witwatersrand Township Estate and Finance Corporation, "Deed of Lease" for stand 567, Jeppestown, October 11, 1895; copy in author's possession from vault of Johannesburg Registrar of Deeds.

25   Leasehold Commission, *Report*, 10; *Tulk v. Moxhay*, Lord Chancellor's Court (1843-60); all ER Rep 9, December 22, 1848; *Renals v. Cowlishaw* (1875 R. 89); Chancery Division 9 Ch D 125, April 10, 1878; *Norwood Township Syndicate v. Dawson*, Transvaal Supreme Court, April 6, 1910, *Transvaal Law Reports* (Grahamstown, South Africa: African Book Co., 1911), 235-43.

26   Quotation from a typical township lease, copy in author's possession from vaults of Johannesburg Registrar of Deeds; 1912 figures from author's calculation based on information in Leasehold Commission, *Report*, 42-113; 1947 data from Witwatersrand Land Titles Commission, *Report* (Pretoria: Government Printer, 1947), 3:4-5. Also see Asiatic Land Laws Commission, *Report* (Pretoria: Govern-

ment Printer, 1939), 7–8, for information on some of the townships without these restrictions.

27 The best overall source for the early activities of the associations are the Rate-payers files (RP) of the HPCF. A group called the Ratepayers United Federation existed as early as 1908 ("Ratepayers Associations," *Transvaal Leader*, October 15, 1908, HPCF RP). After 1918, the JFRA published its proceedings in the *Municipal Magazine*, which it shared with the Transvaal Municipal Association (see *Municipal Magazine*, February 1, 1918, 3–5). On the ambiguous foundation of the Ratepayer Party, see "Ratepayers Call for Terminal Station," *Mail*, September 23, 1924; "Orange Grove Incident," *Star*, September 24, 1924; and "Municipal Slogans," *Mail*, September 24, 1924, all in HPCF RP. Also see Maud, *City Government*, 85, 96–97.

28 Johannesburg Municipality, *Mayor's Minute*, 1910, ix; 1935-36, 190.

29 CM 1905, 26; Johannesburg Municipality, *Mayor's Minute*, 1906, ix; 1907, 97; 1913-15, 81; 1916-17, 78, 85; 1917-18, 72; 1918-19, 71. "Native Housing," *Star*, September 7, 1918; Norren Kagan, "African Settlements in the Johannesburg Area, 1903-1925" (master's thesis, University of Witwatersrand, 1978), 55.

30 Campbell, *Songs of Zion*, 153–54; Lionel Curtis to Johannesburg Town Clerk (Richard Feetham), December 14, 1905, in TAB SNA 301 NA 3738/05; [Lionel Curtis], *Native Locations* (Pretoria: Government Printing Office, 1904), TAB LD 269 AG846/04.

31 "Social Danger," *Star*, November 2, 1912; TAB AG 138 21 995/06; Kagan, "African Settlements," 32–38.

32 Quotation from CM, 1912, 410–11; Kagan, "African Settlements," 39–41; Mike Sarakinsky, "Alexandra: From 'Freehold' to 'Model' Township" (PhD diss., University of Witwatersrand, 1984).

33 Transvaal Asiatic Land Tenures Act Commission, *Report*, 87–90; Asiatic Land Laws Commission, *Report*, 6–16; Gandhi, *Collected Works*, 4:130–31; 5:340; 6:225, 258.

34 *Debates of the Second Session of the Legislative Assembly of the Transvaal* (Pretoria: Wallach's, 1908), quotations on 1470–71. Section 62 of the final version of the Townships Act as interpreted by the governor in Government Notice (Transvaal) No. 640 of 1909 gave the government the right to confiscate all land transferred in violation of restrictive covenants without compensation for buildings or improvements. See H. S. L. Polak to Government of India, in Gandhi, *Collected Works*, 11:573; Transvaal Leasehold Commission, *Report*, 28, 42–117.

35 Department of Native Affairs, *Report*, 1913-18 ([UG 7 1919] Cape Town: Cape Times, Government Printers, 1919), 16–17; T. R. H. Davenport, "The Beginnings of Urban Segregation in South Africa: The Natives (Urban Areas) Act and Its Background" (Grahamstown, South Africa: Institute of Social and Economic Research, 1971), 8–10.

36 CM, 1916, 652–75; "Commission on Black Peril," *Leader*, June 6, 1912; "Menace of the Slums," *Star*, July 25, 1917; both in HPCF NA.

37 Johannesburg Municipality, *Mayor's Minute*, 1904, 7–9; Jho. T. Pascoe to J. de Villiers in NASA TAB CS 729 11787; "The Black Peril," *Star*, September 21, 1908; "Proposed Coloured Township," *Leader*, December 12, 1908, HPCF NA; "Ratepayers' Meeting," *Leader*, March 1, 1911, HPCF RP; "Land for Coloured People," *Leader*, March 19, 1912; "Municipal Locations," *Daily Mail*, June 10, 1912, in HPCF NA; "Indignation and Contempt," *Daily Mail*, October 1, 1913; "Asiatics in the Suburbs," *Daily Mail*, March 4, 1913, HPCF RP; "The Voice of the People," *Evening Chronicle*, June 26, 1912; "Native Housing," *Star*, July 20, 1917; "Menace of the Slums," *Star*, July 25, 1917, all HPCF NA; "Native Housing and Slums," *Daily Mail*, January 17, 1918, HPCF RP; CM, 1916, 655; CM, 1918, 310; Kagan, *African Settlements*, 71–80; Arnold Benjamin, *Parktown, 1892-1972: A Social and Pictorial History* (Johannesburg: Studio Thirty

Five, 1972), 16–17; "Native Housing Problem," *Daily Mail*, February 28, 1918; "The Newlands Location," *Star*, June 19, 1918; both in HPCF NA; "The Grievances of Newlands," *Daily Mail*, March 1, 1919; "Newlands Ratepayers," *Star*, March 1, 1919, HPCF RP; CM, 1919, 384.

38    Lagden to Wyndham and Curtis in TAB SNA 143 NA 1486/03; CM, 1905, 493; "Native Grievances," *Star*, September 16, 1919, HPCF NA; CM, 1919, 177. Even Charles Porter, who repeatedly vouched for the health of Klipspruit, admitted the triangular huts had to go and that the separate latrine buildings were inadequate to serve the small population ("Klipspruit Location: Inspection by M.O.H.," November 17, 1920, in TAB SGJ 78 A197); "Mortality of Infants," *Mail*, October 8, 1919, HPCF NA; Davenport, "Beginnings of Urban Segregation," 6–8.

39    Parnell, "Johannesburg Slums," 17–33; Patrick Duncan, "Suggestions for a Native Policy" (Johannesburg: Central News Agency, 1912), 11; Department of Native Affairs, *Report*, 1919–21 ([U.G. 34-1922] Cape Town: Cape Times, Government Printers, 1922), 13–14; "Slums and Native Housing," June 5, 1919, HPCF RP; "Native Housing," *Star*, September 7, 1918, HPCF NA; Kagan, "African Settlements," 74–80; *Municipal Magazine*, February 1922; *Municipal Magazine*, November 1922.

40    "Black Peril," *Leader*, August 10, 1912; "Black Peril," *Daily Mail*, August 21, 1912; "Prohibition and Colour," *Leader*, August 21, 1912; all HPCF NA; CM, 1916, 601, 652–75; CM, 1917, 386–87; "Canteens for Natives?" *Daily Mail*, December 23, 1918; "Canteens for Natives," *Daily Mail*, August 22, 1918; "Women's Reform Club," *Daily Mail*, August 24, 1918; "Fair Play and Justice," *Daily Mail*, August 29, 1918; all in HPCF NA.

41    "Commission of Native Strike Minutes of Evidence," TAB MJB A823, 1918; "Native Housing," *Star*, September 7, 1918; "Means to Voice Their Wishes," *Mail*, September 7, 1918; "The Moffat Report," *Star*, September 9, 1918; Native Grievances," *Mail*, September 10, 1918; all in HPCF NA. On the Klipspruit riot: "Native Trouble," *Star*, March 24, 1919; "Serious Row at Klipspruit," *Mail*, March 24, 1919; "Native Menace" (two articles with same title on same day), *Star*, March 31, 1919. The pass protests and the disturbances at the courthouse can be followed in the *Star* and *Mail* from March 31 to April 26, 1919, and the Klipspruit Commission hearings ran from August 26 through October 8, 1919, in HPCF NA; the Anti Asiatic Congress ran from August 13 to September 9, 1919, in HPCF Asiatic Affairs file (AA); the Vrededorp riot ran from March 1 through March 4, 1920; and the Malay Location petition ran in *Mail* from March 3, 27, 30, June 9, July 7, September 23, 1920; *Star*, June 8, 1920; all in HPCF NA; *Municipal Magazine*, March 1925, 5. Also see Fredrickson, *Black Liberation*, 140–41.

42    "For Town Natives," *Star*, June 21, 1920, HPCF NA; Parnell, "Johannesburg Slums," 50–51.

43    R. V. Selope Thema, "The Race Problem," *Guardian*, September 1922, in Karis and Carter, *Protest to Challenge*, 213.

44    Native Affairs Commission, *Reports*, 1921–23 (Cape Town: Cape Times Ltd., Government Printers, 1921–23); Interdepartmental Committee on the Native Pass Laws (Godley Commission) (Cape Town: Cape Times Ltd., Government Printers, 1922); Select Committee on Native Affairs, *First Report* (Cape Town: Cape Times Ltd., Government Printers, 1923); *Report Debates of the House of Assembly as Reported in the Cape Times* (Pretoria: State Library, 1969), vol. 8 (1923), February 8, 53; Parnell, "Johannesburg Slums," 48–51.

45    "The Native Problem," *Leader*, November 18, 1912; "The Sewerage Farm Location," *Star*, January 26, 1918; "Slums and Native Housing," *Daily Mail*, July 5, 1918; "Council and Housing," *Star*, December 1, 1918; "The Location Problem," *Daily Mail*, January 21, 1918; "A Broken Reed," *Daily Mail*, July 7, 1918; "Our Flimsy Hold,"

*Daily Mail*, July 10, 1918; all in HPCF NA; Keith S. O. Beavon, *Johannesburg: The Making and Shaping of the City* (Pretoria: University of South Africa Press, 2004), 99; Norman Herd, *1922: The Revolt on the Rand* (Johannesburg: Blue Crane Books, 1966), 16.

46   Transvaal Local Government Commission ("Stallard Commission"), *Report* (Pretoria: Government Printing and Stationary Office, 1922), 47-50; "The Kenilworth Meeting," *Daily Mail*, April 20, 1912; "Black Peril and Compounds," *Leader*, September 11, 1912; CM, 1909, 56-57; CM, 1921, 303.

47   Parnell, "Johannesburg Slums," 50-52.

48   Davenport, "Beginnings of Urban Segregation," 13-23; "Parnell, "Johannesburg Slums," 55-60; quotation from Local Government Commission, *Report*, 48.

49   CM, 1920, 502, 760-62; "Klipspruit Location, " *Star*, March 27, 1920; "Klipspruit Location," *Star*, August 31, 1920; "Locations," *Star*, September 2, 1920; "'The Government's Your Father,'" *Daily Mail*, September 4, 1920; "Natives 'Stirred and Astounded,'" *Daily Mail*, September 24, 1920; all in HPCF NA; "Inattentive Councilors and the Location," unattributed news clipping; Charles James, "Report to Parks and Estates Committee re: Committee of Inquiry, Klipspruit," 5-6, in TAB SGJ 78 1557; Johannesburg Municipality, *Mayor's Minute*, 1921-22, 109; 1923-24, 106; 1924-25, 106; CM, February 14, 1922, 80-81.

50   Hertzog to F. W. Bell quoted in Colin M. Tatz, *Shadow and Substance: A Study in Land and Franchise Policies Affecting Africans, 1910-1960* (Pietermaritzburg: University of Natal Press, 1962), 14-15.

## Chapter Ten

1   J. B. M. Hertzog to F. W. Bell, quoted in Colin M. Tatz, *Shadow and Substance: A Study in Land and Franchise Policies Affecting Africans, 1910-1960* (Pietermaritzburg: University of Natal Press, 1962), 14-15.

2   Reginald Horsman, *Race and Manifest Destiny: The Origins of American Racial Anglo-Saxonism* (Cambridge, MA: Harvard University Press, 1981), 25-42, 81-97, 272-97.

3   Dwight W. Hoover, *The Red and the Black* (Chicago: Rand McNally, 1976), 80-108, 141-63; Horsman, *Race and Manifest Destiny*, 189-207; Christoph Strobel, *Testing Grounds of Empire: The Making of Colonial Racial Order in the American Ohio Country and the South African Eastern Cape, 1770s-1850s* (New York: Peter Lang, 2008).

4   John Higham, *Strangers in the Land: Patterns of American Nativism, 1860-1925* (New York: Atheneum, 1965); Andrew Gyory, *Closing the Gate: Race, Politics, and the Chinese Exclusion Act* (Chapel Hill: University of North Carolina Press, 1998); Horsman, *Race and Manifest Destiny*, 208-48; Paul A. Kramer, *The Blood of Government: Race, Empire, the United States, and the Philippines* (Chapel Hill: University of North Carolina Press, 2006), 397-431; Juan Ramon Garcia, *Operation Wetback: The Mass Deportation of Undocumented Mexican Workers in 1954* (Westport, CT: Greenwood, 1980).

5   Eric Foner, *Reconstruction: America's Unfinished Revolution* (New York: Harper and Row, 1988).

6   John Van Evrie, *White Supremacy and Negro Subordination; or, Negroes a Subordinate Race, and (So-Called) Slavery Its Normal Condition; with an Appendix, Showing the Past and Present Condition of the Countries South of Us* (1868; repr., New York: Garland, 1993), 168-75, 330; Leon Litwack, *North of Slavery: The Negro in the Free States, 1790-1860* (Chicago: University of Chicago Press, 1961), 64-152; Thomas Lee Philpott, *The Slum and the Ghetto: Neighborhood Deterioration and Middle-Class Reform, Chicago, 1880-1930* (New York: Oxford University Press, 1978), 117.

7   Carole T. Emberton, "The Politics of Protection: Violence and the Political Culture of Reconstruction" (PhD diss., Northwestern University, 2006).

8   C. Vann Woodward, *The Strange Career of Jim Crow*, 3rd ed. (New York: Oxford University Press, 1974); J. Morgan Kousser, *The Shaping of Southern Politics: Suffrage Restriction and the Establishment of the One-Party South, 1880–1910* (New Haven: Yale University Press, 1974).

9   Gary Gerstle, *American Crucible: Race and Nation in the Twentieth Century* (Princeton: Princeton University Press, 2001), 14–43; Kramer, *The Blood of Government*, 87–158; Gail Bederman, *Manliness and Civilization: A Cultural History of Gender and Race in the United States, 1880–1917* (Chicago: University of Chicago Press, 1995), 170–216.

10  Eric Paul Roorda, "Dessaraigando la tierra de clubes: La extinción de la 'colonia americana' en La Habana," *Secuencia* 60 (2004): 111–34 (my thanks to the author for supplying a translation of this article); Rosalie Schwartz, *Pleasure Island: Tourism and Temptation in Cuba* (Lincoln: University of Nebraska Press, 1997), 20–30; Thomas H. Hines, "The Imperial Façade: Daniel H. Burnham and American Architectural Planning in the Philippines," *Pacific Historical Review* 41 (1972): 33–53, quotations on 38, 40; David Brody, "Building Empire: Architecture and American Imperialism in the Philippines," *Journal of Asian American Studies* 4 (2001): 123–45; Lewis E. Gleeck Jr., *The Manila Americans (1901–1964)* (Manila: Carmelo and Bauermann, 1977), 33–34, 51, 53, 63, 69, 71, 73; Robert R. Reed, *City of Pines: The Origins of Baguio as a Colonial Hill Station and Regional Capital* (Berkeley: Center for South and Southeast Asia Studies, 1976), 119–60.

11  First quotation from A. Grenfell Price, "White Settlement in the Panama Canal Zone," *Geographical Review* 25 (1935): 9; Juan Gonzales, *Harvest of Empire: A History of Latinos in America* (New York: Viking, 2000), 151–52; Julie Greene, *The Canal Builders: Making America's Empire at the Panama Canal* (New York: Penguin, 2009), 62–74, 151–53, second quotation on 72.

12  Margaret Crawford, *Building the Workingman's Paradise: The Design of American Company Towns* (London: Verso, 1995), 29–45, 61–128.

13  Daniel Nowak, *The Wheel of Servitude: Black Forced Labor after Slavery* (Lexington: University Press of Kentucky, 1978), 29–93; William Cohen, *At Freedom's Edge: Black Mobility and the Southern White Quest for Racial Control, 1861–1915* (Baton Rouge: Louisiana State Press, 1991), 201–98.

14  George Fredrickson, *White Supremacy: A Comparative Study in American and South African History* (New York: Oxford University Press, 1981), 179–98.

15  Charles S. Johnson, *Patterns of Negro Segregation* (New York: Harper, 1943), 117–55; Grace Elizabeth Hale, *Making Whiteness: The Culture of Segregation in the South, 1890–1940* (New York: Pantheon, 1998), 85–240; Woodward, *Strange Career*, 67–110; Joel Williamson, *The Crucible of Race: Black-White Relations in the American South since Emancipation* (New York: Oxford University Press, 1984), 180–258; Edward L. Ayers, *The Promise of the New South: Life after Reconstruction* (New York: Oxford University Press, 1992), 432–37; Glenda Elizabeth Gilmore, *Gender and Jim Crow: Women and the Politics of White Supremacy in North Carolina, 1896–1920* (Chapel Hill: University of North Carolina Press, 1996).

16  Carl H. Nightingale, "The Transnational Contexts of Early Twentieth-Century American Urban Segregation," *Journal of Social History* 39 (2006): 667–75, quotation on 667; Roger Rice, "Residential Segregation by Law, 1910–1917," *Journal of Southern History* 34 (1968): 179–99.

17  Nightingale, "Transnational Contexts," 675–80; Samuel Kelton Roberts Jr., *Infectious Fear: Politics, Disease, and the Health Effects of Segregation* (Chapel Hill: University of North Carolina Press, 2009), 107–38.

18  W. E. B. DuBois, "The Challenge of Detroit," *Crisis*, November 1925, 7–10; Nightin-

gale, "Transnational Contexts," 680-86; Joseph L. Arnold, "The Neighborhood and City Hall: The Origin of Neighborhood Associations in Baltimore, 1880-1913," *Journal of Urban History* 6 (1979): 3-30.

19 Commonwealth of Virginia, *Acts of Assembly*, March 12, 1912, 330-32; Jack Temple Kirby, *Darkness at the Dawning: Race and Reform in the Progressive South* (Philadelphia: J. B. Lippincott, 1972), 108-30; Jeffrey J. Crow, "An Apartheid for the South: Clarence Poe's Crusade for Rural Segregation," in *Race, Class, and Politics in Southern History*, ed. Jeffrey J. Crow, Paul D. Escott, and Charles L. Flynn (Baton Rouge: Louisiana State University Press, 1989), 216-59.

20 Nightingale, "Transnational Contexts," 667-68, 685-86; Herbert Aptheker, *A Documentary History of the Negro People in the United States* (New York: Citadel, 1951), 78-87, 117-20; William B. Hixson, *Moorfield Storey and the Abolitionist Tradition* (New York: Oxford University Press, 1972), 139-42; *Buchanan v. Warley* quoted in Garrett Power, "Apartheid, Baltimore Style: The Segregation Ordinances of 1910-1913," *Maryland Law Review* 42 (1983): 312-13.

21 Letter from Mayor James H. Preston to Real Estate Board of Baltimore City, July 17, 1918, Preston Papers, Baltimore City Archives.

22 For examples, see Chicago Commission on Race Relations, *The Negro in Chicago: A Study on Race Relations and a Race Riot* (hereafter cited as Riot Commission, *Report*) (Chicago: University of Chicago Press, 1922), 465, 562.

23 Philpott, *Slum and the Ghetto*, 27-32, 130-45; National Geographic Society, *Historical Atlas of the United States* (Washington DC: National Geographic Society, 1988), 248-49.

24 Litwack, *North of Slavery*, 168-70; Christopher Robert Reed, *Black Chicago's First Century* (Columbia: University of Missouri Press, 2005), 1:43-57, 178-81, 230-41, 340-48. Elaine Lewinnek, "Better than a Bank for a Poor Man? Home Financing Strategies in Early Chicago," *Journal of Urban History* 32 (2006): 274-301; Margaret Garb, *City of American Dreams: A History of Home Ownership and Housing Reform in Chicago, 1871-1919* (Chicago: University of Chicago Press, 2005), 86-116.

25 "Prejudice, the Ban in Securing Homes," *Chicago Defender*, October 19, 1912; Philpott, *Slum and Ghetto*, 115-46; Allan H. Spear, *Black Chicago: The Making of a Negro Ghetto* (Chicago: University of Chicago Press, 1967), 11-28; Garb, *City of American Dreams*, 177-202.

26 Edith Abbott, *The Tenements of Chicago, 1908-1935* (Chicago: University of Chicago Press, 1936), 363-400; Garb, *City of American Dreams*, 36-59, 186-87; Spear, *Black Chicago*, 74-75, 112-13.

27 Garb, *City of American Dreams*, 186-87; Philpott, *Slum and Ghetto*, 149-51.

28 "To Rout the Saloons," *Chicago Tribune*, October 31, 1893; "Citizens Oppose Negro Neighbors," *Chicago Tribune*, August 22, 1909; "Aroused by Negro Invasion," *Chicago Tribune*, October 13, 1909; Philpott, *Slum and the Ghetto*, 146-200; Spear, *Black Chicago*, 29-50.

29 Riot Commission, *Report*, 119, 121-22, 539, 553 (the author's correction, in brackets, of the commissioner's or the speaker's improperly transcribed Lincoln quotation on 119 is based on the original wording from the Lincoln-Douglas debates).

30 Theresa Runstedtler, *Jack Johnson, Rebel Sojourner: Boxing in the Shadow of the Global Color Line* (Berkeley: University of California Press: 2012), chaps. 4-6; Kevin J. Mumford, *Interzones: Black/White Sex Districts in Chicago and New York in the Early Twentieth Century* (New York: Columbia University Press, 1997), 3-52.

31 Mumford, *Interzones*, 93-120.

32 Quotations from Riot Commission, *Report*, 440-42, 452.

33 Riot Commission, *Report*, 440-42, 452, 661; Garb, *City of American Dreams*, 60-116; Robin Bachin, *Building the South Side: Urban Space and Civil Culture in Chicago*,

*1890-1919* (Chicago: University of Chicago Press, 2004), 254–64; Spear, *Black Chicago*, 201–23; "Negroes Arrive by Thousands; Peril to Health," *Chicago Tribune*, March 15, 1917; Vice Commission of Chicago, *The Social Evil in Chicago: A Study of Existing Conditions* (Chicago: Gunthrop Warren, 1911), 38–39; "In Vice Crusade, Negroes' Part," *Defender*, October 12, 1912; "Urges 'Jim Crow' Rule in Schools," *Chicago Tribune*, February 17, 1912; "No Jim Crow Schools in Chicago," *Defender*, February 24, 1912.

34 The phrase "racist theory of value" is from Charles Abrams, *Forbidden Neighbors: A Study of Prejudice in Housing* (Port Washington, NY: Kennikat Press, 1971), 158. Riot Commission, *Report*, 117–21.

35 *Chicago Real Estate Board Bulletin*, 1917, 315, 551, 623–34; Everett Cherrington Hughes, *The Growth of an Institution: The Chicago Real Estate Board* (1931; repr., New York: Arno Press, 1979), 17; "Segregation of Negroes Sought by Realty Men," *Chicago Tribune*, April 5, 1917; "Black Man Stay South!" *Chicago Tribune*, May 30, 1917; "City Takes Hand in Morgan Park 'Negro Invasion,'" *Chicago Tribune*, July 22, 1917; "Negro Tenants Lower Values, Records Show," *Chicago Tribune*, August 26, 1919. After the Chicago riot in 1919, a second ineffectual effort was made to pass an ordinance in city council: *Journal of the Proceedings of the City Council of Chicago*, August 5, 1919, 1115; "Segregation to Prevent Race Riots Is Urged," *Chicago Tribune*, August 6, 1919; Barbara J. Flint, "Zoning and Residential Segregation: A Social and Physical History, 1910-1940," (PhD diss., University of Chicago, 1977), 310–11.

36 James R. Grossman, *Land of Hope: Chicago, Black Southerners, and the Great Migration* (Chicago: University of Chicago Press, 1989); Florette Henri, *Black Migration: Movement North, 1900-1920* (Garden City, NY: Anchor Press, 1975).

37 Riot Commission, *Report*, 3, 8, 11–17, 55–57, 115, 121–23, 135, 252, 272–80, 536, quotation on 121; William M. Tuttle, *Race Riot: Chicago in the Red Summer of 1919* (New York: Atheneum, 1970), 108–10, 137–40, 153–56, 175–76; Philpott, *Slum and Ghetto*, 151, 167–70.

38 Riot Commission, *Report*, 1–78, 121; Philpott, *Slum and Ghetto*, 170–80.

39 Tim Madigan, *The Burning: Massacre, Destruction, and the Tulsa Race Riot of 1921* (New York: St. Martin's, 2001).

40 On South African racial violence, see chap. 10; Ivan Thomas Evans, *Cultures of Violence; Lynching and Racial Killing in South Africa and the American South* (Manchester: Manchester University Press, 2009), 103–5; Jeremy Krikler, *White Rising: The 1922 Insurrection and Racial Killing in South Africa* (Manchester: Manchester University Press, 2005), 130–50. W. A. Maguire, *Belfast: A History* (Lancaster, UK: Carnegie, 2009), 94–97, 135–43, 197–200; A. C. Hepburn, *A Past Apart: Studies in the History of Catholic Belfast* (Belfast: Ulster Historical Foundation, 1996), 34–46, 113–36, 233–51; Jonathan Bardon, *Belfast: An Illustrated History* (Dundonald, Northern Ireland: Blackstaff, 1982), 144–50, 194–202, quotation on 196.

41 Marc Weiss, *The Rise of the Community Builders: The American Real Estate Industry and Urban Land Planning* (New York: Columbia University Press, 1987), 1–52.

42 A Lexis-Nexis search for American cases citing *Tulk v. Moxhay* and other British precedents resulted in a list of dozens of examples involving land-use covenants that themselves date back to 1822. Some of these include *Parker v. Nightingale* (January 1863) 88 Mass. 341; 1863 Mass. LEXIS 278; 6 Allen 341; *Orne v. Fridenberg* (April 1891) 143 Pa. 487; 22 A. 832; 1891 Pa. LEXIS 939; *Roberts v. Scull* (May 1899) 58 N.J. Eq. 396; 43 A. 583; 1899 N.J. Ch. LEXIS 48; *Sharp v. Ropes* (October 1872) 110 Mass. 381; 1872 Mass. LEXIS 253; and *Korn v. Campbell* 1908 192 N.Y. 490; 85 N.E. 687; 1908 N.Y. LEXIS 899. For a Chicago case, see *Vansant v. Rose* (October 1913) 260 Ill.; 103 N.E. 194; 1913 Ill. LEXIS 1905.

43 Frederick Law Olmsted, "Public Parks and the Enlargement of Towns," *Journal of*

*Social Science* (1871): 3, 8; Olmstead, "Preliminary Report on the Proposed Village of Riverside Near Chicago," *Landscape Architecture* 21 (1931): 257-93; scrapbooks, Roland Park Company Records, Division of Rare and Manuscript Collections, Cornell University, no. 2828, boxes 295, 296: Roberta Mouldry, "Gardens, Houses and People: The Planning of Roland Park, Baltimore," (master's thesis, Cornell University, 1990), pp. 260-322; Weiss, *Community Builders*, pp.17-77.

44 Zeynep Çeylik, *Displaying the Orient: Architecture of Islam at Nineteenth-Century World Fairs* (Berkeley: University of California Press, 1992), 80-88; Alan Trachtenburg, *The Incorporation of America: Culture and Society in the Gilded Age* (New York: Hill and Wang, 1982), 208-35.

45 Carl Smith, *The Plan of Chicago: Daniel Burnham and the Remaking of the American City* (Chicago: University of Chicago Press, 2006), 1-33.

46 Jon A Peterson, *The Birth of City Planning in the United States, 1840-1917* (Baltimore: Johns Hopkins University Press, 2004), 247-49, 308-17; David M. P. Freund, *Colored Property: State Policy and White Racial Politics in Suburban America* (Chicago: University of Chicago Press, 2007), 46-72; Weiss, *Community Builders*, 53-78.

47 Flint, "Zoning and Segregation," 53-71, 176-86, 191-200; Peterson, *Birth of City Planning*, 308-17; Jeffrey M. Hornstein, *A Nation of Realtors®: A Cultural History of the Twentieth-Century Middle Class* (Durham: Duke University Press, 2005), 11-14; Freund, *Colored Property*, 46-54, 76; Weiss, *Community Builders*, 79-106.

48 The plan to transfer the institute to Chicago can be followed in Ely's correspondence with MacChesney from November 28 and 30, 1923, September 2-26, October 21 and 22, 1924, March 6, 1925, October 15, 1925, August 27, 1926. Ely Papers (hereafter EP), Wisconsin Historical Society.

49 Dorothy Ross, *The Origins of American Social Science* (Cambridge: Cambridge University Press, 1991), 98-122, 172-86; Daniel T. Rodgers, *Atlantic Crossings: Social Politics in a Progressive Age* (Cambridge, MA: Harvard University Press, 1998), 97-111.

50 The slogan "Under All is the Land" was inscribed in the institute's logo and can be found in all of its publications; a longer discussion can be found in a letter from Ely to Warren Getz, September 20, 1922, EP. For the institute's advocacy of zoning, see, for example, Richard T. Ely and Edward W. Morehouse, *Elements of Land Economics* (New York: Macmillan, 1924), 86-89.

51 Freund, *Colored Property*, 76-90; Hornstein, *A Nation of Realtors*, 118-55.

52 Seymour Helper, *Zoned American* (New York: Grossman, 1969), 188-53; Flint, "Zoning and Segregation," 300-58; Christopher Silver, "The Racial Origins of Zoning: Southern Cities from 1910-40," *Planning Perspectives* 6 (1991): 189-205; Silver, *The Separate City: Black Communities in the Urban South, 1940-1968* (Lexington: University Press of Kentucky, 1995), 125-62; Freund, *Colored Property*, 54-66; Olmsted quotation on 65.

53 Clement E. Vose, *Caucasians Only: The Supreme Court, the NAACP, and the Restrictive Covenant Cases* (Berkeley: University of California Press, 1959), 5-22; Helen C. Monchow, *The Use of Deed Restrictions in Subdivision Development* (Chicago: Institute for Research in Land Economics and Public Utilities, 1928), 46-71; John W. Wertheimer, *Law and Society in the South: A History of North Carolina Court Cases* (Lexington: University Press of Kentucky, 2009), 43-60; Moudry, "Gardens, Houses and People," 283-84 and note 32; Henry Hubbard, "Land Subdivision Regulations," *Landscape Architecture* 16 (1925): 53-54; Margaret Marsh, *Suburban Lives* (New Brunswick: Rutgers University Press, 1990), 69, 169-73, 180, 184; Dolores Hayden, *Building Suburbia: Green Fields and Urban Growth* (New York: Pantheon, 2003), 61-70; Wendy Plotkin, "Deeds of Mistrust: Race, Housing, and Restrictive Covenants in Chicago, 1900-1953" (PhD diss., University of Illinois at Chicago, 1999), 13-32.

54 *Chicago Real Estate Board Bulletin*, 1917, 624-25.

55  Minutes of meeting on real estate education, November 2, 1923. Papers of the Institute for Research on Land Economic and Public Utilities (IRLEPU), Wisconsin Historical Society, box 11, folder 6. Both MacChesney and NAREB president Herbert U. Nelson attended this meeting.

56  Brunson MacChesney, *General Nathan William MacChesney*, bound typescript of lecture delivered November 29, 1960, at the University of Chicago Law School, 14; Nathan William MacChesney, "Race Development by Legislation," reprint from *Institution Quarterly* 4 (1913): 62–75; Patrick Almond Curtis, "Eugenic Reformers, Cultural Perceptions of Dependent Populations, and the Care of the Feebleminded in Illinois" (PhD diss., University of Illinois Chicago, 1983), 150–51. Ely's relationship with Strong can be followed through their correspondence (EP). Materials he received from the American Eugenics Society are in EP, box 105, folder 11. The letter from Lothrop Stoddard to Ely dated April 9, 1922, suggests that the two followed each other's work closely. Stoddard mentions that Ely was "one of the first ones to see the value of that excellent piece of work, [Paul] Popenoe and [Roswell] Johnson's *Applied Eugenics*" (1918). Ely's own modest contributions to eugenic and social Darwinist theory and his extensive reading of eugenicists like Francis Galton and Karl Pearson are most clearly expressed in his book *Studies in the Evolution of Industrial Society* (New York: MacMillan, 1903), 3–24, 152–88, quotation on 162. Also see his address "The Price of Progress" (1922), 661–62 (EP), which Stoddard praised in his letter. On immigrants and blacks, see his bestselling textbook, *Outlines of Economics*, 4th ed. (New York: Macmillan, 1923), 58–68, quotations on 59, 66. Another bit of evidence that his racism hardened during his Chicago days comes from his personal letters. When Ely moved from Madison, he pointedly brought his white servants with him to replace the black Chicagoans he inherited from the previous owner of his house. As he explained to his cousin, they "had the defects common to their race." Letter to Mrs. Mary Hamilton, November 17, 1926 (EP). For endorsements of the racist theory of value in institute publications, see Richard T. Ely, Michael Rostovtzeff, Mary L. Shine, R. H. Whitbeck, and G. B. L. Arner, *Urban Land Economics* (Ann Arbor: Edwards, Institute for Research in Land Economics, 1922), 113, 118; Frederick Morrison Babcock, *The Appraisal of Real Estate* (New York: MacMillan, 1924), 70–71; Herbert Dorau and Albert Hinman, *Urban Land Economics* (New York: MacMillan, 1928), 309; Monchow, *Deed Restrictions*, 46–71; and Nathan William MacChesney, *Principles of Real Estate Law* (New York: MacMillan, 1927), 586.

57  "Bar 'White Area Sales' to Negro," *Chicago Tribune*, May 5, 1921; A. S. Adams, "Report on the Committee on Code of Ethics," *Proceedings of the General Sessions of the National Association of Real Estate Boards* 17:73–76; Rose Helper, *Racial Policies and Practices of Real Estate Brokers* (Minneapolis: University of Minnesota Press, 1969), 187–262.

58  For cases before 1920, see *Queensborough Land Co v. Cazeaux et al.* 136 La. 724; 67 So. 641; 1915 La. LEXIS 2057; *Los Angeles Investment Co. v. Gary* 181 Cal. 680; 186 P. 596; 1919 Cal. LEXIS 410; 9 A.L.R. 115; *Koehler v. Rowland* (1918) 275 Mo. 573; 205 S.W. 217; 1918 Mo. LEXIS 93; 9 A.L.R. 107; *Parmalee v. Morris* 218 Mich. 625; 188 N.W. 330; 1922 Mich. LEXIS 634; 38 A.L.R. 1180. MacChesney's covenant is reprinted in Philpott, *Slum and Ghetto*, 407–10. The version adopted by the Woodlawn Property Owner's Association is filed in the papers of the NAACP, part 5 group 1, reel 1, frame 1123–31. Plotkin, "Deeds of Mistrust," 18–20.

59  Philpott, *Slum and Ghetto*, 410; Plotkin, "Deeds of Mistrust," 18–20; MacChesney, *Real Estate Law*, 586. The NAREB took up a similar line of argument when it recommended that blacks who did not approve of the association's policies should simply set up their own real estate boards. Helper, *Racial Policies*, 237.

60  Philpott, *Slum and Ghetto*, 127.

61 For a few examples, see Gilbert Osofsky, *Harlem: The Making of a Ghetto, Negro New York, 1890-1930* (New York: Harper and Row, 1963); Francis X. Connolly, *A Ghetto Grows in Brooklyn* (New York: New York University Press, 1977); W. E. B. DuBois, *The Philadelphia Negro* (Millwood, NY: Kraus-Thompson, 1973), 10-45; Robert Gregg, *Sparks from the Anvil of Oppression: Philadelphia's Methodists and Southern Migrants, 1890-1940* (Philadelphia: Temple University Press, 1993); Elizabeth Pleck, *Black Migration and Poverty: Boston, 1865-1900* (New York: Academic Press, 1979); Kenneth Kusmer, *A Ghetto Takes Shape: Black Cleveland, 1870-1930* (Urbana: University of Illinois Press, 1976); David M. Katzman, *Before the Ghetto: Black Detroit in the Nineteenth Century* (Urbana: University of Illinois Press, 1973), 53-80; Howard N. Rabinowitz, *Race Relations in the Urban South, 1865-1890* (New York: Oxford University Press, 1978); Lynell George, *No Crystal Stair: African Americans in the City of Angels* (New York: Verso, 1992).

62 Stanley Lieberson, *A Piece of the Pie: Blacks and White Immigrants since 1880* (Berkeley: University of California Press, 1980), 253-91; Kusmer, *A Ghetto Takes Shape*, 44.

63 St. Clair Drake and Horace R. Cayton, *Black Metropolis: A Study of Negro Life in a Northern City* (1945; repr., New York: Harper and Row, 1962), 201, 383.

64 Thomas J. Sugrue, *Origins of the Urban Crisis: Race and Inequality in Postwar Detroit* (Princeton: Princeton University Press, 1996), 45-46; Ann Durkin Keating, *Building Chicago: Suburban Developers and the Creation of a Divided Metropolis* (Columbus: Ohio State University Press, 1988), 98-126; Freund, *Colored Property*, 92-98; Helper, *Racial Policies*, 220-38.

## Chapter Eleven

1 Eric Hobsbawm, *The Age of Extremes: A History of the World, 1914-1991* (New York: Pantheon, 1994).

2 Thomas Borstelmann, *Apartheid's Reluctant Uncle: The United States and Southern Africa during the Early Cold War* (New York: Oxford University Press, 1994).

3 Christopher R. Browning, *The Path to Genocide: Essays on Launching the Final Solution* (Cambridge: Cambridge University Press, 1992), ix-xii; Donald Niewyk, "Solving the 'Jewish Problem': Continuity and Change in German Anti-Semitism, 1871-1945," *Leo Baeck Institute Year Book* 35 (1990): 335-70.

4 Raul Hilberg, *The Destruction of the European Jews* (1961; repr., New York: New Viewpoints, 1973), 563-629; Leni Yahil, *The Holocaust: The Fate of European Jewry* (New York: Oxford University Press, 1987), 163-64, 363-68.

5 Quotation from Gustavo Corni, *Hitler's Ghettos: Voices from a Beleaguered Society, 1939-1944* (London: Arnold, 2002), 22-23; Christopher R. Browning, *The Origins of the Final Solution: The Evolution of Nazi Jewish Policy, September 1939-March 1942* (Lincoln: University of Nebraska Press, 2004), 25-110.

6 Heydrich quotation from Browning, *Final Solution*, 26; Browning, *Path to Genocide*, 3-58.

7 Corni, *Hitler's Ghettos*, 22-47; Roman Mogilanski, *The Ghetto Anthology: A Comprehensive Chronicle of the Extermination of Jewry in Nazi Death Camps and Ghettos in Poland*, rev. ed., ed. Benjamin Grey (Los Angeles: American Congress of Jews of Poland, 1985), 56.

8 Browning, *Path to Genocide*, 28-58; Browning, *Final Solution*, 167-68; quotation from Corni, *Hitler's Ghettos*, 208 (also see 124).

9 Browning, *Path to Genocide*, 34-42.

10 Browning, *Origins*, 309-73, 430-31, first quotation on 370; second quotation in

Martin Broszat, "Hitler and the Genesis of the 'Final Solution': An Assessment of David Irwing's Theses," *Yad Vashem Studies* 13 (1979): 88.

11  Corni, *Hitler's Ghettos*, 293-329; Israel Gutman, *Resistance: The Warsaw Ghetto Uprising* (Boston: Houghton Mifflin, 1994).

12  Stefan Kühl, *The Nazi Connection: Eugenics, American Racism, and German National Socialism* (New York: Oxford University Press, 1994), 13-96.

13  Browning, *Origins*, 184-93; Hilberg, *Destruction*, 561-72.

14  Hilberg, *Destruction*, 561-72, 586-635.

15  Quotation from *The Correspondence of W. E. B. DuBois*, ed. Herbert Aptheker, 3 vols. (Amherst, MA: University of Massachusetts Press, 1997), 3:39. Mark Mazower, *No Enchanted Palace: The End of Empire and the Ideological Origins of the United Nations* (Princeton: Princeton University Press, 2009), 63.

16  Charles Abrams, *Forbidden Neighbors: A Study of Prejudice in Housing* (Port Washington, NY: Kennikat Press, 1971), 229.

17  H. Morton Bodfish and A. C. Bayless, "Costs and Encumbrance Ratios in a Highly Developed Real Estate Market," *Journal of Land and Public Utility Economics* 4 (1928): 126-27, 131-33; Marc A. Weiss, "Richard T. Ely and the Contribution of Economic Research to National Housing Policy, 1920-1940," *Urban Studies* 26 (1989): 117-18.

18  H. Morton Bodfish, *A History of Building and Loan in the United States* (Chicago: United States Building and Loan League, 1931), 6-18; Bodfish and Bayless, "Costs and Encumbrance Ratios"; Alan Teck, *Mutual Savings Banks and Savings and Loan Associations: Aspects of Growth* (New York: Columbia University Press, 1968), 4-26; Margaret Garb, *City of American Dreams: A History of Home Ownership and Housing Reform in Chicago, 1871-1919* (Chicago: University of Chicago Press, 2005), 46-48; Elaine Lewinnek, "Better than a Bank for a Poor Man? Home Financing Strategies in Early Chicago," *Journal of Urban History* 32 (2006): 274-301; William N. Loucks, *The Philadelphia Plan of Home Financing* (Chicago: Institute for Economic Research, 1929). On building societies in Britain, see Martin Pawley, *Home Ownership* (London: Architectural Press, 1978), 25-38, 65-69. The best account of the role of Ely and Bodfish in promoting building societies is in David M. P. Freund, *Colored Property: State Policy and White Racial Politics in Suburban America* (Chicago: University of Chicago Press, 2007), 103-6. Also see Hornstein, *A Nation of Realtors®*, 118-55; Weiss, "Ely and Housing Policy."

19  David Wheelock, "Government Response to Mortgage Distress: Lessons from the Great Depression," Federal Reserve Bank of St. Louis, Research Division, Working Paper 2008-038A, 2-3.

20  Quotation from Abrams, *Forbidden Neighbors*, 147; C. Lowell Harriss, *History of the Policies of the Home Owners' Loan Corporation* (Washington DC: National Bureau of Economic Research, 1951), 14-40, 49-63; Freund, *Colored Property*, 103-11.

21  Freund, *Colored Property*, 99-129. United States Savings and Loan League, *Fact Book '60* (Chicago: USSLL, 1960), 37; United States League of Savings Institutions, *Savings Institutions Sourcebook* (Chicago: USLSI, 1989), 64-65.

22  William Babcock, "History and Elements of Real Estate Values," typescript of lecture in papers of Institute for Research in Land Economics and Public Utilities (hereafter IRLEPU), Wisconsin Historical Society, box 11, folder 6. On Ely's relationship to Frederick Babcock and information on the firm, see Richard T. Ely, "Housing Research Plans for 1927-29," 11-12, IRLEPU, box 4, folder 18; letter from Babcock to Ely, January 9, 1924, EP.

23  Frederick Morrison Babcock, *The Appraisal of Real Estate* (New York: MacMillan, 1924), 70-71. On the effort to recruit Babcock to the institute, see IRLEPU, box 4, folder 18; Guy Stuart, *Discriminating Risk: The U.S. Lending Industry in the Twentieth*

*Century* (Ithaca: Cornell University Press, 2003), 29–69; Nathan William Mac-Chesney, *Principles of Real Estate Law* (New York: MacMillan, 1927), 586.

24  Federal Housing Administration, *Underwriting Manual: Underwriting and Valuation Procedure under Title II of the National Housing Act with Revisions to April 1, 1936* (Washington DC: Government Printing Office, 1936), 228–33, 284, 289, quotation on 233; Freund, *Colored Property*, 156–59, 208–213; FHA, *The FHA Story*, 10–11; second quotation from FHA administrator James Moffett, in Kenneth T. Jackson, *Crabgrass Frontier: The Suburbanization of the United States* (New York: Oxford University Press, 1985), 213.

25  The reports and maps of the HOLC's city surveys are in City Survey file (CSF), record group 195 (Federal Home Loan Bank Board), National Archives II. Quotation from stamped notice on the cover of "Metropolitan Chicago: Summary of Economic, Real Estate, and Mortgage Finance Survey," CSF, box 84. On the FHA, see Jennifer Light, "Nationality and Neighborhood Risk at the Origins of FHA Underwriting," *Journal of Urban History* 36 (2010): 634–53.

26  In 1927, Ely proposed that the institute conduct community studies on swings in land values to place realtors' advice to clients and bankers' decisions about lending on a scientific basis. Richard T. Ely, "Statement in Regard to Housing Research" (1927) and "Proposal for Continuous Housing Research" (1929), IRLEPU, box 4, folder 18. Ely's collaborator on these studies was Coleman Woodbury, who later served on the FHA's advisory board. The mastermind of the FHA studies was Homer Hoyt, who had more distant ties to the institute (Light, "Nationality and Risk," 635–47).

27  "Residential Security Map, Metropolitan Chicago, Ill.," maps and p. 2 of accompanying typescript text; letters from various institutions to HOLC, thanking the agency for the study; and lists entitled "Sources of Information, Cooperators," "Sources of Information and Assistance," and "Map Consultants"; all in CSF, box 84. Some of other supporters included the Mortgage Bankers Association of America, the Society of Residential Appraisers, the Federal Reserve Bank of Chicago, Dun and Bradstreet, the Chicago Plan Commission, the Chicago Regional Planning Board, and the Chicago Land Use Survey. Quotation from "Building Ghettoes," *Chicago Defender*, September 25, 1937.

28  For a few examples of "Area Description" forms from the South Side of Chicago that treat various "foreign" groups alongside blacks and whites, see D-72, D-74, D-75, D-77, D-78, D-83, and mimeographed description of Hyde Park; interviews with heads of Chicago financial institutions whose loans HOLC purchased, 132–34, 136, 151, 162–63, 170–71, 185; all in CSF, box 84. Compare with David Roediger, *Working toward Whiteness: How America's Immigrants Became White* (New York: Basic Books, 2005), 199–244; Light "Nationality and Risk," 647–60.

29  Division of Research and Statistics, Federal Home Loan Bank Board (hereafter FHLBB), "Metropolitan Chicago: Summary of Economic, Real Estate and Mortgage Finance Survey," 12, CSF, box 84.

30  FHLBB, "Metropolitan Chicago," 3–4, 15. On similar Canadian developments, see Richard Harris and Dorris Forrester, "The Suburban Origins of Redlining: A Case Study, 1935–54," *Urban Studies* 40 (2003): 2661–86.

31  FHLBB, "Metropolitan Chicago," 31.

32  Coleman Woodbury, a public housing advocate and close associate of Ely's at the institute also worked closely with Catherine Bauer. Gail Radford, *Modern Housing for America: Policy Struggles in the New Deal Era* (Chicago: University of Chicago Press, 1996), 59–84; Daniel T. Rodgers, *Atlantic Crossings: Social Politics in a Progressive Age* (Cambridge, MA: Harvard University Press, 1998), 461–68; D. Bradford

Hunt, *Blueprint for Disaster: The Unraveling of Chicago Public Housing* (Chicago: University of Chicago Press, 2009), 15-34.

33 Thomas J. Sugrue, *The Origins of the Urban Crisis: Race and Inequality in Postwar Detroit* (Princeton: Princeton University Press, 1996), 33-88; Arnold R. Hirsch, *Making the Second Ghetto: Race and Housing in Chicago, 1940-1960* (Cambridge: Cambridge University Press, 1983), 42-52.

34 Hunt, *Blueprint for Disaster*, 99-120; Thomas J. Sugrue, *Sweet Land of Liberty: The Forgotten Struggle for Civil Rights in the North* (New York: Random House, 2008), 200-253.

35 Hirsch, *Second Ghetto*, 16-17, 45-46, quotation on 52.

36 Hirsch, *Second Ghetto*, 53-60.

37 Hunt, *Blueprint for Disaster*, 84-97.

38 Hirsch, *Second Ghetto*, 100-134, 212-58; Hunt, *Blueprint for Disaster*, 35-144.

39 Arnold Hirsch, "Searching for a 'Sound Negro Policy': A Racial Agenda for the Housing Acts of 1949 and 1954," *Housing Policy Debate* 11 (2000): 393-41; Hirsch, *Second Ghetto*, 100-134.

40 Hirsch, *Second Ghetto*, 268-75; Sugrue, *Origins of the Urban Crisis*, 47-51; Martin Anderson, *The Federal Bulldozer* (Cambridge, MA: M.I.T. Press, 1964), 7-8, 64-65; Peter H. Rossi and Robert A. Dentler, *The Politics of Urban Renewal* (New York: Free Press, 1961), 224.

41 Karl E. Taeuber and Alma F. Taeuber, *Negroes in Cities: Residential Segregation and Neighborhood Change* (Chicago: Aldine, 1965), 39-40; Anthony Lemon, "The Apartheid City," in *Homes Apart: South Africa's Segregated Cities*, ed. Anthony Lemon (Bloomington: Indiana University Press, 1991), 8, 13; A. J. Christopher, "Port Elizabeth," in Lemon, *Homes Apart*, 51; R. J. Davies, "Durban," in Lemon, *Homes Apart*, 79, 82.

42 Jackson, *Crabgrass Frontier*, 206-15; Freund, *Colored Property*, 134-35, 183-97; Sugrue, *Origins of the Urban Crisis*, 62-72.

43 Hornstein, *A Nation of Realtors*, 134-35; Robert O. Self, *American Babylon: Race and the Struggle for Postwar Oakland* (Princeton: Princeton University Press, 2003), 1-20, 96-132, 256-90.

44 Luigi Laurenti, *Property Values and Race: Studies in Seven Cities* (University of California Press, 1960), 47-68; Melvin L. Oliver and Thomas M. Shapiro, *Black Wealth/White Wealth: A New Perspective on Racial Inequality* (New York: Routledge, 1997), 136-51; Gregory Squires, *Capital and Communities in Black and White: The Intersections of Race, Class, and Uneven Development* (Albany: State University of New York Press, 1994).

45 Hunt, *Blueprint for Disaster*, 104-8.

46 Freund, *Colored Property*, 206-13; Andrew Wiese, *Places of Their Own: African American Suburbanization in the Twentieth Century* (Chicago: University of Chicago Press, 2004).

47 Rodney Davenport and Christopher Saunders, *South Africa: A Modern History* (Houndmills, UK: Macmillan, 2000), 360-61; Deon van Tonder, "'First Win the War, Then Clear the Slums': The Genesis of the Western Areas Removal Scheme, 1940-1949," in *Apartheid's Genesis, 1935-1962*, ed. Philip Bonner, Peter Delius, and Deborah Posel (Johannesburg: Ravan Press, 1993), 317.

48 A. J. van Rensburg, "Pride in Your Profession: A Concise History of the Institute of Estate Agents of South Africa, 1937-1987," *Eiendomsforum-Real Estate Forum*, February 1989, 20-21; March 1989, 10-11; April 1989, 5-6; and September 1989, 19-21; and Stefan Swanepoel, "Looking Back over 50 Years," *Eiendom Forum*, May 1987; both articles generously provided to the author by the institute. Peter Penny, *Economic and Legal Aspects of Real Estate in South Africa* (Cape Town: Juta, 1970), 1n1,

10n12, 31n27; A. J. Jonker, *Property Valuation in South Africa* (Cape Town: Juta, 1984), xnn4-5, 82n16. Jonker relies heavily throughout his book upon studies produced by the American Institute of Real Estate Appraisers (AIREA).

49 T. Dunbar Moodie, *The Rise of Afrikanerdom: Power, Apartheid, and the Afrikaner Civil Religion* (Berkeley: University of California Press, 1975), 1-207; Patrick J. Furlong, *Between Crown and Swastika: The Impact of the Radical Right on the Afrikaner Nationalist Movement in the Fascist Era* (Johannesburg: Witwatersrand University Press, 1991), 3-119.

50 On Vrededorp, see Transvaal Asiatic Land Tenure Act Commission, *Report* (Pretoria: Government Printers, 1934), 90-91. On Curtis, see Charles van Onselen, *Studies in the Social and Economic History of the Witwatersrand, 1886-1914*, vol. 1, *New Babylon* (Harlow, UK: Longman, 1982), 29-30. On Porter, see Sue M. Parnell, "Johannesburg Slums and Racial Segregation in South African Cities, 1910-1937" (PhD diss., University of Witwatersrand, 1993), 26-35.

51 Central Housing Board (CHB), *Report, 1920* (Pretoria: Government Printers, 1921), 4. Figures are from author's calculations based on CHB, *Report, 1936* (Pretoria: Government Printers, 1921), 17, 18.

52 Carnegie Commission, *Report of Investigation on the Poor White Question in South Africa* (Stellenbosch: Pro Ecclesia Printers, 1932).

53 Moodie, *Rise of Afrikanerdom*, 202-7; Ivan Evans, *Bureaucracy and Race: Native Administration in South Africa* (Berkeley: University of California Press, 1997), 66.

54 Moodie, *Rise of Afrikanerdom*, 202-7; Dan O'Meara, *Volkskapitalisme: Class, Capital, and Ideology in the Development of Afrikaner Nationalism, 1934-1948* (Cambridge: Cambridge University Press, 1983), 119-80; Sue M. Parnell, "Shaping a Racially Divided Society: State Housing Policy in South Africa, 1920-50," *Environment and Planning C: Government and Policy* 7 (1989): 261-72; Paul Hendler and Sue Parnell, "Land Finance under the New Housing Dispensation," *South African Review* 4 (1987): 423-31; Katie Mooney, "'*Die Eendsterte Eeuwel*' and Societal Responses to White Youth Subcultural Identities on the Witwatersrand, 1930-1964" (PhD diss., University of the Witwatersrand, 2006), 48-109. Under the 1937 plan, the CHB advanced up to a third of the loans issued under the program, thus granting a government guarantee on the remaining two-thirds or more loaned by the bank. CHB, *Report, 1938* (National Archives of South Africa [NASA], SAB GEM 53/182M) (Pretoria: Government Printers, 1939), 1-5; National Housing and Planning Commission, *National Housing: A Review of Policy and Progress* (Cape Town: Cape Times, 1947), 19, 21; "Housing Position of Railway Staff," NASA SAB SAS 997 P2/42; "Housing Conditions," SAB SAS 1916 R10-W104; "Sub-Economic Housing Schemes: South African Railways and Harbours," SAB VWN 745 SW108/6; "100% Housing Scheme for Public Servants," SAB TES 6886 F/56/150/26; "Report of Special Housing Committee," in *Minutes of the Johannesburg City Council* (CM), 1948, 431-36; 1950, 618-19, 771-72; also see CM, 1937, 1784.

55 Susan Parnell, "Public Housing as a Device for White Residential Segregation in Johannesburg, 1934-1953," *Urban Geography* 9 (1988): 584-602; Mooney, "'*Die Eendsterte Eeuwel*,'" 48-109; G. H. T Hart, "The Evolution of the Spacial Pattern of White Residential Development in Johannesburg" (PhD diss., University of the Witwatersrand, 1974), 237; Emmil J. Jammine, "Assisted Housing Development for Whites, Coloureds and Asiatics in the Main Areas of the Republic, with Particular Reference to the Role Played by Local Authorities" (PhD diss., University of Pretoria, 1968), 330-408.

56 Transvaal Asiatic Land Tenure Act Commission, *Report*, 99-101. On the council deputation to Hertzog (and his return visit to Johannesburg), see Johannesburg Municipality, *Mayor's Minute*, 1927-28, 83; 1928-29, 88.

57 Parnell, "Johannesburg Slums," 41–94; Keith Beavon, *Johannesburg: The Making and Shaping of the City* (Pretoria: University of South Africa Press, 2004), 106–17.

58 Johannesburg Municipality, *Mayor's Minute*, 1928–29, 89; 1929–30, 105–7; 1930–31, 99–100; 1931–32, 108–12; 1932–33, 125–27; 1933–34, 137–41; 1934–35, 147–52; 1935–36, 190–96; 1936–37, 243–56; 1937–38, 247–59, quotation on 256; 1938–39, 239–54; 1939–40, 193–211; 1947–48, 117; CM, 1936, 312, 328–32, 963; 1937, 65–66, 236–37, 738–41, 1153, 1252–54, 1574–75, 1951–55; 1938, 720, 788; 1939, 55–56, 236, 287, 309–11, 371–72, 424–25, 703, 943–44, 1037, 1388–90, 1606–9.

59 Parnell, "Johannesburg Slums," 206–27; Beavon, *Johannesburg*, 93–95, 109–17; Clive M. Chipkin, *Johannesburg Style: Architecture and Society, 1880s–1960s* (Cape Town: David Philip, 1993), 226–41.

60 Davenport and Saunders, *South Africa*, 324–33; quotation from the National Party's "Programme of Principles" of 1913, in Danielus W. Krüger, ed., *South African Parties and Policies, 1910–1960: A Select Source Book* (London: Bowes and Bowes, 1960), 71. On Hertzog and separate development, see Oswald Pirow, *James Barry Munnik Hertzog* (Cape Town: Howard Timmins, n.d.), 195–97. On Jewish immigration restriction, see Furlong, *Crown and Swastika*, 46–69.

61 Moodie, *Rise of Afrikanerdom*, 192–95, 208–10; Davenport and Saunders, *South Africa*, 340–43.

62 Population figures from Johannesburg Municipality, *Mayor's Minute*, 1947–48, 118; Commission of Enquiry into the Disturbances at Moroka, Johannesburg, on the 30th of August, 1947, *Report* (Pretoria; Government Printers, 1948), 10–14, 21–105; Philip Bonner and Lauren Segal, *Soweto: A History* (Cape Town: Maskew Miller Longman, 1998), 20–28; A. W. Stadtler, "Birds in the Cornfields: Squatter Movements in Johannesburg, 1944–1947," in *Labour, Townships, and Protest: Studies in the Social History of the Witwatersrand*, ed. Belinda Bozzoli (1979; repr., Johannesburg: Ravan Press, 2001), 19–48; Kevin French, "James Mpanza and the Sofasonke Party in the Development of Local Politics in Soweto" (master's thesis, University of the Witwatersrand, 1983).

63 Davenport and Saunders, *South Africa*, 353–64; Tom Lodge, *Mandela: A Critical Life* (Oxford: Oxford University Press, 2006), 38.

64 Department of Native Affairs, *Report of the Native Laws Commission* (Pretoria: Government Printers, 1948), 19, 27.

65 Moodie, *Rise of Afrikanerdom*, 259–93, quotation on 273; G. Cronjé, W. Nicol, and E. P. Groenewald, *Regverdige Rasse-Apartheid* (Stellenbosch: Christen- Studenteverenig-ingmaatskappy van Suid-Afrika, 1947); Deborah Posel, *The Making of Apartheid, 1948–1961: Conflict and Compromise* (Oxford: Clarendon, 1991), 23–60; quotations from Herenigde Nasionale Party (Reunited National Party), *Verslag van die Kleurvragstuk-Kommissie* [Sauer Report] (1947), 3, 11.

66 Alan Mabin, "Comprehensive Segregation: The Origins of the Group Areas Act and Its Planning Apparatuses," *Journal of Southern African Studies* 18 (1992): 410; Davenport and Saunders, *South Africa*, 369–74; Verwoerd quotation from Evans, *Bureaucracy and Race*, 59; H. Lever, *The South African Voter: Some Aspects of Voting Behaviour with Special Reference to the General Elections of 1966 and 1970* (Cape Town: Juta, 1972), 163.

67 Davenport and Saunders, *South Africa*, 377–79, 388–94.

68 Quotation from Union of South Africa, *Debates of the House of Assembly (Hansard)* (Cape Town: Unie-Volspers, Parliamentary Printers, 1950), col. 7452; Mabin, "Comprehensive Segregation," 420–23.

69 Union of South Africa, *Debates*, cols. 7442–46, 7450, 7453, 7484–85, 7501, 7512–14, 7556, 7600, 7602, 7631, 7663–65, 7669, 7678–84, 7709, 7757–58, 7771, 7779, 7790, 7797, 7809–22, 7827; Lever, *South African Voter*, 9, 24–28.

70  Evans, *Bureaucracy and Race*, 56-85.

71  Mabin, "Comprehensive Segregation," 426; Evans, *Bureaucracy and Race*, 125-30.

72  Evans, *Bureaucracy and Race*, 122-48; Bonner and Segal, *Soweto*, 28-31; Wilhelm J. P. Carr, *Soweto: Its Creation, Life and Decline* (Johannesburg: South African Institute of Race Relations, 1990), 127-28.

73  CM, 1937, 1251, 1353-56; Van Tonder, "Western Areas," 322-25.

74  Evans, *Bureaucracy and Race*, 152-58; Gordon H. Pirie and Deborah Hart, "The Transformation of Johannesburg's Black Western Areas," *Journal of Urban History* 11 (1985): 387-410; Carr, *Soweto*, 85-89.

75  Posel, *Making of Apartheid*, 61-149; Evans, *Bureaucracy and Race*, 86-118.

76  Evans, *Bureaucracy and Race*, 244-76.

## Chapter Twelve

1  Horace R. Cayton, "Fighting for White Folks?," *Nation*, September 26, 1942, 268.

2  Howard M. Wachtel, *The Money Mandarins: The Making of a Supranational Economic Order* (Armonk, NY: M. E. Sharpe, 1990), 21-88; Dean Baker, Gerald Epstein, and Robert Pollin, "Introduction," in *Globalization and Progressive Economic Policy*, ed. Dean Baker, Gerald Epstein, and Robert Pollin (Cambridge: Cambridge University Press, 1998), 1-34.

3  Edward W. Soja, *Postmetropolis: Critical Studies of Cities and Regions* (London: Blackwell, 2000), 233-322; Manuel Castells, *The Informational City: Information Technology, Economic Restructuring, and the Urban Regional Process* (Oxford: Blackwell, 1991), 7-32; Saskia Sassen, *The Global City: New York, Tokyo, London* (Princeton: Princeton University Press, 1991), 9-10, 245-320; Douglas S. Massey and Nancy A. Denton, *American Apartheid: Segregation and the Making of the Underclass* (Cambridge, MA: Harvard University Press, 1993), 115-47; Loïc Wacquant, *Deadly Symbiosis: Race and the Rise of the Penal State* (Cambridge: Polity Press, 2008); Mike Davis, *City of Quartz: Excavating the Future in Los Angeles* (London: Verso, 1990), 221-64; Anthony Richmond, *Global Apartheid: Refugees, Racism, and the New World Order* (Toronto: Oxford University Press, 1994).

4  Thomas J. Sugrue, *Sweet Land of Liberty: The Forgotten Struggle for Civil Rights in the North* (New York: Random House, 2008), xiii-xviii, 200-252

5  "Reveal Rigid Policy of Segregation at FHA," *New York Amsterdam News*, December 31, 1938.

6  Sugrue, *Sweet Land*, 200-252, 282-85.

7  Sugrue, *Sweet Land*, 414-22; Alan B. Anderson and George W. Pickering, *Confronting the Color Line: The Broken Promise of the Civil Rights Movement in Chicago* (Athens: University of Georgia Press, 1986); David J. Garrow, ed., *Chicago, 1966: Open Housing Marches, Summit Negotiations, and Operation Breadbasket* (Brooklyn: Carlson, 1989).

8  Sugrue, *Sweet Land*, 313-55; Hugh Davis Graham, *Civil Rights and the Presidency: Race and Gender in American Politics, 1960-1972* (New York: Oxford University Press, 1992), 127-31.

9  Sugrue, *Sweet Land*, 433-44; Alexander Polikoff, *Waiting for Gautreaux: A Story of Segregation, Housing, and the Black Ghetto* (Evanston: Northwestern University Press, 2006); William P. Wilen and Wendy Stasell, "*Gautreaux* and Chicago's Public Housing Crisis: The Conflict between Achieving Integration and Providing Decent Housing for Very Low-Income African Americans," in *Where Are the Poor People to Live? Transforming Public Housing Communities*, ed. Larry Bennett, Janet L. Smith, and Patricia A. Wright (Armonk, NY: M. E. Sharpe, 2006), 239-58; Mary Patillo, *Black on the Block: The Politics of Race and Class in the City* (Chicago:

University of Chicago Press, 2007), 181–257; Gregory D. Squires, ed., *From Redlining to Reinvestment: Community Responses to Urban Disinvestment* (Philadelphia: Temple University Press, 1992), 1–37; Alyssa Katz, *Our Lot: How Real Estate Came to Own Us* (New York: Bloomsbury, 2009), 1–26.

10  Folarin Shyllon, *Black People in Britain, 1555–1833* (London; Oxford University Press, 1977); Rozina Visram, *Asians in Britain; 400 Years of History* (London: Pluto, 2002); Ceri Peach, *West Indian Migration to Britain: A Social Geography* (London: Oxford University Press, 1968), 16–36, 83–92; Mike Philips and Trevor Philips, *Windrush: The Irresistible Rise of Multi-Racial Britain* (London: Harper Collins, 1999), 1–44; Rosemary Wakeman, *The Heroic City: Paris, 1945–58* (Chicago: University of Chicago Press, 2009), 145–61; Gérard Noirel, *The French Melting Pot: Immigration, Citizenship, and National Identity*, trans. Geoffroy de la Forcade (1988; repr., Minneapolis: University of Minnesota Press, 1996); Zeynep Çeylik, *Urban Forms and Colonial Confrontations: Algiers under French Rule* (Berkeley: University of California Press, 1997), 45, 81–82, 173–74.

11  Peach, *West Indian Migration*, 16–36, 83–92; Susan J. Smith, *The Politics of "Race" and Residence: Citizenship, Segregation and White Supremacy in Britain* (London: Polity Press, 1989), 49–104; Hervé Vieillard-Baron, *Les banlieues: Des singularités françaises aux réalités mondiales* (Paris: Hachette, 2001), 129–41.

12  Carl H. Nightingale, "A Tale of Three *Global* Ghettos: How Arnold Hirsch Helps Us Internationalize U.S. Urban History," *Journal of Urban History* 29 (March 2003): 257–71; Enzo Mingione, ed., *Urban Poverty and the Underclass: A Reader* (London: Blackwell, 1996); Sako Musterd and Wim Ostendorf, eds., *Urban Segregation and the Welfare State: Inequality and Exclusion in Western Cities* (London: Routledge, 1998); Ronald van Kempen and A. Şule Özüekren, "Ethnic Segregation in Cities: New Forms and Explanations in a Dynamic World," *Urban Studies* 35 (1998): 1631–56; Sako Musterd, "Social and Ethnic Segregation in Europe: Levels, Causes, and Effects," *Journal of Urban Affairs* 27 (2005): 331–48; Ron Johnston, James Forrest, and Michael Poulsen, "Are There Ethnic Enclaves/Ghettos in English Cities?" *Urban Studies* 39 (2002): 591–618; Ceri Peach, "Slippery Segregation: Discovering or Manufacturing Ghettos?," *Journal of Ethnic and Migration Studies* 35 (2009): 1381–95; Hervé Vieillard-Baron, *Les banlieues françaises: Ou le ghetto impossible* (Paris: Edition de l'Aube, 1994); Vieillard-Baron, *Les banlieues*, 129–41; Loïc J. D. Wacquant, "Pour en finir avec le mythe des 'cités-ghettos,'" *Les annales de la recherche urbaine* 52 (1992): 20–30; Loïc Wacquant, "Urban Outcasts: Stigma and Division in the Black American Ghetto and the French Periphery," *International Journal of Urban and Regional Research* 17 (1993): 366–83; Margaret Weir, "Race and Urban Poverty: Comparing Europe and America," *Brookings Review* 11 (1993): 22–27; Eric Fong, "Residential Segregation of Visible Minority Groups in Toronto," in *Inside the Mosaic*, ed. Eric Fong (Toronto: University of Toronto Press, 2006), 51–75; Wendy S. Shaw, *Cities of Whiteness* (Malden, MA: Carlton, 2007).

13  Todd Shepard, *The Invention of Decolonization: The Algerian War and the Remaking of France* (Ithaca: Cornell University Press, 2006), 229–42.

14  See articles collected in Musterd and Ostendorf, *Urban Segregation and the Welfare State*; and Mingione, *Urban Poverty and the Underclass*; Vieillard-Baron, *Les banlieues*, 129–41; Ceri Peach, "Good Segregation, Bad Segregation," *Planning Perspectives* 11 (1996): 379–98; Patrick Simon, "The Mosaic Pattern: Cohabitation between Ethnic Groups in Belleville, Paris," in *Minorities in European Cities: The Dynamics of Social Integration and Social Exclusion at the Neighborhood Level*, ed. Sophie Body-Gendrot and Marco Martiniello (Houndmills, UK: MacMillan, 2000), 100–118; Marco Martiniello, "The Residential Concentration and Political Participation of Immigrants in European Cities," in Body-Gendrot and Martiniello, *Dynamics of Social*

*Exclusion*, 119-28; Eric Fong, "Residential Segregation in Toronto," in Fong, *Inside the Mosaic*, 51-75; Feng Hou, "Spatial Assimilation of Racial Minorities in Canada's Immigrant Gateway Cities," *Urban Studies* 43 (2006): 1191-213; Christiane Droste, Christine Lelévrier, and Frank Wassenberg, "Urban Regeneration in European Social Housing Areas," in *Social Housing in Europe*, ed. London School of Economics and Political Science (LSEPS) (London: LSEPS, 2008), 163-96; Marie-Hélène Bacqué, Yankel Fijalkow, Lydie Launay, and Stéphanie Vermeersch, "Social Mix Policies in Paris: Discourses, Policies, and Social Effects," *International Journal of Urban and Regional Research* 35 (2011): 256-73; Vieillard-Baron, *Les banlieues*, 173-91; Rob Atkinson, "EU Urban Policy, European Urban Policies, and the Neighbourhood: An Overview of Concepts, Programmes, and Strategies" (paper presented at The Vital City EURA conference, Glasgow, 2007, available at http//www.eukn.org/dsresource?objectid=202129).

15 Richard Harris, *Creeping Conformity: How Canada Became Suburban* (Toronto: University of Toronto Press, 2004), 76-83, 133-36; Harris and Doris Forrester, "The Suburban Origins of Redlining: A Canadian Case Study, 1935-54," *Urban Studies* 40 (2003): 2661-86; *Essex Real Estate Co. Ltd. v. Holmes*, Ontario Supreme Court O. J. 296 37 O.W.N. 392 (1930); *McDougall v. Waddell*, Ontario Supreme Court O. J. no 82 (1945); *Bryers and Morris* (1931), O. J. No. 229 40 O. W. N. 572 (1931); *Noble v. Alley*, Supreme Court of Canada S. C. J. no. 34 (1950); Smith, *Politics of "Race,"* 49-104, 146-96; Jeff Henderson and Valerie Karn, *Race, Class and State Housing: Inequality and the Allocation of Public Housing in Britain* (Aldershot, UK: Gower, 1987), 97-184; M. L. Harrison, *Housing, "Race," Social Policy and Empowerment* (Aldershot, UK: Avebury, 1995), 33-81; Richard Skellington and Paulette Morris, *"Race" in Britain Today*, 2nd ed. (London: Sage, 1996), 135-50; Wakeman, *Heroic City*, 42-48, 145-61; Christian Bachman and Nicole Leguennec, *Violences urbaines: Ascension et chute des class moyennes à travers cinquante ans de politique de la ville* (Paris: Albin Michel, 1996), 17-218; Neil MacMaster, "The 'Seuil de Tolérance': The Uses of a 'Scientific' Racist Concept," in *Race, Discourse, and Power in France*, ed. Maxim Silverman (Aldershot, UK; Avebury, 1991), 14-28; Åsa Bråmå, "'White Flight? The Production and Reproduction of Immigrant Concentrations Areas in Swedish Cities, 1990-2000," *Urban Studies* 43 (2006): 1127-46; William Magee, Eric Fong, and Rima Wilkes, "Neighbourhood Ethnic Concentration and Discrimination," *Journal of Social Policy* 37 (2007): 37-61; Peter S. Li, *The Chinese in Canada* (Toronto: Oxford University Press, 1998), 141-56. On white protest against the public housing quotas of the anti-ghetto laws in France, see "Logement social: 44% des communes d'Île-de-France hors la loi," *Libération*, June 26, 2008; Dominique Durand, "Voici, dans l'ordre, le Top 15 des villes 'cancres'" (unpublished manuscript); Husbands, *Racial Exclusionism*, 23-96, 140-48.

16 Nightingale, "A Tale of Three *Global* Ghettos," 265-68. The argument that follows was developed independently from, but resembles that of, William W. Goldsmith in "The Metropolis and Globalization: The Dialectics of Racial Discrimination, Deregulation, and Reform," *American Behavioral Scientist* 41 (1997): 299-310. Thomas J. Sugrue, *The Origins of the Urban Crisis: Race and Inequality in Postwar Detroit* (Princeton: Princeton University Press, 1996), 209-30; Sugrue, *Sweet Land*, 237-43, quotation on 238; Lisa McGirr, *Suburban Warriors: The Origins of the New American Right* (Princeton: Princeton University Press, 2001), 147-86; Becky M. Nicolaides, *My Blue Heaven: Life and Politics in the Working-Class Suburbs of Los Angeles, 1920-1965* (Chicago: University of Chicago Press, 2002), 120-82; Robert O. Self, *American Babylon: Race and the Struggle for Postwar Oakland* (Princeton: Princeton University Press, 2003), 256-90; Matthew Lassiter, *The Silent Majority: Suburban Politics in the Sunbelt South* (Princeton: Princeton University Press, 2006), 1-20, 69-93,

148–74; Kevin Kruse, *White Flight: Atlanta and the Making of Modern Conservatism*, 3–18, 78–104, 161–79 (Princeton: Princeton University Press, 2007).

17  Amy Elizabeth Ansell, *New Right, New Racism: Race and Reaction in the United States and Britain* (New York: New York University Press, 1997), 49–273; Smith, *Politics of "Race" and Residence*, 105–45; Christopher T. Husbands, *Racial Exclusionism and the City: The Urban Support of the National Front* (London: Allen and Unwin, 1983); Véronique de Rudder, Christian Poiret, and François Vourc'h, *L'inégalité raciste: L'universalité républicain à l'épreuve* (Paris: Presses Universitaires de France, 2000); Brooke Jeffrey, *Hard Right Turn: The New Face of Neo-Conservatism in Canada* (Toronto: Harper Collins, 1999); Ghassan Hage, *White Nation: Fantasies of White Supremacy in a Multicultural Society* (London: Routledge, 2000), 27–47.

18  Michelle Alexander, *The New Jim Crow: Mass Incarceration in the Age of Colorblindness* (New York: New Press, 2010); Ruth Wilson Gilmore, *Golden Gulag: Prisons, Surplus, Crisis, and Opposition in Globalizing California* (Berkeley: University of California Press, 2007); Wacquant, *Deadly Symbiosis*; Ken Pease, "Cross-National Imprisonment Rates—Limitations of Method and Possible Conclusions," in *Prisons in Context*, ed. Roy D. King and Mike Maguire (Oxford: Oxford University Press, 1994), 116–30; Douglas C. MacDonald, "Public Imprisonment by Private Means: The Re-Emergence of Private Prisons in the United States, the United Kingdom, and Australia," in King and Maguire, *Prisons in Context*, 29–48; Paul Chevigny, *Edge of the Knife: Police Violence in the Americas* (New York: New Press, 1995); John Solomos, *Black Youth, Racism, and the State: The Politics of Ideology and Policy* (New York: Cambridge University Press, 1988), 173–243; Michael Keith, *Race, Riots and Policing: Lore and Disorder in a Multi-Racist Society* (London: University College London Press, 1993); Didier Lapeyronnie, "Primitive Rebellion in the French *Banlieues*: On the Fall 2005 Riots," in *Frenchness and the African Diaspora*, ed. Charles Tshimanga, Ch. Didier Gondola, and Peter J. Bloom (Bloomington: Indiana University Press, 2009), 21–46; Achille Mbemba, "The Republic and Its Beast: On the Riots in the French *Banlieues*," in Tshimanga, Gondola, and Bloom, *Frenchness and the African Diaspora*, 47–54.

19  Richmond, *Global Apartheid*; Joseph Nevins, *Operation Gatekeeper: The Rise of the "Illegal Alien" and the Making of the U.S.-Mexico Boundary* (New York: Routledge, 2002); Anthony Messina, *The Logics and Politics of Post-World War II Migration to Europe* (New York: Cambridge University Press, 2001); Andrew Geddes, *Immigration and European Integration: Towards Fortress Europe?* (Manchester: Manchester University Press, 2000); Martin A Schain, "The Politics of Immigration in France, Britain, and the United States: A Transatlantic Comparison," in *Immigration and the Transformation of Europe*, ed. Craig A. Parsons and Timothy Smeeding (Cambridge: Cambridge University Press, 2006), 362–92; Ruth Balint, *Troubled Waters: Borders, Boundaries, and Possession in the Timor Sea* (Crow's Nest, N.S.W.: Allen and Unwin, 2005), 125–49.

20  Robert Mark Silverman and Kelly L. Patterson, "The Four Horsemen of the Apocalypse: A Critique of Fair Housing Policy in the USA," *Critical Sociology* 38 (2011): 1–18; National Commission on Fair Housing and Equal Opportunity (NCFHEO), *Report: The Future of Fair Housing* (Washington DC: NCFHEO, 2008), 13; Camille Zubrinsky Charles, "The Dynamics of Racial Residential Segregation," *Annual Review of Sociology* 29 (2003): 167–207; John Iceland, Daniel H. Weinberg, and Erika Steinmetz, "Racial and Ethnic Residential Segregation in the United States, 1980-2000," US Census Bureau, Special Report Series, CENSR-3, available at http://www.census.gov/hhes/www/housing/housing_patterns/pdf/censr-3.pdf; Rima Wilkes and John Iceland, "Hypersegregation in the Twenty-First Century: An Update and Analysis," *Demography* 41 (2004): 23–36.

21  Edward J. Blakeley and Mary Gail Snyder, *Fortress America: Gated Communities in*

*the United States* (Washington DC: Brookings Institution, 1997); Setha Low, "How Private Interests Take Over Public Space: Zoning, Taxes, and Incorporation of Gated Communities," in *The Politics of Urban Space*, ed. Setha Low and Neil Smith (New York: Routledge, 2006), 81–104; Rowland Atkinson and Sarah Blandy, eds., *Gated Communities: International Perspectives* (London: Routledge, 2006); Same Bagaen and Ola Uduku, *Gated Communities: Social Sustainability in Contemporary and Historical Gated Developments* (London: Earthscan, 2010).

22  Neil Smith, *The New Urban Frontier: Gentrification and the Revanchist City* (London: Routledge, 1996); Chris Mele, *Selling the Lower East Side* (Minneapolis: University of Minnesota Press, 2000); Janet L. Smith, "The Chicago Housing Authority's Plan for Transformation," in Bennett, Smith, and Wright, *Where Are the Poor People to Live?*, 93–124; Patricia A. Wright, "The Case of Cabrini Green," in Bennett, Smith, and Wright, *Where Are the Poor People to Live?*, 168–84; Larry Benent, *The Third City: Chicago and American Urbanism* (Chicago: University of Chicago Press, 2010), 159–79: Chris Hamnet, *Unequal City*, 159–87; Jerry Mitchell, *Business Improvement Districts and the Shape of American Cities* (Albany: SUNY Press, 2008); American Civil Liberties Union (ACLU), *Bigger Monster, Weaker Chains: The Growth of an American Surveillance Society* (New York: ACLU, 2003).

23  Wachtel, *Money Mandarins*, 89–203; Susan Strange, *Mad Money: When Markets Outgrow Governments* (Ann Arbor: University of Michigan Press, 1998); Saskia Sassen, "On Concentration and Centrality in the Global City," in *World Cities in a World-System*, ed. Paul L. Knox and Peter J. Taylor (Cambridge: Cambridge University Press, 1995), 63–75; Smith, *New Urban Frontier*, 210–32.

24  William Apgar and Allegra Calder, "The Dual Mortgage Market: The Persistence of Discrimination in Mortgage Lending," in *The Geography of Opportunity*, ed. Xavier de Souza Briggs (Washington DC: Brookings Institution, 2005), 101–26.

25  Jill Quadagno, *The Color of Welfare: How Racism Undermined the War on Poverty* (New York: Oxford University Press, 1994), 89–116.

26  Katz, *Our Lot*, 54–156; Simon Johnson and James Kwak, *13 Bankers: The Wall Street Takeover and the Next Financial Meltdown* (New York: Pantheon, 2010), 120–53.

27  Jacob S. Rugh and Douglas S. Massey, "Racial Segregation and the American Foreclosure Crisis," *American Sociological Review* 75 (2010): 629–51. Thomas M. Shapiro, Tatjana Meschede, and Laura Sullivan, "The Racial Wealth Gap Increases Fourfold," Policy Brief, Institute on Assets and Social Policy, Brandeis University, May 2010, iasp.brandeis.edu/pdfs/racial-wealth-gap-brief.pdf.

28  Margit Tünnemann, "European Cities Responding to the Crisis: A European Perspective" (presentation at URBANPROMO 2009, Venice, November 5, 2009, available at http://www.eib.org/attachments/general/events/margit-tunnemann .pdf).

29  Jon Calame and Esther Charlesworth, *Divided Cities: Belfast, Beirut, Jerusalem, Mostar, and Nicosia* (Philadelphia: University of Pennsylvania Press, 2009), 37–60, 121–43.

30  Janet Abu-Lughod, *Rabat: Urban Apartheid in Morocco* (Princeton: Princeton University Press, 1980), 239–40; Çeylik, *Urban Forms*, 181–95; Lawrence W. C. Lai and Marco K. W. Yu, "The Rise and Fall of Discriminatory Zoning in Hong Kong," *Environment and Planning B: Planning and Design* 28 (2001): 295–314.

31  Garth A. Myers, "Colonial and Postcolonial Modernities in Two African Cities," *Canadian Journal of African Studies/Revue Canadienne des Études Africaines* 37 (2003): 344–57; quotation in William Dalrymple, "The Rubble of the Raj," *Guardian*, November 13, 2004; Jeremy Kahn, "Amnesty Plan for Relics of the Raj," *New York Times*, December 30, 2007.

32  D. P. Chatterjea, "Bidhan Nagar: From Marshland to Modern City," in *Calcutta: The*

*Living City*, ed. Sukanta Chaudhuri (New Delhi: Oxford University Press, 1990), 176-80; Jyoti Hosagrahar, "Heritage, History, and Modernity in Contemporary Indian Urbanism," paper presented at the fourteenth National Conference on Planning History, Baltimore, November 18, 2011; Timothy Mitchell, "Dreamland: The Neoliberalism of Your Desires," *Middle East Report* 210 (Spring 1999), available at http://www.merip.org/mer/mer210/mitchell.html; James Holstun, *Insurgent Citizenship: Disjunctions of Democracy and Modernity in Brazil* (Princeton: Princeton University Press, 2008), 146-202; Theresa P. R Caldeira, *City of Walls: Crime, Segregation, and Citizenship in São Paulo* (Berkeley: University of California Press, 2000), 256-96, quotation on 266; William Langewiesche, "The Mega-Bunker of Baghdad," *Vanity Fair*, November 2007, at http://www.vanityfair.com/politics/features/2007/11/langewiesche200711; Mark L. Gillen, *American Town: Building the Outposts of Empire* (Minneapolis: University of Minnesota Press, 2007).

33  See chapters 3 and 7; Bruce Fetter, *The Creation of Elisabethville, 1910-1940* (Stanford: Hoover Institution Press, 1976), and "L'Union Minière du Haut-Katanga, 1920-1940: La naissance d'une sous-culture totalitaire," *Les cahiers du CEDAF*, vol. 6 (1973); Whyms, *Léopoldville: Son Histoire, 1881-1956,* (Brussels: Office de Publicité, 1956), 21-38; Bernard Toulier, Johan Lagae, Marc Gemoets, *Kinshasa: Architecture et paysage urbains* (Paris: Somogy, 2010), 75-106; Çeylik, *Urban Forms*, 113-81.

34  Mike Davis, *Planet of Slums* (London: Verso, 2006), 70-94.

35  United Nations Human Settlements Programme (UN-HABITAT), *The Challenge of Slums: Global Report on Human Settlements, 2003* (London; Earthscan, 2003), 164-94.

36  William Roger Louis and Ronald Robinson, "The Imperialism of Decolonisation," *Decolonization Reader*, ed. James D. Le Sueur (New York: Routledge, 2003), 49-79; Frederick Cooper, "Conflict and Connection: Rethinking Colonial African History," in Le Sueur, *Decolonization Reader*, 23-45; Frederick Cooper, *Decolonization and African Society: The Labor Question in French and British Africa* (Cambridge: Cambridge University Press, 1996), 386-473.

37  Ananya Roy, "The Gentleman's City: Urban Informality in the Calcutta of New Communism," in *Urban Informality: Transnational Perspectives from the Middle East, Latin American, and South Asia*, ed. Ananya Roy and Nezar AlSayyad (Lanham, MD: Lexington Books, 2004), 147-70; Janice E. Perlman, *The Myth of Marginality: Urban Poverty and Politics in Rio De Janeiro* (Berkeley: University of California Press, 1976), 195-241; Brodwyn Fischer, *A Poverty of Rights: Citizenship and Inequality in Twentieth-Century Rio de Janeiro* (Stanford: Stanford University Press, 2008), 50-89, 213-301; René Colignon, "La lutte des pouvoirs publics contre les 'encombrements humains' à Dakar," *Canadian Journal of African Studies* 18 (1984): 573-82.

38  Perlman, *Myth of Marginality*, 228-29; Rodney R. White, "The Impact of Policy Conflict on the Implementation of a Government-Assisted Housing Project in Senegal," *Canadian Journal of African Studies* 19 (1985): 505, 512; Davis, *Planet of Slums*, 100.

39  Wachtel, *Money Mandarins*, 106-32; UN-HABITAT, *Challenge of Slums*, 34-55; David Harvey, *A Brief History of Neoliberalism* (Oxford: Oxford University Press, 2005), 87-119.

40  UN-HABITAT, *Challenge of Slums*, 45-46; Davis, *Planet of Slums*, 1-19.

41  Davis, *Planet of Slums*, 70-120, figs. on 102; Dorothy J. Solinger, *Contesting Citzenship in Urban China: Peasant Migrants, the State, and the Logic of the Market* (Berkeley: University of California Press, 1999); You-tien Hsing, *The Great Urban Transformation: Politics of Land and Property in China* (Oxford: Oxford University Press, 2010), 1-59; Yan Zhang and Ke Fang, "Is History Repeating Itself? From Urban Renewal in the United States to Inner-City Redevelopment in China," *Journal of Planning Education and Research* (2004): 286-98.

42  John Walton and David Seddon, *Free Markets and Food Riots: The Politics of Structural Adjustment* (Oxford: Blackwell, 1994), 39–45; Hsing, *Great Transformation*, 60–92; UN-HABITAT, *Challenge of Slums*, 151.

43  Shepard, *Invention of Decolonization*, 207–28; Meredith Martin, *The Past Is Another Country: Rhodesia, 1890–1979* (London: Deutsch, 1979); UN Special Envoy on Human Settlement Issues in Zimbabwe, *Report of the Fact-Finding Mission to Zimbabwe to Assess the Scope and Impact of Operation Murambatsvina* (July 18, 2005), at http://ww2.unhabitat.org/documents/ZimbabweReport.pdf; Chris McGreal, "A Lost World," *Guardian*, October 25, 2006.

44  Thomas Bartlett, *Ireland: A History* (Cambridge: Cambridge University Press, 2010), 497–506, 510–27, 554–79; David McKittrick and David Shea, *Making Sense of the Troubles* (Belfast: Blackstaff Press, 2000); Calame and Charlesworth, *Divided Cities*, 61–82; Henry McDonald, "Belfast's Peace Walls Treble after Cease Fires," *Guardian*, July 28, 2009.

45  Tony Kushner and Alisa Solomon, eds., *Wrestling with Zion: Progressive Jewish-American Responses to the Israeli-Palestinian Conflict* (New York: Grove Press, 2003), 13–40; Thomas A. Kolsky, *Jews Against Zionism: The American Council for Judaism, 1942–1948* (Philadelphia: Temple University Press, 1990); Shlomo Sand, *The Invention of the Jewish People*, trans. Yael Lotan (London: Verso, 2009).

46  Stein, *The Balfour Declaration* (London: Valentine, Mitchell, 1961), 23–33, 148–49, 164–65; Walid Khalidi, ed., *From Haven to Conquest: Readings in Zionism and the Palestinian Problem until 1948* (Washington DC: Institute of Palestinian Studies, 1967), xxix–xxxiv, 97–114, 125–42, 165–88, quotation from Zionist leader Theodor Herzl on xxx; Jonathan Schneer, *The Balfour Declaration: The Origins of the Arab-Israeli Conflict* (New York: Random House, 2010).

47  Khalidi, *Haven to Conquest*, 227–36, 255–72, 303–9; Helen Meller, *Patrick Geddes: Social Evolutionist and City Planner* (London: Routledge, 1990), 263–81.

48  Khalidi, *Haven to Conquest*, 227–645; Benny Morris, *The Birth of the Palestinian Refugee Problem Revisited* (Cambridge: Cambridge University Press, 2004), 9–64.

49  Benny Morris, *1948: A History of The First Arab-Israeli War* (New Haven: Yale University Press, 2008), 1–74; Ilan Pappe, *The Ethnic Cleansing of Palestine* (Oxford: Oneworld, 2006), 10–38.

50  On the Nakba and the debate among "new historians" about whether Plan Dalet represented a defensive strategy or an open call to ethnic cleansing, see Morris, *Palestinian Problem Revisited*, x–xx, 65–602; Pappe, *Ethnic Cleansing*, 23–28, 39–224; Salim Tamari, "The Phantom City," in *Jerusalem 1948: The Arab Neighborhoods and their Fate in the War*, ed. Salim Tamari (Jerusalem: Institute of Jerusalem Studies, 1999), 1–9; Nathan Krystall, "The Fall of the New City," in Tamari, *Jerusalem 1948*, 92–153; Khalidi, *Haven to Conquest*, 375–88, 595–600, 850–52; Karen Armstrong, *Jerusalem: One City, Three Faiths* (New York: Ballantine Books, 2005), 398–430.

51  Armstrong, *Jerusalem*, 398–406; Joe Beinin, "The United-States Israel Alliance," in Kushner and Solomon, *Wrestling with Zion*, 41–50.

52  Armstrong, *Jerusalem*, 409–21.

53  Beinin, "U.S.-Israel Alliance"; George W. Ball, *The Passionate Attachment: America's Involvement with Israel, 1947–Present* (New York: Norton, 1992), 19–66, 178–297; Saree Makdisi, *Palestine Inside Out: An Everyday Occupation* (New York: Norton, 2008), 299–318.

54  Makdisi, *Palestine Inside Out*; Eyal Weizman, *Hollow Land: Israel's Architecture of Occupation* (London: Verso, 2007).

55  Armstrong, *Jerusalem*, 421, 429–30; Joseph Dana and Noam Sheizaf, "The New Israeli Left," *Nation*, March 28, 2011; Julia Bacha, *Budrus* (New Vision Films, 2011).

56  T. R. H. Davenport and Christopher Saunders, *South Africa: A Modern History*

479

(London: Macmillan, 2000), 406-25, 449-54, 466-71; Thomas J. Borstelmann, *Apartheid's Reluctant Uncle* (New York: Oxford University Press, 1993), 108-204; Philip Bonner and Lauren Segal, *Soweto: A History* (Cape Town: Maskew, Miller, Longman, 1998), 78-82; Surendra Bhana, "The Tolstoy Farm: Gandhi's Experiment in Cooperative Commonwealth," *South African Historical Journal* 7 (1975): 88-100, quotation on 92.

57   Bonner and Segal, *Soweto*, 82-111, quotation on 111.

58   Ibid., 110-46.

59   Ibid., 128-31, 147-59, quotation on 131; Patrick Heller, "Reclaiming Democratic Spaces: Civics and Politics in Post-Transition Johannesburg," in *Emerging Johannesburg: Perspectives on the Postapartheid City*, ed. Richard Tomlinson, Robert A. Beauregard, Lindsay Bremner, and Xolela Mangcu (New York: Routledge, 2003), 155-84.

# Epilogue

1   Frantz Fanon, *The Wretched of the Earth*, trans. Constance Farrington (1961; repr., New York: Grover Weidenfield, 1963), 37-38.

2   Published work on these subjects is enormous and suggests just how extensive such antisegregationist thinking has become. A few iconic examples include: Michael Omi and Howard Winant, *Racial Formation in the United States: From the 1960s to the 1980s* (New York Routledge & Kegan Paul, 1986); David T. Wellman, *Portraits of White Racism*, 2nd ed. (Cambridge: Cambridge University Press, 1993); David R. Roediger, ed., *Black on White: Black Writers on What It Means to Be White* (New York: Schocken Books, 1998); Elizabeth Ansley, *New Right, New Racism: Race and Reaction in the United States and Britain* (New York: New York University Press, 1997); UN-HABITAT, *State of the World's Cities 2008/2009: Harmonious Cities* (London: Earthscan, 2008), 122-237; UN-HABITAT, "World Urban Forum 5," available at http://www.unhabitat.org/categories.asp?catid=584; Susan S. Fainstein, *The Just City* (Ithaca: Cornell University Press, 2010); Don Mitchell, *The Right to the City: Social Justice and the Fight for Public Space* (New York: Guilford Press, 2003); Lisa Benton-Short and John Rennie Short, *Cities and Nature* (London: Routledge, 2008), 211-57.

3   Observatoire National des Zones Urbaines Sensibles (ONZUS), *Rapport* (2009): 122-42; Ministère de l'Écologie, de l'Énergie, du Développement Durable et de la Mer (MEEDDM), "Benoist apparu presente: Politique du logement social: une nouvelle ambition" (Paris: MEEDDM, Dossier de Presse, February 3, 2010); Marie-Hélène Bacqué, Yankel Fijalkow, Lydie Launay, and Stéphanie Vermeersch, "Social Mix Policies in Paris: Discourses, Policies, and Social Effects," *International Journal of Urban and Regional Research* 35 (2011): 256-73; Christine Lelévrier, "City Policy in France: Social Mix as a Public Answer to Segregation?," *Urban Planning International* 4 (2009): 28-34; Christine Lelévrier, "Les politiques de lutte contre ségrégation: mixité des quartiers ou intégration des populations?," in *Les mécanismes fonciers de la ségrégation, actes du colloque de l'ADEF*, ed. Apprentissages, Didactiques, Évaluation, Formation (ADEF) (Paris: ADEF, 2004), 209-30; Christine Lelévrier, "La mixité dans la rénovation urbaine: dispersion ou re-concentration?," *Espaces et Sociétés* 140-41 (2010): 59-74; Jacques Donzelot et Catherine Mével, "La politique de la ville: Une comparaison entre les USA et la France: Mixité sociale et développement communautaire," *2001 Plus* 56 (2001): 50-51; Jacques Donzelot, "Repenser la politique de la ville," *Le Monde*, February 9, 2010; Johanna Laguerre, "Entre défense des locataires et respect des propriétaires, il faut trouver un juste milieu, a défendu Benoist Apparu," *Le Monde*, October 4, 2010; Ministère de la

Ville, "Le Sénat adopte un budget de politique de la ville au service de la cohésion sociale," available at http://www.ville.gouv.fr/?Le-Senat-adopte-un-budget-de.

4 Christiane Droste, Christine Lelévrier, and Frank Wassenberg, "Urban Regeneration in European Social Housing Areas," in *Social Housing in Europe*, ed. London School of Economics and Political Science (LSEPS) (London: LSEPS, 2008), 163–96; Chris Hamnet, *Unequal City: London in the Global Arena* (London: Routledge, 2003), 121–58; Terence Bendixso, "Push-Pull Forces in the Spatial Organization of Greater London and South-East England," in *Urban Sprawl in Western Europe and the United States*, ed. Harry W. Richardson and Chang-Hee Christine Bae (Aldershot, UK: Ashgate, 2004), 61; Denise Pumain, "Urban Sprawl: Is There a French Case?," in Richardson and Bae, *Urban Sprawl*, 137–58; Angela Hull, *Transport Matters: Integrated Approaches to Planning City-Regions* (London: Routledge, 2010).

5 This line of critique has been most extensively elaborated in France. See Jacques Donzelot, "Repenser la politique de la ville," *Le Monde*, February 9, 2010; Hervé Vieillard-Baron, *Les banlieues: Des singularités françaises aux réalités mondiales* (Paris: Hachette, 2001), 190; Sophie Body-Gendrot and Catherine Wihtol de Wenden, *Sortir des banlieues: Pour en finir avec la tyrannie des territoires* (Paris: Autrement Frontières, 2007), 48–90.

6 Jacques Donzelot and Catherine Mével, "La politique de la ville: Une comparaison entre les USA et la France: Mixité sociale et développement communitaire," *2001 Plus* 56 (2001): 1–51. A good grassroots analysis of US urban policy can be found in Sam Magavern and Partnership for the Public Good (PPG), "Missing the Target: How Economic Development Programs Have Failed to Revive Buffalo's Most Challenged Neighborhoods" (Buffalo: PPG, 2009).

7 Ronald F. Ferguson and William T. Dickens, eds., *Urban Problems and Community Development* (Washington: Brookings Institution, 1999); Peter Medoff, *Streets of Hope: The Fall and Rise of an Urban Neighborhood* (Boston: South End Press, 1994); Katherine Gray, "Land Banks Gain Popularity as a Way to Fight Urban Blight," *USA Today*, July 9, 2009; People United for Sustainable Housing (PUSH Buffalo) and Green for All, "Building a Sustainable City: Green Jobs for Buffalo" (unpublished manuscript, July 2010).

8 For the work of sociologists and planners wrestling with the question of desegregation, see Emily Talen, *Designing for Diversity: Exploring Socially Mixed Neighborhoods* (Oxford: Architectural Press, 2008); and the following collections of essays: David P. Varady, ed., *Desegregating the City: Ghettos, Enclaves, and Inequality* (Albany: SUNY Press, 2005); Xavier de Souza Briggs, *The Geography of Opportunity: Race and Housing Choice in Metropolitan America* (Washington DC: Brookings Institution, 2005); M. Paloma Pavel, ed., *Breakthrough Communities: Sustainability and Justice in the Next American Metropolis* (Cambridge, MA: MIT Press, 2009). On New Urbanism, see Emily Talen, *New Urbanism and American Planning: The Conflict of Cultures* (New York: Routledge, 2005). On Obama's transport policy, see Alyssa Katz, "The Reverse Commute," *American Prospect* (July/August 2010): 17–20. On integrating transport more broadly, see Moshe Givoni and David Bannister, eds., *Integrated Transport: From Policy to Practice* (New York: Routledge, 2010).

9 John Iceland and Kyle Anne Nelson, "Hispanic Segregation in Metropolitan America: Exploring the Multiple Forms of Spatial Assimilation," *American Sociological Review* 78 (2008): 741–65; John Iceland, "Beyond Black and White: Residential Segregation in Multiethnic America," *Social Science Research* 33 (2004): 248–71; Daniel Altschuler, "Immigrant Activists Regroup," *Nation*, December 20, 2010, 14–18.

10 UN-HABITAT, *The Challenge of Slums: Global Report on Human Settlements 2003* (London: Earthscan, 2003); a list of the many researchers and officials who contributed to the report can be found in the acknowledgements section, viii–xvii; UN-

HABITAT, *The Right to the City: Bridging the Urban Divide. Report of the Fifth Session of the World Urban Forum* (Rio de Janeiro, March 22–26, 2010, available at http://www .unhabitat.org/categories.asp?catid=584), quotations on 18, 20.

11  Jockin Arputham, "Developing New Approaches for People-Centred Development," *Environment and Urbanization* (2008): 319–37, available at http://www.sdinet .org/; quotation transcribed by author from "Rose Molokoane—Winner of Outstanding Achievement Award," http://www.youtube.com/watch?v=BA3KNnNX414.

12  Patrick Bond, *Elite Transition: From Apartheid to Neoliberalism in South Africa* (London: Pluto Press, 2000), 89–154; Jo Beall, Owen Crankshaw, and Susan Parnell, *Uniting a Divided City: Governance and Social Exclusion in Johannesburg* (London; Earthscan, 2002), 65–109; Richard Tomlinson, Robert A. Beauregard, Lindsay Bremner, Xolela Mangcu, "The Postapartheid Struggle for an Integrated Johannesburg," in *Emerging Johannesburg: Perspectives on the Postapartheid City*, ed. Richard Tomlinson, Robert A. Beauregard, Lindsay Bremner, Xolela Mangcu (New York: Routledge, 2003), 3–20; Patrick Heller, "Reclaiming Democratic Spaces: Civics and Politics in Posttransition Johannesburg," in Tomlinson, Beauregard, Bremner, and Mangcu, *Emerging Johannesburg*, 155–84; Bond, "Johannesburg's Resurgent Social Movements," in *Challenging Hegemony: Social Movements and the Quest for a New Humanism in Post-Apartheid South Africa*, ed. Nigel Gibson (Trenton, NJ: Africa World Press, 2006), 114–28; Bond, "Globalisation/Commodification or Deglobalisation/ Decommodification in Urban South Africa," *Policy Studies* 26 (2005): 337–58, quotation on 345.

13  Shack/Slum Dwellers International (SDI) website, http://www.sdinet.org/. For the complexities of grassroots claims to urban citizenship, see James Holstun, *Insurgent Citizenship: Disjunctions of Democracy and Modernity in Brazil* (Princeton: Princeton University Press, 2008), 271–314.

14  Quotation transcribed by author from "Rose Molokoane—Winner of Outstanding Achievement Award," http://www.youtube.com/watch?v=BA3KNnNX414.

# Index

as welfare state, 362–63; white racial zones, 254; in World War II, 367–68. *See also* apartheid; *and names of cities*
South African Institute for Racial Relations, 369
South African Native Affairs Commission, 244–45, 247, 248, 277–78; rural native locations proposal, 248–49
South African Native National Congress, 235. *See also* African National Congress
South African Party, 261
South African Republic. *See* ZAR (Zuid Afrikaansche Republiek)
South Asia, *zenana* in, 43
Southeast Asia, foreign merchant districts of, 30
Soviet Union: during Cold War, 333; Hitler's claims regarding Bolsheviks and Jews, 335, 338
Soweto, 231, 233, **376, 378**; anti-apartheid movement in, 419–20; Black Local Authority, 419–20; Civic Association, 419; Meadowlands Township, 375, **378**; Orlando Township, 365–69, **368**, 372, 374; naming of, 378–79; origins in Klipspruit Native Location, 259; Southwestern Townships, 231, 259, 371, 375, 379, 429. *See also* Klipspruit Native Location
Soweto Accord, 420
Spain: colonialism in the Americas, 49–51; colonialism in the East, 57–59; Dutch conflict with, 59; exile of Jews from, 34–35; fascism in, 362; ghettos in, 33–34; Inquisition in, 34–35; "negro" used by Spanish, 66, 67; religious politics of, 33–34; "white" used by Spanish, 67
Spanish Town, Jamaica, slave yards in, 53
sporting events, cross-race, 266, 271–72, 304–5
sprawl: constraining, 427; plans to constrain, 425; of suburbs, 385, 423
Stallard, F. C., 292–93, 361; Hope Woolith (farm), 292; and influx control, 252–53; leadership of Transvaal Local Government Commission, 292–93; Stallard Doctrine, 252–53; Stallardists, 295, 358, 365
Standard State Zoning Enabling Act, 323
Stations of British India. *See* hill stations and cantonments

steering. *See* racial steering by real estate agents
Stephens, Dr. J. W. W., malaria research of, 173, **175**, 176
sterilization laws, 324, 344; of Nazis, 334, 340; in United States, 340
Sterndale, Reginald, in Calcutta, 106
St. Louis (Missouri): North St. Louis ghetto in, 329; segregation ordinance passed in, 306; zoning in, 321
St. Louis (Senegal), self-rule in, 173
Stoddard, Lothrop: German Reich's "racial betterment" encouraged by, 339–40; on immigration restriction, 157; *The Revolt against Civilization*, 325
Storey, Moorfield, legal battle against racial zoning ordinances by, 387
Strangers' districts. *See* merchant districts
Strong, Josiah, 325
Stuyvesant, Peter, city wall decreed by, 51
suburbs: in Batavia, 97; of Cairo, 404; garden-city suburbs, 404; of Giza, 404; of Johannesburg, 275–76, 280, 365; in London, 96, 97–98, 102, 125; in Madras, 97, 98; in Manila, 97; mortgage practices aiding development, 355; opposition to fair housing laws, 394; post-World War II development of, 354–55; property tax in, 355; of Rio, 404; in Rome, 41, 96; of São Paulo, 404; in South Africa, 266, 267; sprawl of, 385, 423; zoning laws favoring low-density developments, 354
Sumer, 25; foreign merchant districts of, 28; separate temple districts in, 22–23
sumptuary laws, 34, 39
Surat, British merchants in, 61
surveyors. *See* land surveyors
Swahilis, in foreign merchant communities, 55
Sweden, plans to constrain sprawl in, 425
Sydenham, Thomas, miasmatic theory of disease by, 88–89
Sydney, bubonic plague in, 167

Tagore, Dwarakanath, 105
Tagore, Rabindranath, 105
Tamil, in Madras, 66
taxation, and deduction on mortgage interest payments, 355
tax rates. *See* property tax

Yale, Elihu: as governor of Madras, 62, 69, 86–87, 98; London real estate owned by, 102
Yersin, Alexandre, bubonic plague research of, 165, 166–67
Yokohoma, 143
Yorubaland, segregation by clan in, 41–42

Zanzibar, plan for residential segregation in, 181
ZAR (Zuid Afrikaansche Republiek), 230; British political power in, 241; Law 3 of 1885, 255, 256, 371; segregation of urban public space, 269–70; social welfare policies of, 362; voting rights in, 239

Zaria (Nigeria), residential segregation in, 179, 215
*zenanas*, 87; in South Asia, 43
Zimbabwe, political voice of African majorities, 411
zoning laws, 321–22; Advisory Committee on Zoning, 323; in Baltimore, 324; in Chicago, 322; and class segregation, 323–24; inclusionary laws, 389; in Los Angeles, 321–22; in New York City, 322; racial segregation implemented using, 323–27, 330; Standard State Zoning Enabling Act, 323; in suburbs, 354; *Zoning Primer*, 323